RISK MANAGEMENT AND INSURANCE PLANNING

2016

Published by:
KEIR EDUCATIONAL RESOURCES
4785 Emerald Way
Middletown, OH 45044
1-800-795-5347
1-800-859-5347 FAX
E-mail customerservice@keirsuccess.com
www.keirsuccess.com

All efforts have been made to ensure the accuracy of the contents of this material. However, should any errors be detected, Keir Educational Resources would greatly appreciate being informed of them. We will post all corrections and clarifications on the updates page on our Web site at www.keirsuccess.com.

Information in this material is subject to change without notice. No part of this material may be reproduced or transmitted in any form or by any means or for any purpose without the express written permission of Keir Educational Resources.

"Topic List for CFP® Certification Examination Copyright © 2011, Certified Financial Planner Board of Standards, Inc. All rights reserved. Used with permission."

"Certified Financial Planner Board of Standards, Inc. owns the marks CFP®, CERTIFIED FINANCIAL PLANNER™, and CFP (with flame logo)®, which it awards to individuals who successfully complete initial and ongoing certification requirements."

ISBN PRINT 978-1-937404-89-5
ISBN EPUB 978-1-945276-04-0

INTRODUCTION

For over 40 years, Keir Educational Resources has helped hundreds of thousands of insurance and financial professionals to obtain their professional designations. Over the last 20 years, Keir has produced supplemental study materials to help students complete the required courses at local universities and colleges in order to qualify to sit for the CFP® Certification Examination. Keir also has comprehensive review materials for the CFP® Certification Examination that have helped thousands of students to pass the CFP® Certification Examination.

While working with numerous program directors and instructors from universities and colleges across the country, Keir Educational Resources frequently receives requests for a book that can serve as the primary textbook for each course that is required by CFP Board Registered Programs. Program directors and instructors involved with these programs are frequently looking for textbooks focused specifically on the topics and learning objectives outlined by CFP Board. **Keir is pleased to offer textbooks designed specifically for each of the courses included in CFP Board Registered Programs. Keir also offers a Case Studies book that can be used in the Financial Planning Development Course.**

Keir designed this textbook using our well proven methodology of structuring each book to follow the topic list provided by the CERTIFIED FINANCIAL PLANNER™ Board of Standards. We have used this methodology for over 10 years to help thousands of students pass the CFP® Certification Examination. The topic list is the current basis for the CFP® Certification Examination, along with the Student-Centered Learning Objectives released by CFP Board in 2015, is the basis for student learning in Registered Programs. This textbook covers Risk Management and Insurance Planning (Topics 22 – 32). **Since we designed this textbook to follow the CFP Board's topic list and Learning Objectives, we are confident that students and instructors will find this unique format to be the most effective way to learn the skills required of a successful financial planner. While written with CFP Board Registered Programs in mind, this Risk Management and Insurance Planning textbook is comprehensive and flexible enough to be used in non-CFP Board programs as well.**

This textbook also includes over 400 multiple choice questions and case questions to help reinforce learning. The multiple choice questions included in this textbook cover the four cognitive levels of questions used on the CFP® Certification Examination: (1) Knowledge/Comprehension, (2) Application, (3) Analysis/Synthesis, and (4) Evaluation. Although there is more emphasis in the CFP® Certification Examination on higher level cognitive questions, a student needs to master lower level knowledge and comprehensive questions in order to master the application, analysis, and evaluation questions.

The CFP® Certification Examination includes comprehensive cases and mini-cases. To provide the experience of working on cases, we have included cases with multiple choice questions in Appendix A at the end of this textbook. Each of the topics contains a table identifying cases and questions covering material in that particular topic. Students should read the case in Appendix A and attempt to answer the case questions identified for that topic. The cases range from a few paragraphs to full blown 5 to 10 pages of facts and financial data. The short cases are similar to mini-cases and allow students to start to develop their ability to answer case questions. The full blown cases provide students with the same level of difficulty as the comprehensive cases on the CFP® Certification Examination.

Although most of the multiple choice questions in this textbook were written by Keir Educational Resources, some of the questions have appeared on past CFP® Certification Examinations and are reprinted here with permission.

EDITORIAL BOARD

John Keir, J.D., Chairman of the Board and Editor-in-Chief, received a B.A from Williams College and a J.D. from Villanova University School of Law. Mr. Keir practiced law in Philadelphia, including a federal court clerkship and public service in the District Attorney's office, before joining Keir Educational Resources in 1989. Mr. Keir has been writing and editing materials for the company primarily in insurance, risk management, claims, securities law, retirement planning, and estate planning. Mr. Keir is the primary author of Keir's Series 6 Study Program.

Sherri Donaldson, CFP®, ChFC®, MSFS, CASL®, CAP®, Editor and Lead Instructor, received her B.S. in Business from The Pennsylvania State University and a Master of Science in Financial Services from The American College. Ms. Donaldson started her career in financial services with Nationwide Retirement Solutions working in the retirement plans field, after which she moved into a position as a Financial Specialist with Nationwide Insurance. In 2001, Ms. Donaldson began working with M&T Securities as a Financial Consultant, then in 2003 moved into a training position with M&T Investment Group. As a Senior Training Specialist, Ms. Donaldson was responsible the company's internal CFP® training program, where she administered and instructed the undergraduate courses required for candidates to be eligible to sit for the CFP® Certification Examination, as well as instructing elective courses for the ChFC® designation, and other advanced designations. She was also responsible for developing and instructing training courses on advanced planning topics such as business succession planning and insurance, estate, and retirement planning for small business owners. In 2007 Ms. Donaldson began working as an independent contractor for Keir as an instructor for CFP® exam review courses. Over the next five years, she also worked for Keir on various writing and editing projects related to CFP® coursework and FINRA licensing. Ms. Donaldson joined Keir full time in 2012. She has over 25 exam cycles of experience helping students to pass the CFP® Certification Exam.

Mr. Keir and Ms. Donaldson serve as the Editorial Board of the following nine college textbooks related to the CFP® Certification Examination and education:

General Financial Planning Principles
Risk Management and Insurance Planning
Investment Planning
Tax Planning
Introduction to Financial Planning

Retirement Savings and Income Planning
Estate Planning
Financial Plan Development
Practical Applications for your Calculator

They are also the editors and authors of Keir's Comprehensive Review materials for the CFP® Certification Examination.

TABLE OF CONTENTS

<u>**Title**</u>   <u>**Page**</u>

Risk Management and Insurance Planning (Topics 22-32)

Topic 22:	Principles of Risk and Insurance	22.1–22.55
Topic 23:	Analysis and Evaluation of Risk Exposures	23.1–23.14
Topic 24:	Health Insurance and Health Care Cost Management (Individual)	24.1–24.85
Topic 25:	Disability Income Insurance (Individual)	25.1–25.37
Topic 26:	Long-Term Care Insurance (Individual)	26.1–26.32
Topic 27:	Annuities	27.1–27.50
Topic 28:	Life Insurance (Individual)	28.1–28.76
Topic 28B:	Life Insurance (Individual) (Part B)	28B.1–28B.20
Topic 29:	Business Uses of Insurance	29.1–29.55
Topic 30:	Insurance Needs Analysis	30.1–30.13
Topic 31:	Insurance Policy and Company Selection	31.1–31.19
Topic 32:	Property and Casualty Insurance	32.1–32.82

Appendix A

Black Hills P&L Case	Appendix A – 1
Brodinski Case	Appendix A – 4
Haurilick Case	Appendix A – 10
Beals Case	Appendix A – 16
Mocsin Case	Appendix A – 28
Loudon Case	Appendix A – 36
Connor Case	Appendix A – 47
Seidelhofer Case	Appendix A – 68
Loomis Company Case	Appendix A – 87
Michael and Diana Eastman Case	Appendix A – 91
Gary and Judy Parker Case	Appendix A – 101

Appendix B – Sample Life Insurance Declarations Page   Appendix B – 1

Appendix C – Sample Summary of Benefits and Coverage   Appendix C – 1

Appendix D – Sample Employee Notice and Consent Form   Appendix D – 1

Appendix E – Sample Life Insurance Needs Analysis Form   Appendix E – 1

Appendix F – Sample Statement of Policy Cost and Benefit Information   Appendix F – 1

Appendix G – Selected Facts and Figures and 72 Topics List   Appendix G – 1

Glossary   Glossary – 1

Index   Index – 1

Keir Review Course
for the CFP® Certification Examination

Live or Online Virtual Review Classes
Price: $600 + $450 for Basic Package (Purchase both and save $50)

Are you eligible to sit for the **CFP® Certification Examination**? Looking for a **live review class** location? Keir offers classes in three formats:

1. Keir Instructor-Led Classes
2. Affiliate-Led Classes, Implementing Keir Study Materials
3. Keir Online Virtual Class Review

Visit www.KeirSuccess.com to find details about all of our class locations, and learn about our highly effective THINK LIKE A PLANNER^{SM} method of study.

RISK MANAGEMENT AND INSURANCE PLANNING

Topics 22–32

[**Note:** This textbook, along with the other Keir textbooks (General Financial Planning Principles, Investment Planning, Tax Planning, Retirement Savings and Income Planning, and Estate Planning), is structured to follow CFP Board's 72 Principal Topics list. Risk Management and Insurance Planning consists of Topics 22-32 in that list. Therefore, this publication, rather than being broken into chapters and starting with chapter 1, will be presented as Topics 22-32.]

 800-795-5347

RISK MANAGEMENT AND INSURANCE PLANNING

Principles of Risk and Insurance (Topic 22)

CFP Board Student-Centered Learning Objectives

(a) Explain the risk management process.

(b) Provide examples of the four primary risk management techniques available to clients.

(c) Describe how insurers use risk pooling to pay for losses incurred by policyholders.

(d) Explain the factors that affect policyholder premiums and recommend appropriate methods for reducing household insurance costs.

Principles of Risk and Insurance
 A. *Purpose and benefits of risk management and insurance* 22.2
 B. *The Risk Management Process* 22.3
  1. *Step 1: Establish the risk management objectives* 22.3
  2. *Step 2: Gather information to identify the loss exposures* 22.4
  3. *Step 3: Analyze and evaluate the loss exposures and the risk management techniques available* 22.7
  4. *Step 4: Develop a plan, selecting the best risk management techniques to achieve the objectives* 22.8
  5. *Step 5: Implement the plan* 22.9
  6. *Step 6: Monitor the plan* 22.10
 C. *Risk management techniques (Responses to risk)* 22.10
  1. *Risk avoidance* 22.10
  2. *Risk reduction* 22.11
  3. *Non-insurance transfer* 22.11
  4. *Retention* 22.11
  5. *Insurance transfer* 22.12
  6. *Choosing risk management techniques based on loss severity and frequency* 22.13
  7. *Three basic rules of risk management* 22.14
 D. *Insurance Definitions and Concepts* 22.15
  1. *Definitions* 22.15
  2. *Law of large numbers* 22.16
  3. *Insurable risks: ideal risk characteristics* 22.18
  4. *Adverse selection* 22.19
   a. *Underwriting* 22.19
  5. *Self insurance* 22.20

    E.   The Insurance Industry 22.20

        1.   Types of producers in the marketing of insurance...................22.20

        2.   Functions of agents and brokers...22.22

    F.   Legal aspects of insurance..22.23

        1.   The principle of indemnity 22.23

            a. Subrogation...22.23

            b. Actual cash value 22.24

            c. Other insurance provision 22.24

        2.   Settling disputes among the parties to an insurance contract ..22.25

            a. Waiver...22.25

            b. Estoppel..22.25

            c. The parol evidence rule 22.25

            d. Nonwaiver provision...22.25

            e. Misrepresentation 22.26

            f. Reformation..22.26

        3.   Insurable interest 22.26

        4.   Contract requirements 22.27

        5.   Void versus voidable contracts 22.29

    G. Insurance contracts...22.29

        1.   Characteristics of insurance contracts 22.29

            a. Principles of utmost good faith...22.30

        2.   Insurance policy components...22.32

            a. Declarations...22.32

            b. The insuring agreement 22.32

            c. Exclusions 22.32

            d. Conditions...22.32

            e. Riders and endorsements 22.33

        3.   Policy ownership..22.33

        4.   Beneficiary Designations...22.33

    H. Policyholder premiums and strategies to reduce household

        insurance costs..22.33

PURPOSE AND BENEFITS OF RISK MANAGEMENT AND INSURANCE

A significant element of the planning process involves identifying potential obstacles to goals and threats to accumulated wealth. As financial planning clients achieve more success in their lives and careers, there is often a tendency to forget the importance of protecting assets and of safeguarding income. Many individuals fail to realize the impact that the added cost of a long-term disability, major illnesses, long-term care, or property losses can have on their family relationships as well as financial resources.

Risk management and insurance planning are part of a well-developed financial plan and when properly designed can lessen the impact of potentially catastrophic life events. By performing a thorough analysis of a client's loss exposures (losses that might occur), the planner and client are able to work together proactively to employ the best and most efficient methods for dealing with loss exposures.

THE RISK MANAGEMENT PROCESS

The risk management process is a process for identifying and measuring risks (possibilities of loss) and for making decisions on how to deal with those risks. It involves a series of six steps an individual or business can follow to manage risk. The six steps are similar to the six steps in the financial planning process (see the definitions section at the end of this topic for more details on the financial planning process). The steps are adjusted to apply specifically to risk management. The risk management process requires the following steps:

1) Establish the risk management objectives
2) Gather information to identify the loss exposures
3) Analyze and evaluate the loss exposures and the risk management techniques available
4) Develop a plan, selecting appropriate risk management techniques to achieve the objectives
5) Implement the plan
6) Monitor the plan

The acronym EGADIM can be used to help remember these six steps.

Large businesses frequently hire full-time risk managers to manage business loss exposures on a regular and continuing basis. Individuals and small businesses, on the other hand, often rely on financial planners, insurance brokers, or consultants to assist periodically with the process. In this textbook, our focus will be primarily on risk management for individuals and families.

Step 1: Establish the Risk Management Objectives

In personal financial planning, the risk management objectives are typically to protect assets, earning capacity, human life value, and health of the client. Objectives may also include less tangible aspirations, such as providing peace of mind or protecting family relationships. For example, a parent who plans to leave a family business to the child who works in the business might choose to leave life insurance death benefits of equal value to a child who is not working in the business in order to prevent animosity between siblings. Sometimes, the risk management objective may be simply to meet legal requirements, such as with the purchase of required auto liability insurance.

Initially, an individual's risk management objectives will tend to be somewhat general, e.g., protect assets and income. Greater specificity is provided in the later steps of the risk management process. Specificity becomes possible for the client and financial planner as more information is gathered and as more analysis is provided concerning the client's situation.

Step 2: Gather Information to Identify the Loss Exposures

In the risk management process, the information gathering step requires a planner to make use of a broad net to catch as many of the potential loss exposures as reasonably possible. The financial planner cannot assist a client with loss exposures until they are identified, so it is important to uncover and identify exposures that can impact the client's risk management objectives.

At this stage of the process, loss exposures are defined as potential reductions in value, without regard to probability. In other words, for now we are more concerned about what *could* happen than what is *likely* to happen. Perils are causes of loss, such as a fire that burns the house down. Losses may be direct or indirect results of the peril. For example, the cost to rebuild the house following a fire is a direct loss as a result of the peril of fire. An indirect loss from the same fire would be the cost incurred for temporary living arrangements while the house is being rebuilt. In some cases, indirect losses may occur without direct losses; for example, a family may incur expenses for temporary living arrangements when forced to evacuate due to the threat of wild fires in the area. The fires may not actually reach the home and destroy it, but the cost of temporary living arrangements is still incurred.

Gathering information to identify exposures can be approached in a number of ways. Businesses may use checklists, questionnaires, operation flow charts, financial statements, and on-site inspections of the plant, its equipment, and general layout of operations to help in identifying the entity's various exposures to loss.

Individuals and families may use checklists, survey forms, questionnaires, financial statement analysis, personal inspections, or contract analysis to assist with identifying loss exposures. Using one or more of these systematic approaches will help to avoid overlooking potential losses.

Identifying loss exposures through financial statement analysis involves a review of the Statement of Financial Position to identify property loss exposures and a review of the Statement of Cash Flows to identify income loss exposures. Each item on the statement is examined to determine potential loss exposures for that item. As an example, a review of the simplified Statement of Financial Position for Jane Buck (below) might look as follows:

Exhibit 22 – 1
Analysis of Statement of Financial Position for Loss Exposures

Account	Perils Exposed To	Consequences
Cash (on hand)	Fire Burglary	Loss of cash
Retirement Assets	Superannuation (outliving assets in retirement) Diminishing health	Insufficient income to support needs Need/cost of long-term care
Primary Residence	Fire Vandalism Water damage Trees in close proximity Injury of others on premises	Loss of use/cost of repair Reduction in value/cost of repair Cost to repair or replace Cost to repair dwelling due to damage from falling trees Medical costs to be paid
Boat	Damage to boat Damage to property of others Injury of others or self	Loss of use/cost of repair Cost to repair or replace Medical costs to be paid
SUV	Damage to vehicle Damage to property of others Injury of others or self	Loss of use/cost of repair Cost to repair or replace Medical costs to be paid
Jewelry	Fire Burglary Misplacement	Loss of value/cost to replace Loss of value/cost to replace Loss of value/cost to replace

Jane Buck
Statement of Financial Position
As of December 31, 20XX

Assets

Cash & Cash Equivalents

Cash on hand	$ 15,000
Checking account	40,000
	$ 55,000

Retirement Assets

401(k)	$ 440,000
Roth IRA	210,000
	$ 650,000

Use Assets

Residence	$ 350,000
Boat	47,000
SUV	28,000
Jewelry	25,000
Household items	175,000
	$ 625,000

Total Assets	**$1,330,000**

Liabilities

Short-term Liabilities

Chase credit card	$ 3,000
HSBC credit card	5,300
	$ 8,300

Long-term Liabilities

Boat loan	$ 18,000
SUV loan	20,000
Student loan	28,000
Mortgage on residence	198,000
	$ 264,000

Total Liabilities	**$ 272,300**
Net Worth	**$1,057,700**
Total Liabilities and Net Worth	**$1,330,000**

The above analysis of the Statement of Financial Position may be combined with property inspections to obtain a more complete view. For example, an inspection of the primary residence may reveal old and decaying trees very near to the dwelling. These inspections are often performed by an insurance agent or consultant with specialized knowledge of perils involving those particular assets.

The use of contract analysis to identify loss exposures might include analyzing contracts such as rental agreements.

Another method of systematically identifying loss exposures is to break them down into personal loss exposures, property loss exposures, and liability loss exposures. For the category of "Property Loss Exposures," for example, a survey form might ask the following questions:

- Do you own a home?
- When was the cost to rebuild or replace the home analyzed?
- Are there any collectibles or high value items within the home?
- Are there any collectibles or high value items located elsewhere?
- How is the home heated?
- Is the electrical wiring up to code?
- Do you own a secondary residence or property?

This approach of reviewing each of the three broad categories of loss exposures (personal, property, and liability) is discussed in more detail in Topic 32 of this textbook.

Class Exercise 22 – 1

Students should review the Personal Balance Sheet for the Loudon case in Appendix A of this textbook, and brainstorm questions to ask the client and discussion points that may help to identify potential loss exposures.

Step 3: Analyze and Evaluate the Loss Exposures and the Risk Management Techniques Available

Each loss exposure must be measured in terms of frequency (how often is it likely to occur) and severity (how much is it likely to cost). This analysis will help to determine the best method for managing the risk. For example, a loss exposure that is low frequency and low severity means it rarely occurs, and when it does occur, it doesn't result in a significant amount of economic loss. These risks can be easily dealt with from emergency funds or regular income. More severe potential losses may be dealt with through insurance or other methods to be discussed in the next section.

Another method that can be used for analysis is to look at maximum possible versus maximum probable losses to evaluate the size of losses and focus on techniques for dealing with the losses depending on severity (this method is discussed in more detail in Topic 32 of this textbook).

Step 4: Develop a Plan, Selecting the Best Risk Management Techniques to Achieve the Objectives

After analyzing the entity's exposures to loss, the planner should identify the alternatives available for handling the important or serious loss exposures, and then the planner should select the appropriate technique or techniques for handling these exposures.

There are two broad categories of risk management techniques: risk control and risk financing. Risk control includes avoidance and reduction. Reduction of risk or reduction of possible losses may be achieved by loss prevention (iron bars for all windows prevent burglaries) and loss reduction (fire extinguishers and sprinkler systems don't prevent fires, but they minimize the severity of any fire that does occur). Risk financing includes transfer and retention. These risk management techniques are discussed in greater detail in the next section of this topic.

An example of some of the recommendations for Jane Buck from the risk assessment in Exhibit 22-1 might appear as follows:

	Risk Management Audit Recommendations For Jane Buck June 15, 20XX	
Risk Problem Area	**Recommendation**	**Action Plan**
1. Excess cash on hand (homeowner insurance limits coverage of cash to $200)	Limit cash kept in home to $200	Jane will move all cash except $200 to checking account
2. Insufficient liquid assets to cover the cost of long-term care in retirement	Purchase long-term care insurance	Planner will set up joint meeting with insurance specialist
3. Primary residence is underinsured for dwelling replacement	Increase coverage in homeowner policy to cover full replacement cost of dwelling	Jane will contact her property-casualty agent
4. Inconsistent deductibles in home and auto coverage (homeowner policy with $250 deductible and auto policy with $1,000 deductible)	Increase deductible on homeowner policy to $1,000	Jane will contact her property-casualty agent
5. Lack of umbrella liability coverage (liability coverage in home, auto, and boat policies of $100,000 is insufficient for an individual with over $1 million of net worth)	Purchase $2 million umbrella liability insurance policy and ensure that the underlying coverages in home, auto, and boat policies meet the requirements of the umbrella	Jane will contact her property-casualty agent
6. Swimming pool is not enclosed inside a fence (liability)	Install a fence to surround swimming pool	Jane will contact company to install fence

Step 5: Implement the Plan

Once a plan has been decided upon for each risk exposure, it must then be implemented. If insurance is selected, new policies must be applied for or current policies updated. Implementation may also require the assistance of other professionals.

Step 6: Monitor the Plan

The final step in the risk management process is the ongoing responsibility to monitor the operation of the techniques selected and correct any shortcomings.

RISK MANAGEMENT TECHNIQUES (RESPONSES TO RISK)
]

The types of risks we are identifying and assessing in the risk management process are "pure" risks. With "pure" risks, there is only a chance of loss or no loss, with no possibility for gain. Some risk exposures are speculative in nature, meaning there is a chance of loss, no loss, or gain. Speculative risks are dealt with in Keir's Investment Planning textbook.

The tools available for dealing with "pure" risk exposures are as follows:

- Avoidance
- Reduction
- Non-insurance transfers (risk sharing)
- Retention
- Transfer to insurance company

Two of these techniques (avoidance and reduction) are used to control risks, two techniques (retention and insurance transfers) are used to finance risks, and one technique (noninsurance transfers) can be used either for risk control or risk financing.

Risk Avoidance

Risk avoidance is a negative technique for handling risk because avoidance means: (a) refraining from doing something (for example, refraining from buying a car or putting a swimming pool in the yard), (b) discontinuing the doing of something (discontinuing manufacture of a particular product), or (c) disposing of something (selling one's dynamite factory). Risk avoidance restrains an individual from engaging in any risky activity or owning anything that might cause financial loss for the owner.

Obviously, there are limitations to the use of avoidance because carried to an extreme, total avoidance would mean one would not produce anything to sell, and one would not travel anywhere or otherwise expose oneself to the possibility of bodily injury or liability suit.

> *"A ship is always safe at the shore – but that is NOT what it is built for."*
> **Albert Einstein**

Risk Reduction

Reduction of risk requires efforts in either of two ways: lower the probable loss frequency (loss prevention, example: burglar-proof windows) or lower the probable loss severity (loss control, example: sprinkler system). Safety programs, fire departments, night security guards, and burglar alarms are measures that will typically accomplish risk reduction both by preventing losses before they occur and by controlling losses after they occur. For example, fire departments will undertake measures to inspect properties to prevent fires, and they will fight fires to reduce the amount of damage resulting.

Non-insurance Transfer

A non-insurance transfer of risk shifts the risk of loss or shifts the financial consequences of a loss to someone else. The transfer will be to someone other than an insurance company. For example, a hold-harmless agreement in a lease will require that the tenant accept all responsibility for injuries occurring on the rented premises.

This method of dealing with risk is also sometimes referred to as risk sharing. An example of risk sharing is the corporation. The investments of a large number of persons are pooled, each bearing only a portion of the total risk. Insurance is another device designed to deal with risk through sharing losses, but is treated as a separate category from non-insurance transfers.

Retention

Retention means keeping the risk, in whole or in part. The collision deductible in auto insurance is a form of retention because the insured pays for the loss to the extent of the deductible. When an entity does not take positive action to avoid, reduce, or transfer a risk, the possibility of loss associated with that risk is retained.

Retention may be voluntary or involuntary. Voluntary risk retention is characterized by recognition that the risk exists, and there is a conscious assumption of the future losses that may occur. The decision to retain an exposure to loss is voluntarily made because there are no alternatives that are more attractive.

Involuntary risk retention takes place when the individual exposed to loss does not recognize the existence of the exposure; or if the exposure is recognized, the individual is not able to avoid it, reduce it, or transfer it. For example, many people do not recognize that continuous exposure to the sun may cause skin cancer. One might argue that the lifeguard at the Florida beach may recognize the risk and involuntarily accepts the risk. Actually, the lifeguard voluntarily accepts the risk in order to keep the job. He or she is not kept at the beach as a prisoner. Under involuntary risk retention, the entity or individual retains the financial consequences of the possible loss without realizing that he or she is doing so.

Retention is advisable when the exposure presents low severity and low frequency of losses. The deductible on car insurance is appropriate because it represents an infrequent loss and a relatively small expense.

Insurance Transfer

Risk may be transferred to someone more willing and able to bear the risk. Insurance is one method of shifting or transferring risk. In consideration of a specific payment (the premium) by the insured party, the insurance company agrees to indemnify the insured (up to a certain limit) for losses that may occur.

Practice Question

Parents decide that their son should not buy a car to take to college, and they will not buy additional car insurance. What risk management technique have the parents employed?

  A. Retention
  B. Avoidance
  C. Reduction
  D. Noninsurance transfer

Answer:
The decision not to buy the car will result in avoidance of the risk exposure arising from ownership and operation of the car.
The answer is B.

It should also be noted that the techniques for managing risk can be applied independently or can be combined in various ways. For example, a homeowners insurance policy is often purchased as a means of dealing with the risk of a fire destroying the home. That homeowner policy will contain a deductible, which is a partial retention of loss (and helps to reduce the premium for the insurance policy by eliminating the administrative burden of small claims). The homeowner may also have a sprinkler system or fire extinguishers in the house to help reduce the size of the loss should a fire occur. The combination of risk management techniques helps to create a more efficient plan for dealing with risk.

Choosing Risk Management Techniques Based on Loss Severity and Frequency

As mentioned previously, each loss exposure should be evaluated in terms of both frequency and severity. The basic rules regarding the severity and frequency of loss are as follows:

(a) When the severity of the potential loss is high, retention is not realistic.

(b) When the probability of loss is high, insurance becomes too costly.

(c) The most appropriate tools for dealing with those risks marked by high severity and high frequency are avoidance and reduction.

(d) Reduction may be used when it is possible to reduce the potential severity or the probability of occurrence to a manageable level; otherwise, the exposure should be avoided.

(e) Risks characterized by high frequency and low severity are best dealt with through retention and reduction. High frequency indicates that transfer is likely to be costly. Therefore, the entity would be well-advised to retain the exposure but implement loss prevention and loss reduction techniques to minimize the aggregate amount of retained losses.

(f) Risks with high severity and low probability of occurrence are most appropriately dealt with through insurance. The earthquake exposure is a good example. The liability exposure is another good example.

(g) Risks characterized by low severity and low frequency are best handled through retention.

The large-loss principle means buying insurance to cover a large potential loss before buying insurance coverage for the smaller exposures. In accordance with the large-loss principle, a family should not buy disability insurance to pay for lost days at work from minor illnesses such as head colds. Instead, the family should use its scarce premium dollars to increase coverage for a longer period of disability, such as 60 or 90 days. The use of deductibles is an example of the application of the large-loss principle. The insured uses scarce premium dollars shrewdly, reducing costs through increased deductibles but purchasing higher limits to cover potentially large losses.

EXHIBIT 22 – 2 Primary Risk Management Technique Based on Loss Severity and Frequency		
	Low Frequency	**High Frequency**
Low Severity	Retention	Reduction Noninsurance transfer
High Severity	Insurance	Avoidance (Catastrophic risk)

Three Basic Rules of Risk Management

As planners and clients assess the various methods of dealing with risk, there are three basic rules of risk management that should be kept in mind:

1) An individual should not risk more than he or she can afford to lose. The most important factor in determining which risks to retain is the maximum potential loss to which the person would be exposed if the risk were to be retained in full. Thus, it is rational to retain the risk of collision on a $1,200 jalopy but to fully insure the liability exposure which could amount to $100,000 or more. An individual's maximum retention should vary directly with its financial resources. A client with huge resources can retain exposures that an ordinary person should insure. In addition, the magnitude of loss that can be afforded by an individual will vary over time, depending on the resources that would be available at the time of loss.

2) Consider the odds. The greater the probability of a loss occurring, other things being equal, the greater is the pressure to do something about the exposure. However, usually other things are not equal. Therefore, the financial planner should consider both the probability of loss and the severity of the potential loss. This means we are back to the basic concept that (in most cases) individuals should insure low-probability, high-severity losses. For high-probability, low-severity exposures, a planner should seek some approach other than insurance. In most cases, the higher the probability of loss, the less appropriate is insurance as a device for dealing with the exposure. For example, insuring normal wear and tear of car tires would be irrational for most families because the family would have to pay premiums to cover the cost of tires plus an amount for an insurance company to handle claims and earn a profit. The family would do better just to buy new tires when needed.

3) Don't risk a lot for a little. This rule is used, for example, where the potential loss might not result in bankruptcy, but where transfer might still be desirable. Thus, a client would not leave uninsured a $150,000

home to save the small premium. Neither should a client elect to save the $500 premium for a $1 million umbrella liability policy. It is probably advisable to determine the actual level of retention for each risk individually on the cost-benefit basis implied in this rule.

INSURANCE DEFINITIONS AND CONCEPTS

When insurance is chosen to deal with risk, it will be important for the planner to have a working knowledge of insurance industry vocabulary and concepts.

Definitions

Definitions for some common insurance terms are provided below.

- Risk—Though many definitions are used by different authors for different purposes, in connection with insurance, we define risk as the possibility of loss. Risk, therefore, is a possibility of an adverse deviation from a desired outcome.

- Policyowner—The policyowner is the individual or entity that owns and has the legal rights regarding an insurance policy. The policyowner may or may not be the person who is insured under the contract. For example, a husband may own a life insurance policy that pays out a death benefit upon the death of his wife (the insured).

- Insured—The insured is the person or organization whose life or property is covered under an insurance contract.

- Peril—A peril is a cause of loss, such as fire, collision, death, disability, or legal liability.

- Hazard—A hazard is a condition that increases the likelihood of loss or increases the size of the loss if one occurs. A can of lighter fluid near a fireplace is a hazard. A loose board in a stairway is a hazard. A faulty engine in a Boeing 737 is a hazard. We should also distinguish physical hazards, moral hazards, and morale hazards.

  - Physical hazard—A physical hazard is a physical condition of property that creates or increases the probability of loss. Examples of physical hazards that increase the probability of loss from the peril of fire are the type of construction (wood frame versus cinder block and steel) and the occupancy of the building (restaurants and bowling alleys are prone to fire loss).

- Moral hazard—A moral hazard refers to the increase in the probability of loss arising out of or associated with the character weakness of people. It is a dishonest tendency on the part of an insured that may induce that person to attempt to defraud the insurance company. A dishonest person may intentionally cause a loss or may exaggerate the amount of a loss in an attempt to collect more than the amount to which he or she is entitled.

- Morale hazard—A morale hazard refers to indifference on the part of the person exposed to loss as to whether a loss occurs and/or the size of the loss. In other words, a morale hazard comes from an insured's attitude of carelessness rather than from dishonesty. Poor housekeeping practices, slovenly disregard for trash and vermin, and general failure to police the premises suggest the existence of a morale hazard.

Practice Question

Which of the following is <u>not</u> a hazard?

- A. A hurricane
- B. Exaggeration of injuries
- C. Driving over the speed limit
- D. Bare electrical wires in a house

Answer:

A hurricane is a peril or cause of loss, not a hazard. The exaggeration of injuries is a moral hazard; driving over the speed limit is a morale hazard, and bare electrical wires are a physical hazard.

The answer is A.

Law of Large Numbers

"While nothing is more uncertain than a single life, nothing is more certain than an average duration of a thousand lives."
Elizur Wright

Insurance entails pooling of risks and transferring them to an insurer to replace uncertainty (a possible large loss) with certainty (a known, modest premium cost). Insurance companies reduce risk for individuals by pooling exposures to loss. The insurance company also reduces risk for itself by pooling together a large number of exposure units. For a large number of insured exposure units, losses in the aggregate are highly predictable.

The law of large numbers specifies that as more units are exposed to loss, the greater will be the predictability of future loss results. This law is basic to the operation of insurance. If the outcome is highly predictable, there is little risk for the insurer because there will be only a small variation from the expected outcome. If we tossed 50 coins one at a time, we probably would not have 25 heads and 25 tails. But, if we tossed a single coin 5 million times, the number of heads would be very close to 2.5 million. Through the combination or pooling of a large number of similar exposure units, a reasonably accurate estimate of the cost of future losses can be made. On the basis of this accuracy, it is possible for the insurer to assume the possibility of loss for each exposure unit and yet have very little possibility of loss for itself. Thus, for insurance to work well, the insurer needs a large number (mass) of similar (homogeneous) exposure units.

For insurance companies, the law of large numbers has two applications. First, the predictions of future losses (for premium-setting purposes) must be based on the prior loss experience of a large number of exposure units. Otherwise, premiums will lack credibility. Second, there must be a large number of exposure units accepted and charged the established premium. If an insurer had only a small number of insured entities or a small number of exposure units, its actual loss experience would likely deviate significantly from its expected or predicted loss experience. By pure chance, the occurrence of a catastrophic peril in one geographic area (for example, a major earthquake) could result in serious losses. However, if the insurer has a large number of widely spread exposure units, the unique occurrence becomes merged in the overall experience. Thus, the overall loss experience will be reasonably close to the overall expected loss experience.

The "law of large numbers" is the basis of insurance because the larger the number of exposure units to which the estimate is applied, the better the chance that actual experience will approximate the estimate of probable losses. Insurance companies base their rates on the expectation of future losses. Thus, they must be concerned with the extent to which actual experience is likely to deviate from predicted results. For the insurance company, risk (or the possibility of financial loss) is measured by the potential deviation of actual from predicted results, and the accuracy of prediction is enhanced when the predictions are based on and are applied to a large number of exposure units.

Practice Question

On the basis of the law of large numbers, one can expect that from a larger number of exposure units:

    A. Future losses will be reduced overall.
    B. Future losses will be less frequent.
    C. Future losses will be more similar.
    D. Future losses will be more predictable.

Answer:
The law of large numbers holds that with more exposure units, the future losses will be more predictable.
The answer is D.

Insurable Risks: Ideal Risk Characteristics

While only "pure" risks (those with outcomes of loss or no loss, and with no possibility of gain) are insurable, not all "pure" risks are insurable. An insurable risk or loss exposure should ideally have the following characteristics:

1. The risk is a "pure" risk (insurance protects against pure risk, which involves loss or no loss, e.g., the fire risk to a house is that it burns or does not burn; insurance does not protect against speculative risk, which involves gain, loss, or no loss, e.g., the market risk for a house is that the price will rise, fall, or remain unchanged.)
2. There are a large number of homogeneous individuals or exposure units subject to loss (so that future losses are reasonably predictable)
3. Losses are accidental for the insureds (insurance is not appropriate for losses that are certain to occur, for example, fading of paint or depreciation of machinery.)
4. Losses are definite as to cause, time, and place, and measurable in terms of dollar amount (insurance does not cover sentimental value, for example.)
5. Probable loss frequency and severity are calculable
6. No incalculable catastrophe potential exists for the insurance company (The peril must be unlikely to damage or destroy a large percentage of the exposure units at the same time. For loss sharing to be a rational concept to apply, only a small percentage of the insured exposure units should experience losses in the same time period.)

Practice Question

Which of the following statements describes a characteristic of an insurable risk?

    A. Losses are indefinite in amount.
    B. Losses have the potential to be catastrophic.
    C. The probable frequency of losses can be calculated.
    D. The probable severity of losses cannot readily be estimated.

Answer:
For a risk to be insurable, the losses need to be definite and measurable. Insurers do not want to cover catastrophic losses because they will lose too much money. The loss severity and frequency should be calculable, so a premium to cover losses can be calculated.
The answer is C.

Adverse Selection

In all lines of insurance, there is a tendency for those who are most susceptible to loss to be the ones most interested in obtaining insurance to cover it. In other words, people who know they are likely to have a claim are more motivated to seek or continue insurance to a greater extent than are the better risks. People with health impairments seek life insurance. Homeowners in river valleys seek flood insurance. If the insurance company does not carefully control adverse selection, insurance premiums based on past loss experience will not be adequate to cover present or future losses. One of the main purposes of underwriting in an insurance company is to reduce adverse selection against the insurer.

Underwriting

To minimize adverse selection, the insurance company uses a professional staff of underwriters. The underwriting department is the selection and classifying department. The underwriting department passes judgment on each application for insurance coverage to determine whether the exposure to loss can be accepted at standard rates, what rate should be charged if there is an above-average expectation of loss, or whether the application should be rejected. In some cases, the underwriting department is encouraged to be liberal in accepting applications because the high yield available in the investment markets means the company can make enough extra investment income to pay the higher loss ratio that is inevitable when underwriting is more liberal.

The work of the underwriting department should include the following activities: (a) Obtain a large number of homogeneous exposure units for each specific classification. The large number is necessary if loss experience is to be maintained at the expected level. If only a few exposure units are accepted, loss experience by pure chance may deviate substantially from expected loss experience. (b) Avoid exposure to the catastrophe hazard (avoid too many exposure units in the hurricane belt or in the Mississippi River valley if flood insurance is offered). (c) Minimize adverse selection by selecting each exposure unit very carefully. Remember, if the underwriting department doesn't select carefully, it will be selected against. (d) Reject any applicant that appears to pose a moral hazard.

The insurance agent and broker can be helpful in the underwriting process. They can provide a preliminary screening of applicants. Certainly, the marketing team should not put its own self-interest ahead of sound selection of applicants. A few bad risks can be devastating to an insurer's profitability. The obvious problem is that the agent wants the commission, and the applicant is pushing the agent to get the applicant's exposure covered by insurance. There is a dangerous conflict of interest.

Property and liability insurers often do post-selection underwriting that is not possible in life insurance. The property and liability policy can be terminated by the insurer at any time with written notice to the insured. The life policy is noncancellable by the insurance company. The property and liability insurer may place an insured in a higher-rated classification, insist on a higher deductible, reduce the limits of coverage, or cancel the policy. Some states now have laws prohibiting the cancellation of auto liability insurance after the policy has been in effect for a certain minimum period. Some states require the insurance company to provide the policyholder with advance notice if renewal is to be denied. These laws are designed to give the policyholder adequate time to acquire a replacement for the existing coverage.

Information used in underwriting insurance is typically obtained from the following six sources: (1) the application and any pertinent appended documents; (2) affidavits submitted by the agent or broker; (3) routine and detailed investigations when such seem warranted; (4) insurance bureaus and associations (for example, life insurance companies have access to the Medical Information Bureau (MIB), an all-industry association that accumulates and provides medical information relative to life insurance applicants); (5) actual medical examinations for life insurance applicants and on-premises inspections for property insurance applicants; and (6) outside agency reports such as driving records from the DMV or the insured's credit score.

Self-Insurance

An individual or business may decide to self-insure its risks of loss, which means losses will be paid, not by buying insurance, but by setting up a fund or designating assets to pay these losses. The risk of loss is retained because there is no transfer of risk to an insurance company through the purchase of an insurance policy.

THE INSURANCE INDUSTRY

Types of Producers in the Marketing of Insurance

Marketing of insurance is approached differently from the marketing of other retail products because the protection offered by insurance is an intangible product. The purchaser of jewelry can hold the piece of jewelry in his hand and see the beauty of it. The purchaser of insurance just gets a paper contract that represents the protection. Marketing insurance, therefore, requires that consumers be educated and that advice be offered as to the best type of policy and policy provisions for a given exposure. This education and advice is provided by insurance producers. There are many types of insurance producers marketing insurance, and we list here the major types of producers:

(a)   General agents assist the insurer in performing its marketing functions. In life insurance, a pure general agency would be owned by the general agent, who would be granted an overriding commission that provides funds to pay a commission to the sales people and salaries to the office staff. A life insurance general agency should be contrasted with a branch office, which is owned and operated by the insurer. In property and liability insurance, the general agent takes some responsibility for underwriting and claims administration. When the general agency is specialized in the handling of particular property or liability lines, the underwriting function becomes an extremely important part of the general agency's overall duties.

(b)   An independent agent generally represents several property and liability insurers, has his or her own office staff, and can afford to spend as much effort on keeping business as getting it. Commonly, the agent has some claims payment authority. The unique status of the independent agent

> *"Show business is my life. When I was a kid I sold insurance, but nobody laughed."* **Don Rickles**

enhances his or her ability to help select insurers and provide other services for clients.

(c)   A captive agent represents exclusively one insurance company and its affiliates.

(d)   A broker is a person who is legally the agent of the insurance buyer. Although he or she represents the buyer, the broker is paid a commission by the insurance company.

🔑 KEY SUMMARY 22 – 1
Agent versus Broker

- **An agent legally represents the insurance company**
- **A broker legally represents the insured**

(e)   Surplus or excess-line brokers are persons licensed to acquire property and liability coverage for the insured beyond what the usual local (domestic) regulations allow. Brokers so licensed are responsible for carrying out the local regulations specifically applicable to these special transactions; very important among these is collection of the local premium tax. A surplus agent is a person performing the same functions but doing so as a representative of the insurer.

(f)   A career agent is a life insurance agent representing one or a few insurers. Career agents usually are supported by an agency in the form of office space, help, education, and training programs.

(g)   A personal producing general agent (PPGA) is a life insurance general agent who is engaged primarily in personal selling, rather than agency building. Frequently, the PPGA receives an expense allowance from the insurance company.

Functions of Agents and Brokers

Several of the functions of agents and brokers are described below.

(a)   A property and liability insurance agent usually is allowed to bind (make the policy effective immediately) the insurance company; a life insurance agent may not bind the company.

(b)   The agent's relationship to the insured is as a representative of the insurance company. The agent owes no obligation or loyalty to the insured except as a professional practitioner.

(c)   The agent is first and foremost a representative of the insurance company. Thus, the agent must be loyal to the company.

(d)   A broker usually may not bind the insurer because the broker is not an agent of the company.

(e)   A broker represents the insured in finding the best coverage or price by working with several insurers.

(f)   A broker is not an agent of the insurance company (except, in some states, for purposes of collecting the premium). Brokers solicit business from clients and place the business most favorably for their clients.

Under the implied powers principle, courts have ruled that the agent has those powers that the public can reasonably expect him or her to have. This is so even though the company expressly may not have granted the agent those powers. Thus, if a property-liability insurance agent binds the insurance company to a risk, the company is bound until it cancels the contract. A principal (the insurance company), however, would not be obligated to pay an insured's loss if there were no evidence that an agency relationship existed between the company and the agent. If there is no express authority (authority that is spelled out in the agent's contract), implied authority (authority in addition to any express authority and necessary so that the agent can perform the duties for which he has been hired), or apparent authority (authority that a reasonably prudent person would believe that the agent has), the principal may not be legally obligated to perform under the contract.

Ratification occurs when a principal adopts an agent's unauthorized act, such as accepting a contract entered without authority from the principal. An insurer may elect to accept an application for life insurance even though the agent was not authorized to take the application. For example, if an agent wrote an application and took a check for the first premium from an overage applicant and if the agent submitted the application to an insurance company, that company, by accepting the premium, has ratified the act of the agent and would be liable for any loss.

Knowledge on the part of a broker is not assumed to be knowledge on the part of the company. Legally, a broker represents the applicant, not the insurance company. Therefore, a life insurance company can void a policy issued to an applicant based on an application submitted by a broker if the company can prove misrepresentation and fraud that was known to the broker but was not known to the life insurance company. However, knowledge on the part of an agent is assumed to be knowledge also of the life insurance company. The life insurance agent represents the company. The agent is the agent of his or her principal – the life insurance company. Thus, the life company is bound to a contract when an agent knowingly encourages an applicant to misrepresent his or her poor health. However, a company can avoid a life insurance policy on grounds of misrepresentation that is discovered prior to the expiration of the "contestable period," which is normally the first 2 years the contract is in force. After that 2 year contestable period, the life insurance company can no longer void the policy.

LEGAL ASPECTS OF INSURANCE

The insurance policy is a legal contract entered into by an insurance company with an applicant or policyowner. In this section, we will identify some rules that arise from the legal requirements for an insurance contract.

The Principle of Indemnity

An insurance policy is a contract of indemnity because the insured is entitled to payment only to the extent of the financial loss incurred. The principle of indemnity states that insurance should restore the insured to roughly the same financial position as existed prior to the occurrence of the loss. The insured should neither profit nor sustain a loss.

Subrogation

Due to the principle of indemnity, property-liability insurance contracts provide for subrogation. Subrogation is a common-law right of the insurer after paying an insured's loss to acquire the legal rights of the insured against any third party responsible for the loss. This right of the insurer is also specifically stated in the "subrogation clause" of the typical property insurance policy. For example, the insurer pays for collision damage under the automobile policy and then has subrogation rights against the negligent third party. In this situation, the insurance company steps into the legal shoes of the insured after paying the amount of the loss caused by the negligent third party. Thus, the insurer's subrogation right preserves the principle of indemnity by preventing the insured from receiving a double payment: one from the insurance company and the second from the negligent third party who caused the loss.

Practice Question

Under property and casualty insurance, what is meant by "subrogation"?

- A. The insured has an obligation to cooperate with the insurer in defending a claim.
- B. After paying a claim, an insurer can obtain reimbursement from a third party.
- C. An insured cannot recover from the insurer, more than the value of the loss.
- D. An insurer can void the policy if an applicant has concealed facts.

Answer:

The right of subrogation is the insurer's right, after paying an insured's claim, to recover from a third party who caused the loss to the insured.

The answer is B.

Actual Cash Value

Actual cash value (ACV) of the loss is the maximum reimbursement that will be provided the claimant under most property insurance contracts. In most cases, ACV is the property's replacement cost minus physical depreciation (not the depreciation the accountant shows in the financial statements). This arrangement assures enforcement of the principle of indemnity because the insured is not provided with new property as a replacement for old property. Depreciation of old property is recognized, and the insured is reimbursed accordingly.

Other Insurance Provision

The "other insurance" provision is a typical provision in property insurance policies and provides that the insurer will pay the percentage of any loss that the amount of the policy's coverage bears to the total amount of coverage by all insurers. Thus, the insured cannot purchase multiple policies and hope to profit if damage to the insured property occurs.

Settling Disputes Among the Parties to an Insurance Contract

Occasionally, disputes will arise between the policyowner and the insurance company issuing the policy. Below are a number of legal doctrines that may apply to such disputes:

Waiver

A waiver is a voluntary (or intentional) surrender of a known legal right. When an insurance agent issues a policy with the knowledge that a policy condition is being violated, the agent is said to have waived that particular policy condition. This is so because knowledge of the agent is imputed to the insurance company.

Estoppel

Estoppel occurs when there has been conduct by one party that leads a second party to believe, reasonably, that a right will not be asserted, and the second party acts in reliance on such reasonable belief. The doctrine of estoppel holds that a right cannot subsequently be asserted to the detriment of that second person. For example, an insurer only smiles when a construction company tells the insurer that the company is storing dynamite in one of its buildings. The insurer would be estopped from denying coverage for storage of hazardous materials if the dynamite explodes and the ensuing fire destroys the building. The insurer's smile led the insured to believe such storage would be acceptable.

The Parol Evidence Rule

The parol evidence rule is sometimes the basis for settling disputes involving contracts because the parol evidence rule specifies that the written contract is the last word in an agreement between two parties. This rule is often said to apply only to oral agreements, but it actually applies to any agreement, oral or written, that has not been incorporated into the final agreement. All previous agreements between the parties are assumed to be included in the written contract. Evidence cannot subsequently be introduced to show that the parties intended to include some additional agreement in the contract. Each party had an opportunity to include everything he or she required in the contract before it was signed. Therefore, the contract as written will be binding on both parties. For this reason, policyowners should review the insurance contract carefully to ensure that all coverage discussed is included in the written contract.

Nonwaiver Provision

In the insurance contract, the insurer may include a nonwaiver provision that states that the insurer's agent may not make promises to the insured without the insurer's approval. Since the insured must read the contract carefully, he or she must know if all that the agent promised is or is not included in the insurer's contract. With such a provision, any dispute over what the agent promised will generally be settled in the insurer's favor unless the court rules that the agent modified or canceled the waiver provision.

Misrepresentation

An insurance policy may be rescinded if it can be proved that one party misrepresented material information in the preparation of the insurance contract. The misrepresented information must be material (important) to the contract in order for the contract to be voidable.

Reformation

Reformation involves the changing of an existing contract, not the creation of a new contract. When a written contract fails through mutual mistake or fraud to state the parties' actual agreement, a court can by reformation correct the writing to state the real intent of the parties.

Insurable Interest

Insurable interest requires that the person to whom insurance proceeds will be paid should stand to suffer an economic loss from the occurrence of the peril. For example, a homeowner has an insurable interest in his or her home because he or she would suffer a financial loss if the home was damaged or destroyed. A creditor also has an insurable interest in the life of a debtor because the creditor might not collect the amount of the loan if the debtor dies before repaying the debt.

In property insurance, the insurable interest in the property insured needs to exist at the time of the loss. Thus, a person may continue to hold a policy that insures a home he or she plans to sell. However, if the home burns after the person signed an agreement to sell the property, he or she no longer owns the property and would suffer no loss. Accordingly, since he or she had no insurable interest at the time of the fire, he or she would collect nothing from the insurer.

In life insurance, the insurable interest in the insured life must exist only at the time the policy becomes effective (the inception of the policy). Thus, a creditor may have an insurable interest in the life of the debtor at the time the policy is issued. However, the creditor may keep the policy in effect after the debtor repays the loan even though the creditor would suffer no loss if the debtor should die.

In property insurance, the insurable interest must be based on a financial interest in the property. In life insurance, however, the courts recognize an insurable interest based on a family relationship even though the policyowner would derive no financial benefit from the continued life of the insured. The courts hold that an insurable interest can be based solely on love and affection. All courts recognize an insurable interest between spouses. However, not all courts go beyond that. Some do include brothers and sisters, but most do not include cousins.

While a property-liability contract cannot be transferred without the insurance company's consent, ownership of a life insurance policy can be transferred, and the new owners need not have an insurable interest.

⏰ **REMEMBER:** INSURABLE INTEREST IS REQUIRED AT THE INCEPTION FOR A LIFE INSURANCE POLICY, BUT INSURABLE INTEREST IS REQUIRED AT THE TIME OF LOSS FOR A PROPERTY-LIABILITY POLICY.

Contract Requirements

From a physical standpoint, the basic components of an insurance contract may be thought of as the declarations, definitions, insuring agreements, conditions, exclusions, miscellaneous provisions, and endorsements or riders. These components of the insurance contract will be discussed in more detail later in this topic.

From a legal standpoint, the components of a valid insurance contract are the offer and acceptance, consideration, legal object, competent parties, and legal form.

- Offer and acceptance—There must be a definite, unqualified offer by one party, and this offer must be accepted in its exact terms by the other party. In property-liability insurance, the offer is made by the prospect when he or she makes application for coverage and (usually) pays the premium. The offer is accepted when the agent binds coverage or when the policy is issued. The property-liability insurance binder can be written or oral (telephone, for example). Thus, a temporary property-liability insurance contract does not have to be a written contract; the oral binder is effective to provide coverage. In life insurance, the usual situation is that the applicant makes the offer through the application and payment of the first premium. The agent gives a conditional receipt for the first premium. The "conditional receipt" specifies that coverage applies immediately, on the condition that the underwriters would have accepted the application as applied for (for example, at standard non-tobacco rates). The insurer accepts by issuing the policy as applied for. Note that the agent does not have the authority to bind the insurer in life insurance.

- Consideration—The consideration for a contract is that which is given or received by a party as an inducement for the completion of the contract. For insurance contracts, the consideration provided by the applicant is the premium plus the statements in the application. The consideration given by the insurer is the promise to pay valid claims submitted for losses. (Note: Since the conditional receipt in life insurance only applies if the application would be accepted by underwriters "as applied for", it is common practice for the agent to collect the premium based on standard underwriting even when the applicant is in excellent health and likely to qualify for a preferred rating.

By doing so, should death occur during the underwriting process, it is more likely that the application would have been accepted "as applied for" based on standard qualifications. If the applicant does, in fact, qualify for a preferred rating, the excess premium collected is returned.)

- Legal object—For an insurance contract to have a legal object, it must have a legal purpose. Generally, an insurable interest at the time of the loss satisfies the legal purpose for a property-liability insurance contract. In life insurance, an insurable interest at the policy's inception fulfills the requirement.

- Competent parties—The basic principle is that some parties are not capable of understanding the contracts into which they enter. Therefore, courts have ruled that incompetent parties are not bound by such agreements. A minor's contracts are usually voidable at his or her option. Many states have reduced the legal age for purposes of negotiating a contract for insurance. Therefore, if the applicant resided in one of the states permitting a reduced legal age for insurance, the minor applicant who met the minimum requirement could negotiate a binding contract.

- Legal form—Insurance contracts must use language that at least approximates that prescribed by state law. The insurer must also follow the proper procedure for filing and gaining state approval of its contracts.

Practice Question

When does life insurance coverage become effective?

    A. The insured signs the application.
    B. The insurance company issues the policy.
    C. The insurance agent delivers the policy and collects the first premium.
    D. The insured does not cancel the policy within the cancellation period.

Answer:
A life insurance contract is in force when the agent delivers the policy and collects the first premium. The policy will also be in force where the insured pays the first premium with the application. In that case, a conditional receipt is given to the insured, and the policy is effective from the date of application if the applicant is insurable.
The answer is C.

Void versus Voidable Contracts

The difference between a void and a voidable contract:

- A void contract is not a contract at all, but rather an agreement without legal effect because it lacks one of the requirements specified by law for a valid contract. It cannot be enforced by either party. For example, a contract having an illegal object is void, and neither party can enforce it.

- A voidable contract is one that, for reasons satisfactory to the court, may be set aside by one of the parties. It is binding unless the party with the right to avoid it elects to avoid it. Thus, a voidable contract between an adult and a minor may be fulfilled by both parties to the mutual benefit of both parties. A contract an adult makes with a minor child is voidable by the child, but is not voidable by the adult.

INSURANCE CONTRACTS

Characteristics of Insurance Contracts

There are seven characteristics of insurance contracts that help to make them distinguishable from other types of contracts:

(1)   Property insurance contracts are contracts of *indemnity*. With an indemnity policy, the insurer promises to reimburse the insured only to the extent of the insured's covered financial loss. Life insurance policies are not contracts of indemnity; instead, they are "valued policies." This means the insurer agrees to pay the face amount of the policy, regardless of the value of the life that is lost. Some property insurance policies are valued policies. Such property insurance policies may not preserve the principle of indemnity because they pay the policyowner the face amount, regardless of the policyowner's actual financial loss.

(2)   The property insurance contract is a *personal* contract. This means that the policy is personal to the insured and may not be assigned to anyone else without the approval of the insurer. It is as important for the insurer to pass judgment on the moral character and financial position of its insured as it is for the insurer to pass judgment on the condition of the property insured. The life insurance policy is not a personal contract. It may be assigned to anyone the policyowner chooses. Thus, a life insurance policy may be assigned to a creditor as security for a debt.

(3)   Contracts may be unilateral or bilateral. Under the terms of a unilateral contract, only one party makes a promise. Under the terms of a bilateral contract, both parties make promises that are legally enforceable. The insurance

contract is a *unilateral* contract. Only one party (the insurer) is legally bound to do something. The insured makes no promise to do anything. Of course, if the insured does not pay the renewal premium, the policy will be canceled. Also, there are policy conditions the policyowner must meet in order to obtain the policy benefits promised by the insurer.

(4)   The insurance contract is a contract of *adhesion*. This term means the insurance policy is written by one party (the insurer), and the second party (the insured) adheres (or accepts) the contract as written, or the insured rejects the contract (refuses to purchase the policy). The policy is not drawn up through negotiations. The insured may choose not to purchase the policy, but if purchased, the policy must be accepted as it is written. The insured usually cannot alter the language or rewrite any provisions of the policy. Because the insurer chooses the policy language, the courts interpret any ambiguous language against the insurer. Courts assume that the insurer had every opportunity to make the language suit the insurer's interests, and the insured merely adhered to the policy terms. Consequently, the insurer suffers for any ambiguity.

(5)   The insurance contract is an *aleatory* contract. An aleatory contract contains a promise and obligation to perform that depends on an uncertain event. An insurance contract is aleatory because the insured may receive benefits only in the event a loss occurs. Insurance and gambling contracts are aleatory. These contracts do not involve an exchange of equal values, and the party who will benefit more from the contract will be determined by chance. Insurance differs from gambling contracts due to the requirement of an insurable interest. The insurance contract enables one to avoid a loss, not make a gain. On the other hand, a typical sales contract is commutative. Both parties will receive equivalent benefits.

(6)   The insurance contract is a *conditional* contract because one party (the insurer) has to perform only if certain conditions are met. The insured must fulfill all the applicable conditions of the policy. For example, a disability insurance policy may specify that benefits will continue to be paid on the condition that a physician recertifies every six months that the insured remains disabled.

(7)   The insurance contract is a contract of *utmost good faith*. Both parties must behave honestly. However, the concept of utmost good faith probably has greater application to the honesty of the insured. In making its decision whether to insure and how to rate an applicant, the insurer relies on the complete truthfulness of the applicant in providing information concerning the loss exposure. If the information provided by the applicant is false or incomplete, the insurer may be able to avoid the contract on grounds of breach of warranty, misrepresentation, or concealment.

Principles of Utmost Good Faith

The following insurance principles are significant to the concept of utmost good faith:

(a)   Misrepresentation. A misrepresentation is an untrue statement. If the misrepresentation is material, it usually is grounds for voiding an insurance policy. For property insurance policies, the insurer may refuse to pay a claim on grounds of misrepresentation whenever the loss occurs. However, for a life insurance policy, the misrepresentation must be discovered within the one- or two-year contestable period. Otherwise, the life insurance policy is valid, despite the misrepresentation of the applicant-policyowner.

(b)   Warranty. A warranty is a statement made by an applicant and contained in a property-liability insurance policy which, if untrue, renders the policy voidable by the insurer. For most insurance policies, a warranty must be in writing and be a part of the insurance contract. The law concerning warranties is not applicable in life insurance. State laws require that the life insurance policy must state that all statements by the applicant will be construed to be representations and not warranties. The courts today are tending to hold that property insurance contracts may not be avoided because of a breach of warranty or misrepresentation unless the violation caused the loss or increased the risk which caused the loss. Such decisions are obviously more favorable for the insured.

(c)   Concealment is the failure to disclose known material information. The information omitted is considered material if the disclosure of the information would have led the insurer to make a different underwriting decision. The failure of the insured to disclose material facts constitutes concealment. A willful concealment (intent to defraud the insurer) is grounds for voiding an insurance policy. The insured has an obligation to disclose extraordinary facts within the scope of his or her knowledge. The difficulty of establishing willful concealment (intent to defraud) makes it difficult for the insurance company to void an insurance policy on the grounds of concealment.

Practice Question

Which of the following principles does not apply to the usual insurance contract?

A. Aleatory contract
B. Bilateral contract
C. Contract of adhesion
D. Indemnity contract

Answer:
An insurance contract is an aleatory contract, a contract of adhesion, and an indemnity contract. It is unilateral rather than bilateral.
The answer is B.

Insurance Policy Components

In order for the financial planner to analyze and evaluate existing insurance policies, a basic knowledge of the components of the policy will be required. Typical components of the insurance policy which the planner will likely want to review include the declarations, the insuring agreement, exclusions, conditions, and riders and endorsements.

Declarations

The declarations section of an insurance policy will clearly identify the insured, the location, the condition of the property to be covered under property-casualty insurance (or the individual to be covered for life and health insurance), and the other specifics of the coverage, such as the date the policy went into force, the term (time-frame) of the coverage, and the dollar amount of coverage that is provided. The declarations page is usually found at the beginning of the policy. An example of a declarations page from a life insurance policy can be found in Appendix B of this textbook.

The Insuring Agreement

The purpose of the insuring agreement in an insurance policy is to set forth the coverage provided by the policy. It is in this section that the company promises to pay for covered losses.

Exclusions

The purpose of exclusions in an insurance policy is to remove from coverage various perils, hazards, properties, persons, locations, and types of losses the insurer does not wish to cover. Some exclusions exist because the losses are uninsurable; for example, loss as a result of war could be catastrophic for the insurance company and is typically an excluded peril in property insurance. Several exclusions exist to avoid duplication of coverage with other types of policies; for example, the health insurance policy might exclude occupational injuries, which are covered under workers' compensation insurance. Other exclusions remove coverage because the loss exposure does not apply to most applicants on a broad basis; for example, most homeowner policies do not provide coverage for boats, but those who need that coverage can add it through an endorsement to the policy. These exclusions help to reduce the premium, but should be reviewed carefully in case the insured does need coverage for the excluded losses.

Conditions

The purpose of conditions in an insurance policy is to set forth, in detail, the duties and rights of both parties. Some conditions relate to the duties of the insured in the event of loss. Other conditions are designed to protect the insurance company from adverse loss experience because of increases in hazards within the control of the insured. Conditions are also used to provide the ground rules for the continuance of the insurance agreement. For example, the payment of the renewal premium is a condition for continuance of coverage.

Riders and Endorsements

Riders and endorsements are provisions that are added to the policy to modify or clarify the coverage. The term "rider" is typically used with life and health insurance policies, and the term "endorsement" is typically used with property-casualty policies. Riders and endorsements often require payment of an additional premium because they are adding to the coverage or modifying it in a way that is favorable to the insured.

Policy Ownership

Property and casualty policies are owned by the insured because the insured must have an insurable interest at the time of the loss. Other kinds of insurance such as life, disability, and health insurance can be owned by persons other than the insured. For example, employers often purchase these kinds of insurance coverage for employees.

Beneficiary Designations

Designations of beneficiaries are primarily important for life insurance and annuities and will be discussed under the topics dealing with those products.

POLICYHOLDER PREMIUMS AND STRATEGIES TO REDUCE HOUSEHOLD INSURANCE COSTS

The risk management process will likely reveal a large number of loss exposures that will need to be addressed within the plan. While those loss exposures that fit into the category of low frequency and high severity may be ideally dealt with through insurance, the funds available for purchasing coverage may be limited. The planner will need to work with clients to prioritize loss exposures and determine ways to reduce premium costs to achieve adequate protection at an affordable price.

One approach might be to break down the insurable risks into those the client deems essential to cover, those desirable to cover, and those the client chooses not to cover. Which risks are essential or desirable to cover may be largely based on assessment of severity and frequency, but the planner will also need to factor in the risk tolerance level for the individual client. The client's psychological assessment of the risk will vary from person to person and from situation to situation. For example, one client who has provided care for an aging parent may feel that long-term care insurance is essential because the client does not want her children to go through the physical and emotional strain of care-giving that she went through. Another client may feel that long-term care insurance is not desirable at all.

Once it has been determined which risks are essential and desirable to cover with insurance, the planner and client can then look at the amount of coverage needed and assess methods available to reduce premiums. The amount of coverage that is needed may be affected by employee benefits that provide coverage (for example, group term life insurance or disability insurance), the coverage need may be affected by social insurance programs that provide some coverage (for example, Social Security or unemployment insurance), and the need may be affected by accumulated wealth that is available to cover all or a portion of the loss exposure.

In general, a client can reduce insurance costs by eliminating duplicate coverage and by increasing deductibles. Additional ways premiums might be reduced for various types of insurance include the following actions:

1) Homeowner insurance: install fire extinguishers and alarm system in the home, insure both home and auto with the same insurer, remove trees that are too near the house, improve your credit score.
2) Auto insurance: buy older, less expensive cars, take teenagers for driving classes, ask for good student discounts, pay premiums annually instead of monthly, buy anti-theft devices, airbags, and anti-lock brakes, maintain a clean driving record, improve your credit score.
3) Life insurance: stop smoking, do not participate in high risk hobbies like skydiving or motocross racing, pay premiums annually instead of monthly, use term insurance to cover temporary needs, maintain a healthy weight.
4) Disability insurance: increase the elimination period, integrate with Social Security, reduce the benefit period, buy group insurance (many professional organizations offer group DI to members).

Students may be surprised to see "improve your credit score" listed as a way to reduce insurance premiums. What does credit score have to do with insurance? A credit score is an analysis of an individual's credit history which is most frequently used for securing a loan. A credit score looks at payment history, amount of available credit, amount of debt, and length of credit history to arrive at a numerical ranking or "credit score". Similarly, insurance company underwriters can assess an "insurance score," and part of the insurance score comes from an assessment of how a person manages his or her financial affairs. Actuarial studies have shown the insurance score to be a good predictor of insurance claims, which helps underwriters determine which applicants may be higher or lower risks in terms of claim filing. The insurance company will charge a higher premium to those more likely to file a claim. As a result, establishing good credit can improve the insurance score and reduce insurance costs. Clients can increase their credit score by paying bills on time, not obtaining more credit than needed, and keeping the balances on credit cards as low as possible.

DEFINITIONS

The Financial Planning Process – Financial planning is a six-step process that is used to develop comprehensive strategies to assist clients in achieving their goals and objectives. The six steps in the financial planning process are:

1. Establish and define the client-planner relationship
2. Gather information, including goals and priorities
3. Analyze and evaluate the client's current financial status
4. Develop and present the financial plan
5. Implement the financial plan
6. Monitor the plan

APPLICATION QUESTIONS

1. Which of the following perils best meets the ideal requirements for an insurable risk?

   A. Sickness
   B. Flood
   C. Nuclear radiation
   D. Lightning
   E. Unemployment

2. (Published question released December, 1996)

Regarding the characteristics of insurance, which of the following is/are fundamental?

   (1) Probability (possibility and predictability of a loss)
   (2) Law of large numbers
   (3) Transfer of risk from individual to group
   (4) Insurance is a form of speculation

      A. (1) and (2) only
      B. (1), (2), and (4) only
      C. (1), (2), and (3) only
      D. (4) only
      E. (1), (2), (3), and (4)

3. (Published question released November, 1994)

Conditions that increase either the frequency or severity of loss are called:

   A. Subrogation
   B. Risks
   C. Hazards
   D. Perils
   E. Extenuating circumstances

4. For which of the following loss exposures is the insurance technique best suited, based on loss frequency and loss severity?

    A. Damage in coastal North Carolina due to hurricanes
    B. Breakage of eyeglasses
    C. Losses of a grocery store owner due to shoplifters
    D. Burning out of household light bulbs
    E. Legal liability for bodily injury in an auto accident

5. Which of the following is (are) consistent with the principle of indemnity?

    (1) Settlement of property losses on an actual cash value basis
    (2) Award of damages for pain and suffering
    (3) Payment of the face amount of a life insurance policy at the death of the insured

    A. (1) only
    B. (1) and (2) only
    C. (1) and (3) only
    D. (2) and (3) only
    E. (1), (2), and (3)

6. Which of the following persons has (have) an insurable interest?

    (1) A small business owner in the life of a key employee
    (2) A homeowner in his or her household contents
    (3) The operator of a private plane in the safety of his or her passengers

    A. (1) only
    B. (2) only
    C. (3) only
    D. (1) and (2) only
    E. (1), (2), and (3)

7. Jack, while burning leaves in his back yard, negligently causes the neighbor's house to catch fire. The neighbor collects for the damage from his own homeowners policy. The insurer then brings action against Jack for reimbursement under which of the following principles?

    A. Insurable interest
    B. Subrogation
    C. Utmost good faith
    D. Apparent authority
    E. Estoppel

8. Which of the following is an example of noninsurance transfer as a method of treating pure risk?

    A. Ann installs double locks on all the doors in her home.
    B. Ben turns in his driver's license when his eyesight fades severely.
    C. Clare, a landlord, includes a hold-harmless agreement in the lease of her premises to a tenant.
    D. Don keeps a portable fire extinguisher in his car.
    E. Ellen includes a high deductible in her major medical coverage.

9. What is the main responsibility of the underwriting department of a life insurance company?

    A. To guard against adverse selection
    B. To set a limit on the amount of insurance issued
    C. To set adequate insurance rates
    D. To avoid exposures that could result in loss

10. Charlie loans $10,000 to Dave. As security for the loan, Charlie takes out and pays the premiums for a $10,000 life insurance policy on Dave, naming Charlie as beneficiary. Dave eventually repays the loan. Charlie keeps the policy in force. Then, Dave dies. In this situation, the policy's death proceeds will be paid to:

    A. Dave's estate
    B. Charlie
    C. Dave's family
    D. The state
    E. No one

11. A 17-year old boy has bought a car for $1,000. His parents have consulted you on the best risk management techniques to use for property and liability loss exposure in connection with the car. Which of the following recommendations is most appropriate?

    A. Insurance for both the property loss exposure and the liability loss exposure

    B. Avoidance for the property loss exposure, reduction for the liability loss exposure

    C. Retention for both the property loss exposure and the liability loss exposure

    D. Retention for the property loss exposure, transfer for the liability loss exposure

12. (Published question released December, 1996)

Temporary insurance coverage, contingent on an applicant's ability to present evidence of insurability, can be provided by:

    A. Evidence of consideration
    B. Conditional receipt
    C. Delivery of contract
    D. Initial premium payment

13. Which of the following statements concerning insurance agents and brokers is correct?

    A. A broker represents the insurance company and owes a duty of loyalty to both insured and insurer.

    B. The broker's knowledge of the risk is binding on the insurer, not the insured.

    C. An independent agent's knowledge of the risk is not attributed to the insurer.

    D. An insurance company agent owes a duty of loyalty to the insurer, not to the insured.

14. Which of the following statements concerning insurable interest are correct?

    (1) Insurable interest with life policies is required at the time of issuance.
    (2) Insurable interest with property and liability policies is required at time of a loss.
    (3) Insurable interest with life policies is required at the time policy proceeds are paid.

      A. (1) and (2) only
      B. (2) and (3) only
      C. (1) and (3) only
      D. (1), (2), and (3)

15. An insurance broker is characterized by which of the following?

    (1) An independent contractor
    (2) Represents the insured
    (3) Can bind the insurer

      A. (1) and (2) only
      B. (1) and (3) only
      C. (2) and (3) only
      D. (1), (2), and (3)

16. The process by which the risk manager achieves his or her risk management goals should involve all the following steps, EXCEPT:

      A. Determine objectives.
      B. Identify and evaluate exposures to loss.
      C. Consider alternatives and select from among the feasible risk-treatment devices.
      D. Arrange insurance for catastrophic exposures to both pure and speculative risks.
      E. Evaluate and review results of decisions implemented.

17. Match the terms or phrases in the left column with the appropriate definition in the right column.

A.	Risk	1.	A cause of loss
B.	Hazard	2.	Loss costs are predictable
C.	Peril	3.	Loss is fortuitous
D.	Accidental loss	4.	Something that increases probability of loss
E.	Calculable loss	5.	Possibility of an adverse deviation from a desired outcome

18. Which of the following would be an example of a peril?

    A. A defective step on a basement stairway
    B. A can of gasoline placed near a fireplace
    C. A collision between a freight train and a school bus
    D. An aged and rotten tree leaning toward a homeowner's garage roof

19. All the following statements concerning the basic rules of risk management are correct, EXCEPT:

    A. A firm's maximum retention should vary directly with the magnitude of its financial resources.
    B. The higher the probability of loss, the more appropriate is insurance as a device for dealing with the exposure to loss.
    C. One rule admonishes us not to risk a lot for a little. This rule would suggest that a twenty-eight-year-old with three children dependent on him or her should certainly own some life insurance.
    D. Even if the probability of occurrence of loss is fairly low, the decision as to how to handle the exposure should be made largely on the basis of the financial severity of the potential loss.

20. Insurance is highly suitable as a technique for dealing with which of the following?

    (1) Losses that are high in frequency and low in severity
    (2) Losses that are low in frequency and low in severity

    A. (1) only
    B. (2) only
    C. Both (1) and (2)
    D. Neither (1) nor (2)

21. Which of the following statements concerning the elements of an insurable risk are correct?

(1) The smaller the number of units exposed to the peril of fire, the more predictable the actual number of future fire losses.
(2) Future losses must be definite as to time of occurrence and as to dollar amount.
(3) Future losses must be fortuitous.
(4) The rule against subrogation should be equally applicable to hazards and perils.

    A. (1) and (2) only
    B. (2) and (3) only
    C. (1), (2), and (3) only
    D. (1), (2), (3), and (4)

22. All the following are examples of losses for Bernice that are accidental in nature for her, EXCEPT:

    A. A tidal wave engulfs her vacation home.
    B. A thief burglarizes her principal residence.
    C. The tires on her car gradually wear out.
    D. Her home depreciates in value due to a zoning change.

23. Insurers must be vigilant to minimize adverse selection. Which of the following statements concerning the importance of the elements of an insurable risk for a property insurer intent on minimizing adverse selection are correct?

(1) Selecting only homogeneous exposure units excludes some exposure units whose loss probabilities are substantially higher than the average for the class.
(2) Excluding catastrophic exposures excludes exposures where there is a high probability that the occurrence of an insured peril will cause losses for many exposure units at the same time.
(3) Requiring losses to be fortuitous means the insured must have no opportunity to hasten the occurrence of an insured peril.
(4) Requiring losses to be definite as to time and amount is designed to reduce the morale hazard.

    A. (1) and (2) only
    B. (2) and (3) only
    C. (1), (2), and (3) only
    D. (1), (2), (3), and (4)

24. To minimize adverse selection and assure sound insurance operations, the underwriting department of an insurance company would strive to achieve which of the following?

(1) Obtain a large number of homogeneous exposure units for each specific classification of exposure units.
(2) Avoid exposure to the catastrophe hazard.
(3) Have agents and brokers participate in the underwriting process by providing a preliminary screening of applicants.

    A. (1) only
    B. (1) and (2) only
    C. (1) and (3) only
    D. (2) and (3) only
    E. (1), (2), and (3)

25. All the following statements concerning the various methods of handling risk are correct, EXCEPT:

    A. Incorporating hold harmless agreements into transactions involve transfer of risk.
    B. Subcontracting is an example of risk avoidance.
    C. Loss control can be implemented, whether the exposure is retained or insured.
    D. By building more units, a large motel chain may actually reduce the uncertainty concerning future fire losses.

26. The alternative methods of handling risk include which of the following?

(1) Avoidance and retention
(2) Hazard reduction and loss reduction
(3) Risk transfer and risk reduction

    A. (1) only
    B. (2) only
    C. (3) only
    D. (1) and (2) only
    E. (1), (2), and (3)

27. Mr. and Mrs. John Public own a home valued at $120,000 and an automobile valued at $7,000. The most practical method for this family to use to handle these exposures would be:

    A. Avoidance of the exposures
    B. Hazard reduction and loss reduction
    C. Risk shifting or transfer
    D. Risk reduction

28. Why is the law of large numbers important to the sound operation of insurance?

    A. Because it is vital to the principle of indemnity
    B. Because it is vital to the predictability of losses
    C. Because it is vital to the marketing success of all insurers
    D. Because it helps to enforce the principle of subrogation

29. Effective operation of the law of large numbers requires which of the following?

    (1) A large volume of homogeneous exposures
    (2) A large group of insureds with widely different risk characteristics

    A. (1) only
    B. (2) only
    C. Both (1) and (2)
    D. Neither (1) nor (2)

30. Which of the following are the two items that are involved in the dual application of the law of large numbers by insurance companies?

(1) The larger the number of perils insured, the better will be the predictability of future hazards.

(2) The larger the number of exposure units from which loss experience data is gathered, the more accurate will be the predictability of future losses.

(3) The larger the number of exposure units, the more predictable will be both the hazards and the perils involved in future losses.

(4) The larger the number of exposure units insured, the closer actual losses will be to predicted losses.

    A. (1) and (2) only
    B. (1) and (3) only
    C. (1) and (4) only
    D. (2) and (3) only
    E. (2) and (4) only

31. Which of the following is (are) in the category of examples of adverse selection?

(1) Helen wants to stay in the hospital for a few extra days to enjoy the peace and quiet and to make sure she is fully recovered from her illness.

(2) Belinda, a very careful driver but a very cautious person, wants both liability and physical damage automobile insurance.

    A. (1) only
    B. (2) only
    C. Both (1) and (2)
    D. Neither (1) nor (2)

32. Which of the following are among the basic rules that a business entity should apply to the severity and frequency of its property loss exposures?

(1) Retention is not realistic for high-severity loss exposures.
(2) The most appropriate tools for dealing with those loss exposures marked by high severity and high frequency are avoidance and reduction.
(3) Exposures that are characterized by high frequency and low severity are best handled through insurance.
(4) Exposures that are characterized by low severity and low frequency are appropriate for retention.

    A. (1) and (2) only
    B. (1), (2), and (4) only
    C. (2), (3), and (4) only
    D. (1), (2), (3), and (4)

33. Before an insurance contract comes into existence, which of the following must be present?

(1) Agreement (offer and acceptance)
(2) Competent parties
(3) Written policy
(4) Legal purpose and consideration

    A. (1) and (2) only
    B. (1), (2), and (4)
    C. (2), (3), and (4) only
    D. (1), (2), (3), and (4)

34. The legal requirement that there be consideration before an insurance contract comes into existence refers to:

    A. Thoughtfulness on the part of the agent in presenting the details of the insurance coverage
    B. Cooperation on the part of the prospective insured in answering the questions on the application
    C. The premium that is the sole consideration to be provided by the insured before coverage can begin
    D. The provisions and stipulations in the policy and the premium specified

35. Which of the following statements concerning insurance contracts with minors is (are) correct?

   (1) Only the minor may avoid the contract – the insurer must perform its contractual obligation in the absence of a disaffirmation by the minor.

   (2) Generally, a minor may disaffirm an insurance contract the same as any other contract.

   (3) Many states have specific statutes binding minors to their contracts for life and health insurance.

     A. (1) only
     B. (2) only
     C. (3) only
     D. (1) and (2) only
     E. (1), (2), and (3)

36. Adherence to the principle of indemnity means which of the following?

     A. The insurer will pay the face amount of a life insurance policy, regardless of the cause of death.
     B. The insured can profit from his or her insurance coverage if he or she has two identical fire insurance policies.
     C. The insurer will reimburse the insured only to the extent of the insured's financial loss.
     D. The insurer does not have to rely on the insured's representations contained in the application for insurance.

37. Which of the following would generally be the LEAST helpful to the insurance company in preserving adherence to the principle of indemnity?

     A. Application of the principle of insurable interest
     B. Loss settlements on the basis of actual cash value
     C. The use of valued policies
     D. The use of subrogation

38. Which of the following statements concerning voidable and void contracts is (are) correct?

    (1) A contract is voidable if the contract may be set aside or disaffirmed by one of the parties.

    (2) A contract is void if it lacks one of the legal requirements for a valid contract.

    (3) A voidable contract may be fulfilled by both parties to the mutual benefit of both parties.

      A. (1) only
      B. (1) and (2) only
      C. (1) and (3) only
      D. (2) and (3) only
      E. (1), (2), and (3)

39. Which one of the following statements concerning property insurance contracts is correct?

    A. A property insurance contract is considered to be bilateral because it is between two parties – the insurer and the insured.

    B. In a property insurance contract, the insurer makes no legally enforceable promises until a covered loss occurs.

    C. Although a property insurance contract is personal, it is really the property and not the person that is being insured.

    D. Property insurance contracts are contracts of indemnity, but life insurance contracts are not contracts of indemnity.

40. Which of the following types of contracts is so named because it permits one party to receive potential benefits greatly in excess of the benefits received by the other party?

    A. A contract of adhesion
    B. An aleatory contract
    C. A contract by estoppel
    D. A contract with subrogation rights

41. Which of the following statements concerning the nature of the insurance contract is (are) correct?

(1) The insured can usually negotiate the wording of the provisions in an insurance contract.

(2) The insurance contract is offered to the typical insured on a take-it-or-leave-it basis. Therefore, it is considered to be a contract of adhesion.

(3) Because insurance is a contract of adhesion, ambiguities are resolved in favor of the insured.

    A. (1) only
    B. (2) only
    C. (1) and (2) only
    D. (2) and (3) only
    E. (1), (2), and (3)

42. Which of the following statements describes the correct application of the doctrine of insurable interest for property insurance purposes?

    A. The insured's financial insurable interest in the property is the maximum amount payable to him or her for any insured loss.

    B. The insured may receive the actual cash value (ACV) of the property in case of a total loss, even if his or her insurable interest is for a lesser amount (provided, of course, that the amount of coverage is at least equal to the ACV of the property).

    C. A person may insure a neighbor's home and profit from the indemnity provided by the property insurance coverage.

    D. The courts recognize that people have a sentimental attachment to family heirlooms and permit insurance coverage in excess of the person's actual financial interest in the property.

For practice answering case questions related to Topic 22, please answer the following questions in the cases included in Appendix A at the back of this textbook.

Case	Questions
Black Hills P&L	1
Brodinski	
Haurilick	
Beals	1
Mocsin	
Loudon	
Connor	1 and 2
Seidelhofer	1, 2, and 3
Loomis Company	
Michael and Diana Eastman	
Gary and Judy Parker	1, 2, 3, 4, and 5

ANSWERS AND EXPLANATIONS

1. D is the answer. A is not always definite and measurable or completely accidental for the insured. B and C present severe catastrophe potentials. E is not always accidental and presents possible catastrophic losses for an insurer.

2. C is the answer. (4) is incorrect because insurance deals with an existing risk of loss, rather than creating a risk of loss.

3. C is the answer, by definition. Snow and ice on the walk is a hazard because it increases the probability of an occurrence of a loss. A snow storm is a peril because it is a loss-producing agent. Stepping on the walk is a risk because risk is the possibility of loss. Subrogation is the right of the insurance company after it pays an insured the amount of a loss to collect from a third party that caused it. If the insured's house caught on fire while the neighbor was burning leaves, the insurance company will pay the insured for the loss and then sue the neighbor under the right of subrogation to recover the amount it paid the insured.

4. E is the answer. Insurance works best for exposures that represent low loss frequency and high loss severity, as in E. A represents high loss frequency and high loss severity. B and C represent moderate loss frequency and low loss severity. D represents high loss frequency and low loss severity.

5. A is the answer. (2) is not designed to place the individual in about the same financial condition as he or she was in prior to the loss since pain and suffering are not financial losses. (3) is not correct because the face amount may have little relationship to the size of the loss incurred by the beneficiary due to the insured's death.

6. E is the answer. An insurable interest is present when the individual stands to lose, usually financially, by the occurrence of a peril. In A, the loss might be reduced earnings of the firm. In B, it is the reduction in the value of the contents. In C, the potential loss might be from liability for negligence.

7. B is the answer, by definition. It refers to the right of the insurer to take over Jack's right of action against the neighbor who caused the loss to Jack and, therefore, to Jack's insurer.

8. C is the answer. A and D are examples of loss reduction. B is an example of avoidance. E is an example of partial retention, together with insurance.

9. A is the answer. Adverse selection is present in all lines of insurance. Underwriting attempts to minimize it so that the rates established by the actuarial department for the coverage will be adequate. Part of the underwriting process may be to limit the amount of coverage or to reject some applicants whose loss exposures are excessive.

10. B is the answer. The fact that Charlie did not have an insurable interest at the time of the loss will not preclude him from recovering the death proceeds.

11. D is the answer. The property loss exposure is low because the car is only worth $1,000, so this exposure should be retained. The insurance is not worth the premium expenditure. The liability exposure can be enormous, so insurance is appropriate to transfer the potential financial responsibility.

12. B is the answer. When life insurance is sold, the agent can take a check for the first premium and issue a conditional receipt. This receipt provides temporary coverage but does not constitute the insurance company's acceptance of the application. The insurer accepts the applicant's offer to enter into a contract by issuing the policy. The delivery of the contract, therefore, is the coverage requested and not temporary coverage. The initial premium is paid by the applicant so it does not signify temporary coverage by the insurer. A check is evidence of consideration but it does not provide any temporary coverage. The conditional receipt provides the temporary coverage.

13. D is the answer. The insurance company agent and the independent agent represent the insurance company and owe a duty of loyalty to the insurance company, not to the insured. An insurance broker represents the insured and owes a duty of loyalty to the insured.

14. A is the answer. Insurable interest must exist at the time of the loss in property-liability insurance, but only at the time of issuance for a life insurance contract.

15. A is the answer. (3) is incorrect. The broker represents the applicant/insured for most purposes and so is not able to bind the insurer.

16. D is the answer. D is not one of the steps in the process of achieving an entity's risk management goals because insurance generally is not appropriate for speculative risks. A, B, C, and E are all among the steps.

17. 1-C, 2-E, 3-D, 4-B, 5-A, all by definition.

18. C is the answer. A peril is a cause of loss. The collision in C is actually the only cause of loss in the four situations. All of the other three are hazards.

19. B is the answer. B is not a correct statement because the higher the probability of loss, the more appropriate is retention and budgeting or perhaps avoidance if the loss is both high frequency and high severity. If the probability of loss is high, the purchase of insurance would be too much a case of exchanging premium dollars for loss dollars with the insurance company. This is why normal, predictable wear and tear is not an appropriate exposure to be insured.

20. D is the answer. Losses that are low in severity usually do not need to be covered by insurance. High-severity, low-frequency losses are most suitable for the insurance technique.

21. B is the answer. (1) is not a correct statement. The larger (not smaller) the number of units exposed to the peril of fire, the more predictable will be future fire losses. (2) and (3) are both correct statements. They are both requirements for an exposure to loss (risk) to be commercially insurable. (4) is not correct. (4) is a nonsense statement.

22. C is the answer. Wearing out of the tires is an expected loss, not an accidental one. (A sudden blowout of a tire, however, would be accidental for her.) A, B, and D are all accidental as far as she is concerned, even though the losses in B and D arose from someone else's deliberate action.

23. C is the answer. (1), (2), and (3) are correct statements. (4) is not a correct statement because definiteness of time and occurrence and amount of loss is designed to reduce the <u>moral</u> hazard, <u>not</u> the <u>morale</u> hazard.

24. E is the answer. All three statements are correct. (3) is correct even though there is a conflict of interest on the part of the agents and brokers. Despite the conflict of interest, agents and brokers can be helpful by providing a preliminary screening of applicants.

25. B is the answer. Subcontracting transfers the risk to someone else. This is not avoidance. Avoidance means the entity exposed to the loss gets rid of the exposure, but not by passing the exposure on to someone else. A, C, and D are correct statements. C is correct because the entity can take steps to improve both loss prevention and loss reduction, whether the exposure to loss is retained or insured. D is correct because the larger the number of exposure units, the more predictable are future losses (the law of large numbers).

26. E is the answer. All three of the items are alternative methods of handling risk of loss.

27. C is the answer. The purchase of adequate automobile and homeowners insurance is the most practical method for the Public family to use to handle these two exposures to loss.

28. B is the answer. The law of large numbers is important to the sound operation of insurance because loss data must be obtained for a large number of exposure units to make loss prediction accurate and reliable. Second, a large number of exposure units must be insured in order to have actual losses approximately equal the predicted or probable losses.

29. A is the answer. Not only must there be mass and homogeneity in the statistical group, there must also be mass and homogeneity in the insured group. Therefore, (2) is incorrect.

30. E is the answer. The law of large numbers depends on a large number of exposure units because the larger the number of exposure units from which loss experience data is gathered, the more accurate will be the predictability of future losses. The larger the number of exposure units insured, the closer actual losses will be to predicted losses. With a larger number of exposure units, it is the losses and not the hazards and perils involved in future losses that will become more predictable.

31. D is the answer. Adverse selection is a tendency for those most likely to have losses to want to obtain and retain insurance to cover those losses. Neither of these cases reflects that tendency.

32. B is the answer. (3) is not a correct statement. Insurance is generally not appropriate for high-frequency and low-severity type losses. This would mean exchanging dollar losses each year with the insurance company, plus an additional percentage for administration expenses. Retention and proper budgeting are appropriate for such losses.

33. B is the answer. (3) is not necessary. A written property insurance policy need not be provided for the applicant. An oral contract may be arranged between the parties. In fact, an oral binder (although temporary) is the equivalent of a contract in property and liability insurance. (1), (2), and (4) must all be present in order to have an insurance contract come into existence.

34. D is the answer. The provisions and stipulations in the policy are the consideration given by the insurer. The consideration given by the insured is the premium paid plus the statements in the application.

35. E is the answer. All three statements are correct.

36. C is the answer. A is not a correct statement because a life insurance policy is not a contract of indemnity. The face amount of the policy may be considerably less than the financial loss that occurs when a person dies. A 30-year-old person has substantially greater value to the family or business firm than the typical 90-year-old, but both lives may be insured for $100,000. B is not correct because the two property insurance companies would share the financial loss. The principle of indemnity requires that the insured be paid the amount of the financial loss, not more, not less. D is not correct because the representations of the insured-applicant have nothing to do with the principle of indemnity. The principle of indemnity is accurately summarized by C.

37. C is the answer. The use of valued policies could result in either over-indemnity or under-indemnity. A valued policy means the insurer and the insured agree on the value of the property item at the time the policy is issued. The value of the item may increase or decrease after the policy is issued. Also, a life insurance policy is a valued contract. The life insurance policy is not a contract of indemnity. The life insured may be worth more or less than the face of the policy. A, B, and D function to help preserve the principle of indemnity – to assure reimbursement for the insured equal to the amount of the loss, no more and no less.

38. E is the answer. All three statements are correct.

39. D is the answer. D is a correct statement, but A, B, and C are not correct statements. An insurance policy is a unilateral contract, not bilateral. Only the insurance company makes a binding promise. The insured makes no binding promises. The insurer promises to indemnify the insured in case a covered loss does occur. This promise is legally binding before any loss occurs. The property insurance policy really is insuring the person (the insured) and not the property. It is the insured that is made financially whole after a covered loss occurs.

40. B is the answer. By definition, an aleatory contract is one in which one party may (but not necessarily will) receive benefits greatly in excess of the benefits received by the other party. In an insurance contract, the insured may receive $100,000 in benefits, yet pay only a $1,000 premium.

41. D is the answer. (1) is not a correct statement because the applicant-insured usually must accept the insurance policy as it is written. There is no opportunity for the applicant-insured to change policy provisions. Some large corporate buyers of insurance are permitted to tailor-make their policies – but not the usual homeowner. (2) and (3) are correct statements.

42. A is the answer. B is an incorrect statement because the insured may only receive the dollar value of his or her insurable interest. Otherwise, the insured is gambling by purchasing insurance. This is against public policy. C is an incorrect statement because the insured also would be using insurance for gambling purposes. D is not a correct statement. The courts do not permit the purchase of property insurance to insure sentimental values. Only the property's ACV or its replacement cost is insurable.

Analysis and Evaluation of Risk Exposures (Topic 23)

CFP Board Student-Centered Learning Objectives

(a) Identify and measure liability, automobile, homeowner's, flood, earthquake, health, disability, long-term care, and life risks.

(b) Explain maximum possible and maximum probable loss amount to a client.

Analysis and Evaluation of Risk Exposures
    A. Identifying, analyzing, and evaluating risk exposures......................23.1
    B. Maximum possible and maximum probable loss 23.2
    C   Personal risk exposures 23.3
        1. Death...23.3
        2. Disability..23.3
        3. Poor health...23.3
        4. Unemployment 23.4
        5. Superannuation (retirement)..23.4
    D. Property risk exposures 23.4
    E. Liability risk exposures...23.5
        1. Negligence...23.5
        2. Intentional torts...23.6
        3. Strict liability 23.6
    F. Definitions..23.7

Identifying, Analyzing, and Evaluating Risk Exposures

As described in Topic 22, the second step of the risk process requires the planner and client to work together to identify loss exposures; then, in the third step, the planner will analyze and evaluate those loss exposures. This third step also requires the planner to evaluate the risk management techniques available to deal effectively and efficiently with each loss exposure.

To ensure that no loss exposures are overlooked, it is helpful to develop a systematic approach to identifying them. One common approach used in risk management planning for individuals and families is to look at several categories of loss exposures and determine which are present in each client's situation.

The principal loss exposures confronting a typical household can be divided into personal, property, and liability exposures. An analysis of loss exposures in each category will identify all possible losses that might occur. Those loss exposures must then be evaluated in terms of maximum *possible* and maximum *probable* losses to determine whether insurance coverage or some other risk management technique is needed to deal with the exposure. Along with the maximum possible and maximum probable analysis, which tends to be rather objective, the planner must also consider the more subjective aspects of exposures, such as the client's level of tolerance for each particular risk (or level of aversion to the risk, as the case may be).

A client's level of risk tolerance will also be a factor in determining the appropriate amount of insurance and the policy deductibles. It is often helpful for clients to view the cost of insurance premiums as a starting point for deciding how best to handle each insurable loss exposure (remember not all risks are insurable). If the premium seems high, the planner and client may want to look for a different alternative.

In cases where insurance already exists, the planner must evaluate the existing coverage to determine whether there are any gaps in coverage that must be closed and whether the existing coverage is working efficiently to accomplish the planning and risk management objectives.

MAXIMUM POSSIBLE AND MAXIMUM PROBABLE LOSS

Identification of risk exposures simply seeks to recognize what is possible. Evaluation of risk exposures requires an additional step: an analysis of what is likely.

The maximum possible loss is the worst that *could* happen, while the maximum probable loss is the worst that is *likely* to happen. Maximum possible loss is typically estimated for property loss exposures rather than liability loss exposures because property values and exposures can generally be estimated with greater accuracy. Liability loss exposures tend to be more unpredictable. The maximum possible loss is usually estimated for each separate location and for each peril. For example, a planner will want to estimate the maximum possible loss for fire at the client's home and then separately for any vacation home or business location. The planner might then estimate the maximum possible loss for windstorm or theft at the same locations.

> *"When you have exhausted all possibilities, remember this: you haven't."*
> **Thomas Edison**

The maximum probable loss is often much less than the maximum possible loss. The maximum possible loss from windstorm may be a total loss of the building and contents, but the maximum probable loss may be significantly less due to improved construction techniques or early warning devices. Maximum probable loss from fire might be reduced by fire alarms, sprinkler system, or proximity to a fire station. Maximum probable loss from theft might be reduced by a burglar alarm, safe, or video cameras.

In some cases, the maximum possible loss may be so extremely unlikely to occur that it is not worth spending the extra premium dollars to cover it. Part of the risk management process will be to weed out the extremely unlikely losses and to concentrate on those that are more probable. For example, a client who lives in the mountains may consider the possibility of flood losses to be so unlikely as not to be worth coverage. A client who lives in a flood plain or near a river will likely have a different evaluation of this risk.

Class Exercise 23 – 1

In this role-play exercise, students will practice explaining the risk management process, including a description of maximum possible and maximum probable loss to a client. Other students in the class will be asked to evaluate. A sample evaluation form is provided on Keir's instructor web site.

PERSONAL RISK EXPOSURES

Personal loss exposures include loss of income and/or loss of accumulated assets due to death, disability, poor health, unemployment, or old age.

- For death, the personal exposure includes illness costs, funeral costs, estate administration costs, state death taxes, federal estate taxes, desired gifts and bequests, and the economic value of the human life, meaning the present value of the lost income for the support of the surviving spouse, dependent children, and others.

- For disability, losses include medical care costs, long-term care costs, costs of needed services, and lost income.

- For poor health, the risk is that an individual will require medical care costs and other services and will sustain a loss of income due to inability to work.

- For unemployment, there is lost income and extra costs of obtaining new employment.

- For old age (superannuation), the personal exposure is lost income and extra expenses of a retirement lifestyle or health care.

One measure of the risk exposure from death is the mortality rate. *Mortality* rates or death rates rise as age increases, so a life insurer's claims costs will increase for older insured groups. In the absence of a leveling technique, premium costs for individuals will rise as the insured group grows older.

A measure of the risk exposure from disability is the *morbidity* rate, or rate of disability. Morbidity rates have a tendency to rise as age rises, though not in a steady progression from age to age as do mortality rates. Morbidity rates have only a minor impact on life insurance costs, affecting only such supplementary coverage as waiver-of-premium and accidental death and dismemberment benefits.

PROPERTY RISK EXPOSURES

Property loss exposures involve reduction in value, extra costs to replace, perhaps lost income, and perhaps costs associated with loss of use.

Consider such properties as the following:

- Dwelling and its contents
- Other structures on the premises
- Real and personal property (personal property is property that is not real estate) off premises
- Intangible property, such as contract rights, intellectual assets, good will
- Property held as a bailee, e.g., golf clubs stored in the garage for a friend
- Autos, boats, planes, recreational vehicles, high-value items

In many cases, the client will already have some form of property insurance and the planner must start by reviewing existing insurance coverage. The planner will need to determine that the policy provides coverage for the important exposures previously identified. Details regarding analysis of homeowners, auto, liability, and business insurance will be provided later in this topic.

> *"Risk is trying to control something you are powerless over."*
> **Eric Clapton**

LIABILITY RISK EXPOSURES

Liability loss exposures arise from activities that can give rise to lawsuits, damage awards (monetary, specific performance, injunction), fines, costs of defense, and court costs. Liability can arise from a wide range of activities including the following:

- Owning, renting, or taking custody of property
- Owning, using, or maintaining autos, recreational vehicles, boats
- Employing domestics
- Engaging in business activities
- Engaging in hobbies
- Keeping pets
- Serving alcohol
- Caring for children of others
- Committing intentional torts (libel, slander, trespass, invasion of privacy, etc.)

As can be seen from the list above, clients are very likely to have exposure to liability losses. Careful evaluation of these liability loss exposures is an important part of financial planning since liability damage awards can be very high dollar amounts. While clients may feel that the probability of a claim is negligible, the low cost of insurance versus the high potential cost of a liability claim makes umbrella liability insurance an extremely attractive risk management tool.

When analyzing and discussing liability loss exposures, a planner will need to have a basic understanding of liability concepts, such as negligence, intentional torts, and strict liability. Liability is imposed on persons who cause losses due to their negligence or intentional torts or as a result of engaging in activities that carry strict liability.

Negligence

Negligence is failure to exercise ordinary care. Ordinary care is the degree of care that a reasonable man of ordinary prudence would exercise in the same or similar circumstances. This standard of care is established to protect others from unreasonable risk of harm.

In order to prove liability for the tort of negligence, four elements are required: (1) a duty that is owed, (2) a breach of the duty, (3) injury or damage occurring as a result of the breach, and (4) the breach is the proximate cause of the harm.

Example:

Russell backed out of his driveway without looking and backed into an oncoming car. Russell will face liability for negligence because the four elements of the tort of negligence can be shown: (1) he had a duty to exercise ordinary care in backing out of his driveway, (2) he failed to exercise ordinary care in that he failed to look while backing out, (3) he caused damage to the car owned by the other driver, and (4) his failure to look was the proximate cause of the accident and damages.

Intentional Torts

Intentional torts are wrongful actions performed intentionally and causing injuries or damages. These torts generally fall into three categories: (1) interference with personal rights, (2) interference with property rights, and (3) business torts. Assault and battery, invasion of privacy, false imprisonment, libel, and slander are examples of intentional torts that interfere with personal rights. Trespass, conversion, and nuisance are examples of intentional torts that interfere with property rights. Unfair competition and fraud are examples of business torts.

Strict Liability

Strict liability is liability imposed without regard to fault. Even though a person intended no harm and was not negligent, he can be held liable for certain torts. Strict liability applies most often to products that are unreasonably dangerous to users. For example, even though a company designed and manufactured a car without negligence, the company will be responsible to owners who are injured because the car is unreasonably dangerous and catches on fire in an accident.

Strict liability is often treated as equivalent to absolute liability. Absolute liability applies to the keeping of wild animals and to ultra-hazardous activities such as blasting, crop spraying, and holding water in a reservoir or irrigation pond. The high risk of harm to others requires that the person engaging in the activity be absolutely liable for any injuries.

An employer's liability for workers' compensation benefits is also essentially without regard to fault and treated under principles of strict liability. The employer is required to pay lost wages and medical and rehabilitation expenses to injured workers for injuries and diseases related to employment.

DEFINITIONS

Bailee – A bailee is a person who is entrusted with possession of personal property for a particular purpose and on the understanding that the property will be returned to its owner. For example, a customer brings clothes to the laundry and leaves the clothes with the laundry owner for cleaning. There is an implied understanding that the clothes still belong to the owner and will be returned to him. The laundry is the bailee of the clothes, and the owner is the bailor.

APPLICATION QUESTIONS

1. Carl is a 40-year-old highly successful surgeon with a wife and two children. Carl and his family live in a beautiful home in an exclusive neighborhood, and he and his wife each drive Jaguar convertibles. Carl owns a high-powered speedboat and flies his own private plane. He is also the sole source of support for his aged mother. Which of the following are the two largest loss exposures confronting Carl and the family.

(1) Lost income due to Carl's death
(2) Loss of the plane due to a tornado
(3) Loss of the home in a fire
(4) Liability arising out of Carl's profession and the use of the cars, boat, or plane
(5) Long-term care costs for Carl's mother

    A. (1) and (4) only
    B. (1) and (5) only
    C. (2) and (3) only
    D. (2) and (5) only
    E. (3) and (4) only

2. Terry rents a room in her house to a college student. In the event that the house is seriously damaged by a fire or other peril, which of the following losses, in addition to the actual cash value of the damaged home, is Terry likely to encounter?

(1) Lost income
(2) Extra living costs
(3) Extra costs to replace the damaged property

    A. (1) only
    B. (2) only
    C. (3) only
    D. (1) and (3) only
    E. (1), (2), and (3)

3. Sam bought a house on an acre of land and paid the seller $200,000. The house has a garage, and Sam parks his Ford truck in the garage. The truck has a market value of $15,000. Sam's wife keeps her jewelry at the house, and the jewelry is worth $20,000. Which of the following statements concerning the maximum possible loss for Sam at his house is correct?

A. The maximum possible loss for fire will include the house but not the Ford truck.
B. The maximum possible loss for theft will include the jewelry and the house.
C. The maximum possible loss for windstorm will include the truck but not the jewelry.
D. The maximum possible loss for flood will include the truck and the jewelry.

4. Which of the following statements concerning maximum possible loss and maximum probable loss is correct?

A. Maximum possible loss for fire will be reduced by fire alarms.
B. Maximum probable loss for theft will be reduced by video cameras.
C. Maximum possible loss for flood will be increased by removing a levee at the river.
D. Maximum probable loss for windstorm will be increased by use of improved construction techniques.

5. Which of the following is a personal risk exposure?

A. Unemployment
B. Owning and using an auto
C. Negligence
D. Renting an apartment

6. Which of the following is a liability risk exposure?

A. Superannuation
B. Slander
C. Poor health
D. Costs to replace real estate

7. Which of the following is generally the most attractive risk management tool to recommend to clients for dealing with liability risk exposures?

    A. Umbrella policy
    B. Health policy
    C. Disability policy
    D. Workers' compensation policy

8. The legal principles of strict liability apply to which of the following?

    A. Intentional torts
    B. Intangible property
    C. Workers' compensation
    D. Unfair competition

9. Which of the following are intentional torts?

    (1) Invasion of privacy
    (2) Negligence
    (3) False imprisonment
    (4) Libel and slander

        A. (1) and (2) only
        B. (2) and (3) only
        C. (1), (3), and (4) only
        D. (1), (2), (3), and (4)

10. Which of the following is (are) among the causes of or sources of legal liability?

    (1) Absolute liability
    (2) Intentional tort
    (3) Negligence

        A. (3) only
        B. (1) and (2) only
        C. (1) and (3) only
        D. (2) and (3) only
        E. (1), (2), and (3)

11. All the following statements concerning the elements that must be proven to establish tort liability for negligence are correct, EXCEPT:

A. There is a duty owed the plaintiff.
B. There is a failure to act in accordance with the duty owed.
C. Damage or loss occurs.
D. The damage or loss must be significant (usually interpreted to mean in excess of $1,000).
E. The damage or loss results from the breach of the duty owed.

For practice answering case questions related to Topic 23, please answer the following questions in the cases included in Appendix A at the back of this textbook.

Case	Questions
Black Hills P&L	
Brodinski	
Haurilick	
Beals	
Mocsin	
Loudon	
Connor	3 and 4
Seidelhofer	4 and 5
Loomis Company	
Michael and Diana Eastman	
Gary and Judy Parker	6, 7, 8, 9, and 10

ANSWERS AND EXPLANATIONS

1. A is the answer. Carl's largest single monetary "asset" is his ability to earn a significant income for his family over the next 20 or more years. This far exceeds the value of his home, boat, plane, cars, or other tangible property. It even exceeds the high cost of long-term care for his aged mother. The other, and perhaps even greater, loss exposure Carl faces is legal liability, which is of virtually unlimited magnitude. A judgment against him for negligence could cost him most of his accumulated assets and much of his future income.

2. E is the answer. Terry is likely to lose the rental income from the student and to incur extra costs for alternate housing and restaurant meals. Also, the replacement cost is likely to exceed the ACV of some of the damaged property.

3. D is the answer. The maximum possible loss is the worst that can happen. In this question, the losses are for items of property. A fire could destroy the house, truck, and jewelry, so that they would be a total loss. A flood or windstorm could also destroy all of these items. The peril of theft can cause loss of the jewelry and truck but not the house.

4. B is the answer. Maximum possible loss is the worst that can happen, but the maximum probable loss is the worst that is likely to happen. The use of anti-theft devices, alarms, and video cameras can reduce the amount of the damage and loss that occurs from theft, so that the maximum probable loss from theft is reduced. Fire alarms and other warning devises can reduce loss from fire and reduce the maximum probable loss but not the maximum possible loss. Removing a levee may increase the probability of flood damage, but the maximum possible loss from flood will still be the same. Improved construction techniques can reduce maximum probable loss from the peril of windstorm.

5. A is the answer. Personal risk exposures include death, disability, poor health, and unemployment. Property risk exposures include the ownership or possession of a dwelling and its contents, real and personal property, intangible property, cars, boats, planes, and other valuable items. Liability loss exposures arise from activities that can give rise to lawsuits and damage awards due to negligence, intentional torts, or strict liability.

6. B is the answer. Liability arises from actions or activities in which there is a loss resulting from negligence, intentional torts, or strict liability. Torts can involve interference with personal rights or property rights. Slander is an intentional tort involving interference with personal rights. Thus, slander is an example of a liability risk exposure. Superannuation is loss of income due to an individual growing old and losing the ability to perform in employment. It is a personal risk exposure. Poor health is also a personal risk exposure. Costs to replace real estate are a property risk exposure.

7. A is the answer. An umbrella insurance policy provides liability coverage that is generally in addition to the coverage provided in other insurance, such as homeowners or car insurance. It provides additional liability coverage with high limits such as $1 or $2 million and is relatively inexpensive. The low cost and high limits of coverage make umbrella coverage a very attractive risk management tool. Health and disability insurance do not provide liability coverage. Workers' compensation insurance is of more limited value since it is for business owners who have employees.

8. C is the answer. The principles of strict liability apply to workers' compensation benefits because workers are entitled to benefits without regard to fault of the employer or employees. The employer must pay lost wages and medical and rehabilitation expenses to injured workers. Strict liability does not apply to intangible property which is property such as good will, contract rights, and intellectual assets. Unfair competition is an intentional tort and is not governed by principles of strict liability.

9. C is the answer. (2) is not an intentional tort. (1), (3), and (4) are all intentional torts.

10. E is the answer. All three items are torts that can be sources of legal liability.

11. D is the answer. D is an incorrect statement. The damage or loss does not have to exceed $1,000. A, B, C, and E are all valid elements that must be proven in order to establish tort liability for a negligent act.

Health Insurance and Health Care Cost Management (Individual)
(Topic 24)

CFP Board Student-Centered Learning Objectives

(a) Compare and contrast group and individual health insurance alternatives, including fee for service and managed care health plans.

(b) Incorporate expected retiree health costs in a client's retirement plan, in consideration of household financial resources, existing or future coverage under group insurance plans, and Medicare.

(c) Explain alternatives for acquiring health coverage including COBRA and Medicaid.

A. **Health Insurance and Health Care Cost Management**	**24.3**
B. **Health Insurance Policy Types**	**24.3**
1. *Hospital, surgical, and physicians' expense insurance*	24.4
2. *Major medical insurance*	24.5
a. *Internal limits*	24.5
b. *Deductibles*	24.5
c. *Aggregate deductible*	24.6
d. *Coinsurance*	24.6
e. *Cap on insured's payments*	24.6
3. *Comprehensive major medical policy*	24.7
a. *Exclusions*	24.8
1.) *Affordable Care Act Impact on Coverage and Exclusions*	24.9
4. *Comparison of policies*	24.9
a. *Control of utilization and costs*	24.10
C. **Managed Care Plans**	**24.10**
1. *Managed care plans*	24.10
2. *Health maintenance organizations (HMOs)*	24.11
3. *Preferred provider organizations (PPOs)*	24.12
4. *Point-of-service (POS) plans*	24.13
D. **Health Savings Accounts**	**24.13**
1. *Health Savings Accounts (HSAs)*	24.13
2. *Rules for Health Savings Accounts (HSAs)*	24.13
3. *Archer Medical Savings accounts (MSAs)*	24.15
4. *Health reimbursement arrangements (HRAs)*	24.16
E. **Health Insurance for Seniors**	**24.16**
1. *Medicare*	24.16
a. *The Medicare program*	24.17
b. *Funding Medicare*	24.17
c. *Eligibility*	24.18

        d. Traditional Medicare – Parts A and B 24.21
            1.) Out-of-pocket costs for Medicare Parts A and B.............24.22
        e. Medicare Part C – Medicare Advantage.............................24.23
        f. Medicare Part D – prescription drug benefits.......................24.24
        g. Taxation of Medicare premiums and benefits.......................24.24
    2. Medigap coverage...24.25

F. Medicaid **24.27**
    1. Transfers to reduce assets..24.28
    2. Long-Term Care Insurance Partnership Program......................24.28

G. Taxation of Premiums and Benefits for Individual Health
**   Insurance Policies**...**24.29**
    1. Taxation of premiums and benefits for individuals and
       self-employed individuals..24.29
    2. Additional Medicare tax and Medicare tax on investment income...24.30

H. Health Care Reform...**24.30**
    1. 2010 health care reform...24.30
    2. ACA minimum essential coverage for individuals 24.32
    3. The Health Insurance Marketplace 24.33
        a. Premium tax credits..24.33
        b. Open Enrollment...24.34
        c. Comparing policies in the Marketplace...............................24.35
    4. Marketplace or non-marketplace?...24.35
    5. Embedded versus non-embedded deductible 24.36
        a. Embedded deductible..24.37
        b. Non-embedded deductible..24.38
    6. Embedded versus non-embedded MOOP 24.40

I. Group Medical as an employee benefit...............................**24.45**
    1. Employee benefit analysis...24.45
    2. Group medical insurance policy types....................................24.45
        a. Traditional indemnity (fee-for-service).............................24.45
        b. Managed care 24.45
        c. Consumer-directed health plans.......................................24.45
    3. The mechanics of group health insurance 24.46
        a. Coordination of benefits 24.47
        b. Regulation of employer-provided health insurance................24.49
             1.) Self-funded plans...24.49
             2.) Summary Plan Descriptions and
                Summary of Benefits and Coverage.................................24.50
             3.) Mental Health Parity 24.51
             4.) Family Medical Leave Act (FMLA) 24.51
        c. Tax advantages of employer-provided health plans................24.52
    4. Health Care Reform and employer-provided coverage................24.53
        a. Upcoming changes...24.55
             1.) Employer shared responsibility 24.55
             2.) Small employers...24.56

J. **COBRA and HIPAA** *24.58*
    1. Continuance and convertibility *24.58*
    2. COBRA *24.58*
    3. HIPAA *24.61*
    4. Continuation *24.62*
K. **Other Employee Benefits** *24.62*
    1. Cafeteria Plans *24.62*
    2. Flexible spending accounts (FSAs) *24.63*
    3. Voluntary employees' beneficiary associations (VEBAs) *24.64*
    4. Dental insurance *24.65*
    5. Vision insurance *24.66*
L. **Planning for Health Care Costs in Retirement** *24.66*
    1. Planning for health care costs in retirement *24.66*
        a. Assumptions *24.68*
M. **Definitions** *24.69*

HEALTH INSURANCE AND HEALTH CARE COST MANAGEMENT

For individuals and families, poor health presents a substantial risk of catastrophic losses. Most financial planning clients will deal with this risk by employing a combination of risk management techniques, including risk reduction (for example, regular exercise or a healthy diet), risk transfer (for example, medical insurance), and risk retention (for example, the deductible in the health insurance policy). The annual and lifetime cost of health care, including insurance premiums, deductibles, coinsurance amounts, and items not covered by insurance, can take a significant portion of a family's budget, especially during the retirement years.

In order to analyze and evaluate individual health care coverage, planners will need to have an understanding of the various types of policies and the potential out-of-pocket costs. The planner will also need to be able to advise clients regarding gaps in coverage and ways to obtain the most appropriate coverage at an affordable cost.

HEALTH INSURANCE POLICY TYPES

Medical expense coverage is provided by several different types of organizations. We will begin with the main coverages provided by commercial insurance companies and Blue Cross and Blue Shield plans. The four basic types of coverage are hospitalization insurance, surgical expense coverage, physician's expense coverage, and major medical coverage.

Hospital, Surgical, and Physicians' Expense Insurance

A basic hospital, surgical, and physicians' expense policy provides benefits as described below:

Hospital expense coverage pays primarily for room and board in a hospital. Up to a fixed amount per day is paid while the person is hospitalized, along with certain miscellaneous expenses incurred while in the hospital (for example, X-rays, lab tests, and medicines). General nursing care is also covered. There is usually a limit on the number of days of coverage for each hospital stay. There may also be internal limits for some benefits, such as a maximum number of convalescent care days, a maximum number of X-rays per claim, or a maximum dollar amount for maternity benefits. When written by Blue Cross, hospital service benefit contracts provide service, not cash, to the insured. The service typically takes the form of up to a specified number of days of care in a semiprivate room plus all other necessary services provided by the hospital. Blue Cross pays the hospital under a contract, and the hospital agrees to accept the contract amount as the full charge for the care it provides.

Surgical expense coverage pays according to a schedule that lists covered surgical procedures and the amount that will be paid for each procedure. Some policies pay the full fee of the surgeon, up to the level of the UCR (usual, customary, and reasonable) charges, which are the amounts billed by surgeons for the same procedure in the same geographic area. In Blue Shield plans, the surgeon's services are provided to the insured, much as hospital services are provided under Blue Cross plans.

Physicians' nonsurgical coverage pays mainly the doctor's charges when the person is being treated in a hospital or in the doctor's office. There are limits on the amount payable per doctor visit or per day, and sometimes, there is a limit on the number of visits per period of illness that will be covered by the policy. Blue Shield provides similar coverage, also on a service basis, not a cash basis.

Major Medical Insurance

A major medical expense policy may be written by a commercial insurer or by the Blues, and provides broad coverage of almost all types of medical expenses, whether incurred in or outside a hospital. Prior to the 2010 Health Care Reform, these policies were designed for catastrophic medical care costs and, therefore, had a high limit of liability, such as $1 million per illness or per lifetime. As of September 23, 2010, new health insurance plans and plans renewed after this date may no longer include annual or lifetime limits.

"Supplementary" major medical coverage is superimposed on a basic hospital-surgical-medical plan while "comprehensive" major medical coverage is a stand-alone plan.

The major medical policy has few exclusions, but does have a number of policy features that will impact the potential out-of-pocket expenses a client may need to cover when an injury or illness occurs. These features include internal limits, deductibles, coinsurance amounts, and stop-loss limitations.

Internal Limits

Some major medical policies contain a cost-sharing provision called an internal limit. An internal limit specifies the maximum amount of certain expenditures that the insurer will pay. It sets a limit on a specific coverage. For example, the insurer may set an internal limit of $500 on the amount it will pay per day for hospital room-and-board charges or for such charges in an intensive care unit of a hospital.

Deductibles

Major medical policies will have an initial deductible, perhaps $500, $1,000, or even $2,000 per illness, accident, or calendar year and per person or per family. This deductible requires the insured to bear the first set of covered charges before the insurance company is liable for any benefit payments. The reason for a deductible is to hold down premium costs by eliminating small claims and the expenses associated with them.

A "corridor" deductible may be used when a supplemental major medical plan has been added to a basic medical expense plan. The corridor deductible will apply after the basic plan's benefits are exhausted and before the supplemental major medical plan's benefits are available. For example, suppose the insured had a basic medical expense policy with a $20,000 limit and a supplemental major medical policy with a $300 corridor deductible. If the insured had $25,000 of medical bills, the basic medical expense policy would pay $20,000, and the remaining $5,000 of expenses would be paid by the supplemental major medical policy after subtracting the $300 corridor deductible.

Aggregate Deductible

In some medical expense policies, an aggregate deductible limits the maximum of a series of deductibles that will be applied during a specified period. For example, a medical expense policy may have a $500 deductible per family member per year, not to exceed $1,000 in the aggregate for the family during the year. If each member of the family incurs over $500 of medical expenses, the family will be required to pay only the $1,000 aggregate deductible amount, and the insurer will pay the remaining expenses.

Coinsurance

Another type of cost-sharing provision is the coinsurance provision found in virtually all major medical policies. This provision specifies that the insurance company will be responsible for only a specified percentage, such as 80%, of covered medical expenses in excess of the deductible. The other 20% must be borne by the insured. The amount borne by the insured may be referred to as a percentage participation.

Cap on Insured's Payments

One other provision that is noteworthy is the provision found in many major medical policies that places a cap on the amount that the insured will be called upon to pay during any one illness or, perhaps, during any one calendar year. In some policies, the cap is the maximum amount of medical expenses to which the coinsurance clause will be applied. Some policies allow the deductible to be included in the cap, but other policies do not. The cap on an insured's payments may also be called a stop-loss or an out-of-pocket maximum. Each policy must be examined carefully to understand how the maximum is computed.

Exhibit 24 – 1, below, shows the allocation of medical expenses under a typical major medical expense policy in which there is a deductible, an 80% coinsurance provision, and a cap that limits the out-of-pocket expenses of the insured.

EXHIBIT 24 – 1
Who Pays Medical Costs with Supplemental Major Medical Expense Coverage

← Deductible →	← Coinsurance → 80%/20%	← Beyond cap or → stop-loss
Insured pays 100%	Insured pays 20%	Insured pays 0%

Practice Question

The Marconi family has a major medical expense policy covering all members of the family – Allen, June, and their son David. The plan has a per person $500 calendar year deductible, and the insurer will pay 80% of the next $5,000 per person, then 100% of additional medical expenses. During the year, the family had the following medical expenses:

    Allen $7,000
    June $8,000
    David $6,000

What will the insurer pay under the policy?

    A. $16,500
    B. $18,500
    C. $19,500
    D. $20,500

Answer:
The Marconi family must pay three deductibles of $500 and three coinsurance amounts of 20% x $5,000 = $1,000. The Marconis pay $1,500 + $3,000 = $4,500, so the insurer will pay $16,500.
The answer is A.

Class Discussion 24 – 1

Having a good understanding of policy features, benefits, and cost-sharing provisions allows the planner to analyze the potential out-of-pocket costs the client may need to cover.

As a group, discuss how to determine the minimum amount of emergency funds a client should have to cover health care costs if his or her major medical policy has a $1,000 deductible, 80/20 coinsurance, and stop-loss limit of $5,000.

Comprehensive Major Medical Policy

A comprehensive major medical policy combines, in one policy, the features and coverage provisions of a basic policy with a major medical policy. Instead of a large initial deductible, however, the comprehensive policy may have a lower initial deductible, such as $100 or $200 or a similarly sized corridor deductible.

Practice Question

Donna has a comprehensive major medical policy that has a $100 annual deductible and 20% percentage participation. The policy pays 100% after out-of-pocket costs reach $5,000. If Donna incurs bills of $300 for an illness and then $7,000 for an injury, what will the insurer pay?

    A. $3,160
    B. $5,760
    C. $6,160
    D. $7,200

Answer:

The deductible will be subtracted from the first illness, and the insurer will pay 80% of the remaining $200, or $160. Donna will pay $140. The insurer will pay 80% of the $7,000, or $5,600, and Donna will pay $1,400. She has not yet paid $5,000 out-of-pocket, so the insurer still pays 80%. The out-of-pocket provision is different from an 80%/20% coinsurance provision because the deductible is included. The insurer only pays 100% when the insured's total costs have reached $5,000. In this case, the insurer will pay a total of $5,760.
The answer is B.

Exclusions

Some typical exclusions found in medical expense insurance policies include expenses due to the following:

- Intentionally self-inflicted injury
- While outside the U.S. or Canada
- Covered by workers' compensation
- War or any act of war
- Covered by a government agency
- Suicide or attempted suicide, while sane or insane
- Alcoholism or drug addiction (limited benefits are sometimes provided)
- Cosmetic surgery (except when necessitated by injuries)
- Eyeglasses
- Eye refractions
- Dental expenses
- Rest cures
- Active duty in the military
- Hearing aids
- Participating in a riot or rebellion
- Custodial care
- Routine physical examinations

Affordable Care Act Impact on Coverage and Exclusions

As a result of the Affordable Care Act, all qualified health insurance plans must cover the following 10 essential health benefits:

1. Outpatient services, such as doctor visits or tests done outside a hospital
2. Emergency services
3. Hospital stays
4. Pregnancy and baby care
5. Mental health and substance abuse services, including behavioral health treatment
6. Prescription drugs, including generic and certain brand-name drugs
7. Rehab and habilitative services (those that help people recover from an accident or injury and those that help people with developmental issues)
8. Lab tests
9. Preventive and wellness services (along with those that help people manage chronic conditions, including chiropractic care)
10. For children only, dental and vision services

(**Note:** Some health plans were grandfathered when the ACA rules came into effect and may not cover these 10 essential health benefits, so each policy must be examined carefully.)

Comparison of Policies

The appropriate type of medical expense coverage for a client depends on many factors. However, a basic hospital, surgical, and physicians' expense policy has important disadvantages, including low benefit maximums, several separate maximums for separate categories of expenses, and coverage only for hospital confinements. These disadvantages make these policies unattractive for most financial planning clients.

The comprehensive major medical policy as just described is an indemnity policy (also known as a fee-for-service type policy), allowing the insured to choose any doctor or hospital with payment being made according to the cost of services received. Managed care plans, as described below, are designed to reduce health care costs through a variety of methods which may include a focus on preventive care, controls on inpatient admissions and length of stay, or restrictions on which medical services providers the insured may choose. In some cases, managed care plans only include coverage for services received from providers in a limited geographical area. This particular limitation may have a great impact on planning clients who have vacation homes in other states, who frequently visit friends and relatives in other states, or who travel for business or pleasure.

Planners should also note that most policies, whether major medical, managed care, or Medicare, exclude coverage for care received in a foreign country.

Clients planning to travel internationally will need to investigate the purchase of international travel insurance or Medicare Supplement policies that provide coverage in foreign countries.

Control of Utilization and Costs

Because of the high and continuously rising cost of medical care, medical coverage plans are increasingly using several provisions to control utilization and costs. For example:

    (a)   High deductibles and coinsurance requirements

    (b)   Increasing use of coordination of benefits provisions to reduce duplicate coverage of the same expenses, especially when a dependent child is covered under both Dad's group coverage and Mom's group coverage

    (c)   Requiring second opinions before surgery is covered

    (d)   Requiring preadmission certification or permission of the insurer before hospitalization as an inpatient is covered

    (e)   Case management to control medical care costs for the treatment of serious health impairments, such as AIDS, cancer, or heart disease. A long-term program of treatment designed to reduce expenses is authorized by the insurer. Such a program might involve greater use of home care or hospice services instead of a long hospital stay.

These cost control measures should also be taken into consideration when analyzing a policy. While some clients will view these as a fair trade-off for lower premiums or co-pay amounts, other clients may be willing to pay more to retain greater flexibility.

MANAGED CARE PLANS

Managed Care Plans

Managed care plans are health care organizations that emphasize cost control. One method of controlling costs is to promote preventive care. For example, many chronic health conditions, such as diabetes and high blood pressure, can be prevented from getting worse if they are diagnosed and treated early. Another method of controlling costs is to negotiate contracts with health care providers and medical facilities that agree to provide services for a reduced fee.

The principal types of managed care plans are health maintenance organizations (HMOs), preferred provider organizations (PPOs), and point-of-service (POS) plans. The type of managed care plan will determine how care is accessed and received, as well as the amount of out-of-pocket costs for each type of service. Plans with reduced choices typically cost less than plans that offer greater flexibility.

Health Maintenance Organizations (HMOs)

HMOs are organizations of medical care providers that operate under a contract to provide medical care service to members. HMOs can be for-profit or not-for-profit and can be sponsored by insurance companies, the Blues, physicians, hospitals, labor unions, or even consumer groups. HMOs emphasize both cost control and preventive care.

The typical services provided under HMO plans are physician services, outpatient services at a hospital, inpatient health services in a hospital, diagnostic laboratory services, home health services, and perhaps even services for such items as vision care, dental care, and mental health care. The HMO emphasis on preventive medical care typically means full coverage for care such as annual physicals and routine mammography so that illnesses and diseases may be detected and treated early, avoiding higher costs later on. The insured pays a flat monthly fee to the HMO for all covered services from participating physicians and perhaps also a small copayment, such as $15, per visit.

HMOs operate under three basic types of plans. In the staff practice plan, salaried doctors and other medical care professionals are employees located in a common facility owned by the HMO. Insureds under the HMO plan thus go to this facility for their medical care. Under the group practice type of HMO, there is usually one site where all of the medical care providers are located, but this site is owned by the medical care providers, rather than by the HMO. Also, the medical care providers usually are not salaried employees of the HMO. Under the individual practice association type of HMO, individual medical care practitioners are members of the plan and work out of their own offices. They contract with the HMO to serve HMO plan participants, receiving a flat annual fee, called a capitation fee, for agreeing to provide medical service. The flat capitation fee is paid, regardless of the extent or complexity of the service provided to a patient, thus serving to discourage physicians from providing unnecessary medical treatment. Some HMOs combine the features of more than one of these basic types of plans.

One of the most important disadvantages of an HMO is the limited range of choices that the plan participant has as to where he or she may receive medical care. In most circumstances, the hospital or the physician must be a member of the HMO in order for the plan participant to be eligible for medical care from that provider (except for cases of true emergencies). Those insured under an HMO will typically have a "primary care physician" who serves as gatekeeper, authorizing coverage of costs of specialist care when he or she deems it necessary.

Some states have "any willing provider" laws requiring the HMO to allow subscribers to use other providers who, while not under contract with the HMO, are willing to comply with the HMO's standards and to accept its contractual prices for services provided to subscribers.

One of the great advantages of HMOs is that the service provided is broad and deep, and minimal use is made of deductibles and coinsurance provisions.

Preferred Provider Organizations (PPOs)

A preferred provider organization is an association of medical care practitioners that contracts with an insurer or employer to offer medical care services to insureds at discounted prices. The participants are free to use the services of any medical care practitioner, but lower deductibles and lower coinsurance requirements are used to persuade the individual to obtain medical care from members of the PPO. The members of the PPO, in turn, are willing to offer care at a reduced cost to the employer or insurance company, in return for the large volume of business that the sponsoring employer or insurance company will direct to the PPO practitioners.

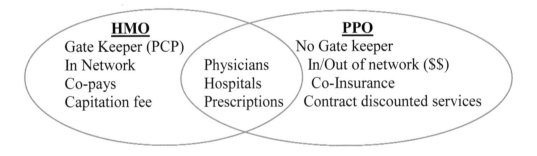

Practice Question

Your client works at a company that gives employees a choice of health care plans between a health maintenance organization (HMO) and a preferred provider organization (PPO). What should you tell the client is the main difference between these two types of plans?

- A. The HMO will be less expensive for the client than the PPO.
- B. The client will generally receive more preventive care with the PPO than with the HMO.
- C. The client's choice of health care providers will generally be more limited with the HMO than with the PPO.
- D. The deductibles and co-pay will generally be lower with the PPO than with the HMO.

Answer:

The HMO will be less expensive than the PPO if the client is able to use the care providers accessible through the HMO, but if the client has to go outside the HMO network for much of his care, the costs could be greater with the HMO. HMOs emphasize preventive care and annual physicals more than do the PPOs. The client's choice of health care providers is generally more limited with the HMO than with the PPO because the client will not be reimbursed when going for care outside the HMO network. The deductibles and co-pay are generally lower with the HMO than with the PPO.

The answer is C.

Point-of-Service (POS) Plans

A point-of-service plan combines many of the aspects of traditional medical expense insurance with those of an HMO and/or a PPO. At the time medical treatment is needed, the covered individual decides whether to receive care within or outside the network arranged by the POS plan. Expenses incurred outside the network are reimbursed as if the individual were covered under a traditional insurance plan, with fairly high deductible and copayment provisions.

HEALTH SAVINGS ACCOUNTS

Health Savings Accounts (HSAs)

One of the newer concepts in health care coverage is creating a consumer directed health plan called a health savings account or HSA. This plan combines a high deductible medical expense insurance policy with a savings account. Insureds decide how much of their savings will be spent on health care and, therefore, are given an incentive to minimize the initial health care costs each year. The financial incentive is often combined with an increase of access to decision making tools to assist consumers with choosing higher-quality care at lower costs. Insureds with consumer-directed health care plans may be more likely to participate in wellness programs and to do more research on alternatives for receiving care. For example, insureds may research the quality and cost of going to an urgent care center versus the emergency room for non-life-threatening ailments.

Rules for Health Savings Accounts (HSAs)

Individuals covered under a high-deductible health plan are eligible to make tax-deductible contributions to health savings accounts. A high-deductible health plan (HDHP) for a family in 2016 has an annual deductible of at least $2,600 and a limit on annual expenses (excluding premiums) of up to $13,100. For an individual plan, the deductible and annual expenses required under the plan are 50% of the amounts listed above for the family plan. An HDHP may, however, provide preventive care benefits without a deductible or with a deductible less than the minimum annual deductible. Before establishing an HSA it is a good idea to verify with the insurer that the plan qualifies, or to check the declarations page of the policy for the words "qualified high-deductible health plan" or a reference to IRC Section 223.

Financial planning clients who are married should also be aware that they will be ineligible for an HSA if they are covered under any other health plan. Ineligibility applies even to a spouse's non-HDHP or a spouse's FSA (flexible spending account – see page 24.63) that is permitted to be used for the client's medical expenses. If the FSA is limited to paying only the client's dental and vision expenses and the client is not covered under the spouse's health insurance policy, then the client may still be eligible for an HSA as long as the other HSA rules are met.

One advantage of an HSA is that the contributions are an above-the-line deduction, so taxpayers need not itemize their tax deductions to benefit from an HSA. In 2016, deductible contributions are limited to:

(1) $3,350 for individual coverage
(2) $6,750 for family coverage

For those 55 or older, the annual limit is increased by $1,000 in 2016.

Individuals enrolled in Medicare are not allowed this deduction (Medicare is not a high deductible plan). The full amount may be contributed and deducted regardless of the actual amount of the deductible or maximum out-of-pocket expenses.

HSAs are individually owned, and are not required to be sponsored by an employer, although employers may contribute to them through a cafeteria plan. An HSA can be opened through banks, insurance companies, or other approved IRA (individual retirement account) trustees or custodians. Being individually owned means that, even if the employer contributed to the HSA on an employee's behalf, upon termination of employment, the HSA still belongs to and is controlled by the employee.

When an individual or family changes health plans part way through the year and no longer qualifies for an HSA, a portion of the contribution that was previously made may be subject to taxation, plus a 10% penalty.

Another advantage of HSAs is that earnings on the contributions to an HSA are not taxed currently, and distributions used to pay for qualifying medical expenses are tax-free. Qualified medical expenses include:

- Medical expenses for the client and any dependents that are not reimbursed by health insurance policy
- COBRA health insurance premiums
- Long-term care premiums
- Health insurance premiums if the client is receiving unemployment compensation

Distributions will be tax-free even if used after the individual has become eligible for Medicare. Distributions not used for medical expenses are subject to income tax and a 20% penalty. The penalty is not assessed if the individual account owner is age 65 or older, disabled, or deceased. This means that retirees age 65 or older who remain healthy through their lives and into their retirement years will be able to access the dollars in the HSA account for other retirement goals by paying the income tax on the earnings, but without penalty. It is possible for healthy individuals to accumulate significant amounts inside the HSA through both annual tax deductible contributions and earnings in the account. HSAs, similar to IRAs, can be invested in many different types of investment vehicles such as savings accounts, money market funds, bank CDs, stocks, bonds, or mutual funds. The choice of investment vehicle must, of course, be made with caution as to the level of risk associated with it. It would be wise to keep at least enough for one or two years of maximum out-of-pocket expenses in a safe and non-fluctuating investment.

The Tax Relief and Health Care Act of 2006 added the flexibility for a taxpayer to roll over FSA and HRA funds into an HSA when the employee switches to a health insurance plan that is compatible with the HSA provisions. In addition, a taxpayer now has the ability once during his or her lifetime to roll over funds from an IRA into the HSA, up to the yearly HSA contribution limit. The taxpayer will not be allowed to deduct these rolled over amounts, but will be allowed to access these funds for health care expenses. In the event that the taxpayer becomes ineligible for an HSA account within 12 months of these rollovers, the rolled over amount will be subject to income taxes and penalty.

HSA accounts allow a beneficiary to be named to receive the HSA funds in the event of death of the account holder. A beneficiary who is a surviving spouse will be permitted to roll the HSA funds to their own HSA account. If the beneficiary is a non-spouse, the account is distributed and is taxable to the beneficiary. In the event there is no beneficiary named, the account will be distributed and taxed to the estate.

Archer Medical Savings Accounts (MSAs)

The Archer MSA, also called just Medical Savings Account (MSA), was a pilot program that preceded health savings accounts. No new Archer MSAs are now permitted, but those in existence may continue to operate. Like HSAs, the Archer MSAs are designed to accompany high-deductible health plans.

Eligibility is limited to self-employed persons and employees of small employers with 50 or fewer employees.

If the employer makes contributions to the Archer MSA, the contributions are deductible by the employer and are not income to the employee. If the employee makes contributions, the employee can deduct these contributions from his or her income. If contributions are within specified limits, the earnings are not subject to current taxation. Any distributions from an Archer MSA for medical expenses are excluded from income. Distributions not used for medical expenses are subject to income tax and a 20% penalty. The penalty is not assessed if the individual is age 65 or older, disabled, or deceased.

Health Reimbursement Arrangements (HRAs)

A health reimbursement arrangement (HRA) can serve an employer as a supplement or substitute for medical expense insurance for employees. The HRA reimburses employees for medical expenses as claims are submitted. One advantage of the HRA is that it can cover medical expenses not ordinarily reimbursed by medical insurance. Any medical expenses paid will be tax-deductible for the employer, and as long as the plan is not discriminatory, reimbursement will be tax-free to the employee. The plan can be fully funded by insurance; it can be partially insured, such as with stop-loss coverage; or it can be unfunded.

An HRA set up as a savings account can provide for the employer to credit the employee's account for a specified amount annually. Contributions to an account are deductible by the employer, up to a certain amount. If the employee does not use the entire credit in a year, it continues to build from year to year. When employment terminates, the unused funds in the account revert to the employer.

HEALTH INSURANCE FOR SENIORS

Medicare

There are currently over 49 million people covered by Medicare with enrollment expected to rise to 80 million by 2030. Medicare is the primary insurance for those age 65 and older, but few rely on Medicare as their only source of health care coverage.

(http://www.aarp.org/content/dam/aarp/research/public_policy_institute/health/who-relies-on-medicare-factsheet-AARP-ppi-health.pdf)

The Medicare Program

Medicare benefits are medical expense benefits for persons who are age 65 or over and for certain disabled persons who have not yet reached age 65.

Medicare is actually made up of four separate programs:

- Part A coverage is for inpatient hospital care, skilled nursing care, home health care services, and hospice care.

- Part B is for doctors' services, medical supplies provided by a doctor in his or her office, drugs administered by a physician, outpatient hospital services, the costs of home health care visits, and many other services.

- Part C is a Medicare Advantage plan offered by private companies, but approved by Medicare. These plans cover all Medicare services, but may also offer additional coverage.

- Part D provides prescription drug coverage.

Funding Medicare

Social Security and Medicare are financed through a system of partial advance funding. This funding requires tax receipts sufficient not only to cover current benefit costs, but also to prepay some of the expected future benefit costs. Reserves for future benefits, however, are quite small. The Medicare reserves are especially small and may be nonexistent by 2026.

Medicare benefits are paid for by taxes on earnings: 1.45% of earnings for employees (matched by the employer) and 2.9% on self-employment income. Employer contributions to Social Security and Medicare are tax-deductible and not taxable to the employee. Employee contributions are not deductible.

The 2010 Health Care Reform includes two Medicare tax increases starting in 2013. The first increase is an additional 0.9 percent Medicare tax on **earned income** above $200,000 for single taxpayers and $250,000 for families. This 0.9 percent tax does not apply to distributions from qualified retirement plans such as IRAs, 401(k) plans, 403(b) plans, and 457 plans. The second increase is a 3.8 percent Medicare tax on **net investment income** for single taxpayers with an AGI above $200,000 and joint taxpayers with an AGI above $250,000.

In spite of these new taxes, much uncertainty remains about the long-term viability of Medicare. Most of the ways in which the future financial stability of the plan may be maintained are politically unpopular. They include raising the tax rates, using more general tax revenues to further subsidize the programs, reducing allowable payments to service providers, and increasing the taxes on benefit payments. Other suggestions have been to increase the rate of return earned by the tax and premium revenues, reducing benefits, increasing the minimum age for some benefits, adding a means test as an eligibility criterion, and increasing Medicare deductibles and co-pay requirements.

While Part A benefits are provided at no cost to eligible persons, Part B requires a premium payment.

The Part B monthly premium is based on the taxpayer's modified adjusted gross income (AGI) and filing status. The basic premium is $121.80 per month in 2016. The tables below summarize the monthly premiums required in 2016 by filing status and modified AGI. Note that the AGI used is the client's AGI 2 years prior (in other words, there is a 2 year look-back on AGI), so clients considering taking lump-sum distributions from qualified retirement plans or conversions of traditional to Roth IRAs should be aware of the effect an increase in AGI from these events may have on their Medicare Part B premiums. It may be a good strategy to complete these transactions in the year prior to the year in which the client turns age 63 to avoid the issue.

	Filing Status and Modified AGI	
Premium	Single	Married Filing Jointly
$121.80	$0 to $85,000	$0 to $170,000
$170.50	$85,001 to $107,000	$170,001 to $214,000
$243.60	$107,001 to $160,000	$214,001 to $320,000
$316.70	$160,001 to $214,000	$320,001 to $428,000
$389.80	$214,001 or higher	$428,001 or higher

	Filing Status and Modified AGI
Premium	Married Filing Separately
$121.80	$0 to $85,000
$316.70	$85,001 to $129,000
$389.80	$129,001 or higher

Additional out-of-pocket costs for insureds under Medicare are discussed below.

Eligibility

Eligibility for Medicare requires that the person be age 65 or older and be entitled to retirement benefits under Social Security or the Railroad Retirement program. Civilian federal employees also are generally eligible for Medicare at age 65. Part A is provided to these individuals at no charge. Spouses over 65 who are eligible for Social Security benefits based on their spouse's earnings are also covered. Those under 65 who receive Social Security disability payments for 24 months are covered, as well. And a person who is fully or currently insured under Social Security, as well as his or her spouse and dependent child(ren), and who requires renal dialysis or a kidney transplant is also covered. Anyone 65 years of age or older who does not meet the foregoing eligibility requirements can enroll voluntarily in Part A. A person who enrolls voluntarily must pay a monthly premium and must also enroll in Part B. Persons 65 or older are eligible for Medicare benefits even if they continue to work.

Everyone eligible for the no-cost Part A coverage is also able to purchase Part B coverage by paying a monthly premium. Those receiving Social Security benefits prior to age 65 are automatically enrolled in Medicare Parts A and B at age 65 and will receive a Medicare insurance card in the mail three months before turning age 65. Those not yet receiving Social Security benefits at age 65 will need to enroll for Medicare during the Initial Enrollment Period (IEP) beginning three months before the month of the 65th birthday and ending three months after the month of the 65th birthday (seven months total). Enrollment can be done at www.ssa.gov, by calling the Social Security administration, or visiting the local Social Security office. Clients should be encouraged to enroll in the three months prior to the month of the 65th birthday so that coverage will begin on the first day of the month of the 65th birthday (unless the birthday is on the first of the month, then benefits begin the first day of the prior month). For example, if a client's birthday is on August 15th, coverage will begin August 1st, but if the client's birthday is August 1st, coverage will begin July 1st. If enrollment is done in the month the client turns age 65 or in the three months following, coverage will be delayed for 1 to 3 months after enrollment.

Part B is a negative election, meaning that when you apply for Part A, you automatically get Part B as well unless you opt out of it. Anyone who does not apply for Part B when he or she is initially eligible can apply later, during general enrollment periods, which are the first three months of each year. A person who delays enrollment, however, will pay premiums, increased by 10% for each 12-month period that the person was eligible and did not enroll. A person who has continuous group coverage from age 65 until retirement can enroll up to eight months after group coverage ends and not be subject to premium increases. The eight months applies from the time of termination of the employer coverage regardless of whether COBRA is elected (COBRA continuation is discussed on page 24.58)

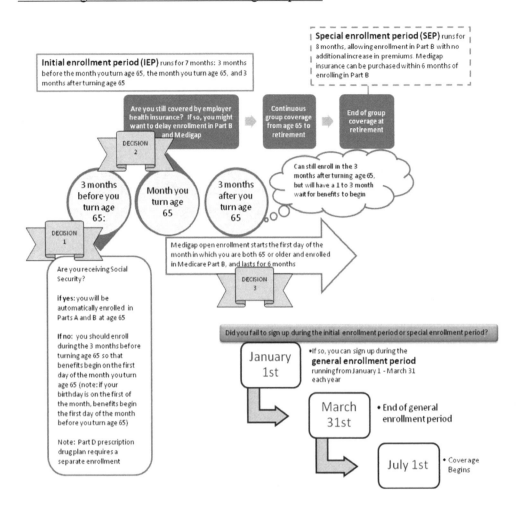

Practice Question

Which of the following persons are eligible for Medicare Part A benefits without paying a monthly premium?

(1) A person, age 63, who took early retirement
(2) A person, age 42, who has just begun receiving Social Security disability benefits
(3) A person, age 67, who is entitled to Social Security benefits as a spouse
(4) A person, age 65, who is not eligible for Social Security benefits but wants to enroll in Medicare

    A. (1) and (2) only
    B. (2) and (3) only
    C. (2) and (4) only
    D. (3) and (4) only

Answer:

A person taking early retirement is not eligible for Medicare until age 65, so retirees need to find medical insurance to cover them until age 65. A person who is disabled can receive Medicare benefits after receiving Social Security disability benefits for two years. A person who is 65 and who is entitled to Social Security benefits as a spouse is eligible for Medicare. A person who is not otherwise covered can also voluntarily enroll.

The answer is D.

Traditional Medicare – Parts A and B

Medicare Part A (in 2016) covers hospital room-and-board charges for up to 90 days, subject to a deductible, as well as a coinsurance requirement for days 61-90. When a patient enters the hospital, a "benefit period" is initiated. The patient must pay an initial deductible of $1,288 which covers the first 60 days in the hospital. A daily co-insurance amount of $322 must be paid by the patient for days 61-90. If the patient is still in the hospital beyond 90 days, Medicare no longer pays. Each individual does, however, have 60 lifetime reserve days which can be used if they are in the hospital beyond 90 days. The lifetime reserve days require a coinsurance payment of $644 per day, and once those days are used they are no longer available should the patient be in the hospital beyond 90 days at another time. Each benefit period ends when the patient has been out of the hospital for 60 consecutive days. Once one benefit period ends, if the patient must be admitted to the hospital again later, a new benefit period starts over with the payment of $1,288 to cover the first 60 days. There is no limit on the number of benefit periods that can be triggered during a lifetime.

Also covered under Part A are hospital charges for general duty nursing, hospital equipment, drugs and biologicals, use of the operating room, diagnostic or therapeutic services, and blood transfusions (subject to a deductible or replacement requirement for the first three pints).

Medicare Part A also provides benefits for care in a skilled nursing facility if medically necessary, following at least three days of hospitalization. Care is paid for in full for 20 days, and a coinsurance of $161 per day applies for days 21-100. In addition, Medicare Part A pays some benefits for medically necessary care by a home health care agency and for hospice care for the terminally ill.

Medicare Part B provides medical insurance coverage for doctors' visits, including home health care visits not covered by Part A. The benefits are subject to a $166 (in 2016) annual deductible and require the insured to pay 20% of all charges above the deductible. Part B only covers drugs administered by a doctor and does not currently cover any prescription drugs.

For planning purposes, we are often more interested in what is *not* covered than what *is* covered, since we need a plan to fill in any gaps.

Part A does not cover hospital stays beyond 90 days (if all lifetime reserve days have been used). Part A also excludes services provided outside the U.S., its territories, and its possessions. It also covers only up to 100 days of skilled nursing care, and only following at least 3 days of hospitalization.

Medicare Part B excludes prescription drugs not administered by a doctor. It does not cover services provided outside the U.S., its territories, and its possessions. Part B does not cover routine physical exams (except as required by the Affordable Care Act), routine eye exams, dental care, hearing aids, or eyeglasses. It also excludes luxury elective services, custodial care, elective cosmetic surgery, services covered by workers' compensation, and services provided free in a federal facility.

Part A and Part B both exclude coverage for the first 3 pints of blood when a blood transfusion is needed.

Out-of-Pocket Costs for Medicare Parts A and B

In addition to understanding eligibility, services, and exclusions, planners must also consider the out-of-pocket costs that clients covered under Medicare may pay. Medicare has deductibles and coinsurance amounts for both Part A and B. In 2016, individuals covered by Medicare Part A will pay out-of-pocket:

- $1,288 for a hospital stay of 1-60 days
- $322 per day for days 61-90 of a hospital stay
- $644 per day for days 91-150 of a hospital stay
- All costs of the stay after it exceeds 150 days
- Nothing for the first 20 days at a skilled nursing facility
- $161 per day for days 21-100 at a skilled nursing facility
- All costs for days over 100 at a skilled nursing facility (Medicare does not cover any of the costs of care that is primarily custodial.)
- Nothing for home health care prescribed by a doctor if the insured is confined to his or her house
- Nothing for hospice care for terminal illness
- 20% of the cost of durable medical equipment
- 100% of the cost of care received in a foreign country. Since Medicare does not cover care in a foreign country, clients planning to travel abroad during retirement should be advised to purchase international travel insurance or a Medigap policy that covers this gap.

Part B has a $166 (2016) per year deductible and a 20% copayment after the deductible is reached for covered physician services, including surgeon fees and physical therapy. The copay is 20% for outpatient mental health, and limits apply to most physical and occupational therapies. Laboratory tests are covered without a copayment. The copayments above may be higher if the physician used has not agreed to accept the amount approved by Medicare for a particular service as payment in full. There is no stop-loss associated with these costs.

New emphasis on preventive medical care has pushed Medicare to waive deductibles and copayments on some preventive care, such as mammograms, pap smears, cancer screening, flu vaccinations, and a yearly wellness visit.

Medicare Part C – Medicare Advantage

Medicare Advantage (also called Medicare Managed Care Plan), Part C, is an option whereby those eligible for the traditional Medicare program can instead elect coverage under an HMO plan, PPO plan, medical savings account, private fee-for-service plan, or a private contract with a physician.

When enrolling in a Medicare Advantage Plan, the Part B premium is still paid, along with a premium for the Part C coverage, which will vary based on the deductibles, coinsurance, co-pay, and maximum out-of-pocket limits of the plan chosen. Medicare Advantage Plans may be limited to only doctors who are in the network, or may allow the covered individual to see doctors outside of the network as well, but with a higher out-of-pocket cost. Medicare Advantage Plans are required to offer at least the same benefits as Parts A and B (they will never have less coverage than Parts A and B), although most plans offer greater coverage and also include prescription drug coverage. This plan eliminates the need for Medigap coverage.

Over the past decade, the percentage of Medicare enrollees choosing Medicare Advantage Plans has nearly doubled, from 16% to over 30%. **One feature that makes Medicare Advantage Plans attractive for planning purposes is that they have an annual maximum-out-of-pocket amount. Although that amount may increase each year, it still eliminates a large portion of the unknown potential costs of medical care for retirees, allowing planners and clients to develop a "worst case scenario" for planning purposes.** The Medicare Advantage plans also tend to have lower premiums than Medigap policies, and may offer additional benefits, such as dental and vision. For retirees who plan to travel frequently, however, the limitation of needing to see doctors who are in the network may be too restrictive since many networks are confined to a particular geographic region.

Medicare beneficiaries can switch to Medicare Advantage from Parts A and B, or switch from Medicare Advantage to Parts A and B, or switch between Medicare Advantage Plans during open enrollment periods each year, which run from October 15th through December 7th.

Medicare Advantage plans with high deductibles can be combined with a Medicare Medical Savings Account (MSA) in which the plan deposits money into the account to be used to pay health care costs before the deductible is met.

Individuals entitled to Medicare benefits cannot contribute to health savings accounts (HSAs).

Medicare Part D – Prescription Drug Benefits

The Medicare Modernization Act of 2003 provides a prescription drug benefit for qualified retirees. Any person who is enrolled in Medicare Parts A or B is eligible for the Medicare Prescription Drug Plan (Part D). While persons receiving Social Security checks are automatically enrolled in Medicare Parts A and B, **enrollment in the Part D prescription drug plans is not automatic and is separate from enrollment in Parts A and B.** In general, retirees will enroll by applying directly to the prescription drug plan that they select. Enrollment is voluntary, but there is a penalty for delaying. For every month that enrollment is delayed, the premium will increase by 1%.

The Medicare Part D law enacted by Congress provided for an average monthly premium of $39 for the standard plan. The actual premium charged varies among the plans offered and may be more or less than $39, depending on the plan benefits and copayments.

Part D coverage can be offered through stand-alone plans or through HMO plans. The HMOs have offered Medicare Part A and B coverages through Medicare Advantage plans, and these plans are able to offer the prescription drug benefit, as well. An individual who elects a Medicare Advantage plan cannot also have a stand-alone plan.

For those retirees who have purchased a Medigap policy with prescription drug coverage, the coverage provided by Medicare is better, so the Medigap policies are not "creditable." The Medigap policies are labeled H, I, and J and are no longer offered. For those policies still in effect, the insurer must reduce the premium if the policyowner enrolls in a Medicare Part D plan.

Seniors can go to www.medicare.gov/find-a-plan to view plans available in their area and can enter the prescription drugs they take to see what is covered.

Taxation of Medicare Premiums and Benefits

Premiums for Medicare Part B are deductible in the same way as other medical expenses, as itemized deductions subject to the 10% of adjusted gross income (AGI) floor. Self-employed individuals, however, may deduct Medicare premiums above-the-line.

Editor's Note: The medical expense deduction floor increased from 7.5% to 10% beginning in 2013. However, if the taxpayer or spouse reaches age 65 or older by the end of the year, they will be permitted to use the 7.5% floor through 2016.

Benefits received under Medicare are tax-free.

Part D subsidies will be excluded from a retiree's gross income, but the prescription drug expenses can still be claimed as a deduction.

Medigap Coverage

For those Medicare beneficiaries who want to fill in the gaps created by many of the limitations or exclusions specified in the Medicare program, additional coverage, so-called Medigap (also called Medicare Supplement) insurance, is available from many carriers at additional cost. There are strict federal guidelines for these coverages, which outline only 10 different plans that can be offered. Each plan covers different amounts of the gaps in Medicare coverage. The plans are named using the letters A through N (plans E, H, I, and J are no longer offered), and plan coverages are standardized. This simplifies comparing the costs of various insurance company coverages because all carriers offering Plan D, for example, will provide the same benefits. Also worth noting is that Medigap policies only work with traditional Medicare (Parts A and B), and not with Part C (Medicare Advantage).

Medicare supplemental insurance (Medigap) must provide the following basic benefits:

(1) Hospitalization – pays the coinsurance for days 61-90 under Part A, the 60-day lifetime reserve, and an additional 365 days after Medicare benefits end.

(2) Medical expenses – pays the coinsurance for physician and medical service charges under Part B.

(3) Blood – pays for the first 3 pints of blood each year.

In addition to basic benefits, Medigap plans can offer any of the following benefits not covered by Medicare:

- Coinsurance for days 21-100 at a skilled nursing facility
- Hospital inpatient deductible under Part A
- Deductible under Part B
- Physician and medical service charges exceeding the amount approved by Medicare
- 80% of emergency care charges in a foreign country
- At-home assistance with daily living

- Preventive care

An individual who is at least 65 years of age can buy any Medigap policy during the 6-month period after enrolling for Medicare Part B. A person cannot be turned down for health reasons, and insurers cannot exclude coverage of preexisting conditions for more than 6 months. Affordable Care Act rules prohibiting exclusion of pre-existing conditions do not apply to Medigap policies. ACA rules are discussed beginning on page 24.30.

The Plan A Medigap policy will only pay for basic benefits. The other plans cover basic benefits and the additional benefits as shown in the following chart:

EXHIBIT 24 – 2
Medigap Plans

Benefits	B	C	D	F	G	K	L	M	N
Days 21-100 at skilled nursing facility		✓	✓	✓	✓	50%	75%	✓	✓
Deductible – Part A	✓	✓	✓	✓	✓	50%	75%	50%	✓
Deductible – Part B		✓		✓					
Excess physician and medical service charges				✓	✓				
Emergency care in a foreign country		80%	80%	80%	80%			80%	80%

*After you meet your out-of-pocket yearly limit and your yearly Part B deductible ($166 in 2016), the Medigap plan pays 100% of covered services for the rest of the calendar year.	Out-of-Pocket Limit*	
	4,960	2,480

Note: Plans E, H, I, and J are no longer offered.

Plan F also offers a high-deductible plan. Enrollees must pay for costs up to $2,160 before the plan will make any payments.

The government mandates that all Medigap policies of the same letter (A, B, C, D, F, G, K, L M or N) offer the same coverage to make it easier for seniors to determine which policy they need. The government rules do not require all premiums be structured in the same way, so selecting a policy letter does not mean that shopping is simplified to just looking for the lowest premium.

Policies that are "community rated" charge the same monthly premium to everyone, regardless of age, but premiums may increase due to other factors (e.g., inflation, underwriting, etc). These policies tend to be the least expensive over the course of a lifetime.

Issue-age-rated policies base the premium on age at issue. The premiums will not increase based on age, but may go up based on other factors.

Attained-age-rated policies base the premium on current age each year. These will be less expensive when clients are younger, but premiums will go up each year. Generally, premiums will begin to be higher than other types of policies around age 70 – 75.

The best time to purchase Medigap insurance is during open enrollment, which is the 6 month period beginning on the first day of the month in which you are both 65 or older and enrolled in Medicare Part B. For policies purchased during this time, there is no medical underwriting based on health, although there can be up to a 6 month waiting period for coverage for preexisting conditions. This waiting period can be reduced or eliminated if you had prior creditable coverage. Many types of health care coverage will qualify as prior creditable coverage. Each month of prior coverage reduces the waiting period for coverage of preexisting conditions by one month, so if prior coverage lasted at least 6 months, there will be no wait. However, there cannot be a break in coverage for more than 63 days. A preexisting condition is one that was diagnosed or was being treated within the 6 month period before the date that coverage starts. Policies purchased during the open enrollment period will not have a higher premium based on health.

If you have group health coverage through an employer or union, you may want to wait to take the action of enrolling in Part B of Medicare and purchasing a Medigap policy. This delay makes sense when the employer plan provides similar coverage. When your employer coverage ends, you will get a chance to enroll in Part B without a late enrollment penalty, and your Medigap open enrollment period will start at that time as well.

MEDICAID

Medicaid is the nationwide program (administered by the individual states) that provides medical benefits for those without resources to pay. Generally, Medicaid is not a topic discussed much with the average financial planning client because a planner's goal is usually to build wealth and avoid circumstances that would qualify clients for Medicaid.

One area where Medicaid benefits are more likely to be discussed is that of long-term care planning. While Medicare will not pay for long-term care, Medicaid will pay for long-term care for those who are eligible. Medicaid should only be looked at as a last resort because the facilities that accept the lower reimbursements paid by Medicaid have been shown to provide lower levels of care. A planner who wants the best for his or her clients will generally be able to find better alternatives than planning to qualify for Medicaid.

Because Medicaid is a state-administered program, the exact eligibility requirements vary among the states. In general, to qualify for Medicaid, clients must pass both income and asset tests. For Medicaid to pay the expenses of nursing home care, a recipient's income (after reducing it by the amounts for the support of the noninstitutionalized spouse and dependents and other medical expenses) must be insufficient to pay for the nursing home costs. No income solely attributable to the noninstitutionalized spouse is counted.

Further, a patient must use all but $2,000 of nonexempt assets for payment of medical expenses, including the nursing home costs, before he or she is eligible for Medicaid. Those assets which are specifically exempt include:

- Home, if used by dependents
- Personal property
- Life insurance with little or no cash value
- Retirement accounts that cannot be withdrawn in a lump sum
- Assets used in a business or for the production of income

All other assets must be used to provide care before Medicaid will pay. The asset test also applies to spouses of patients, who may keep one-half of nonexempt assets up to a state maximum (usually under $100,000), with the rest required to be spent on care.

Transfers to Reduce Assets

Transfers to children or friends and transfers in trust in order to reduce the assets of the patient will make patients ineligible for Medicaid if done within 5 years before admission to a nursing home. Any transfer for less than fair consideration will disqualify the patient for a time equal to the amount transferred, divided by the average monthly cost for nursing home care in the patient's state. Congress has repeatedly sought to remove opportunities for elderly persons to preserve wealth through Medicaid planning in which the cost of long-term care was passed to taxpayers. Consequently, planners will find Medicaid planning increasingly difficult. One notable exception to the Medicaid asset spend-down rules, however, is the Long-Term Care Partnership program.

Long-Term Care Insurance Partnership Program

Under a state and federal government partnership program, private insurance companies can offer long-term care insurance policies that provide asset protection from Medicaid reimbursement. A Partnership qualified policy includes an "asset disregard" for Medicaid to the extent of the total amount of benefits received under the long-term care policy. For example, in order to be eligible for

Medicaid, an individual must spend down all assets except approximately $2,000. If an individual buys a long-term care policy that provides $150,000 of lifetime benefits and then requires Medicaid benefits, the individual will be allowed to retain $150,000 of assets in addition to the $2,000 that does not need to be spent down to obtain Medicare benefits.

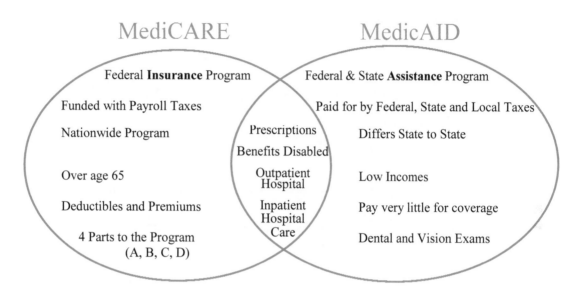

MediCARE

Federal **Insurance** Program

Funded with Payroll Taxes

Nationwide Program

Over age 65

Deductibles and Premiums

4 Parts to the Program
(A, B, C, D)

Prescriptions

Benefits Disabled

Outpatient Hospital

Inpatient Hospital Care

MedicAID

Federal & State **Assistance** Program

Paid for by Federal, State and Local Taxes

Differs State to State

Low Incomes

Pay very little for coverage

Dental and Vision Exams

Class Discussion 24 – 2

Is it ethical for a planner to assist clients with their impoverishment as a strategy for "Medicaid planning"?

TAXATION OF PREMIUMS AND BENEFITS FOR INDIVIDUAL HEALTH INSURANCE POLICIES

Taxation of Premiums and Benefits for Individuals and Self-Employed Individuals

An individual who is not self-employed may deduct the premiums for medical expense insurance on Schedule A of IRS Form 1040; however, an actual deduction will be allowed only to the extent that the premiums and non-reimbursed medical expenses exceed 10% of the insured's adjusted gross income. However, if the taxpayer or spouse reaches age 65 or older by the end of the year, they will be allowed to use the 7.5% threshold through 2016.

For a self-employed person, a deduction for medical expense insurance premiums may be taken on the first page of IRS Form 1040 (above-the-line) in determining the adjusted gross income. The amount of this deduction is 100% of the premiums.

Benefits paid by medical expense insurance normally are free of income tax, but there are a few exceptions. Benefits are taxable if they are in excess of any expenses incurred. They are also taxable if the insured deducted the medical expenses and then in the following year received payment of benefits for the same expenses. For example, if the insurance company denied a claim, the insured deducted those expenses, and then the following year the insurance company paid the claim, the payment would be taxable income for the insured.

Health Savings Accounts are a tax-advantaged approach to medical insurance as discussed previously in this topic.

Additional Medicare Tax and Medicare Tax on Investment Income

The 2010 Health Care Reform includes two Medicare tax increases starting in 2013. The first increase is an additional 0.9 percent Medicare tax on earned income above $200,000 for single taxpayers and above $250,000 for families. This 0.9 percent tax will not apply to distributions from qualified retirement plans such as IRAs, 401(k) plans, 403(b) plans, and 457 plans. The .9% tax may also be referred to as the hospital insurance (HI) tax. It is paid by the employee who earns wages working for a business (not by the business), and is on only the employee portion of the self-employment tax for those who are self-employed.

The second increase is a 3.8 percent Medicare tax on net investment income (including interest, dividends, annuities, royalties, certain rents and certain other passive income) for single taxpayers with an AGI above $200,000 and joint taxpayers with an AGI above $250,000. The tax is imposed on the lesser of an individual's net investment income for the tax year or modified adjusted gross income in excess of $200,000 ($250,000 for married couples filing a joint return and $125,000 for married couples filing a separate return). This surtax on unearned income applies to individuals, estates, and non-charitable trusts.

HEALTH CARE REFORM

2010 Health Care Reform

Health Care Reform (the Patient Protection and Affordable Care Act, commonly called the Affordable Care Act (ACA)) signed into law during 2010 will

dramatically change health care for most individuals over the next few years. The act has proved controversial and numerous members of Congress would like to repeal or revise the laws. Assuming the rules remain unchanged, the key provisions of the ACA include:

2010

- Elimination of (1) discrimination against children with pre-existing conditions and (2) lifetime coverage limits.
- Children now allowed to be covered on their parents' insurance until age 26.

2011

- Flexible spending accounts (FSAs), health savings accounts (HSAs) and health reimbursement accounts (HRAs) may no longer reimburse individuals for over the counter medicines unless prescribed by a doctor.
- Penalty on nonqualified distributions increased to 20% for both HSAs and Archer Medical Saving Accounts (MSAs).

2013

- Individual taxpayers with more than $200,000 of **earned income** and families with more than $250,000 of **earned income** will pay an additional 0.9% in Medicare tax.
- Individual taxpayers with AGI above $200,000 and joint filers with AGI above $250,000 will pay 3.8% Medicare tax on **investment income**.
- FSA contributions limited to $2,500 per year.
- 10% AGI threshold for deducting medical expenses as an itemized deduction.

2014

- All individuals must have minimum essential coverage or they will pay a per person penalty of up to 1% of income (minimum amount of $95) in 2014. The penalty increases to 2% of income in 2015 (minimum amount of $325) and 2.5% of income in 2016 (minimum amount of $695 indexed for inflation). The penalty for children under age 18 or in college is 50% of the above amounts. The combined family penalty will be limited to 300% of the individual penalty for the year.
- Employers with 50 or more employees will be required to provide minimum essential coverage for employees or have to pay an additional tax of up to $2,000 per employee per year. **Editor's Note:** The employer mandate provision has been delayed until 2015.

2018

- Insurers of group insurance plans with high dollar health insurance premiums over $10,200 for individual coverage and $27,500 for family coverage (indexed for inflation) will pay a 40% excise tax starting in 2018. The insurance company can pass this excise tax to the insured individual by increasing the premiums. **Editor's Note**: The excise tax on these so-called "Cadillac plans" has been the subject of much criticism and numerous attempts at repeal. In 2015 the Appropriations Act set a two-year delay (so that the excise tax goes into effect for tax years beginning after December 31, 2020), and removed the tax from the list of nondeductible taxes so that employers may deduct the tax payment from gross income as a business expense. Planners advising businesses that offer high dollar health plans should be aware that it is likely that additional attempts to repeal the tax are likely over the next few years before it goes into effect, so there is still some uncertainty about when and if the excise tax will occur

ACA Minimum Essential Coverage for Individuals

Starting in 2014, each individual will be required to have minimum essential health coverage for each month of the year, qualify for an exemption, or pay a penalty when filing his or her federal income tax return. The payment applies to individuals of all ages, including children (the adult claiming the child as a dependent on his or her tax return is responsible for paying the penalty if the child does not have minimum essential coverage or an exemption).

The following lists a few of the types of coverage that are considered minimum essential coverage:

- Employer-sponsored coverage (including COBRA coverage)
- Coverage purchased in the individual market, including a qualified health plan offered by the Health Insurance Marketplace (also known as an Affordable Insurance Exchange)
- Medicare Part A coverage and Medicare Advantage plans
- Medicaid coverage
- Children's Health Insurance Program (CHIP) coverage
- Certain types of veterans health coverage administered by the Veterans Administration
- TRICARE
- Self-funded health coverage offered to students by universities for plan or policy years that begin on or before Dec. 31, 2014 (for later plan or policy years, sponsors of these programs may apply to the Department of Health and Human Services (HHS) to be recognized as minimum essential coverage)

Exemptions from the requirement to obtain minimum essential coverage include groups such as religious sects opposed to insurance, those whose income is below the minimum threshold for filing a tax return, and those with short coverage gaps of less than 3 months during the year, among others. Additional details may be found at http://www.irs.gov/uac/Individual-Shared-Responsibility-Provision.

It should be noted that some of the exemptions require certification from the Health Insurance Marketplace while others are claimed on the income tax return.

The Health Insurance Marketplace

In order to increase health care coverage and affordability, the Affordable Care Act contained a provision for the establishment of Health Insurance Exchanges (also known as Health Insurance Marketplaces). The exchanges are meant to create an organized and competitive market in which individuals may purchase health insurance. The exchanges offer a variety of certified health insurance plans to choose from and provide information about each plan to help consumers understand and compare their options. Some Marketplaces are operated by the states (such as California and Maryland), while others are run for the states by the federal government (www.healthcare.gov).

To be eligible to shop for insurance in an exchange, the person must be a resident of the state where that Marketplace is located, must be a U.S citizen or lawfully present in the U.S., and may not be incarcerated. While anyone meeting these requirements can purchase coverage in the Marketplace, not everyone will qualify for premium tax credits.

Premium Tax Credits

Beginning in 2014, taxpayers with moderate incomes who purchase health insurance coverage through the Health Insurance Marketplace may be eligible for a Premium Tax Credit. In addition to meeting income guidelines, qualifying health insurance must be purchased through the Health Insurance Marketplace, the insured must be ineligible for coverage through an employer or government plan (including Medicare and Medicaid), the taxpayer must file jointly with their spouse if they are married, and the taxpayer cannot be claimed as a dependent by another taxpayer.

The premium subsidies were designed to assist millions of Americans who could not otherwise afford health insurance. It is estimated that 19 million people will receive premium subsidies by 2019.

In order to be eligible, the taxpayer's household income for the year must be at least 100% but less than 400% of the Federal Poverty Line (FPL) for the taxpayer's family size. For example, in 2016, a family of two with income between $15,930 and $63,720 was between 100% and 400% of the FPL, and that family would qualify for a premium tax credit (the lower the income within the range, the higher the credit amount). For a family of four, the range is $24,250 to $97,000.

Those who are eligible to receive the premium credit can choose to have some or all of it paid directly to the insurance company in 2016 in order to reduce current premiums, or to receive the credit when filing their 2016 income tax return in 2017.

Open Enrollment

In general, enrollment in non-group health plan coverage in the Marketplace can only be done during the Open Enrollment period. The Open Enrollment period for 2016 coverage was scheduled for November 1, 2015, to December 17, 2015, but was extended through January 31, 2016. The open enrollment period for 2017 and beyond is scheduled to run from November 1, 2016 to January 31, 2017.

Generally, once the open enrollment period has ended, individuals and families will not be able to enroll in Marketplace health plans until the next open enrollment period. An exception is available, however, if certain changes in circumstances occur during the year. In that case, there will be a special 60-day opportunity to enroll in health plans through the Marketplace outside of the open enrollment period. Events that may trigger the special enrollment opportunity include:

- Loss of eligibility for other coverage such as loss of employer provided coverage due to termination of employment or a student's loss of student health coverage due to graduation. There is, however, no special enrollment period granted if health insurance is lost due to the insured not paying his premiums.

- Addition of a dependent such as a spouse upon marriage or the birth of a child. No special enrollment period will be granted due to pregnancy, however.

- Divorce or legal separation.

- Loss of dependent status, such as a child covered under a parent's plan reaching age 26.

- Moving to another state or outside of the health plan's service area.

- Exhaustion of COBRA coverage (discussed later in this topic). Note, however, that simply choosing not to pay COBRA premiums any longer does not trigger a special enrollment period. If a client decides that COBRA premiums are too expensive, he or she will need to stay on COBRA until the next Marketplace open enrollment period begins. Only exhaustion of COBRA benefits triggers the special enrollment period. COBRA coverage is discussed in more detail on pages 24.58-24.61.

- For those enrolled in a Marketplace plan, income increases or decreases large enough to change the individual's or family's eligibility for subsidies.

Comparing Policies in the Marketplace

As mentioned previously, one of the goals of the Marketplace is to make it easy to compare various health plans. One item of comparison will, of course, be costs. Plans offered on the exchange may be managed care plans, so a comparison of doctors, hospitals, care facilities, and pharmacies who are participating providers should also be considered, along with how any medications that are taken regularly are treated under each plan. Every plan sold in the Marketplace is required to provide a link on the Marketplace web site so that consumers are able to search the plan's health provider directory to find out whether their health providers are included.

Each plan offered on the exchange will also provide information regarding deductibles, co-pays, co-insurance, and maximum out-of-pocket costs. Preventive health services must be covered entirely with no cost to the insured.

To make cost comparisons easier for insureds, the Marketplace has categorized health plans as Bronze, Silver, Gold, or Platinum. Bronze plans have the highest deductibles and greatest cost sharing, which means the insured will pay a higher portion of any health care bills. The cost sharing amount in Silver plans will be a bit lower than Bronze plans. Gold plans tend to have even lower cost sharing, and Platinum plans have the lowest deductibles, co-pays, and other costs to the insured. In general, it should be expected that the lower the cost sharing is, the higher the premium will be. Also, any potential cost-sharing assistance is based on the benchmark Silver option (bought within the Marketplace).

A good place to start is to have the client request records of past treatment from his doctors (some doctors make this information available to patients online under a secure patient account) to determine frequency and level of use. While the past does not guarantee similar results for the future, clients with ongoing health issues will be better able to assess which plan will provide the necessary benefits with a cost-sharing structure that fits the client's budget.

Marketplace or Non-Marketplace?

The ACA created the Marketplace and gave consumers the option to purchase coverage in a manner similar to group plans. Some of the basic features within the Marketplace include: plans must provide comprehensive (essential) benefits, coverage cannot be denied because of pre-existing health conditions, nor can rates be increased on an individual basis (i.e., rate increases cannot be based on either pre-existing conditions or gender). Consumers automatically receive preventative services at no additional cost.

Consumers still have the option to buy coverage outside of the Health Insurance Marketplace, but in doing so, may face a different cost and benefit environment. One of the major differences is that non-Marketplace coverage does not provide premium tax credits or cost-sharing help. This can be a significant factor for people who meet the income limits (income between 100 percent and 400 percent of the federal poverty level for tax credits; income between 100 percent and 250 percent for cost-sharing help).

The four metal plan tiers (bronze, silver, gold, and platinum) are available within or outside the Marketplace Exchanges. Regardless of the tier, consumers may have greater choice of provider networks when they get coverage using non-Marketplace options, which may provide a strong reason to look outside the Marketplace. That said, each of the tiers must meet the ACA essential health benefit requirements. Generally, policies purchased through private insurers (i.e., non-Marketplace) tend to have at least slightly higher premiums, but may also provide additional provider options. The decision to look inside or outside the Marketplace can impact consumer satisfaction and potential expense. However, knowing the options will help the planner guide clients as they make those decisions.

Attempting to predict future health care needs for a client who has always enjoyed good health may be a bit daunting, but knowing the health care plan's maximum out-of-pocket expenses enables a planner to evaluate a best-case scenario, a worst-case scenario, and an in-between scenario. This approach aligns with the "maximum possible and maximum probable" analysis discussed in Topic 23.

Embedded Versus Non-Embedded Deductible

All health care policy deductibles have one general purpose, to reduce insurer expenses for common treatments by introducing cost-sharing measures. In this case, the cost sharing comes in the form of a deductible amount that the covered individual(s) must pay before the insurance policy makes any payments. So a person who incurs a $2,000 medical expense, and has a $3,000 deductible, will have to pay the entire $2,000. That amount will be applied to the deductible, but $1,000 of the remaining deductible amount still must be paid before the insurance policy will make any payments. It's not inconceivable for a person with a high deductible amount to pay virtually all medical care expenses for the year out of pocket. While the deductible may not apply to certain types of preventive care, as required by the Affordable Care Act, but it would apply to all other covered expenses.

Traditionally, medical care reimbursement policies had only one type of deductible, albeit with several variations. This was true whether the policy covered only one individual or included one or more family members. Individual policies still operate in the same way, but family policies normally do not. Today, a policy that covers family members may have either an embedded or a non-embedded deductible.

Embedded Deductible

Family plans with an embedded deductible actually have two deductible types: an individual deductible and a family deductible. The individual component allows each covered individual in the family to satisfy the deductible for their own medical expenses, and begin receiving reimbursements from the policy before the family has collectively met their deductible. The family component relates to the family as a whole, and is the amount of covered expenses that the family must meet before moving beyond the deductible.

Embedded Deductible Example 1:

The Jones family has a health care plan with an embedded deductible. The individual annual deductible amount is $2,300, and the amount for the family is $4,600. After the deductible has been satisfied, the coinsurance is 80/20. The only medical expenses for the year were for Dad, who had a skiing accident resulting in $6,500 of covered medical expenses.

The family's combined expenses total $6,500. Here's how they paid the deductible:

	Expenses	Deductible (paid by family)	Amount Subject to Coinsurance
Dad	$6,500	$2,300	$4,200
Mom	$0	$0	$0
Daughter	$0	$0	$0
Son	$0	$0	$0
Total	$6,500	$2,300	$4,200

The total paid by the Jones family is $2,300 + $840 = $3,140

Embedded Deductible Example 2:

The Johnson family has a health care plan with an embedded deductible. The individual annual deductible amount is $2,300, and the amount for the family is $4,600. After the deductible has been satisfied, the coinsurance is 80/20. The family was in a boating accident where all four family members required varying amounts of medical intervention. The family incurred the following expenses:

Dad: $3,200
Mom: $1,850
Daughter: $800
Son: $650

Because their plan has an embedded deductible, there are two components. First, once the entire family's deductibles total $4,600, they collectively move into the next level of coverage. Second, until they meet the collective family deductible, individual family members can move to the next coverage level after meeting the individual deductible amount of $2,300.

In this example, only Dad has met the individual deductible amount of $2,300, so the final $900 of his expenses moves into the next coverage level. At this point, the family still has to meet an additional $2,300 deductible amount to satisfy the aggregate family deductible. The family's combined expenses total $6,500. Here's how they paid the deductible:

	Expenses	Deductible (paid by family)	Remainder (paid by insurer)
Dad	$3,200	$2,300	$900
Mom	$1,850	$1,850	$0
Daughter	$800	$450	$350
Son	$650	$0	$650
Total	$6,500	$4,600	$1,900

The total paid by the Johnson family is $4,600 + $380 = $$4,980

Non-Embedded Deductible

Plans having a non-embedded family deductible do not embed or insert the individual deductible option into the family deductible amount. As a result, the insureds must satisfy the entire family deductible amount before the policy will help pay for any individual's medical expenses. One family member can meet the entire deductible or it may require several family members to do so. Either way, there is no cost sharing coverage until the family has met its entire deductible.

Non- Embedded Deductible Example 1:

Let's revisit the Jones family (from Example 1 under the embedded deductible), and change from an embedded to a non-embedded deductible. The change will make the family pay the total $4,600 before the insurer will make any payment.

The deductible amount for the family is $4,600, and there is no individual amount. After the deductible has been satisfied, the coinsurance is 80/20. The only medical expenses for the year were for Dad, who had a skiing accident resulting in $6,500 of covered medical expenses.

The family's combined expenses total $6,500. Here's how they paid the deductible:

	Expenses	Deductible (paid by family)	Amount Subject to Coinsurance
Dad	$6,500	$4,600	$1,900
Mom	$0	$0	$0
Daughter	$0	$0	$0
Son	$0	$0	$0
Total	$6,500	$4,600	$1,900

The total paid by the Jones family is $4,600 + $380 = $4,980

Note that with the embedded deductible, the total paid by the Jones family was $1,840 less. A planner will need to understand how to evaluate the policy in order to recommend an appropriate emergency fund for the client or assist the client with decisions regarding which type of policy to select. In some cases, there may be a single family member who is likely to have higher medical expenses than others during the year, making the embedded deductible more attractive for that family.

Non-Embedded Deductible Example 2:

Now, let's revisit the Johnson family (from Example 2 under the embedded deductible) and change from an embedded to a non-embedded deductible. The change will make the family pay the total $4,600 before the insurer will make any payment.

The deductible amount for the family is $4,600, and there is no individual amount. The family was in a boating accident where all four family members required varying amounts of medical intervention. The family incurred the following expenses:

Dad: $3,200
Mom: $1,850
Daughter: $800
Son: $650

Because their plan has a non-embedded deductible, it only has the aggregate family deductible component. After the entire family's expenses total $4,600, they collectively move into the next level of coverage. Until that point, the insurer will make no payments.

The family's combined expenses total $6,500. Here's how they paid the deductible:

	Expenses	**Deductible (paid by family)**	**Remainder (paid by insurer)**
Dad	$3,200	$3,200	$0
Mom	$1,850	$1,400	$450
Daughter	$800	$0	$800
Son	$650	$0	$650
Total	$6,500	$4,600	$1,900

The total paid by the Johnson family is $4,600 + $380 = $$4,980

Embedded Versus Non-embedded MOOP

The ACA has a provision limiting maximum out-of-pocket expenses (MOOP). Beginning January 1, 2016, all non-grandfathered plans must include a MOOP that is no higher than $6,850 individual and $13,700 family. These amounts are indexed annually, and represent the most a policy-holder will have to pay during the policy period (e.g., one year). The MOOP includes the deductible, along with any other cost sharing, such as copays and coinsurance. However, the MOOP does not have to include premium payments or amounts charged by non-network providers. Unlike in previous years, plans must now include a provision that, once any individual has expenses exceeding the individual MOOP amount (e.g., $6,850), the plan must pay the excess of covered expenses for that individual, regardless of whether the family MOOP has been met. This is quite similar to how embedded deductibles function. With these regulations, it should be relatively easy to determine annual expense maximums, but that is often not the case, and is a good reason for the financial planner and client to review coverage and likely expenses.

In practice, embedded and non-embedded MOOPs function in the same way as their deductible counterparts. This means, among other things, that the determination of whether a MOOP is embedded or non-embedded only applies to policies covering the primary insured and at least one other family member. Also, one family member with high enough expenses can meet the entire family's MOOP amount. Let's look at some examples of how this would work for a family of four.

Example: Embedded MOOP

Assume the expenses listed below include the deductible, copays, coinsurance and all other covered costs. Also assume an individual MOOP of $6,850 and a family MOOP of $13,700.

Family members Jeff, Lizzy, Gregory, and Tamara have the following medical expenses during the year (Jeff and Gregory were also injured in a car accident later in the year):

	Expenses	Out-of-Pocket (paid by family)	Remainder (paid by insurer)
Jeff	$2,000	$2,000	$0
Lizzy	$3,500	$3,500	$0
Gregory	$7,000	$6,850	$150
Tamara	$9,000	$1,350 *	$7,650
Jeff	$8,000	$0	$8,000
Gregory	$6,000	$0	$6,000
Total	$35,500	$13,700	$21,800

* At this point, Gregory has met his embedded individual MOOP, and the family has met the total MOOP.

Example: Non-embedded MOOP

The Anderson family has a policy with an individual MOOP of $6,850 and a non-embedded family MOOP of $13,700. Assume the expenses listed below include the deductible, coinsurance, and all other covered costs. They had the following medical expenses during the year:

	Expenses	Out-of-Pocket (paid by family)	Remainder (paid by insurer)
Dad	$14,000	$13,750 *	$250
Mom	$10,000	$0	$10,000
Daughter	$500	$0	$500
Son	$1,200	$0	$1,200
Total	$25,700	$13,750	$11,950

* At this point, Dad has single-handedly met the family MOOP, and no further out-of-pocket payment is required. This payment situation would have been true whether the family had either an embedded or a non-embedded MOOP.

Let's look at the Anderson family again and assume they had different covered medical expenses during the year.

	Expenses	Out-of-Pocket (paid by family)	Remainder (paid by insurer)
Dad	$7,500	$7,500	$0
Mom	$4,000	$4,000	$0
Daughter	$3,000	$2,250 *	$750
Son	$1,750	$0	$1,750
Total	$ 16,250	$13,750	$2,500

* At this point, the family has met their MOOP, and no further out-of-pocket payment is required.

One final note, regardless of the plan or MOOP provisions, without special endorsements or exemptions, ACA plans do not reimburse expenses incurred outside the U.S. This means any plan holder who will be traveling outside this country should explore reasonable options in the event they incur medical expenses in a foreign location. It may be possible to make arrangements for expatriate plans when a U.S. citizen is transferred or otherwise chooses to live outside this country, but the specific rules are unclear and, therefore, should carefully be explored.

Practice Question

Diego and Maria have two children – Patti and Tomas. Diego and Maria work at a small (30 employee) accounting firm, and have no health care coverage as an employee benefit. They purchased a Silver plan through their Marketplace Exchange to cover their family's health care needs. Most years they wonder whether they need the coverage, but not this year. Each of the family members has incurred medical expenses, with Diego starting things off. In February, Diego was injured skiing, breaking his collar bone and one of his legs. Between the emergency room and follow-up care, Diego's portion of the medical bills totaled $10,000.

Their health care coverage is as follows:

- Embedded Silver plan: (but they earn too much for premium assistance or tax breaks)
- MOOP Individual: $6,850
- MOOP family: $13,700

How much of Diego's medical expenses will the insurer have to pay (non-grandfathered plan in 2016)?

- A. $3,150
- B. $6,850
- C. $10,000
- D. $13,700

Answer:

Diego ski injuries: $10,000: Individual MOOP $6,850; Family MOOP $13,700, but the insurer must pay the remainder of Diego's expenses after he reached his personal (embedded) MOOP. Diego pays $6,850 to reach his MOOP, and the plan pays remainder of covered expenses.

Total medical expenses: $10,000
Total embedded MOOP for Diego $6,850
Total policy payment: $3,150

The answer is A.

Practice Question

Bill and Nancy have one child – Sarah. Bill and Nancy are self-employed, and decided to purchase a Gold plan, and do so outside the Marketplace Exchange. They chose this route because they know the agent and also want greater flexibility in choosing medical professionals. Bill, Nancy, and Sarah have incurred the following medical expenses this year:

- Nancy: Has started experiencing a general sense of being unwell in January that continued throughout the year . . . fatigue, getting sick regularly, weight gain and as a result, clinical depression. Total expenses so far for medication, doctor visits, testing and the like have added up to $3,000.
- Sarah: Was in an auto accident in May. Everyone was OK, but Sarah had to be treated at the emergency room. Expenses for the ER and follow-up treatment totaled $5,000.
- Bill: Could no longer delay back surgery, so he scheduled it for July. The surgery worked as anticipated, but the total bill for care was $70,000.

Their health care coverage is as follows:

- Non-Embedded Gold plan
- MOOP Individual: $6,850
- MOOP family: $13,700

What is the total amount of out-of-pocket expense Bill and Nancy will have to pay for all family members?

A. $6,850
B. $13,700
C. $14,850
D. $21,700

Answer:
Bill and Nancy purchased a plan with a non-embedded deductible/out-of-pocket expense. As a result, the family in this scenario must satisfy the entire family deductible before any payment by the insurer. Nancy and Sarah's bills totaled $8,000, leaving $3,750 of Bill's expenses to be paid by Bill and Nancy thereby reaching the family out-of-pocket amount. From that point, the remainder of Bill's expenses should be paid by the insurer.
The Answer is B.

GROUP MEDICAL AS AN EMPLOYEE BENEFIT

While the Affordable Care Act is attempting to make medical expense insurance available to more Americans through the Health Insurance Marketplace beginning in 2014, most people who have medical insurance are still covered by an employer-paid plan.

Employee Benefit Analysis

Medical expense insurance as an employee benefit is usually highly valued by employees and their families. The high cost of medical treatment makes a health plan an important benefit for an employer to offer to attract and retain employees. The tax advantages to employers and employees make the employer-paid plan a cost-effective way to provide the coverage. Nevertheless, the rising cost of health insurance has increasingly made the coverage burdensome or unaffordable for many small businesses.

Group Medical Insurance Policy Types

Group medical expense insurance provided as an employee benefit may be any of the policy types mentioned earlier during the discussion of individual plans.

Traditional Indemnity (Fee-for-Service)

The traditional indemnity plan provides group medical insurance similar to the major medical coverage discussed earlier in this topic. The plans reimburse employees for necessary medical expenses, with few exclusions, but the plans contain cost-sharing features, such as deductibles and coinsurance.

Managed Care

Health insurance for employees may be provided under a managed care option in order to help control costs for both the employee and the employer. Managed care policies can be prepaid plans where the employer pays the provider of services in advance for future services, such as in an HMO. Managed care policies may also be offered as postpaid plans where services are paid for after they have been provided, such as with a PPO.

Consumer-Directed Health Plans

Consumer-directed health plans (CDHPs) are becoming a very popular way for employers to reduce the cost of providing health care benefits to employees. The use of a CDHP provides for significant premium savings for the employer, who will frequently use part of that premium savings to contribute to the employee's HSA account in order to assist the employee with the high deductible. Another nice advantage to the employee is that if the employee remains healthy for a number of years and does not spend the money in the HSA account, it accumulates earnings, and none of the contributions or earnings are forfeited upon termination of employment.

As CDHPs have become more popular, many large employers have begun offering a variety of health and wellness activities for employees. For example, the employer may sponsor a worksite health fair where screenings and educational seminars are offered to employees free of charge. Some large companies also encourage employees to establish support groups for things like weight management or smoking cessation. Online tools, such as risk assessments for various types of chronic conditions, are also becoming more readily available. Of course, all of these little perks are nice, and a great way for employers to encourage workers to maintain a healthier lifestyle, but they only work if employees choose to participate in them. Some employees may hesitate to participate due to concerns about the privacy of their health information. In order to make the programs more attractive, some employers offer financial incentives to employees who participate.

Additional information regarding workplace wellness programs can be found in the 2013 research report sponsored by the Department of Labor and Department of Health and Human Services, available online at:

http://www.dol.gov/ebsa/pdf/workplacewellnessstudyfinal.pdf

The Mechanics of Group Health Insurance

When offering group medical insurance to employees, the employer does have some flexibility regarding which employees are eligible for coverage. For example, coverage might only be offered to full-time employees (excluding part-time) who have worked for the company for at least 60 days (the probationary period whereby the company has the opportunity to ensure that the employment relationship is likely to last long-term before any employee benefits are offered).

Most large employers will allow the employee to choose from multiple types of policies such as traditional indemnity, an HMO, or a PPO type of policy, or among choices with different deductibles and coinsurance amounts. Employees may also be permitted to choose coverage for self-only, self plus spouse, or family (covering the employee, spouse, and all dependents). These selections typically must be made during an open enrollment period; for example, employees may have to choose their benefits for the upcoming year during October of the current year. When new dependents are added during the year (for example a child is born), there will be a limited time period (usually 31 days) following the event to add that dependent, and coverage will commence as of the date the dependent becomes eligible.

Dependent coverage is typically the same as the coverage for the employee, and eligible dependents are the spouse and any children under the age of 26 (including step-children, adopted children, and those born out of wedlock). Children under age 26 can remain on their parent's plan even if the child is married, does not live with the parents, is not financially dependent on the parents, or is eligible to enroll in his or her own employer's plan.

While group plans are not required to offer health benefits to an employee's domestic partner (unmarried same-sex or heterosexual partners), many plans do make the benefits available. Clients involved in domestic partnerships should be advised to check with their human resources department or health plan administrator for benefit availability. Some companies may set requirements such as a minimum time frame (e.g., 12 months) that the couple has been together, or may require proof of financial interdependence (e.g., a copy of a joint lease or joint mortgage).

When a domestic partner becomes covered under a plan, there are some federal tax implications that the client should be aware of. If the employer pays any part of the health insurance premium for the domestic partner, the employee will be taxed on that amount. An employee who will be taxed for additional premiums may wish to have increased taxes withheld from their paycheck to avoid a larger tax bill at the end of the year. When a domestic partner does not have health insurance coverage available through their own employer, paying the additional taxes for dependent coverage through the employee's group plan is still likely to be more cost efficient than obtaining an individual policy. If the domestic partner does have coverage available through their own employer, then the planner will need to help evaluate the coverage offered under each group plan versus the dependent coverage of a domestic partner.

Since the overturn of Section 3 of the Defense of Marriage Act (DOMA) in 2013, same-sex married couples are treated the same as heterosexual married couples under federal tax rules. When a same-sex spouse is covered under an employer-provided health insurance plan, the additional premiums paid for that coverage may be paid on a pre-tax basis, the same as for a heterosexual spouse.

Coordination of Benefits

When an individual is covered under more than one group plan, the coordination of benefits (COB) provisions will apply to determine which policy is the primary payer of any claims, and which policy is the secondary payer. These provisions are designed to ensure that the total benefits paid from all policies do not exceed 100% of the allowable expenses incurred.

While coordination of benefits provisions may vary, the approach proposed in the model legislation drafted by the National Association of Insurance Commissioners (NAIC) is frequently used. States typically adopt some or all of the model legislation. Some of the more common coordination provisions are described below. Note that in each case, the plan designated as the primary plan will pay benefits without regard to other insurance.

- A plan that covers the person as an employee is primary to a plan that covers the person as a dependent. For example, husband and wife both have health insurance coverage through their employers that covers both husband and wife. The plan through husband's employer is primary for him and secondary for the wife. The plan through the wife's employer is primary for her and secondary for her husband.

- The plan covering a person as an active employee, or as a dependent of, an active employee is primary to a plan covering the person as a retired or laid-off employee.

- A plan covering a person as an employee, retiree, or dependent of an employee or retiree is primary to COBRA coverage. (COBRA coverage is a continuation of group insurance following termination of employment and is discussed in this text on page 24.58.)

- A person covered as a dependent of an active employee, who also has retiree coverage from their previous employer, and is covered under Medicare will have primary coverage as a dependent of an active employee, Medicare pays second, and then the retiree coverage last (because retiree coverage is meant to supplement Medicare).

- Coverage for dependent children of divorced or separated parents may be determined by court decree. In the absence of a court decree stating otherwise, coverage for dependent children is treated as follows:

  ➢ For a dependent child whose parents are married, or unmarried but living together, the plan of the parent whose birthday (month and day only, not year) is earlier in the calendar year is primary. For example, if the father's birthday is June 6th and mother's birthday is September 2nd, then the father's plan is primary and the mother's plan is secondary.

  ➢ If the dependent child's parents are divorced, separated, or are not living together, and there is no court decree allocating responsibility for the child's health care coverage, then the order of benefits is as follows: the plan covering the custodial parent is primary, followed by the plan covering the custodial parent's spouse, then the plan covering the non-custodial parent, and lastly the plan covering the non-custodial parent's spouse. The custodial parent is the parent awarded custody of the child by a court decree, or in the absence of a court decree, the parent with whom the child resides more than one half of the calendar year.

Practice Question

John Delanie's employer provides group medical expense insurance covering the family, including his wife Elisa and their son David. Elisa's employer also provides a group plan covering the family. The plans both have typical coordination of benefits clauses. If Elisa and David are injured in an accident and have eligible medical expenses, what benefits will the group plans pay?

    A. John's plan will pay half of David's costs, and Elisa's plan will pay the rest.
    B. Elisa's plan will pay all of the costs.
    C. John and Elisa's plans will each pay 50% of all costs.
    D. Elisa's plan will pay for her expenses, but John's plan will pay for David's expenses if John's birthday is celebrated before Elisa's.

Answer:
Under typical coordination of benefits clauses, Elisa's group plan will pay all of her medical expenses because her policy will be primary. Although she is covered under John's group policy, that dependent coverage for Elisa will be secondary. David is covered as a dependent under both policies, so the policy for the employee with the earlier birth date on the calendar will be primary.
The answer is D.

Regulation of Employer-Provided Health Insurance

In many cases, the employer offering health insurance coverage will contract with, and pay premiums to, a health insurance company that provides the benefits and administration and also assumes all claims risk. This type of structure is called a fully insured group plan.

Group health insurance is regulated at both the federal and state level. States are primarily responsible for regulating insured group plans, but the Affordable Care Act (ACA) gives the federal government some control over various provisions, such as waiting periods for coverage to begin and certain preventive services the plan is required to cover.

Self-Funded Plans

Some large employers, usually those with at least several hundred employees, may choose to self-fund their group health plan by setting aside a pool of money to be used to pay claims of employees as they arise. Since this shifts the risk for paying claims to the employer, many of these plans will choose to partially insure by purchasing a policy, called a stop-loss policy, to cover claims above a certain threshold. Self-insured plans often have a contract with a third-party administrator to handle the administrative functions and claims. For this reason, the employee may not even realize that the plan is self-funded. Self-funded plans are not regulated at the state level, so they do not have to meet requirements imposed by state law when a state mandates coverage for certain medical services or treatments.

Self-funded plans have to meet nondiscrimination rules (under Section 105(h) of the tax code) that are not currently imposed on fully insured plans. Self-funded plans must ensure that the plan does not discriminate in favor of highly compensated individuals (HCIs) in regard to eligibility or benefits. If discrimination does occur, the HCI will be taxed on the excess benefits he or she received from the plan above those received by non-HCIs. For purposes of Section 105(h), a highly compensated individual is one of the top five highest paid officers, a greater than 10% shareholder, or in the top 25% highest paid employees. A discussion of how these discrimination tests are conducted and details of the tax calculation for HCIs in discriminatory plans is beyond the scope of this textbook.

While fully insured health plans do not currently have to meet the same nondiscrimination rules as self-insured plans, fully insured health insurance offered through cafeteria plans must meet the nondiscrimination provisions of cafeteria plans under Section 125 of the tax code. Also worth noting is that the tests for nondiscrimination and definition of highly compensated individual for cafeteria plans are different from those used for self-funded plans.

Summary Plan Descriptions and Summary of Benefits and Coverage

All employer-provided health plans, including both fully insured and self-funded plans, are also federally regulated by the Department of Labor under the Employee Retirement Income Security Act of 1974 (ERISA). ERISA grants employee-participants certain rights, such as the disclosure of important plan information (provided via a Summary Plan Description), timely and fair processing of benefit claims, the right to elect temporary continuance of group health coverage after losing coverage (see COBRA later in this topic), the right to a certificate evidencing health coverage under the plan, and the right to recover benefits due under the plan.

The Summary Plan Description (SPD) is one of the most important documents for the planner and client to review. The plan administrator is legally required to provide the SPD to participants free of charge. This SPD is the document that tells participants how the plan operates and what benefits are provided, including information about when an employee becomes eligible to participate in the plan, how services and benefits are calculated, and how to file a claim. If, for some reason, the client is unable to obtain a copy of the SPD from the plan's administrator, they can request a copy from the DOL's EBSA (Employee Benefits Security Administration).

Class Exercise 24 – 1

As a group, the class can explore the DOL's EBSA website to become familiar with the types of useful information about employer-provided health plans that is found there: http://www.dol.gov/ebsa/

Final regulations issued jointly by the Departments of Health and Human Services, Labor, and Treasury (the Agencies) on Feb. 9, 2012, require that, effective September 23, 2012, participants receive a Summary of Benefits and Coverage (SBC) that is presented in clear language and in a uniform format to help consumers to better understand the coverage they have and allow them to compare their coverage options across different types of plans. In addition employees must also receive a copy of the Uniform Glossary, which provides standard definitions of terms commonly used in health insurance coverage. The SBC does not replace the SPD, but may reference the SPD in its footnotes. Additional information regarding SBCs can be found on page 24.50, and an example of a completed SBC from the Department of Labor (www.dol.gov) is provided in Appendix C of this textbook.

Mental Health Parity

The Mental Health Parity and Addiction Equity Act prohibits large group employer-funded plans (covering over 50 employees) from imposing financial requirements (such as co-pays or deductibles) or treatment limitations on mental health and substance use disorder benefits in a way that is more restrictive than those imposed on other medical benefits.

Family Medical Leave Act (FMLA)

The Family Medical Leave Act allows eligible employees to take unpaid, job-protected leave for certain family and medical reasons. While on leave, the employee can continue group health insurance coverage as if he or she were not on leave.

Eligible employees are entitled to 12 weeks of unpaid leave for the birth of a child, adoption of a child, to care for a family member (spouse, child, or parent) who has a serious health condition, or for a serious health condition that makes the employee unable to perform his or her essential job functions. Twenty-six weeks of leave is available during any 12 month period for the employee to provide care for a covered military service member who is a member of the employee's family (spouse, child, parent).

Tax Advantages of Employer-Provided Health Plans

As an employee benefit, none offers more tax advantages than health insurance paid for by the employer. When the employer pays all or a portion of the premium, the employer is permitted a tax deduction for the premiums paid (as long as total compensation is reasonable). Although this is an economic benefit to the employee, which typically requires that the employee be taxed on that amount, tax law provides that for health insurance premiums, this economic benefit is not taxable income to the employee.

When the health insurance plan is contributory, meaning employees share in the cost of premiums, the share of premiums paid by employees is typically withheld from their paychecks on a pretax basis. In addition, any benefits received from the plan are also tax-free to the employees. If employees pay their share of the premiums after-tax, then the premiums can be added together with their other qualified medical expenses that were not reimbursed by insurance, and can be deducted as itemized deductions on Schedule A of their income tax returns; however, only the total expenses above 10% of adjusted gross income will be deductible.

For self-employed individuals (sole proprietors, partners in a partnership, LLC members, and greater-than-2% S-corporation owners) who do not have an employer-provided health plan available through another employer or spouse's employer, premiums paid by the business on behalf of the owner will first be taxable income to the owner, and will then be deductible as an above-the-line tax deduction on the owner's federal income tax return (Form 1040). The deduction for health insurance premiums, however, cannot exceed the earnings from the business (for example, if the business produced a loss for the year, no premium deduction will be permitted). For greater-than-2% S-corp. owner-employees, the premiums will be included as taxable income on the owner-employee's W-2, and are then deducted above the line on the Form 1040.

Practice Question

Jill's employer has set up a health insurance plan, and her employer takes $100 contributions per month from each employee's pay check for the cost of the plan. The total cost of coverage is $5,500 annually for Jill's family. Jill had surgery this year, and the insurer paid $4,000 of the expenses. What are the income tax consequences of the health care expenditures for Jill?

    A. Jill will report no income for the coverage and benefits, and she can deduct her contributions.

    B. Jill will report no income for the coverage and benefits, but she cannot deduct her contributions.

    C. Jill will report no income for the coverage, but she must report benefits as income and can deduct her contributions.

    D. Jill will report income for the cost of the coverage less her contributions, but she will not report the benefits as income.

Answer:

The cost of a health plan paid by the employer is not taxable income to the employee, so Jill does not report income for the employer's payment. The employer can deduct the cost of the health plan, and an employee does not report income for this benefit. The benefits paid by the plan are also not income to Jill. Jill cannot deduct the contributions because they are taken out of her pay. In other words, Jill is not taxed on this income taken out of her pay, so she cannot take a deduction for it.

The answer is B.

Health Care Reform and Employer-Provided Coverage

As mentioned earlier in this topic, the 2010 Health Care Reform will dramatically change health care coverage over the next few years. A number of provisions from the Affordable Care Act that apply to group health plans have already been implemented. Other provisions will be phased in over the next several years. When discussing the rules of the ACA, however, it should also be noted that some plans are considered "grandfathered plans," and portions of the ACA are not applicable to these plans.

Some provisions of the Affordable Care Act already in effect have benefitted insureds by eliminating any annual or lifetime limits on essential benefits, by prohibiting preexisting condition exclusions (effective September 23, 2010 for enrollees under age 19 and effective January 1, 2014 for all other enrollees), and by permitting children to remain covered under a parent's policy up to age 26 regardless of whether the child is a dependent of the parent or is a student. Non-grandfathered fully-insured and self-insured plans must also provide coverage for certain preventive services with no coinsurance and no deductible.

In addition, the ACA maximum out-of-pocket expense limitations take effect for policy years beginning in 2014. In 2016, the annual limit on out-of-pocket costs is $6,850 for self-only coverage or $13,700 for family coverage. These dollar amounts will increase annually.

The ACA also permits the use of "rewards" under health-contingent wellness programs offered in connection with group health plans. Rewards are generally limited to 30% of the cost of coverage, although the maximum permissible reward for wellness programs designed to prevent or reduce tobacco use is 50% (in essence, this creates a tobacco premium surcharge of up to 50%). If these incentive plans are used, reasonable alternatives must be provided in order to avoid prohibited discrimination.

As mentioned previously, the ACA requires that all eligible employees receive a copy (in print or electronic form) of a Summary of Benefits and Coverage (SBC) by the first day of any open enrollment period. This Summary is intended to make it easier for employees to understand and compare health plan choices. The SBC is required to contain the following elements:

- A description of the coverage, including the cost-sharing, for each category of benefits
- The exceptions, reductions, or limitations on coverage
- The cost-sharing provisions of the coverage, including deductible, coinsurance, and copayment obligations
- Renewability and continuation of coverage provisions
- A coverage facts label or coverage examples (common benefits) showing scenarios for having a baby (normal delivery) or for managing Type 2 diabetes (routine maintenance, well-controlled)
- A statement that the SBC is only a summary and that the plan document, policy, or certificate of insurance should be consulted to determine the governing contractual provisions of the coverage
- A contact number to call with questions and an Internet web address where a copy of the actual individual coverage policy or group certificate of coverage can be reviewed
- An Internet address (or other contact information) for obtaining a list of the network providers, an Internet address where an individual may find more information about the prescription drug coverage under the plan or coverage, and an Internet address where an individual may review the Uniform Glossary, and a disclosure that paper copies of the Uniform Glossary are available
- A uniform format (four double-sided pages in length, and 12-point font)

Upcoming Changes

For group health plan (including both insured and self-insured plans) years beginning on or after January 1, 2015, the maximum time an otherwise eligible employee can be required to wait before coverage becomes effective is 90 calendar days, following a maximum 30 day orientation period. For example, if the employee begins work on September 15th, the 30 day orientation period ends on October 14th (as measured by adding one month and subtracting one day) and group health insurance coverage must begin no later than January 13th (the 91st day from the end of the orientation period).

Today, only self-insured plans have nondiscrimination rules, but the ACA includes a provision requiring fully insured plans not to discriminate in favor of highly compensated employees as to either eligibility or benefits. This provision of the ACA was originally set to take effect in 2010, but has been delayed indefinitely. Employers offering fully insured plans will want to watch for any provision setting an effective date because the penalty for non-compliance is steep – an excise tax of $100 per day, for each person discriminated against.

Employer Shared Responsibility

On Feb. 10, 2014, the IRS and Treasury issued final regulations on the Employer Shared Responsibility provisions under section 4980H of the Internal Revenue Code. The shared responsibility rules will begin in 2015 and will apply only to employers who employ at least 50 full-time employees or a combination of full-time and part-time employees that is the equivalent of 50 full-time employees. A full-time employee is defined as one who works an average of at least 30 hours per week.

The Employer Shared Responsibility rules require these employers to offer affordable health coverage providing at least a minimum level of coverage to 95% or more of full-time employees and their dependents, or the employer will be subject to a shared responsibility payment of $2,000 per full-time employee (minus up to 30); but only if at least one full-time employee receives a premium tax credit for purchasing individual coverage in the Health Insurance Marketplace. Many insurance companies offering employer-provided insurance provide a calculator on their website that can be used to estimate the amount of shared responsibility payments.

The majority of businesses will fall below the 50 full-time equivalent employees and will, therefore, not be subject the Employer Shared Responsibility provisions.

Additional details regarding shared responsibility payments can be found at:

https://www.irs.gov/Affordable-Care-Act/Employers/Employer-Shared-Responsibility-Provisions

Beginning in 2016, large employers (with 50 or more full-time equivalent employees as defined under the Shared Responsibility provision) will also be required to report prior year information regarding coverage offered to full-time employees, including whether the coverage met the minimum value requirements. These reports must be submitted to the IRS and a statement provided to all full-time employees.

In order to meet the minimum value requirements, the plan must cover at least 60% of the total allowed cost of benefits under the plan. In other words, the plan must be designed in such a way that it would be expected to pay at least 60% of the total cost of medical services for a standard population, leaving 40% or less of the costs to be paid by the employees. Thus, if the deductibles, copays, and other out-of-pocket costs for employees were more than 40% of the total costs of medical services, the plan would not meet the minimum value requirements. The IRS and Department of Health and Human Services (HHS) have produced a minimum value calculator that employers, insurance companies, third-party administrators, or other entities can use to input plan information such as deductibles and co-pays and receive a determination as to whether the plan provides minimum value.

Small Employers

Beginning in 2014, small employers (those with 50 or fewer full-time employee equivalents) may be eligible to purchase insurance plans through the Small Business Health Options Program (SHOP) Marketplace operating in each state. An FTE Calculator is available to help small employers identify whether they qualify to purchase coverage through SHOP.

The SHOP marketplace was designed to help these small businesses provide health coverage to their employees, and the employer will be required to cover all full-time employees who work over 30 hours per week on average in order to purchase coverage through SHOP. Many states also require that at least 70% of full-time employees enroll in the SHOP plan (Arkansas, Iowa, NH, NJ, SD, TX all require 75%, TN 50%), although that requirement may be waived if coverage is purchased during the open enrollment period from November 15th to December 15th each year. If these participation rates are not reached, the small employer may choose to (1) change the offer of coverage, perhaps to contribute more toward the employee's insurance premiums to encourage more of them to participate, (2) enroll during open enrollment (November 15 – December 15) when the participation requirement is waived, or (3) withdraw the offer of coverage. An employer who chooses to withdraw the offer of coverage can reapply at any time during the same calendar year.

While the health insurance plans offered through the SHOP exchange are also generally available in the market outside of SHOP, it is important to note that businesses with fewer than 25 employees may qualify for tax credits, but only if insurance is purchased through SHOP.

Also worth noting is that self-employed individuals who do not have any employees may purchase coverage through the Health Insurance Marketplace, but are not permitted to purchase coverage through SHOP.

Small employers who are eligible to purchase coverage through SHOP will have the ability to choose from four levels of coverage, and can also choose the amount the employer will pay toward employee premiums. In addition, coverage can start in any month of the year. Those enrolled by the 15th of the month will begin receiving coverage on the first of the following month.

Finally, a small business health care tax credit may be available to employers with fewer than 25 employees with average annual wages of employees falling below $51,800 (in 2016). The employer must pay a uniform percentage of premium for all employees that is at least 50% of the total premium cost. The maximum credit is 35% of premiums paid, with any premium costs not covered by the credit remaining a tax deductible expense for the business. The credit can only be claimed in two consecutive years. To help small businesses determine whether they are eligible for the credit, a Small Business Health Care Tax Credit Estimator is available on the Taxpayer Advocate Service website at:

http://www.taxpayeradvocate.irs.gov/calculator/Instructions/TheEstimator.htm

Another estimator is available on the Healthcare.gov website at:

https://www.healthcare.gov/shop-calculators-taxcredit/

Class Discussion 24 – 3

Aside from meeting the ACA rules for mandated coverage, what are some of the advantages to employers of sponsoring group health care coverage for employees?

COBRA AND HIPAA

Employer-provided health coverage will typically cease when employment is terminated, but health coverage can also cease when an employee loses eligibility for coverage (for example, the employee reduced hours to part-time) or when a dependent ceases to qualify as a dependent (for example when a divorce occurs or when a child reaches age 26). It is important for planners to be able to advise a client on alternatives when employer-provided coverage is no longer available.

Continuance and Convertibility

When an individual loses eligibility for group insurance through an employer, the employee can elect to continue the group coverage under the COBRA rules, or can convert to an individual policy. The conversion privilege is usually available for 31 days after the termination of the group coverage. The individual coverage can be purchased without evidence of insurability and without exclusion of preexisting conditions. Employees can usually convert both their own coverage and the coverage of dependents. If an employee elects to continue group coverage under COBRA, the same privilege to convert to an individual policy must be made available for 31 days after the COBRA-continuation coverage ends.

Another option when employer coverage is lost may be to adjust the other spouse's employer-provided coverage to extend coverage to the spouse who recently lost coverage. For example, if husband and wife are each covered under their own employer's group plan and husband loses his group coverage, a special enrollment may be available under the wife's employer-sponsored plan to add the husband.

With the Affordable Care Act's elimination of exclusions for pre-existing conditions, the urgency to convert to an individual policy to preserve insurability and avoid exclusion of pre-existing conditions may be reduced. Remember, however, that a policy must be purchased through the Health Insurance Marketplace within 60 days of loss of coverage from the group plan (or COBRA). Missing the 60 day special enrollment period will require the client to wait until the next open enrollment period for the Marketplace.

COBRA

The Consolidated Omnibus Budget Reconciliation Act (COBRA) is federal legislation requiring some employers to offer terminated employees the right to purchase medical expense insurance coverage at group rates. COBRA covers virtually all types of group plans that fall into the "health" plan category (for example, medical, vision, and dental plans), except long-term care plans.

The following employers are not required to provide continuation coverage for their employees:

- Employers with fewer than 20 employees
- Churches
- Government employers

An eligible employee may elect "continuation coverage" under COBRA during the 60-day period immediately after the later of two dates: (1) the date the coverage for the person terminates, or (2) the date the plan administrator notifies a qualified beneficiary of the beneficiary's right to continue coverage.

A "qualifying event" is one of the four types of changes in an employee's or dependent's status that makes him or her eligible for continuation coverage under COBRA. The four types of changes are:

1. Termination of employment, except for gross misconduct

2. Reduction in the employee's work hours to such an extent that he or she is no longer eligible for coverage

3. The loss of coverage by a dependent because of the employee's death, divorce, legal separation, or eligibility for Medicare

4. The loss of dependency status by children of employees (for example, attainment of the maximum age limit of 26)

The following persons are "qualified beneficiaries" eligible for continuation of group coverage under COBRA (if a "qualifying event" has occurred):

(1) A covered employee
(2) A covered employee's spouse
(3) A covered employee's dependent children

The plan administrator is required to notify all eligible beneficiaries within 14 days of knowledge of a qualifying event. The employer has 30 days to notify the administrator when a qualifying event occurs. In some cases, such as divorce, the employer may not be aware that a qualifying event has occurred, in which case the employee must notify the employer within 60 days or no COBRA coverage will be available.

If an employee takes leave under the Family and Medical Leave Act but then does not return to work, the qualifying event under COBRA is treated as occurring on the last day of the leave.

The election period for COBRA starts on the date of the qualifying event and must last at least 60 days from the time the beneficiary receives notification from the administrator. Each of the qualified beneficiaries can choose COBRA continuation independently. When the election for coverage is made, coverage is retroactive to the date of the qualifying event. If coverage is initially waived and medical expenses are incurred during the 60 day election period, the waiver can be revoked and coverage will begin retroactively to the day of the qualifying event, so that those recently incurred medical expenses will be paid by the plan. Of course, this also means premiums must be paid retroactively, but if the medical expenses are significantly higher than the total premiums, it can be a large savings to the insured.

Some planning clients who are losing coverage due to a job change will have a probationary period before becoming eligible for coverage under the health plan of the new employer. If the client is healthy and will be eligible for the new coverage before the 60-day COBRA election period ends, he may decide to wait and see if he has any medical expenses before electing COBRA. If no or low costs are incurred before the new coverage begins, the client will have saved the cost of the premiums. If the client ends up with significant medical costs during that 60 day timeframe, he can elect COBRA retroactively. Care must be used when employing this strategy, however, because if the client has any pre-existing conditions and there is a period of more than 63 days between the old health plan coverage and the new health plan coverage, the new plan may be permitted to exclude coverage for preexisting conditions for up to 6 months.

Termination of employment will make the affected employees eligible for 18 months of continuation coverage, while other "qualifying events" permit 36 months of coverage. If termination is due to disability, the employee must be permitted to continue coverage for 29 months.

Planners should make particular notice of the 18 month limit for retirement (termination of employment). The average retirement age in the U.S. is 62 but retirees are not eligible for Medicare until age 65, which could mean a substantial gap in health insurance coverage for retirees who choose, or are forced, to retire early.

During the period of the continuation coverage, the employer may require the employee to pay up to 102% of the cost of the continued coverage (150% for disabled employees after 18 months).

When the maximum period for continuation coverage terminates, an employee must be able to exercise the conversion rights that are otherwise available under the plan, or, as an alternative, will be eligible for the special 60-day enrollment period in the Healthcare Marketplace.

Employees age 65 and older who have chosen not to enroll in Medicare Part B due to the employer-provided coverage should generally not elect COBRA coverage at termination of employment and should instead enroll in Medicare Part B. This enrollment is recommended because failure to enroll in Medicare Part B within 8 months of termination of employment will cause the Part B premium to be permanently increased, and because COBRA premiums are typically more expensive than Medicare Part B premiums.

🔑 **KEY SUMMARY 24 – 1**
COBRA Coverage

When must the COBRA election be made?	Within 60 days of health plan coverage ending
Who can make an election?	Employee, spouse, or dependent
What are qualifying events for an employee?	Termination (except for gross misconduct)
What are qualifying events for dependents?	Employee's death, divorce, legal separation, or Medicare eligibility, or a child is no longer dependent
What is the premium for continued coverage?	Maximum of 102% of the cost to the employer
What coverage must be provided?	Identical coverage as under the employer's plan
How long does coverage continue?	18 months for a terminated employee 29 months for a disabled employee 36 months for others

---

HIPAA

Prior to the 1996 passing of the Health Insurance Portability and Accountability Act (HIPAA), individuals with pre-existing conditions often were fearful of changing jobs because of at least temporary loss of health care coverage with their new employers. To solve the problem, HIPAA specified that if a person was covered by health insurance and had met the requirements in that plan for the coverage of preexisting conditions, he or she no longer needed to meet the requirements of a new employer's group health insurance plan with respect to preexisting conditions. Also, group plans may not exclude coverage for preexisting conditions for more than 12 months for those who enroll when they first become eligible to do so (18 months for late enrollees). Furthermore, only those preexisting conditions that are manifested within the six months prior to the enrollment date may be subject to this exclusion.

Other aspects of the HIPAA are dealt with in the discussion of long-term care in Topic 26 of this textbook.

Continuation

In addition to the requirements of COBRA and HIPAA, some employers offer continued coverage for certain employees, such as retirees, disabled employees, or surviving family members of a deceased employee. In addition, some state laws require continuation of coverage in situations not covered by COBRA, such as employers with fewer than 20 employees.

In the past, it was common for continuation of group coverage to be offered to retirees, although accounting rule changes have made it unattractive for employers to continue to offer such coverage (see FASB rule 106 for additional details). Many employers who do still offer retiree health care coverage have amended their plans to allow them to terminate the plan at any time, making it an unreliable source of coverage for the retiree.

OTHER EMPLOYEE BENEFITS

Cafeteria Plans

A cafeteria plan is an employee benefit program which, within stated limits, permits employees to design their own benefit packages by allocating a predetermined number of dollars among available options. The choices or options available under cafeteria plans permit employees to write their own employee benefit programs to meet their unique individual needs. However, the law requires the employer to offer at least one cash benefit. The cash benefit offered can be actual cash or some benefit the employee purchases (after taxes) with his or her elected cash amount and one or more so-called "statutory nontaxable benefits" (for example, group life insurance and health insurance).

Cafeteria plans can now offer health savings accounts as part of their menu of choices. Employers who make contributions to the health savings accounts for employees must make comparable contributions for all participating employees.

Within the limits allowed by law, employers can deduct contributions, and employees can exclude the amount contributed from gross income.

A cafeteria plan is prohibited from offering a pension or other retirement plan, a deferred-compensation plan, educational assistance, employee discounts, or noncash fringe benefits. However, a cafeteria plan may offer a 401(k) plan with employer matching contributions. A cafeteria plan can offer group term life insurance, but not cash value life insurance. Cafeteria plans also cannot offer long-term care insurance as a tax-free benefit. If the cafeteria plan includes the long-term care insurance, the premiums will be treated as taxable income to the employee.

Whenever an employee elects to receive cash, the cash received is includible in the employee's gross income. If the plan is discriminatory, the value of any benefits provided to a highly-paid employee by the employer is includible in the employee's gross income.

Flexible Spending Accounts (FSAs)

A flexible spending account is a type of cafeteria plan and must meet the rules prohibiting discrimination in favor of highly-compensated employees. The FSA may exist along with a cafeteria plan or as a stand-alone plan. Under a flexible spending account plan, the employee elects a reduction in compensation and requests those dollars be allocated to the purchase of a specific benefit. The benefits that can be provided include the following:

- Health insurance premiums and payment of medical expenses not covered under a health insurance plan, such as co-pays and coinsurance payments, eyeglasses, and dental care
- Expenses for dependent care
- Parking
- Mass transportation

The maximum salary deferral for a health care FSA in 2016 is $2,550. Salary reductions must be made before the compensation is earned. The elections to reduce salary for a flexible spending account are made annually before the beginning of the year for which the reduction will be effective.

Salary reduction occurs for each benefit, and unused amounts allocated to one benefit cannot be reallocated to another benefit. If the money allocated to each benefit is not used by the end of the year, it is forfeited. However, money allocated to parking and mass transportation is not forfeited and can be paid out as additional compensation the following year.

Starting in 2005, employers were permitted to revise their flexible spending accounts to allow employees up until March 15th of the following year to spend the funds. Beginning in 2014, as an alternative, IRS Notice 2013-71 permits an employer, at its option, to amend its § 125 cafeteria plan document to provide for the carryover to the immediately following plan year of up to $500 of any amount remaining unused as of the end of the plan year in a health FSA. This option only applies to plans that have not been amended to allow employees up to March 15th of the following year to spend the funds. The carryover of up to $500 does not count against or otherwise affect the indexed $2,550 salary reduction limit applicable to each plan year.

The dollars allocated by the employee to purchase specific benefits in the flexible spending account are not includible in the employee's gross income and are not treated as wages for Social Security taxes. The reduction in an employee's salary can reduce income taxes, and if the employee's income will be reduced below the Social Security wage base, Social Security taxes will also be reduced. An employer's payroll taxes may also be reduced.

While the use-it-or-lose-it feature on a health FSA may seem unfavorable, the significant tax savings makes them very attractive for payment of recurring medical expenses such as prescription drugs taken on a regular basis, annual eye exams and eyeglasses or contact lenses, routine dental visits, etc.

Voluntary Employees' Beneficiary Associations (VEBAs)

Voluntary employees' beneficiary associations (VEBAs) are set up as funding arrangements for employee benefits and are not employee benefit plans in themselves. Income of a VEBA is tax-exempt when it complies with IRC Secs. 501(c)(9) and 505, and the employer is permitted to deduct the firm's annual contribution. Thus, an employer may make use of a VEBA to advance the time for deduction of benefit contributions.

The purpose of a VEBA as set forth in IRC Sec. 501(c)(9) is to provide "life, sickness, accident, and other" benefits designed to "safeguard or improve the health of a member... against a contingency that...impairs a member's earning power." A VEBA may be used to provide a funding vehicle for a liberal list of employee benefits. In addition to life, sickness, and accident benefits, the employee may receive vacation, child care, legal services, severance, education, job training, and supplemental unemployment compensation benefits. A VEBA is not permitted to provide retirement benefits, commuting benefits, or miscellaneous fringe benefits.

A VEBA enables an employer to provide more benefit security and to prefund more tax-deferred benefits than under a qualified plan or a self-insured plan. A VEBA permits the employer to deduct contributions and to avoid taxation for investment income earned on those contributions. Under a self-insured plan, the employer is only permitted to deduct actual benefit payments.

The dollar value of benefits provided and the employer's contribution to the VEBA are not included in employees' gross income. The employer may deduct each dollar contributed to a VEBA when the plan is structured as an employee welfare plan and the plan qualifies as a multi-employer trust.

Employees have the option of becoming members of the VEBA, and membership is voluntary. Membership is available also to the employees' designated beneficiaries.

Employees of a common employer are eligible to become members. The usual nondiscrimination rules apply.

Noncurrent employees (e.g., former employees or retirees) may become members of a VEBA, but the number of such "nonemployees" cannot exceed 10% of the total membership.

Some VEBA benefits may be funded by insurance, but those that are not may create a large, uncertain expense and funding problem for the employer. On the other hand, the IRS has shown growing concern regarding employers overfunding the plans in order to control their taxation (especially with small employers). Many VEBA trusts are established by labor unions in order to remove the liability for health plans from their accounting books.

Dental Insurance

A method of cost containment used with many employer-provided health care plans involves carving out certain types of coverage to be managed under a separate contract or to be subcontracted to another medical expense provider specializing in that area. Common examples include prescription drug coverage, vision benefits, mental health benefits, and dental insurance.

Group dental plans are provided by insurance companies, dental service plans, Blue Cross-Blue Shield, managed care plans, and employer self-funding. Group dental insurance contracts are typically similar to group medical expense contracts and may be incorporated into a group major medical contract. Eligibility for dental coverage is usually the same as for medical expense coverage, although the probationary period may be longer. Some insurers may require evidence of insurability before coverage becomes effective.

Dental plans differ from medical expense plans in paying benefits for routine diagnostic procedures and preventive treatment. Dental insurance plans pay for most dental expenses, including treatment of gum diseases and orthodontics.

Scheduled plans pay benefits from the first dollar up to a specified maximum, while nonscheduled plans pay the reasonable and customary expense. Nonscheduled plan benefits are subject to deductibles and coinsurance, but diagnostic and preventive services are often covered in full. Combination plans offer features of both scheduled and nonscheduled plans.

Dental HMOs typically have no deductibles and are more likely to pay in full for services. Most plans, except for dental HMOs, have a calendar-year benefit limit, and nearly all plans have overall maximums.

There is seldom a conversion privilege with dental insurance as there is with medical expense insurance. Dental coverage, however, is subject to the COBRA continuation rules.

Vision Insurance

Most group vision coverage is provided under a carve-out benefit plan. The plans may be offered by insurance companies, Blue Cross-Blue Shield, HMOs, PPOs, or state optometric associations. Some plans provide benefits according to a schedule that sets the amounts to be paid for eye examinations, lenses, and frames. Other plans pay benefits on a service basis rather than setting a maximum. Vision plans do not pay for eye surgery or for treatment of eye diseases because a medical expense plan will cover these expenses.

Vision care plans are also subject to COBRA continuation rules.

PLANNING FOR HEALTH CARE COSTS IN RETIREMENT

Planning for Health Care Costs in Retirement

Planning for the cost of health care in retirement is a challenging task. The cost of health care is one of the major unknown expenses that retirees will face. The retiree may be fortunate enough to maintain good health throughout the retirement years. On the other hand, for many retirees, health care costs represent a significant portion of retirement spending.

A recent study from the non-profit Employee Benefit Research Institute (EBRI) indicates that Medicare covers approximately 62% of the cost of health care services for retirees age 65 and older. According to the EBRI research, a large part of out-of-pocket expenses for retirees comes from the cost of prescription drugs, and those costs can vary dramatically. In order for a female retiring at age 65 to have a 50% chance of having enough money to pay for her health care expenses (Medigap premiums, Medicare Part B premiums, Medicare Part D premiums, and out-of-pocket prescription drug expenses) through average life expectancy for a woman, she would need to have $86,000 ($65,000 for a man) set aside to cover these costs, based on median prescription drug expenses. To have a

90% chance of having enough money, she would need $139,000 ($122,000 for a man) to cover median prescription drug expenses. Should the woman be in the 90th percentile of prescription drug expenses, these numbers jump to $124,000 for a 50% chance ($96,000 for a man), and $195,000 for a 90% chance ($172,000 for a man) of having enough.

(http://www.ebri.org/pdf/notespdf/EBRI_Notes_10_Oct-13_RetSvgs-IRAs.pdf)

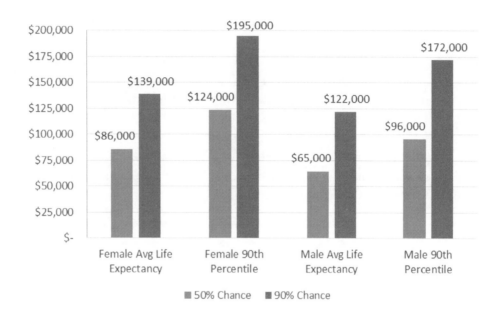

Financial planners will be called upon to assist clients with decisions regarding Medicare and Medigap policies and continuation of employer insurance. The planner will need to estimate the costs of health care and incorporate them into the retirement plan. These costs include premiums, deductibles, co-pays, and costs not covered by insurance.

Retirees who have contributed to an HSA and been healthy enough to avoid utilizing it for medical expenses over a significant time period will have a nice-sized pool of tax-free money to be used to cover health care costs during the retirement years. If the employee is lucky enough to remain healthy throughout retirement, the money remaining in the HSA can be used for other expenses. Remember that there is no 20% penalty if money is withdrawn from the HSA after age 65 (although income taxes will be due on the funds that are withdrawn from the account).

As clients age, additional capital expenditures may also be necessary to enable them to remain in their home. Examples include replacing steps with ramps, replacing tubs with showers, installing handles in bathrooms, and moving washers and dryers, bathrooms, and bedrooms to the first floor of the home. These additional costs may be significant and should be estimated and included in the retirement plan.

Assumptions

Calculating financial needs in retirement requires assumptions regarding inflation rates, which are often based on historical CPI figures. For retiring clients, health care costs represent a significant percentage of spending, and the inflation rate for health care tends to be significantly higher than the CPI-U (Consumer Price Index for Urban Consumers) figure that is most frequently referred to. The Bureau of Labor Statistics publishes CPI-M for medical inflation, as well as CPI-U, and some planners prefer to use a blended inflation statistic when estimating retirement income needs.

A client's level of risk tolerance will also be a factor in determining the appropriate types and amount of insurance for healthcare. The planner will need to seek the client's input concerning assumptions about healthcare cost inflation to be used in preparing the analysis and evaluation of the client's current and expected financial situation. In addition, an analysis of insurance coverages, premiums, and maximum annual out-of-pocket costs in the insurance policy may allow the planner to estimate a "worst case scenario" for annual cash flow needs to pay for health care expenses in retirement.

Class Discussion 24 – 4

What types of information does a planner need to gather in order to evaluate the client's health insurance and health care cost management choices?

DEFINITIONS

Above-the-Line Deductions – In the formula for calculating income taxes, certain deductions, called above-the-line deductions, may be used to reduce the taxpayer's adjusted gross income. Above-the-line deductions may be taken by all taxpayers who qualify for them, regardless of whether they choose to take the standard deduction or itemized deductions later in the tax return.

Adjusted Gross Income (AGI) – In the formula for calculating income taxes, the adjusted gross income is total income minus certain deductions (called above-the-line deductions). Adjusted gross income is the last line on the front of the Form 1040 and the first line on the back of the Form 1040.

Blue Cross/Blue Shield – The Blue Cross and Blue Shield Association is a national federation of 37 independent, community-based and locally operated Blue Cross® and Blue Shield® companies. Blue Cross and Blue Shield companies offer a variety of insurance products in all 50 U.S. states and across various market segments including large employer groups, small businesses, and individuals.

Consumer-Directed Health Care Plan – A consumer-directed health care plan combines a high deductible insurance policy with a Health Savings Account (HSA).

Deduction – In calculating income taxes for the year, deductions are certain types of expenses incurred throughout the year that taxpayers are permitted to use to reduce income. Deductions may be broken down into above-the-line deductions and below-the-line deductions. For below-the-line deductions, taxpayers can choose to take a standard deduction amount, or they can choose to itemize deductions, such as qualified mortgage interest, state and local income taxes, and charitable contributions.

Itemized Deductions – Itemized deductions are specified expenses that individual taxpayers can use to reduce taxable income for the year. Among other expenses, itemized deductions include the ability to deduct qualified medical expenses to the extent that they exceed 10% of the taxpayer's adjusted gross income for the year (7.5% of AGI if the taxpayer or spouse is over age 65 as of the end of the tax year).

Multi-Employer Trust – A multi-employer trust is established by a group of employers to provide tax advantaged benefits for employees and owners. When established to provide healthcare and other benefits for the welfare of employees, they may be referred to as Multiple Employer Welfare Arrangements (MEWAs).

Self-Employment Tax – Self-employment tax includes both the employee and employer portion of the Social Security and Medicare tax. Individuals who are self-employed include sole proprietors, partners in a partnership, and LLC members.

Social Security Currently Insured Status – In order to be eligible to receive benefits under Social Security, a worker must be currently or fully insured. Currently insured status allows a deceased, retired, or disabled worker to receive limited benefits. To be currently insured, a worker must have earned 6 of the last 13 credits available (a worker can earn a maximum of 4 credits per year, and one credit is earned for each $1,260 earned in 2016).

Social Security Fully Insured – In order to be eligible to receive benefits under Social Security, a worker must be currently or fully insured. Fully insured status allows a deceased, retired, or disabled worker to receive a full range of benefits. To be fully insured, a worker must have earned 40 credits during their lifetime (a worker can earn a maximum of 4 credits per year, and one credit is earned for each $1,260 earned in 2016).

Social Security Wage Base – Workers who have earned income and self-employed individuals are required to pay Social Security taxes on income up to the wage base. For 2016, the wage base is $118,500.

State High Risk Pools – State high risk pools are programs that were set up in 35 states from 1976 to 2009 to assist uninsurable individuals. The health care reform act of 2010 provided additional funding to all 50 states to either expand existing programs or to create new programs. States can choose to continue to run their own programs or can defer to the federal government to run their programs.

Stop-Loss Insurance for Self-Insured Plans and HRAs – Stop-loss insurance provides protection against catastrophic or unpredictable losses for employers who have chosen to self-insure their health care plans for employees. Under the stop-loss policy, the insurance company will become liable for losses over a certain dollar amount (the deductible).

TRICARE (formerly CHAMPUS) – TRICARE is a health insurance plan offering civilian benefits for military personnel, military retirees, and their dependents.

APPLICATION QUESTIONS

1. Bonnie, a diabetic, has a typical basic hospital, surgical, and physicians' expense policy. Which of the following medical expenses incurred by Bonnie is <u>not</u> likely to be covered by this policy?

    A. The surgeon's fee when Bonnie had her gallbladder removed
    B. The ongoing costs of Bonnie's insulin for treatment of her diabetes
    C. The hospital's charge for use of the operating room for Bonnie's gallbladder operation
    D. The hospital's charge when Bonnie was treated in the emergency room as an outpatient when she broke her ankle
    E. The cost of general duty nursing care Bonnie received in the hospital during the few days after her gallbladder surgery

2. Which of the following are among the characteristics of major medical insurance?

    (1) Many exclusions
    (2) Internal limits for hospital room-and-board charges
    (3) High initial deductible
    (4) High corridor deductible

    A. (1) and (2) only
    B. (1) and (3) only
    C. (2) and (3) only
    D. (3) and (4) only
    E. (1), (3), and (4) only

3. Terry Jackson has a major medical policy with a $500 initial deductible per illness, an 80% coinsurance requirement, and an internal limit of $500 per day for hospital room-and-board costs. During a recent hospital stay of four days, Terry incurred the following bills:

Hospital room-and-board charge	$2,600
Hospital lab fees and tests	$4,400
Surgeon's fee	$2,800

How much of Terry's medical bills will be paid by the major medical insurer?

A. $5,110
B. $5,790
C. $6,180
D. $6,960
E. $7,440

4. Beverly Thompson has a typical comprehensive major medical insurance policy. Which of the following medical expenses that Beverly incurred recently is (are) likely to be covered by this policy?

(1) Replacement of eyeglasses she broke while playing tennis
(2) Treatment for food poisoning in the emergency room of a hospital
(3) A face-lift to remove old-age wrinkles from her face

A. (1) only
B. (2) only
C. (3) only
D. (1) and (2) only
E. Neither (1), (2), nor (3)

5. Deductibles are used in major medical policies for which of the following reasons?

(1) To reduce premium costs
(2) To reduce malingering
(3) To eliminate small claims
(4) To lower administrative costs

A. (1) and (2) only
B. (1) and (3) only
C. (2) and (4) only
D. (1), (3), and (4) only
E. (2), (3), and (4) only

6. The coinsurance or percentage participation requirement in a major medical policy is designed for which of the following purposes?

    (1) To increase the policy's stop-loss
    (2) To reduce moral hazard
    (3) To eliminate small claims

        A. (1) only
        B. (2) only
        C. (3) only
        D. (1) and (2) only
        E. (2) and (3) only

7. Hal's comprehensive major medical policy has a $5,000 "stop-loss" limit. The primary purpose of this limit is to:

    A. Limit Hal's coverage to claims that exceed the specified amount
    B. Limit Hal's total benefits to the specified amount
    C. Limit Hal's out-of-pocket costs for a given claim
    D. Limit the amount to which the insurer may raise Hal's annual premium
    E. Limit Hal's benefit amount for rehabilitation costs

8. Jerome Guiffray has a major medical policy with a $250 deductible, 80% coinsurance, and a $4,000 cap on his total out-of-pocket cost (excluding the deductible). Jerome had bills of $200 for visits in the first part of the year and then had bills of $3,750 for a prolonged illness near the end of the year. What amount of medical expenses will Jerome have to pay for the year?

    A. $250
    B. $790
    C. $990
    D. $1,050

9. As a result of a recent hospitalization, Linda's hospital bill was $9,000, including $250 for flowers ordered from the hospital florist shop. How much will Linda's major medical insurer pay if the policy has a $500 deductible and an 80 percent coinsurance provision?

    A. $6,600
    B. $7,000
    C. $7,875
    D. $8,750
    E. $9,000

10. (Published question released January, 1999; updated)

Which of the following is a benefit currently provided by Medicare?

A. Hospice benefits for terminally ill patients
B. A stop-loss limit for annual medical expenses in excess of $2,500
C. Coverage for custodial care
D. Full coverage for prescription drugs that can be self-administered

11. Raymond is 65 years of age and is eligible for Social Security benefits. Which of the following statements concerning his eligibility for Medicare benefits is correct?

A. If Raymond signs up for Part A, but not Part B, he cannot sign up for Part B later.
B. If Raymond is enrolled automatically for Part A, the premiums will be lowest for Part B if he signs up at age 65.
C. If Raymond signs up for Part B later, the premium will be the same as at age 65.
D. If Raymond declines Part A and Part B, he will be able to sign up at any time.

12. Which of the following statements concerning Medicare benefits available to those over 65 are true?

(1) Medigap coverage is available to cover costs not paid for by Medicare, but only under federal guidelines.
(2) A patient pays deductibles for hospital stays, but nothing for home health services.
(3) Part A of Medicare coverage is optional for those covered by Social Security and requires a monthly premium.
(4) Options for those covered by Medicare include Medicare HMOs and Medicare MSAs.

A. (1) and (2) only
B. (2) and (4) only
C. (3) and (4) only
D. (1), (2), and (4) only
E. (1), (2), (3), and (4)

13. A client has asked about long-term care in the event of a lengthy illness. Which of the following programs will pay for more than 100 days of nursing home care?

    A. Medicare, Part A
    B. Medigap policy, Plan E
    C. Medicaid
    D. Medicare, Part B

14. (Published question released December, 1996)

Under the Consolidated Omnibus Budget Reconciliation Act (COBRA), an employer is required to extend medical plan coverage to eligible members of the employee's family if the employee:

    (1) Dies
    (2) Retires
    (3) Divorces
    (4) Terminates employment (prior to retirement)

        A. (1), (2), and (3) only
        B. (1) and (3) only
        C. (2) and (4) only
        D. (4) only
        E. (1), (2), (3), and (4)

15. Under which of the following circumstances is an employer not required to extend medical plan coverage to an employee or his or her dependents under COBRA?

    A. The employee quit to take a job with another employer.
    B. The employee took leave under the Family and Medical Leave Act and then did not return to work.
    C. The employee was terminated for gross misconduct.
    D. The employee was terminated in a corporate reorganization.
    E. The employee was terminated for negligence in performance of his or her duties.

16. Harold is married and works for an airline that has medical insurance with an HSA and a profit-sharing plan. Harold is considering whether to make contributions to an IRA or to his HSA. Harold is age 55 and earns $175,000 AGI annually. Which of the following statements is most appropriate for a recommendation to Harold?

    A. Harold should fund the IRA because he is close to retirement, and the HSA is only for medical expenses.

    B. Harold should fund the HSA because contributions are deductible for the HSA, but are not deductible for the IRA.

    C. It makes no difference because distributions from both the IRA and HSA are subject to income tax, but are not subject to any penalties after age 59½.

    D. It depends on whether Harold will have medical expenses exceeding 10% of AGI for the year.

17. Which of the following group benefit plans offered by an employer for employees is <u>NOT</u> subject to the continuation rules under COBRA?

    A. Vision care plan

    B. VEBA

    C. Dental plan

    D. Major medical plan

18. All the following statements concerning the MSA program are correct, EXCEPT:

    A. It is different from Health Savings Accounts (HSAs).

    B. It pays part of the medical expenses of participants not covered by the participant's health plans.

    C. It requires the imposition of a high deductible.

    D. A person would be disqualified if he or she had either an individual disability income policy or a long-term care insurance coverage.

    E. A penalty is imposed if the participant makes an excess contribution.

19. All the following statements concerning HSAs are correct, EXCEPT:

    A. HSA distributions used by the participant-taxpayer for the family's medical expenses are excluded from the taxpayer's gross income.

    B. Any HSA distributions not used for medical expenses are subject to federal income taxes.

    C. If HSA contributions are less than the prescribed limits, the account earnings are included in the account holder's gross income for federal income tax purposes.

    D. If one spouse has an FSA at work, neither spouse is eligible to contribute to an HSA.

    E. Contributions will be deductible even if individuals do not itemize.

20. All the following statements concerning Voluntary Employee Beneficiary Associations (VEBAs) are correct, EXCEPT:

    A. The employer may deduct contributions for federal income tax purposes.

    B. The employer avoids taxation on the investment income earned on contributions.

    C. The employee may be provided retirement and miscellaneous fringe benefits.

    D. Noncurrent employees may become members of a VEBA.

21. Which of the following statements concerning the typical VEBA is (are) correct?

    (1) Membership is voluntary.

    (2) Discrimination in favor of highly-compensated employees is not permitted.

    (3) Employees may receive vacation, child care, legal services, education, and job training benefits.

        A. (1) only
        B. (1) and (2) only
        C. (1) and (3) only
        D. (2) and (3) only
        E. (1), (2), and (3)

22. Which of the following can be found in the Summary of Benefits and Coverage for a group health plan?

(1) Cost-sharing provisions of the coverage, including deductible, coinsurance, and copayment obligations

(2) An internet address (or other contact information) for obtaining a list of the network providers, and Internet address where an individual may find more information about the prescription drug coverage under the plan

(3) Any exceptions, reductions, or limitations on coverage

    A. (1) only
    B. (1) and (2) only
    C. (1) and (3) only
    D. (2) and (3) only
    E. (1), (2), and (3)

23. John and Alice Smith have a 9-year-old son, Greg. John and Alice recently got divorced, and Greg will be living primarily with Alice, although he will spend every Wednesday, every other weekend, and 1 week of each month in June, July, and August with John. The Child Support Agreement requires John to provide health insurance for Greg and to pay for 70% of any out-of-pocket costs. Alice has health insurance coverage available through her employer and has decided to purchase the coverage for herself plus one dependent (Greg), since the additional cost to her is minimal. Which of the following is true if Greg has a skateboarding accident and breaks his arm?

    A. Alice's policy will be primary because she is the custodial parent.
    B. John's policy will be primary because he is required to provide coverage under the terms of the support agreement.
    C. The policies will split the cost evenly after both deductibles have been paid.
    D. The policies will split the costs, with John's policy paying 70% and Alice's policy paying 30%.

24. Ron and Sandy have come to your office to discuss some retirement planning issues. Ron will be turning age 65 in 5 months and Sandy is currently 63. Ron hasn't started collecting Social Security benefits yet because he is still working, and he is unsure whether he will retire this year or wait a few more years. Sandy has never worked outside the home. As long as he continues to work, Ron will have health insurance for both himself and Sandy through his employer with a $250 annual per person deductible, a 90% coinsurance, and a stop-loss limit of $5,000. Ron's share of the premium is $50 per pay. Many of their retirement questions have to do with Medicare and health insurance because both Ron and Sandy have existing health issues. All of the following statements are proper advice for you to give Ron and Sandy, EXCEPT:

A. Ron should sign up for Medicare three months before the month of his 65th birthday.

B. Ron should delay enrollment in Medicare Part B until he is no longer covered under his employer's health plan.

C. Sandy will be eligible for Medicare as a spousal benefit when Ron turns age 65.

D. If Ron retires from his job in the next 2 years, Sandy will be able to purchase health insurance without evidence of insurability from the Healthcare Marketplace within 60 days of losing the employer-provided coverage.

25. Wessel and Antoinette are shopping for health care coverage as they prepare for the birth of their first child in March. Neither earns much money, but they both recognize the need for the coverage, especially with the new baby. Together, their income only reaches 133 percent of the Federal Poverty Line for this year. If Wessel and Antoinette want premium assistance from the ACA to help them pay for health care coverage, what is the best purchase option from their state's Marketplace Exchange?

A. Bronze plan

B. Silver plan

C. Gold plan

D. Platinum plan

26. Dan and Deborah, along with their two children, are on a vacation touring several South American countries. They are having a wonderful experience, until they all start to get sick. The doctor from whom they received initial care explained many rivers and lakes are not considered safe for visitors in which to boat or swim. They have done both several times. As a result, the family required a short hospital stay and medication to address their health problems. The care helped them to get well, but the total bill, split into four equal sections, was $10,000, which they had to pay on site. Upon their return to the U.S., Dan submitted the receipts with a request for reimbursement from their insurer.

Here is a summary of their coverage.

Gold Plan, with an embedded deductible/MOOP
MOOP Individual: $6,850
MOOP family: $13,700

All medical care fit under the essential services and urgent care guidelines, so there should not be any additional cost sharing. Of the $10,000, what amount did the insurer reimburse?

A. $0
B. $3,150
C. $5,000
D. $10,000

For practice answering case questions related to Topic 24, please answer the following questions in the cases included in Appendix A at the back of this textbook.

Case	Questions
Black Hills P&L	
Brodinski	1 and 2
Haurilick	
Beals	
Mocsin	
Loudon	
Connor	5 and 6
Seidelhofer	6 and 7
Loomis Company	
Michael and Diana Eastman	
Gary and Judy Parker	11, 12, 13, 14, and 15

ANSWERS AND EXPLANATIONS

1. B is the answer. The cost of the insulin is not covered since the policy focuses on charges by hospitals, surgeons, and physicians visiting patients in hospitals.

2. C is the answer. (1) is incorrect because these policies provide broad coverage with few exclusions. (4) is incorrect because corridor deductibles usually are not high and are found only in comprehensive major medical policies.

3. D is the answer. The covered medical expenses are $2,000 for hospital room-and-board charges ($500 x 4 days), $4,400 for lab fees and tests, and $2,800 for the surgeon, for a total of $9,200. From this, the $500 deductible is subtracted, leaving a balance of $8,700. The insurer will pay 80% of this amount, or $6,960.

4. B is the answer. Eyeglasses and elective cosmetic surgery are both typically excluded.

5. D is the answer. (2) is incorrect. Deductibles do nothing to induce the insured to recover quickly once a health insurance policy has begun paying benefits.

6. B is the answer. The coinsurance requirement does not affect the size of the policy's stop-loss limit, nor does it eliminate small claims. It does, however, discourage malingering, a form of moral hazard.

7. C is the answer. The purpose of the limit is to cap the amount that Hal will have to bear himself.

8. C is the answer. After the $250 deductible, the insurer will pay 80% of the bills until Jerome has paid $4,000. After the stop-loss of $4,000 is reached, Jerome will pay nothing. In this case, Jerome must pay 20% of $3,700, plus the deductible of $250, for a total of $990.

9. A is the answer. The flowers are not a covered medical expense. The coinsurance clause means the insurer pays 80% of the amount by which the covered medical expenses, $8,750, exceed the $500 deductible. ($8,750 – $500) x 0.8 = $6,600.

10. A is the answer. Hospice care is specifically covered under Medicare. However, there is no benefit for care that is primarily custodial. Only skilled care is covered. There is limited payment for short-term stays in a skilled nursing facility, but only for conditions that required hospitalization. Further, Medicare does not have any stop-losses on the amount patients must pay. This is especially burdensome for those whose physicians do not accept the amount allowed under Medicare as payment in full. Starting in 2006, Medicare covers a portion of prescription drugs.

11. B is the answer. A person who is eligible for Social Security benefits will be automatically enrolled for Medicare unless they sign a form electing not to be covered. If a person enrolls in Part A, the person can enroll later in Part B, but only during specified periods each year. If a person enrolls during one of the general enrollment periods (January to March each year), coverage will become effective in July of that year. The premiums will increase for delayed enrollment.

12. D is the answer. Part A (hospital coverage) covers all those eligible for Social Security, without any payment of premiums. Part B is optional and requires the payment of premiums. Medigap coverages come in only a limited number of combinations, mandated by federal regulations. These plans pay for various costs not covered by Medicare, such as copayments and prescriptions. Home health care is covered 100%, while hospital stays require deductible payments by patients. Medicare HMOs and MSAs are being offered in an attempt to lower the cost of Medicare coverage.

13. C is the answer. Medicare does not provide for more than 100 days of skilled nursing care. This coverage is under Part A. Part B does not provide any nursing care. Medigap policies do not provide long-term care and limit the skilled nursing care to 100 days under Plans C to J. Medicaid will pay for long-term care for those persons who are eligible under both the income and asset tests.

14. E is the answer. COBRA requires that group health plans must permit employees and certain beneficiaries to elect to have their current health insurance coverage extended at group rates for up to 36 months following the occurrence of a "qualifying event" that results in the loss of coverage for a "qualified beneficiary." (1), (2), (3), and (4) are all "qualifying events."

15. C is the answer. An employee is eligible for continuance of coverage when terminated unless the termination is for gross misconduct. Negligence would not be sufficient to preclude continuance of coverage under COBRA.

16. B is the answer. Harold cannot deduct the contributions to an IRA because he is an active participant in an employer-sponsored retirement plan (the profit-sharing plan), and his income is above the limits. The contributions to the HSA are deductible above-the-line, so he does not need to be concerned about the amount of his itemized medical expenses. Harold can actually contribute more to the HSA for family coverage than to an IRA. Distributions for qualified medical expenses can be made from an HSA, without tax or penalty, at any time, but for other uses, the distributions are subject to income tax and penalty before age 65. In other words, after age 65, the funds in the HSA are treated the same as the funds in an IRA, so there is no advantage then to the IRA. The HSA has the advantage of not being subject to the minimum distribution rules that apply to the IRA.

17. B is the answer. Although VEBA plans are able to provide benefits to terminated employees, VEBAs are not subject to COBRA. Medical expense plans, vision plans, and dental plans are subject to continuation under COBRA rules. If a client elects COBRA, the client will pay 102% of the premiums for the insurance coverage.

18. D is the answer. Although a participant is prohibited from having other medical expense coverage, a participant may own nonmedical expense insurance. A, B, C, and E are correct statements.

19. C is the answer. C is not a correct statement. Under the circumstances described, the account earnings would not be included in the account holder's gross income for federal income tax purposes. A, B, D, and E are correct statements. Statement D is true because if the spouse with the high-deductible plan is "covered by other health insurance" he or she is not eligible for an HSA, and one spouse being covered by an FSA is treated as both spouses being covered. An exception is if the FSA is "limited purpose" (covers dental and vision only).

20. C is the answer. Employees may not be provided retirement or miscellaneous fringe benefits. A, B, and D are correct statements. Note that the number of noncurrent employees that may become members of a VEBA cannot exceed 10% of the total membership.

21. E is the answer. All three statements are correct.

22. E is the answer. All of the items listed can be found in the Summary of Benefits and Coverage for a group health plan.

23. B is the answer. When parents are divorced or separated, the policy of the parent required to provide coverage under the terms of the Child Support or Separation Agreement (or by court decree) will provide primary coverage. The policy of the other parent will be secondary.

24. C is the answer. A spouse of a covered worker is eligible for Medicare starting at the spouse's own age 65, not when the worker turns age 65. Answer choice A is true because Ron is not yet receiving Social Security benefits, he will not automatically be enrolled in Medicare at age 65. He must contact the Social Security Administration to enroll. Since there is no premium for coverage under Part A, he should enroll for Part A beginning at age 65 even if he is still working and covered under his employer's health plan. Answer choice B is correct because Ron's share of the premium under his employer plan is less than the cost of Part B of Medicare and the employer plan provides coverage that requires just a 10% coinsurance from Ron with a maximum out-of-pocket cost of $5,000, while Medicare Part B would require a 20% coinsurance with no stop-loss limit. Since Ron is covered under creditable coverage at work, he should be able to enroll in Medicare Part B with no increase in premium as long as he enrolls within 8 months of termination of group coverage.

25. B is the answer. Individuals may purchase any of the four plan types. However, those wanting premium assistance must purchase a Silver plan through their Marketplace Exchange.

26. A is the answer. Plans do not reimburse medical expenses incurred outside the U.S. Therefore, although the family would have had 100 percent coverage in the U.S., their actual reimbursement is zero.

Disability Income Insurance (Individual) (Topic 25)

CFP Board Student-Centered Learning Objectives

(a) Describe differences between short-term and long-term disability plans and identify the policy provisions that should be included in privately-purchased disability policies.

(b) Create a plan for meeting individual disability income needs, in consideration of household financial resources, and existing coverage under employer plans, Social Security, and disability income insurance options.

(c) Calculate the tax implications of paying for and receiving disability benefits.

A. **The Need for Income Replacement**...**25.2**
   1. *Social Security disability benefits*...*25.3*
   2. *Disability income insurance policies*...*25.5*
B. **Analyzing Disability Income Policies**...**25.6**
C. **Individual Disability Income Policies**..**25.6**
   1. *Exclusions*...*25.6*
   2. *Probationary period*...*25.7*
   3. *Definitions of disability*...*25.7*
   4. *Elimination period*..*25.8*
   5. *Benefit period*..*25.9*
      a. *Short-term versus long-term coverage*..................................*25.9*
   6. *Benefit amount*..*25.9*
   7. *Underwriting of disability income policies*...............................*25.10*
   8. *Renewability provisions*...*25.11*
   9. *Other Policy Provisions*..*25.12*
      a. *Presumptive disability*..*25.12*
      b. *Recurrent disability*...*25.12*
      c. *Waiver-of-premium provision*..*25.12*
      d. *Misstatement of age*..*25.13*
      e. *Facility of payment*...*25.13*
      f. *Relation of earnings to insurance*.......................................*25.13*
      g. *Change of occupation*...*25.13*
D. **Riders to Disability Income Policies**...**13.14**
   1. *Partial disability*..*25.14*
   2. *Residual disability*..*25.14*
   3. *Guaranteed Insurability Option (GIO)*....................................*25.15*
   4. *Cost of living adjustment (COLA)*..*25.15*
   5. *Social Security rider*..*25.16*

    E. **Taxation of premium and benefits for individual disability insurance** **25.17**
    F. **Disability insurance as an employee benefit** **25.17**
        1. *Definition of disability* 25.19
        2. *Exclusions* 25.19
        3. *Short-term disability and sick pay plans* 25.19
        4. *Social Security offset* 25.20
            a. *Social Security disability backpay* 25.20
    G. **Taxation of employer-sponsored group disability** **25.21**
        1. *Taxation for partners and S-corporation owners* 25.22
    H. **Employee benefit analysis** **25.23**
    I. **Creating a plan for disability income needs** **25.24**
        1. *Selecting an insurance company* 25.26

THE NEED FOR INCOME REPLACEMENT

Stop for a moment to consider all of the things that are important to you. What comes to mind? Perhaps it is your family, a feeling of security, assets that you have accumulated, or the comfortable lifestyle that you enjoy. Now, what is it that makes all of those things possible? While it may not be the only factor making those important things possible, your ability to earn an income is certain to be one of the primary contributors. Without that income you may not be able to make the house or car payment, you may have to spend down your invested assets or retirement savings, and your family may have to adjust to a lower standard of living. During your working years, the income you earn is the "roof" on your financial house – it protects everything inside that is important to you.

The probability of a 30 year old male being disabled for at least 90 days before age 65 is 19.6% (28.6% for female), according to the 1985 Commissioners Individual Disability Income Table A[1]. Of course, the actual odds of disability vary from person to person based on factors like age, chronic health conditions, and lifestyle choices such as smoking, diet, and exercise, but the risk of disability is one that has the potential to be catastrophic to financial planning clients.

Planners and clients must also keep in mind that disability is a two-edged sword. One edge cuts into and may drain the life blood of the family's income when the wage earner is unable to work. The second edge of the disability sword may cut into both the family income and the family's accumulated savings because of increased medical expenses.

In spite of the catastrophic potential, disability income protection is one of the most overlooked personal risks and is likely to be a weakness in the client's financial plan. People have a tendency to protect all of their other assets – houses, cars, boats, jewelry, etc. – but often forget to protect (or make a conscious decision not to protect) their most valuable asset – their ability to earn an income. Some planning clients will recognize the risk of disability, but assume that Social Security Disability Income (SSDI) or employer-provided disability benefits will be enough to maintain their lifestyle without really understanding how these programs work or the amount of monthly benefits they could expect to receive.

Using a SWOT (strengths, weaknesses, opportunities, and threats) analysis of existing disability income protection may be helpful when analyzing the risk.

Some common sources of disability income include Social Security, employer-provided plans, and individual DI insurance.

Social Security Disability Benefits

Social Security is often the core disability protection a client will currently have in place. Many Americans believe that they do not need additional DI insurance because Social Security will be there for them in the event of a disability and provide all that they need. A SWOT analysis will quickly reveal the short-comings of this strategy.

To be eligible for Social Security disability income payments, clients will need to be both "fully" and "disability" insured. To be fully insured, individuals must have either 40 credits (they can earn up to 4 credits per year) or have a number of credits equal to the number of years from age 21 to age at disability, with a minimum of 6. To be disability insured, a client must have a minimum amount of

---

[1] This 1985 Commissioners table is the most recent data available, but the National Association of Insurance Commissioners has listed working with the Society of Actuaries and American Academy of Actuaries to replace the table as an important goal of 2014.

work under Social Security *recently* (we don't need the details here, just a basic understanding of this concept).

In order to avoid fraudulent and frivolous claims, and to weed out malingerers, the Social Security definition of disability is very strict and requires the inability to engage in *any* substantial gainful employment (defined as the ability to earn $1,090 per month in 2015). In addition, the disability must be expected to last at least one year or result in death.

This definition of disability is difficult to meet. In fact, less than 40% of initial applications get approved (http://www.ssa.gov/policy/docs/statcomps/di_asr/). There is an appeal process, but depending on the area of the country, it can take anywhere from 6 months to 2 years to get a hearing. In the meantime the disabled worker still needs to make the house payment, car payment, and eat. There are some attorneys who specialize in Social Security Disability claims who may help clients draft "dire need" letters (e.g., "If I don't get my hearing soon, they are going to foreclose on my house, or I will no longer be able to afford my medication.") that may help to get the hearing scheduled sooner, and an inquiry from the client's Congressman might also help, but for planning purposes, we need to prepare for a potentially lengthy wait. Even if you assume the client could eventually qualify, your client would still need income from another source for a minimum of 2 years just in case the application gets denied and must be appealed.

If the client does qualify for SSDI payments, other members of the family such as a spouse (who is age 62 or older or who is caring for a child under age 16) of the disabled worker, and children under age 18 (19 if still in high school) may also qualify for benefits.

Class Exercise 25 – 1

Work in groups to complete a SWOT analysis for Social Security Disability Income benefits.

SSDI SWOT ANALYSIS			
STRENGTHS	WEAKNESSES	OPPORTUNITIES	THREATS

In addition to the potentially long time to receive benefits, clients can expect a shortfall in income following a disability. This shortfall will need to be covered elsewhere, and clients will generally prefer an insurance policy with a more liberal definition of disability. Clients can create an account and view the estimated amount of disability benefits they would receive at www.ssa.gov.

Disability Income Insurance Policies

Disability income policies are designed to replace a portion of a worker's earned income when the worker is unable to work because of injury or sickness. The benefit paid is a fraction of the income the worker earned prior to the disability. Usually, the person has to be totally disabled for benefits to be paid. The cause of the disability is not a factor (though some policies exclude occupational injuries and illnesses).

Disability income insurance is important to both the single person and the family breadwinner because the insurance replaces income the person would have earned if he or she had remained healthy.

For most families, replacement of income for injury or sickness requires a disability income insurance policy. Some policies pay benefits only for accidental injury. Most policies (and certainly the most desirable policies) pay benefits for both accidents and sickness.

Sticker shock is one of the biggest reasons many clients do not purchase individual DI policies. Premiums tend to seem expensive in comparison to other types of insurance. Keep in mind that the premium directly reflects the risk. DI policies are priced this way due to the high probability of benefits being paid for a disability. It will often be up to the planner to work with clients to structure the policy to fit the budget while still providing necessary protection.

ANALYZING DISABILITY INCOME POLICIES

In order to analyze disability income (DI) policies, planners need to have a good understanding of the various components of a DI policy and of how provisions in these policies affect coverage and premiums.

One of the first details to be analyzed in an individual DI policy is whether it provides coverage for accident, illness, or both. Policies that cover accidents only are rather inexpensive, but the majority of disability claims arise from illness; so a policy that covers only accidents will leave the client with a major planning weakness.

Premiums for disability protection are based on age, health, occupation, and avocation, as well as the features and provisions of the policy. As we discuss the features and provisions of DI policies, be sure to pay close attention to the effect on premiums, and ways to maintain adequate coverage while keeping the cost affordable.

INDIVIDUAL DISABILITY INCOME POLICIES

Exclusions

There are generally only a few exclusions in individual disability income policies. These exclusions include war, self-inflicted injuries, work-related injuries, and preexisting conditions.

A preexisting condition is a disabling physical condition for which the insured sought treatment before the disability income policy was issued. Such preexisting conditions are usually excluded from coverage under individual disability income policies.

Some states allow policies to exclude injuries or sickness that results from alcoholism or drug addiction, while other states do not allow such exclusions.

Some disability income policies, particularly short-term policies covering blue-collar industrial workers, exclude illnesses or accidents resulting from occupational exposures. In most cases, such occupational disabilities are covered by workers' compensation laws. Double payment would only encourage the feigning of disabilities, and insurers do not want to encourage dishonesty. Policies excluding occupational disabilities are known as nonoccupational policies. Long-term policies, which are written and issued mostly for professional and other white-collar insureds, often provide benefits for both occupational and nonoccupational disabilities.

Probationary Period

The probationary period is the period of time after issuance of a disability insurance policy, usually fifteen to thirty days, during which no sickness coverage is effective. Thus, the provision will deny coverage for a sickness that was in the incubation stage when the policy was issued. The probation period helps to protect the insurance company from paying for preexisting conditions. Note that coverage still applies during the first few days for any bodily injuries arising out of accidents.

Definitions of Disability

One of the key features to assess in a disability policy is the definition of total disability. No benefit is payable if the injury or sickness is not disabling. The way total disability is defined can range from a very strict definition to a very liberal one.

From the standpoint of providing the most protection for the client, the best definition is "own occupation". This is the most liberal definition of disability because it will provide disability income benefits if the client is unable to perform his or her own occupation. For example, if a surgeon developed arthritis in his hands and could no longer perform surgery, he would be eligible to receive benefits from the policy. The benefits would be payable even if the surgeon were now able to serve as the department head or teach courses at medical school and could make the same amount of money (or more). From the insurance company's standpoint, this definition is likely to result in numerous long-term claims; therefore, it is the most expensive definition in terms of premium charged.

The client will find that the worst definition to have is "any occupation". This definition is similar to the Social Security definition in that benefits can only be received if you are unable to engage in *any* occupation. If a surgeon could work at the local Walmart, he would no longer qualify for benefits. Policies with this strict definition of disability are generally not used in individual policies.

Fortunately, there are also several definitions that fall in between the two extremes. One such definition is the "modified any occupation", also known as the "education, training, or experience" definition. Under this definition insureds will receive benefits when their disability keeps them from engaging in any occupation for which they are qualified due to education, training, or experience. If the surgeon could not perform surgery but could work as department head or teach, he would no longer receive benefits. But if he could only work as a greeter at Walmart, he would receive benefits.

The split definition may be even more appealing to that surgeon than the education, training, or experience definition. A split definition starts out as own occupation (often referred to as simply "own occ") for a period of time (usually 2 years), then switches to the modified any occupation (education, training, or experience) definition.

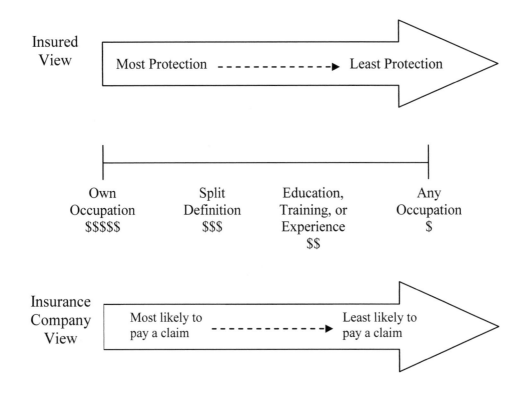

Elimination Period

The elimination period is the amount of time the insured must be disabled before benefits are payable. It serves a similar purpose to a deductible in a medical insurance policy in that it requires the insured to cover small claims out-of-pocket and helps to reduce the cost of the premium. By denying replacement of income for a period of time, the insurer can also deter the insured from feigning disability to enjoy a paid vacation.

The elimination period may be 30, 60, 90, or 120 days. The longer the elimination period, the lower the premium, but keep in mind that the insured needs to be able to cover expenses during this time, so the maximum elimination period should be determined by the amount of emergency funds the client has available. Some clients may also have short-term disability income coverage or sick-leave time at work, which might allow for a longer elimination period in the individual policy (as long as employment is not expected to change, which could mean loss of those short-term benefits).

Benefit Period

Planners should also be aware of the benefit period for individual disability policies. The benefit period is the length of time benefits will continue to be paid. The longer the benefit period, the higher the premium.

Ideally, the benefit period will continue to age 65 as a full replacement for lost income to retirement age. In order to control the premium cost, some clients may prefer a shorter benefit period; perhaps 20 years to make sure the mortgage can be paid off or to see the kids through college, or 10 years to match the time until they would be eligible for early retirement at age 55.

Lifetime benefit periods are available with some insurers and for some occupations. Shorter benefit periods are also available.

Policies for some clients may have limitations on the length of benefit period the insurer will allow due to the insured working in an occupation that is dangerous or requires difficult physical labor.

Short-Term versus Long-Term Coverage

Disability income policies may be broadly classified as short-term and long-term. Some companies provide short-term benefits for a maximum of six months. However, more and more companies are extending the benefit period covered under their "short-term" policies to a maximum of one or two years.

Long-term disability coverage refers to a disability income policy whose benefit period is longer than 6 months, often 5 years, 10 years, or longer, and perhaps as long as until age 65. A few long-term policies provide lifetime replacement of income for disabilities caused by accident. The longer benefit period for accidents is available because of the lesser moral hazard associated with accidents. When long-term coverage is preferred by the purchaser over short-term benefits, the price differential is often a determining factor. However, for some occupations, insurers will not write benefit periods in excess of five years.

Benefit Amount

Ideally, planners would like to cover as much of the client's income as possible, but insurers will limit the disability benefit to something less than 100% for several reasons. First, there is a moral hazard created when someone can stay at home and make the same income as when going to work. Some insureds may see this benefit as a good reason to intentionally injure themselves. Moreover, insureds who were legitimately disabled may malinger, so lower benefits help to create an incentive to return to work.

Second, the premiums on individual DI policies are paid with after-tax dollars, but benefits are received income tax-free. If the insured's effective federal tax rate is 20%, then they can receive 20% less income from the DI policy and still have as much money in their pocket as when they were working.

Underwriting of Disability Income Policies

Careful underwriting is of critical importance for insurers in disability income insurance, particularly because of the high degree of moral and morale hazard that is potentially present.

The occupational classification into which the insured falls is important in the underwriting process. Applicants are assigned to an underwriting class based on job title and description of job duties performed. For example, a job title of "construction project manager" might have different underwriting classes and premiums, depending on whether the primary duties involve work on construction sites (wearing a hardhat), or coordinating subcontractors by calling them from the office. Underwriting standards are also sometimes more liberal for professionals than for blue-collar workers, it being assumed (not always correctly) that professionals are more motivated and stable in their work.

Underwriting will require an earnings history, typically for the past two years, and it will require medical history. Underwriting for medical history is more complicated for disability policies than for life insurance policies. For life insurance, the concern is only with medical conditions that could kill, but for disability policies underwriters look at a much larger list of potential illnesses and injuries. Underwriters will also consider factors about personal habits and lifestyle; for example, they may ask whether you travel outside of the country, whether you are a pilot, or whether you have ever been arrested.

Clients should be forewarned that by the time the underwriting process is completed it is unlikely that they will be offered the most desirable choices of policy provisions. For example, even though they may have a condition that would require a short elimination period, the insurer may offer only a longer elimination period; or perhaps the insurer may offer only a limited benefit period for the particular occupation. In factoring the maximum benefit that will be offered, the underwriters may also consider other coverage available (for example, group disability and Social Security) in order to ensure that the total combined benefit amount remains below the pre-disability earnings. Insurance companies may have different underwriting requirements, so applying for benefits with multiple companies may allow the client to compare the coverage and benefits actually available to them. For example, some insurance companies prefer to underwrite white-collar occupations and will place numerous restrictions on policies for blue-collar workers, while another company might be much more liberal in their offerings for blue-collar workers.

Class Discussion 25 – 1

How would you evaluate the amount of disability income protection that is needed for a client?

Renewability Provisions

Evaluating a disability policy will also require an understanding of the renewability provision, which describes the insured's right to continue the policy from year-to-year or, conversely, the insurer's right to cancel the policy.

If a disability policy is guaranteed renewable, the policy owner can keep it in force by paying the premium as it comes due, until reaching a certain age. The insurance company is not permitted to cancel or rewrite any policy provisions, but the insurer may increase premiums for the entire classification of policy owners in which the insured was placed when the policy was issued.

A better policy for the insured is one that is noncancellable. A noncancellable policy guarantees the insured the right to renew the disability income policy for a stated number of years or to a stated age, with the premium at renewal guaranteed. The insurer has no right to cancel the policy or to increase premiums.

Other renewability provisions, such as conditionally renewable, optionally renewable, or cancellable, should generally be avoided. With a conditionally renewable policy, the insurer has the right to terminate the contract by not renewing it under certain conditions stated in the contract. The insured always has the right to cancel, but the insured's renewal right is limited because under certain conditions, the insurer may refuse to renew the policy. When a policy is renewable at the company's option (optionally renewable), the company has the right to cancel the insured's policy at the end of the policy term (usually each year). The insured is at the mercy of the insurer's decision. A cancellable policy may be terminated by the insurer at any time during its term. Thus, the insured has no right to continue the policy if the insurer elects to cancel or refuse to renew.

Financial planners will want to ensure that the policy is either noncancellable or guaranteed renewable so that the client is assured of being able to continue the policy as long as it is needed to protect income. While noncancellable is preferable to guaranteed renewable, it will also have a higher premium. This trade-off should also be evaluated.

Other Policy Provisions

Presumptive Disability

Many disability policies describe specific injuries that will qualify the insured for permanent total disability status. Total disability will be presumed when the individual suffers loss of sight, loss of speech, loss of hearing, or loss of use of both hands, both feet, or one hand and one foot. If an individual recovers, however, the individual is no longer presumed disabled, and the presumptive-disability benefits will end.

Recurrent Disability

The purpose of a recurrent disability clause is to differentiate between two separate disabilities and a continuation of the same disability. The distinction is important in that, if the two losses constitute two separate disabilities, two waiting periods and two benefit maximums are applicable, whereas if the two losses are deemed to be one disability, only one waiting period and one benefit maximum apply. The typical recurrent disability clause specifies that if within six months of a total disability, the insured sustains a subsequent period of disability from the same or a related cause, the second disability will be deemed a continuation of the first one. Otherwise, it will be deemed a new disability, regardless of the cause.

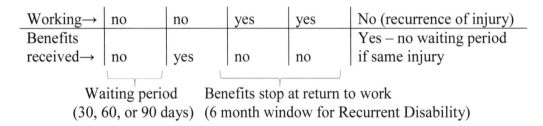

Working→	no	no	yes	yes	No (recurrence of injury)
Benefits received→	no	yes	no	no	Yes – no waiting period if same injury

Waiting period   Benefits stop at return to work
(30, 60, or 90 days)   (6 month window for Recurrent Disability)

Waiver-of-Premium Provision

Under the typical waiver-of-premium provision in a disability income contract, the insurer agrees to waive the premium after the insured has been continuously and totally disabled for some period, such as 90 days. The insured must pay the premiums during the 90-day elimination period, but if the 90 days are passed, the waiver becomes effective retroactively, so that any premiums paid during that period are refunded to the insured.

Misstatement of Age

Misstatement of age is a policy provision requiring an adjustment in the amount of coverage when the insured has misstated his or her age. The coverage is adjusted to provide the benefit that the premium paid would have purchased if the age had been stated correctly. Under this provision, the disability policy owner is protected because the contract is not voidable when the age of the insured is misstated. Instead, the amount payable is adjusted to provide an equitable benefit. Thus, the clause protects both the insurer and the insured.

Facility of Payment

Under the facility of payment clause, the insurer may pay the policy's death benefit up to $1,000 to any relative by blood or marriage of the insured or beneficiary whom the company believes is entitled to receive the money. A disability income policy may provide a death benefit because of the inclusion of Accidental Death and Dismemberment coverage in the policy. There may be other benefits payable following the insured's death. The facility of payment provision is designed to relieve the insurer of the problem of finding an authorized and legitimate payee for a small amount of death benefits.

Relation of Earnings to Insurance

The relation of earnings to insurance clause, sometimes called the average earnings clause, states that if at the time disability occurs, the total disability income provided by all policies exceeds the insured's earned income, or average earned income for the preceding two years (whichever is greater), the income benefits under the policy will be reduced proportionately. The clause is designed to protect the insurer from the moral hazard where the disability benefits payable exceed the normal income of the insured. Disability income insurers are exposed to a moral hazard because people often prefer to receive insurance benefits rather than work.

Change of Occupation

The change of occupation provision permits the insurer to reduce the benefit payable in the event the insured changes to a more hazardous occupation. The benefit is reduced to the amount the premium paid would have purchased at the more hazardous employment classification. If the insured changes to a less hazardous occupation, the premium is reduced, but the benefit remains the same.

Practice Question

Larry Pugh, age 42, has requested a recommendation for a disability income insurance policy. Larry earns $60,000 annually and has a family of four, i.e., a wife and two children. Which of the following policies will provide the best coverage?

    A. A split definition, with a 30-day elimination period
    B. Any occupation definition, with a 30-day waiting period
    C. An own occupation definition, with 60-day waiting period
    D. An own occupation definition, with 30-day elimination period

Answer:
The own occupation definition is more liberal than the any occupation definition. The own occupation definition is better than the split definition. A shorter elimination or waiting period is preferable to a longer one.
The answer is D.

RIDERS TO DISABILITY INCOME POLICIES

Riders are features that can be added to the policy. Some riders enhance the benefits and require an extra premium; other riders are designed to reduce the premium.

Partial Disability

A partial disability benefit applies to most accident and some sickness benefits, and promises to pay a reduced benefit if the insured can perform some but not all the important daily duties of his or her occupation. A policy's partial disability benefit is typically 50% of the total disability benefit. The benefit is usually paid for only a short time, and usually only following a period of total disability. Six months is the most common benefit period.

Residual Disability

Residual disability benefits are designed to make up income lost because a continuing disability that is less than total prevents the insured from working at full-income capacity. Residual disability is typically measured by the ratio of a person's reduction in earnings after recovery from total disability to his or her earnings before disability. Thus, the residual disability coverage will provide a benefit that is the same percentage of the maximum policy benefit as the percentage reduction in the insured's earnings. For example, if a $40,000 income is reduced to $28,000, this is a 30% reduction. The insured's monthly insurance benefit would be 30% of the promised maximum benefit. Residual disability is often permanent. Therefore, benefits may continue for the maximum benefit period of the basic coverage – perhaps for the insured's lifetime.

Not all policies will have partial or residual benefits available, and these coverage provisions will affect the premium cost, so planners and clients will need to evaluate the benefits from this coverage with the added premium.

Practice Question

Tanya, age 38, is considering a disability income insurance policy. Which one of the following policy provisions should be recommended to her as the most important?

    A. Own occupation definition of disability
    B. Any occupation definition of disability
    C. Partial disability benefit
    D. Residual disability benefit

Answer:

The definition of disability determines when benefits are payable, so it is more important than other provisions. The definition is also more important than the amount of benefits or the selection of an elimination period. The most favorable definition is own occupation.

The answer is A.

Guaranteed Insurability Option (GIO)

The guaranteed insurability option rider (also known as a future increase option) allows the benefit to be increased periodically if income has gone up, but does not require proof of insurability with each increase. Proof of the increase in income will be required. This may be a good feature to add if the client believes income will increase substantially but is concerned about insurability in the future. This rider will add to the cost of the premium, and the premium for the additional benefit amount will be based on attained age.

Cost of Living Adjustment (COLA)

We mentioned earlier that ideally we would choose a benefit to age 65 or lifetime. What if you were disabled at the age of 40 and continued to be disabled continuously to age 65? Not only is inflation a problem because you keep getting the same income for 20

> *"Inflation is when you pay fifteen dollars for the ten-dollar haircut you used to get for five dollars when you had hair."* **Sam Ewing**

years, but you also missed the opportunity to advance in your career and reap the reward of a higher salary. For an extra premium, a COLA rider can be added so that after benefit payments start, they can increase in future years. Some policies base the increase on CPI, others increase based on a fixed percentage each year. Some policies, however, will put a cap on the total increase (for example, the cap might be double the original benefit). Adding a COLA rider will increase the premium of the policy.

Social Security Rider

The Social Security rider can be added for an additional premium. A Social Security rider provides benefits when an individual is disabled under the policy definition but does not qualify as disabled for Social Security.

There are two main reasons that insurers offer the Social Security rider. First, the rider can provide benefits to a disabled individual while an application for Social Security benefits is pending. Approximately 60% of applications are denied initially, and the hearing and appeal process can take more than a year. Even if the initial application is accepted, there is a 5 month waiting period. The rider can provide benefits during this interim period. Second, the rider can replace benefits that are not paid when a Social Security claim is denied. The amount of benefits that an insurer will be willing to provide under a disability policy typically takes into account the Social Security disability benefits. When an insurer's underwriting limit for a disability policy is set at 60% of the insured's earnings, this limit is based in part on the likelihood that some earnings will be replaced by Social Security. If the Social Security benefits are not paid, then the insured will want additional benefits. The rider can act as a supplement to provide these benefits.

Insurers offer different kinds of Social Security riders, so it is important to read the policy to determine what benefits will be provided. A rider may be written to provide benefits only until the Social Security benefits begin, or the rider may provide benefits only after the Social Security Administration denies the claim. A rider may specify that no benefits will be paid if the insured receives any Social Security benefits, even a small amount, or the rider may provide that the insurer will only reduce the amount of benefits by the amount of the Social Security payments.

Some insurers provide a Social Insurance Rider that provides for benefits to be affected not only by Social Security but also by workers compensation benefits.

Example:

A client buys a disability income policy with a base benefit of $4,000 per month and a Social Security rider that will pay a supplement of $700. If the client is disabled, but does not qualify for Social Security benefits, the rider will pay an additional $700 per month. The combination of the $700 from the rider plus the $4,000 base benefit from the disability policy will provide a total of $4,700 per month of income.

TAXATION OF PREMIUM AND BENEFITS FOR INDIVIDUAL DISABILITY INSURANCE

Premiums for individually owned disability income insurance are not deductible by an individual under any circumstance.

For individual disability income insurance, benefits normally are free of income tax. The tax-free treatment of benefits is one reason for the amount of benefits from a disability policy to be less than the client's full gross income amount. If a client makes gross income of $4,000 per month but has an effective tax rate of 25%, the net amount the client has available to spend each month is $3,000 (25% x $4,000 = $1,000 that is paid in taxes). The client, therefore, can maintain the same standard of living with a benefit that is less than 75% of gross income.

DISABILITY INSURANCE AS AN EMPLOYEE BENEFIT

A common planning mistake for clients is the belief that group disability coverage at work is all that they need, without really knowing how the policy works. It is important for planners to be able to evaluate the group coverage and identify any weaknesses that may exist. Planners should also remind clients that the employer controls the policy and can reduce benefits, or if clients change employers, this coverage may no longer be available. In many cases, the individual DI policy should be the base of the disability protection plan, and the employer-sponsored group disability should serve as a supplement.

While the focus here will be on employer-sponsored group insurance, students should also be aware that group rates on DI insurance are often available through professional organizations and can offer significant cost-savings over an individual policy. As long as the client remains in good standing with the professional organization, the client can continue the policy, even when changing employers.

Group disability benefits are split into short-term and long-term coverage. While most employers will offer both, it is possible to offer one without the other, so planners should not assume that if a client says they have DI coverage at work that it means that they have both short and long-term coverage.

Short-term benefits typically start after a short period of disability, usually a week or two. During the first two weeks the employee may be using sick days or vacation days, or the employer may offer a sick-leave plan. Once benefits start under the short-term coverage, they will typically continue for a period of 6 months (although plans may vary).

Long-term (LT) benefits are usually coordinated with short-term (ST) benefits so that if the ST benefit period is 6 months, the LT elimination period is 6 months and benefits for disabled employees can flow smoothly from one and then the other. Long-term benefits are often payable until normal retirement age or even to death, but will, of course, cease if recovery occurs (the employee no longer meets the definition of disabled).

Also note that disability income benefits are one of the few employee benefits that allow employers to discriminate and offer a higher level of benefits to executives while still being allowed a tax deduction, so it will be very common to find several different levels of benefits within the group plan. If a planner works with several employees of the same company, the planner will likely find that these employees have different disability benefits, so a planner should try not to make assumptions without verifying the coverage, length of employment, number of years the employee was an officer, etc. For example, a company may offer benefits at 50% of salary for full-time salaried employees (while hourly employees are not covered), but 60% of salary for officers, and anyone VP or above gets 80% of salary for the number of months equal to the number of years they have been a VP or above. That is the beauty of being able to discriminate.

Planners and clients will need to consult the Summary Plan Description (SPD) for disability benefits to determine precisely what type of coverage is offered, as well as the amount. Generally, individual policies are not issued, the sponsoring employer will have a master contract, and employees are given a certificate of coverage and an SPD that outlines the details of the coverage.

Some group policies will also have a dollar cap on the amount that can be received. For example, the group policy might pay a maximum monthly benefit of $5,000. This maximum is to avoid making it likely that executives who earn high salaries will simply adjust their lifestyles to live on 60% or 75% of their former high salaries; there should always be incentive to go back to work. For those not subject to the dollar cap, benefits of 50 to 70 percent of the employee's pre-disability income are typical.

The short- and long-term coverage is usually provided through insurance policies, but sick-leave plans are generally self-funded by the employer.

Definition of Disability

The definition of disability frequently used for group long-term disability plans is the so-called "qualified for" definition or "educated and trained for". This definition requires "the total and continuous inability of the employee to engage in any and every gainful occupation for which he or she is qualified or shall reasonably become qualified for by reason of training, education, or experience." This definition is more liberal than the Social Security definition, but not as liberal as the "regular occupation" or "own occupation" definition found in many individual disability policies. While a more liberal definition might be used in plans limited to selected executives, it is not generally used in plans widely available to employees.

Exclusions

The typical exclusions under group long-term disability policies are: (a) disabilities occurring when the employee is not under the care of a physician, (b) disabilities resulting from self-inflicted injuries, and (c) disabilities occurring prior to an employee's eligibility for coverage under the employer's plan.

Short-Term Disability and Sick Pay Plans

In addition to their long-term disability plans, most employers have a short-term disability plan that continues the employee's compensation for a limited period of time prior to the commencement of the long-term benefit (assuming there is a long-term plan). Plans providing benefits for disabilities extending beyond six months are labeled "long-term plans."

The short-term plan is typically in two parts. The first part is the employer's continuation of the employee's regular pay for a short time. No insurance is involved. This is followed by three to six months of short-term plan benefits, which are typically financed by insurance.

Some employers provide a special short-term benefit plan for selected executives. Such benefit plans are exempt from the anti-discrimination laws. Thus, the employer is free to determine which executive employees will be eligible, the terms and conditions of coverage, and the level of benefits to be provided.

Social Security Offset

To avoid providing employees with benefits that exceed their usual earnings, employers usually integrate long-term disability income benefits with benefits and income from other sources. The employee's benefits under a group disability plan will be reduced when benefits are received from Social Security, workers' compensation, retirement plans, other insurance paid for by the employer, and any earnings from employment. Most state laws do not permit reduction in benefits due to individual disability policies purchased by the employee.

With some plans, integration with Social Security is determined only from what the disabled employee receives from Social Security (primary insurance amount). Under other plans, if there are dependents, integration may be based on the total benefit received by the employee's family.

Disability benefits may be reduced in part or in full by Social Security benefits. Under a full-integration approach (also known as substitution), the group long-term disability benefits are reduced to the full extent of the Social Security benefits. In this situation, the group benefits are a substitute for Social Security unless or until Social Security becomes available.

Under a dual-percentage approach, the group disability benefits are based on different percentages of the employee's earnings, depending upon whether other sources are available or not. For example, when no other sources are available, the employee might receive 50% of earnings; but when other sources are available, the employee can receive benefits until they reach 70% of earnings. Employers can adopt plans with different integration formulas, depending upon their budgets and objectives.

It is also common for group benefits to be offset by other types of social insurance and for workers' compensation.

Social Security Disability Backpay

As discussed previously, Social Security disability applications are rarely approved with the initial application. The appeals and hearing process often takes one to two years to complete, but for those who eventually do get approved, the benefits are paid retroactively to the 6th month of disability. This creates a lump sum payment for past-due benefits, commonly referred to as "backpay".

If Social Security disability benefits are delayed, a long-term disability plan pays full benefits up until the point where the Social Security Administration approves the application. When the insured finally receives the Social Security payments, some of the insurance benefits may need to be repaid to reflect the offset that should have occurred. It will be important for the planner and client to check the terms of the long-term disability policy (both individual and group) to determine whether it includes a clause requiring excess payments made by the insurance company to be repaid. Most companies will require full payment immediately when the lump-sum amount is received from Social Security, although some insurance companies will be willing to reduce future payment amounts until the debt is paid off. Some policies also factor in lump-sum SSDI payments made to other family members (such as a spouse or child) when calculating the amount to be repaid.

The insurance company issuing the long-term disability policy will typically require the insured to sign a Social Security Reimbursement Agreement, and will require that the insured apply for Social Security disability when the insurance company payments begin.

If an attorney is hired to assist with the SSDI application and appeals process, it is typical for the attorney to charge up to 25% of the backpay amount as a fee. The backpay amount is normally reduced in determining the actual dollar amount owed to the insurance company.

Class Discussion 25 – 2

What documents and types of information do you need to gather to analyze a client's group disability coverage?

TAXATION OF EMPLOYER-SPONSORED GROUP DISABILITY

The same income tax treatment is accorded short-term plans and long-term plans. The employer may deduct premium payments, as well as direct compensation payments when there is no insurance involved.

The employee incurs no federal income taxes for disability income insurance premiums paid by the employer. Insurance premiums paid by the employer also escape both the employee's Social Security tax and the employee's unemployment insurance tax (FICA and FUTA taxes).

If the employer pays all premiums under the plan, benefit payments must be included in the employee's gross income but are subject to Social Security and Medicare taxes for only a limited period (usually 6 months). Benefits offered under cafeteria plans, however, are generally not subject to FICA taxes, even during the first 6 months.

If the employee contributes a portion of the premiums and pays for them with after-tax dollars, then the portion of the benefits attributable to employee contributions is received tax-free.

Example:

Tom Jackson's employer, Melon Co., pays for 70% of the premiums on his group disability insurance, and Tom pays the other 30% with an after-tax deduction from his paycheck. Melon Co. will take a tax deduction for its share of the premium payment, and Tom will not be taxed on this amount, even though it is of economic benefit to him. Since Tom has avoided tax on the premium payment made by Melon Co., any benefits from the policy will be taxable, and he cannot get tax-free benefits for the portion of the benefit funded by the premium payment from Melon Co. So if Tom's benefit payment is $1,000 per month, he will be taxed on 70% of that amount ($700). Since Tom paid his 30% share of the premiums with after-tax dollars, he has not received any tax advantage for that 30% of the policy yet, therefore, 30% ($300) of each benefit payment will be tax free.

Some employers will allow employees the choice of paying their share of premiums pre-tax or after-tax. If the employee chooses to pay with pre-tax dollars, it will make the benefits taxable. Since the employee's share of the group premium is usually minimal, and the likelihood of disability and its impact so great, it is almost always better to pay with after-tax dollars.

Taxation for Partners and S-Corporation Owners

For a partnership and S corporation, the premiums for disability coverage on a partner and greater-than-2% shareholder are deductible by the business. The amount of the premiums paid, however, will be added to the taxable income for the partner or over-2% shareholder. The benefits paid to the partner or S corporation shareholder will not be subject to income tax.

EXHIBIT 25 – 1		
Tax Consequences for Disability Income Insurance		
Type of Contract	**Are premiums deductible?**	**Are benefits taxable?**
Individual owns policy and pays premium	No	No
Employee owns policy, and employer* pays premium	Yes, by employer (No, for employee)	Yes
Business expense policy, and business pays premium	Yes	Yes
Policy to fund buy-sell agreement (entity or cross-purchase)	No	No

* If employer is a partnership or S corporation, the employer can deduct the cost, but premiums are additional income to an employee who is a partner or >2% shareholder. Benefits are not taxable to the partner or s-corp. owner.

Business overhead disability insurance and policies to fund buy-sell agreements are discussed in Topic 29.

EMPLOYEE BENEFIT ANALYSIS

There may be times when the financial planner is working with a business owner  to determine which, if any, employee benefits should be offered to employees and how those benefits should be structured. In deciding whether to offer a disability income plan to employees, an employer must consider the trade-off between paying the premiums and paying employees a bonus that can be used for the premiums on individual coverage. This evaluation is especially important when the employer chooses to offer the DI only to a select group of executives.

While the employee pays no income tax on premiums paid by the employer, the disability benefits from an employer-paid plan are taxable to the employee. If no disability occurs, the employee avoids taxes with the employer paying the premiums; but if a disability occurs, the employee will have a larger tax bill.

On the other hand, the employee must pay income taxes each year on any bonus and receives no deduction for paying the premiums on a disability policy. The disability benefits, however, will be received tax-free. If an executive expects tax rates to rise in the future, the option of receiving disability income tax-free may be attractive. Moreover, the additional taxes from the bonus might be alleviated by providing a "double bonus" plan that pays the income taxes. Thus, if a disability occurs, the bonus approach may be more beneficial.

To calculate the double bonus amount, take the premium and divide it by (1-tax bracket). For example, if the premium is $3,000 and the executive is in the 35% tax bracket, then you would take 3,000/.65 = $4,615. By providing a bonus of $4,615 to the executive, the executive will then have enough additional net income to purchase the insurance policy and pay the additional taxes due on the bonus.

Another thing to remember is that if the client is a small business owner and the business is structured as a pass-through entity (partner in a partnership, >2% owner in an S-corp, or LLC member) the business can take a tax deduction for the premiums paid, but it will show up as income for the owner. This tax treatment also applies to health insurance premiums, but health insurance premiums can be deducted above-the-line for these owners. DI premiums are not deductible by the individual taxpayer. Double bonuses generally do not help owners of pass-through entities due to the flow-through of taxation (it does for their employees, just not for the owners). Owners of C-corps are treated the same as other employees, so the double bonus will work for them.

When working with small business owners, also remember that insurers will usually set a limit on the amount of disability insurance they will issue for a given person, and that limit includes disability insurance purchased for uses such as nonqualified deferred compensation, keyperson insurance, group plan, individual policy, business overhead, etc). The key is that when underwriting an individual policy, insurers usually look at how much group coverage there is, but when they underwrite group policies, insurers generally do not have individual underwriting considerations or the ability to ask about existing individual policies. So a small business owner who is also an employee of the business can typically obtain more coverage by purchasing the individual policy first and then putting the group policy in place for the business. The owner could end up with more coverage than the insurer would ordinarily issue for an individual.

CREATING A PLAN FOR DISABILITY INCOME NEEDS

In creating a plan to address disability income needs, the planner should consider household financial resources, existing coverage under employer plans, the likelihood of qualifying for Social Security disability benefits, and individual disability income insurance options.

Household Financial Resources

In determining the amounts and types of coverage for disability income insurance, the planner will want to ask the following questions concerning financial resources:

- How strongly does the family rely on this income? Is it the income of a single parent supporting 3 kids, or is it the part-time wages earned by a spouse used to provide extra spending and vacation money?
- With current emergency funds, how long could the family continue to pay expenses before a hardship is incurred?
- Which of the current expenses are fixed and essential and which may be delayed or reduced during a period of disability?
- What additional expenses might be incurred as a result of the disability (e.g., will the client continue to be covered under the employer group health plan, or will the client eventually need to convert to an individual policy; will the client need to pay someone else to mow the lawn)? What expenses might be reduced as a result of the disability (e.g., the expense of parking in the parking garage at the office)?
- What other sources of income may be available in the event of disability?
- If assets will need to be liquidated to replace income, which assets are most advantageous to liquidate?
- What are the investment and tax consequences of selling assets or withdrawing funds from accounts, including CDs, life insurance, annuities, retirement accounts, brokerage accounts, and real estate?
- What collateral may be used for loans and what is the availability of credit?

Existing Coverage Under Employer Plans:

The planner will want to ask the following questions about employer disability income plans:

- What is the elimination period for short-term and long-term disability?
- How long is the benefit period?
- What percentage of salary is covered, and is it integrated with Social Security?
- What is the definition of disability?
- If I leave this employer, is the coverage portable?
- Will benefits received be taxable or tax-free?

Social Security Disability:

The following points are important to review with the client when considering disability income protection:

- The rules for qualifying for Social Security disability benefits are strict.
- There is a 5-month waiting period before benefits start.
- Projections are available at ssa.gov to evaluate the potential amount of disability income the client may qualify for.

Individual DI Policy Options:

- Individual DI allows the client and planner the flexibility to design the policy to meet the client's needs (employer DI requires the employee to accept what is offered).
- Premiums for individual DI can be high for certain types of occupations, short elimination periods, long benefit periods, and high income replacements.
- Policies should be guaranteed renewable or non-cancelable (a cancelable policy is a weakness in the plan).
- Benefit periods should be to retirement age, or as long as the client can afford to purchase.
- Elimination periods should be no longer than the period of time emergency funds will cover.
- The definition of disability should be more liberal than the Social Security definition.
- Clients close to or in retirement should not buy additional disability income insurance and should terminate existing policies.

Despite the danger of losing coverage when the client moves from one employer to another, many clients and planners like to use the group coverage as the "base" of the plan because of the lower premiums for group versus individual policies. If the group benefits are adequate to cover current expenses, but additional income is needed for COBRA health insurance premiums or funding retirement contributions to stay on track, or to pay for additional medical expenses, etc., there will still be a need for additional coverage. This additional insurance should be provided through an individual policy. Some insurers offer a rider so a retirement contribution is made in addition to the stated disability income amount, to ensure that a period of disability does not derail the client's plans for saving for retirement.

Selecting an Insurance Company

Once the planner and client have determined that an individual disability policy is needed, they should, of course, evaluate the policy features and provisions available through different insurance companies.

When recommending a particular insurer for the client, the planner should evaluate its:

(a)   Financial safety
(b)   Occupational classification system
(c)   Specific products offered
(d)   Attitude toward writing disability income coverage generally
(e)   Underwriting philosophy and standards
(f)   Claims-paying reputation
(g)   Efficiency in processing applications

APPLICATION QUESTIONS

1. Which of the following statements concerning individual disability income policies is <u>not</u> correct?

A. They usually contain a waiting or elimination period.
B. They usually cover both accident and sickness.
C. They usually replace all of the disabled insured's lost earnings.
D. They have more than one definition of disability.
E. They may be written to cover only nonoccupational disability.

2. Burton has a disability income policy that pays $4,000 per month for total disability. Burton's normal earnings are $6,000 per month. He is now back to work after a period of total disability, but he is able to work only on a part-time basis at a salary of $4,000 per month. In this situation, which of the following statements are correct?

(1) If Burton's disability income insurance included a partial disability benefit, he would collect $2,000 per month from it.
(2) If Burton's disability income policy included a residual disability benefit, he would collect $1,333 per month from it.
(3) If Burton's disability income policy contained a recurrent disability clause, he would collect $4,000 per month from it.

    A. (1) and (2) only
    B. (1) and (3) only
    C. (2) and (3) only
    D. (1), (2), and (3)
    E. Neither (1), (2), nor (3)

3. Bruce Wickham, a college professor of chemistry, is interested in obtaining disability income insurance since his university does not offer such coverage. In order to keep the cost of coverage down, which of the following recommendations should be made to Bruce?

(1) Buy a policy with the "own occupation" definition of total disability.
(2) Accept only a policy that will replace 100% of his regular salary.
(3) Obtain a policy that pays lifetime benefits.

    A. (1) and (2) only
    B. (1) and (3) only
    C. (2) and (3) only
    D. (1), (2), and (3)
    E. Neither (1), (2), nor (3)

4. (Published question released January, 1999)

A successful architect wants to purchase disability income insurance. She is concerned about becoming totally disabled, but also about a reduction in income if she is obliged to reduce her workload because of a less-than-total disability. To satisfy these concerns, which of the following should be included in her disability income coverage?

    A. Residual disability benefits
    B. A change-of-occupation provision
    C. Dismemberment benefits
    D. A relation of earnings-to-insurance provision

5. Marvin was a radio reporter until he lost his voice box last year due to throat cancer. Now, he works in a newsroom writing and editing news stories. He has contacted you because his insurance company will not pay disability income benefits. What is the most likely explanation for the insurer's refusal to pay benefits?

    A. The elimination period has not run.
    B. The policy is guaranteed renewable rather than noncancellable.
    C. The policy contains a presumptive disability clause.
    D. The policy uses an "any occupation" definition of disability.

6. Clarence Hardy is an employee at the Drake Candy Corporation, an S corporation. Clarence and other employees are covered under a disability income plan that will pay him 50% of his $96,000 salary if he becomes disabled. The company adds the pro rata cost of the plan to each employee's W-2. Clarence is in the 25% income tax bracket. What is the amount of monthly disability benefits Clarence will receive after tax if he remains in the same tax bracket when disabled?

    A. $2,250
    B. $3,000
    C. $3,500
    D. $4,000

7. (Published question released December, 1996)

Typically, when group long-term disability income insurance premiums are paid by a C corporation, all disability benefit amounts received by an employee are:

A. <u>Not</u> includible in the income of the employee for federal tax purposes, without regard to any other sources of income
B. Includible in the income of the employee for federal tax purposes, without regard to any other sources of income
C. <u>Not</u> includible in the income of the employee for federal tax purposes if any portion of the benefit is reduced/offset by other income
D. Includible in the income of the employee for federal tax purposes if any portion of the benefit is reduced/offset by other income
E. Includible in the income of the employee for federal tax purposes unless he or she is over age 65

8. What is the usual federal income tax treatment of the employer's premium payments under a group long-term disability income insurance plan?

A. The amount of the premium payments is excluded from the employee's income, regardless of whether the plan is discriminatory.
B. The amount of the premium payments is fully included in the employee's income if the plan is discriminatory.
C. The amount of the premium payments is included in the employee's income to the extent the plan will replace more than 50% of an employee's earnings.
D. The amount of the premium payments is excluded from the employee's income only if the plan is nondiscriminatory.

9. Cook Electric Company is a small electrical supply company with 25 employees, 5 of whom are salaried. The company is considering adding a group long-term disability income insurance plan and would like a recommendation. The company wants a plan that will be cost-effective, will not result in additional current income taxes for employees, and will be tax-efficient for the company. Which of the following statements would be appropriate for a recommendation of a plan?

    A. Cook should adopt a plan with a definition of disability so that benefits will be paid for as long as the employee is unable to perform his or her regular occupation.

    B. Cook should limit the plan to salaried employees and provide for full integration with Social Security and workers' compensation benefits.

    C. Cook should establish a double bonus plan so employees can purchase individual disability income policies.

    D. Cook should establish a bonus plan for salaried employees to buy individual policies and a group plan that provides benefits equal to 50% of earnings, without integration for unsalaried employees.

10. Many insurance companies in their disability income policies now use a "split definition" of disability. Which of the following is how this split definition is generally stated?

    A. Inability to perform any occupation, followed by inability to perform his or her own occupation

    B. Inability to perform any occupation for which qualified, followed by inability to perform his or her own occupation

    C. Inability to perform his or her own occupation, followed by inability to perform any occupation for which reasonably suited

    D. Inability to perform any occupation, followed by inability to perform any occupation for which reasonably suited

11. Which of the following policy definitions of disability will be most favorable for the insured?

    A. Inability to perform any occupation for which fitted by education, training, or experience

    B. Inability to perform his or her own occupation for five years, and then inability to perform any occupation for which fitted by education, training, or experience

    C. Inability to perform his or her own occupation for two years, then inability to perform any occupation for which fitted, but, in fact, does not engage in any occupation

    D. Inability to perform his or her own occupation

12. Which of the following statements concerning the residual disability benefit clause in a disability income policy is (are) correct?

    (1) It actually pays the equivalent of a partial disability benefit for a few days.
    (2) The benefit is typically paid only after the insured recovers from total disability.

      A. (1) only
      B. (2) only
      C. Both (1) and (2)
      D. Neither (1) nor (2)

13. Which of the following statements concerning the waiting (elimination) period in an individual disability income policy is (are) correct?

    (1) It serves much the same purpose as a deductible in property insurance.
    (2) It denies coverage for injuries that occur during the first few days after the policy is issued.
    (3) It eliminates coverage for the "sniffle" type disability and helps to reduce the moral hazard.

      A. (1) only
      B. (1) and (2) only
      C. (1) and (3) only
      D. (2) and (3) only
      E. (1), (2), and (3)

14. What underwriting requirement do insurers impose when offering the insured a disability income policy with a guaranteed insurability option?

      A. Evidence of insurability at the time of each increased benefit
      B. Evidence of actual increases in the CPI or in some other price index
      C. Evidence of actual earned income for the insured, adequate to justify larger benefit amounts
      D. Evidence of increases in the size of the insured family

15. Henry is the owner of a disability income policy he purchased individually. Which of the following statements concerning the federal income tax treatment of this policy is (are) correct?

(1) Since the premium payments are a type of medical expense, they are deductible for Henry like his other medical expenses.
(2) Since the benefit payments are designed to replace a portion of Henry's lost earned income, they are taxed to Henry like earned income.

    A. (1) only
    B. (2) only
    C. Both (1) and (2)
    D. Neither (1) nor (2)

16. Mark International wants to add a disability plan to their employee benefits program. Which of the following definitions of disability will help to minimize the premiums?

    A. Any occupation
    B. Educated and trained for
    C. Own occupation
    D. Qualified for

17. Bob broke his leg skiing earlier this year. Bob collected $10,000 from his short-term disability plan paid for solely by his employer. How much does Bob have to include in his gross income?

    A. $0
    B. $5,000
    C. $8,500
    D. $10,000

For practice answering case questions related to Topic 25, please answer the following questions in the cases included in Appendix A at the back of this textbook.

Case	Questions
Black Hills P&L	
Brodinski	3, 4, 5, and 6
Haurilick	
Beals	2
Mocsin	
Loudon	1 and 2
Connor	7 and 8
Seidelhofer	8 and 9
Loomis Company	
Michael and Diana Eastman	
Gary and Judy Parker	16, 17, 18, 19, and 20

ANSWERS AND EXPLANATIONS

1. C is the answer. Insurers usually limit benefit amounts to some fraction, such as two-thirds, of the insured's normal earnings.

2. A is the answer. (1) is correct because a partial disability benefit is usually 50% of the total disability benefit. (2) is correct because a residual disability benefit is a percentage of the total disability benefit that equals the percentage reduction in earnings. Burton's earnings were reduced by 1/3, from $6,000 to $4,000, so he would collect 1/3 of the $4,000 total disability benefit. (3) is incorrect because the recurrent disability clause has no application in this situation.

3. E is the answer. The "own occupation" definition creates the highest cost of coverage, all other things being equal. Bruce is unlikely to find an insurer that will replace 100% of his earnings, but if he does, the high benefit amount will increase the premium cost. Likewise, lifetime benefits create the highest cost of coverage, all other things being equal. Therefore, (1), (2), and (3) would all be very imprudent recommendations to make to Bruce.

4. A is the answer. A residual disability benefit will pay a portion of the total disability benefit based on the reduction in the insured's earnings after a return to part-time work.

5. D is the answer. The disability occurred last year, so the elimination period has most likely run. Elimination periods are typically 60 to 120 days. The question does not mention that the policy was not renewed, so the issue is not over the policy renewal provisions. The loss of speech could give rise to a presumptive disability, so the failure to pay benefits suggests that the problem is not arising from the presumptive disability provision. The problem could be from the definition of disability because Marvin is able to work in a job for which he is qualified by his education, training, and experience. If the policy defined disability in terms of drop in income, this definition would also result in no benefits for Marvin.

6. D is the answer. The disability income benefits are excluded from income because Clarence pays the premiums for the policy. The company adds the premium cost to income, so the employees are actually paying for the coverage.

7. B is the answer. When group long-term disability income insurance premiums are paid by a C corporation, the employee must include benefit amounts received in his or her gross income for federal income tax purposes. Thus, A, C, D, and E are incorrect.

8. A is the answer. When group long-term disability insurance is paid for by the employer, the amount of the premium payments is excluded from the employee's income even though the plan is discriminatory.

9. B is the answer. Cook's plan can be cost-effective if it limits the group to salaried employees and if the plan is integrated with Social Security and workers' compensation. Since Cook will be paying the premiums, employees will not have additional income taxes, and Cook will be able to deduct the payments. While the benefits will be subject to income tax, the employees will not have additional taxes currently. Choice A is not correct because this definition of disability is more liberal than the usual definition in long-term disability plans. Choice C is incorrect because Cook will be paying the double bonus to all employees and will not be obtaining a cost-effective alternative. Choice D is incorrect because the bonus plan for salaried employees will mean additional taxes for them, and the lack of integration of the group plan for unsalaried employees will not be cost-effective.

10. C is the answer. It is the only statement that correctly describes the usual split definition of total disability.

11. D is the answer. All the other definitions are more severe or more restrictive than D. D is the most liberal of all the definitions of disability.

12. B is the answer. (1) is not a correct statement. Residual disability is usually more permanent than a few days. Residual disability is the reduction in earnings that persists after the person returns to work. (2) is a correct statement.

13. C is the answer. (1) and (3) are correct statements. (2) is a definition of a probationary period, not a waiting or elimination period.

14. C is the answer. The insurer wants to be sure that the increased benefits are consistent with the insured's earned income. Excessive benefits relative to the insured's earned income may motivate the insured to feign disability. When one can obtain a larger income by being disabled than by working, one may give some thought as to how to become disabled. A, B, and D are not underwriting requirements that disability income insurers impose.

15. D is the answer. The premiums are not deductible, and the benefit payments are not taxable.

16. A is the answer. The any occupation definition of disability will keep the premiums low as the benefits under the policy are lower. The most expensive policy will include the own occupation definition. Educated and trained for definition will generate a higher premium than any occupation but a lower premium than the own occupation definition. Educated and trained for is the same definition as qualified for.

17. D is the answer. Bob must include 100% of the disability premiums since his employer paid the entire premium.

Long-Term Care Insurance (Individual) (Topic 26)

CFP Board Student-Centered Learning Objectives

(a) Identify activities of daily living that can trigger the need for long-term care.

(b) Develop an appropriate long-term care insurance plan based on needs, financial resources, policy coverage, and cost.

A. **The Need For Long-Term Care Planning** **26.2**
B. **Paying For Long-Term Care Expenses** **26.2**
C. **Methods For Handling The Long-Term Care Need** **26.3**
D. **Long-Term Care Insurance (LTCI)** **26.5**
    1. LTCI as part of the financial plan *26.5*
    2. Designing an LTCI policy *26.6*
    3. LTCI laws – HIPAA rules and NAIC model legislation *26.6*
E. **LTCI Policy Features and Provisions** **26.9**
    1. Eligibility and underwriting *26.9*
    2. Eligibility to receive benefits *26.10*
    3. Covered services *26.10*
    4. Waiting (elimination) periods *26.12*
    5. Benefit periods *26.13*
    6. Benefit amount *26.13*
        a. Reimbursement versus indemnity *26.14*
    7. Waiver-of-premium *26.14*
    8. Inflation protection *26.14*
    9. Nonforfeiture benefits *26.15*
    10. Renewability provisions *26.16*
    11. Cost *26.16*
F. **Taxation of Long-Term Care Insurance Premiums and Benefits**... **26.17**
G. **Paying for LTCI Premiums From Other Plans** **26.18**
H. **Group Long-Term Care Insurance** **26.19**
I. **Long-Term Care Insurance Partnership Program** **26.20**
J. **Life Insurance for Long-Term Care** **26.21**
    1. Life insurance with long-term care riders *26.21*
K. **Continuing Care Retirement Communities (CCRCs)** **26.22**
L. **Definitions** **26.24**

THE NEED FOR LONG-TERM CARE PLANNING

There are many reasons financial planners should include long-term care planning in their portfolio of skills. One reason is simply the demographics of the U.S. population. The over-65 population in the U.S. continues to grow rapidly as a percentage of the total population. Also, almost 40% of those who are over age 65 will likely need care in a nursing home for some period of time.

Almost 5% of Americans over age 65 already reside in nursing homes, and another 12% are disabled but live at home. Each year, almost 2 million people spend some time in a nursing home, and a large portion of nursing home expenses are paid by the patients or their family members.

> *"The population of people 85 and older is expected to increase from 5.7 million in 2011 to 14.1 million in 2040."* - **2014 Medicare & You, National Medicare Handbook**

The high cost of nursing home care, typically from $40,000 to $75,000 or more per year, is another major factor pointing to the need for long-term care planning. This high potential cost is likely to have a significant impact on a client's overall financial plan, and long-term care needs should be included as an integral part of each retirement and estate plan.

PAYING FOR LONG-TERM CARE EXPENSES

Long-term care expenses are paid from public and private sources. Public sources include Medicaid, Medicare, and Veterans' benefits, and private sources include long-term care insurance, personal savings, investment portfolios, annuities, reverse mortgages, and life insurance.

Robert Wood Johnson Foundation's Health Policy Snapshot from February 2014 (http://www.rwjf.org/content/dam/farm/reports/issue_briefs/2014/rwjf410654) reveals that approximately 62% of long-term care spending in 2011 came from Medicaid, just under 5% came from other public sources such as Medicare and the Department of Veterans Affairs, and approximately 32% came from private resources including out-of-pocket and long-term care insurance.

Veterans' benefits are not discussed in detail in this text, but planners should be aware that government funds may be available to help disabled veterans and their spouses pay for personal care services provided at home or in a VA nursing home. Additional information can be found at www.va.gov.

METHODS FOR HANDLING THE LONG-TERM CARE NEED

There are a number of ways to deal with the need for long term care, and it is likely that a financial plan will ultimately include a combination of several methods. Unfortunately, many planning clients become fixated on one method that they expect will always work and, consequently, fail to consider alternatives. It will be the planner's responsibility to ensure that clients take a realistic view of the methods available to find the right combination. Below, we have noted some of the most common misconceptions, along with some information for correcting them.

Misconception 1: "My spouse or children will care for me."

In a perfect world, we might plan for a spouse or child to provide any care that is needed; unfortunately, many events and circumstances can undermine such plans. Most long-term care needs arise later in life, when the spouse and adult children are retired and may be dealing with health issues of their own. Family members may be prevented from providing the care that is needed on a daily basis. Children who are healthy enough to provide the care may be in a different geographic region or may be in the peak earning years of their careers. Asking those children to become full-time caregivers may be asking them to give up their careers and their own retirement security, and may even require them to sell their homes and to move. Moreover, providing care on a full-time basis is both physically and emotionally strenuous, and can have a negative impact on the relationships among family members.

Misconception 2: "Medicare will cover it."

An important fact to keep in mind is that Medicare does not cover custodial (non-medical) care. Medicare does provide limited benefits for skilled nursing care (24-hour care with medical staff on duty), but only up to 100 days. The skilled nursing benefit will only be available if the patient enters the skilled nursing facility within 30 days following at least a 3-day inpatient hospital stay, and a licensed physician must certify that the person requires skilled nursing care. The skilled nursing care facility must meet the standards established for "participation" under Medicare law. Medicare will pay for the first 20 days in full, after which there will be an out-of-pocket co-pay of $161 per day (in 2016) for the next 80 days. After 100 days, Medicare will no longer provide coverage.

Misconception 3: "My medical expense insurance will cover it."

Medical expense insurance generally does not cover long-term care, although some Medigap policies do cover the Medicare Part A co-pay for days 21-100. See Topic 24 for a list of Medicare Supplement policies providing this coverage.

Misconception 4: "I will give away all of my assets to qualify for Medicaid."

There is a five year look-back for assets transferred directly to family members or into a trust, so giving away assets in order to qualify for Medicaid would need to be done well in advance of the actual need for care. Unlike Medicare, Medicaid may provide custodial services either in a facility or at home. Rules as to covered services and eligibility vary from state-to-state. Each state's Medical Assistance Office is the best resource to determine exactly what the eligibility requirements are within that state, but generally assets will need to be reduced to a level that leaves the client impoverished, which is likely to be a very uncomfortable situation for financial planning clients. The federal government also requires states to recover from a patient's estate the amount Medicaid spent on behalf of an institutionalized long-term care patient. Some estates are exempt, such as those where there is a surviving spouse; however, recovery may be made after the death of the surviving spouse.

In addition, most care facilities only accept a limited number of Medicaid patients, and some facilities do not accept Medicaid at all, so it may be difficult to get into the most desirable care facility in a given geographic area. A better solution is to purchase a long-term care insurance policy under the Partnership for Long-Term Care programs offered in most states. Partnership programs are discussed on page 26.20.

While financial planning clients may utilize some of the methods discussed in this section, many clients still feel that a level of risk attaches to these methods. For example, the spouse might be able to provide care for a period of time or Medicare may pay initially, but these alternatives leave some potential gaps. Many planning clients will find the purchase of a long-term care insurance policy to be the most effective means of protecting against the risk of needing care for an extended period of time. Even those who have accumulated enough wealth to pay for the high cost of care without insurance often prefer to purchase insurance to preserve assets to pass on to the next generation.

After making the case for long-term care insurance, we should also point out, however, that only about 7% – 8% of Americans have purchased long-term care insurance policies. Long-term care insurance, like any other financial services product, is not right for everyone. Long-term care insurance premiums can be prohibitive to those in the middle class and may require a significant percentage of retirement income. The general rule of thumb is that LTCI premiums should be no more than 7% of income, although this rule will, of course, vary from client-to-client depending on other expenses, such as medical insurance, housing expenses, and other out-of-pocket expenses. The effect of potential increases in premium must also be factored in (see renewability provisions on page 26.16 for additional details on premium increases).

One thing to keep in mind is that many middle-class senior citizens have sacrificed some retirement savings to pay for children to attend college. Those children who are now prospering in their careers may be more than willing to fund the cost of long-term care insurance for their parents. The child may want the peace of mind from knowing that a parent can be cared for in a high-quality care facility or at home, whichever is most desirable, and alleviate the difficult position the child might otherwise have to face in choosing between caring for parents or continuing a career.

Class Discussion 26 – 1

Should children be held legally liable for paying a parent's nursing home bill under filial responsibility laws?

See the article regarding a Pennsylvania court decision (based on PA statute) at:

http://www.forbes.com/sites/feeonlyplanner/2012/08/13/new-financial-burden-for-boomers-forced-to-pay-parents-long-term-care-bill/

LONG-TERM CARE INSURANCE (LTCI)

LTCI as Part of the Financial Plan

Some planners consider long-term care insurance (LTCI) to be part of estate planning because the insured is protecting assets for heirs instead of depleting them for custodial care. Other planners consider long-term care insurance to be part of retirement planning because the insured is providing funding for the risk that custodial care will be required during retirement. In reality, it is important to consider long-term care in connection with both parts of the financial plan.

For retirement planning, the long-term care exposure is different from and in addition to the superannuation exposure because superannuation (living longer than expected) does not imply incapacity; consequently, the two exposures are handled by different retirement planning strategies. Nevertheless, the cost of providing care, either through personal funds or the premiums for long-term care insurance, must be factored into the retirement spending plan.

Even if, after considering the need for long-term care insurance, the client ultimately declines to purchase LTCI, it is good practice for the financial planner to document the discussion and the client's decision. This documentation will help to protect the planner from later suit by the client's heirs who might claim the planner neglected to advise the client to buy LTCI.

Designing an LTCI Policy

The cost and amount of protection provided by the LTCI policy can vary greatly based upon the structure of the policy. It will be important for the planner to assist the client in understanding how the policy works, what services are covered, and which policy features should be included.

When designing a policy for a client, the planner should take into consideration all of the following details:

- Factors that affect premiums
- Partnership program coordination
- Liquid assets available to pay for care
- Asset protection for heirs
- Family history
- Client risk tolerance/aversion

Premiums can vary based on factors such as age, health, and marital status at the time of application. Married applicants may be offered lower premium rates due to the potentially shorter duration of claims, because the spouse is able to provide care for a period of time. Premiums also vary based on the selections the client makes for the benefit period, elimination period, and daily benefit amount.

LTCI Laws – HIPAA Rules and NAIC Model Legislation

Long-term care insurance is a relatively new insurance product in that it has only been available for about 35 years (versus life insurance, which has been around for hundreds of years). When reviewing existing policies, it is important to understand that some significant changes have come about in the way policies are structured, and policies issued prior to 1997 are likely to have coverage gaps. Some of the early private LTCI policies provided benefits only if the insured person required "skilled nursing care." If the physician would not certify that the insured needed "skilled nursing care," the insured person would not be eligible for the benefits of a long-term care facility. As it turns out, only about 5% of the persons who required long-term care could be certified as needing full-time skilled nursing care.

Another cause for discontent in the early years of long-term care insurance was the common policy requirement that the insured be hospitalized for a minimum number of days before the insurer would pay for long-term care. This requirement eliminated one-half of the people otherwise eligible and needing long-term care. Statistics from the National Care Planning Council confirm that slightly less than 50% of nursing home admissions involve patients who move directly from a hospital to a nursing home facility. Fortunately, most insurers have now deleted the prior hospitalization requirement from long-term care policies.

In the late 1980's, the National Association of Insurance Commissioners (NAIC) created a Long-Term Care Insurance Model Act to establish standards for long-term care insurance policies, to protect applicants from unfair or deceptive sales practices, and to facilitate public understanding and comparison among LTCI policies. The model legislation has been updated frequently throughout the years, and most states have adopted it in some form.

The Health Insurance Portability and Accountability Act (HIPAA) of 1996 led the way to much more comprehensive policies and added a number of requirements that are a great benefit to insureds and policy owners. Most policies issued today will be HIPAA qualified policies and will, therefore, qualify for certain tax advantages (discussed on page 26.17). HIPAA contains the following requirements for long-term care insurance policies (details of these requirements will be discussed later):

(a)   A requirement that policies be either noncancellable or, at least, guaranteed renewable

(b)   A maximum limit of six months on the time during which preexisting conditions may be excluded, together with a maximum look-back period of six months, relating to pre-existing conditions

(c)   Limitations on exclusions in long-term care insurance policies

(d)   Requirements for continuation or conversion for those who are covered under group policies

(e)   A requirement that someone other than the policyholder receive a notice of policy termination due to nonpayment of premium, as well as a requirement that a lapsed policy be reinstated if proof of cognitive impairment or loss of functional capacity is provided to the insurer as the reason for the lapse

(f)   Prohibition of post-claims underwriting

(g)   Minimum standards applicable to benefits for home health care and community health care

(h) A requirement that specified inflation protection benefits be offered

(i) Prohibition of policies requiring prior hospitalization or prior institutionalization in order to qualify for nursing home care, as well as prohibition of requiring prior nursing home care in order to qualify for home health care benefits

(j) A requirement that a nonforfeiture benefit be made available

The Health Insurance Portability and Accountability Act of 1996 also provides the following consumer protection standards relating to long-term care insurance companies:

(a) A requirement that insurers establish a process to ensure against inappropriate replacement of existing long-term care insurance policies

(b) A requirement that insurers report lapse rates, replacement sales, and denied claims each year

(c) A requirement that advertising materials used by insurance companies be filed with the state regulatory authority

(d) A requirement that insurers establish marketing standards to prevent twisting, high-pressure sales tactics, and "cold lead" advertising

(e) A requirement that agents make reasonable efforts to determine the appropriateness of a recommended policy for the particular insured

(f) A requirement that prospective purchasers be given an outline of coverage, as well as an approved shopper's guide

(g) A requirement that group certificates include a description of the policy's principal benefits and exclusions

(h) A requirement that a full refund of premium be paid up to 30 days after the policy is purchased, if requested

(i) A requirement concerning disclosure and reporting for accelerated death benefits that are subject to the NAIC's Long-Term Care Insurance Model Act and Regulation

(j)   A requirement of a defined incontestability period, as well as a requirement that conditions be spelled out for rescission of the policy by the insurance company

LTCI POLICY FEATURES AND PROVISIONS

Eligibility and Underwriting

Some insurance companies have a minimum age of 40 for writing LTCI policies, but many will write policies beginning at age 18 or at any age. Most companies have a maximum age of approximately 84 to 89 years for issuing a policy.

While the health of the insured is important for underwriting long-term care policies, planners will find that underwriting considerations for LTCI are unique in comparison to underwriting for other types of insurance, such as life or disability. Insurers may make use of cognitive questionnaires in addition to physical exams since cognitive impairment is one of the most important issues for LTCI. Depending on a client's age and history, this may be as simple as a telephone interview, or may require an in-person interview.

Underwriters are also likely to be more concerned with an applicant's physiological age (age as measured by health and function) than chronological age (number of years since birth). Musculoskeletal issues (such as osteoporosis) and recent physical therapy can throw up red flags, as can combinations of medical histories, such as diabetes combined with heart disease. Even something as simple as taking multiple medications may cause the underwriter to seek additional information because of the potential for drug interactions that may adversely affect intellectual capacity or physical ability. Some insurance companies may be more liberal than others in underwriting certain conditions, so it may be beneficial to review policies from several different insurers. Some insurance companies will also offer preferred health discounts.

> *"Old age is always 15 years older than I am."* – **Francis Bacon**

Most policies specify that benefits will not be paid for a preexisting condition for which treatment was recommended or received within 6 months of the purchase of the coverage, or for alcohol or drug addictions within 2 years of the purchase of coverage.

The best age at which to purchase a policy is often in the 50's to early 60's when the client is likely to be healthy enough to qualify, premiums will be low, and preferred health discounts may be available. Some companies will also offer premium discounts if both husband and wife purchase policies, and some companies allow spouses to use "shared benefits." For example, if husband and wife each purchased a policy providing benefits for 2 years, and wife needed care and used up all of her 2 years of benefits, she could then draw against the benefits from the husband's policy (assuming he was not yet using his benefits). When working with married clients, it is a good idea to ask the insurer whether discounts for shared benefits are available.

Eligibility to Receive Benefits

LTCI is designed to provide benefit payments when the insured is in need of long-term care. The insured's eligibility for benefits is determined by the policy's benefit triggers. In older long-term care policies, the trigger was a period of prior hospitalization before benefits became payable under the long-term care policy. In more modern policies, however, activities of daily living (ADLs) are the trigger.

ADLs are usually described in the policy and may include activities such as dressing, eating, bathing, transferring (e.g., moving from a bed to a wheelchair), and toileting or maintaining continence. These 6 ADLs are the most common trigger found in modern LTCI policies because they are specifically identified in HIPAA. In order for a policy to be tax qualified, it must list at least 5 of these 6 ADLs, and must define physical impairment as inability to perform at least 2 of the ADLs without substantial assistance from another person. Since elderly people typically require assistance with bathing before they need help with other ADLs, a policy that does not list bathing as an ADL may be slower to pay benefits. Some policies also include ambulating (walking) as an ADL to trigger benefits; however, ambulating is not an ADL identified by HIPAA for tax-qualified policies.

Benefit triggers rely on a physician certification that the insured is expected to be unable to perform at least 2 of the 5 or 6 listed activities of daily living (ADLs) for 90 days or longer. Benefits may also be triggered by severe cognitive impairments that require substantial supervision to protect the individual from threats to health and safety, such as senile dementia, Alzheimer's disease, or Parkinson's disease (these are often referred to as "organic" cognitive impairments). Some cognitive impairments such as alcohol or drug addiction are often excluded from coverage, and some mental illnesses (considered "nonorganic" psychiatric impairments, such as schizophrenia) may also be excluded from coverage.

Covered Services

Several types of services may be covered by LTCI policies, including care in a skilled nursing facility, care in an intermediate nursing facility, custodial care, home health care, adult day care, and respite care to provide temporary replacement for those who are caring for incapacitated individuals. These various types of long-term care require caregivers with different levels of skill, and each level demands a price commensurate with the technology and professionalism required. Modern LTCI policies cover the cost of care across the full range of settings.

Skilled nursing care is the highest level of care. The insured resides in the skilled nursing facility and is provided with 24-hour care by a registered nurse who is under a licensed physician's supervision. This care is the most comprehensive level of care and, of course, the most expensive.

An intermediate care facility provides a level of care that is between skilled care and custodial care. While skilled care may not be needed, there may be medical issues rising above the capacity of a custodial environment. Intermediate care facilities will have fewer nurses per 100 persons than skilled care facilities.

Assisted living facilities, like intermediate care facilities, provide assistance with activities of daily living and limited health care for those who do not require the level of medical care of a skilled nursing facility.

Custodial care provides unskilled assistance with personal needs. The insured does not need medical care, just help with daily life. The main services and functions provided are food preparation, food service, bathing, and moving patients from bed to chair and subsequently chair to bed.

Home health care is just what it says – care that is provided in the insured's home. Many insureds prefer to live in their own home as long as possible, and the home health care coverage of an LTCI policy allows them to do just that. Home care is encouraged wherever possible for the convenience and happiness of the person, as well as for its cost-effectiveness. In some cases, a daily visit to the person's home by a nurse is necessary. In other cases, a nurse comes only once or twice a week. One question that is often asked about home care in an LTCI policy is whether the policy will pay a relative to care for the insured at home. Most policies will only pay a relative who is licensed to provide care, so a planner must be sure to clarify this requirement with the insurer if it is an issue.

Adult day care is similar to child day care – it provides a safe environment with activities and meals for the insured while the primary caregiver is at work during the day.

Caregivers often experience depression and a decline in physical health. Serving as a caregiver can be very mentally, emotionally, and physically challenging. It is important for the caregiver to have a respite from providing care on a regular basis. Most modern long-term care policies provide respite care as a covered service.

LTCI policies may also offer a bed reservation benefit. The reason for a reservation benefit is that the cost of an empty bed at a facility is high, and many high-quality skilled and intermediate care facilities have waiting lists of individuals who would like to move into the facility when a bed opens up. This demand means that if a resident leaves the facility for a period of time, perhaps to spend a couple of weeks at home with family over the holidays or due to hospitalization, there is a risk that the facility will place another patient in the open bed. The bed reservation benefit allows for the institutionalized individual to have a short-term absence without fear of losing his or her place in the institution. Bed reservation benefits are typically limited to 15 or 30 days.

Alzheimer's facilities (also called Alzheimer's Special Care Units (SCUs)) are designed to meet the unique care needs of individuals with Alzheimer's disease or severe dementia. In some cases the SCU is a floor in another facility where dementia patients are grouped together and offered specialized activities.

Waiting (Elimination) Periods

When choosing a LTCI policy, the planner will need to assist the client with decisions regarding the length of the elimination period. The elimination period is the length of time that care must be received before the policy will pay benefits. It works like a deductible, allowing the policy owner to self-insure for a short period of time to eliminate small claims and, thereby, control the cost of the policy. The longer the elimination period, the lower the premium.

As with selecting the disability insurance elimination period, selecting the LTCI elimination period requires some planning. Typical waiting periods are 0 to 180 days. The client should have enough liquid assets available to cover costs during the entire elimination period. If the current cost of care in the client's geographic region is $200 per day, and a 90 day elimination period is selected, the client would need a minimum of $18,000 of liquid assets to cover the elimination period. Also factor in that the client is purchasing the policy many years before the need will arise, and the cost of care will be increasing, so if the average cost of care is $200 per day today, and increases at a rate of 4% for the next 15 years, the cost will rise to $360 per day. This means the client would need to have $32,400 in liquid assets available at that time.

Another element to be analyzed in the policy is how care received at home will be counted toward the elimination period. Some policies may use actual days (3 days of care = 3 days), while other policies may count any care received during a week as a full week. Another important question to ask is whether care received by family members counts toward the waiting period if a doctor certifies that care is needed. Some policies may not count days where care is provided by an unlicensed family member.

Benefit Periods

Planners will also need to assist clients with selection of an appropriate benefit period for the policy. The benefit period is the length of time the policy will continue to pay for services. The benefit period can range from one year to lifetime (depending on the age at which the policy is purchased), although many insurance companies have stopped offering lifetime benefit options. Two, three, and five years are the most commonly selected benefit periods.

Some clients will choose 2 or 3 years as the benefit period based on statistics showing that the average stay in a nursing home is about 2 years. Some will choose 5 years thinking that if they transfer all of their assets to the kids the day they start care, they can outsmart the Medicaid 5-year look-back rules. If the goal is to eventually qualify for Medicaid, the planner and client should look at a Long-Term Care Partnership policy, as discussed on page 26.20 of this text.

Another way to determine the appropriate length of the benefit period is to consider family history, personal health history, and risk tolerance (or aversion). Clients with a history of longevity in the family are more likely to need care for longer periods of time. If that longevity is combined with an aversion to Medicaid, the client is likely to desire a much longer benefit period. Other clients may already have health issues or come from a family that generally does not live long and may not have an aversion to Medicaid. These clients would be willing to accept a shorter benefit period. Also keep in mind the longer the benefit period, the higher the premium.

Benefit Amount

Another important decision in structuring the LTCI policy is the selection of the benefit amount, which is the daily maximum that will be paid from the policy. The amount may range from as low as $50 to above $300 per day. Of course, the higher the daily benefit, the higher the premium.

The planner should do some research to determine the average daily cost for home health aides, custodial care, and skilled care in the client's geographic area. These costs vary widely in different parts of the country. Each year, Genworth conducts a "Cost of Care Survey" and makes information about costs of various levels of care throughout the country available on their website at: https://www.genworth.com/corporate/about-genworth/industry-expertise/state-maps.html.

Some policies will also allow the applicant to select a home health benefit of 50%, 75%, or 100% of the institutionalized daily benefit amount.

Reimbursement Versus Indemnity

The daily benefit amount selected within the LTCI policy may work in one of two ways: as a reimbursement or as an indemnity.

Policies that use the reimbursement approach will pay for actual expenses incurred for the insured's care. These policies, in effect, create a pool of money to be used for long-term care expenses. For example, if a $250 daily benefit is chosen with a benefit period of 3 years, then the pool of money available is $250 x 365 days x 3 years = $273,750. Some days the expenses may be more than the daily benefit amount (in which case the payment will usually be limited to the daily maximum amount to ensure that the benefits last at least as long as the benefit period), and some days the actual expenses may be less. If expenses are less than the daily amount for a period of time, then the benefits may actually last longer than the selected benefit period.

A policy using the indemnity (a.k.a., per diem) approach will pay the selected daily benefit for each day care is received, regardless of the amount of actual expenses incurred. An indemnity policy will never last longer than the benefit period selected.

Waiver-of-Premium

Premiums for LTCI policies are typically payable for life. In the past, insurance companies offered limited pay policies, such as 10-pay or to-age-65, but many have stopped offering them. Policyholders normally do not have to continue to pay premiums while benefits are being paid. The waiver-of-premium provision usually eliminates the need for premiums six months after benefit payments have begun, but some waiver-of-premium provisions are more liberal and will eliminate premiums 90 days after the insured has qualified for benefits.

Inflation Protection

Recall that planners will most often recommend purchase of a policy when clients are in their 50's to early 60's, but the need for care will likely not come for another 20 or 30 years. In order to be tax-qualified, HIPAA requires that LCTI policies offer the option of purchasing an inflation protection rider (also called an inflation protection endorsement). Some state laws mandate a certain amount of inflation protection be built into the premium, in other states inflation protection is a rider that is added to the policy for an extra premium. The inflation protection rider will allow the daily benefit amount to increase over time, and the increase can be based on simple or compound inflation with varying percentage increases available.

A simple inflation protection rider at 5% would increase the benefit by 5% of the initial daily benefit every year. For example, with a $100 initial daily benefit amount, the benefit would increase by $5 each year so that after 10 years, the benefit amount is $150 per day.

A compound inflation protection rider at 5% would increase the benefit by 5% using compounding (each year the increase is 5% of the previous year's daily benefit amount). So with an initial daily benefit of $100, after 10 years the new daily benefit would be $163.

$100	Year 2	Year 3	Year 4	Year 5	Year 10	Year 20
Simple 5%	$105.00	$110.00	$115.00	$120.00	$150.00	$200.00
Compound 5%	$105.00	$110.25	$115.76	$121.55	$162.89	$265.33

Rather than an automatic increase under simple or compound inflation, some policies provide inflation protection by way of a guaranteed purchase option. With this endorsement, the insured is periodically offered the ability to increase the daily benefit amount without proof of insurability. If an increase is elected, the benefit will increase and the premium will also increase to reflect the additional benefits purchased at the insured's current age. If not elected, no change in premium will occur until the next periodic increase is permitted and elected.

When added as an endorsement to the LTCI policy, the premium for compound inflation protection will be higher than the premium for a simple inflation protection rider. The age of the insured at the time of purchase will likely dictate which is appropriate, simple or compound. For older applicants (approximately age 70-75 or older), simple inflation protection may be adequate; however, for younger applicants, compound inflation will be necessary to ensure that the daily benefit keeps up with increases in costs over the long period of time before benefits are needed.

Nonforfeiture Benefits

Long-term care insurance is similar to homeowners insurance in that it does not build cash value. If a claim occurs while the policy is in force, benefits will be paid; however, if no claims are made, the insurer will pay no benefits. Some clients may be concerned about the possibility that they will decide many years from purchase that they do not want to keep, or cannot afford to keep, the policy in force. Nonforfeiture benefits may take the form of a reduced paid-up amount of insurance (meaning a smaller benefit amount with no additional premium payments being required). Alternatively, the nonforfeiture benefit may consist of a return of all premiums paid, minus all claim payments.

Some states have a contingent nonforfeiture benefit so that if premiums increase by a certain percentage the insured can choose to take the benefits that the current premium would now purchase, or they can choose to take a paid up policy with a shorter benefit period.

Renewability Provisions

HIPAA requires that LTCI policies be either guaranteed renewable or noncancellable in order to receive the best tax advantages. A policy that is guaranteed renewable allows the insured to continue coverage, and denies the insurer the right to cancel coverage as long as premiums are paid. The insurance company can, however, increase premiums for a guaranteed renewable policy, as long as it is an increase for the entire class of insureds and is approved by the state's Insurance Commission. Clients and planners should be aware of the possibility of a rate increase. In 2012 many insurers applied for and received permission to increase rates on LTCI policies by as much as 40%. While such large increases may not be typical, it is worth doing some research in advance of the purchase of a policy. Some state insurance departments provide historical information regarding rate increases for the various insurance companies permitted to sell LTCI policies within the state. The insurance company can also provide its historical premium increase information upon request.

Policies that are noncancellable do not allow the insurance company to increase rates; however, these policies will have higher initial premiums than guaranteed renewable policies.

Cost

The cost of a LTCI policy varies considerably from insurance company to insurance company. It also depends, of course, upon the level of benefits, the elimination period, the length of the benefit period, and the age of the insured when the coverage takes effect. To cite some typical examples, however, a policy paying $100 per day of benefits with a 90-day elimination period and a 3-year benefit period might cost between $700 and $1,050 for a 55-year old male. The same coverage might cost $900 to $1,150 per year at age 60 and $1,300 to $1,650 at age 65. Adding inflation protection can increase the premium by 25% – 40%, but is an important feature, especially for young (under age 75) applicants.

The policy's outline of coverage is a good place to look to compare the features of various policies before making a decision. Decisions should not be made purely on cost due to the vast differences in the ways in which policies can work. It is, of course, also a good idea to check the financial stability of the insurance company (see Topic 31 in this textbook for additional information regarding ratings of insurance companies).

TAXATION OF LONG-TERM CARE INSURANCE PREMIUMS AND BENEFITS

A qualified long-term care insurance contract is a traditional LTCI policy (not a hybrid life/LTCI policy) that meets a number of requirements for income tax purposes.

Policies issued before January 1, 1997 were grandfathered under the Health Insurance Portability and Accountability Act of 1996, and are considered tax-qualified policies. Policies issued January 1, 1997 or after may be tax qualified policies if they follow the provisions set forth under HIPAA. In addition to the requirements described on pages 26.7-26.9, above, certain requirements must be met in order for a long-term care insurance policy to qualify for favorable federal income tax treatment under HIPAA. These requirements are as follows:

(a)   Except for per-diem policies, long-term care insurance policies may pay for only "qualified long-term care services," as defined by the tax Code.

(b)   Covered services must be required by a chronically ill person.

(c)   Services must be provided as prescribed by a licensed health care practitioner.

(d)   Policies must be guaranteed renewable and may not include a nonforfeiture benefit in the form of a cash surrender value.

(e)   Policies must offer a nonforfeiture benefit.

(f)   Policies must coordinate with Medicare and Medicare supplement policies. (This requirement does not apply to per-diem-based policies.)

Policies issued after January 1, 1997 that are tax qualified will typically have a statement on the declarations page of the policy identifying it as a tax-qualified policy.

A qualified long-term care policy, then, receives some degree of favorable federal income tax treatment. The premiums are deemed by the IRS to be health insurance premiums and can be added together with other qualified medical expenses (as discussed in Topic 24 of this textbook) on Schedule A Itemized deductions. To the extent that the total qualified medical expenses exceed 10% of adjusted gross income (7.5% through 2016 if the taxpayer or spouse is age 65 or over), a deduction is permitted. However, the maximum amount of LTCI premiums that can be added as a medical expense is limited to a specified amount per year, based on the covered person's age. The same dollar limits apply to self-insured individuals (sole proprietors, partners in a partnership, and LLC members when the LLC is taxed as a sole proprietor or partnership), although self-employed individuals get the advantage of deducting premiums above-the line.

2016 Dollar Limits for Deductibility of LTCI Premiums
For Employees on Schedule A
And Self-Employed Individuals (above-the-line)

Age of Covered Person	Premium Deduction Limit
40 or under	$390
Above 40 but not above 50	$730
Above 50 but not above 60	$1,460
Above 60 but not above 70	$3,900
Above 70	$4,870

These dollar limits are subject to inflation adjustments each year.

In addition to the tax advantage of deductible premiums, benefits received from LTCI policies are generally tax-free. Benefits from reimbursement policies will be tax-free because they reimburse for actual expenses. Per diem benefits from indemnity policies are tax-free up to $340 (for 2016).

C-corporations offering LTCI coverage to employees (including owners who work for the corporation) may take a corporate tax deduction for premiums (not subject to dollar limitations based on age).

When LTCI is offered as a group benefit to employees, an employer can deduct contributions, and the contributions are not taxable income to employees. Generally, employees will receive the benefits under the qualified long-term care contract tax free.

PAYING FOR LTCI PREMIUMS FROM OTHER PLANS

Long-term care insurance premiums may not be paid for with funds from a Flexible Spending Account (FSA), nor can long-term care insurance be offered inside a cafeteria plan. However, under a Health Savings Account (HSA), LTCI premiums are an eligible medical expense (see topic 24 for additional details on HSAs).

🔑 **KEY SUMMARY 26 – 1** **Long-Term Care**	
	What long-term care benefits are provided
Medicare	– Skilled nursing facility not covered after 100 days – No benefits for custodial care
Medical Expense Insurance	– No custodial care or home health care benefits – Nursing care may be for a limited period or amount
Life Insurance	– Accelerated death benefit or viatical settlement available for terminal or chronic illness – Policy loans to pay long-term care costs – Long-term care rider
Long-Term Care Insurance	– Benefits for custodial care, home health care, and skilled nursing facility – Purchaser selects limits, benefit periods, elimination period, and other features

GROUP LONG-TERM CARE INSURANCE

Many employer-sponsored LTCI plans are not actually group insurance plans. A true group plan would permit all members of the group to enroll. Employer-sponsored plans can discriminate regarding eligibility and use individual underwriting, or they can be true group plans making everyone in the group eligible and have limited underwriting. It is common for LTCI to be offered as an executive benefit to a select group of employees.

When employers offer group LTCI on a more extensive basis, the plan is usually limited to full-time employees, and employees must pay the entire cost or a portion of the cost.

One of the disadvantages of a group plan is that in many cases the employer selects the plan features, such as the elimination period, benefit period, and benefit amount; whereas, individually owned long-term care insurance policies can be tailor-made for longer waiting periods, longer benefit payment periods, nursing care at home, and even waiver of premium. Some group policies do allow for customization, so it is important to find out all of the details of the group policy being offered. One advantage of a group policy is the potential for a group discount on the premium. Some group plans also allow employees to purchase policies for their spouses or other family members.

The choice between a group program and a premium bonus plan to a group of selected executives would justify keen analysis by the employee benefit advisor, with a complete census of employees and their family members.

Long-term care coverage is not subject to the COBRA rules but can be continued as an individual policy upon termination of employment.

LONG-TERM CARE INSURANCE PARTNERSHIP PROGRAM

As the cost of long term care continues to increase beyond amounts that are affordable to most Americans and the elderly continue to represent a greater percentage of the population, state Medicaid programs will face exponentially increasing costs to assist with long term care needs. Ordinarily, qualification for Medicaid requires that the individual or couple spend down all of their assets to the point of being impoverished.

In an effort to encourage more people to purchase private long term care insurance and relieve some of the burden on Medicaid, most states (all but 7) have entered into the Partnership for Long Term Care program. The program establishes special eligibility rules that allow individuals who purchase private LTCI protection to qualify for Medicaid payments for long term care after the insurance policy pays for the initial period of care. The program, therefore, allows people to protect some of their assets to be passed on to heirs.

A partnership qualified policy includes an "asset disregard" for Medicaid to the extent of the total amount of benefits received under the long-term care policy. For example, in order to be eligible for Medicaid, an individual must spend down all assets except approximately $2,000. If an individual buys a long-term care policy that provides $150,000 of lifetime benefits and then requires Medicaid benefits, the individual will be allowed to retain $150,000 of assets in addition to the $2,000 that does not need to be spent down to obtain Medicare benefits.

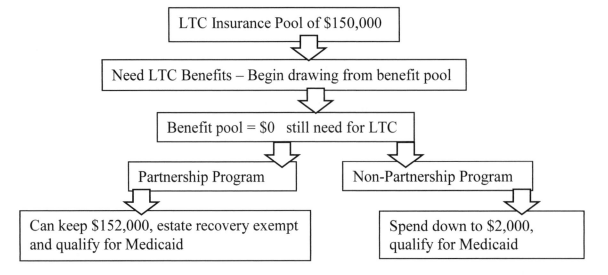

Not all LTCI policies are partnership qualified, so it is important to understand the rules of the partnership program within the client's state. Partnership qualified policies must be tax qualified, contain certain consumer protections, and must include an inflation adjustment for applicants under age 75 in most states. The insurance company will provide notice in writing (a separate letter or in the policy declarations) that the policy is a partnership qualified policy. If a separate letter is sent, it should be kept in a safe place along with the policy.

Planners can check with the state's insurance commission (many states also have separate LTCI partnership websites) for state-specific requirements. Some states also offer alternatives to the asset disregard plan. If there is a possibility the client may want to receive care in a different state, perhaps to be closer to children who have moved to another area, it is also a good idea to check whether the states offer reciprocity if the client moves (reciprocity means that the asset protection moves along with them).

LIFE INSURANCE FOR LONG-TERM CARE

In some cases, life insurance policies can be useful ways to cover the costs of long-term care. Accelerated death benefits that may be available in a life insurance policy are discussed in Topic 28. Another approach is to enter into a viatical settlement agreement. In such an agreement, the owner of a life insurance policy sells it to an outside party or company for a negotiated percentage of the death benefit. Proceeds from the sale are used to finance the needed long-term care. The buyer of the policy keeps it in force and collects the proceeds when the insured dies. Additional treatment of viatical settlements is provided in Topic 28. Policyowners can also access cash to pay long-term care costs by borrowing from their life insurance policy cash value.

A disadvantage of both accelerated death benefits and viatical agreements is that the death proceeds will be reduced or eliminated when the insured dies. Consequently, the original need that gave rise to the life insurance will not be met. A further disadvantage of viatical settlements is the questionable ethics sometimes practiced by the policy purchasers. These persons or companies have no insurable interest in the insured, but are willing to take a gamble that the insured will die soon.

Life Insurance with Long-Term Care Riders

A long-term care rider can be added to some life insurance policies. These hybrid policies are often viewed as a middle ground for those who are concerned about long-term care, but who don't like the fact that a traditional long-term care policy works like a homeowner policy in that if you have a claim you get reimbursed, but if you never have a claim you don't get anything back at the end. By purchasing a life insurance policy with a long-term care rider, either the insured will receive a payout for long-term care or the beneficiary will receive the death benefit. If the insured uses only a portion of the death benefit, then the remaining amount will be paid to the beneficiary. But planners and clients should be aware that using the policy for long-term care will reduce or eliminate the death benefit.

Life insurance policies with long-term care riders can come in two forms: reimbursement or indemnity. A reimbursement rider provides reimbursement for long-term costs actually incurred; whereas, an indemnity rider will pay out a set dollar amount per week or month once benefits are triggered (for example, 2% of the death benefit per month). One advantage to the indemnity rider is the flexibility of receiving that set dollar amount, which can be used to pay *any* expenses rather than being limited to just a reimbursement for qualified expenses.

The triggers to receive benefits under the long-term care rider are typically similar to the triggers in traditional long-term care policies (unable to perform 2 or 3 from a list of 5 or 6 activities of daily living). The benefits received from the policy will generally be income tax free, but the premiums are not tax deductible. The hybrid policies are typically single-premium policies. Planners and clients should keep in mind that the premium will reflect a cost for both long-term care and the death benefit, so the purchase of these policies will make more sense for a client who needs or has a desire for both elements. Other important planning considerations are that the hybrid policies do not qualify as long-term care insurance under the Partnership plans in many states, and most will not offer inflation protection since the amount of long-term care benefits is based on the fixed death benefit amount.

One advantage to purchasing the life policy with long-term care rider is that the life insurance premiums are generally fixed (or are a single-premium amount); whereas, most traditional long-term care policies are guaranteed renewable, meaning that the premiums can, and often do, increase if the insurer increases the premium for the entire class of insureds. This factor may make it difficult to plan for the insurance expense. While traditional long-term care policies can be non-cancelable, meaning that the premiums will not increase, fewer insurers are offering those types of policies, and the original premium amount will, of course, be higher.

CONTINUING CARE RETIREMENT COMMUNITIES (CCRCs)

Continuing care retirement communities (CCRCs), also called life-care communities, are another option in planning for long-term care needs, and clients may ask financial planners to assist them with selecting and arranging these homes.

A CCRC typically starts out with individuals or married couples living independently in a single-family home, apartment, or condominium. As care needs progress, they may then move into a multi-unit dwelling where custodial care is provided, an intermediate care facility, and finally to a skilled nursing facility within the CCRC. The decision to become part of the CCRC, therefore, will be made while the client is still healthy and not yet in need of care.

Residents of a CCRC should expect to pay an entrance fee which can vary from a small amount to tens of thousands of dollars, along with a monthly fee, which can be as low as a few hundred dollars to several thousand dollars depending on what is included. Services may include some meals, housekeeping, yard maintenance when in the single-family dwelling, some types of health care, linen services, transportation services, or use of on-site recreational facilities.

The following are some of the elements that the planner and client will want to assess before a decision to enter a CCRC is made:

- Is the entrance fee refundable (in full or in part) if the clients change their minds? While it may seem ideal at first, situations may change abruptly. For example, if husband and wife move into the community together and one of them dies, the survivor may wish to move somewhere closer to other family members.
- Does the monthly fee (in the same amount or a differing amount) apply when moving from independent living to assisted living or a nursing home?
- Exactly what does the monthly fee cover, and what is specifically excluded from coverage under the monthly fee?
- Are there additional fees for the use of on-site recreational facilities?
- What is the policy for fee increases?
- Does the CCRC offer or require the purchase of long-term care insurance?
- What is the financial strength and viability of the CCRC? Especially in cases where a very large up-front fee is paid, the clients will want to be sure the facility does not end up in bankruptcy just at the time when the client is most in need of care.

DEFINITIONS

Above-the-Line Deductions – In the formula for calculating income taxes, certain deductions, called above-the-line deductions, may be used to reduce the taxpayer's adjusted gross income. Above-the-line deductions may be taken by all taxpayers who qualify for them, regardless of whether they choose to take the standard deduction or itemized deductions later in the tax formula.

Adjusted Gross Income (AGI) – In the formula for calculating income taxes, the adjusted gross income is total income minus certain deductions (called above-the-line deductions). Adjusted gross income is the last line on the front of the Form 1040 and the first line on the back of the Form 1040.

Cold Lead Advertising – Cold lead advertising is the use of a marketing method that fails to clearly disclose that the purpose of the marketing is to solicit insurance and that contact will be made by an insurance agent. Cold lead advertising is a prohibited sales practice.

Deduction – In calculating income taxes for the year, deductions are expenses incurred throughout the year that taxpayers can use to reduce income. Deductions may be broken down into above-the-line deductions and below-the-line deductions. For below-the-line deductions, taxpayers can choose to take a standard deduction amount, or they can choose to itemize deductions, such as qualified mortgage interest, state and local income taxes, and charitable contributions.

Incontestability Period – The incontestability period is the period of time, usually 2 years, after which an insurance company is no longer permitted to contest a claim based on information provided on the application.

Itemized Deductions – Itemized deductions are specified expenses that individual taxpayers can use to reduce taxable income for the year. Among other expenses, itemized deductions include qualified medical expenses to the extent that they exceed 10% of the taxpayer's adjusted gross income for the year (7.5% of AGI if the taxpayer or spouse is age 65 or over as of the end of the tax year).

Recission by the insurance company – Recission refers to an insurance company's ability to void a policy.

Twisting – Twisting refers to the sales practice of an agent knowingly making misleading statements or incomplete comparisons of policies in order to induce the prospective client to buy a different policy. Twisting is a prohibited sales practice.

APPLICATION QUESTIONS

1. (Published question released November, 1994)

A client, age 70, a widower with <u>no</u> close relatives, has crippling arthritis. The client is unable to walk and is confined to a custodial nursing home. Which of the following programs is (are) likely to pay benefits towards the cost of the nursing home?

(1) Medicare may pay for up to 100 days of care after a 20-day deductible.
(2) Long-term care insurance may pay part if coverage of the facility type is broad enough.
(3) Private medical insurance may pay part if it is a comprehensive major medical policy.
(4) Medicaid may pay if the client has income and assets below state thresholds.

    A. (1), (2), and (3) only
    B. (1) and (3) only
    C. (2) and (4) only
    D. (4) only
    E. (1), (2), (3), and (4)

2. A taxpayer who itemizes may take a deduction for which of the following types of individually owned insurance policies?

(1) Long-term care insurance
(2) Disability income insurance
(3) Major medical expense insurance
(4) Life insurance with a long-term care rider

    A. (3) only
    B. (1) and (4) only
    C. (1) and (3) only
    D. (2) and (3) only

3. Jake and Sally are considering buying a long-term care policy on Sally's mother in case they ever have to place her in a long-term care facility. Which of the following steps can Jake and Sally take to hold down the annual premium cost of this coverage?

    A. Select a fairly long waiting or elimination period.
    B. Wait a few years before obtaining the coverage.
    C. Add an inflation protection rider.
    D. Select a policy with a lengthy list of ADLs, any two of which will trigger coverage.
    E. Choose a policy that has a lifetime benefit period.

4. Which of the following are among the ways in which a life insurance policy can be used to help finance the cost of the insured's long-term care?

    (1) Add an accelerated death benefits option to the policy.
    (2) Enter into a viatical settlement agreement.
    (3) Enter into a structured settlement agreement.
    (4) Create a policy loan against the cash value.

        A. (1) and (2) only
        B. (2) and (3) only
        C. (3) and (4) only
        D. (1), (2), and (4) only
        E. (2), (3), and (4) only

5. Which of the following statements concerning the prior hospitalization requirement in long-term care insurance policies is (are) correct?

    (1) This requirement was included in almost all early policies.
    (2) Statistics indicate that approximately 95% of persons admitted to nursing homes move directly from a hospital to a nursing home.
    (3) Today, very few policies have a prior hospitalization requirement.

        A. (1) only
        B. (1) and (2) only
        C. (1) and (3) only
        D. (2) and (3) only
        E. (1), (2), and (3)

6. Which of the following statements concerning the significance of ADLs is (are) correct?

(1) Complete inability to perform two of the ADLs listed in the policy typically means the insured is eligible for the benefits provided by the policy.
(2) For all policies, the requirement is inability to perform. A mere recognizable impairment of ability to perform does not make a person eligible for benefits.

    A. (1) only
    B. (2) only
    C. Both (1) and (2)
    D. Neither (1) nor (2)

7. Which of the following services is LEAST likely to be covered by a recently issued long-term care insurance policy?

    A. Respite care for the insured to relieve home care givers temporarily
    B. Home health care for the insured by a relative not licensed to provide care
    C. Health care for the insured in an assisted living facility
    D. Health care for the insured in a skilled nursing facility

8. Which of the following statements concerning advantages of a hybrid life insurance policy containing a long-term care rider is correct?

    A. If the policy is used for long-term care, it will not reduce the death benefit.
    B. The premium is fixed and cannot increase as can the premium on a long-term care policy.
    C. The policy will qualify for the Long-Term Care Partnership Program in most states.
    D. The trigger for benefits is much less restrictive than the trigger in a traditional long-term care policy.

9. Which of the following statements concerning premiums paid by individuals for long-term care insurance is correct?

A. Premiums are fully deductible for federal income tax purposes.
B. Premiums paid for long-term care plus other medical expenses are fully deductible if the total exceeds the 10% threshold before any deduction is allowed.
C. Only limited amounts of long-term care premiums may be included as medical expenses.
D. Premiums paid by individuals for long-term care are never deductible to any extent.

10. Which of the following statements concerning the federal income tax treatment of the financing of long-term care insurance coverage is correct?

A. Such financing under a cafeteria plan is not permitted.
B. A person's coverage may be paid through a medical care flexible spending account.
C. The benefits of such insurance coverage are fully included in the recipient's gross income.
D. Long-term care contracts are subject to the rules of COBRA.

For practice answering case questions related to Topic 26, please answer the following questions in the cases included in Appendix A at the back of this textbook.

Case	Questions
Black Hills P&L	
Brodinski	
Haurilick	
Beals	
Mocsin	
Loudon	
Connor	9
Seidelhofer	10 and 11
Loomis Company	
Michael and Diana Eastman	
Gary and Judy Parker	21, 22, 23, 24, and 25

ANSWERS AND EXPLANATIONS

1. C is the answer. (1) is incorrect because Medicare does not cover stays in custodial nursing homes. (3) is incorrect because a comprehensive major medical policy covers medical care costs, not custodial care costs. Below is the CFP Board of Examiner's response to a candidate's question regarding this exam item:

The clarification on why (3) above is incorrect is that a comprehensive major medical policy would pay for treatments for the arthritis but not for the custodial care which is required because he cannot perform the functions of daily living: i.e., dressing, feeding, bathing, etc.

2. C is the answer. Premiums for long term care insurance and for major medical expense insurance are deductible as medical expenses. Premiums for individually owned disability income insurance are not deductible, but benefits are received tax-free. Life insurance policies with long-term care riders are not considered qualified long-term care insurance. The premiums for life insurance are not deductible, although benefits received by reason of death or as a payout on the long-term care rider are generally income tax-free.

3. A is the answer. A lengthy waiting period will hold down the cost. All the other options will increase the annual premium cost. In B, the premium rises with age. C and E serve to increase the benefit amount. D will make it easier for Sally's mother to qualify for benefits.

4. D is the answer. (3) is incorrect. A structured settlement may involve the use of an annuity. It does not normally involve a life insurance policy.

5. C is the answer. (2) is not a correct statement. Statistics indicate approximately 50% of the people admitted to nursing homes move directly from a hospital. (1) and (3) are correct statements.

6. A is the answer. (2) is not a correct statement. Many policies provide that recognizable impairment of ability to perform two ADLs is sufficient to qualify an insured for the policy's benefits. (1) is a correct statement.

7. B is the answer. Most long-term care insurance policies will only pay a relative who is licensed to provide health care. The other kinds of care are paid for by most modern long-term care policies.

8. B is the answer. With a hybrid life insurance policy, the premium is fixed and will not increase, but the premium for a long-term care policy can and usually will increase over time. If a hybrid policy is used for long-term care, it will reduce the death benefit. A hybrid policy will not qualify for the Partnership Program. The trigger for benefits under the long-term care rider to a hybrid policy will usually be similar to the trigger in a traditional long-term care policy.

9. C is the answer. Limited amounts of premiums paid may be included in medical expenses. But, only total medical expenses in excess of the 10% threshold are deductible. A, B, and D are not correct statements. B is not correct because there are limits on the amount of long-term care premiums that are deductible.

10. A is the answer. B is not correct. Such an expense may not be paid through a medical care flexible spending account. C is not correct. The insurance benefits are not included up to a maximum amount per day subject to annual adjustments for cost of living. D is not correct. Such contracts are not subject to COBRA rules.

Annuities (Topic 27)

CFP Board Student-Centered Learning Objectives

(a) Explain the characteristics of an annuity including contribution and distribution options and differentiate between immediate and deferred annuities.

(b) Compare and contrast annuities (fixed and variable) with other investment alternatives, including an analysis of costs, contract terms, and taxation.

Annuities
- A. *What is an Annuity and How is it Useful?* 27.2
  - 1. *What is an annuity?* 27.2
  - 2. *The parties to the contract* 27.3
  - 3. *Deferred annuities: two phases* 27.4
  - 4. *Uses of annuities* 27.4
- B. *Classifying Annuities* 27.5
  - 1. *Immediate annuity versus deferred annuity* 27.6
  - 2. *Single-premium annuity versus periodic-premium annuity* 27.6
  - 3. *Single life annuity versus joint life annuity* 27.7
  - 4. *Pure annuity versus refund annuity* 27.7
  - 5. *Qualified annuity versus nonqualified annuity* 27.8
  - 6. *Fixed annuity versus variable annuity* 27.8
- C. *Annuitization Options* 27.9
  - 1. *Straight life annuity* 27.9
  - 2. *Refund annuities* 27.9
    - a. *Life with cash refund* 27.10
    - b. *Life with installment refund* 27.10
    - c. *Life with period certain* 27.10
    - d. *Period certain* 27.10
  - 3. *Temporary annuity* 27.11
- D. *Annuity Fees and Charges* 27.11
- E. *Fixed Annuities* 27.13
- F. *Variable Annuities* 27.14
  - 1. *Accumulation phase* 27.14
  - 2. *Annuitization phase* 27.15
  - 3. *Riders to variable annuities* 27.15
  - 4. *Advantages of variable annuities* 27.16
  - 5. *Disadvantages of variable annuities* 27.17
- G. *Equity-Indexed Annuities* 27.17
- H. *Regulation of Annuities* 27.19
  - 1. *CFP Board requirements* 27.20
  - 2. *FINRA scrutiny of VAs* 27.20

I.   Taxation of Qualified Annuities 27.21
J.   Taxation of Nonqualified Annuities 27.22
     1.   Accumulation period.. 27.22
          a.   Withdrawals after age 59½.................................. 27.22
          b.   10% penalty tax on early distributions 27.23
          c.   Aggregation rules.. 27.24
     2.   Annuitization period.. 27.24
     3.   Section 1035 exchange... 27.26
          a.   Tax-free distributions to pay for long-term care insurance .27.26
K.   Rules for Distributions to Beneficiaries........................... 27.27
L.   Nonnatural Owners of Annuities 27.28
M.   Structured Settlements 27.29
     1.   Damages 27.29
N.   Using Annuities in Retirement Planning to Overcome the
     Superannuation Problem 27.30
O.   Qualified Longevity Annuity Contracts (QLACs).............. 27.31
P.   Hybrid Annuity/Long-Term Care Products 27.32
Q.   Evaluating Annuities.. 27.33
     1.   Financial strength of the issuing insurance company 27.33
     2.   Bonus rates.. 27.33
     3.   Guaranteed minimum withdrawal benefits (GMWBs)............. 27.34
     4.   Timing of annuitization... 27.34
     5.   Avoid anchoring... 27.34
     6.   Should I annuitize or just take withdrawals?................. 27.36
     7.   Other general information 27.37
R.   Definitions.. 27.38

WHAT IS AN ANNUITY AND HOW IS IT USEFUL?

What is an Annuity?

An annuity is a series of periodic payments that continue for a specified period of time. The term "commercial annuity" refers to a financial product sold by life insurance companies and designed to provide payments over a fixed period of time or for the duration of one or more lives. The person on whose life payments are based is called the annuitant.

Annuities and life insurance policies are sometimes viewed as bets made by insurance companies on how long a person will live. If the person lives a long time, the insurance company "wins" the bet on a life insurance policy because the insured must pay more premiums. But the insurance company "loses" the bet on the annuity because it must make more payments to the annuitant who lives a long time. The point of this comparison is that life insurance and annuities provide different protection. Whereas life insurance provides for the surviving family members when an insured "dies too early", an annuity provides for the annuitant who "lives too long." This problem of living too long so one outlives one's assets is a major concern for

> *"I'm just one of the lucky people. I have no other reason for my longevity."* – **Johnny Mathis**

many financial planning clients when discussing retirement planning and is sometimes referred to as the longevity risk or the superannuation problem.

How can an insurance company guarantee income for life, no matter how long the annuitant lives? Insurance companies receive a premium when the annuity contract is purchased and then make payments for the life of the annuitant. Insurance companies are able to guarantee income for life because some annuitants will die earlier than expected, and the unused portion of their premium can be used to make the payments to those who live longer than expected. This annuity benefit is similar to the risk pooling concept used with other insurance products.

It is interesting to note that the mortality tables used to measure the life expectancy of annuitants differ from the tables used to measure the life expectancy of insureds under a life insurance policy. In fact, the mortality tables for annuitants indicate a longer life expectancy than those for life insurance. This difference makes logical sense since those most likely to seek annuities that guarantee income for life are those most likely to have longer than average life expectancies. While people with health problems tend to apply for life insurance, those with good health and a family history of longevity will tend to apply for annuities.

Because these commercial annuities are viewed as a retirement savings vehicle providing a needed service to retirees, the current tax law allows them some favorable tax treatments, which will be discussed later in this topic.

The Parties to the Contract

With an annuity, there are two parties to the contract: the owner and the insurance company. The owner is the person who has the right to make decisions involving the contract, such as the selection of payment options. An annuity may name an annuitant who may or may not be the same person as the owner. An annuitant who is not also the owner is not a party to the contract. The annuitant is the person who receives the payments when the contract is annuitized. Annuitizing the contract means that the insurance company makes the periodic payments. If the annuity contract promises to make payments for life, the benefits will continue as long as the annuitant lives.

A beneficiary is named in the annuity contract to receive a death benefit or any unpaid value in the annuity at the death of the owner or annuitant. The owner has the right to change the person named as the beneficiary. Death benefits are generally paid when the owner or annuitant dies before the contract is annuitized. Unlike life insurance death benefits, the death benefits from annuities are taxable. Naming someone other than the estate of the deceased owner as the beneficiary has the advantage of avoiding probate; however, the annuity will still be subject to estate taxes.

Deferred Annuities: Two Phases

Deferred annuities have two distinct phases: the accumulation phase and the annuitization phase (also called the distribution phase or the liquidation phase). During the accumulation phase, either a single premium or multiple premium payments are invested in the annuity. Under flexible premium contracts, multiple deposits are made over a period of time. Any interest, dividends, or gains on investments are added to the accumulation account.

The annuitization phase begins at the start of the payout of benefits. In the annuity phase, the annuity value is initially based upon the premiums deposited plus any amounts accumulated during the accumulation phase. During the annuity phase, no more premiums are invested, but income earned on investments continues to be added to the account, and benefits are paid to the annuitant.

The biggest advantage of deferred annuities is that earnings accumulate tax-deferred during the accumulation phase.

Uses of Annuities

Annuities may be suitable for several types of clients. A client who has already accumulated a significant amount of money may wish to liquidate that sum in a scientific manner. This client can buy an annuity that will produce income as long as the client is alive and will not be disrupted by business reversals or unwise investments.

On the other hand, a client who has not yet accumulated a significant sum of money may find an annuity an attractive vehicle for periodically saving money. The client might buy a flexible premium deferred annuity and make periodic premium payments, or the client might purchase single-premium deferred annuities each time he or she comes into a substantial block of money, such as a bonus, inheritance, or capital gain.

Annuities are frequently used as a vehicle to accumulate additional funds for retirement after a person has made the maximum contributions allowed to retirement plans. A client who has taken full advantage of the deferral provided by a 401(k) and an IRA may also make unlimited after-tax contributions to an annuity. The guaranteed income for life can be a very attractive feature for a client who wants to avoid outliving assets.

Charities offer Charitable Gift Annuities where a donor makes a donation to the charity, and the charity promises to pay the donor a fixed payment stream for life. The charity can insure its obligation to make the payments for life by purchasing an annuity from a life insurance company. If the donor gives the charity $100,000 and the charity pays $60,000 for an annuity from the insurance company, the charity no longer has to worry about the risk of the donor living so long that the funds are exhausted (it knows it has $40,000 to work with), and the donor also has peace of mind from knowing that a large insurance company with superior investment knowledge is guaranteeing the annuity payments.

Practice Question

For which of the following uses can a planner appropriately recommend that a client purchase a life annuity outside a retirement plan?

    (1) Tax deductible contributions
    (2) Tax deferred growth
    (3) Overcome fear of running out of income in client's retirement
    (4) Provide family income after client's death

        A. (1) and (2) only
        B. (2) and (3) only
        C. (3) and (4) only
        D. (2), (3), and (4) only

Answer:
Contributions to purchase an annuity outside a retirement plan are not tax deductible. The growth in the annuity is tax deferred. The life annuity is used appropriately to deal with the danger of running out of income in retirement. To provide a family with income after death, life insurance is more appropriate than an annuity.
The answer is B.

CLASSIFYING ANNUITIES

There are a number of different ways in which annuities can be classified. For example, annuities can be classified as immediate or deferred, and they can be classified as single premium or flexible premium. A particular annuity, then, might be called a single premium immediate annuity (SPIA), a single premium deferred annuity (SPDA), or a flexible premium deferred annuity (FPDA).

The following are some ways in which annuities can be classified:

Immediate Annuity Versus Deferred Annuity

Annuities may be classified according to the starting date for the payout.

In an immediate annuity, the payment stream begins one payment interval after the annuity is purchased. Payment intervals may be monthly, quarterly, semi-annually, or annually. For example, an immediate annuity paying $5,000 per month would make its first benefit payment one month after purchase. The more frequent the payment period, the lower the benefit will be because the cost to the insurance company is higher with more frequent payments.

Deferred annuities start their payout more than one interval after the initial purchase. Often, working people buy annuities with the plan that the payments will begin years later at retirement. For example, Sam, age 50, may purchase a $5,000 per month annuity today with a lump-sum payment to the insurer and arrange to have the benefit payments begin when Sam plans to retire at age 60.

Single-Premium Annuity Versus Periodic-Premium Annuity

Annuities can also be classified by the time at which the purchase price is paid, all at once or over a period of time.

In a single-premium annuity, the purchase price is paid in a lump sum, as in the case of Sam in the previous example. An annuity purchased with a single premium could be a deferred or an immediate annuity.

In a periodic-premium annuity (also called flexible-premium annuity), the purchase price is spread over several months or, more often, several years. An annuity purchased with more than one premium can only be a deferred annuity since an immediate annuity requires all premium payments to have been made just prior to the start of the first distribution.

Practice Question

Which of the following products cannot be offered by insurance companies as a fixed or variable annuity?

    A. Single premium, immediate annuity
    B. Single premium, deferred annuity
    C. Periodic premium, immediate annuity
    D. Periodic premium, deferred annuity

Answer:

A periodic premium annuity must be offered as a deferred annuity and cannot be offered as an immediate annuity. An immediate annuity begins with the annuitization phase, and no additional premiums can be added to an annuity after the beginning of the annuitization phase.

The answer is C.

Single Life Annuity Versus Joint Life Annuity

Annuities may be classified according to whether they cover one life or more than one life.

In a single life annuity, the duration of only one annuitant's life determines how long the benefit payments will continue.

In a joint life annuity or a joint-and-survivor life annuity, the lives of two annuitants are involved. (Three or more annuitants would be rare.) In a joint life annuity, benefit payments continue only until the first of the two annuitants dies.

> *"When a man retires, his wife gets twice the husband but only half the income."*
> **– Chi Chi Rodriguez**

In a joint-and-survivor life annuity, benefit payments continue while either of the two annuitants is alive. Frequently, this type of annuity is arranged to provide a smaller periodic benefit to the survivor after the first death. The amount that will continue to the survivor then also becomes part of the description. For example, a joint-and-75% survivor annuity pays a fixed amount periodically while both annuitants are alive and then 75% of that amount to the survivor after the death of one of the annuitants. A joint-and-survivor annuity is frequently used by husband and wife to ensure guaranteed income for life for both of them. A joint-and-survivor annuity is required for qualified retirement plan distributions when the participant is married (although it can be changed with notarized spousal consent).

Joint-and-survivor annuities may also be useful for single individuals with disabled dependent children or other dependent family members. The payments can continue after the individual's death to the dependent family member or to a trust for the family member.

Pure Annuity Versus Refund Annuity

Annuities may be pure, single-life annuities, or they may have a refund or period certain feature.

Under the pure life annuity involving only one annuitant, benefit payments are made for as long as the annuitant lives, but no benefit payments are made after the annuitant's death.

A refund annuity offers a refund of premiums when the annuitant dies sooner than expected and the benefit payments have been less than the amount of premiums.

The older the annuitant is the greater will be the difference in payment amount for a pure annuity versus a refund annuity. For example, according to quotes from immediateannuities.com, a 75-year-old male investing $100,000 could receive a life annuity paying $757 per month or a life with installment refund annuity paying $640 per month (a difference of $117 per month). An 80-year-old male investing $100,000 could receive $908 per month as a life annuity, or $725 per month under a life with installment refund annuity (a difference of $183 per month). The increase in the difference is due to the fact that an older annuitant will have a shorter life expectancy requiring the pure life annuity payments to increase greatly with the age of the annuitant, but the installment refund annuity is based only in part on life expectancy, so payments increase more slowly.

Qualified Annuity Versus Nonqualified Annuity

Annuities are also classified according to whether they are qualified or nonqualified.

Qualified annuities are those that are funded with pre-tax dollars, such as from deductible traditional IRA contributions or those held within qualified retirement plans. Because the contributions to the annuity have not yet been taxed, all payments received will be fully taxable.

Nonqualified annuities are funded with after-tax dollars, but earnings during the accumulation phase are tax-deferred. When the contract is annuitized, part of each payment will be taxable (the part representing a distribution of earnings), and part will be tax-free (the portion representing a distribution of principal that has been previously taxed).

Fixed Annuity Versus Variable Annuity

Annuities are often classified according to how the periodic benefit payment is determined: fixed or variable.

In fixed annuities, the periodic payment is a specified number of dollars. Variable annuities have a payout that varies corresponding with the investment success of a chosen portfolio.

ANNUITIZATION OPTIONS

The amount of each payment from the annuity contract will be based on several factors, including the age of the annuitant at the time the contract is annuitized, the amount invested in the contract, current market conditions, mortality rates, and the annuitization (distribution) option selected. The following annuitization options are frequently available, each serving a unique purpose: straight life annuity (either single or joint life), life with cash refund, life with installment refund, life with period certain, period certain, and temporary.

Straight Life Annuity

In a pure or straight life annuity, the annuitized payments continue only until death, with nothing payable thereafter. For a straight life annuity, the older the annuitant is when the payout starts, the larger will be each periodic payment, all other factors being equal.

A pure or straight life annuity has the advantage of assuring the annuitant a lifetime income he or she will not outlive. The pure life annuity provides a greater monthly payout to the annuitant than any other payout arrangement because forfeiture of principal by those annuitants who die prematurely will increase the payout to annuitants who survive.

> *"I advise you to go on living solely to enrage those who are paying your annuities. It is the only pleasure I have left."* – **Voltaire**

The disadvantages of a pure or straight life fixed annuity include the lack of protection against inflation and the lack of liquidity resulting from the requirement that the principal sum cannot be withdrawn after the annuity contract enters the annuitization phase. Some annuitants are also hesitant about taking the risk of "losing the bet" – in other words, what if they die early and must forfeit the remaining principal? For this reason, straight life annuities are recommended primarily for those who are not concerned about leaving an inheritance to heirs, or who have planned other methods of wealth transfer. For example, if a client's goal is to leave $100,000 to his child upon death, he might purchase a life insurance policy with a $100,000 death benefit, and then can invest more of the remaining funds to obtain the higher payment stream of a life annuity.

Refund Annuities

Clients who are concerned about forfeiting any remaining principal upon death may wish to consider a refund annuity instead of a life annuity. A refund annuity promises to pay the designated beneficiary the difference between the total premiums paid into the annuity and the benefit payments made to the annuitant prior to death. Some refund annuities pay only a portion of the difference. The refund may be a lump sum or may be paid in continued monthly benefit checks.

Life With Cash refund

A life annuity with cash refund feature will pay the annuitant as long as he or she lives, but the insurer promises that if the annuitant dies before receiving some portion of the principal paid into the annuity, a cash refund will be paid. A beneficiary will receive a lump sum payment equal to the principal amount promised minus the amount received by the annuitant.

Life With Installment Refund

A life annuity with installment refund feature will pay the annuitant as long as he or she lives, but promises that if the annuitant dies before receiving some portion of the principal paid into the annuity, an installment refund will be paid. A beneficiary will receive periodic installment payments equal to the principal amount promised minus the amount received by the annuitant.

Life With Period Certain

Under the life annuity with period certain, benefit payments are made for the lifetime of the annuitant, but if death occurs before the expiration of a specified number of years, the payments will continue to a designated beneficiary for the remainder of the minimum period. For example, a life annuity with 10-year certain makes four annual payments before the annuitant dies. The named beneficiary will receive an additional six annual payments to complete the 10-year certain. If, however, the annuitant had lived beyond 10 years, no additional payments would be made to the beneficiary.

The longer the guarantee period is, the more costly it is, resulting in a lower level of benefit payments.

Period Certain

A period certain annuity promises that the payments will continue for a fixed period of time. Notice that the word "life" does not appear here, so there is no contingency based on anyone's life. The payout period is simply a stated period of time, for example 5 years or 10 years.

A period certain may be selected when the client needs a certain dollar amount over a given period of time and wants to ensure that the income is available each year to fund that goal. For example, perhaps a client decided to retire at age 60 but, realizing he will not be eligible for Medicare until age 65, wants to set aside a sum of money today that will pay him an amount equal to his annual health insurance premium payment for each of the next 5 years. By investing in a period certain annuity, no matter what happens with his investment portfolio, he knows without a doubt that the health insurance premiums will be funded.

Temporary Annuity

In a temporary annuity, benefit payments continue for the shorter of a specified number of periods or until the annuitant dies. Nothing is payable after the end of the specified period or after the annuitant's death.

Practice Question

Which of the following annuity distribution options will provide the largest monthly benefits for a given premium?

    A. Straight life annuity
    B. Joint and survivor annuity
    C. Life annuity with refund feature
    D. Life annuity with period certain

Answer:
The straight life annuity will provide the largest monthly benefit for a given premium. The joint and survivor annuity will provide benefit payments for two lives, but there is an additional cost for the insurance company of providing these benefits for two lives instead of one. The additional cost will reduce the size of the benefits that can be paid for the life annuity. The life annuity with refund feature and life annuity with period certain provide features that will require the insurer to incur additional costs. The payments of a refund and of the period certain benefits require a reduction in the amount that can be paid as a life annuity.
The answer is A.

ANNUITY FEES AND CHARGES

Annuity contracts must be read carefully to ensure that both the planner and the client understand the fees and charges that are involved since there are a number of different types of fees and charges that may be found in the various types of annuities.

Mortality and expense (M&E) fees cover the guarantees made in the contract. The mortality fee covers the promise to pay income for life as well as a death benefit. The contract may also state a guaranteed maximum expense rate, for which a fee is charged. These fees are stated as a percentage of the contract value each year.

Insurance companies may also share administrative or maintenance fees to cover the cost of record-keeping and mailing of reports or forms. It is also common to have an extra fee for annuities that are IRAs due to the additional reporting burden of the IRA. These fees are typically stated as a flat dollar amount per year.

Some annuities will have a front-end load to cover up-front expenses, such as sales commissions, marketing, and set-up costs.

Nearly all contracts will have a surrender charge (also called a back-end load) that is assessed if the contract is surrendered in a short period of time. These surrender charges can be significant and can last 5, 10, or even 15 years, so they must be carefully evaluated prior to the purchase of the annuity. The percentage rate of the surrender charge will typically decline over time. For example, the charge may be 6% if surrendered after one year, 5% after two years, 4% after three years, 3% after four years, 2% after five years, 1% after six years, and 0% after seven years. In some annuities, the surrender charge remains fixed for a period of time and then drops to zero. The amount of the surrender charge can vary greatly from contract-to-contract, in some cases being as low as 1% or 2% and in other contracts as high as 15% or more.

Example:

Year 1	Year 2	Year 3	Year 4	Year 5	Year 6	Year 7
6%	5%	4%	3%	2%	1%	0%

Most contracts will provide a list of contingencies, such as admittance to a nursing home, under which the surrender charge will be waived. Some contracts also allow up to 10% of the contract to be withdrawn in a partial surrender each year without a surrender charge being incurred.

With variable annuities, an investment management fee will be charged for managing the assets within the subaccounts. This fee is deducted from the account and is reflected in a reduced rate of return for each subaccount. While this fee is not paid directly by the client, the client should understand that he or she is paying it indirectly.

Sometimes, particularly with variable annuities, the fees are described in terms of basis points (abbreviated bps, and pronounced as "bips" by those in the industry). A basis point is 1/100th of 1%. So a fee of 40 basis points is equal to .40%, while a fee of 100 basis points is equal to 1%.

Many annuities, especially variable annuities, allow the contract to be customized by adding various riders, each of which adds an additional fee. One criticism of variable annuities is the potentially high fees, commonly around 2%, which is substantial.

FIXED ANNUITIES

In a traditional fixed annuity, the benefit payments are known in advance, based on guaranteed cost elements with respect to mortality, expenses, and interest credits. The benefit payments will initially include return of principal and investment income. After annuitants outlive their life expectancy, payments consist of the survivorship or insurance benefit. Some annuities are participating, which means they may pay a dividend, so dividends may enhance benefit amounts.

Premiums paid into a fixed annuity will be placed in the general account of the insurance company where they are invested in a portfolio of bonds, mortgages, and other types of conservative investments. A minimum guaranteed interest rate, typically 1.5% or 2%, will be credited to the annuity account on an annual basis, but the insurance company typically pays a higher rate based on current market conditions. Because the insurance company guarantees a minimum rate to the investor, the insurance company will bear that investment risk in the general account portfolio.

One of the biggest advantages of the fixed annuity is the guarantee of a known, fixed income for life. Oddly enough, this is also one of the biggest disadvantages of the fixed annuity because fixed income streams paid over a period of 20 or 30 years will be subject to purchasing power risk. In other words, as inflation causes prices to increase, the same fixed income will not buy the same goods.

Practice Question

Which of the following contribute to the determination of annual payments received by an insurer's group of life annuitants?

    (1) Return of principal
    (2) Investment income
    (3) Return of expense loading
    (4) Survivorship or insurance benefit

        A. (1) and (2) only
        B. (1), (2), and (4) only
        C. (1), (3), and (4) only
        D. (2), (3), and (4) only

Answer:
(1), (2), and (4) are all sources of funds from which payments can be made to those annuitants in the specific group who continue to live. The survivorship or insurance benefit is paid to those annuitants who live beyond their life expectancy. (3) is not a source of funds because there is no return to the annuitant of any excess loading (except perhaps through the dividend formula of a participating contract).
The answer is B.

VARIABLE ANNUITIES

A variable annuity contract does not guarantee a fixed payment each period; rather, payments vary directly with the results achieved on the account in which the premiums are invested, usually a combination of common stock and bond portfolios. If the investment account does well, benefit amounts will rise; but if the investment account loses money, the benefit amounts can fall.

The proponents of variable annuities emphasize that, over the long term, dividends and market prices of common stocks tend to vary directly with changes in the cost of living, increasing the annuitized payment amount and allowing the client to maintain purchasing power during the distribution period.

Accumulation Phase

Premiums paid during the accumulation phase of an annuity are used to purchase accumulation units in the investment account. The valuation of each unit is determined by dividing the total market value of all assets in the account by the number of accumulation units outstanding. Since the value of each unit is constantly changing, the number of units purchased with each additional deposit will vary. Reinvested dividend distributions from the selected investments are used to purchase additional units.

The purchaser of a variable annuity usually may elect to place his or her dollar contributions in one or more subaccounts within the investment account. The decision regarding which subaccounts to choose will depend on the purchaser's willingness to take risks and his or her emphasis on safety and security. These investment options or subaccounts, are also called separate accounts, because they are segregated from the general account of the insurance company. Separate accounts resemble mutual funds in many aspects, but may have higher management fees than similar mutual funds.

The subaccount investment options may be numerous and diversified; for example, an annuity investor may be able to choose among several types of stock portfolios (large company stocks, small company stocks, portfolios that focus on growth or on income), multiple bond portfolios (long-term, short-term, government, corporate), and multiple specialty portfolios (real estate, health care stocks, emerging markets, etc). Because annuity cash values grow on a tax-deferred basis, one advantage of the variable annuity is that clients can make adjustments to their investment selections as their goals and needs change without incurring tax on the sale of the units of one subaccount when the money is moved to another subaccount.

Annuitization Phase

When entering the annuitization (liquidation) period, the accumulation units are exchanged for annuity units. The annuitant usually may elect either a fixed monthly payout or a variable monthly amount. When the variable payout is selected, the insurance company determines the number of benefit payment units the annuitant is to receive each month. This number of units is determined from the dollar amount in the annuitant's account at the start of the liquidation period, the life expectancy of the annuitant, and the payout arrangement selected by the annuitant.

The value of the benefit payment unit is determined by dividing the value of the total assets supporting the benefit payment units by the total number of benefit payment units outstanding. The monthly payment is the current value of the benefit payment unit multiplied by the number of benefit payment units to be paid to the annuitant each month. This payment will vary as the value of each unit fluctuates based on the investment performance of the underlying subaccounts.

Monthly Payment = # of units x Current Value of 1 Unit

Riders to Variable Annuities

Variable annuities come with the ability to add a lot of bells and whistles by way of riders added to the contract. Each additional rider adds to the cost of the contract, so planners and clients should carefully evaluate the impact of each rider on total return versus its potential benefits. Only a few of the most common riders will be mentioned here.

The standard death benefit paid during the accumulation phase is usually the higher of the current market value or the gross premiums paid. One popular rider to a variable annuity is an enhanced death benefit rider which promises that if the annuitant dies during the accumulation phase, the death benefit paid to the beneficiary will be the greater of the current account value or the highest anniversary value, and some riders add in a third value based on a specified percentage increase (such as 4%) per year. The cost of the rider can vary from 35 basis points in some contracts to 115 basis points in others.

A Guaranteed Minimum Income Benefit (GMIB) rider promises a minimum future income when the contract is annuitized. It typically requires a waiting period of at least 10 years before the contract is annuitized, and cannot be withdrawn as a lump sum. The annuity payment is derived from a benefit base, which is typically the amount of premiums compounded at a specified interest rate. This minimum provides protection in case the value of the subaccounts falls drastically. Some GMIBs allow the benefit base to be "stepped up" to the account balance if the latter is higher at certain policy anniversaries. When utilized, the payment amount, in most cases, will be fixed, so the ability to keep up with inflation is lost, and there may be restrictions on the underlying investment options that may be selected. The cost for this benefit is typically 60 to 80 basis points per year. Some insurance companies guarantee that this cost will not increase, but with other companies the charges may be increased, so it is important to review the prospectus to determine both how the feature works and how the costs may change. The variable annuity prospectus is the document that outlines all of the rules and features of the contract.

A Guaranteed Minimum Withdrawal Benefit (GMWB) rider does not require annuitization to receive the benefits. The GMWB guarantees the owner's investment at a minimum, and it may guarantee the investment amount plus an interest component. The GMWB promises the minimum amount even if the annuity cash values fall to zero. Like the GMIB, it does not guarantee a lump sum value, so the owner takes withdrawals over a period of time. Unlike the GMIB, there is usually no waiting period before the withdrawals can begin. The cost of the GMWB rider is typically 70 – 95 basis points, with prospectus maximums of up to about 120 basis points (meaning that the cost may be increased in the future, but not above the stated maximum).

Many variable annuities offer a variation of the GMWB that guarantees partial withdrawals of limited amounts for the owner's lifetime or the joint lifetime of the owner and spouse. These are called Guaranteed Lifetime Withdrawal Benefits or GLWBs.

The living benefit riders available in variable annuities are continuously being enhanced, modified, and changed, and they are becoming increasingly complex. Marketing materials tend to provide very limited information, so it is imperative for planners to read and understand the prospectus for each variable annuity before making a recommendation on the purchase of the contract or the addition of a rider.

Advantages of Variable Annuities

The advantages of variable annuities are:

- Some hedge against inflation

- Tax-deferral for investment income during the accumulation period and to some extent during the liquidation years
- Professional management of the investment dollars
- Dollar-cost averaging
- Diversification

Disadvantages of Variable Annuities

The primary disadvantages of variable annuities as compared to fixed annuities are the investment risk, the complexity, and the potentially high costs and fees. Under the fixed annuity, the insurance company assumes the investment risk; however, with a variable annuity there is no minimum guaranteed interest rate, and the contract can lose value when the underlying subaccount investments are in the down stage of a market cycle. The complexity comes from the insertion of investment portfolios similar to mutual funds into an annuity framework. The total cost of a variable annuity can be substantial, with fees including sales charges, management fees, insurance costs (mortality and expense fees), administrative fees, premium taxes, fees for riders, and surrender charges.

EQUITY-INDEXED ANNUITIES

Equity indexed annuities are somewhat complex in that they are fixed annuities but have the appearance of variable annuities. An equity-indexed annuity offers the guaranteed minimum interest credits of a traditional fixed annuity, but it offers an additional potential return based on the growth of a specified index of common stocks, such as the S&P 500 index. So an equity-indexed annuity will have more risk and greater potential return than a fixed annuity, but will have less risk and less potential return than a variable annuity.

Another complexity found in equity-indexed annuities is that only a specified percentage, called the participation rate (always less than 100%), of the gain in the index is taken into account in determining the return to the owner of the annuity. The time for measuring the index can vary from contract-to-contract, so it is important to understand how the increase in the index will be measured. Some contracts will use a simple point-to-point measurement: the change from where the index stands on the date of purchase versus where it is one year from that date. Other contracts may look at the index at various points in time and use a high water mark over a period of several years.

If the index decreases in value, a minimum guaranteed interest rate will be credited to the account (typically between 1% and 3%, with the caveat that it is paid on 90% of the total payments made into the contract).

The contract should be read carefully, because the amount of interest may be reduced by the charging of an asset fee (sometimes called a spread or margin). For example, if the spread is 2% and the gain in the index is 10%, then 8% will be used as the gain in the index. The contract may also specify a cap on the interest that can be credited to the account.

Example:

Homer buys an equity-indexed annuity that has a guaranteed minimum rate of 2% and a participation rate of 75% of the increase in the S&P 500 index over a 1-year period. The interest crediting is capped at 9%. On the day Homer purchases his annuity, the S&P 500 index is at 1800, and one year later the index is at 2050, an increase of 13.88%. With a 75% participation rate, Homer may be expecting to be credited with 10.42% interest (.75 x 13.88 = 10.42); however, the contract caps his interest at 9% so he will be credited with a 9% rate.

Another point to be aware of is that some contracts allow the insurance company to change the participation rate, interest cap, or the spread at each policy anniversary. Also, if the contract is terminated before the end of the interest-crediting term the index credit is lost. Due to this loss potential and the surrender fees involved, equity-indexed annuities should be viewed as long-term investments.

An indexed annuity may or may not be considered a security and registered with the SEC, although most of them are not. Those not registered with the SEC are regulated as fixed annuities by state insurance departments.

EXHIBIT 27 – 1
Comparison of Fixed and Variable Annuities

	FIXED	VARIABLE
Benefits	Fixed amount is paid monthly, quarterly, or annually.	Amount paid each period varies with the investment results of separate accounts.
Investment of Premiums	Premiums are invested in the insurer's general account.	Premiums are invested in separate accounts.
Assets	General account assets are mostly fixed-income.	Owner selects among investment options, similar to stock or bond mutual funds.
Investment Returns	A fixed return is guaranteed during accumulation and payout years.	Returns depend on the success of separate accounts; there is no guarantee.
Risk	Insurer assumes the investment risk.	Owner assumes the investment risk.
Votes	Owner has no voting rights for investment policies or adviser.	Owner has voting rights for investment policies and adviser.

REGULATION OF ANNUITIES

As with all financial products, planners have an obligation to ensure that any annuity recommended to a client is suitable for that client based on the client's financial status, investment objectives, tax status, risk tolerance, and time horizon, along with the advantages and disadvantages of the product itself.

Since annuities are sold by life insurance companies and are considered an insurance product, each state's insurance commission (department) is responsible for regulating the insurers and contracts issued within their state.

The NAIC has developed model regulations for both annuity suitability and annuity disclosures.

While fixed annuities are regulated by the state insurance commission, they are not regulated by FINRA or the SEC because they are not considered securities.

For SEC purposes, variable annuities are securities, and anyone selling a variable annuity must hold a FINRA Series 6 or 7 license as well as the insurance license. A variable annuity must be sold with a prospectus, which will describe how the annuity works as well as the fees and risks. Before recommending a variable annuity to a client, the planner should read the prospectus and ensure that he or she fully understands all of the information provided within it. The prospectus must be delivered to the client at or before the time of sale, and the client should also be encouraged to read it and understand all of the elements of the contract.

CFP Board Requirements

Those planners who are CFP® certificants, will be required to provide documentation of plan recommendations and any applicable product disclosures to the client. When recommending a variable annuity or variable life product, the client must receive a current prospectus. In addition, the planner will need to disclose any additional compensation that he or she may receive upon sale of the annuity product, including commissions and/or any trailing commissions from 12b-1 fees within the variable product.

FINRA Scrutiny of VAs

In recent years FINRA has been viewing many variable annuity sales, especially those to seniors, with scrutiny. While variable annuities can be a good match for the right client, they also present a temptation to unscrupulous financial advisors due to their high commission payout rates. FINRA's investor alert on variable annuities can be viewed at:

http://www.finra.org/web/groups/investors/@inv/documents/investors/p125846.pdf

FINRA has also shown recent concern for potential abuses involving a Section 1035 exchange from variable annuities into equity-indexed annuities. Again, there are valid reasons for making these changes, but the potential for abuse is high. Section 1035 exchanges are discussed on page 27.26.

TAXATION OF QUALIFIED ANNUITIES

An employee's accrued benefits under a qualified retirement plan are paid out under one of the qualified pension plan's various annuity forms or annuity options. The full amount of each benefit payment is included in the employee's gross income if the plan is noncontributory (the employee has no cost basis because only pre-tax dollars were put into the plan). If the plan is contributory (employee has cost basis because after-tax dollars were put into the plan), part of each payment is excluded, and part is included in the employee's gross income upon distribution from the plan.

EXHIBIT 27 – 2
Taxation of Contributory and Noncontributory Plans

Noncontributory Plans
Full amount of each payment is *included* in gross income.

Contributory Plans
Part of each payment is excluded, and part is included in gross income.

The excluded portion of each payment to the retired employee is determined by dividing the employee's total investment in the contract (the employee's cost basis) by the expected number of payments as set forth in the following government table:

Annuitant's Age at Annuity Starting Date	Number of Payments (Divide Cost Basis by Number)
Age 55 and below	360
Age 56-60	310
Age 61-65	260
Age 66-70	210
Age more than 70	160

For joint and survivor annuities:

Combined Ages at Annuity Starting Date	Number of Payments (Divide Cost Basis by Number)
110 and below	410
111 – 120	360
121 – 130	310
131 – 140	260
141 and higher	210

This method of determining the monthly exclusion amount is to be used for all qualified plan annuity distributions that commence after November 18, 1996. If the annuitant receives his or her cost basis in benefit payments, any additional benefit payments are included in full in the taxpayer's gross income.

 K Study Tip – **The tax rules for employee annuities (from qualified plans and tax-sheltered annuities) provide a "simplified" method, using the government tables to determine expected return.**

TAXATION OF NONQUALIFIED ANNUITIES

Accumulation Period

Non-qualified annuities have their own set of tax rules. Generally, the accumulation inside annuities grows on an income-tax-deferred basis. Be careful not to be taken in by statements that annuities grow tax-free, however. Eventually, the growth will be taxed.

When withdrawals are made during the accumulation period (without annuitizing), they are taxed on a last-in-first-out (LIFO) basis, meaning that earnings are distributed first, followed by return of cost basis (the amount of premiums paid into the policy less any prior distributions treated as basis). The earnings are subject to ordinary income tax, plus a 10% premature distribution penalty if the annuitant is under age 59½.

Withdrawals After Age 59½

Generally, when some of the accumulated funds are taken out of an annuity and the payment is not part of a periodic distribution plan, **the amount withdrawn is subject to income tax at ordinary income rates to the extent that there is a gain in the contract.**

Example:

- Bill invested $50,000 in his deferred annuity.
- At age 65, when the annuity had grown to $70,000, Bill withdrew $25,000.

Since the gain in the annuity was $20,000, that portion of the withdrawal is subject to income tax. The other $5,000 is considered a distribution of principal and is not subject to tax. This is called the last-in, first-out (LIFO) form of taxation. It applies to annuities purchased and/or funded after August 13, 1982.

For annuities purchased on August 13, 1982, or earlier, the first-in, first-out (FIFO) method is used. If the annuities in the above example were purchased before August 13, 1982, there would be no income tax. In fact, except with the case of annuitization, there will not be income taxes paid on that annuity until more than the $50,000 investment is withdrawn. With these older annuities, the principal is removed before any earnings are removed.

10% Penalty Tax on Early Distributions

The above example assumed that distributions were taken out during or after the year in which the annuitant reached age 59½. The same law that created the differing taxation of distributions added a 10% federal excise tax for withdrawals taken before the year in which the annuitant turned 59½. The excise tax applies to any non-periodic annuity distribution made from an annuity that was purchased or funded on or after August 14, 1982, but it applies only to that part of the distribution that is subject to income tax.

☞ **K Study Tip** – The 10% penalty for withdrawals prior to age 59½ applies *only* to the part of the distribution subject to income tax.

In our first example, where $25,000 was withdrawn, if Bill was age 57 at the time of withdrawal, not only would $20,000 be added to his income for tax purposes, but he would also have to pay a $2,000 excise tax.

For those under age 59½, the penalty can be avoided by entering the annuitization period rather than taking a withdrawal. The 10% penalty is also waived upon the death or disability of the owner, or when distributions are made as substantially equal periodic payments following the rules of Section 72(q) of the tax code. There is also no 10% penalty for distributions from an annuity purchased as a qualified funding asset from a personal injury settlement (see structured settlements on page 27.29 for more information on these annuities).

Aggregation Rules

To prevent the manipulation of tax rules, the IRS will treat all annuities purchased from the same insurer in the same year by the same policyholder as a single contract. For example, Ken purchases an annuity for $5,000, and it grows to $6,000. Ken wants to take a withdrawal (partial surrender of $500, which will be treated by the IRS as a distribution of earnings and taxed as ordinary income. If, instead, Ken had purchased 5 different policies for $1,000 each, at the same rate of earnings each policy would grow to $1,200 (the total of all policies being $6,000). Now, if Ken withdraws his $500 from just one contract, he will only pay tax on $200, with the other $300 treated as a return of principal. The IRS views this as an abusive strategy and, to prevent its use, treats all annuity contracts purchased in the same year from the same insurer as a single contract for tax purposes.

Annuitization Period

When the accumulation period ends and the annuity is turned into a stream of periodic payments, part of each payment is taxable income, and part is not taxable. A calculation must be done to determine which portion of each payment is to be excluded from taxable income. The method of distribution will determine the specific calculation to be done.

If the annuity payments are for a specified number of periods or a specified amount of income that results in the number of payments being known, simply divide the cost, or basis, of the annuity by the number of payments. The result is the amount of each payment that is excluded from income for tax purposes and is referred to as the excludable amount.

For a fixed annuity, if the annuity is for the life of the annuitant, the basis (investment in the contract) is divided by the expected return (total value of the payments) to get the percentage of each payment that is to be excluded from income for tax purposes. This percentage is known as the exclusion ratio. The expected return is calculated by multiplying one year of payments by the life expectancy multiple found in IRS annuity tables I-III for pre-July 1, 1986 annuities and tables V-VII for annuities funded after June 30, 1986. Tables I-III are gender specific, and Tables V-VII are unisex. However, if the individual outlives these tables, the entire annuity payment will be taxable, as the taxpayer would have already recovered his or her basis.

Example:

Harold is 65 years of age and will begin to receive benefits from an annuity he bought for $40,000 in 1990. The payments will be $6,000 annually, and Harold's life expectancy is 20 years. The total value of payments expected under the contract are:

$6,000 x 20 years = $120,000

The investment in the contract of $40,000 is divided by the expected return of $120,000, so the exclusion ratio is:

$40,000/$120,000 = 1/3

Each payment of $6,000 will consist of $2,000 of tax-free return of capital and $4,000 of ordinary income.

> ### 🔑 KEY SUMMARY 27 – 1
> **Calculating the Exclusion Amount for a Non-Qualified Fixed Annuity**
>
> **(1) If the annuity is for a fixed period, the number of payments is known.**
>
> $$\text{Exclusion amount} = \frac{\text{Basis}}{\text{\# of payments}}$$
>
> **(2) If the annuity is for life, the number of payments is not known.**
>
> $$\text{Exclusion \%} = \frac{\text{Basis}}{\text{Expected return}}$$
>
> **Note:** Basis = Investment in the contract

For a variable annuity, because the expected distribution amount is not known, the investment in the contract is divided by the number of years of expected payout (either life expectancy or a period of years) to determine an excludible dollar amount for each payment received. If one of the variable payments happens to fall below the exclusion amount, a new exclusion amount is recalculated based on the remaining life expectancy or remaining period of years of payout. Like fixed annuities, once the investment in the contract has been fully recovered, all payments will be fully taxable as ordinary income.

After the death of the owner the gain within an annuity will eventually be taxed as ordinary income (unless the annuity is a Roth IRA, which allows qualified distributions to be made tax-free if all of the rules are followed). There is no step-up in basis for an annuity upon death of the owner or annuitant, so beneficiaries who receive a death benefit from an annuity will be responsible for paying the tax on the earnings in the contract.

 REMEMBER: *GAINS IN COMMERCIAL ANNUITIES WILL EVENTUALLY BE TAXED AS ORDINARY INCOME (NO STEP-UP IN BASIS).*

> ☞ ***K Study Tip* – Distributions from a commercial annuity will consist of tax-free return of capital and ordinary income, but no capital gain.**

Section 1035 Exchange

An annuity can be exchanged for another annuity in a tax-free exchange under Section 1035 of the tax code. The annuitant must remain the same under the old and new annuity contracts, and the transfer must be completed as a trustee-to-trustee transfer between the insurance companies. If any amount is distributed to the owner of the contract, it will be irrevocably treated as a taxable distribution.

A portion of the funds in an annuity contract can also be transferred to a new annuity contract in a nontaxable partial exchange.

A Section 1035 exchange should not be done without appropriate cost-benefit analysis, keeping in mind factors such as the implications of starting a new surrender charge period under the new annuity contract.

Tax-Free Distributions to Pay for Long-Term Care Insurance

Under a provision of the Pension Protection Act of 2006, beginning in 2010 nonqualified annuity distributions used to pay for qualified long-term care insurance (LTCI) premiums are income tax-free.

For deferred annuities, the tax-fee treatment is accomplished through a partial Section 1035 exchange from the nonqualified annuity to the LTCI issuer. Each partial exchange will reduce the earnings and basis of the annuity pro rata.

Income from a nonqualified SPIA paid to the LTCI carrier is treated as a partial assignment of income in a 1035 exchange and is also tax-free.

In both cases the funds must be paid directly from one insurance company to the other, and other 1035 exchange rules, such as the requirement that the contracts be for the same insured, must also be followed.

While the annuity-to-LTCI transfer is tax-free, planners should remain aware of any surrender charges that may be due if the amount of the LTCI premium is greater than any free withdrawal amount (typically 10% can be withdrawn each year without a surrender charge, but that amount can vary from contract-to-contract).

It should also be noted that not all LTCI carriers accept 1035 exchanges, so a little research may be needed before policies are selected. Also note that the Section 1035 exchange to LTCI is only available for nonqualified annuities. Qualified annuities are not permitted to be used.

RULES FOR DISTRIBUTIONS TO BENEFICIARIES

When the owner of a deferred annuity dies before benefit payments begin, the beneficiary will generally be paid a death benefit that is the account balance or the amount of premiums paid. To the extent that there is gain in the contract, the beneficiary will have to report this gain as ordinary income. If there is substantial gain in the contract, the beneficiary can extend the income-tax-paying period by choosing a life annuity, a distribution over life expectancy, or an annuity with a specified number of installments shorter than life expectancy, but this election must be made within 60 days of the owner's death and the first distribution must be taken by the first anniversary of the owner's death.

In the event that the owner and the annuitant are different persons and the owner dies, the following rules apply:

1. If the annuity has not begun payments, then the entire interest must be distributed within 5 years after the owner's death.

2. If annuity payments have begun, the remaining amount in the contract must be distributed at least as rapidly as under the method of distribution in effect at the time of the owner's death. (Note that the person receiving the annuity payments has not died, so the insurer remains obligated to make payments to the annuitant, but the annuity owner has died.)

3. When the beneficiary is the surviving spouse of the owner, then the spouse can treat the annuity as his or her own, and the spouse can delay distributions as could the owner. In other words, the surviving spouse steps into the

deceased owner's shoes and continues the contract as if he or she were the original owner.

4. When the beneficiary is not an individual (for example, an estate, a trust, a partnership, or a corporation), the 5 year rule must be followed and the entire interest must be distributed within 5 years after the owner's death. For example, if Joe is the owner of an annuity and he names a testamentary trust created in his will as the beneficiary of the annuity contract, then the entire value of the annuity must be distributed within 5 years of Joe's death.

It is good practice to also name successor or contingent beneficiaries in case the primary beneficiary predeceases the owner.

NONNATURAL OWNERS OF ANNUITIES

Corporations once had the same tax-deferral as individuals with annuities. **Now, a corporation must report any earnings or accruals in an annuity as ordinary income in the year in which it is credited to the contract.** This rule applies to any "nonnatural person," except trusts acting as agents for natural persons.

Practice Question

The Anderson Plastics Corporation purchased an annuity to fund a supplemental executive retirement plan for its officers. The purchase price was $80,000, and the gain that accumulated during the year was $10,000. The plan will not pay benefits until the officers retire. What amount of this gain is taxable in the current year?

    A. The company must report $10,000 of the gain as ordinary income.
    B. The accumulation in the annuity is tax-deferred, so the company reports none of the gain.
    C. The officers must report the gain as income in proportion to their expected benefits.
    D. The company must report the $10,000 as capital gain.

Answer:
The Anderson Plastics Corporation is a nonnatural person, so it must report the internal buildup in the annuity as ordinary income. The same rule applies to variable and fixed annuities.
The answer is A.

STRUCTURED SETTLEMENTS

A structured settlement is an agreement under which someone who is entitled to receive a large, lump-sum payment of money decides, instead, to accept periodic sums of money. Frequently, structured settlements arise as ways of compensating a party who has been injured, such as in an auto accident or a medical malpractice claim. Often, an annuity is purchased by an insurance company that has insured the defendant to provide a benefit that is a long-term solution for the claimant in lieu of a lump-sum settlement. The annuity contracts are specifically tailored to meet the needs of the injured or wronged party.

Advantages of structured settlements:

- Financial security for the injured or aggrieved person
- Benefit payments that match cash needs in amount and timing
- Professional management of the funds
- Income tax advantage since the payments, both principal and interest, are injury damages and so are tax-free. In contrast, if the claimant received the lump sum and invested the entire amount, the earnings would be taxable.

Disadvantages:

- The insurer issuing the annuity might become insolvent, causing payments to the injured or aggrieved party to be delayed and subject to limits imposed by the state guaranty fund.
- The actual cash needs, in amount or timing, might exceed those anticipated when the structured settlement agreement was finalized.

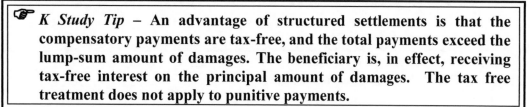 *K Study Tip* – An advantage of structured settlements is that the compensatory payments are tax-free, and the total payments exceed the lump-sum amount of damages. The beneficiary is, in effect, receiving tax-free interest on the principal amount of damages. The tax free treatment does not apply to punitive payments.

Damages

Damages are a monetary amount paid in settlement or awarded to a party for an injury or harm. Damages may be **compensatory** (to pay for actual financial losses sustained and perhaps to compensate for pain and suffering, disfigurement, etc.) or **punitive** (to punish the tortfeasor for an especially malicious or callous act of wrongdoing).

Compensatory damages for personal physical injuries or physical sickness are generally not subject to income taxes, but punitive damages are taxable. Damages in a wrongful death action are deemed compensatory and not taxable.

Employment discrimination claims and damage to reputation do not involve physical injuries, so the damages are taxable. Emotional distress by itself does not involve physical injuries, so these damages are taxable. When emotional distress requires medical care, however, the amounts paid for medical care can be excluded from income.

Practice Question

Which of the following damages received for claims must be reported as taxable income?

(1) Punitive damages
(2) Damages for pain and suffering
(3) Damages for wrongful death
(4) Damages for emotional distress

    A. (1) and (2) only
    B. (1) and (4) only
    C. (3) and (4) only
    D. (1), (2), and (4) only

Answer:
Damages for pain and suffering and wrongful death are compensatory damages for physical injuries and are not taxable. Punitive damages and damages for emotional distress are taxable.
The answer is B.

USING ANNUITIES IN RETIREMENT PLANNING TO OVERCOME THE SUPERANNUATION PROBLEM

One of the biggest unknown factors in retirement planning is how long a client will live. Some planners attempt to deal with the problem of longevity by assuming long life expectancies, such as age 95 or 100. Using such long life expectancies, however, means that clients with modest savings may be compelled to sacrifice lifestyle during their retirement years to make sure the money lasts, "just in case" they live to be centenarians.

> *"You can be young without money but you can't be old without it."* – **Tennessee Williams**

One solution to this problem of trade-offs is immediate annuities. Clients nearing retirement are asked to identify essential expenses (budgetary items that must be paid, like insurance premiums and mortgages) and discretionary items (such as travel and gifts). Since essential expenses are those that must be paid on a timely basis, guaranteed lifetime incomes, such as Social Security and pension income, are designated to pay these expenses. If there is a shortfall (more essential expenses than guaranteed income), an immediate annuity is purchased to provide enough additional guaranteed lifetime income to cover those expenses. Other investment assets, then, produce the money for paying discretionary expenses, and these assets can be managed as part of a diversified portfolio. Moreover, if the portfolio is having a bad year, some discretionary expenses might have to be deferred until a later time when the portfolio returns are more substantial.

Another way annuities can be used in retirement planning is to put aside a sum of money in a deferred annuity with the intention of annuitizing at a later age, perhaps age 80 or 85, if the client is still alive at that time and has a better idea of health and other factors likely to affect continued longevity. The advantage of waiting is the higher payout amount based on age. For example, according to immediateannuities.com, a 65-year-old male with $100,000 to invest in a single-life immediate annuity starting in 6 months would receive approximately $550 per month, while an 80-year-old would receive approximately $900 per month.

The more risk-averse clients are, the more likely they are to choose to annuitize sooner rather than later.

A third way to use annuities in retirement planning to maintain lifestyle while taming the threat of longevity is to use a variable annuity with a Guaranteed Minimum Withdrawal Benefit rider. Research has shown that by adding a Guaranteed Minimum Withdrawal Benefit rider to a variable annuity, annuitants can take a higher level of payments for life with very little risk, so a retired person may not need to sacrifice lifestyle for longevity.

QUALIFIED LONGEVITY ANNUITY CONTRACTS (QLACs)

Many retirees like the concept of using a lump sum to buy a deferred annuity earmarked to be annuitized when they reach a certain age, such as 75 or 80. This strategy for ensuring that the retiree does not outlive his or her income becomes problematic, however, when the majority of retirement savings is inside a qualified defined contribution retirement plan, such as a 401(k), because qualified retirement plans have required minimum distributions (RMDs) beginning at age 70½. Being required to start withdrawals at age 70½ eliminates the ability to wait until a later age to see how things look.

On July 1, 2014, the Treasury issued final regulations allowing the purchase of "longevity annuities" inside qualified defined contribution plans (including 401(k)s, 403(b)s, and 457 plans). The regulations permit retirees to allocate up to the lesser of $125,000 or 25% of the employee's account balance to the purchase of a "qualifying longevity annuity contract," or QLAC. The dollar amount is set to increase with inflation. The 25% limit is separately determined for each plan in which the employee participates.

For IRAs (as opposed to qualified defined contribution plans), the amount of premiums paid for the QLAC may not exceed the lesser of $125,000 or 25% of the aggregate account balances as of December 31st of the year before the calendar year in which the QLAC premium is paid.

A QLAC is a deferred annuity set to begin at an advanced age, but no later than age 85.

Prior to annuitization, the value of the QLAC is excluded from the account balance used to determine required minimum distributions (RMDs).

In order to be qualified, the QLAC must follow certain rules, including the commencement of the annuitized payment no later than age 85. Contracts are permitted to offer a return of premium (ROP) feature both before and after the annuity start date such that a lump sum death benefit may be paid to a beneficiary to the extent that the premium payments made with respect to the QLAC exceed the payments made to the employee under the QLAC. When a QLAC is providing a life annuity to a surviving spouse, it may also provide a similar ROP benefit after the death of both the employee and the spouse. When a beneficiary receives payment from the QLAC it will follow the same tax and distribution rules as other qualified plan inheritances.

Variable and indexed annuities are not permitted to be QLACs. In addition, QLACs are not permitted to offer a cash surrender value.

HYBRID ANNUITY/LONG-TERM CARE PRODUCTS

One of the newest types of annuity products on the market is a hybrid annuity/long-term care product where a qualified long term care (LTC) rider is attached to an annuity.

Clients who do not wish to pay for traditional LTC insurance might have a particular sum of money they plan to save toward potential long-term care expenses. That lump sum can be placed in an annuity with a LTC rider that would provide a higher long-term care benefit if needed. For example, the annuity product might double or triple the benefit if needed for LTC expenses. If LTC is not needed, the annuity can be used to provide income similar to a traditional annuity product. Most insurers will have a minimum, such as $50,000, that must be contributed to the contract, so clients will need to have a substantial amount of savings to be able to afford to set aside this amount outside of their regular income-producing portfolio in retirement. In addition, hybrid policies typically do not qualify for state LTC partnership programs as discussed in Topic 26.

Clients who already have an existing traditional annuity and wish to change to a hybrid policy may be able to do so under a Section 1035 tax-deferred exchange if the rules of the 1035 exchange are followed.

When comparing hybrid products to traditional LTC insurance, the traditional LTC policy will typically offer higher benefits for each premium dollar; however the traditional LTC policy pays nothing if there is never a need for long-term care. Whether the traditional or hybrid policy is better for the client will depend on each client's unique circumstances, goals, perceptions, and risk tolerance level.

Another factor to evaluate is the alternative of investing the lump sum elsewhere. Could the investment returns be used to purchase a traditional LTC policy that will pay a higher benefit amount, without tapping into the principal amount invested? If so, the LTC benefit is higher and may qualify for the partnership program, plus the principal sum is still available to pass to heirs. Of course, with a traditional policy you also have to be prepared for potential premium increases. Again, it comes down to client preferences and risk tolerance, and in some cases to a straightforward desire for simplicity.

EVALUATING ANNUITIES

Financial Strength of the Issuing Insurance Company

Since the strength of guaranteed income for life is only as great as the insurance company making the promise, planners should carefully evaluate the financial strength of a company before recommending one of their annuity products. One method of evaluation is to look at the company's ratings by independent agencies such as A.M. Best, Standard and Poors, Moody's, and Fitch. Topic 31 of this textbook provides additional details regarding evaluation of insurance companies.

Bonus Rates

Some fixed annuities will offer a "bonus" interest rate for a short period of time, followed by interest being credited at a current rate in later years. When evaluating these bonus features, a planner should consider how long the bonus rate will apply, the rate after it expires, how withdrawals may affect the rate (in some cases withdrawals will reduce the bonus rate either prospectively or retroactively), and whether the contract can be terminated without a surrender charge after the bonus rate expires. For example, the contract may state that if the renewal rate is 2% lower or more, the contract can be terminated without a surrender charge. If the contract is surrendered, however, the owner will pay taxes on the earnings (plus a 10% penalty if under age 59½).

A planner should always ask to see the company's renewal rate history, which may provide a better idea of whether the rates typically drop to the guaranteed minimum rate (usually 1.5% or 2%) after the bonus period expires, or whether they renew at rates above the minimum. For many fixed annuities, the bonus rate will be offset by increased expenses, so the long term rate is no different.

Guaranteed Minimum Withdrawal Benefits (GMWBs)

GMWBs can be a beneficial feature for the right client, but can also be very tricky. Planners should read the prospectus and ensure that they understand and can communicate all of the rules and features. If the rider is too complicated for the planner to understand, it will also be too complicated for the client to understand, and should be avoided.

Timing of Annuitization

Since payments increase from annuities beginning at later ages, higher dollar amounts can be made available by delaying the decision to annuitize. Delaying also allows an opportunity to evaluate ongoing health issues that may affect life expectancy. Clients who are particularly risk averse, however, may choose to annuitize sooner rather than later.

Since current interest rates impact the amount of the annuity payments, clients will typically be offered higher payouts during higher interest rate environments. So in low rate environments, if clients can hold off on annuitizing for a few years until interest rates rise, they will have both the advantage of higher age and higher rates.

Avoid Anchoring

Anchoring is a behavioral characteristic in which a person becomes fixated on one particular piece of information to the exclusion of everything else. When evaluating whether an annuity is a good fit for a client's particular financial need, all elements should be examined and weighed.

For example, let's take a client, Jill, who is a CPA who wants to evaluate a variable annuity versus investing in a mutual fund. Based solely on after-tax returns, Jill will likely find the mutual fund to be more attractive.

If Jill invests $100,000 in a variable annuity with an expense ratio of 2% per year and the investment return is 12% per year, in 15 years, she will have an account value of $417,725. This value can be found using a financial calculator's time-value-of-money function with the following variables:

PV = 100,000
N = 15
I = 10% (12% investment return minus 2% expenses)
Solve for FV

If Jill is in the 28% tax bracket, her net after-tax amount received is $328,762. [$317,725 gain x (1-.28)] + $100,000 = $328,762.

Had Jill invested in an index mutual fund with a .5% expense ratio, the account would grow to $511,826, found on the financial calculator as follows:

PV = 100,000
N = 15
I = 11.5 (12% investment return minus .5% expenses)
Solve for FV

If Jill is in the 28% marginal tax bracket, her capital gain tax rate is 15%, so the net after-tax amount received is $450,052. [$411,826 gain x (1 − .15)] + $100,000 = $450,052.

Focusing on just the taxes, however, ignores all of the other features of a variable annuity. What if, for example, Jill doesn't live another 15 years? What if she dies 2 years later when the market has plunged and her account value is down to just $55,000? With the mutual fund, Jill's husband or children would get $55,000. But with the variable annuity, the heirs would get a minimum of $100,000 (perhaps more if an enhanced death benefit rider was purchased).

Or what if Jill wants to use this income to purchase long-term care insurance? The annuity can be used to make partial 1035 exchanges to pay the premium on the qualified LTCI policy on a tax-free basis, whereas mutual fund gains used for the premiums will be taxed.

Or what if Jill needs guaranteed income for life? There is no guarantee with the mutual fund. Other elements could also be explored, and it could very well be that in the end the annuity is not the right choice for Jill, but the point is that all of the various elements of Jill's life situation, as well as the policy fees and features, need to be evaluated together.

Should I Annuitize or Just Take Withdrawals?

The owner of an annuity will have the option of taking withdrawals from an annuity instead of annuitizing. The owner could take withdrawals as the money is needed rather than accepting the periodic payments.

The pros and cons of annuitization versus withdrawals from a variable annuity depend on many factors, such as the amount of money invested, the length of time the money is invested, the growth of the annuity, the owner's risk tolerance, the annuitant's need for annuity payments, and the income tax bracket of the annuitant-owner. The age and health of the annuitant and his or her life expectancy will also be important in making the decision. The owner should also consider what assets are held outside the variable annuity.

For purposes of simplicity, assume that the owner-annuitant has invested $100,000 in the variable annuity at least 10 years ago and is past the surrender charge period, the annuity has doubled in value, and the annuitant is over age 59½ so no 10% penalty will be involved.

First, the owner-annuitant should consider the tax implications. With a withdrawal, the LIFO rule of taxation applies. If the owner withdraws $25,000, it will all be taxable ordinary income due to the earnings in the annuity. If the annuitant is in a high tax bracket, this withdrawal could give rise to substantial additional tax. With annuitization, a portion of the distribution will be tax free return of investment, so the tax consequences are much lower.

Second, if the annuitant needs a lot of money from the annuity, then a withdrawal may be needed regardless of income tax consequences. The annuitization will generally set payments at an amount that is based on life expectancy. So, it will be important to determine whether the annuitant needs or wants a life income or has immediate needs for cash.

Third, with annuitization, the payments will continue to the annuitant for life whereas withdrawals are likely to deplete the amount in the annuity and could mean the annuitant runs out of money prematurely.

Fourth, if the annuitant will live past his or her life expectancy, the total amount that will be paid to the annuitant after annuitization is likely to be higher than the amount that can be withdrawn. Part of what is paid with an annuity comes from the early deaths of other annuitants. Thus, the annuitants who are the survivors will benefit by receiving what does not have to be paid to the deceased annuitants.

Fifth, there are costs of an annuity to pay for the additional risks taken by the insurance company, but the annuitant will probably find that the benefit of an assured life income is worth these costs. Nevertheless, an owner may believe that the costs are not worthwhile and may not need the life income and will want to take withdrawals and invest the proceeds separately.

Sixth, with annuitization, the owner will be giving up the flexibility of making withdrawals. The owner's ability to give up this flexibility by annuitizing may depend on what other resources are available.

Seventh, annuitization may affect the owner's ability to leave any of the money in the annuity to heirs if death comes earlier than expected.

Eighth, a planner may need to consider the possibility that the annuitant will want to preserve Medicaid eligibility. Withdrawals might be taken from the annuity and given to a spouse who does not need nursing home care. The community spouse can buy an SPIA and receive income without it being counted for Medicaid eligibility.

Other General Information

- Fee-based planners can offer no-load annuities that do not pay a commission and often do not have a surrender charge.

- Due to the lack of liquidity in annuities, clients should always maintain sufficient liquidity outside of an annuity.

- While annuities do avoid probate, they do not avoid estate taxes. Many clients get confused on this issue and mistakenly believe that probate and estate taxes are one and the same.

DEFINITIONS

12b-1 fees – A 12b-1 fee is an annual distribution or marketing fee that may be assessed in the subaccounts of variable annuities and mutual funds. 12b-1 fees can also be used to provide ongoing compensation to sales agents.

401(k) Plan – A Section 401(k) plan is a defined contribution qualified retirement plan established by an employer and allows employees to save money for retirement in a tax-advantaged way through payroll deductions. Employers typically match a portion of employee contributions as a way to encourage employees to contribute.

403(b) Plan – A Section 403(b) plan is a retirement plan established by tax-exempt organizations (employers described in Sec. 501(c)(3) of the IRC) and public school districts, and the plan allows employees to save money for retirement in a tax-advantaged way through payroll deductions.

457 Plan – A Section 457 plan is a retirement plan established by governmental units, agencies, and tax-exempt organizations, and the plan allows employees to save money for retirement in a tax-advantaged way through payroll deductions.

Capital Gain Tax Rates – When property is held longer than one year and is sold for a gain, it receives special tax treatment as a capital gain rather than being taxed as ordinary income, which is taxed at the taxpayer's highest marginal tax bracket. The long-term capital gain rate is 15% for most taxpayers (0% for those in the 10% and 15% marginal brackets; 20% for those in the 39.6% marginal bracket.

Defined Contribution Plan – A defined-contribution plan is a qualified retirement plan established by an employer in which individual accounts are established for participating employees, and the employer contributes a percentage of each employee's compensation. Benefits are based on amounts contributed to each participant's account and the returns earned on the accounts.

Dollar Cost Averaging – Dollar cost averaging is an investment strategy requiring an investor to make purchases of the same dollar amount at regular intervals, such as monthly or quarterly. Rather than investing a lump sum in the market all at once when the market may be at a high point, investments are spread over time to reduce the risk of buying at the wrong time. By investing at regular intervals, some dollars are invested when market prices are higher, and some dollars are invested when market prices are lower, creating the potential for a lower average cost per unit (share). Dollar cost averaging does not, however, eliminate the risk of loss.

Estate Tax – An estate tax is a tax imposed on a decedent's right to transfer property to heirs and beneficiaries at death.

FINRA (Financial Industry Regulatory Authority) – FINRA is a self-regulatory organization whose members are broker-dealers. FINRA oversees broker-dealers and writes and enforces rules for sales of securities and for those who sell them. Anyone who represents buyers or sellers of securities must register with FINRA under the sponsorship of a broker-dealer.

Individual Retirement Account (IRA) – An IRA is a retirement savings vehicle that can be set up by individuals with earned income, and the IRA provides special tax advantages. Individuals are limited in the amount they can contribute.

Marginal Tax Rate – U.S. income taxes are imposed on a progressive tax scale, which means that the higher the income, the higher the amount of tax that is paid. Taxpayers pay first at 10%, then 15%, 25%, 28%, 33%, 35%, and 39.6%. A taxpayer's marginal tax rate is the highest rate applied to their income, and represents the tax that will be paid on the next dollar of income for that year.

NAIC (National Association of Insurance Commissioners) – The NAIC is a national organization of state officials who are responsible for regulation and supervision of insurance in the 50 states. Although the NAIC has no official power, it has been effective in fostering uniformity in insurance laws and regulations among the states. The NAIC prepares model acts that can be used by states for regulation of insurance and through the preparation of these model acts the NAIC encourages uniformity in state laws.

Ordinary Income Tax Rates – Ordinary income tax rates are the rates assessed on income that is not treated as a capital gain. Taxpayers add all of their ordinary income, such as wages and business income, for the year, subtract certain allowable reductions, and pay tax at progressive rates as income increases: first at 10%, then 15%, 25%, 28%, 33%, 35%, and 39.6%.

Probate – Probate is the legal process through which a decedent's will is validated, claims against the estate are paid, and assets are distributed to beneficiaries.

Qualified Retirement Plans – Qualified retirement plans are retirement plans established by employers in order to receive special tax treatment, such as the ability to deduct contributions made to the plan and tax-deferred growth prior to when distributions are made to employees. In order to receive the special tax treatment, certain rules must be followed.

SEC (Securities and Exchange Commission) – The SEC is the government agency holding primary responsibility for enforcing securities laws and regulating stock exchanges and other key participants in the securities industry.

APPLICATION QUESTIONS

1. A typical professional basketball player in the NBA should consider the purchase of annuities having which of the following characteristics?

(1) Deferred
(2) Variable
(3) Level periodic premiums
(4) Immediate

    A. (1) and (2) only
    B. (1) and (3) only
    C. (2) and (3) only
    D. (3) and (4) only
    E. (1), (2), and (3) only

2. Which of the following statements describes the operation of a life annuity with no period certain?

    A. The emphasis is on a specific method for the creation of an adequate fund.
    B. The annuitant receives a lifetime income, but all payments cease at death.
    C. Because of the interest factor, an annuitant is assured of receiving back more than he or she paid in.
    D. In the absence of the period certain, the annuitant may outlive the payout period.

3. Which of the following statements concerning types of annuities is <u>not</u> correct?

    A. In a deferred annuity, if the insured dies during the accumulation period, a death benefit is payable.
    B. In an equity-indexed annuity, the principal may be guaranteed, while interest credited is based on the performance of the stock market.
    C. In a cash refund annuity, benefit payments will at least equal the purchase price of the contract.
    D. In a variable annuity, the value of the accumulation units is fixed, while the value of the annuity units during the liquidation period fluctuates.

4. Margaret Dyer, age 63, has inherited $250,000 from her mother and wants to use the money as a retirement fund. Since her family has long life expectancy, she is concerned about running out of money in her old age. What kind of annuity is most appropriate for Margaret?

    A. Straight life annuity
    B. Life annuity with refund feature
    C. Life annuity with period certain
    D. Temporary annuity

5. Which of the following statements concerning the variable annuity is <u>not</u> correct?

    A. A high percentage of the funds available for investment is typically invested in common stocks or other equities.
    B. It is possible that prices for investments in a variable annuity will fail to parallel the cost of living.
    C. The amount of the monthly payout is to some extent a function of mortality expectations.
    D. Most insurers base their payouts on the performance of the S&P 500 stock index.

6. Pedro was seriously injured in an auto accident and was awarded $750,000 in damages. Instead of accepting the money in a lump sum, Pedro's attorney worked out with the defendant's attorney an arrangement under which Pedro would receive the following amounts:

    – $100,000 in cash now
    – An income of $10,000 per month, starting after one month and continuing for 5 years
    – A lump-sum payment of $350,000 at the end of the fifth year, concurrent with the final $10,000 income check

The arrangement worked out between the two sides in this case is called:

    A. A temporary annuity
    B. A pure life annuity
    C. A structured settlement
    D. A like-kind exchange
    E. A Crummey arrangement

7. If 9% annually (0.75% monthly) represents a fair rate of return to Pedro in the preceding question, was he being treated adequately?

    A. Yes, because he received exactly the equivalent of $750,000.
    B. Yes, because he received more than the equivalent of $750,000.
    C. No, because he received less than the equivalent of $750,000.
    D. No, because he received exactly the equivalent of $750,000.
    E. Yes, because he received more than $750,000.

8. Which of the following statements concerning the federal income tax treatment of monetary settlements is (are) correct?

    (1) Under a structured settlement, the portion of each payment received that represents interest is taxed as income, while that represented by principal is tax-free.
    (2) Damages received because of employment discrimination are taxable as income.
    (3) Punitive damages are tax-free for the recipient.

        A. (1) only
        B. (2) only
        C. (3) only
        D. (1) and (2) only
        E. (2) and (3) only

9. Ted Danlow's foreign car repair shop was destroyed by a fire that started in a defective piece of equipment. Ted carried insurance on the building and is planning to rebuild in a year. Ted sued the manufacturer of the defective equipment for damages, including loss of profits and goodwill. The manufacturer has offered to settle. Which of the following statements concerning the settlement Ted Danlow will receive is correct?

    A. If Ted wants to rebuild, a structured settlement will be preferable to a lump-sum payment.
    B. If the insurance proceeds for the building exceed its original cost, Ted will have a taxable gain for the year.
    C. The amount of the settlement paid to Ted for the loss of profits will not be taxable income.
    D. The amount of the settlement paid to Ted for the loss of goodwill is not taxable income.

10. An annuitant pays $60,000 for a pure or straight life annuity whose annual payments are $6,000. The annuitant has a life expectancy of 16 years. How much of the $6,000 annual payment is included annually in the annuitant's gross income?

    A. $1,368
    B. $1,750
    C. $2,250
    D. $2,634
    E. $3,118

11. Ken purchased a nonqualified variable annuity for $40,000 and annuitized it this year when it was worth $75,000. The payments received by Ken this year will consist of what amounts?

    (1) Tax-free return of capital
    (2) Capital gain
    (3) Ordinary income

        A. (1) and (2) only
        B. (1) and (3) only
        C. (2) and (3) only
        D. (1), (2), and (3)

12. Which of the following statements describes the operation of a life annuity with no period certain?

    A. The emphasis is on a specific method for the creation of an adequate fund.
    B. The older the annuitant is when he or she receives the first annuity payment, the greater will be the amount of each payment.
    C. The annuitant will receive more in payout regardless of the age payments begin.
    D. In the absence of the period certain, the annuitant may outlive the payout period.

13. Which of the following statements indicates the rationale of the variable annuity?

    A. Common stock prices can be expected to increase a certain percent each year.

    B. Dividends and market prices of common stocks over the long term tend to vary directly with changes in the cost of living.

    C. Conventional annuities are now obsolete because of the built-in inflationary factors in the U.S.

    D. The cost of living varies each year with the level of common stock prices.

14. Henry is a financial planner whose client, Bernice, is a widow. Bernice is 67 years old and about to retire, but is concerned about outliving her money since her parents both lived into their 90's. Henry has discussed the idea of a life annuity with Bernice, but she is concerned that if she were to die sooner than expected, the amount she invested might be lost. She would prefer an investment that would at least provide something for her grandson if she were to die in a short period of time without receiving back her total premiums. Which of the following is an appropriate recommendation for Henry to make to Bernice?

    A. A 10-year period certain annuity

    B. A hybrid annuity/long-term care policy

    C. A life annuity with cash refund

    D. Henry should not recommend annuities because experts such as Suze Orman say they are poor investments

15. All of the following are requirements for Qualified Longevity Annuity Contracts (QLACs), EXCEPT?

    A. A maximum of $125,000 may be used to purchase the QLAC

    B. A QLAC is purchased in an IRA or defined contribution retirement plan

    C. In order to be qualified, a QLAC must be annuitized no later than age 85

    D. In order to be qualified, a QLAC must be a variable annuity

16. All of the following are true regarding the use of annuities in retirement planning, EXCEPT?

    A. Hybrid annuity/LTC contracts will qualify for all states' long-term care partnership programs

    B. A hybrid annuity/LTC contract allows for tax-free distributions to pay for qualified long-term care expenses

    C. A Section 1035 partial exchange can be used to make tax-free distributions from a nonqualified annuity to pay premiums on a qualified long-term care insurance contract

    D. A life annuity can overcome the superannuation problem

For practice answering case questions related to Topic 27, please answer the following questions in the cases included in Appendix A at the back of this textbook.

Case	Questions
Black Hills P&L	
Brodinski	
Haurilick	
Beals	
Mocsin	
Loudon	
Connor	10 and 11
Seidelhofer	12 and 13
Loomis Company	
Michael and Diana Eastman	
Gary and Judy Parker	26, 27, 28, 29, and 30

ANSWERS AND EXPLANATIONS

1. A is the answer. (1) is correct. The annuity should be deferred since the player has no need for income while still earning a living playing basketball. Also, (2) is correct since inflation could erode the purchasing power of the annuity over the possibly long period before benefit payments are needed. (3) is incorrect because the player has only a few years in which he can afford premiums for a large annuity contract. (4) is incorrect because (1) is correct. In summary, the player should buy a single-premium, deferred, variable annuity in each of his years as a highly-paid player in the NBA.

2. B is the answer. All life annuity payments stop at death. A is not a correct statement. The emphasis is on the liquidation of the fund or the actuarial spreading of the fund (however created) over the probable life span of the age group of which the annuitant is a member. C is not a correct statement. If a life annuity with no period certain is selected, the purchaser may die within a few months and, therefore, receive only a small part of what he or she paid the insurance company for the annuity. D is not a correct statement. A life annuity, with or without a period certain, will pay the annuity amount for as long as the annuitant lives. The period certain means only that if the annuitant dies after only a few months of receiving a monthly check, the insurance company will continue payments for the remainder of the period certain.

3. D is the answer. The value of both the accumulation units and the annuity units fluctuates.

4. A is the answer. The straight or pure annuity will last for Margaret's lifetime and will provide the largest periodic payments for a given investment amount. She will not outlive the payments, regardless of her longevity. She could outlive the temporary annuity and she would not receive as large payments if she selects the period certain or refund feature.

5. D is the answer. The payout provided by a variable annuity is determined primarily by the investment performance of the assets acquired by the insurance company to fund the variable annuity contracts outstanding. The payout is not based on any index, such as the S&P 500 stock index. A, B, and C are correct statements.

6. C is the answer, by definition. A and B are incorrect because although the settlement includes an annuity (a temporary one, not a life annuity), the annuity is not the entire settlement. D and E are income tax planning techniques that are unrelated to structured settlements.

7. B is the answer. Compute the present value of the payments Pedro will receive, discounted at a 0.75% rate of interest. The present values are:

$100,000 now	$100,000
59 end-of-period payments of $10,000	475,347
$360,000 at the end of the 60th month	229,932
Total	$805,279

8. B is the answer. (1) is incorrect because these payments are totally tax-free, both principal and interest. (3) is incorrect because punitive damages are taxable as income to the recipient.

9. D is the answer. Damages for loss of goodwill are treated as payment for loss of capital and are not taxable. The loss of profits is treated as a loss of income, so the damages paid for this item are taxable. The insurance proceeds are not taxable because Ted is planning to rebuild. In an involuntary conversion such as the destruction of Ted's shop, the taxpayer does not recognize gain where the property will be replaced with property of equal or greater value. A structured settlement will not be preferable for Ted because he wants to rebuild and will need the money immediately for the costs of starting his business. Ted cannot afford to take payments over many years.

10. C is the answer. The annuitant's cost for the contract is $60,000, and the expected total return is $96,000 ($6,000 per year for 16 years). The exclusion ratio is 62.5%, which is determined by dividing the cost for the contract ($60,000) by the anticipated return ($96,000). The excluded amount of each annual payment is determined by multiplying the annual return of $6,000 times the exclusion ratio of 62.5%, which gives an excluded amount of $3,750. The amount included is the total annual return ($6,000) minus the excluded amount ($3,750), which gives an included amount of $2,250.

11. B is the answer. The annuity payments will consist of tax-free return of capital and ordinary income until the capital investment is recovered.

12. B is the answer. The older the person is when he or she receives the first annuity payment, the shorter the probable period of survivorship. Therefore, the insurance company can pay out more dollars to such people each month, all other factors being equal. A is not a correct statement. The emphasis is on the liquidation of the fund or the actuarial spreading of the fund (however created) over the probable life spans of the age group of which the annuitant is a member. C is not a correct statement. If a life annuity with no period certain is selected, the purchaser may die within a few months and, therefore, receive only a small payout. D is not a correct statement. A life annuity, with or without a period certain, will pay the annuity amount for as long as the annuitant lives. The period certain only means that if the annuitant dies after only a few months of receiving a monthly annuity check, the insurance company will continue payments for the remainder of the period certain.

13. B is the answer. Note that there is no guarantee that dividends and market prices of common stocks will vary directly with changes in the cost of living, but this is the rational basis for the variable annuity. A, C, and D do not indicate the rationale of the variable annuity.

14. C is the answer. A life annuity with cash refund will guarantee Bernice receives payments for the rest of her life, no matter how long she lives, but if she dies before receiving back an amount equal to her premium payments, the difference between her total premiums and the amount she received will be paid as a lump sum to her beneficiary. The 10-year period certain annuity will not provide a guaranteed life income for Bernice so it would not be appropriate. A hybrid annuity and long term care policy is not the best recommendation because Bernice has not stated a need for long term care coverage and has not asked about long term care policies.

15. D is the answer. Variable and indexed annuities are not permitted to be QLACs. All of the other statements are true regarding the rules for Qualified Longevity Annuity Contracts.

16. A is the answer. Hybrid annuity/LTC contracts generally will not qualify for a state's long-term care partnership program; only traditional long-term care policies will qualify. B and C are true statements. In answer choice D, the superannuation problem refers to the risk of outliving one's money. A life annuity overcomes that problem by guaranteeing an income that cannot be outlived.

Life Insurance (Individual) (Topic 28)

CFP Board Student-Centered Learning Objectives

(a) Explain the underwriting factors commonly used in the life underwriting process. [Also see Topic 31 in this textbook]

(b) Differentiate between term, whole life, variable, universal, and VUL policies and select the most appropriate type of coverage to match a client's specific circumstances.

(c) Calculate a client's insurance needs using alternative approaches, including the capital needs, human life value, capital retention, income retention, and income multiplier methods. [See Topic 30]

(d) Recommend whether a policy should be replaced based upon quantitative and qualitative factors.

(e) Describe common life insurance termination options.

(f) Recommend life insurance purchase and benefits distribution options based upon needs, financial resources, and cost.

A. Life Insurance Uses and Benefits	**28.3**
B. Life Insurance Premiums	**28.4**
1. Mortality	*28.5*
2. Interest	*28.5*
3. Expenses	*28.5*
4. Policy reserves	*28.6*
5. Net amount at risk	*28.6*
6. Types of policies	*28.7*
C. Term Insurance	**28.7**
1. Renewal and conversion	*28.7*
2. Decreasing term insurance	*28.8*
3. Advantages and disadvantages of term life insurance	*28.9*
D. Whole Life Insurance	**28.11**
1. Premiums on whole life policies	*28.11*
2. Cash values	*28.13*
3. Advantages and disadvantages of whole life policies	*28.13*
E. Variable Life Insurance	**28.15**
1. Separate accounts	*28.15*
2. Inflation hedge	*28.16*
3. Advantages and disadvantages of variable life insurance	*28.16*
4. Regulation of variable life insurance	*28.17*

F. **Universal Life Insurance** **28.18**
    1. *Unbundling the elements of the policy* 28.18
        a. Flexible death benefits 28.19
    2. *Advantages and disadvantages of universal life insurance* 28.20
G. **Variable Universal Life Insurance** **28.21**
H. **Endowment Life Insurance** **28.22**
I. **Survivorship Life Insurance** **28.23**
J. **The Life Insurance Contract** **28.23**
    1. *Declarations page* 28.23
    2. *Contractual provisions* 28.24
    3. *Designating beneficiaries* 28.27
        a. Primary and contingent 28.27
        b. Named beneficiaries and class beneficiaries 28.27
        c. Revocable versus irrevocable beneficiaries 28.29
    4. *Common disaster clause* 28.29
K. **Policy Riders** **28.29**
L. **Dividends** **28.31**
    1. *Dividend options* 28.31
M. **Interest Crediting Methods** **28.32**
N. **Nonforfeiture Options** **28.33**
O. **Settlement Options** **28.35**
P. **Policy Illustrations** **28.36**
Q. **Policy Replacement** **28.37**
R. **Viatical Settlements** **28.38**
    1. *Viatical settlement or accelerated benefits* 28.38
    2. *Tax rules – Section 101(g)* 28.39
    3. *Planning* 28.41
    4. *Ethical issues* 28.42
S. **Other Strategic Uses of Life Insurance** **28.43**
    1. *Pension maximization* 28.43
    2. *Installment note protection* 28.43
    3. *Charitable giving* 28.43
    4. *Business uses* 28.44
T. **Life Insurance as an Employee Benefit** **28.44**
    1. *Group term life insurance* 28.44
        a. Nondiscrimination rules 28.45
    2. *Contributory versus noncontributory plans* 28.45
    3. *Dependent coverage* 28.46
    4. *Tax treatment* 28.46
    5. *Group Permanent insurance* 28.47
        a. Group universal life insurance programs 28.47
        b. Group/ordinary plan 28.47
    6. *Conversion analysis* 28.48
    7. *Portability of GULPS* 28.48

U. Group Carve-Out Life Insurance..**28.48**
   1. Premium bonus plan..*28.48*
   2. Death-benefit-only plan..*28.49*

LIFE INSURANCE USES AND BENEFITS

The death of a family member, friend, or business associate typically results in emotional distress for survivors. Psychologists tell us that those suffering the loss of a loved one, and those diagnosed with terminal illnesses, will go through 5 stages of grief: (1) denial and isolation, (2) anger, (3) bargaining, (4) depression, and (5) acceptance. The order of the stages and the length of time each person spends in each stage vary from individual to individual, and may be expressed with different levels of intensity.

Imagine a young surviving widow with school-age children who is not only dealing with the grief of losing a husband, but also trying to help her children to adjust to the loss of a father. If this young wife is your planning client, the last thing you want to do is deliver even more bad news: "I'm sorry but you cannot afford to continue living in your current house without your husband's income." While life insurance death benefits do not ease the emotional and physical loss, they can ease the burdens for surviving family members, allow them time to go through the stages of grief, and give them options. Where there is money, there are choices. Where there is no money, there are few choices.

There are a million similarly heart-wrenching situations that could apply to clients of any age. Life insurance, then, is designed to provide financial protection for survivors (family, friends, charity, business associates, and even pets) when an insured dies. Most often, life insurance will be used to replace a portion of the insured's future earning power that would be used to support dependents if the insured had lived. Another way to view it is that life insurance is designed to replace a person's economic value.

Undoubtedly, people can provide different kinds of economic value to their families. The economic value of a husband who earns a paycheck every week is generally not hard for the family to determine. On the other hand, the economic value of a stay-at-home parent who does not earn a paycheck may be more difficult to calculate. The economic value of a stay-at-home parent includes the "services" provided to the family and is at least equal to the cost of hiring someone to provide those services when the parent is not able to do so. Of course, we realize that there is really no way to value a human life, but we must attempt to assign some sort of economic value for insurance purposes. A detailed discussion of methods of calculating the appropriate amount of death benefit can be found in Topic 30 of this textbook.

In addition to providing for loved ones and paying end-of-life expenses (such as funeral and final illness expenses), there are many other personal risk exposures that can be eliminated by appropriate use of life insurance. Moreover, life insurance can be purchased to accomplish a variety of goals, including the following:

- To provide for orderly disposition of a business interest by means of a buy-sell agreement (discussed in detail in topic 29).
- To make gifts to charities (church, school, or other charitable organizations).
- To create a memorial or endowment in honor of the deceased.
- To fund special goals, such as college education for children or grandchildren.
- To build cash value that can be spent for retirement.
- To cover the life of a debtor who owes the client money (For example, the client sold a business and is receiving installment payments. If the debtor dies prematurely, life insurance will assure that the client receives full payment.)
- To pay estate taxes and estate settlement expenses.

Life insurance provides numerous benefits, along with the obvious replacement of income. Because life insurance serves a valuable social and economic function, it has very favorable income tax treatment. Life insurance death benefits are generally received free of income taxes, and cash values grow on a tax-deferred basis. A detailed discussion of the taxation of life insurance can be found in Topic 28B of this textbook.

LIFE INSURANCE PREMIUMS

An insurance company begins the process of setting the premium for a particular life insurance policy by determining gross premium. To arrive at the gross premium amount, the insurance company will make assumptions regarding expected mortality costs, interest earnings, and expenses. The gross premium can be determined using the following formula:

Gross Premium = Mortality Costs – Interest Earnings + Expenses

Mortality costs and expenses will increase the gross premium amount, while interest earnings decrease the gross premium amount. Net premium is the gross premium less expenses, so once gross premiums are calculated, the net premium can be determined based on just the first two of these elements: mortality costs and interest earnings.

Mortality

The mortality rate is a measurement of the number of deaths in a given population over a period of time. Actuaries who are skilled in mathematics and statistics are employed by insurance companies to create mortality tables showing mortality rates by age and sex. The mortality rate for a given age is found by dividing the number who die at that age by the number alive at the start of that age. The law of large numbers requires the insurance company to write policies on a large number of similar risks (for example, a group of 35 year-old males), and the total premiums collected from the group must create a fund large enough to provide the death benefits for the few who die each year.

Death rates rise as age increases; hence, claims costs for a given group of insured people will rise. In the absence of a leveling technique, premium costs will also rise as the insured group grows older. Morbidity rates, which are rates of disability also calculated by actuaries at insurance companies, have a tendency to rise with age, though not in a steady progression from age to age as do mortality rates. Morbidity rates have only a minor impact on life insurance costs, affecting only such supplementary coverages as waiver-of-premium and accidental death and dismemberment benefits (discussed later in this topic under policy riders).

Interest

Life insurance policies are generally expected to be long-term contracts. In other words, a policyowner will purchase a policy at a young age and continue to pay premiums for 30, 40, or more years until death occurs. The premiums collected by the insurance company will be invested during that period of time, and will be earning interest. The interest rate is the assumed rate of interest the insurer will earn on its investment of premiums until each claim is paid.

Expenses

Some expenses of a life insurer vary with the size of the premium, such as agent commissions and premium taxes (an excise tax that the states assess to life insurance companies or to policyowners, based on gross premiums). Other expenses vary with the amount of insurance, such as the costs of underwriting, including medical examination and evaluation of character. Still other expenses are the same for each policy, regardless of its premium or amount, such as premium billing costs and policy issuance expenses. Most of a life insurer's expenses are incurred in the first policy year. The expenses are much lower in each renewal year; however, most life insurance is sold on a level premium basis. Consequently, the insurer's loading (the amount added to the premium to cover the cost of expenses) in the level premium is very inadequate in the first year to meet expenses and more than adequate to meet each renewal year's expenses. If a policy lapses after only a year or two, the life insurer will lose money because it will not have had time to recoup its high first-year expenses. Consequently, lapse rates, particularly early lapse rates, have an impact on the cost of life insurance.

Incidentally, the high first-year expenses of a life insurer are the main reason policy dividends and nonforfeiture values (the amount the policyowner receives if the policy is surrendered) are usually nonexistent or very small in the early policy years. It is also the reason many life insurers add a one-time policy fee to the premium in the first policy year.

Policy Reserves

For insurers, reserves are amounts of money held to pay future claims for death benefits. The reserve on a life insurance policy at any point in time is the difference between the present value of future benefits and the present value of the future net premiums. Accumulation and investment of reserves are governed by state law because reserves provide safety that the insurer will be able to pay death benefits.

At a policy's inception, there is no reserve because the net single premium, which is the present value of the future benefits, is the actuarial equivalent of the future net level premiums. Once the policy starts running, however, a reserve arises because: (a) the present value of future benefits rises as the date of death gets closer and (b) the present value of future net level premiums declines because fewer premiums remain to be paid.

Net Amount at Risk

Life insurance policies that have a cash value were traditionally designed such that the accumulated reserves will equal the death benefit amount at age 100. Newer policies use the 2001 CSO (Commissioners Standard Ordinary) mortality table that runs to age 120, with policy maturity, then, at age 121. As the cash value increases, it becomes part of the death benefit, reducing the "net amount at risk" for the insurance company. The net amount at risk is the amount of insurance that the company is providing at any given time.

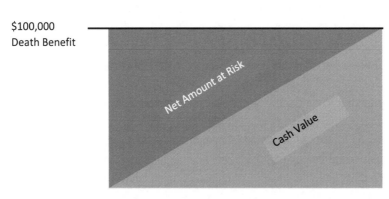

$100,000 Death Benefit

Net Amount at Risk

Cash Value

Policy Year

Types of Policies

There are numerous types of life insurance policies that are available for purchase today, and new products and features appear in the marketplace on a regular basis as insurance companies continually attempt to create attractive and competitive policies. In this book we will focus on just the principal types of life insurance policies, including term, whole life, variable life, universal life, and variable universal life. Each of these policy types will have some unique features, and each will have both advantages and disadvantages associated with it. In this topic, we will stick to general information about each type of policy, then in Topics 30 and 31 we will discuss how to choose among them for the various goals and risk tolerance levels of clients.

TERM INSURANCE

Term insurance pays the face amount of the policy when the insured dies during the term of the policy. It provides protection for a definite but limited period of time. If the insured survives the term, the policy expires, unless the policy is renewable or convertible. Most term insurance policies are both renewable and convertible.

Renewal and Conversion

Renewable policies allow the policyowner to extend the period of coverage for an additional term, but only up to a certain age (usually to age 65 or 70). For example, if a 10 year term policy is purchased, it expires after 10 years, but can be renewed for another 10 year term at that time, without evidence of insurability. A yearly renewable term policy can be renewed each year.

The premium for term insurance is low per $1,000 of coverage during the early years because protection is not provided during the years of high mortality. The premiums for yearly renewable term life insurance will increase each year, but the increases are greater as the insured grows older. When level, renewable, term insurance is purchased, the premium will remain the same for the entire term (for example 10, 15, or 20 years), but will increase based on attained age at each renewal. This ability to renew without insurability causes adverse selection for the insurance company because those in poor health are likely to renew, even at higher rates. When these level term policies are issued, they provide the policyowner with the guaranteed rate for the current period, but also contain a list of guaranteed rates at which the policy can be renewed. These rates may not be the actual rate assessed at the time, but represent a guaranteed maximum. An example appears in the chart below.

ART vs level Premium Sample Illustration

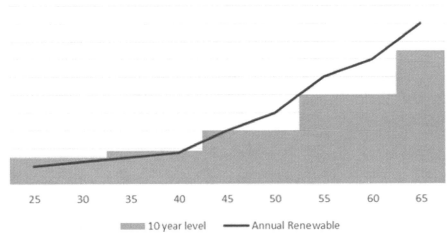

In addition to being renewable, most term insurance policies are also convertible into permanent cash value policies, such as whole life or universal life policies. As with renewability, no evidence of insurance is required. The time period during which conversion is permitted will be stated in the term policy; for example, a 10 year term policy might be convertible from years 2 through 8. In some cases, the term policy is converted to a new permanent policy based on the insured's attained age at the time of conversion. In order to reduce the amount of the premium, some companies allow the new permanent policy to be issued using the age of the insured at the time the term policy was purchased (called a retroactive or original age conversion). These conversions will, however, require a large lump-sum initial deposit in order to bring the policy's cash value (and reserves) up to the level of a permanent policy purchased at that younger age.

Decreasing Term Insurance

Yearly renewable term insurance often provides a level amount of death benefit from year to year, and this term insurance is often required by creditors to protect them in the event of the debtor's death prior to the debt being repaid. Other kinds of term insurance may have increasing or decreasing amounts of insurance, and a substantial amount of term insurance is decreasing term. This kind of insurance is used to insure that a mortgage will be paid off in the event of an owner's death. With decreasing term insurance, there is a decreasing death benefit to match the principal reduction in the amortization schedule of the mortgage; however, it is only the death benefit that decreases over time – premiums are typically level.

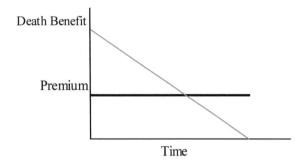

A comparison of decreasing term versus level term is warranted when insurance is being purchased to cover a loan repayment. In many cases the extra premium for a level death benefit will be minimal, making the level death benefit a more logical choice.

Advantages and Disadvantages of Term Life Insurance

Term life insurance offers the following advantages:

- The cost per unit of coverage is low. Since the protection is provided for only a limited time, the premium payer is not paying the high cost of protection provided by permanent policies during the years of expected high mortality, for example, after age 65.

- Since the agent's commission is a percent of the premium, the low-premium on a term policy means the policy owner is buying protection at low commission charges.

- State premium taxes are low because the premium is low.

- Various term lengths are available and can be matched with client needs that have a set time-frame. For example, if the client wishes to ensure that a college fund will be available for his newborn child, a 20-year term policy would provide him with the desired protection at a low premium cost.

- The convertibility feature provides flexibility for clients whose goals change over time. For example, where a policy was originally purchased for college, as in the example above, then after the child has finished college, the client may want to convert to a permanent policy to leave a substantial sum to his favorite charity upon his death.

Term life insurance may have the following disadvantages:

- Protection is provided for only a temporary period unless the policy owner elects to renew or convert.

- Renewal requires a high premium at the higher ages and is unavailable beyond some maximum age.

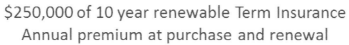

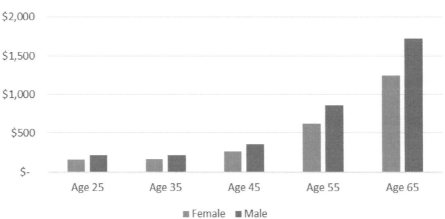

- Term insurance builds no cash value; therefore, there is no savings/investment element, and no ability to borrow from the policy.

- Term insurance involves substantial adverse selection because of the renewal and conversion features. It is debatable to what extent this adverse selection increases the cost of term insurance. The adverse selection arises because there is a strong tendency for those in poor health to renew or convert their term insurance. Those in good health are likely to drop their term coverage at the end of the coverage period.

- The policy owner loses the tax shelter available to owners of permanent life insurance.

Practice Question

Which of the following statements concerning yearly renewable term insurance is (are) correct?

(1) It provides protection for one year at a time.
(2) It builds up a cash value to provide cash that might be used for a child's education.

    A. (1) only
    B. (2) only
    C. Both (1) and (2)
    D. Neither (1) nor (2)

Answer:

There is no cash value in a yearly renewable term policy.

The answer is A.

WHOLE LIFE INSURANCE

Whole life insurance provides protection against loss due to the insured's death, no matter when death occurs, even at a very advanced age. Unlike yearly renewable term insurance, which is pure insurance (no cash value component), whole life insurance builds a cash value within the policy. Since mortality is lower in the early policy years (younger ages), the insurer receives more in premium payments during those years than is needed to pay death benefits and operating costs. The excess premium builds the cash values for the surviving insured-policyowners. That cash value works to prepay future premiums so that the annual premium payment can remain level even while the actual cost of insurance is increasing.

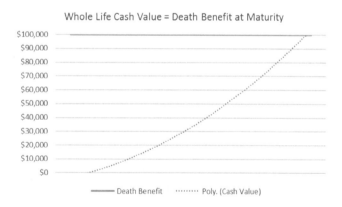

Whole life policies are characterized by their numerous guarantees. The amount of the premium is guaranteed throughout the entire premium-paying period (although it may not always be a level amount). The death benefit is guaranteed, and the cash value amounts and interest earnings are also guaranteed.

Premiums on Whole Life Policies

There are two broad forms of premium structure in whole life insurance policies: (a) straight whole life policies, and (b) limited-payment whole life policies.

A straight whole life policy (also called an ordinary life policy) provides protection for the whole of life, with a level premium calculated on the assumption that it will be payable for the whole of life. While level premiums are the most common way to structure whole life premiums, one problem that is created by a level premium is that younger insureds, for example, recent college graduates, may not be able to afford the premiums. Many insurance companies offer modified whole life policies in which the premium can start off at a lower, level amount and then increase to a higher level amount a few years later (presumably when the insured has advanced in a career and has higher income). Another possibility is a graded policy in which the premium starts out low and gradually increases over a few years until it reaches a higher level amount. These policies are alternatives that provide permanent insurance without requiring a young insured to purchase term insurance (the lowest cost policy) and convert later.

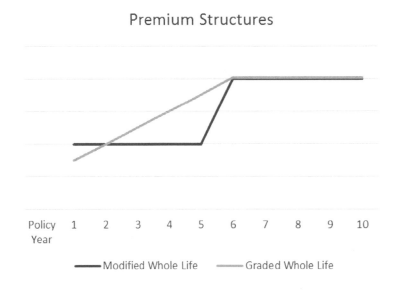

Premium Structures

Policy Year 1 2 3 4 5 6 7 8 9 10

Modified Whole Life   Graded Whole Life

Limited-pay whole life insurance is a form of whole life insurance with premiums payable only for a limited number of years; for example, a 20-pay whole life policy would be paid up after 20 level, annual premium payments have been made. Another common example is a to-age-65 policy, where premiums cease at age 65. With this kind of policy, a policyowner can avoid premium payments during retirement. The policy becomes a paid-up policy at the end of the stipulated premium-paying period. Thus, protection is provided for the whole of life, but premiums are paid for only a limited period. Since fewer premium payments are made, each premium will be a higher dollar amount than with straight life.

The most extreme form of limited-pay policy is the single-premium whole life (SPWL) policy in which only one, large payment is made, and no further premiums are due even though the policy provides coverage no matter how long the insured lives. The single premium is the amount a policyowner would pay to have the policy fully paid at issue date. When market rates of interest are high, the payment of a single premium can be an attractive investment because the cash value will earn a higher rate of interest and the earnings grow tax deferred inside the policy. Unfortunately, the favorable tax treatment of lifetime benefits for traditional whole life insurance has been lost with SPWL policies, because they will always be treated by the IRS as modified endowment contracts (MECs), as discussed in detail in Topic 28B of this textbook. The death benefit, however, remains free of federal income taxes.

Cash Values

As mentioned previously, the policyowner pays premiums higher than the actual amount needed to cover the mortality costs in the early years of a whole life policy, creating a cash reserve that will earn interest. Premiums paid to the insurance company for whole life (and universal life) policies are invested in the life insurance company's general account. This general account provides the money to pay the guaranteed death benefit and guaranteed cash values.

The investment income earned on the policy's cash value helps to keep the annual premium low (or zero) in the later years. The growth in the cash value is tax deferred.

Whole life policies are designed such that the cash value will equal the death benefit amount when the policy matures at age 121 (or age 100 for older policies). In effect, at that point, the insurance company will no longer have a net amount at risk, because the cash value will have fully funded the death benefit.

Prior to the time that the policy matures, the policy's cash value may be obtained by the policyowner by way of loans. Borrowing from the cash value has the advantage of not requiring loan underwriting, and the interest rate is typically very low. The disadvantage is that if the insured dies while loans are outstanding, the death benefit will be reduced to cover the loans.

The amount of cash value available for loans will be stated in the policy. Typically, no loan is available in the first 2 or 3 years due to the high cost of issuing the policy and the inadequate time for recovering those costs. The amount available for loan will depend on the policy provisions and will vary based on the type of policy.

Advantages and Disadvantages of Whole Life Policies

Whole life insurance offers the following advantages:

- It provides permanent protection. The policy never has to be renewed or converted.

- It provides permanent protection at the smallest initial outlay. A level premium for a straight whole life policy is lower than that for any other permanent policy. Of course, the limited-payment whole life policies require higher premiums than the straight whole life policies.

- It combines savings with protection. The premiums exceed the cost of insurance in the early years, so cash value accumulates in the policy.

- It provides substantial flexibility. After maturity, the proceeds may be distributed under one of the various settlement options provided in the policy. Before maturity, a policyowner may borrow the cash values as a premium loan or for an emergency fund; or the policyowner may surrender the policy and accept one of the nonforfeiture options discussed later in this topic on page 28.33, or the cash surrender value may be used to purchase an annuity.

- The cash value can be used as collateral for credit purposes. The policy may be pledged for a loan or held as security for payment.

- The permanent protection and its guarantees make whole life insurance a good funding source for special needs trusts. For example, parents of a child with Down Syndrome might establish such a trust for the care of their child after the parents have passed away.

Whole life insurance may have the following disadvantages:

- The payment of premiums can extend over a long period of time. For a straight whole life policy, the premiums are calculated on the assumption that they are payable for the lifetime of the insured. In addition, the premium is initially higher than for a term policy. Limited-payment policies do not always solve the problem of the extended premium-paying years because the higher premium may make the policy unaffordable.

- During periods of inflation, the cash values tend to lose purchasing power. Whole life policies share with other permanent life insurance policies the limitation that there is generally no hedge against inflation.

Practice Question

Which of the following statements concerning a whole life insurance policy is correct?

    A. The premium increases annually as the age of the insured increases.
    B. The policy may be surrendered for its cash value only on premium payment dates.
    C. The policy provides permanent protection and never has to be renewed or converted.
    D. As the policy's cash value increases, the face amount of the policy payable declines.

Answer:
The premium remains level for the entire premium-paying period, often the lifetime of the insured, so A is not a correct statement. The policy may be surrendered for its cash value at any time, so B is not a correct statement. D is not a correct statement because the face amount of the policy does not change as the policy's cash value increases.
The answer is C.

VARIABLE LIFE INSURANCE

Variable life products are insurance policies that invest the cash value into a securities portfolio similar to a mutual fund. The owner's rate of return, therefore, varies according to the performance of the underlying portfolio. Although the cash value will fluctuate based on investment returns, the death benefit is still guaranteed. Thus, variable life products are hybrids: part insurance and part security.

The primary benefit of a variable life product is a potentially higher rate of return than more conservative investments, such as bonds or the insurance company's general account. The primary risk of variable life products is that the actual rate of return may, in fact, be lower than that of standard insurance policies.

Separate Accounts

As with variable annuities (discussed in topic 27), variable life insurance policies require that the insurance company invest the policyowner's cash value in a separate account, rather than in the company's general investment account. The funds in this separate account are then invested into various subaccounts similar to mutual funds, each separately managed, and each with a specific investment objective. This separate account requirement is the primary characteristic that differentiates variable products from traditional fixed insurance products.

Since variable products invest in separate accounts similar to mutual funds, the variable products are regulated by the SEC as securities. Variable products must be registered like other securities, and representatives who sell them must be registered with FINRA.

Inflation Hedge

Variable life insurance provides for the policy's death benefit to vary with the investment experience of the separate account maintained by the insurer, but there is always a guaranteed minimum amount. For example, a policy may have a guaranteed minimum death benefit of $100,000, and if the subaccounts perform well, the death benefit can increase.

In the early years of variable life insurance, the investments available were primarily common stocks and other equities. It was hoped that common stock prices would increase as inflation increased, and hopefully, the death benefit would increase as the family's need for life insurance protection increased. During the 1970s, however, inflation increased, but common stock prices did not increase. Today, most companies issuing variable life policies offer the policyowner several investment options. At a minimum, most companies make at least three different separate accounts available: (a) a common stock fund, (b) a bond fund, and (c) a money market fund; although most policies offer many more than three choices. The policyowner may elect to allocate the policy's cash value among the available funds in any desired proportion.

Advantages and Disadvantages of Variable Life Insurance

Variable life insurance offers the following advantages:

- To the extent the growth of the investments in the separate accounts keep up or exceeds the rate of inflation, the insured has protection against the risk of living costs increasing.

- Variable life provides the policy owner with a choice of investments as compared to conventional whole life, which is funded primarily by fixed-dollar investments (for example, bonds and real estate mortgages).

Variable life insurance may have the following disadvantages:

- The cost may be higher than for conventional whole life policies because of the increased administrative expense and the additional regulatory requirements imposed by the SEC and FINRA.

- There is no guarantee of a minimum investment yield as promised under conventional whole life policies; therefore, variable life insurance would not be appropriate for the insurance buyer who wants specific and guaranteed future cash values. (However, variable life policies do guarantee a minimum death benefit, which is usually the initial face amount.)

Regulation of Variable Life Insurance

Because variable life insurance is both insurance and investment, it is regulated by both the state insurance departments and the federal government. Agents selling variable life insurance must hold both a life insurance license and a FINRA (series 6 or 7) license, and will be required to deliver a prospectus to the client at or before the time of sale. The prospectus contains a variety of information about the policy, including administrative charges and other fees, state premium taxes, surrender charges (which typically apply for 10 to 15 years), and information about the subaccount portfolios such as investment choices, objectives, historical performance, restrictions on investments, and other relevant information.

In addition to these rules, those licensed agents who are also Certified Financial Planners™ must disclose to clients any commissions or 12b-1 fees that they or their firm may receive upon the sale of a variable life insurance policy.

Practice Question

Which of the following statements concerning variable life insurance is (are) correct?

(1) The cash surrender values vary according to investment experience.
(2) The death benefit will not vary with investment experience.

    A. (1) only
    B. (2) only
    C. Both (1) and (2)
    D. Neither (1) nor (2)

Answer:
Cash value and death benefit will vary with the investment experience of the separate accounts in variable life insurance. These two characteristics help define variable life insurance.
The answer is A.

UNIVERSAL LIFE INSURANCE

Universal life (UL) insurance is a flexible premium life insurance policy that permits the policy owner to vary premium payments within limits and change the death benefit from time to time. If the policyowner wants to increase the death benefit, satisfactory evidence of continued insurability will need to be provided to the insurer.

The popularity of universal life is due not only to its flexible payment feature but also to its offering permanent insurance at premiums that are typically much less for young families than the premiums on whole life. The flexible premium payments allow the owner to pay in more in some years and less in other years, and even skip payments altogether in some years. For example, owners might pay in extra premiums prior to their children reaching college age, then stop all premiums during years the kids are in college, then start paying again after the children have graduated and are no longer dependents. The policyowner may not, however, pay more in dollars in a given year than the maximum the insurer establishes for that year. The reason for this rule is to prevent the policyowner from paying in too much money and thus running afoul of the government's rule concerning a reasonable relationship between the policy's death benefit and the accumulation fund. In other words, the government requires that there always be some insurance aspect to the policy, so the insurance company has to make sure that policy owners don't "overfund" the cash value to the point where there is no longer a net amount at risk to the insurance company.

Unbundling the Elements of the Policy

Universal life "unbundles" the life insurance product, meaning that the cash value and death benefit are separated. This unbundling makes the universal life policy more transparent than the whole life policy because a policyowner is shown the cost for mortality charges and expenses, as well as the rate at which cash value accumulates. These elements are not shown in "bundled" contracts such as whole life policies. With a whole life policy, the policyowner pays a fixed premium, and the cash values increase at a guaranteed schedule, so the insurer does not show the mortality charges, expenses, or interest rate credited on cash value. Variable life and variable universal contracts are similarly "unbundled."

With a universal life policy, a fixed percentage of the gross premium is allocated to the insurer's expenses. The remainder is credited to the policy's cash value. Interest is added to the cash value monthly at money market rates of interest, and the cash value is reduced by the charges for mortality costs. Interest credited depends on the insurer's investment success, but typically has a low guaranteed minimum (such as 2%). Because of variations in the insurer's investment results, it is not possible to predict actual future cash values.

The separation of the various pieces of the policy is what allows the flexibility in a universal life policy. After the first year, the policy owner can pay in more or less in premiums, because as long as there is an adequate cash value, the mortality and expense fees can still be paid from the policy. Unbundling also allows the cash value to be accessed by way of withdrawals, rather than just through loans.

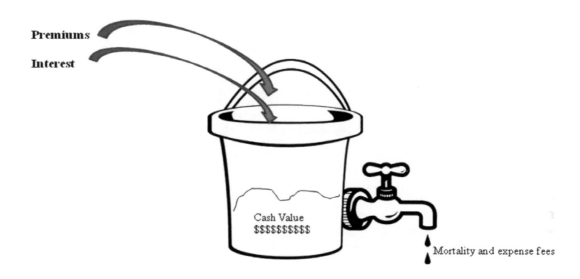

Withdrawals from life insurance policies that are not modified endowment contracts (MECs) are taxed on a first-in-first-out basis. In other words, when there is a withdrawal, a tax-free return of premium occurs first, then after all premium dollars have been withdrawn, earnings come out and are taxed as ordinary income. Policyowners are still permitted to take loans from universal life policies, and these loans are not taxable as well.

Flexible Death Benefits

This unbundling of the elements of the universal life policy also allows for flexibility in the death benefit. Universal policies have been developed with different designs so this flexibility can be provided in different ways.

Under one design of UL, a level death benefit is provided until the policy's cash value exceeds this amount, at which point the death benefit increases. This policy works similarly to a whole life policy in that the cash value becomes part of the death benefit, gradually reducing the insurance company's net amount at risk. For example, if the original death benefit is $100,000 and the cash value has grown to $30,000, the insurance company's net amount at risk is only $70,000. As a result the mortality cost, or cost of insurance, will be reduced. These policies may be referred to as Type I or Type A policies. Clients seeking to grow cash value as quickly as possible would choose this form of death benefit.

Under a second design of UL policy (Type II or Type B), the death benefit is a minimum level amount plus the policy's increasing cash value. Because the insurer's net amount at risk is constant, the mortality expense will continuously increase with age. For example, in a Type II policy with an original death benefit of $100,000 and a cash value that has grown to $30,000, the death benefit is $130,000, and the policy owner will still be paying mortality fees on the original $100,000 of insurance protection. For this policy, the cash value will grow more slowly than in the Type I policy because the mortality costs are not declining. A Type II policy, then, is a better choice for someone who is less concerned about building cash value, and more concerned about increasing the death benefit amount.

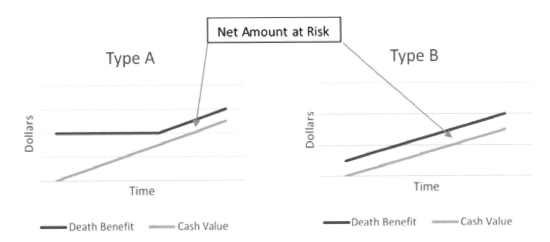

Advantages and Disadvantages of Universal Life Insurance

Universal life insurance may be used for the same purposes as whole life insurance and other cash value policies. Universal life can have the following specific benefits:

- The policy's cash value earns interest on the basis of current market rates.

- As compared to non-life-insurance products, there is the advantage of tax-deferred investment income. This tax advantage has always been true for life insurance cash values, so the favorable tax treatment is not an innovation made possible by universal life. What is new is the larger cash value the policyowner can achieve by increasing the premium payments.

- Universal life provides the policyowner with considerable flexibility. After payment of the first premium, the policyowner can "coast" by skipping a payment now and then. The cost of the insurance protection and expenses are taken out of the policy's cash value.

- Cash value can be accessed through both withdrawals and loans.

Universal life insurance can have the following disadvantages:

- The universal life policyowner ends up with neither the most competitive insurance coverage nor the most competitive savings vehicle. The rate of return available in the money market may be less than could be earned by life companies using conventional life insurance company investments. Therefore, the future yield potential is uncertain.

- The flexibility of universal life also can be viewed as a limitation. With the flexible premium, the semi-compulsory form of saving that traditional whole life policies generate for policyowners is lost.

- It is possible that policyowners will be tempted to move from one insurer to another looking for higher rates of return.

VARIABLE UNIVERSAL LIFE INSURANCE

Variable universal life insurance (VUL) combines a standard universal life policy with the investment characteristics of variable life insurance. A variable universal life insurance policy, then, combines most of the flexibility features of universal life insurance with the investment flexibility of a variable life insurance policy. The flexibility features available to the owners of variable universal life insurance include: (a) premium payment flexibility after the first year, (b) choice of either a level death benefit or an increasing death benefit, (c) partial withdrawals of cash at any time, (d) policy loan at any time, (e) choice of a limited number of portfolios as the investment vehicle, and (f) the right to switch cash values among the various investment portfolios without charge (Note: Some policies limit the number of changes permitted each calendar quarter or each year.).

As with variable life, variable universal life insurance is regulated as both an insurance product and an investment, requiring the agent to be both insurance licensed and FINRA (series 6 or 7) licensed. VUL policies are also sold with a prospectus and require disclosures by those who are CFP® professionals.

EXHIBIT 28 – 1 Comparing Types of Life Insurance			
Product	**Death Benefit**	**Premiums**	**Cash Value**
Term life (yearly renewable)	Fixed, level	Increase	None
Whole life (ordinary)	Fixed, level	Fixed, level	Guaranteed, fixed rate of accumulation
Universal life	Adjustable	Flexible	Rate of interest varies above minimum
Variable life	Adjustable	Fixed	Owner chooses among investments; no guarantee
Variable universal life	Adjustable	Flexible	Owner chooses among investments; no guarantee

ENDOWMENT LIFE INSURANCE

An endowment life insurance policy pays the named beneficiary the face amount at the insured's death, or it pays the policyowner the face amount at the end of a specified term of years. If the insured has not died by the end of the specified term, the policy's cash value is equal to the death benefit, and the policy reaches maturity.

An endowment policy is a high savings-investment contract that can be used for accumulating cash for any number of purposes, including a college education and a retirement fund, but endowment life insurance is high-cost protection per $1,000 of coverage.

Because endowments typically have a very large savings component in comparison with the protection component, the Tax Code views most endowments as savings instruments, not life insurance policies. Consequently, most endowments do not qualify for the same favorable tax treatment accorded other life insurance policies. Sales of endowment policies have been very limited since they lost their tax advantages in 1984. (See Topic 28B for more information on tax treatment.)

SURVIVORSHIP LIFE INSURANCE

A survivorship (second-to-die) life insurance policy pays the face amount only at the death of the second of two specified insureds, often spouses. The policy is useful: (a) for providing funds to pay the estate taxes on the estate of the second spouse to die; (b) as a way to conserve funds for one's children and grandchildren after the death of a husband and wife; and (c) as a way of transferring property to a charity after the death of the second spouse. A survivorship life policy may be written as a term life, whole life, universal life, or variable universal life policy.

The underwriting of a second-to-die policy looks at the health of both insureds, but more weight is given to the mortality outlook on the healthiest of the two insureds since the policy does not pay until the second death. A spouse who is borderline as to insurability may be able to acquire second-to-die insurance when other coverage would not be available. Of course, if the healthier spouse is still alive when the unhealthy spouse dies, no death benefit will be paid, so it does not provide income for the surviving spouse. It can, however, provide for children or grandchildren after both spouses have died, or provide funding for special interests, such as creating an endowment in the name of both spouses.

> *"Not having to worry about money is almost like not having to worry about dying."* – **Mario Puzo**

Details of estate planning are beyond the scope of this textbook; however, we want to mention the importance of survivorship life in estate planning. Many estate plans are designed so no estate taxes will be paid upon the first spouse's death, and these taxes are deferred until the second spouse's death. This kind of planning makes survivorship life insurance an ideal policy to fund payment of estate taxes at the second spouse's death.

THE LIFE INSURANCE CONTRACT

In order for financial planners to help clients understand how their policies work and what the potential benefits are, planners will need to know about policy provisions.

Declarations Page

As mentioned in Topic 22 of this textbook, the declarations page of the policy is a good place to look for an outline of the most pertinent information regarding the policy. The declarations page will typically include all of the following information:

- The name of the insurance company
- The name of the owner of the policy
- The name of the insured
- The policy number
- The date of issue
- The face amount of the policy
- The name of the beneficiary
- The type of insurance (for example, term or whole life)
- A statement about the free-look provision (the owner typically has 10 days to review the policy and return it for a full refund of premium if she does not wish to keep the policy)

An example of a declarations page from a life insurance policy can be found in Appendix B of this textbook.

Contractual Provisions

Some policy provisions are required by state law, while other provisions are considered optional.

Most life insurance policies include the following provisions:

- Insuring agreement – Payment of the face amount of the policy will be made upon receipt of proof of the insured's death.

- Entire contract – This provision states that the policy and the application attached to the policy and any riders constitute the entire contract between the parties. In other words, parol evidence (extrinsic evidence) may not be introduced to show that the terms of the policy are other than as written.

- Effective date – Life insurance policies can be backdated to take advantage of lower rates at a younger age. Backdating usually does not exceed six months and requires payment of premiums back to that date.

- Ownership – The applicant, the insured, and the policyowner of a life insurance policy can be different persons. The ownership clause in a life insurance policy states that the person designated as the owner has the right to assign or transfer the policy, receive the policy's cash value and dividends, and borrow against the policy's cash value. The purpose of the ownership clause in a life insurance policy is to make it clear who is the owner of the policy. The clause becomes important when someone other than the insured is the policyowner. The policyowner may be the beneficiary, or the owner may be the insured's business partner or anyone to whom the former policyowner elects to transfer the policy and its valuable rights.

- Premium payment – The more often the premium is paid during the year, the higher the premium that is payable per year. The insurer incurs expenses and loss of interest when premium payments are spread over the full year.

- Grace period – Coverage continues even if the premium payment is late, as long as the premium is paid within the 31-day grace period (for universal life policies with a flexible premium, the grace period may be 60 or 61 days). No reinstatement is necessary. If death occurs during the grace period, the overdue premium payment will be subtracted from the death benefit.

- Misstatement of age and sex – If an error of this kind is made, the life insurance policy will be adjusted to reflect the amount of coverage that the premium paid would have purchased at the correct age and sex.

- Incontestable clause – The incontestable clause is a provision required by law and stating that the insurer has only two years from the date of policy issue to challenge the validity of a life insurance policy. The purpose of the incontestable clause is to deny the life insurance company the right to contest the validity of a life insurance policy after a reasonable period of time when evidence to meet the contest may have disappeared or may be difficult to obtain. It would be unfair, for example, for the insurer to deny a widow's claim for the policy proceeds when the insured (who usually has the best knowledge of all the facts) is six feet underground and unable to assist in defeating the insurer's challenge. After the two year period has elapsed, the company cannot challenge the policy; however, the company can challenge the validity of a claim. For example, if death caused by flying a private plane is excluded, the insurer can deny payment of a death claim if death is caused by the excluded activity. There are also certain situations in which the incontestable clause will not apply because the policy is treated as being void from the time of its inception. For example, an insurer can contest a policy in the circumstances that the policy was purchased with the intent to murder the insured, the policy was lacking insurable interest at the inception of the policy, or the policy was obtained by fraudulent impersonation (e.g., the insured's healthy twin sister took the medical exam in place of the unhealthy insured).

- Suicide clause – The suicide clause provides that if the insured dies due to suicide, whether sane or insane, in the first one or two years after the policy is issued, the insurer's obligation will be simply to refund the premiums paid.

- Loan provisions – The policy will specify the terms applicable to policy loans. Without credit checks, the policyowner can borrow 90% to 100% of the cash value, and the interest rate that accrues on the borrowed funds can be a fixed rate or a variable rate. Technically, the insurer is permitted to delay lending for up to 6 months, but it is extremely uncommon for a delay to occur. There is no repayment schedule or requirement, and any unpaid interest is added to the loan balance. If the insured dies, the insurance company deducts the loan balance from any death benefit. If the policy is terminated, the loan is deducted from the cash surrender value.

- Automatic premium loan – With some whole life policies, the insurer gives a policyowner an automatic loan when the premium is delinquent. The policy will stay in force as long as the cash value can pay premiums. This provision may be particularly beneficial for policy owners who are developing dementia who may forget to make the premium payment, or for an owner experiencing significant health issues who is hospitalized or disabled for a period of time and forgets or is unable to make the premium payment.

- Assignment – Ownership of a life insurance policy may be transferred to someone else, even to a person who does not have an insurable interest in the life of the insured. The assignment provision states the conditions under which the insurance company will honor the assignment. The company must be informed of any assignment. It assumes no responsibility for the validity of the assignment. There are two types of assignment: absolute assignment and collateral assignment. In an absolute assignment, a policyowner transfers all control of and rights in the policy to a third party. Collateral assignment is a transfer of some ownership rights to provide security for a debt.

- Reinstatement – Due to the policy provision allowing reinstatement, a policyowner can revive a life insurance policy even after the grace period has expired and the premium has not been paid. Usually, for the insurer to reinstate the policy, all back premiums must be paid, and the insured must present proof of insurability. A policy surrendered for its cash value may not be reinstated except by special permission of the insurer.

- Exclusions – The usual exclusions in a life insurance policy are suicide and war. Suicide is usually excluded for only one or two years after inception of the policy to avoid the hazard of a person contemplating suicide when buying life insurance. War is sometimes excluded in policies newly issued to persons who are likely to be exposed to hostile action under war conditions. Life insurance policies issued during peace times do not exclude war-related deaths.

- Beneficiary designation – The policyowner may name anyone as beneficiary, even a person without an insurable interest. The policyowner has to decide whether the beneficiary designation will be revocable or irrevocable. A revocable designation may be changed at any time by the policyowner. An irrevocable designation may only be changed (or the policy assigned) with the consent of the beneficiary.

Practice Question

Victor Cartier's doctor told him that he most likely had only three years to live after his heart attack. Victor will sell his business and live comfortably on the income from his investments. Which of the following provisions of his whole life policy would be of most concern to Victor?

A. Incontestable clause
B. Reinstatement clause
C. Grace period
D. Misstatement of age

Answer:
The change in Victor's health will likely make him uninsurable, so Victor will not be able to reinstate the policy if it lapses for failure to pay premiums within the grace period. The change in his health does not affect the other provisions. *The answer is B.*

Designating Beneficiaries

Primary and Contingent

The primary beneficiary of a life insurance policy is the person or persons designated to receive the death benefit, but the right to the death benefit is lost if the primary beneficiary dies before the insured.

The contingent beneficiary of a life insurance policy is the person or persons designated to receive a life insurance policy's death benefit if the primary beneficiary dies prior to the death of the insured. Also, in the rare circumstance where the primary beneficiary murders the insured, most states have enacted slayer statutes that prohibit the primary beneficiary from receiving the death benefit, in which case the contingent beneficiary would then receive the policy proceeds.

Named Beneficiaries and Class Beneficiaries

Beneficiaries may be named individually or by class. Named beneficiaries are identified by their names. Class beneficiaries are not identified by name. For example, "grandchildren of the named insured" would be a class designation for the beneficiaries. In class beneficiary designations, it is sometimes difficult to ascertain whom the policyowner intended for beneficiaries, especially where the composition of the group has changed since the designation was made. There could also be questions as to how far-reaching the class is. For example: Does "my children" include step-children, or children given up for adoption? Because of the potential ambiguity, it is often advisable to name beneficiaries and to review them frequently. It is a good practice for a planner to include a review of beneficiaries during each annual review meeting with the client.

If class beneficiaries are used, they may be designated as *per capita* or *per stirpes*. *"Per stirpes"* means by the root or stock. *Per stirpes* distribution means the property passes to the issue as though their immediate ancestor had divided the property equally among them. For example, under *per stirpes* distribution, if a decedent's two children each had two children, the children would each receive one-half of the proceeds, and the grandchildren would receive nothing. If one of the decedent's children had died before the decedent, the two children of that predeceased child would share their parent's one-half interest. Thus, the two grandchildren would receive one-quarter of the proceeds, and the surviving child would receive one-half. *Per stirpes* is also called right of representation.

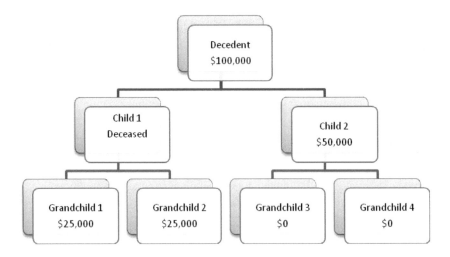

Per capita means "by the head" or by each person. Per capita distribution means all issue share equally regardless of their degree of relation. Thus, if a decedent is survived by only one of two children and by four grandchildren, the one child and four grandchildren would each take a one-fifth interest.

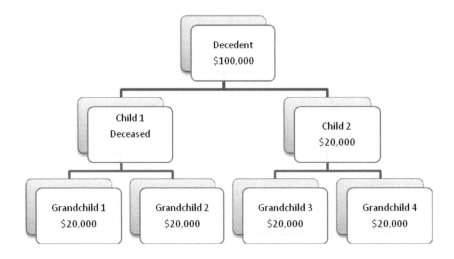

Revocable Versus Irrevocable Beneficiaries

A revocable beneficiary of a life insurance policy is the person designated to receive the death proceeds, but the policyowner retains the right to change the beneficiary designation at any time. The revocable beneficiary has a "mere expectancy." The policyowner is in full control. The revocable beneficiary, however, does acquire a full legal interest in the policy's death proceeds at the moment of the insured's death.

An irrevocable beneficiary designation cannot be altered by the policyowner without the permission of the beneficiary. The policyowner has relinquished the right to change the beneficiary designation, acquire a policy loan, surrender the policy, or assign the policy. In other words, the owner shares his or her ownership rights with the irrevocably designated beneficiary.

Common Disaster Clause

Most policies contain a common disaster clause which states that the primary beneficiary must survive the insured by a specified period, such as 60 or 90 days, in order to receive the policy proceeds. Otherwise, the policy proceeds will be paid as though the primary beneficiary had died before the insured.

POLICY RIDERS

Riders are provisions or endorsements that are added to a life insurance policy in order to amend the policy. Riders may be used to increase or decrease benefits, waive a condition, or amend the original contract in some specific way. The terms "rider" and "endorsement" are synonymous. Riders that add benefits will typically have an additional premium cost associated with them. Presented below is a brief summary of the more common riders that may be added to life insurance policies.

- The waiver-of-premium rider stipulates that in the event the policyholder becomes totally and permanently disabled before some age, such as age 60 or age 70, premiums on the contract will be waived during the continuance of any disability that lasts beyond a specified period of time, usually six months. During the disability, the policy's death benefit will remain unchanged, and cash value can continue to grow.

- The double indemnity rider pays twice the policy's face amount if death is due to accident. It is favored by some because of its low premium and because of the relatively high probability of death from accidental causes in the younger years, as compared to natural causes. Those who oppose the provision argue that double indemnity is not a wise purchase because one is gambling on the cause of death. The probability of death from an accident is very low, even at the younger ages. One's family is really not going to need twice as much in death benefit if one dies as a result of an accident rather than from natural causes.

- The guaranteed insurability option or guaranteed purchase option gives the policyowner the right to buy additional specified amounts of insurance at specified dates or events, without the insured having to prove insurability. A typical option permits the insured to purchase additional life insurance at three-year intervals, beginning with the policy anniversary nearest his or her age 25 and terminating with the anniversary nearest his or her age 40. The amount obtainable at each specified anniversary may be limited to the face of the original policy or a smaller set dollar amount, such as $10,000. The inclusion of this option makes sense for a young family likely to have additional children, or for a family whose future income can be expected to rise considerably. Where the needs and the premium-paying capacity of the family are expected to increase, the use of the guaranteed purchase option makes sense.

- A long-term care (LTC) rider may be added to some life insurance policies for an additional premium. This rider commits the insurer to a daily, weekly, or monthly dollar benefit for long-term care if the insured is unable to perform a specific number (two or three) of the activities of daily living (ADLs). (Additional information on life insurance with long-term care riders can be found in Topic 26 of this textbook).

- Accelerated death benefits may be provided by riders to life insurance policies, or they may be included in the policy without additional premium charge. The benefit is a discounted value of the life insurance policy's death benefit, payable in the event of certain contingencies other than death. Among the contingencies are terminal illness (typically defined as an illness where death is expected within one or two years), the insured's contracting one of a listed group of dread diseases, or the insured's taking up permanent residence in a nursing home.

Practice Question

If a whole life policy has a waiver-of-premium rider and the policyholder becomes disabled, which of the following statements are correct?

(1) The insurance company will pay the full amount of the premium.
(2) The cash value is frozen at the time the insured becomes disabled.
(3) The death benefit remains the same.
(4) The death benefit will be partially taxable due to the insurance company paying the premium.

    A. (1) and (2) only
    B. (1) and (3) only
    C. (2) and (3) only
    D. (3) and (4) only

Answer:
With a whole life policy that has a waiver-of-premium rider, the insurance company will pay the entire premium in the event of the policyholder's disability. The death benefit remains the same. The death benefit is not taxable as a result, and cash value can continue to increase.
The answer is B.

DIVIDENDS

If a life insurance contract is a "participating policy", a portion of the premium may be returned to the policyowner in the form of a dividend. The amount of the dividends will depend on the insurance company's earnings for the year. Because they are a return of premiums paid, dividends are not taxable income to the policyowner.

Dividend Options

Life insurance policy dividends payable under participating policies may be taken in cash, applied toward the payment of the policy's current premium, applied to the purchase of paid-up additions to the policy, left on deposit with the insurance company to accumulate at interest, or used to purchase term insurance.

The cash option would be an advantage over the other options when the family anticipates that it will have need of the funds and does not need additional life insurance.

The premium payment option is an advantage when the family wishes to have its life insurance at the lowest possible cash outlay and believes that it helps the family's budgetary process to have part of the premium paid through the use of policy dividends.

The use of dividends to purchase additional units of life insurance is an advantage when the family believes it needs additional life insurance. The additional insurance is acquired at net cost (no loading for expenses) with significant savings realized for the family and without the need to provide evidence of insurability.

The use of the dividend deposit option (also called the accumulate at interest option) is an advantage when the family wishes to build an emergency fund or a savings fund for an unscheduled purpose and believes that the discipline of the annual withholding of the dividends would be appropriate.

The use of the dividend to purchase term insurance (sometimes called the fifth dividend option) allows the purchase of additional death benefits under a term insurance policy. The term insurance available is usually equal to the policy's cash value. The fifth dividend option is an advantage if the policy's cash value is borrowed for any purpose. Finally, the family may use the option to increase the amount of life insurance protection, whether the cash value has been borrowed or not.

Some insurance policies in the past had been described as "vanishing premium" policies based on the premise that at some point the expected dividends would be high enough to cover the cost of all remaining premiums for the life of the policy. This language is no longer permitted to be used in illustrations where the dividend payments are not guaranteed.

INTEREST CREDITING METHODS

Inasmuch as interest credits are a significant factor affecting the cost of life insurance, it is important to understand how interest is computed by the insurer for the effect it will have on dividends and a policy's cash value. Two of the most common interest crediting methods are:

- Portfolio method – Here, the rate used is based on that earned by the insurer on its overall assets or a specified subdivision thereof.

- Investment generation ("new money") method – Here, the rate used is based on the rate earned by the insurer on those assets or a specified subdivision thereof that were invested or reinvested in the most recent year or the most recent specified number of years.

It can be seen, then, that if interest rates have been rising, the new money rate will exceed the portfolio rate. The reverse is true if interest rates have been declining.

It may also be important to understand whether the rate being used is a gross rate or a net rate. Among the elements subtracted from the gross rate to derive the net rate are investment expenses, income taxes, and other expense charges. Further, it may be important to understand whether capital gains of the insurer (realized, unrealized, or both) are included in the interest rate. Other considerations of importance are whether different interest rates are used by the insurer for new vs. old policies of a particular type, for policies of different types, and for encumbered vs. unencumbered portions of the policy's savings element (in other words, if part of the cash value has been borrowed by way of a policy loan, there may be a different interest rate credited to that portion of the cash value). Also of importance in policy illustrations is the matter of how the interest being used compares with the rate actually earned by the insurer in recent years.

NONFORFEITURE OPTIONS

Nonforfeiture options refer to the alternative ways that a policyowner may receive the policy's cash value upon surrender of the policy. The term "nonforfeiture" means that the policyowner does not give up or forfeit the policy's cash value if he or she elects to terminate the policy on some date prior to death. The following nonforfeiture options are available for the cash value of life insurance policies:

(1)   Lump sum payable in cash. The standard nonforfeiture law requires that a surrender value be made available in cash, but the law also permits a company to delay or postpone payment of the policy's cash value for a period of six months after surrender of the policy. Insurers almost never delay payments for this period.

(2)   Paid-up policy of a reduced amount. In lieu of obtaining the surrender value in cash, the policy owner may elect to receive a reduced amount of paid-up life insurance that will pay a death benefit under the same conditions as the face amount of the original policy.

(3)   Paid-up extended term insurance. The amount of the term insurance will be the same as the face amount of the original contract, but the period of coverage will be only for the time span found in a printed table in the policy, and is determined by the attained age of the insured and the magnitude of the cash value.

Orignal Policy was $100,000

Practice Question

Which of the following statements concerning the nonforfeiture options with a whole life policy is correct?

  A. The insurance company must pay the insured the cash value promptly upon request.
  B. The policy will automatically make a loan to pay any delinquent premium.
  C. The policy will provide extended term insurance in the same face amount as the original policy.
  D. The policy will provide a paid-up life policy in the face amount of the original policy.

Answer:

The nonforfeiture option to pay the cash surrender value will allow the insurer to delay the payment for up to 6 months. The automatic premium loan is not a nonforfeiture provision. The nonforfeiture provisions include the extended term option, which will provide term insurance in the face amount of the original policy. The nonforfeiture provision for a paid-up life policy will be for an amount less than the face amount of the original policy.

The answer is C.

SETTLEMENT OPTIONS

Settlement options determine how the proceeds of the policy will be distributed upon the death of the insured. The usual choices available to the beneficiaries are: (1) to have the proceeds paid in a lump sum, (2) to have the proceeds distributed as periodic income of some fixed amount for as long as the capital sum and investment income permit, (3) to have the proceeds distributed over a fixed number of months or years, (4) to have the proceeds invested by the insurance company and receive just the earnings on the account until the beneficiary elects to have the proceeds distributed (commonly called the interest only option), and (5) to have the proceeds annuitized to be paid as a life income to the beneficiary, perhaps with a minimum period certain or refund feature, as discussed in topic 27 of this textbook.

EXHIBIT 28 – 2
Life Insurance Policy Options

Nonforfeiture Options	Settlement Options	Dividend Options
-Cash surrender	-Lump-sum cash	-Cash
-Paid-up permanent policy	-Fixed-amount installments	-Reduced premium
(reduced death benefit)	-Fixed-period installments	-Accumulate at interest
-Extended term policy	-Interest only	-Paid-up additions
	- Annuity options (straight, refund, period certain)	-1-year term insurance

---

Practice Question

Which of the following is a settlement option for a whole life insurance policy?

    A. Interest-only
    B. Accumulate at interest
    C. Paid-up additions
    D. Paid-up reduced amount

Answer:
Accumulate at interest and paid-up additions are dividend options. Paid-up reduced amount is the nonforfeiture option of permanent life insurance with a reduced death benefit. The interest-only option is a settlement option.
The answer is A.

POLICY ILLUSTRATIONS

A policy illustration is a projection of the financial results that can be achieved with a life insurance policy. The projection is often based on assumptions about premium payments, investment earnings, and dividends. Generally, illustrations help to educate applicants on how a life insurance policy will work, and these illustrations are typically the main source of financial information provided to applicants concerning a new policy.

Multiple-year policy illustration sheets are almost always used in the sale of large amounts of permanent life insurance. When properly used, policy illustrations can help a prospective purchaser understand how complex life insurance policies work. Illustrations can also help to demonstrate how sensitive a policy is to changes in such cost factors as mortality, expenses, and interest.

There are many kinds of policy illustrations. Illustrations often have several columns showing the policy year, annual premium, cash values, and death benefit. Usually, each policy year is shown on a separate line for 10 or 20 years and at key ages, such as ages 60, 65, and 70. Illustrations may show dividends and may make projections using dividends to buy paid-up additions or to reduce future premium payments. Some illustrations compare different policies, but illustrations are not an adequate way to compare costs. Since illustrations can make use of different assumptions, the projections are not always accurate for purposes of comparisons among policies.

Policy illustrations can be misused in the life insurance sales process to mislead prospective purchasers. One such misuse is to compare, without adjusting for the time value of money, amounts to be paid by the policyowner in one or more time periods, with amounts to be received by the policyowner in one or more other time periods. Another misuse is to base the illustration on overly optimistic (or undisclosed) assumptions concerning future mortality and expense charges and interest credits or the future marginal federal income tax bracket of the policyowner. A third misuse of policy illustrations arises when policy values that are not guaranteed by the insurer are not clearly differentiated from those that are guaranteed.

If an illustration assumes a tax rate, it should use a marginal tax rate that is the same as the applicant's. Illustrations based on tax rates differing greatly from the applicant's are misleading and could be deceptive sales practices.

The NAIC has adopted model regulations for life insurance illustrations that have been enacted in many states. These regulations do not apply to variable life or to annuities. The regulations require illustrations to include identifying information, and they require certain disclosures. In addition, the regulations prohibit insurers and agents from describing nonguaranteed items (such as dividends) in a way that implies that the items are guaranteed. They prohibit use of the term "vanishing premium" or a similar term that implies the policy will become paid up when a portion of future premiums are projected to be paid from nonguaranteed items. An illustration must also be accompanied by a summary describing the features and columns used. The summary must state that actual results may be more or less favorable than what is shown.

It is also worth noting that a planner reviewing existing life insurance policies owned by a client can (and should) have the client request an in-force policy illustration from the issuing insurance company. This illustration will allow the planner and client to monitor the performance of the policy versus what was expected, enabling them to correct any potential problems before they occur. For example, in a UL policy the interest rates actually earned may be less than originally expected, requiring additional premium payments to be made.

POLICY REPLACEMENT

Replacement of one life insurance policy with another, whether with the same or a different insurer, often works to the disadvantage of the policyowner. The disadvantages of replacement include the fact that the policyowner again has to pay the high first-year expenses of the new policy through a policy fee, reduced or no dividends for a period of time, and reduced or no nonforfeiture values for a time. Other disadvantages include the fact that the incontestability clause and the suicide clause begin running anew. A further disadvantage is that the premium for the new policy, which is based on the insured's attained age, may be higher than that for the old policy, whose premium is probably based on an earlier attained age. A major advantage of policy replacement inures to the replacing agent, inasmuch as he or she is eligible for a high first-year commission.

Policy replacements have often been based on deception on the part of the replacing agent. When this is the case, replacement is called "twisting," a practice that is illegal in every state.

In recent years, however, policy replacements sold honestly have sometimes proven to be in the best interests of the policyowner. Due to higher interest rates and improved mortality experience, as well as sometimes more liberal policy wording, a policyowner may be in a better position under a new policy than under the one it replaces.

Most states regulate policy replacements in order to protect consumers against unfair treatment by insurers and agents. The regulations usually require the following:

- Disclosure by the agent to his or her insurer as to whether the policy being applied for will replace another policy.

- Notification by the agent to the applicant of the importance of comparing carefully the benefits and costs of the new and old policy, perhaps by consulting with the original selling agent or insurer.

- Notification to the original insurer stating that a policy replacement is being considered by its policyowner and providing information about the proposed new policy.

- Notice by the replacing insurer to the policyowner of a 20-day "free-look" period to examine the new policy without penalty.

- Delivery by the original insurer or agent to the policyowner, within 20 days, of specified information about the old policy, prepared in accordance with the disclosure regulation.

VIATICAL SETTLEMENTS

If the insured does not meet the requirements for an accelerated death benefit but still needs money for medical or other costs, a viatical agreement may be appropriate and valuable. In a viatical settlement, a policyowner who is terminally ill or chronically ill transfers a life insurance policy to a third party for a lump-sum payment. The payment is determined by discounting the value of the death benefit to be paid when the insured dies, and the discounts can be substantial due to the uncertainty of projecting an insured's life expectancy. In most cases the offer is for only 50% to 85% of the face value.

A viatical settlement is typically provided by a company of investors who are referred to as the viatical settlement provider or the viatical company. The policyowner is the viator. The policyowner will assign the policy to the viatical company, and the viatical company will collect the death benefit at the insured's death. Since there is no requirement of an insurable interest at the time of the assignment or at the insured's death, the viatical company is able to collect the policy proceeds.

Viatical Settlement or Accelerated Benefits

Typically, a viatical settlement is sought by a policyowner who cannot obtain accelerated benefits from the insurance company. For example, a policyowner with AIDS or similar disease may have need of the money during his or her lifetime to pay for medical expenses or special treatment. Many insurance policies offer accelerated benefits when an insured is diagnosed with a terminal illness, and such accelerated benefits will generally be more advantageous for the policyowner than a viatical settlement. An insured who is chronically, but not terminally, ill may not be eligible to receive benefits under an accelerated benefit rider, however, making the viatical settlement a suitable option.

Generally, there are no restrictions on the use that a policyowner may make of accelerated benefits or of the proceeds of a viatical settlement (although some restrictions may apply under viatical settlements for chronically, rather than terminally, ill insureds in order to receive proceeds free of tax).

Practice Question

Which of the following statements describes a viatical settlement?

- A. The policyowner settles a lawsuit against the insurer for damages from cancellation of a life policy.
- B. The policyowner obtains accelerated benefits under a life policy due to a terminal illness.
- C. The policyowner who had no insurable interest in the insured's life obtains payment of a death benefit.
- D. The policyowner who has a terminal illness assigns a life policy to a third party for a lump-sum payment.
- E. The policyowner who receives accelerated benefits from a life policy for chronic illness excludes the payments from income.

Answer:

In a viatical settlement, a policyowner who is terminally ill or chronically ill transfers a life insurance policy to a third party for a lump-sum payment. The payment of accelerated benefits by an insurance company to an insured who is chronically or terminally ill is not a viatical settlement. While a viatical settlement and accelerated benefits can be excluded from income, this income tax rule is not the definition of a viatical settlement.

The answer is D.

Tax Rules – Sec. 101(g)

Under Section 101(g) of the Code, accelerated benefits and payments from a viatical settlement are treated as though the benefits were paid by reason of the death of the insured. Since death benefits from life insurance are generally received free of income tax, the accelerated benefits and viatical settlement will also be received income-tax-free. It should be noted, however, that in order for a viatical settlement to be tax-free, the purchase of the policy must be made by a "qualified viatical settlement provider". To be a qualified viatical settlement provider, the company must meet several rules including being licensed in the state in which the insured resides and following certain provisions of the NAIC's Viatical Settlement Model Act. Section 5 of the Model Act sets forth standards of evaluation for reasonable payments under the viatical settlement as shown in the chart below.

Insured's Life Expectancy	Minimum Percentage of Face Value (less outstanding loans) received by the viator
Less than 6 months	80%
6 - 12 months	70%
12 - 18 months	65%
18 - 25 months	60%
25 months or longer	Greater of cash surrender value or accelerated death benefit available in the policy

Companies that are not qualified viatical settlement providers may offer substantially less than these amounts. Qualified companies will use these as minimum guidelines, but the actual offer may vary among companies. A policyowner considering a viatical settlement should obtain quotes from several companies before making a decision.

The benefits received from sale to a qualified viatical company during the insured's lifetime are tax-free under the following conditions:

- The insured is terminally ill; or
- The insured is chronically ill.

A person is terminally ill if a physician certifies that the individual has an illness or condition that can reasonably be expected to result in death in 24 months or less.

A person is chronically ill if within the past 12 months, a health care practitioner has certified that the individual has been unable to perform, without substantial assistance, at least two activities of daily living for at least 90 days. A person is also chronically ill if substantial supervision is required to protect that person from threats to health and safety due to cognitive disability. For chronically ill insureds, the advance on the death benefit is tax free to the extent such payment is used for costs incurred by the payee (that are not compensated for by insurance or otherwise) for qualified long-term care services provided for the insured.

The accelerated benefits and viatical settlement are income-tax-free, not only to an insured, but also to a policyowner who is not an insured, such as where a spouse or family member owns the policy. If a policy is transferred for value, as it will be to a viatical provider, the gain obtained by the viatical company will be subject to income tax under the transfer-for-value rules (to be discussed in Topic 28B of this textbook).

> ☞ **K Study Tip** – **The same income tax rules apply to accelerated benefits paid by a life insurance company and to the payment from a qualified viatical settlement company. In either case, the policyowner can be eligible for the income tax exclusion.**

If an insured receives accelerated benefits and then lives beyond the 24 months, the insured does not then become subject to income tax liability on the benefits. The terminal illness or chronic illness condition need only be satisfied at the time of payment to the policyowner.

Planning

Most insurance policies offer accelerated benefits when death is expected within 12 months, although some may be shorter, such as 6 months, and others may be longer, such as 24 months. The income tax laws provide the exclusion of benefits from income for payments where life expectancy is 24 months or less. Viatical settlement providers may be willing to enter into a viatical settlement where life expectancy is longer than 24 months. A viatical settlement, therefore, may be appropriate for an insured who has a terminal illness, but who is expected to live longer than 24 months and who will need the money for medical or other expenses, or for an insured who is chronically, rather than terminally, ill.

In cases where the accelerated death benefit is limited, such as 50% of the death benefit amount, a combination of the accelerated benefit and sale to a qualified viatical company may yield additional income. For example, a client with a life expectancy of 12 months who has a policy with a $100,000 death benefit that is limited to 50% payout for accelerated benefits could take the full $50,000 of accelerated benefits, leaving a remaining death benefit of $50,000. With a life expectancy of 12 months, the viatical company may offer to pay the insured 70% of the remaining $50,000 death benefit.

Before deciding on a viatical settlement, the policyowner should also keep in mind that the policy death benefits will no longer be available to fund the goal for which the policy was originally purchased. The viatical settlement is usually the choice of last resort when all other sources of income have been exhausted.

🔑 KEY SUMMARY 28 – 1
Comparison of Viatical Settlements and Accelerated Benefits

	Viatical settlements	*Accelerated Benefits*
▪ Who pays policyowner?	Third-party purchaser	Insurance company
▪ What is paid to policyowner?	Portion of death benefit	Portion of death benefit
▪ Who receives death benefit?	Third-party purchaser	Beneficiary
▪ What is tax treatment?	Benefits are tax-free if insured is terminally or chronically ill; transfer-for-value rule applies to viatical company	Benefits are tax-free if insured is terminally or chronically ill
▪ What are limiting factors?	Payment received may be low in comparison to the death benefit amount; death benefit is no longer available to support dependents after death of the insured	Only for insured expected to die in 6 to 24 months; death benefit is no longer available to support dependents after death of the insured

---

Ethical Issues

Insurance companies and regulators have been concerned about viatical settlements due to the lack of insurable interest of the viatical company and due to the increased risk that insureds will be the targets of foul play. Moreover, insureds need to be advised that once a policy is transferred in a viatical settlement, they will have no control over subsequent transfers. Some state laws require viatical companies to advise potential viators that they may be able to obtain accelerated benefits from their own insurer. Investors who participate in viatical companies need to be warned that the investment in viatical settlements is highly speculative.

OTHER STRATEGIC USES OF LIFE INSURANCE

Due to the ability to leverage premium dollars (a small premium buys a large death benefit), life insurance has many strategic uses. We will briefly mention a few of the more frequently used strategies here, although numerous others exist.

Pension Maximization

At retirement, clients who have a pension available through their employer will be asked to choose a form of distribution for the pension. Qualified retirement plan rules will require the selection of a joint-and-last-survivor annuity if the client is married, unless the spouse signs a waiver allowing for another payout selection. The joint-and-survivor annuity ensures that a surviving spouse is not left destitute at the death of the retired worker.

A joint and survivor annuity for two spouses will provide less monthly income, however, than a straight (or pure) life annuity for only one spouse. Alternatively, the male client might elect a straight (or pure) life annuity for himself (a male life will receive larger life income than a female per $1,000 invested). To protect his spouse, the client uses some of the increased monthly income to purchase life insurance on his own life to provide a life income for his spouse in case of premature death. The cost of the life insurance for a male client will obviously be a factor to consider carefully.

Installment Note Protection

A client retiring from a successful personal business may sell the business to a daughter, son, relative, or business associate in an installment sale where regular monthly payments are made over a period of years, rather than a single lump-sum. Monthly income is assured if the purchaser continues to live in good health. To protect this income, the business seller should buy both life insurance (term life to match the length of the installment note) and disability income insurance on the purchaser-debtor.

Charitable Giving

Clients who are charitably inclined often use life insurance to leverage donations to charities upon death. For example, a client who plans to make a bequest of $100,000 to a charity could use the $100,000 to purchase a single-premium life insurance policy providing a death benefit of 2 or more times that amount (depending on age and other underwriting factors). The increased death benefit could be used to increase the bequest to the charity, or could be used as wealth replacement (replacing the wealth left to the charity) for the family. Or, instead, a life policy with a $100,000 death benefit could be purchased for an amount less than $100,000, leaving additional assets for heirs.

Business Uses

Business uses of life insurance are discussed in detail in topic 29 of this textbook, but are outlined briefly here.

A closely held business is exposed to loss at the death of a valuable key person whose contribution to the success of the business will be difficult to replace. Purchase of a life insurance policy with the business as the beneficiary will decrease the financial strain on the business during the period of time it takes to hire and train a replacement, and can defray some of the costs of recruiting a new employee.

When a partner in a business dies, the remaining partners must liquidate the partnership and pay the estate the fair market value of the deceased partner's interest. Similarly, in a closely held corporation, a buyout of the deceased owner's business interest may be required to continue the business because the deceased owner's family has no interest in working in the business. Life insurance to fund a prearranged buy-sell agreement is ideal. The death that creates the need for the funds for the buyout provides the funds.

> **Class Discussion 28 – 1**
>
> Should clients purchase life insurance policies on their minor children?

LIFE INSURANCE AS AN EMPLOYEE BENEFIT

Group Term Life Insurance

In addition to individual life insurance, a large amount of life insurance is sold on a group basis. The most common form of group life insurance is group term life insurance. The coverage is based on yearly renewable term insurance, and it is the lowest-cost group life insurance. There is a master contract between the insurer and the employer, and the individual employees receive certificates evidencing their coverage.

Benefits must not discriminate in favor of "key employees" and must be based on a formula that precludes individual selection. The most typical formula for group term life insurance is to establish a multiple of salary – 1 times, 1½ times, or 2 times salary. Second choice is a four-category set group term insurance amount, with no group being more than 10 times the lowest amount, and established categories based on job classifications. For example, a doctor's office might establish the limits as follows:

Physicians	$120,000
Physician's Assistants	$60,000
Nurses	$30,000
Office Staff	$15,000

Nondiscrimination Rules

To be nondiscriminatory, a group term life insurance plan must meet one of the following four criteria:

- The plan must benefit at least 70% of employees.
- No more than 15% of participants can be "key employees."
- The plan must benefit a nondiscriminatory classification of employees.
- The plan is part of the employer's cafeteria welfare plan for the firm's employees.

The group term life insurance coverage is issued without evidence of insurability. When an employee leaves the employer, the group coverage can be converted, within 31 days of termination of employment, to an individual cash value policy, without the need to provide evidence of insurability.

Clients who may otherwise have trouble being underwritten for life insurance due to health issues should be advised to take maximum advantage of group life insurance available without evidence of insurability.

In most states, an employee can make an assignment of the group life insurance contract. Any assignment must be in writing and filed with the insurance company.

Contributory Versus Noncontributory Plans

Group life insurance, group health insurance, and pension plans can be contributory or noncontributory. The difference between noncontributory and contributory plans is that with a noncontributory plan, the employer finances the entire cost and with a contributory plan, the employer and the employee share the financing of the plan. Noncontributory plans assure a high percentage of participation, reduce adverse selection, help to keep administration expenses low, and are preferred by employees because of the favorable income tax treatment of the premium payments. Employers, however, tend to provide a larger amount of life insurance coverage under their plans when the employees are making a contribution to the cost.

Dependent Coverage

Some group plans cover the employee's spouse and children, usually for a small amount, such as $2,000. Group term life insurance coverage up to $2,000 on a spouse or dependent is considered a *de minimis* fringe benefit and is not taxable to the employee. An employee can often purchase additional coverage on a contributory basis, and there will be no income tax consequences. The employee is automatically the beneficiary of dependent coverage. There is usually a conversion privilege with the dependent coverage on the spouse, but not for children.

Tax Treatment

Premiums can be deducted by the employer, and the cost of up to $50,000 of group term life insurance is excluded from the taxable income of employees. If the employer pays the premiums for more than $50,000 of coverage, the premiums are deductible for the employer, but the cost of the excess coverage is taxable income to the employee. The exclusion for the cost of $50,000 of group term life insurance is not available where the employee is a sole proprietor, partner, or more than 2% shareholder of an S corporation.

If the employer insists on adopting a discriminatory group term life insurance plan, the full group premium charged by the insurance company becomes taxable to the employee and appears on his or her W-2 for the year.

If the plan is not discriminatory, any group insurance coverage in excess of $50,000 is taxed to the employee at a rate per thousand, established by the Government in Section 79 of the Internal Revenue Code. It is called the Government Table I. The rates in Table I are level for each five years of attained age and increase even into retirement if the group insurance is kept in force.

Table 1 Cost Per $1,000 of Protection For 1 Month

Age	Cost
Under 25	$ .05
25 through 29	.06
30 through 34	.08
35 through 39	.09
40 through 44	.10
45 through 49	.15
50 through 54	.23
55 through 59	.43
60 through 64	.66
65 through 69	1.27
70 and older	2.06

Group Permanent Insurance

A group life insurance plan can include insurance with a permanent benefit such as a cash value policy. A policy provides a permanent benefit if it provides economic value over more than one policy year. The cost of the permanent benefit paid by the employer is taxable income to the employee. The premiums are deductible by the employer as a business expense, provided the employee's rights to the insurance are nonforfeitable when premiums are paid.

Group Universal Life Insurance Programs

Group universal life programs (GULPs) provide employees with the advantages of individual universal life policies, as well as the advantage of group underwriting. Universal policies allow variation in the timing of premium payments and cash buildup from investment return. They can also provide coverage beyond retirement. Group underwriting provides reduced costs, coverage without evidence of insurability, and convenience to employees.

GULPs can be part of a group insurance plan, but since the cost of permanent insurance is taxable income to employees when an employer pays the premium, the GULPs are usually set up for employees to pay the premiums. The coverage is often obtained through a trustee, so the coverage is not deemed to be carried by the employer and thus is not subject to Sec. 79 of the Code.

Group/Ordinary Plan

In a group/ordinary plan, employees have the option of group term or a combination of group term and permanent insurance. The employer pays for the term insurance, and the employee pays for the whole life or for most of the whole life coverage.

Conversion Analysis

Group term insurance contracts contain a conversion privilege allowing employees to buy an individual life policy from the insurance company, without evidence of insurability. The employee must apply for conversion within 31 days after termination of employment. The face amount of the individual policy cannot exceed the amount of the coverage under the group contract, and the employee can generally select any kind of policy offered by the insurer except term insurance. The premium is determined by the employee's attained age on the date of conversion.

If an employee is insurable, the rates for a conversion policy may be higher than rates available from another insurer, so an employee should check rates of other insurers. The permanent insurance obtained by conversion may cost more than the employees want to spend, and term insurance will generally be less costly. In addition, certain supplementary coverage, such as disability benefits, may not be available under conversion policies but can be obtained by buying a policy from another insurer.

If an employee is uninsurable, the conversion policy will be an important option to exercise, and the employee may want to convert to the largest amount of coverage available. Factors that will affect the underwriting of individual policies include tobacco use, age, hazardous occupations or avocations, and health issues such as high blood pressure, history of cancer in the recent past, diabetes, heart disease, family health history, sleep apnea, obesity, high cholesterol, etc.

Portability of GULPs

With a GULP, an employee who terminates or retires can continue the universal life coverage, and there is no conversion. The insurer will bill the employee directly for the premiums. The employee also has the option of terminating the coverage and withdrawing the cash value or taking one of the policy settlement options.

GROUP CARVE-OUT LIFE INSURANCE

Premium Bonus Plan

With a group carve-out plan, the employer selects a group of employees for coverage on a discriminatory basis. The employer can offer executives better benefits by removing them from the group term life insurance plan. The group term life plan may also avoid being discriminatory by not including the executives. The employer can use a bonus plan (under Sec. 162 of the tax code) to pay for the coverage in a carve-out plan. The employer's cost for the plan is deductible.

The higher rates of Table I for highly-paid executives have encouraged many employers to adopt, for insurable executives, some form of permanent insurance which the employer helps the executive buy – deducting the individual policy premium as an ordinary and necessary business expense under Revenue Code Section 162. If the key executive is also a stockholder or a key executive whose total compensation may be questioned as being excessive, the premium payment by the employer may not be deductible.

While a bonus is always taxable to the covered executive, the employer may decide to pay a dual bonus – that is, pay gross income to the executive in an amount that will pay the tax on the bonus and leave enough after taxes to pay the premium.

The employee typically owns the policy and names his or her own personal beneficiary. For estate planning purposes, the policy may instead be owned by an irrevocable trust. In most cases the policy will be under complete control of the executive and will be portable if employment is terminated. In some cases, however, to encourage the executive to stay with the company for at least a certain period of time, a restrictive endorsement may be attached to the policy.

Insurability is typically required for a small group of selected executives, but many insurance companies look upon these risks as very favorable and will consider "bundle" underwriting so that moderately special risk insureds may be given standard premium policies. This is balanced by the executives who may be "super select" risks.

Death-Benefit-Only Plan

Some employers believe that a way to accomplish the group carve-out objective and tie the employed executive even closer to the company is to insure the executive with a company-owned policy and enter into a supplemental agreement to pay a death benefit to an employee who dies in service. There is no portability of the policy in this scenario except what the employer and employee may negotiate at the time of termination or retirement.

Under this arrangement, the death benefits would be received by the company, and any payments to the employee's beneficiary would be taxed as income in respect of a decedent (Revenue Code Section 691) because there is no longer an exclusion for employer payments to a beneficiary after the employee's death. The death benefit would not be part of the executive's estate since the policy was owned by the employer (unless the insured executive was a controlling shareholder of the company). Due to the death benefit avoiding federal estate taxes, this design makes death-benefit-only plans attractive to highly-compensated employees who have large estates.

APPLICATION QUESTIONS

1. Which of the following statements concerning limited-payment life insurance is <u>not</u> correct?

   A. It may apply to a whole life policy.
   B. It provides lifetime protection.
   C. Premiums may be level.
   D. "Paid-up" means the same as "matures."

2. You have just sold Anne a whole life policy and pointed out to her that, in addition to providing death benefit protection, the policy builds up a cash value. Anne asks you where the cash value comes from. What should you tell her?

   A. The net premium is greater than the mortality costs of the early years.
   B. The interest rate actually earned exceeds the assumed interest rate.
   C. Insureds who discontinue their insurance contribute to a surplus fund.
   D. The mortality table used shows higher mortality than actual mortality.
   E. You will have an actuary call her to explain it.

3. Which of the following statements concerning universal life insurance is <u>not</u> correct?

   A. It is a flexible-premium policy.
   B. It provides lifetime protection.
   C. It separates the protection and savings components.
   D. It prohibits cash withdrawals.
   E. The cash value is credited with market interest rates.

4. Which of the following statements concerning universal life insurance is (are) correct?

(1) The policy's cash value appreciates on the basis of current investment yields, rather than yields available when the policy was issued.

(2) The annual increase in the policy's cash value attributable to investment income is not currently included in the policyowner's gross income for tax purposes.

(3) The policyowner might elect to pay premiums for five years and then pay no premiums for two years with no decrease in the amount of his or her life insurance coverage.

    A. (1) only
    B. (1) and (2) only
    C. (1) and (3) only
    D. (2) and (3) only
    E. (1), (2), and (3)

5. Steve Brown, age 35, has a wife and two children. He feels that they are not able to save any of what they earn. He would like a recommendation for a life insurance program that would help them. What kind of policy would be most appropriate for Steve?

    A. Whole life
    B. 15-year level term
    C. Universal life
    D. Variable universal life

6. In which of the following types of life insurance products are the funds supporting the contract invested as part of the insurer's general account?

(1) Universal life insurance
(2) Variable annuities
(3) Whole life insurance
(4) Variable universal life insurance

    A. (1) only
    B. (2) only
    C. (3) only
    D. (1) and (3) only
    E. (2) and (4) only

7. Sam Wright, age 60, has related the story of a friend who owned a whole life policy issued by a company that went bankrupt. The cash value was reduced and restricted for many years. Sam is interested in additional permanent life insurance but wants to know if there is a way to avoid this problem. What type of policy would be most appropriate to address these concerns?

    A. Universal life
    B. Variable universal life
    C. Limited-pay whole life
    D. Endowment life

8. Which of the following statements concerning the second-to-die policy is <u>not</u> correct?

    A. It is also called survivorship life.
    B. It pays half the death benefit at the first death and the other half upon the second death.
    C. It is usually whole life, but it may be term or universal insurance.
    D. It is often used in estate planning.

9. Which of the following statements concerning the grace period provision in a life insurance policy is correct?

    A. Even if the policyowner waits eight months to pay a premium, he or she may reinstate the policy without evidence of insurability.
    B. The grace period is six months in most companies.
    C. If the insured dies during the grace period without having paid the premium, the full death proceeds are paid to the beneficiary.
    D. Insurers permit payment of the premium within the grace period with no questions asked.

10. Which of the following statements concerning the incontestable clause is correct?

    A. An incontestable clause is an optional provision in a life insurance contract.
    B. An incontestable clause permits an insurer to contest a policy during the contestable period.
    C. A two-year incontestable clause makes the misstatement of age clause inapplicable after two years.
    D. A two-year incontestable clause makes an aviation exclusion rider ineffective after two years.
    E. The incontestable clause applies even for nonpayment of premium.

11. In her application for insurance on her own life, Dolores understated her age by two years in order to obtain a lower rate. At her death, the misstatement of age provision in a life insurance policy will result in which of the following?

    A. The payment of death proceeds that the premium paid would have purchased if the age had been correctly stated

    B. An increase in the death proceeds since the age has been understated

    C. A denial of the claim

    D. No change in the amount of the death proceeds, but an adjustment of the premium

12. Which of the following statements concerning the rights of a beneficiary in a life insurance policy is <u>not</u> correct?

    A. A revocable beneficiary has a mere expectancy.

    B. An irrevocable beneficiary has a vested right.

    C. The policyowner may exercise all of the ownership rights under the policy, without the consent of the revocable beneficiary.

    D. The policyowner has the right to assign the policy to whomever he or she wishes, without the consent of the beneficiary, whether the beneficiary has been designated revocably or irrevocably.

    E. At time of death of the insured policyowner, the rights of a revocable beneficiary are no different from those of an irrevocably designated beneficiary.

13. (Published question released November, 1994)

Which of the following statements about assignments is (are) true?

    (1) An absolute assignment is an irrevocable transfer of all ownership rights, which can be accomplished through a sale or gift.

    (2) A collateral assignment is a temporary transfer of some or all of the ownership rights, on the condition that such rights revert to the assignee.

    (3) A collateral assignment is a temporary transfer of some or all of the ownership rights whereby such rights revert to the assignor upon satisfaction of agreed upon conditions.

    (4) A collateral assignment is a temporary transfer of some or all of the ownership rights, on the condition that such rights revert to the insurance company upon satisfaction of agreed upon conditions.

    A. (1), (2), and (3) only

    B. (1) and (3) only

    C. (2) and (4) only

    D. (4) only

    E. (1), (2), (3), and (4)

14. (Published question released November, 1994)

Which of the following is (are) true regarding the ownership of life insurance?

(1) A policy can only be issued to the insured.
(2) Generally, assigning a policy requires proof that the insured is still "insurable," meaning still in good health.
(3) Only a person with an insurable interest, generally a relative, a business associate, or lender, can be named as a beneficiary.
(4) The policyowner can assign (transfer) ownership of the policy to whomever he or she chooses, even if the assignee has <u>no</u> insurable interest.

    A. (1), (2), and (3) only
    B. (1) only
    C. (2) and (4) only
    D. (4) only
    E. (1), (2), (3), and (4)

15. Harry and his wife both die in a common accident, within minutes of each other. Harry's life insurance policy has a 30-day common disaster provision and his wife is the named beneficiary. In this case, the proceeds of the policy on Harry's life will be paid to which of the following?

    A. Harry's estate
    B. Harry's wife's estate
    C. The courts to determine who should receive the money
    D. The state, since no one is entitled to the money

16. Ben has named Jerry as primary beneficiary of Ben's life insurance policy and Tom as the contingent beneficiary. In which of the following ways do the rights of Jerry differ from the rights of Tom?

(1) If Jerry is living when the insured dies, Tom has no legal right to any of the life insurance lump-sum death proceeds.
(2) The only circumstances under which Tom would have any legal right to the lump-sum death proceeds would be if Jerry predeceases the insured.

    A. (1) only
    B. (2) only
    C. Both (1) and (2)
    D. Neither (1) nor (2)

17. Which of the following statements concerning life insurance policy riders is (are) correct?

    (1) The waiver-of-premium provision really provides a limited amount of disability income for the insured policyowner.

    (2) The accidental death provision provides for an increased death benefit if death results from an accident.

    (3) The guaranteed insurability option permits the insured policyowner, at stated intervals, to purchase specified amounts of additional life insurance, but only if evidence of insurability can be provided.

    A. (1) only
    B. (1) and (2) only
    C. (2) and (3) only
    D. (1), (2), and (3)

18. Which of the following statements concerning participating life insurance is (are) correct?

    (1) Participating policies overcharge the policyowner because the insurer expects to return to the policyowner each year some of the overcharge.

    (2) Companies selling participating life insurance are so confident of their dividend-paying capacity that many companies are now guaranteeing their dividends.

    A. (1) only
    B. (2) only
    C. Both (1) and (2)
    D. Neither (1) nor (2)

19. (Published question released December, 1996)

Bruce, age 55, is the beneficiary of his mother's $200,000 life insurance policy. The insurer has requested him to select a settlement option for payment of the proceeds. What factors should he consider before making the decision?

(1) His current income needs
(2) His asset management ability
(3) His net worth
(4) His estate planning goals
(5) His tax liability on the $200,000

    A. (1), (2), (3), and (5) only
    B. (2) and (4) only
    C. (1) only
    D. (3), (4), and (5) only
    E. (1), (2), (3), and (4) only

20. Ken and Lyn are a retired married couple with no children and no other source of income except Social Security. They have accumulated substantial cash values in their life insurance policies. Which of the following would be the most appropriate way to take the cash values?

    A. Interest-only
    B. Joint-and-survivorship income
    C. Installments for a fixed period
    D. Installments of a fixed amount
    E. Reduced amount of paid-up insurance

21. Why does the straight or pure life-income settlement option provide the life insurance beneficiary with a larger life income than any of the period-certain life-income options?

    A. Those beneficiaries who live only a short time provide funds to sustain the benefits for the fortunate survivors.
    B. The straight life-income option has a higher rate of interest guaranteed.
    C. The period-certain benefit is discounted for the disability risk.
    D. The federal income tax bite is greater for the period-certain option.

22. Jack is the insured under a $100,000 whole life insurance policy. Jack's planner has recommended that the policy be replaced with a new $100,000 universal life policy on Jack. If this replacement takes place, which of the following will result?

    A. Jack's new policy will cover suicide immediately.
    B. Jack's new policy will be incontestable immediately.
    C. Jack's new policy will constitute a taxable event under the Internal Revenue Code.
    D. Jack's new policy's premium will be based on his attained age.

23. John, who is seriously ill, is thinking about entering into a viatical agreement. Which of the following statements concerning a viatical agreement is (are) correct?

    (1) It is usually created only if the insured has less than 60 days to live.
    (2) It usually pays the insured something less than the life insurance policy's face amount.

        A. (1) only
        B. (2) only
        C. Both (1) and (2)
        D. Neither (1) nor (2)

24. Which of the following statements concerning a viatical settlement is correct?

    A. The viator must use the payments from the settlement for medical expenses.
    B. The viatical company is prohibited from transferring the life policy to another third party.
    C. The viatical settlement requires a transfer to a third party with an insurable interest.
    D. If an insured regains health after such settlement, the payments in prior years must then be reported as income.
    E. The discount on the death benefit that can be paid by a viatical company is not limited by law.

25. David learned that he had contracted HIV and is not expected to live more than 5 years, but is still able to perform all activities of daily living. He has a life insurance policy with a face value of $400,000 that he could sell to a viatical company for $200,000. On the policy, David had paid premiums of $2,000 each year for 15 years, and the cash value is $26,000. What capital gain will David have to report if he sells the policy to the viatical company?

    A. $0
    B. $26,000
    C. $170,000
    D. $174,000

26. Dana Williams owns a $100,000 life insurance policy insuring her husband's life. Dana's husband James has a terminal illness and is expected to die within 36 months, but is still able to perform all activities of daily living. Dana is considering a viatical settlement or applying for accelerated benefits. Which of the following statements concerning the income tax consequences of a viatical settlement or accelerated benefits for the Williams is (are) correct?

    (1) A lump sum paid in a viatical settlement to Dana currently will be received income-tax-free.
    (2) A lump sum paid to Dana in a viatical settlement when a doctor certifies that James is expected to die within 24 months will be received income-tax-free.
    (3) Accelerated benefits paid by the insurer to Dana when a doctor certifies that James is expected to die in less than 12 months will be received income-tax-free.
    (4) If a viatical provider agrees to make periodic payments to the Williams as needed for medical expenses over the next three years, the payments will be ordinary income.

        A. (1) only
        B. (1) and (2) only
        C. (2) and (3) only
        D. (3) and (4) only
        E. (1), (2), and (3) only

27. (Published question released December, 1996)

In group life insurance plans provided by employers, which of the following statements about the conversion privilege is (are) true?

(1) The policy may be converted from a term policy to an individual permanent life policy.
(2) The policy may be converted from a permanent product to a term product.
(3) The policy may be converted if the insured provides evidence of insurability.
(4) At conversion, the billing is switched to the insured.

    A. (1) and (4) only
    B. (1), (2), and (3) only
    C. (1), (2), (3), and (4)
    D. (2) and (3) only
    E. (4) only

28. (Published question released January, 1999)

Your client's employer has recently adopted a group universal life insurance plan. The advantages of such a plan for your client typically include all of the following, except that:

    A. It allows employees to borrow or withdraw cash.
    B. It provides an opportunity to continue coverage after retirement.
    C. The entire premium cost is borne by the employer.
    D. It provides flexibility in designing coverage to best meet individual needs.

29. The Arthur Reynolds Company (ARCO) is a medium-sized Indiana machine tool company located 100 miles south of Chicago. The Company has three key executives whose retention by the Company is considered to be important to the Company's future growth and expansion of operations. The board of directors is considering several special employee benefit plans that could be implemented to make continued service with ARCO attractive for the three executives. Which of the following statements concerning benefit plans being considered by the ARCO board of directors is (are) correct?

(1) Three $100,000 ordinary life insurance policies would provide capital accumulation and estate liquidity for each of the three families.
(2) The attitude of ARCO's board of directors toward portability of any benefit plan established would likely parallel that of the three executives.
(3) Evidence of insurability is usually required for small group carve-out plans.

A. (1) and (2) only
B. (2) and (3) only
C. (1) and (3) only
D. (1), (2), and (3)

30. When John Grant died, his company wanted to pay his widow Joan a death benefit. What is the maximum amount that the company can pay as a death benefit to Joan Grant that will not have to be included in gross income?

A. $0
B. $5,000
C. $10,000
D. $50,000
E. $75,000

31. Allison Quinn, age 43, is an employee of BizzCo Corporation and earns an annual salary of $95,000. Allison has recently been informed that the company is implementing a group term life insurance plan and will pay the premium for an amount of coverage equal to her salary. What are the tax implications of this benefit for Allison?

A. Allison will not be taxed on the benefit as long as the plan is nondiscriminatory.
B. Allison will pay tax on an additional $5.00 of income.
C. Allison will pay tax on an additional $4.50 of income.
D. Allison will pay tax on an additional $54.00 of income.
E. Allison will pay tax on an additional $114.00 of income.

32. Which of the following statements concerning the nature of term insurance is correct?

    A. It provides protection for only a limited period of time.
    B. It usually builds cash values in the later years.
    C. It is convertible only with evidence of insurability.
    D. It is renewable for another term at no increase in premium.

33. Which of the following statements concerning yearly renewable term insurance is (are) correct?

(1) It provides protection for one year at a time.
(2) It builds up a very high cash value.

    A. (1) only
    B. (2) only
    C. Both (1) and (2)
    D. Neither (1) nor (2)

34. All the following statements concerning term life insurance are correct, EXCEPT:

    A. It provides temporary protection.
    B. It is usually not renewable.
    C. It is usually convertible.
    D. It usually has no cash value.

35. All the following statements concerning whole life insurance are correct, EXCEPT:

    A. It provides lifetime protection.
    B. It may be limited-payment life.
    C. Premiums do not increase with age.
    D. It lacks cash surrender values.

36. Which of the following statements concerning the level premium method of buying permanent life insurance is (are) correct?

(1) In the early years, the premium payer is paying more than the annual pro rata mortality cost for the members of the group.

(2) The investment income earned on the policy's cash value helps to keep the annual premium low in the later years.

(3) Since the annual increase in the policy's cash value attributable to investment income is not currently included in the policy owner's gross income for tax purposes, part of the premium is really paid by Uncle Sam.

    A. (2) only
    B. (1) and (2) only
    C. (1) and (3) only
    D. (2) and (3) only
    E. (1), (2), and (3)

37. Which of the following is (are) among the advantages of owning variable life insurance instead of a conventional whole life policy?

(1) To the extent that the market prices and annual yields of common stocks keep up with inflation, the needs of the policy owner's family are better protected against inflationary increases in living costs.

(2) The policy owner and family have the benefits of the same guarantees that traditionally have been associated with whole life plus increased investment diversification provided by the variable life policy.

    A. (1) only
    B. (2) only
    C. Both (1) and (2)
    D. Neither (1) nor (2)

38. Which of the following statements concerning the disadvantages of universal life insurance is (are) correct?

(1) The future yield potential for the policy owner is uncertain.
(2) The semi-compulsory regular savings feature of conventional whole life insurance is lost.
(3) Since the cash value is invested primarily in common stocks and other equities, it is exposed to all the risks of such investments.

   A. (1) only
   B. (1) and (2) only
   C. (1) and (3) only
   D. (2) and (3) only
   E. (1), (2), and (3)

39. All the following statements concerning variable universal life insurance are correct, EXCEPT:

   A. There are several investment options.
   B. There is no minimum guaranteed rate of interest.
   C. The policy owner may not invest in money market funds.
   D. The investment risk falls upon the policy owner.

40. Endowment insurance is designed for achieving which of the following?

(1) Providing a mechanism to save for old-age retirement
(2) Providing a hedge against the possibility of the saving period being cut short by death
(3) Providing low-cost protection during a temporary period
(4) Providing a fund for a specific purpose, such as a child's education

   A. (1) and (2) only
   B. (1), (2), and (4) only
   C. (1), (3), and (4) only
   D. (2), (3), and (4) only

41. Which of the following statements concerning the incontestable clause is correct?

    A. An incontestable clause prohibits the company from challenging a claim for any reason.

    B. If the policy has a two-year incontestable clause, the company can challenge it if the insured dies within two years.

    C. A two-year incontestable clause makes the misstatement of age clause inapplicable after two years.

    D. An incontestable clause prohibits the company from contesting the policy until the expiration of the contestable period.

42. Which of the following are typical settlement options for life insurance death proceeds?

    (1) Installments for a fixed period
    (2) Installments for a fixed amount
    (3) Extended term insurance
    (4) Life income with period certain

    A. (1) and (2) only
    B. (1), (2), and (3) only
    C. (1), (2), and (4) only
    D. (2), (3), and (4) only

43. The most common type of group life insurance is:

    A. Dependents' group life
    B. Group survivors income
    C. Group paid-up life
    D. Group term life
    E. Group ordinary life

44. Which of the following is a major characteristic of group term life insurance?

    A. The premium is based on the level of the employee's annual wage earnings.

    B. The cost is higher than for an individual term policy because of adverse selection.

    C. The coverage is generally issued without evidence of insurability.

    D. The amount of coverage is determined by a formula that, unfortunately, too often invites adverse selection.

    E. The primary reason for the low cost is the lower mortality that can be expected among the working population.

45. Which of the following is a common characteristic of group life insurance?

    A. Benefits are based on a formula that relates benefits to the Consumer Price Index.

    B. A master contract exists between the insurer and the employee.

    C. Either the employer or the employee pays the full premium cost.

    D. Individual employees receive certificates as evidence of their insurance coverage.

    E. A terminating employee has no opportunity to convert his or her coverage.

46. Which of the following statements concerning dependents' group life insurance is (are) correct?

    (1) It typically provides each dependent of the employee the same amount of coverage as is available to the employee.

    (2) The spouse's coverage is usually convertible on the same basis as the employee's coverage.

    (3) Dependents' coverage may be available even if the employee has no group coverage.

    A. (1) only

    B. (2) only

    C. (1) and (2) only

    D. (1) and (3) only

    E. (1), (2), and (3)

47. Which of the following statements concerning group ordinary life insurance is (are) correct?

(1) The employer pays for the group term component.

(2) The employee and employer may share the cost of the ordinary whole life component.

(3) Recent changes in the federal tax laws have increased the attractiveness of this coverage for employees.

    A. (1) only
    B. (1) and (2) only
    C. (1) and (3) only
    D. (2) and (3) only
    E. (1), (2), and (3)

48. Which of the following statements concerning group universal life insurance is correct?

    A. The employer and the employee usually share the premium payment.

    B. Since there is a group master contract, the insurer does not issue an individual policy to each participant.

    C. Because the amount of coverage is greater per employee than for the conventional individual universal life policy, the cost per $1,000 of coverage is greater.

    D. Some insurers issue coverage to a participant without requiring a medical exam.

    E. The higher commissions paid to agents per $1,000 of coverage tends to increase the cost of the coverage.

49. Which of the following statements concerning a group carve-out plan is (are) correct?

(1) The coverage is available on a discriminatory basis.

(2) The employer deducts the premium cost, which is not taxable income for the employee.

(3) A double bonus plan can overcome the executive's dislike of the taxation of the policy premium.

    A. (1) only
    B. (1) and (2) only
    C. (1) and (3) only
    D. (2) and (3) only
    E. (1), (2), and (3)

50. In determining the amount of group life insurance coverage for its employees, an employer would logically consider which of the following factors?

    (1) The value of the employees to the firm
    (2) The individual preferences of each employee
    (3) The employees' need for protection
    (4) The employees' ability to contribute to the cost of the plan

        A. (1) and (2) only
        B. (2) and (3) only
        C. (1), (2), and (3) only
        D. (1), (3), and (4) only
        E. (1), (2), (3), and (4)

51. To qualify for favorable federal income tax treatment for the employer and the employee, an employer-sponsored group life insurance plan must meet all the following requirements, EXCEPT:

    A. The coverage must be term insurance, not to exceed $50,000.
    B. The amount of coverage must be determined on some basis that precludes individual selection of the amount.
    C. Participation eligibility must be nondiscriminatory.
    D. The employee may request coverage equal to twice his or her salary as long as this amount does not exceed $50,000.

52. If the cost of the first $50,000 of employer-provided group term life insurance is to be excluded from the gross income of all participating employees, which one of the following conditions must the plan meet?

    A. The plan must provide a death benefit that is included in the gross income of the employee's designated beneficiary.
    B. The insurance must be provided under a policy in which the employees have a proprietary interest.
    C. The government's Table I rates must be used to calculate all premiums for the group insurance provided.
    D. The plan must not discriminate in favor of key employees as to eligibility or benefits.
    E. The employee must be permitted to select the amount of his or her coverage.

53. "C" is an employee of F Corporation, with an annual salary of $60,000. "C's" employer provides $90,000 of group term life insurance. "C" is required to contribute monthly $0.15 per $1,000 of coverage. The IRS Uniform Premium Table shows $.60 as the monthly cost per $1,000 for the coverage. How much is included in "C's" annual gross income for the benefits received from his or her employer's group life insurance coverage?

   A. $0
   B. $126
   C. $153
   D. $240
   E. $288

54. "D" is an employee of R Corporation, with an annual salary of $75,000. The employer has a noncontributory group permanent whole life policy, covering "D" for $100,000. "D's" rights in the premiums are vested in the year the premiums are paid by the employer. "D" has designated his or her spouse "W" as beneficiary. Under these circumstances, which of the following is included in "D's" gross income for federal income tax purposes?

   A. The entire cost of the coverage
   B. The cost of the coverage in excess of $50,000
   C. The annual increase in the policy's cash value
   D. The cost of the term insurance in excess of $50,000 plus the amount of the annual increase in the policy's cash value

55. "G" is an employee of S Corporation, with an annual salary of $40,000. "G" is covered under his or her employer's noncontributory group life insurance policy. The policy provides both $60,000 of group term coverage and $40,000 permanent coverage. Under these circumstances, which of the following must be included in "G's" gross income?

   (1) The cost of $10,000 of group term life insurance
   (2) Any policy dividends "G" receives
   (3) The cost of the permanent benefits

      A. (1) only
      B. (1) and (2) only
      C. (1) and (3) only
      D. (2) and (3) only
      E. (1), (2), and (3)

For practice answering case questions related to Topic 28, please answer the following questions in the cases included in Appendix A at the back of this textbook.

Case	Questions
Black Hills P&L	
Brodinski	7, 8, 9, and 10
Haurilick	
Beals	3
Mocsin	1
Loudon	2
Connor	12 and 13
Seidelhofer	14 and 15
Loomis Company	
Michael and Diana Eastman	
Gary and Judy Parker	31, 32, 33, 34, and 35

ANSWERS AND EXPLANATIONS

1. D is the answer. Paid-up means no additional premiums are required. Maturity means that the face amount is payable on death or as an endowment.

2. A is the answer. Since mortality is lower in the early years than in the later years for the whole group of insured lives, the insurer has more dollars received from premium payments than are needed to pay death benefits in the early years. The excess dollars build the cash values for the surviving insured-policyowners. B may or may not be true, but if B is true, it is not the primary reason for policy cash values. C may also be true, but surplus belongs to the insurance company and its owners, not to the insureds. D may also be true, but this is not the primary reason for policy cash values. If you chose E as the answer, you need to do more studying about the level premium method of providing life insurance protection.

3. D is the answer. Cash withdrawals are permitted, without interest, but with a reduction of the death benefit.

4. E is the answer. All three statements are correct.

5. A is the answer. Whole life will have fixed premiums that will force Steve to pay premiums and build cash value. The policy is permanent, so it will last for his lifetime. The premiums can be varied with universal and variable universal policies, so Steve will not always be forced to save. Term life does not build cash value.

6. D is the answer. Only the funds supporting variable annuities and variable life insurance are invested through an insurer's separate accounts (sub accounts). For all other individual contracts, the funds are invested as part of the general account.

7. B is the answer. With a variable policy, the cash value is invested in separate accounts and is not subject to the claims of creditors against the insurance company. With whole life and universal life, the cash value is invested in the insurer's general account and is subject to claims of creditors. Endowment policies also invest the cash value in the insurer's general account but do not have the tax advantages of other policies.

8. B is the answer. The death proceeds are paid only upon the death of the insured who is the last to die.

9. D is the answer. In order to reinstate a life insurance policy, all back premiums must be paid, with interest, and insurability must be shown. The grace period is usually 31 days long. If the insured dies during the grace period, the insurer may deduct the unpaid premium from the proceeds.

10. B is the answer. The clause is mandatory, not optional. Also, the misstatement of age clause and the aviation exclusion rider supersede the incontestable clause. The clause does not apply to nonpayment of premium.

11. A is the answer. B and C incorrectly describe the effect on the death benefit. D is incorrect because the premium is not adjusted. The death benefit is adjusted.

12. D is the answer. The policyowner must obtain the consent of the irrevocably designated beneficiary if the policyowner wishes to assign the policy. A, B, C, and E are correct statements.

13. B is the answer. (1) is correct, by definition. (2) is incorrect because a collateral assignment entails eventual return of the transferred rights to the assignor. Therefore, (3) is correct, and (4) is incorrect.

14. D is the answer. (1) is incorrect because the policyowner need not be the insured. (2) is incorrect because a life insurance policy is freely assignable. (3) is incorrect because a life insurance beneficiary need not have an insurable interest.

15. A is the answer. The proceeds will be payable to Harry's estate because his wife failed to outlive him by at least 30 days.

16. C is the answer. Both (1) and (2) correctly distinguish the rights of the primary beneficiary from the rights of the contingent beneficiary.

17. B is the answer. (1) is a correct statement because the premium amount is really the amount of the disability income payable. (2) is a correct statement because the death benefit increases if death occurs within 90 days of the accident. (3) is not a correct statement because evidence of insurability is not required.

18. A is the answer. (1) is the only correct statement. (2) is not correct because life companies are forbidden by law from guaranteeing their dividends.

19. E is the answer. (5) is not correct because the $200,000 of death proceeds are not taxable income.

20. B is the answer. Their primary need is for income that they cannot outlive. The joint-and-survivorship arrangement will provide an income until the second death. Most insurers will allow cash values to be taken as a life income through their use to buy an annuity.

21. A is the answer. Those who elect the straight or pure life-income option and then die within a short time leave no continuing benefit for anyone. The life insurance company actuary can determine the probability of survival or death for a large group of beneficiaries. Those who die do not receive the full amount of their death proceeds. What the dead people do not receive can be given to those who survive.

22. D is the answer. The new policy will have a new suicide exclusion and a new contestable period, so A and B are incorrect. C is incorrect because the replacement involves one life policy for another life policy on the same life.

23. B is the answer. (1) is incorrect. The agreement often is created because the insured's life expectancy exceeds the length of time, such as six months, for which the insurer will make accelerated death benefits available.

24. E is the answer. The discounts that can be offered in viatical settlements are not regulated. Only offers from "qualified viatical settlement providers" are governed by the NAIC minimum offer percentages. In addition, there is no limit on the transfer of the life insurance policy after the policyowner enters into an assignment with a viatical company. The insured has no control over subsequent transfers. Benefits that are received tax-free are not later made taxable due to a change of health. The policyowner is not required to use the payment from a viatical settlement for medical expenses. No insurable interest is required when a third party obtains an existing policy in a viatical settlement.

25. C is the answer. For life insurance proceeds to qualify for the exclusion, the taxpayer must be terminally ill or chronically ill. David does not qualify as terminally ill until he has only 24 months to live. He is also not chronically ill since he is still able to perform all activities of daily living. Since David will live as much as 5 years and does not meet the definition of chronically ill, the proceeds will not be eligible for the exclusion. His gain is the difference between the sale price and the premiums paid. If David had only 24 months to live, or been unable to perform at least 2 ADLs, the sale proceeds from the life insurance policy would be received by the policyowner free of income tax. The cash value does not make any difference in the taxation of the policy.

26. C is the answer. The tax-free receipt of accelerated death benefits applies to insurance policies and viatical settlements. If the insured has a terminal illness and is certified to have a life expectancy of less than 24 months, the benefits are received free of income tax. Likewise, if the insured is chronically ill and the policy is sold to a qualified viatical settlement provider, the payment received is free of income tax. The insured need not own the policy for the benefits to be income-tax-free. Thus, the payments made when James has a life expectancy of 36 months are not received free of income taxes, whereas payments when life expectancy is 24 months or less will be. The payment over three years would be taxed as a capital gain.

27. A is the answer. (2) is incorrect because conversion must be to permanent insurance. (3) is incorrect because evidence of insurability is not required.

28. C is the answer. A group universal life insurance plan (GULP) is permanent insurance, so the policy will build up cash value which can be borrowed, and it will continue after the employee's retirement. The universal policy is flexible in allowing premium payments to be altered to fit individual needs. Typically, a GULP is set up to take advantage of group underwriting for employees, but the employees pay the premiums. If the employer were to pay the premiums, the employees would have additional taxable income. Since there is no tax advantage to the employer paying, the GULPs are typically set up for employees to pay the premiums.

29. C is the answer. (2) is not correct because the ARCO board would be opposed to portability because the board would like to use the employee benefit plan as an inducement for the three executives to remain with ARCO. (1) and (3) are correct statements.

30. A is the answer. The entire amount of a death benefit must be included in gross income. There is no longer an exclusion which used to allow an employer to give $5,000 tax free to the deceased employee's family.

31. D is the answer. Employees are taxed on group term life insurance premiums paid for by the employer on death benefits over $50,000. The amount of additional income is calculated using the Table 1 cost of insurance, which shows the monthly cost per $1,000 of death benefit. Since Allison is age 43, the monthly cost from Table 1 is 10 cents per $1,000 of death benefit over $50,000. The employer is paying for an extra $45,000 of coverage so 45 x .10 x 12 = $54.

32. A is the answer. B is not correct. There usually are no cash values. C is not correct because evidence of insurability is not required either to renew or convert a term insurance policy. D is not correct because an increase in premium is required at each renewal because of the higher attained age.

33. A is the answer. There is no cash value in a yearly renewable term policy.

34. B is the answer. Term life insurance is usually renewable.

35. D is the answer. Cash values are an integral part of whole life insurance.

36. E is the answer. All three statements are correct.

37. A is the answer. (2) is not a correct statement because there are no investment guarantees for variable life insurance policies. (1) is a correct statement.

38. B is the answer. (3) is not a correct statement because for a conventional universal life policy, the cash value is invested primarily in medium- and short-term instruments. (1) and (2) are correct statements.

39. C is the answer. The policy owner has his or her choice, usually including a stock fund, a bond fund, a balanced fund, a global fund, a real estate fund, and a money market fund.

40. B is the answer. (3) is not correct. Endowment life insurance is high-cost protection. An endowment policy is a high-savings investment contract, but it provides protection at a high premium per $1,000 of coverage. Endowment insurance is appropriate for achieving (1), (2), and (4). (1), (2), and (4) are all objectives that can be achieved by the use of endowment insurance. However, the unfavorable income tax treatment of endowments has rendered them virtually obsolete in the marketplace.

41. B is the answer. If the policy has a two-year incontestable clause, the company can challenge it if the insured dies within two years. The incontestable clause prohibits challenges to the policy after the contestable period; it does not prohibit the company from denying claims that are not covered by the policy. The misstatement of age clause and the death of the insured within two years are exceptions to the incontestable clause.

42. C is the answer. (3) is not a settlement option that is typically available for life insurance death proceeds. Extended term insurance is not a settlement option. It is an optional use of the policy's nonforfeiture value. (1), (2), and (4) are all settlement options typically available for a life insurance policy's death proceeds.

43. D is the answer. Group term life insurance is the most common type of group life insurance due to the relatively inexpensive premiums and the employee being the insured life.

44. C is the answer. A is not correct. The premium is based on the cost of yearly renewable term insurance. B is not correct. The cost is lower than for an individual policy because of the economies of scale inherent in all group insurance. The fixed costs of marketing and administration can be spread over hundreds, or even thousands, of employees covered under one master contract. D is not correct. The benefit formula that determines the amount of coverage for each employee is designed to preclude employee selection of the coverage amount. This prevents, rather than invites, adverse selection. E is not correct. Actual mortality is high, not low, because of the lack of medical exams.

45. D is the answer. A is not correct. Benefits are based on a formula that relates benefits to the employee's wages, position, or length of service. B is not correct. The master contract is between the insurer and the employer. C is not correct. It is not common for the employee to pay the full cost because this would be a deterrent to 100% participation. To encourage participation, the employer pays part or all of the premium cost, which helps to assure participation of the young and healthy employees. E is not correct. A terminating employee may convert his or her group coverage to an individual cash-value policy, without providing evidence of insurability.

46. B is the answer. (1) is not a correct statement because the amount of coverage typically available to a dependent is less than the coverage available to an employee. (3) is not a correct statement because, normally, dependent coverage is written only with group coverage on the employee. (2) is a correct statement.

47. B is the answer. (3) is not a correct statement because the unfavorable tax treatment of group ordinary life insurance has made it unattractive for most employees. (1) and (2) are correct statements.

48. D is the answer. A is not a correct statement. The employee usually pays the full cost; there is no cost-sharing by the employer. B is not a correct statement. The insurer does issue an individual policy to each participant. C is not a correct statement. The cost is less per $1,000 of coverage for the group policy because of the economies of scale available. E is not correct. Agent commissions per $1,000 of coverage are lower than those for individual policies.

49. C is the answer. (2) is not a correct statement because the premium paid by the employer is included in the employee's gross income. (1) and (3) are correct statements.

50. D is the answer. (2) is not correct. (2) should never be a factor in determining the amount of group life insurance for an employee. If given a choice, the employees in poor health would select the maximum permitted, while those young employees in good health would select only small amounts of coverage or none at all. (1), (3), and (4) are all factors the employer would logically consider.

51. D is the answer. D is an incorrect statement because an employee cannot select the amount of coverage he or she would like. The amount must be determined by some formula or some method that prevents adverse selection. If the amount were arbitrarily determinable by each employee, those in poor health would all select $50,000. Those in good health would tend to select lesser amounts. A, B, and C are correct statements.

52. D is the answer. A is not an acceptable condition. The death benefit must not be included in the beneficiary's gross income. B is not an acceptable condition. The employees must not have any ownership rights or proprietary interest in the master contract. C is not an acceptable condition. The Table I rates only apply to calculating the income tax on amounts of group term life insurance over $50,000 on any employee. E is not an acceptable condition. This would result in excessive adverse selection, as emphasized previously.

53. B is the answer. The cost of the $40,000 excess insurance is $288 ($.60 x 40 x 12) minus $162 paid by "C" ($.15 x 90 x 12). $288 – $162 = $126.

54. A is the answer. If no part of the coverage qualifies as group term life insurance, the full amount of the premiums must be included in "D's" gross income.

55. E is the answer. All three items are included in "G's" gross income.

Life Insurance (Individual) (Part B) (Topic 28B)

CFP Board Student-Centered Learning Objectives

(a) Explain the tax treatment of life insurance premiums and proceeds.

A. Income Taxation of Lifetime Benefits from Life Insurance 28B.1
    1. Premiums 28B.1
    2. Dividends 28B.2
    3. Loans 28B.2
    4. Withdrawals 28B.2
        a. Determining basis 28B.3
    5. Definition of life insurance 28B.3
    6. Surrender 28B.4
    7. Tax-free exchange – Section 1035 .... 28B.4
    8. Life Settlements 28B.5
B. Income Taxation of Life Insurance Death Benefits 28B.6
    1. Transfer-for-Value Rule 28B.6
C. Modified Endowment Contracts (MECs) 28B.7
    1. 7-Pay test for a MEC 28B.8
    2. Taxation of lifetime benefits in MECs 28B.9
    3. Section 1035 exchanges of MECs 28B.10
D. Definitions 28B.12

INCOME TAXATION OF LIFETIME BENEFITS FROM LIFE INSURANCE

Premiums

As a general rule, premiums paid for the purchase of life insurance policies are not deductible on a payer's income tax return.

An exception to this rule applies when a divorce occurs and one spouse is paying the premium on a policy owned by the other spouse under the terms of an alimony decree. For example, a husband is paying alimony to his wife. Because the wife is dependent on this income, the wife is named as the policyowner of a life insurance policy insuring the life of the husband, and the wife is also named as the beneficiary. The husband, however, is required to pay the premiums under the terms of the alimony decree. The premiums are treated as additional alimony income to the wife (as though the husband had paid cash to the wife, and the wife used it to pay the premium), and the premiums are deductible by the husband as additional alimony payments. On the other hand, if the husband maintained ownership of the policy but was required to name the wife as irrevocable beneficiary, the premium payments would not be treated as alimony, and would not be income tax deductible by the husband.

A second exception to the rule that premiums are not income tax deductible applies to the payment of premiums on a policy for which a charity is the owner and beneficiary. In this case, the premiums are treated as a cash contribution to the charity. The deductibility of charitable contributions is limited based on the donor's adjusted gross income. A detailed explanation of these limitations is beyond the scope of this textbook, but planners should be aware that the advice of a tax professional is advisable. It is also worth noting that merely naming a charity as an irrevocable beneficiary is not enough to allow the premiums to qualify as a deductible contribution; the charity must actually own the policy and have the policyowner rights, including access to cash values.

As discussed in Topic 28, an employer is permitted to pay for up to $50,000 of group term life insurance on behalf of an employee, and the premium is not taxable to the employee (as long as the plan is nondiscriminatory). If the employer pays for more than $50,000 of group term life insurance, the Table 1 cost of the excess coverage will be reported on the employee's W-2 form and will be taxable income.

Dividends

Life insurance policy dividends are not taxed like dividends on stock. The IRS treats a policy dividend as a return of excess premium. As long as the cumulative dividends paid to a policyowner do not exceed the cumulative premiums paid, the dividends are free of income tax. When the dividends exceed the cumulative premiums paid, the policyowner must report subsequent dividends as ordinary income for tax purposes.

When a policyowner elects to allow dividends to accumulate at interest with the insurance company, the dividend will remain tax-free, but the interest earned will be taxable each year.

Loans

Generally, policy loans do not create a taxable event unless the policy is a MEC (discussed below).

Withdrawals

The growth of cash values inside a permanent life insurance policy is fully income-tax-deferred. When the owner makes a withdrawal from the cash value of a life policy, the withdrawn amounts are treated as a nontaxable return of basis first, followed by taxable earnings. This is called the FIFO (first-in-first-out) method of income taxation. No tax is owed until the withdrawal amount exceeds the owner's basis, and the basis is generally the total amount of premiums paid. Thus, if an owner uses the withdrawal feature of a universal life policy, no tax is owed until the amount withdrawn exceeds the premiums paid. A typical withdrawal strategy for UL policies is to take tax-free withdrawals until all basis is recovered, then any further distributions from the policy are borrowed as tax-free loans. It should be kept in mind, however, that outstanding loans reduce the death benefit paid upon the death of the insured.

The rule is different for a policy that is a MEC (modified endowment contract, as discussed later in this topic). The rule is also different for a withdrawal from a policy when there is a reduction in the policy's death benefit during the first 15 years of the policy. In both of these circumstances, the withdrawal is treated as income to the extent of earnings under the policy.

When income or gain must be reported from a withdrawal or other distribution, it is reported as ordinary income. In this respect, life insurance and annuities are similar in that investment gains on the contracts are not treated as capital gains, but as ordinary income.

Determining Basis

The basis in the contract is the amount that can be recovered tax-free when withdrawals are taken from the policy or when the policy is surrendered. The total premiums paid for a policy, less the cost of certain riders (e.g., waiver of premium riders and accidental death riders), are the starting point for determining basis.

Remember, however, that dividends are treated as a tax-free return of premium. In calculating basis, then, any dividends paid in relation to the policy will reduce the basis.

Definition of Life Insurance

Because of perceived and actual abuses of the income tax advantages granted to life insurance cash values, Congress passed legislation restricting these tax advantages by adopting a new definition of life insurance. The legislation created two tests to determine whether a policy would qualify as life insurance. Failure to consistently meet one of these tests resulted in the policy losing the tax status of life insurance, so the growth in cash value would not be deferred but would be taxable annually. The tests are as follows:

- The cash value accumulation test provides that the cash value cannot at any time exceed the net single premium that would have to be paid at that time to fund all future benefits from the policy.
- The guideline premium test and cash value corridor test must both be met as an alternative to the cash value accumulation test. Congress created a series of guideline single premiums and guideline level premiums. The details of these tests are quite complex, but planners will not need to calculate them because insurance companies provide this information.

These tests were intended to prevent people from using life insurance primarily as an income tax avoidance device. The result was that many forms of life insurance that met specific needs were eliminated. Prior to the legislation, endowment policies were often purchased to provide funds for college, weddings, home buying, and retirement, but this legislation virtually eliminated endowment insurance.

Surrender

When a policy is surrendered for its cash value, the excess of surrender value over the owner's basis is taxable as ordinary income. The basis is the owner's premium payments less dividends. Any loans outstanding are included in the cash surrender value for income tax purposes.

If the cash surrender value is less than the basis, no loss is permitted to be recognized since the difference is assumed to be the cost of the insurance protection.

One potential method for a policyowner to avoid immediate taxation on the full amount of gain in the year the policy is surrendered is to elect to receive the cash surrender value under an installment payment option. If the election to receive installment payments is made within 60 days of surrender, each payment received will consist of a partial tax-free return of basis and part ordinary income. This installment election allows the basis, and the gain, to be spread out over a number of years. If the policyowner dies before the end of the installment period, the contingent payee will continue receiving the payments with the same tax treatment.

Tax-Free Exchange – Sec. 1035

The IRC provides that if an individual wants to trade an existing insurance policy for a different one, that transaction is not treated as a surrender and purchase, but as a tax-free exchange. IRC Sec. 1035 permits this exchange. There are limitations to this privilege. The exchange must occur directly from insurance company to insurance company, and the policies must both have the same insured.

In addition, a policy may not be exchanged where the exchange will eliminate or delay the collection of taxes by the IRS. A life insurance policy may be exchanged for another life insurance policy or an endowment. An endowment may not be exchanged for a whole life policy unless the whole life policy also endows at age 95. A life insurance policy may be exchanged for an annuity, but the reverse is not true. An annuity may be exchanged for a different annuity, but not one that matures at a later date.

	Can be Exchanged For:
Life Insurance	<ul><li>Life insurance</li><li>Endowment</li><li>Annuity</li></ul>
Endowment	<ul><li>Endowment</li><li>Annuity</li></ul>
Annuity	<ul><li>Annuity (new annuity must mature at same date or earlier)</li></ul>

Life Settlements

A life settlement occurs when a policyowner sells the life insurance policy to a third party for more than the cash surrender value, but less than the death benefit value. In most cases, the insured is neither terminally nor chronically ill (in which case accelerated benefits or a sale to a qualified viatical settlement provider would be more advantageous). The owner simply does not want the policy any longer and determines that he or she may be able to sell it for a larger amount than could be obtained through surrendering the policy.

The purchaser of the life insurance policy is making the purchase as an investment. Since a reasonable estimate of life expectancy will be needed (after all they have to keep the policy in force and won't collect on their "investment" until the insured actually dies), the policies are typically on an insured who is age 65 or older.

The tax consequences to the seller can vary depending on the facts of the situation, so the planner and client will certainly want to collaborate with a knowledgeable tax professional to determine the tax consequences of such a sale before the client enters into a sale agreement. The sale is part insurance and part investment, so the seller will have some return of basis, some ordinary income (to the extent there would have been ordinary income had the policy been surrendered rather than sold), and potentially also some capital gain (if sale price exceeds surrender value). Revenue Ruling 2009-13 provides guidance on taxation for the seller of a life insurance contract, while Revenue Ruling 2009-14 provides guidance on taxation for the buyer of a life insurance contract.

> **Class Discussion 28B – 1**
>
> Is it ethical for financial planners to assist planning clients to invest in life settlements (purchase life insurance policies on strangers as part of their investment portfolio)?

INCOME TAXATION OF LIFE INSURANCE DEATH BENEFITS

Generally, under Internal Revenue Code (IRC) Section 101(a), the death benefits of life insurance paid by reason of the death of the insured are income-tax-free. This favorable tax treatment also extends to death benefits paid by accident and health insurance, as well as death benefits paid under workers' compensation insurance plans. It does not, however, apply to "death benefits" paid by annuities.

When a settlement option that includes payment of interest is chosen (such as interest-only or fixed period), the portion of the payment that represents interest will be taxable as ordinary income, and the portion representing death benefit will be tax-free.

As mentioned in Topic 28, death benefits paid to terminally or chronically ill insureds are also income tax-free, as long as the rules are met.

Transfer-for-Value Rule

As stated above, IRC Sec. 101(a) provides that the death benefit of life insurance is income-tax-free. The major exception to this provision is the transfer-for-value rule. If a policy is transferred to the wrong party, the death benefit in excess of the total amount paid for the transfer and any subsequent premiums, is received as ordinary income:

Example:

Joe X sells his $100,000 life insurance policy to Company L, a viatical company, for $60,000. Company L pays the $1,000 annual premium for four years before Joe dies. The profit to Company L is calculated as follows:

$$\$100,000 - \$60,000 - \$4,000 = \$36,000$$

This profit is received as ordinary income and is, therefore, fully taxable.

Transfers do not create a transfer-for-value problem when made to the following persons or entities:

- The insured
- A company in which the insured is an officer or shareholder
- A partnership in which the insured is a partner
- A business partner of the insured
- Anyone who received the policy with the same basis as the insured. Persons who would receive the policy with the same basis as the insured include any person who receives the policy as a gift and an ex-spouse who receives the policy as part of a property settlement in a divorce.

Several of these exceptions to the transfer-for-value-rule are useful in planning for buy-sell agreements for business owners. For example, the ability of business partners to transfer existing policies either to each other or to the partnership, is a valuable exception that allows the agreement to be funded without adverse tax consequences. It should be noted, however, that the same flexibility is not available when the business is a corporation. There is no exception to transfer-for-value when shareholders transfer policies to each other. The only exception for a corporation is for the insured (who is an officer or shareholder) to transfer an existing policy to the corporate entity.

If the policyowner is a company and the policy was issued as a key person policy purchased with company assets, the transfer-for-value rule would not apply when the policy is subsequently sold to the insured (often upon retirement of the employee).

Obviously, a violation of the transfer-for-value rule, causing the death benefit to be taxed as ordinary income to the extent it exceeds basis, is not a situation that is likely to make clients happy. The good news is that it can be reversed by a later transfer that falls under one of the exceptions listed above. For example, if the policy were later transferred back to the insured, it would no longer be considered a transfer-for-value.

MODIFIED ENDOWMENT CONTRACTS (MECs)

The advantageous tax treatment of life insurance cash values makes it tempting for investors to purchase policies more for the tax advantages than for the protection of a death benefit. Even after legislation was enacted defining life insurance (as described earlier in this topic), many companies continued to sell single-premium policies. These policies barely met the guideline premium and cash value corridor tests. With short-term interest rates high, the policies performed quite well. These policies were again sold by some insurance agents as tax shelters, rather than life insurance. As a result, Congress passed another law specifically to eliminate the purchase of single-premium life insurance as merely an income tax deferral strategy. These policies are called modified endowment contracts (MECs). The word "endowment" has little relevance to any form of endowment sold by life insurance companies.

With a policy that is a MEC, there is no change to the tax treatment of death benefits. The "punishment" applies when cash value is withdrawn or borrowed or the policy surrendered during the insured's lifetime; thus, single premium policies can still be useful as a means of transferring assets to heirs via the death benefit.

7-Pay Test for a MEC

The basic test to determine whether a policy is a MEC is the 7-pay test. Congress had the IRS create a series of premiums based on the earlier guideline premiums. Each form of insurance has a 7-pay premium for each age and sex combination. If at any time during the first seven years of a life insurance policy's existence, the cumulative premiums exceed the 7-pay premium times the number of years since the issue of the contract, the policy irretrievably becomes a MEC. There is a provision that permits removing the excess premium if done during the year in which it was paid.

A policy may also become a MEC if there are "material" changes made to the contract after June 21, 1988. Unfortunately, this term has not been clearly defined, but as a general rule, a change will be treated as material if it increases benefits under the policy. An increase to the death benefit that requires proof of insurability is a material change. Since increases in death benefit by exercising the options under a guaranteed insurability option do not require evidence of insurability, that change is not material. When a Type II UL policy death benefit increases due to the growth of the cash value, those death benefit increases are also not material changes. Some riders that increase benefits are material changes, but adding a long-term care rider is typically not a material change.

A reduction in benefits in the first 7 years could also cause a previously non-MEC policy to become a MEC. This rule makes sense because otherwise an applicant could evade the MEC rules by originally applying for a policy with a very large death benefit, paying premiums for 4 or 5 years, and then simply reducing the death benefit: voilà, the client has funded a large cash value as a tax shelter. To avoid this "backdoor" access to tax shelter, when a reduction in benefits occurs during the first 7 policy years, a new 7-pay test will be required. The new 7-pay test is calculated as if the policy had originally been issued with the reduced death benefit. The same reapplication of the 7-pay test applies to survivorship life (second-to-die) policies even after the first 7 years.

Any contemplated changes to the policy should be discussed with the issuing insurance company to determine whether the change would cause the policy to become a MEC.

Policies issued before the enactment of the MEC rules are exempt from the penalties as long as there are no material changes after June 21, 1988.

Taxation of Lifetime Benefits in MECs

When a life insurance policy is a MEC, taxes will be applied to the extent benefits are accessed during the insured's lifetime: taking a policy loan or withdrawal, or surrendering the policy. If cash value is taken in any of those ways from a MEC, the distributions will be taxed on a LIFO (last-in-first-out) basis. In other words, the earnings are distributed (and taxed as ordinary income) before any cost basis is recovered. In addition, if the policyowner is under age 59½, a 10% penalty will apply to the distribution of earnings. The 10% penalty does not apply to annuitized payments or to payments received as a result of disability, even if the owner is under age 59½.

When a policy loan from a MEC is taxable, the taxable amount of the loan increases the basis in the policy for calculating taxes on future withdrawals.

Example 1: Dan owns a MEC policy with a $100,000 cash value. He has paid $30,000 in premiums, and no dividends have been paid on the policy. If Dan takes out a $50,000 loan, the full amount will be taxable because earnings come out first (and he has $70,000 of earnings in the policy). If Dan is under age 59½, he will pay a 10% penalty in addition to the ordinary income taxes. Since Dan received a taxable loan of $50,000, his basis in the policy increases to $80,000 (the $30,000 paid in premiums plus the $50,000 taxable loan).

Example 2: Donna owns a MEC policy with a $100,000 cash value. She has paid $70,000 in premiums, and no dividends have been paid on the policy. If Donna takes out a $50,000 loan, she will pay tax on the $30,000 of earnings. If Donna is under age 59½ she will also pay a 10% penalty on the $30,000 of earnings that were distributed. The $20,000 that is nontaxable does not affect her basis in the contract because it is a loan rather than a withdrawal. In other words, it is not treated as a return of her investment that would reduce the basis in the contract; it is not withdrawn, just borrowed. Her new basis in the policy is $100,000 (the original $70,000 basis plus the $30,000 loan she paid tax on).

> *Did you ever notice that when you put the words "The" and "IRS" together, it spells "THEIRS?"* – **Author Unknown**

When a premium payment that is made will cause a policy to become a MEC, the insurance company is permitted to return the premium (plus interest) within 60 days of the end of the contract year in order to prevent the policy from becoming a MEC. Many insurance companies prefer to return the premiums within 60 days of the time it is received by them, rather than holding excess premiums to the end of the year. The company will also often contact the policyowner and explain the tax implications of the excess premium before returning it to the policyowner, just in case the policyowner actually does want the premium dollars to stay in the policy and is willing to accept the MEC treatment.

Section 1035 Exchanges of MECs

Policies that are MECs can still be exchanged tax-free under Section 1035 of the tax code; however, the policy will remain a MEC, even if exchanged for a new policy that would have passed the 7-pay test. The easy way to recall this rule is "once a MEC, always a MEC."

EXHIBIT 28B – 1 Taxation of Life Insurance		
	MEC Policy	**Non-MEC Policy**
Test	Premiums exceed 7-pay test anytime in first 7 years	Premiums less than 7-pay test during first 7 years
Loans (cash value > premiums)	LIFO – Ordinary income; plus if owner under age 59½, 10% penalty tax	Not taxable income
Living proceeds (withdrawal or distributions) (cash value > premiums)	LIFO – Ordinary income; plus if owner under age 59½, 10% penalty tax	FIFO – No income tax until cost basis recovered tax-free
Death benefit	Not taxable income	Not taxable income

Practice Question

Which of the following statements concerning modified endowment contracts (MECs) is not correct?

    A. All single-premium policies issued on or after June 21, 1988 are MECs.
    B. Policies issued on or after June 21, 1988, are MECs if they fail to meet the "7-pay" test.
    C. Withdrawals from MECs are taxed on a FIFO basis.
    D. Classification as a MEC does not affect the tax-free receipt of the policy proceeds by the beneficiary upon the death of the insured.

Answer:

Policies issued on or after June 21, 1988 that fail to meet the "7-pay" test are classified as modified endowment contracts. The "7-pay" test is based on whether or not aggregate premiums paid at any time during the first seven years of the policy exceed the aggregate premiums that would have been paid on a level-annual-premium basis. If so, the policy is a MEC. Thus, any single-premium policy is a MEC. The key tax factor pertaining to MECs is that any withdrawals (loans, withdrawals, surrender) are taxed on a LIFO basis. Consequently, any withdrawal from the policy in excess of the policyowner's basis is includible in current income. If no withdrawals are made from the policy prior to the insured's death, there is no taxable incident, and the proceeds pass to the beneficiary free of tax in the usual fashion.

The answer is C.

DEFINITIONS

Adjusted Gross Income (AGI) – In the formula for calculating income taxes, the adjusted gross income is total income minus certain deductions (called above the line deductions). Adjusted gross income is the amount shown on the last line on the front of the Form 1040 and on the first line on the back of the Form 1040.

Capital Gain Tax – A capital gain occurs when property is sold for a gain. When property is held longer than one year and is sold for a gain it receives special tax treatment as a long-term capital gain rather than being taxed as ordinary income. Ordinary income is taxed at the individual taxpayer's marginal tax bracket, while the long-term capital gain rate is 15% for most taxpayers (0% for those in the 10% and 15% marginal brackets; 20% for those in the 39.6% marginal bracket).

Ordinary Income Tax – Ordinary income tax rates are the rates assessed on income that is not treated as a capital gain. Taxpayers add all of their ordinary income together for the year, subtract certain allowable reductions, and pay tax at progressive rates as income increases: first at 10%, then 15%, 25%, 28%, 33%, 35%, and 39.6%.

W-2 Form – Form W-2 is the income tax form used to report taxable earnings and income tax withheld for an employee of a business. It is mailed to the employee by January 31st of the following calendar year and is used to report earnings and withheld taxes when filing the individual income tax return.

APPLICATION QUESTIONS

1. Which of the following statements about a MEC is (are) correct?

   (1) A policy may be a MEC when it is issued or may become a MEC at a later point in time.
   (2) If the policy becomes a MEC and the excess premium is not withdrawn during the year it was paid, the policy becomes a MEC forever.
   (3) The principal tax penalty associated with a MEC arises if the policy is surrendered or borrowed against prior to age 59½.

   A. (3) only
   B. (1) and (2) only
   C. (1) and (3) only
   D. (2) and (3) only
   E. (1), (2), and (3)

2. Which of the following would be a transfer-for-value for tax purposes when a life insurance policy is transferred for adequate consideration?

   (1) The transferee is the corporation in which the insured is an officer.
   (2) The transferee is the partnership in which the insured is a partner.

   A. (1) only
   B. (2) only
   C. Both (1) and (2)
   D. Neither (1) nor (2)

******

(Two published questions released December, 1996)

John Rivera owns a $300,000 level-term life policy which he purchased five years ago. He has paid premiums of $500/year for the past five years. He also owns a $100,000 whole life policy which he purchased fifteen years ago. He has paid premiums of $2,000 per year for the past 15 years, and now the policy has a cash surrender value of $40,000. Over the years, the whole life policy has paid cash dividends to John. The cumulative dividends paid to John since inception total $5,000.

3. John has decided to cancel his $300,000 level-term policy. Which statement is true?

    A. John has a taxable gain of $2,500.
    B. John has a taxable gain of $297,500.
    C. John would have <u>no</u> taxable gain.
    D. John would have a taxable gain only if he died while the insurance was in force.

4. Assume the same facts as above, but assume that the whole life policy is a participating policy and has paid John $5,000 in dividends since inception. Which statement is true?

    A. The cash dividends received by John to date are taxable.
    B. If John died today, his beneficiary would receive a death benefit of $95,000 from the whole life policy.
    C. The cash dividends received by John to date are treated as nontaxable.
    D. The cash dividends received by John should have been reported as a long-term gain on his personal income tax return in the year they were paid.

******

5. Hal designates his daughter as beneficiary of his life insurance death proceeds in the amount of $10,000. The beneficiary elects to receive the death proceeds under the fixed-period option over a ten-year period. What part of each annual payment will the beneficiary receive free of federal income taxes?

    A. $500
    B. $600
    C. $1,000
    D. $1,200
    E. The full amount

6. Tony Delgado wants to purchase additional life insurance for his wife so she will be provided for in the event of his death. He has an annuity that is worth $95,000 that he purchased for $45,000 in 2007. There is a 6% surrender charge for the annuity. Tony would like to use the annuity to obtain more life insurance coverage. What is appropriate to recommend to him?

    A. Exchange the annuity for a variable annuity in a tax-free exchange.
    B. Annuitize the annuity and use the money to buy life insurance.
    C. Surrender the annuity and use the proceeds to buy additional life insurance.
    D. Exchange the annuity for a whole life insurance policy in a tax-free exchange.

7. Susan Alpert bought a life policy in July 1988 with a single premium. Under these circumstances, which of the following statements is (are) correct?

    (1) Susan can borrow the amount of the policy's investment income without incurring income tax liability.
    (2) If Susan surrenders the policy for its cash surrender value, she is in receipt of taxable income to the extent the policy's cash surrender value exceeds Susan's cost basis.
    (3) If Susan dies after borrowing the policy's cash surrender value, the designated beneficiary will be in receipt of taxable income.

    A. (2) only
    B. (1) and (2) only
    C. (1) and (3) only
    D. (2) and (3) only
    E. (1), (2), and (3)

8. In 2001, Britney bought a single-premium variable life policy with a face value of $100,000. Her premium payment was $32,000. Britney is now 42 years of age, and the cash value of the policy is $65,000. What are the consequences of Britney taking a loan for $25,000 this year?

    A. The loan is not taxable.
    B. The loan is ordinary income.
    C. The loan is ordinary income, plus a 10% penalty will be owed.
    D. The loan is taxable income, but there is no penalty if it is a hardship withdrawal.

9. A viatical settlement company purchased a $250,000 policy for $160,000. It paid additional premiums of $7,000 over the next three years before the insured died. What income must the viatical company report from the policy proceeds in the year of the insured's death?

    A. $0
    B. $83,000 ordinary income
    C. $83,000 capital gain
    D. $90,000 ordinary income

10. If a whole life insurance policy is classified as a modified endowment contract (MEC):

    (1) Its sale will be prohibited by the state insurance commissioner.
    (2) Its federal income tax treatment will be adversely affected.

        A. (1) only
        B. (2) only
        C. Both (1) and (2)
        D. Neither (1) nor (2)

11. Which of the following is (are) among the advantages of most single-premium whole life insurance policies?

    (1) Withdrawals from the policy are taxed on a FIFO basis.
    (2) Withdrawals from the policy are exempt from the 10% penalty tax.

        A. (1) only
        B. (2) only
        C. Both (1) and (2)
        D. Neither (1) nor (2)

12. (Published question released November, 1994)

Which one of the following statements about life insurance products and their tax attributes is correct?

    A. Modified endowment contracts do <u>not</u> provide a tax-free death benefit if the policyholder dies prior to age 59½.

    B. Tax-deferred annuities owned by a corporation are eligible for tax-deferred accumulation.

    C. Permanent life insurance owned by a pension plan is 100% income-tax-free to the beneficiary of the plan.

    D. If a person purchased a life and 20-year term-certain immediate annuity at age 50, there would be <u>no</u> premature distribution penalty.

    E. Policyholders of single-payment deferred annuity contracts purchased prior to 1987 may withdraw funds tax-free from their policy up to basis.

For practice answering case questions related to Topic 28B, please answer the following questions in the cases included in Appendix A at the back of this textbook.

Case	Questions
Black Hills P&L	
Brodinski	
Haurilick	
Beals	
Mocsin	
Loudon	
Connor	14 and 15
Seidelhofer	16 and 17
Loomis Company	
Michael and Diana Eastman	
Gary and Judy Parker	36, 37, 38, 39, and 40

ANSWERS AND EXPLANATIONS

1. E is the answer. All three statements about a MEC are correct.

2. D is the answer. Where the transfer of a life insurance policy is made in return for receipt of some valuable consideration, the transfer-for-value rule applies, with certain exceptions. In essence, where a transfer for value is made, the new policyowners will be liable for tax on the amount of the death proceeds minus the total of the consideration paid for the policy and the net premiums paid by the new policyowner. The exceptions to the application of the transfer-for-value rule include:

(a) A transfer to the insured
(b) A transfer to a partner of the insured
(c) A transfer to a partnership in which the insured is a partner
(d) A transfer to a corporation in which the insured is a shareholder or an officer
(e) A transfer in which the purchaser's basis is determined in whole or part by the seller's basis

3. C is the answer. John will receive nothing when he cancels the term policy, so there is no gain.

4. C is the answer. Cash dividends from a life insurance are generally treated as a return of principal and are not taxable income. The dividends also do not reduce the death benefit payable, as would a loan.

5. C is the answer. The amount to be received free of tax is the full face amount of the policy, which, in this case, is $10,000. The beneficiary chooses to receive this sum on a fixed-period option over 10 years. The nontaxable portion each year is, therefore, $1,000, the face amount of the policy ($10,000) divided by the payment period (10 years). Amounts received annually in excess of $1,000 are taxable to the beneficiary.

6. B is the answer. An annuity cannot be exchanged tax-free for a life insurance policy under Section 1035 of the Code. An annuity can be exchanged tax-free for a variable annuity, but this exchange does not acquire more life insurance for his wife. A surrender will result in the loss of the surrender charge. By annuitizing, Tony can obtain the benefits without a surrender charge and can use the annuity payments to pay premiums each year.

7. A is the answer. A single-premium life insurance policy purchased on or after June 21, 1988, is classed as a modified endowment contract (MEC), and distributions (loans, withdrawals) are taxed on a last-in, first-out (LIFO) basis. Distributions up to the amount of the inside buildup are includible in gross income for tax purposes. Further distributions would constitute a return of capital (nontaxable). Consequently, a surrender of the policy for its cash value would result in taxable income to the contract owner (Susan), amounting to the difference between the cash value and the contract cost (premium paid). (3) is not a correct statement because life insurance proceeds paid by reason of death are not taxable income for anyone.

8. C is the answer. The single-premium policy is a MEC. The loan is a distribution that is treated as ordinary income. Since Britney is under age 59½, she will have to pay the 10% early withdrawal penalty. There is no hardship exception for MECs.

9. B is the answer. The viatical company must report the gain as ordinary income. The amount of the viatical settlement plus the additional premiums are costs and are deducted from the proceeds in determining the gain.

10. B is the answer. Withdrawals from a MEC are taxed on a LIFO basis, meaning that they will consist mainly or entirely of interest earnings, not of principal. Also, if made before age 59½, withdrawals are subject to a 10% penalty tax.

11. D is the answer. (1) is incorrect because withdrawals are taxed on a LIFO basis. (2) is incorrect because withdrawals before age 59½ are subject to the 10% penalty tax.

12. D is the answer. With an immediate annuity, the payments to the annuitant begin as soon as the annuity is purchased. Since the annuitant is under age 59½, the penalty for premature distribution would normally be imposed. The penalty is not imposed, however, if the distribution is based on the life expectancy of the annuitant. In this case, the annuity is a life annuity with a term certain, so it fits within the exception for a distribution based on the annuitant's life expectancy. Thus, no penalty will be imposed. A modified endowment contract will pay a tax-free death benefit in the same way as any life insurance contract. Taxes are imposed when a policyholder attempts to withdraw cash values from a modified endowment contract, and a penalty is imposed if the withdrawal is prior to age 59½. A corporation is not eligible for treatment under the annuity rule, so it must report income on an annuity contract. If a pension plan receives death benefits from life insurance owned by the plan, the distribution to a plan beneficiary will be taxable income just like any other distribution from a pension plan. For a single-payment deferred annuity contract purchased before August 14, 1982, the initial withdrawals will be tax-free because FIFO treatment applies. After the cost basis is withdrawn, any further withdrawals are taxable earnings. For non-qualified annuities purchased after August 13, 1982, withdrawals before the annuity date receive LIFO treatment. Consequently, the first withdrawals are the taxable earnings and then the tax-free investment.

Business Uses of Insurance (Topic 29)

CFP Board Student-Centered Learning Objectives

(a) Recognize the complications of closely owned and/or family owned businesses.

(b) Distinguish the difference between the three types of buy/sell agreements and appropriate uses.

   i. *The Cross Purchase Agreement*
   ii. *The Entity Purchase Agreement*
   iii. *The Wait and See Agreement*

(c) Explain the potential financial risk to the company due to the loss of a key employee.

(d) Identify the opportunity to provide non-qualified benefits for business owners and key executives.

   i. Section 162 Executive Bonus Plan
   ii. Non-Qualified Deferred Compensation

A. *Complications of Closely Owned and/or Family Owned Businesses* ...29.3
   1. *Risk of lost income due to disability of the owner* 29.3
   2. *Risk of lost income due to death or disability of a key employee*..29.3
   3. *Ability to attract and retain key/highly skilled employees* 29.3
   4. *Succession planning issues* 29.4
      a. *Strain on the business due to death, disability, or retirement of an owner and lack of a ready market to sell the business* . 29.4
      b. *Lack of diversification*..29.5
      c. *Management/personnel issues* 29.5
B. *Types of Business Entities*..29.6
   1. *Sole Proprietorship*..29.6
   2. *Partnerships*..29.7
      a. *General partnerships* 29.7
      b. *Limited partnerships* 29.8
   3. *Limited Liability Companies (LLCs)* 29.8
   4. *C-Corporation*...29.8
      a. *Corporate alternative minimum tax*...........................29.9
      b. *Accumulated earnings tax*.....................................29.10
      c. *Perpetual life of a C-Corporation* 29.10
      d. *Transferability*...29.10
   5. *S-Corporations*..29.11

C. Buy-Sell Agreements 29.15
    1. Why does a business need a buy-sell agreement? 29.15
    2. Elements of the buy-sell agreement 29.16
        a. Triggering events 29.16
        b. Permitted transferees 29.17
        c. Mandatory purchase or option to purchase.................29.17
        d. Price..29.17
        e. Terms of sale 29.18
        f. Funding 29.18
        g. Additional provisions 29.19
D. Types of Buy-Sell Agreements and Funding with Insurance 29.20
    1. One-way buy-sell agreements 29.20
    2. Cross-purchase agreements...............................29.21
        a. Income tax treatment of cross-purchase agreements..........29.22
    3. Entity purchase (stock redemption) agreements.....................29.23
        a. Income tax treatment of entity purchase
            (stock redemption) agreements 29.24
            1.) Section 101(j) rules for business-owned life insurance....29.24
    4. Choosing between cross-purchase and
        entity purchase agreements................................29.25
    5. Trusteed agreements 29.26
    6. Wait-and-see agreements.................................29.27
    7. Life insurance ownership and transfer of ownership issues.....29.27
E. Key Person Insurance 29.28
    1. Determining the amount of death benefit to be purchased.......29.29
F. Split-Dollar Life Insurance 29.30
    1. Endorsement method versus collateral-assignment method.....29.30
G. Business Overhead Expense Insurance 29.31
H. Section 162 Bonus Plans...................................29.32
    1. Distinction between owner and employee.....................29.32
    2. Operation of a section 162 bonus plan.......................29.32
I. Nonqualified Deferred Compensation 29.33
    1. Types of nonqualified deferred compensation plans 29.33
        a. Salary reduction plans 29.33
        b. Salary continuation plans 29.34
    2. Funding arrangements...................................29.34
        a. Rabbi trusts 29.34
        b. Secular trusts 29.35
    3. Income tax treatment....................................29.35
    4. Use of life insurance to fund plan benefits.....................29.37
J. Definitions..29.40

COMPLICATIONS OF CLOSELY OWNED AND/OR FAMILY OWNED BUSINESSES

We begin this topic with some of the problems that are faced by closely owned and family owned businesses and that can be solved with insurance.

Risk of Lost Income Due to Disability of the Owner

In a large corporation, when employees become disabled and cannot return to work for several months, the employees typically do not need to worry about whether the business will still be operating when they are ready to go back to work. In a small to mid-size business, however, when the owner becomes disabled for a significant period of time, the owner not only has to worry about paying personal expenses for himself and his family, but also has to worry about paying business bills to keep the business operating throughout his recovery.

The individual or group disability policies discussed in Topic 25 of this textbook will pay the owner's personal income needs, but do not provide any money to keep the business operating while the owner recovers. Business overhead expense (BOE) insurance can be used to fill that gap.

Risk of Lost Income Due to Death or Disability of a Key Employee

Closely held and family owned businesses may have a few select employees who are key drivers of business revenue or who have highly specialized skills or technical expertise that is difficult to replace. When such employees become disabled or die, considerable time, expense, and lost revenue may be incurred before replacements are found. Key person life insurance can provide the business with the liquidity needed to locate, hire, and train replacements, and key person disability insurance can help to sustain operations and replace lost revenue while disabled key employees recover.

Ability to Attract and Retain Key/Highly Skilled Employees

Small to mid-size businesses that are closely held or family owned may find themselves at a competitive disadvantage compared to larger competitors in terms of attracting and retaining key and highly skilled employees. Section 162 bonus plans and nonqualified deferred compensation plans may help to make the compensation package more attractive, provide a means to "tie" those key employees to the business, and deter them from leaving.

Succession Planning Issues

Business succession planning encompasses a large number of issues, several of which can be addressed by the use of life and disability insurance. While many financial professionals  equate a buy-sell agreement with succession planning, true succession planning is more broad-based. The goal of business succession planning should be twofold: (1) to ensure a graceful, fulfilling, and lucrative exit for the owner and (2) to position the business to grow and prosper well into the future.

One of the biggest mistakes business owners make is waiting too long to establish an exit strategy. An exit strategy is important to business owners for a number of reasons, including;

- Setting business and personal goals
- Facilitating retirement of the owner
- Controlling how and when the owner exits the business
- Ensuring the survival and growth of the business
- Preserving family harmony
- Reducing family and employee uncertainty
- Maximizing company value
- Minimizing, deferring, or eliminating income and estate taxes

Failure to have a succession plan in place often results in undervaluation of the company, paying more than necessary in taxes, losing control over the exit process, and failing to realize personal, financial, or business goals during the exit process. When family ownership is involved, it is common for emotional factors and family dynamics to outweigh rational decision-making unless a well thought-out plan has already been established.

While a detailed discussion of succession planning is beyond the scope of this textbook, we will address a few issues that can be dealt with through the use of insurance. Those issues include (1) strain placed on the business when an owner retires, becomes disabled, or dies; (2) lack of diversification in the investment and retirement portfolio of the owner; (3) lack of a ready market to sell the business when a sale is desirable or needed; and (4) management and personnel issues arising with the transfer of the business.

Strain on the Business due to Death, Disability, or Retirement of an Owner and Lack of a Ready Market to Sell the Business

In the absence of a pre-arranged plan for transfer of the business interest, a great amount of strain can be placed on the business, the remaining owners, and the family members of a deceased, disabled, or retired owner.

A buy-sell agreement funded with life insurance and disability income insurance guarantees a buyer for a retiring, disabled, or deceased owner's interest. The agreement also fosters the continuation of the business by not allowing the departing owner's interest to fall into the hands of outsiders – persons who may not be qualified to run the business or who may be incompatible with the remaining owners.

Lack of Diversification

 Owners of closely held and family businesses frequently reinvest profits in order to facilitate the growth of the business. When a business owner's wealth consists mainly of the business interest, the result is a serious lack of diversification. While a qualified retirement plan will help to reduce the lack of diversification, many owners are hesitant to establish a qualified retirement plan due to nondiscrimination rules requiring contributions for employees as well as owners. In such a situation, a life insurance retirement plan (LIRP) strategy may be beneficial. A LIRP uses a cash value life insurance policy (often a UL or VUL policy), funded with after-tax premium payments, to build a savings that will grow on a tax-deferred basis. At retirement, withdrawals are taken first (up to the amount of basis in the policy so that the withdrawals are tax-free), then additional tax-free income may be created by taking loans from the remaining cash value. The loans will reduce the death benefit available to heirs, so retirement and estate planning needs must both be considered.

Management/Personnel Issues

With a family owned business, the owner often desires that the business stay in the hands of family members after the original owner is no longer active in the day-to-day operations of the business. Ownership of the business may be transferred by making gifts or by selling ownership interests to family members. Unfortunately, in many cases the new owners do not have the same skills and management ability that the departing owner had. In these situations, it will be imperative for the ongoing success of the business that key non-family personnel remain.

Retention of key employees may be achieved with the use of nonqualified deferred compensation plans, Section 162 bonus plans, as well as non-insurance based strategies. These benefits may also offer a good way for new owners to convey to key employees that their value to the business is recognized.

Another problem that frequently arises when family owned businesses are transferred to the next generation is that the senior family member who built the business may feel the need to treat all children "equally" in providing an inheritance, even though not all children are involved in the business. A business owner who leaves equal ownership interests to all children almost always causes discord.   Those who work in the business will want profits retained in the business to facilitate growth, while those not involved in the business will want profits to be distributed.   One way to resolve this issue is to leave the full ownership in the hands of those children who actually work at the business, and use life insurance to provide an equivalent value for children who do not work in the business.   Most planners, however, recommend a family meeting to discuss this strategy before it is implemented, since a child who runs the business may feel cheated - his inheritance requires work and everyone else got cash. Communication between parents and children is key to any strategy used for succession of the family owned business.

TYPES OF BUSINESS ENTITIES

You will see in this topic that strategies often work for some business entities but not for others. It will be important to keep in mind that strategies will have different levels of usefulness and different tax consequences depending on the business entity. We will not cover all of the various effects of strategies on different entities; instead, we will provide a general overview of select items of interest regarding the entity types. The focus will be on features which affect insurance-based strategies.

In practice, the planner will want to surround himself with a team of experts, including an attorney and a CPA who are knowledgeable in particular planning areas. In many cases, the business owner will already have a team of professionals, such as attorneys and accountants, with whom the owner works on a regular basis.   The planner will want to make use of these professionals, and additional specialists can be added as needed.

> *"Whenever you see a successful business, someone once made a courageous decision"* –
> **Peter F. Drucker**

Sole Proprietorship

A sole proprietorship is a business entity owned by one individual (or in some states, by a husband and wife). Many small businesses start out as sole proprietorships because of the low cost and legal ease of establishing this form of business entity. For both legal and federal income tax purposes, there is no distinction between the business and the owner. Even when a sole proprietorship is conducted under a fictitious name (sometimes called a DBA – "doing business as" name), the business and the owner are only one entity. The owner of the business and the business are treated as one and the same, and the owner has unlimited personal liability for business debts. For federal income tax purposes, the sole proprietor will simply fill out a Schedule C to show the income and expenses of the business and attach the schedule to his own personal income tax return (Form 1040).

Because there is no legal distinction between the owner and the business, the life of the business is generally limited to the life of the owner. In other words, when the owner dies, the business dies with him, except the assets and good name of the business can be transferred to a new owner.

Potential buyers of a sole proprietorship frequently include family members, key employees, or competitors. In some cases, a sole proprietor, in planning for retirement, will hire and mentor a key employee with the intent of selling the business to the employee at retirement.

Partnerships

A partnership is formed when two or more individuals come together to form a business. Partnerships can be structured as general partnerships or as limited partnerships. In either case, the federal income tax treatment is such that the business profits and losses flow through to the owners. In other words, there is no income tax owed by the business itself (although the partnership does file an informational tax return, Form 1065). Instead, the income and expenses of the business flow through to the owners (the partnership sends each owner a Form K-1 showing his or her share of business profits and losses), and each owner reports his or her share of profits and losses on an individual tax return.

General Partnerships

In a general partnership, all partners are general partners, having proportionate control over the management of the business. While a formal partnership agreement (legal document governing the terms of the partnership) is not required to form a general partnership, a written agreement is strongly recommended. An agreement prepared by an attorney will help the partners to avoid potential disagreements that may arise, and can address the fate of the business if one of the partners leaves the business due to death, disability, retirement, or other reasons. The partnership agreement may place restrictions on the sale or transfer of an ownership interest, often requiring the other partners to agree to the transfer. This situation can also be addressed through a separate buy-sell agreement document (to be discussed later in this topic).

General partners are jointly and severally liable for debts of the partnership, meaning that, like a sole proprietor, they have unlimited personal liability for business debts. The joint and several liability, however, actually adds an additional layer of risk, because even though two partners split the business ownership 50/50, when one is not able to pay his share, the other may be required to pay the full amount.

Limited Partnerships

Limited partnerships are structured with at least one general partner and any number of limited partners. The general partners are responsible for the management of the business and are subject to unlimited liability.

A limited partner's liability is limited to his capital contribution to the business, but a limited partner does not have any management control over the business. Limited partnership interests are more easily transferred because they are not subject to the same restrictions on transfers as general partnership interests. In order to achieve limited liability for the limited partners, a formal partnership agreement is required.

Limited Liability Companies (LLCs)

A limited liability company (LLC) is one of the newest and most popular forms of business entity. LLCs are organized under Articles of Organization and governed by an Operating Agreement. Ownership interests are called membership interests, and can be managing or non-managing interests: managing membership interests have control over the management of the business, while non-managing membership interests do not. All states also now allow single-member LLCs as well as multi-member LLCs, and there is no limit on the number of members an LLC may have. One of the biggest advantages of an LLC is that all members generally have limited liability.

For federal income tax purposes, a single-member LLC is considered a disregarded entity and is taxed as a sole proprietorship. LLCs with two or more members can choose to be taxed as a partnership, a C-corporation, or an S-corporation.

The LLC Operating Agreement may restrict transfers of ownership interests, or a separate buy-sell agreement can be used. Potential buyers of business interests include family members, other owners, key employees, and competitors.

C-Corporation

A C-corporation is a business entity in which the business and its owners are separated for both legal purposes and federal income tax purposes. The corporation is established under state law through the filing of Articles of Incorporation, and the operation of the business is governed through the corporate Bylaws. Corporations are characterized by a centralized management because they are managed by a board of directors, who are elected by the shareholders (owners) of the corporation, and the board appoints the officers who conduct the daily operations of the business. In practicality, closely held and family owned businesses owners (shareholders) will often have elected themselves to the board of directors.

The liability of the owners of a corporation is generally limited to their capital contribution. For federal income tax purposes, the corporation is its own tax-paying entity, separate from the owners. A C-corporation files its taxes on a Form 1120, and the corporation is responsible for paying taxes on the profits of the business. When a corporation decides to distribute those profits to owners (as opposed to retaining them within the business for growth), a dividend distribution is made to the owners. Dividend distributions are not tax deductible by the corporation and are taxable income to the owners on their personal income tax returns. This double taxation is one of the disadvantages of the corporate entity.

C-corporations are also subject to some special taxes that do not impact other entities. Two of these special taxes are the corporate alternative minimum tax and the accumulated earnings tax.

Corporate Alternative Minimum Tax

Congress added the alternative minimum tax (AMT) to the Internal Revenue Code to prevent upper-income taxpayers with many deductions from reducing their income tax below a certain minimum level. The AMT is a separate method of computing taxable income, with different rates and exemptions from the regular income tax calculation. The AMT is computed after the regular tax liability, and the taxpayer always pays the higher amount.

In addition to individuals, C-corporations are also subject to the AMT. (Pass-through entities are not subject to the tax since it is assessed to the owners on their individual income tax returns.) C-corporations use an exemption amount of $40,000 and a rate of 20% after calculating their alternative minimum taxable income (AMTI).

To calculate AMTI for a corporation, the corporation's income is increased by 75% of adjusted current earnings (ACE). ACE includes the inside buildup and the death proceeds from a life insurance policy owned by the corporation, such as a policy purchased to fund a buy-sell agreement, a non-qualified deferred compensation plan, or a split-dollar plan, or for key person life insurance. The net effect, then, is that the inside build-up and any death benefits from life insurance owned by the corporation may be subject to tax at a rate or up to 15% (20% tax rate x 75% of ACE being taxed). If the C-corporation will be subject to the corporate AMT, a planner may need to increase the death benefit so the corporation will be able to pay the tax and still have the amount of death benefit needed.

It should be noted, however, that not all C-corporations are subject to the corporate AMT. Small corporations (under $7,500,000 in average receipts over 3 years) are exempt from the AMT, as are corporations in their first year of existence. Also, if a corporation has fewer than 3 years in existence, as long as its gross receipts are less than $5 million, it qualifies for the small corporation exemption. To get a rough idea of whether the corporation might be subject to the corporate AMT based on average gross receipts, a planner can look at line 1 of the corporation's income tax return, Form 1120, to see the gross receipts reported for the year. If the business is nearing the $7.5 million level and growing, it is probably best to plan ahead for the impact of any death benefits that are likely to be paid, such as for key persons, policies funding an entity purchase buy-sell agreement, or a nonqualified deferred compensation agreement. The company can increase the death benefits to provide cash to pay the tax if it is needed.

Accumulated Earnings Tax

Since a corporation might refrain from paying dividends in order to avoid the double tax on corporate income, an accumulated earnings tax is levied on any earnings not distributed to shareholders and exceeding the reasonable needs of the business. If it can be shown that there is a legitimate business need for accumulating earnings within the corporation, the accumulated earnings tax will not be assessed. In addition, the corporation is permitted to retain up to $250,000 of accumulated earnings without showing a reasonable need of the business. If the business is a personal service corporation (e.g., in the fields of health, law, engineering, etc), the maximum that can be retained without showing a reasonable need of the business is $150,000.

The accumulated earnings tax is 20% of excess accumulated earnings (in addition to regular income taxes), so C-corporations have an incentive to distribute income in one form or another.

Perpetual Life of a C-Corporation

Because a corporation exists separate and apart from the owners (unlike a partnership), the corporation does not dissolve when an owner retires, becomes disabled, dies, or leaves the business for any other reason. It should be noted, however, that for closely held and family owned corporations, the original owner leaving the business can still become a death sentence for the business unless a proper succession plan has been put into place.

Transferability

While shares of a corporation are generally thought of as being freely transferable, stock transfers may not in fact be freely transferable when the corporation is closely held or family owned. There may be a restrictive agreement, either as part of the corporate Bylaws or as a separate buy-sell agreement, perhaps limiting transfers only to other family members or requiring agreement among the other shareholders. In some states, in order for those restrictions to be enforced, the shares must be stamped with a notice that they are subject to a restrictive agreement. It is important for such rules to be followed, so working with a knowledgeable attorney will be of great importance to the planning team.

S-Corporations

Like C-corporations, S-corporations are established under state law through Articles of Incorporation, and the operation of the business is governed through the corporate Bylaws. S-corporations are also managed by a board of directors, who are elected by the shareholders (owners) of the corporation. Closely held and family owned S-corporation shareholders will often have elected themselves to the board of directors. Also, as with C-corporations, shareholder liability is generally limited to their capital contribution.

For federal income tax purposes, the S-corporation is a flow-through entity, similar to a partnership. No tax is paid at the entity level, although the S-corporation does file an informational tax return, Form 1120-S. Income and losses flow out to the shareholders on Form K-1, and this information must be reported on the individual shareholder's personal income tax return, Form 1040.

An S-corporation can lose its eligibility for flow-through taxation if it fails to follow certain rules. S-corporations are only allowed to have one class of stock (C-corporations can have more than one class of stock). S-corporations are also limited to a maximum of 100 shareholders (C-corporations have no limit on the number of shareholders). There are also restrictions on who is permitted to own the shares of an S-corporation. Eligible owners include individuals, estates, and certain types of trusts. S-corporation status will be lost if any of the shareholders is a non-resident alien.

Transferability of S-corporation shares is often limited in the bylaws only to eligible shareholders in order to prevent loss of S-corporation status. In addition, closely held and family owned S-corporations may have additional restrictions on transfers, such as only to family members or requiring approval of remaining shareholders. These restrictions could be part of the bylaws or could be in a separate buy-sell agreement document. As with C-corporations, some state laws will require the stock certificates to be stamped with a notice that the shares are subject to a restrictive agreement in order for that restriction to be enforceable.

🔑 **KEY SUMMARY 29 – 1**
Characteristics of Business Entities - Sole Proprietor and Partnership

Factor	Sole Proprietor	Partnership
Owners' Liability	Unlimited personal liability.	Unlimited personal liability, including liability for the acts of partners.
Organization Costs	None needed except for possible local licensing.	No formal agreement is required unless it is a limited partnership. A written agreement is recommended.
Management	Sole owner makes the decisions.	Decisions are made according to the partnership agreement – in the absence of one, partners vote according to their share of profits.
Taxation of Owners	All net income from the sole proprietorship is subject to income tax and self-employment tax, whether or not received by the owner.	All net income of the partnership is allocated to the partners, according to the partnership agreement. It is self-employment income for general partners, but not for limited partners.
Employee/Owner Benefits	Health insurance premiums are 100% deductible. Life insurance premiums on the owner are income to the owner.	Same as for a proprietorship.
Restriction on Owners	None.	None.
Transfer of Ownership	Sale of assets only.	Partnership agreement should govern how transfer takes place and who must approve it; because of the personal involvement of partners, it may be difficult. The seller reports a gain on the difference between the sale price and basis, with special allocation to inventory and receivables.
Risk Protection	None – The owner is liable for all losses; the owner should avoid risky activity and/or should insure.	None – The owners are liable for all losses; owners should avoid risky activity and/or should insure.

🔑 KEY SUMMARY 29 – 2
Characteristics of Business Entities - S-Corporation, LLC, and C-Corporation

Factor	S Corporation	Limited Liability Company	C Corporation
Owners' Liability	Limited personal liability.	Limited personal liability.	Limited personal liability.
Organization Costs	Organized like a regular corporation and filed with the state. The S corporation election must be signed by all shareholders and filed with the IRS.	Articles of Organization must be filed with the state; LLCs are governed by state law.	Articles of Incorporation must be filed with the state, which will require a payment of fees. Legal assistance may be required.
Management	Shareholders elect the board of directors, who, in turn, appoint management to make day-to-day decisions. Shareholders should ratify major decisions.	The owners, called members, choose managers according to the organizational agreement.	Same as for an S corporation.
Taxation of Owners	Owners can be employees of the corporation and receive salary that is taxable to the recipient and deductible to the corporation. Net income is allocated to the shareholders according to their stock ownership and is not subject to self-employment tax.	Members are taxed the same way as partners, if that option is chosen by the LLC.	Owners can be employees and receive taxable income as salary, which is deductible by the corporation. Net income from the corporation is taxed at the corporate level. Shareholders are taxed separately on dividends received.

KEY SUMMARY 29 – 2
Characteristics of Business Entities - S-Corporation, LLC, and C-Corporation

Factor	S Corporation	Limited Liability Company	C Corporation
Employee/Owner Benefits	Employee benefits are nontaxable only for the employees who own less than 2% of stock.	Same as for partnerships.	Owner/employees can be provided with health, disability, and group term life (up to $50,000) with no taxable income to the owner/employee.
Restrictions on Owners	Up to 100 shareholders that are domestic individuals, estates, or certain trusts.	None.	None.
Transfer of Ownership	Generally, ownership can be transferred by a simple sale of stock. Bylaws may restrict sales. Restrictions help ensure compliance with S corporation rules.	The operating agreement should do the same as a partnership agreement.	Same as for an S corporation.
Risk Protection	Owners have limited liability, so they can engage in risky activity.	Owners have limited liability, so they can engage in risky activity.	Owners have limited liability, so they can engage in risky activity.

BUY-SELL AGREEMENTS

 A properly funded buy-sell agreement is an important part of succession planning for owners of closely held and family businesses. The purpose of the agreement is to arrange for orderly disposition of the business interest when a change in ownership becomes necessary, often due to the death, disability, or retirement of an owner.

In some cases, the owner will choose to make gifts of ownership interests to a child or other relative who is interested in taking over the business. In many cases, however, an owner needs to plan for the sale of his or her ownership interest. Ownership in a small business often has little market appeal to anyone other than those already involved in the business. Consequently, the obvious buyers are usually the remaining owners, key employees, or family members.

When working with business owners to establish the buy-sell agreement, the financial planner will need to assemble a team of professionals to ensure that all of the important elements are addressed. An attorney will be needed to draft the document to ensure that the agreement will be enforceable. In addition, in some cases the corporate bylaws, partnership agreement, or LLC operating agreement may contain some form of buy-sell agreement within them. When that is the case, either a new agreement will need to be drafted in such a way as to avoid violating any terms of that existing agreement, or the consent of everyone affected may be required to change the agreement. The attorney will be able to provide guidance on these issues. In addition, a CPA or other tax advisor will likely be needed to advise regarding the income and estate tax implications of transfers under the agreement. Also, an insurance professional will be necessary to provide guidance on the best types of life and disability policies to be used for funding the agreement.

Why Does a Business Need a Buy-Sell Agreement?

Having a funded buy-sell agreement in place is important to the business and to the owners for a number of reasons. A few are listed below.

- The agreement establishes a buyer, and it specifies a formula to determine the sale price. Otherwise, the business may not appeal to buyers on short notice (for example, at the unexpected death of the owner) or may be difficult to value or sell at a fair price when the owner is no longer part of the business.

- The agreement defines the events that will trigger a sale of the business.
- The sale of the business provides liquidity for the estate of a deceased owner.
- The agreement avoids conflicts between heirs and surviving owners (e.g., the remaining owners are not stuck with the surviving spouse of a deceased owner as their new business partner).
- The orderly transfer of the business helps to maintain stability of business operations.
- Having an agreement in place assures suppliers that the business will continue to operate smoothly when an owner leaves the business.
- Having an agreement can improve the creditworthiness of the business.
- The agreement ensures a fair price, and proper funding ensures that resources will be available to pay the agreed-upon price.
- The agreement can ensure that existing owners maintain control and prevent outsiders from becoming owners.
- Having a succession plan and funded buy-sell agreement in place gives employees peace of mind regarding the stability of the company and their jobs. Without such a plan, employees may "jump ship", for example, when the owner becomes disabled, because of the fear that the business will not survive.

Elements of the Buy-Sell Agreement

While the attorney will be responsible for drafting the agreement, the financial planner should have a basic understanding of the most common elements of buy-sell agreements.

Triggering Events

A buy-sell agreement should have a provision that specifies when the buyer must buy and the seller must sell. The event that sets the sale in motion is called the triggering event. The three most common triggering events for buy-sell agreements are death, disability, and retirement of an owner. It is important for disability to be defined clearly in the agreement (or by reference to the definition used in the disability insurance policy used to fund the buy-out for disability), and typically an owner must be disabled for two years or longer before being forced to sell his share of the business under the terms of the agreement.

Other potential triggering events that may be included in the agreement include involuntary transfers, such as divorce or bankruptcy, or a desire to sell before retirement. If divorce is a triggering event, spouses may also be required to sign the agreement. Another triggering event may be worded broadly, such as the "inability to contribute to the ongoing success of the business." Such a provision could cover unusual situations, including incarceration, loss of a professional license, or disappearance.

Some buy-sell agreements may also address disagreements among the owners through a provision called a "push-pull provision", a "Russian roulette clause", a "Mexican stand-off clause", or a "bullet clause". This provision states that if an irreconcilable dispute arises any owner can offer to purchase the interests of the other owners. The offering owner sets the price and terms. The other owners then have a certain amount of time to choose to sell, or instead they can buy out the offering owner at the same price and terms (which usually ensures the offering price will be reasonable).

For this insurance textbook, we are most concerned with the triggering events of death and disability since the buyout can be funded through insurance.

Permitted Transferees

In some cases there may be no limits on who the business can be sold to, but more often with closely held or family owned businesses, the agreement will restrict the sale to remaining owners or list an order for sales to family members, such as the offer to sell must be made first to siblings, then to cousins, then back to the entity.

In some cases existing owners must be offered the opportunity to purchase the shares first, then if they refuse, the shares become freely transferable (a so-called "right of first refusal").

S-corporations should limit transfers to eligible S-corporation shareholders only.

Mandatory Purchase or Option to Purchase

For the three main triggering events (death, disability, and retirement), the agreement will establish that sale and purchase are mandatory. Other triggering events may be optional.

Price

The agreement should establish a formula for determining the sale price, and may have different formulas for different triggering events. For example, if retirement occurs before a certain age, the price may be lower than if retirement occurs at normal retirement age, or the price might be lower if the seller is forced to sell due to the loss of a professional license. For businesses whose value is largely dependent upon client retention (e.g., financial planning practices), the price might be stated as an initial minimum dollar amount with the final sale price determined at a later point in time from the financial performance and client retention achieved by the business after the sale. That approach provides a strong incentive for the retiring owner to plan for a smooth transition of client relationships.

In some cases, the sale price will be stated as a flat dollar amount, such as $1,000,000. This flat price can be problematic, however, because the agreement can quickly become outdated and will need to be updated frequently.

Terms of Sale

Some triggering events, such as retirement, may state that the seller will be paid via an installment sale (regular payments over a number of years) due to the lack of liquid assets to pay a lump sum.

For a sale at death, a buy-sell agreement will typically require a lump-sum payment, but this requirement will usually mean that life insurance must be available for funding. If an owner is uninsurable, an installment sale might be used instead. The mechanics of using life insurance for funding the buyout upon death will be discussed in the next section regarding types of buy-sell agreements.

Sales due to an owner's disability may be set up as a single lump-sum or as an initial, smaller lump-sum followed by installment payments for a period of years. Special disability buy-out insurance policies are available that can be matched to the terms of the buy-sell agreement. These policies typically require at least a 2 year elimination period, so no payments will be made by the policy until the owner has been disabled for two years. This elimination period should be coordinated with the terms of the buy-sell agreement for disability. Forcing an owner to sell when disabled for a shorter period of time is usually not favored by owners due to the high odds of disability and often lengthy recovery periods that follow. It hardly seems fair to force an owner to sell because he suffered multiple broken bones in a skiing accident that took 9 months to heal, but from which he made a full recovery. The 2 year or longer time frame is more appropriate.

Funding

The buy-sell agreement is only effective if funds are available to make the purchase when needed, so funding the agreement is crucial. While funding is theoretically possible by making cash contributions into a fund earmarked for the buyout, accumulating an adequate amount in such a sinking fund usually takes a very long time, is costly, and is probably not the most efficient use of the business's or owners' resources. Accordingly, a sinking fund should be viewed as a last resort to be used only where insurance is not available either because of the type of trigger (e.g., retirement cannot be insured against) or because an owner is uninsurable. The purchase of life insurance and disability buy-out insurance provides an immediate pool of money to fund the buy-out at exactly the time it is needed, and premiums are usually much lower than the savings that would be required to fund the buyout.

When insurance is used to fund a cross-purchase agreement, as described in the next section, the agreement should contain a clause making it a legal obligation for each owner to keep the policies in force by paying the premiums as required by the policy.

Elements of a Buy-Sell Agreement
• Triggering events • Permitted transferees • Mandatory purchase or option to purchase • Price • Terms of sale • Funding

Additional Provisions

A buy-sell agreement might stipulate that the agreement will continue in force for remaining owners after the first owner transfers ownership under the agreement. Aternatively, the agreement might provide that the agreement ends after the first triggering event and the remaining owners must negotiate a new agreement.

A clause may be included in the buy-sell agreement to disallow withdrawals or loans from cash value policies. The agreement may also prohibit the use of the policy as collateral for a loan.

For cross-purchase agreements (each business owner is the owner of a life insurance policy insuring the lives of the other owners), there may be a clause stating what is to be done with the policies after the first owner dies. For example, the agreement may provide that policies insuring the lives of the surviving partners will be retained by the decedent's estate or the decedent's spouse or that policies may be sold to a life settlement company. The agreement might provide that policies can be sold only to the insured or other remaining owners. Such a clause should be drafted with input from a CPA regarding the effect of transfer for value rules on the taxation of the death benefit (transfer for value rules were discussed in Topic 28B of this textbook).

> **EXHIBIT 29 – 1**
> **Transfer-for-Value Rule**
>
> **General Rule:** If a life insurance policy was sold (transferred for value) during the insured's lifetime, the purchaser will report income in the amount of the death benefit less the purchase price and premiums paid.
>
> **Exception:** The full exclusion of a life insurance death benefit from income applies if the purchaser is:
>
> - The insured
> - The insured's partner
> - The insured's partnership
> - A corporation in which the insured is an officer or shareholder
>
> A gift of a policy is not a transfer for value, so the full exclusion from income applies to a gift as well as to a policy transferred as part of a property settlement in a divorce.

The parties to a buy-sell agreement may want to include a clause stipulating the frequency with which the value of the business will be reviewed and updated. For example, the parties may require a review every other year, and may require that additional insurance be purchased if the value has increased by more than a stated amount or percentage.

TYPES OF BUY-SELL AGREEMENTS AND FUNDING WITH INSURANCE

As mentioned in the previous section, there are numerous triggering events that could be listed in a buy-sell agreement. In this section we will focus on setting up life insurance policies to fund a purchase upon the death of a business owner. Disability buy-out policies can be structured similarly.

One-Way Buy-Sell Agreements

When the business is a sole proprietorship (one owner), an LLC with only one member, or a corporation with one buyer (as opposed to shareholders selling to each other), it is possible to have a one-way buy-sell agreement. There is no reciprocity because the buyer does not expect to sell a business to the sole proprietor. The owner will agree only to sell and the buyer will agree only to buy.

Often either a family member or a key employee will have a desire to purchase the business when the owner dies. If that is the case, the buyer will purchase a life policy on the current owner.

Cross-Purchase Agreements

A cross-purchase agreement is a buy-sell agreement among only the respective owners, and the business entity is not a party to the agreement. Each owner commits to buying an agreed upon percentage of the ownership interest of every other owner who dies. The estate of each owner commits to selling his or her ownership interest to the surviving owners. A formula method or set price is usually a part of the contract.

If there are three stockholders, six policies are required. To calculate the number of policies needed in a cross-purchase agreement, take the number of owners times the number of owners minus one [n(n − 1)]. Owner A must own a policy on B and C, owner B must own a policy on A and C, and owner C must own a policy on A and B.

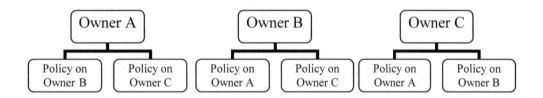

If owner A dies, B and C will collect the death benefits from the policies they own on A's life and will use the proceeds to purchase A's business interest from A's estate.

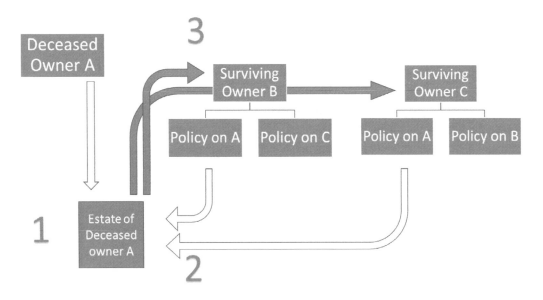

Step 1: Owner A's assets move to the Estate
Step 2: Owners B & C use death benefit proceeds from life policies on A to buy business from A's estate
Step 3: Owner A's business shares are sold and distributed to Owner B and C

In addition, upon A's death, his estate must deal with the policies that A owned insuring the lives of B and C. The buy-sell agreement may stipulate that A's estate will transfer (sell) to B the policy insuring B's life, and the policy insuring C's life is transferred (sold) to C to avoid an awkward "transfer-for-value" problem at the death of the second stockholder. If the business is a partnership, as opposed to a corporation, there is no transfer for value problem if policies are sold to the other owners (e.g., the policy on B is sold to C, and the policy on C is sold to B). Such sales of the policies might be desirable where surviving partners wish to maintain a cross-purchase agreement with each other. The surviving partners will need additional insurance to fund the purchase since each of them now has a greater ownership interest in the business.

Income Tax Treatment of Cross-Purchase Agreements

The premiums paid to purchase insurance required by the buy-sell agreement are not tax deductible, but the death benefits received will be income tax free, as long as a transfer for value problem does not exist.

From the viewpoint of the surviving owners, there is an advantage to the cross-purchase agreement over the entity purchase agreement because of lower income taxes upon the subsequent sale of the business. When the surviving owner receives the death benefit and uses it to purchase the deceased owner's share of the business, the price paid by the surviving owner will provide cost basis in the business interest, and the cost basis will be recovered tax free when the business is sold. This addition of cost basis is sometimes referred to as a "step-up" in basis.

Example:

Bill and Ted started a corporation in which each of them contributed $500,000 in exchange for their shares of stock (to make it simple, let's say they each received 1 share of stock). For income tax purposes, then, they each have a cost basis of $500,000 (which can be recovered tax-free when the shares are sold at a later date). Over time, the business has grown and is valued at $4 million when Bill and Ted decide to enter into a cross-purchase buy-sell agreement. Bill purchases a policy on Ted's life with a $2 million death benefit, and Ted purchases a policy on Bill's life with a $2 million death benefit. A month later Bill dies in a mysterious skiing accident. Ted collects the death benefit (income tax free) and uses it to purchase Bill's share of the business from his estate. Since Ted purchased Bill's share for $2 million, his total cost basis for his 2 shares of stock is now $2,500,000 (the $2 million paid for Bill's share, plus his original $500,000). If Ted decides to immediately sell the entire business (both shares) for $4 million, he will pay income taxes on $1,500,000 of gain ($4,000,000 sale price – $2,500,000 basis). As will be seen in the next section, Ted would have to pay taxes on a much higher amount of gain if the buy-sell agreement had been set up as an entity purchase (stock redemption) agreement.

Event	Bill	Ted
Initial Purchase $1,000,000	$500,000	$500,000
CV of Business $4,000,0000	$2,000,000	$2,000,000
Insurance Policies Purchased	DB of 2 million on Ted	DB of 2 million on Bill
Death of Bill	Ownership interest to Estate	Insurance policy pays death benefit to Ted
Transfer	Ted purchases from Estate	Owns full business
New Cost Basis	–	$2.5 million (initial investment + purchase with Insurance Proceeds)

Entity Purchase (Stock Redemption) Agreements

An entity agreement (or stock-redemption plan for a corporation) is a buy-sell agreement between the partnership (or corporation), acting as a separate business entity, and the individual owners (or stockholders), in which the entity agrees to buy the ownership interest (or stock) from the estate of a deceased owner. The individual owners commit their respective estates to selling their ownership interests to the entity. The agreement usually sets forth the purchase price for the ownership interests or specifies a formula to be used to determine the value of the interests.

A schedule should be appended to the agreement, recording the life insurance policies that are subject to the agreement. There should be a provision in the agreement stating that the life insurance policies are intended to provide funds with which to purchase the interest of a deceased owner. Provision should be made for additions, substitutions, or withdrawals of policies because during the years the agreement is in effect, there may be a need to add additional life insurance policies if the value of the corporation or the partnership increases, or there may be a need for withdrawal of one or more policies if the value of the ownership interest declines.

Income Tax Treatment of Entity Purchase (Stock Redemption) Agreements

The business entity will be the owner and beneficiary of a policy on each owner. Premiums for this life insurance are not deductible by the entity, but the life insurance death benefit proceeds are received income tax-free. Remember, however, that if a C-corporation owns the policy and is the beneficiary of the policy, the corporate alternative minimum tax may apply. If it is likely that the corporate AMT would cause the death benefit to be taxable, the amount of death benefit should be increased by 15% (the maximum tax rate that would apply) in order to ensure that the corporation will have enough cash on hand to pay the AMT taxes as well as to pay the purchase price to the deceased owner's estate. For example, if the agreed-upon purchase price is $600,000, then a death benefit of $705,883 (found by dividing $600,000 by (1 – the tax bracket) = $600,000/.85). If these extra funds are not readily available from the life insurance proceeds or some other source, the corporation may be prevented from making the purchase due to laws in some states that disallow payments to shareholders if the payments will cause retained earnings to fall too low, in order to protect the business's creditors.

Section 101(j) Rules for Business-Owned Life Insurance

Section 101(j) of the tax code sets forth rules regarding employee notice and consent when a business entity wishes to purchase a life insurance policy in which the employee will be the insured and the business will be the owner and beneficiary. In order to retain the income tax-free nature of the death benefit, the business is required, before the contract is issued, to:

1) Notify the employee in writing that the business (policyholder) intends to insure the employee's life, for the maximum face amount for which the employee could be insured at the time the contract is issued.
2) Obtain from the employee written consent to being insured under the contract and to continued coverage after the insured terminates employment.
3) Inform the employee, in writing, that the business (policyholder) will be a beneficiary of any proceeds payable upon the death of the employee.

An example of an Employee Notice and Consent form (sometimes referred to as a Section 101(j) form) can be found in Appendix F of this textbook.

In addition to the notice and consent requirements, one of the following must also apply:

1) At the time the policy is issued, the employee is a key employee (as defined under the law: a director, a 5% or greater owner, one of the 5 highest paid officers, among the 35% highest paid employees, or an employee with compensation of at least $120,000 per year (indexed for inflation under Section 414(q) in 2015)).
2) At the time of death, the employee was still employed with the business at any time during the 12 months prior to death.
3) The death benefit is paid to the insured's heirs.
4) The death benefit is used to purchase the insured's ownership interest in the business from the insured's heirs or estate (e.g., under a buy-sell agreement).

Failure to comply with these requirements will result in the death benefit being taxed as ordinary income, to the extent that it exceeds the employer's cost basis in the policy. Each year that the business continues to own the policy, it will be required to file Form 8925 with its income tax return to report information regarding the policy.

Choosing Between Cross-Purchase and Entity Purchase Agreements

The choice between a cross-purchase agreement and an entity purchase agreement will vary based upon the individual circumstances and goals of the business and its owners.

If the goal is to achieve equity of results (fairness), a cross-purchase plan will be required to accomplish this goal when there is a disproportionate amount of ownership interest held by one participant and/or when there is a wide difference in the ages of the owners. The cross-purchase agreement is needed to accomplish equity of results because the owner paying higher premiums will be the younger owner or the owner with a lower percentage of ownership: the policy on the life of the older owner will have higher premiums due to greater mortality risk, the policy on the life of the owner who owns a higher percentage of the business will be higher due to the higher death benefit required. It is "fair" for the younger, lower-proportion owner to pay higher premiums because he has more to gain or is more likely to be the surviving owner.

Under a stock-redemption or entity type plan, the life insurance premiums are paid out of net income after taxes. The older owners with the largest equity interests will really be bearing (out of their share of retained earnings) the largest percentage of the premium payments. To take more earnings belonging to older and larger percentage owners is unfair because the owners are contributing to buy their own ownership interests. In effect, the older owners are paying premiums out of their shares of earnings to subsidize the younger owners' purchase of their business interests. Thus, the stock-redemption or entity agreement plan produces poor "equity of results" for the old and large owners unless the agreement calls for adjustments.

A stock-redemption plan (entity agreement for a partnership) might be preferred over a cross-purchase plan if there are several owner-participants because this kind of plan would reduce the number of life insurance policies needed. An entity purchase agreement might also be required if there is a disproportionate amount of ownership interest owned by the older participants because the younger participants may be unable or unwilling to pay the sizeable premiums for life insurance coverage for the older owners that would be required under a cross-purchase agreement.

A stock-redemption agreement may also be preferred if the owners individually are in higher income tax brackets than the firm. Since the premiums for the life insurance policies funding the stock redemption agreement will be paid by the firm, the premium dollars are not paid out to the owners as salaries that would be taxed as ordinary income at the owners' respective individual rates. (Sometimes, with a cross purchase plan, firms pay additional salary as a strategy to help cover the premium cost.) Both the firm and the individual owners must pay their life insurance premiums with after-tax dollars, so having the premiums paid by the firm when it is in a lower tax bracket may be of interest.

Trusteed Agreements

To avoid the transfer-for-value problem with a corporation, or if the owners simply want to avoid purchasing separate life insurance policies on one another, they can use a trusteed cross purchase agreement where a trustee takes out the life insurance policy on each owner and the other owners contribute their individual share of the insurance premium.

Trusteed agreements are also useful when the "step up in basis" of a cross-purchase agreement is desirable, but the large number of owners makes a cross-purchase unattractive. For tax purposes, the trustee is treated as a straw man (one with no substance) and the surviving owners are treated as having received the death benefit and purchased the shares of the deceased owner upon death, thus providing them with an increased cost basis.

Wait-and-See Agreements

If the buy-sell agreement has a wait-and-see provision, the surviving owners will typically be given the first opportunity to purchase the shares of the deceased owner as they would under a cross-purchase agreement. If the surviving owners decline the stock, then the corporation has the option (or in some cases is required) to implement a redemption.

The wait-and-see approach could also be used in conjunction with a Section 303 stock redemption (an estate planning strategy where shares are sold back to the corporate entity in an amount equal to the costs of the funeral, taxes, and administrative expenses of the estate to gain an income tax advantage on the shares redeemed). When such an estate planning strategy is combined with the wait-and-see approach, the entity would first purchase the shares being redeemed under the Section 303 redemption, then the surviving owners would be offered the remaining shares under a cross-purchase option, followed by a requirement for the entity to purchase any shares not bought by the surviving owners under the cross-purchase option.

Life Insurance Ownership and Transfer of Ownership Issues

When life insurance is put in place to fund an entity purchase buy-sell agreement, it is essential that if the entity is obligated to buy the business, the entity should own the insurance, the entity should be the beneficiary, and the entity should pay the premiums (and cannot deduct them).

In a cross-purchase arrangement, often used when there is a disparity in ages of the stockholders or in percentage of ownership, the insurance ownership arrangements may become complicated.

The premiums come from the pockets of the owners. A buys a policy on B, and A owns the policy, names himself or herself the beneficiary, pays all the premiums personally, and owns the cash value. B does the same with a policy on A.

As mentioned previously, transfer for value rules may create an adverse tax situation when one shareholder purchases an existing policy on the other shareholder.

Example:

For its stock-redemption plan, the Pharmax Corporation purchased $250,000 life insurance contracts on its two largest stockholders, Harriet and Diane. When the stockholders decided to change the plan to a cross-purchase plan, Diane bought the policy on Harriet for its cash value of $30,000. Diane paid annual premiums of $2,500 for 8 years before Harriet died. Diane can exclude the $30,000 purchase price and the $20,000 ($2,500 x 8) of premiums, for a total of $50,000. She must report ordinary income in the amount of $200,000 ($250,000 – $50,000).

When a C corporation is involved, the transfer-for-value problem can be avoided if A's estate sells the policy owned on B and C to the corporation, which is an exempt transferee. Before A's death, they may have had a cross-purchase agreement. Now they have a cross-purchase and an entity agreement – an entity buy-sell funded by the policies which used to be owned by A.

When a wait-and-see approach is used, the funding may be structured as though there is both an entity agreement and a cross purchase agreement. The entity will own a policy on each owner as would occur with an entity agreement, and each owner will purchase a policy insuring each of the other owners as would occur with a cross purchase agreement. As an alternative, funding can be structured solely as a cross-purchase agreement with insurance policies owned by the individual owners. If the entity is to make the first purchase, the surviving owners can make capital contributions to the business using the proceeds received from the life insurance death benefit so that the entity has the cash available to make the purchase.

KEY PERSON INSURANCE

Key person life insurance is designed to protect a business upon the loss of a key employee. Usually, one or two key people represent the technical genius or creative talent in a  small to mid-size business. The sudden death of such a person can have a disastrous financial effect on the company. It could take years to replace the key employee with someone as talented or with the right synergy for the team. It can weaken the company's credit rating or require the sale of a portion or all of the business if there is no way to cover costs while a replacement person is found.

The tax-free proceeds from a key person life insurance policy can be used to find, hire, and train a replacement; compensate for lost business during the transition;

or finance any number of timely business transactions. In addition, the cash value from a permanent life policy will appear as an asset on the company's financial statements.

The business will own, pay for, and be the beneficiary of the policy. Premiums for key person life insurance are not a deductible business expense, and the death proceeds are received tax-free (unless the business is a C-corporation subject to the alternative minimum tax).

C-corporations should adopt a corporate resolution authorizing the purchase of key employee life insurance to prove cash value build-up is for a reasonable business purpose to avoid the accumulated earnings tax becoming an issue. This precaution is not needed for sole proprietors or partnerships because they are not subject to the accumulated earnings tax. Because the business entity will be the owner and beneficiary of the policy, the rules under Section 101(j), discussed previously in this topic on page 29.24, must be followed. In some cases, however, the employee may be reluctant to allow purchase of the policy for fear that the medical underwriting may reveal health issues they do not want disclosed to the employer.

Determining the Amount of Death Benefit to be Purchased

Valuing the key employee is largely arbitrary, but it can be based on tangible, profit-producing factors. How much financial loss would the business suffer if a key person died last night? Would the death of the key person affect the credit standing of the firm? Would the death of the key person result in a loss of customers?

One way to value the key person is to use a multiple of compensation. This method assumes that the value of the employee is reflected in their compensation package. The appropriate multiple depends on how long it might take to replace that employee.

Another method to value the key employee is calculating a replacement cost. This method factors in the amount of profit that would be lost or need to be replaced, the cost to hire a replacement, and the amount of time it will take to return to the profitability level enjoyed before the death of the key employee.

When the key employee is in a sales position, the value could also be measured by contribution to earnings. There are numerous other ways to value the key employee as well, and life insurance companies are usually willing to assist the planner and client in determining the best and most appropriate method.

Upon retirement, the policy can be sold to the insured key employee, or the cash value can be used to provide a supplemental retirement income to the key employee. If the policy is given, rather than sold, to the key employee, the cash value will be taxable income to the employee, and the business will get a deduction for that amount. If the policy is to be transferred to the insured and the business is a corporation, the corporate board of directors should authorize the transfer. Alternatively, the business can: (1) surrender the policy, (2) take a paid-up policy, or (3) continue to pay premiums and collect the death benefit upon the death of the key employee (assuming 101(j) rules have been met).

SPLIT-DOLLAR LIFE INSURANCE

Under a split-dollar life insurance plan, the employer and employee typically share the premium cost of a whole life insurance policy. Usually, the employer pays the portion of the premium that represents the annual increase in the policy's cash value, and the employee pays the portion of the premium that is attributable to the pure life insurance protection (Table 2001). The employer gets back the amount it pays in premiums when the employee dies and the death benefit is paid out – or when the policy is surrendered for its cash value.

The benefit to the employee is that he or she can obtain the life insurance protection at a reduced cost, but the amount of protection to the employee decreases as the employer's cash value interest increases.

The employer usually advances a portion (or sometimes all) of the premium to the employee and has a lien on the policy cash value and death benefit for the sum of premiums the company has paid on the policy up to the date of death or policy surrender. The agreement typically makes the policy portable if the retiring employee makes the employer "whole" by repaying (without interest) all premium advances.

Endorsement Method Versus Collateral-Assignment Method

The life insurance policy in a split-dollar plan can be owned by either the employer or the employee. Under an endorsement method, the employer owns the policy, and an endorsement is filed with the insurer, prohibiting a change of beneficiary without the insured's consent. Under a collateral-assignment method, the employee owns the policy, but the employee makes an assignment to the employer of benefits, so the employer will receive back its premium payments.

During September 2003, the Treasury issued final regulations on the new tax structure of split-dollar plans. Under these final regulations, split-dollar plans are now taxed one of two ways, depending on who owns the life insurance policy.

If the employee owns the policy, any premiums paid by the employer are treated as loans. In order to avoid any income tax ramifications, the employee must pay the market rate of interest on the loan balance. If the employee pays below the market rate of interest, the employee will have to include in his or her income the difference between the interest due at the market rate and the actual interest paid.

If the employer owns the policy, any premium payments by the employer are treated as providing economic benefit to the employee. Thus, the employee will have to include in his or her income the value of the employee's interest in the policy's cash value. The employee will also have to include the value of the pure insurance protection if the employee does not pay this portion of the premium (Table 2001 cost).

BUSINESS OVERHEAD EXPENSE INSURANCE

Small businesses find business overhead expense (BOE) insurance important to reimburse fixed expenses while the business owner is disabled. The coverage will pay for expenses such as rent, utilities, taxes, and employee salaries. Expenses will be reimbursed up to the maximum monthly limit selected by the insured. The policies are generally short-term, with maximum benefit periods of less than two years and elimination periods of 30, 60, or 90 days. The definition of disability is usually the insured's "regular and own occupation."

Premiums are deductible as business expense, and the benefits are taxable income when received. However, benefits are then used to pay tax-deductible business expenses.

The BOE policy does not replace the owner's earnings, so an individual disability income policy will also be needed to ensure that the owner is able to pay personal expenses during the period of disability.

SECTION 162 BONUS PLANS

As discussed in Topic 28 of this textbook, a Section 162 bonus (carve-out) plan is often used to offer additional life insurance benefits to a select group of executives or key employees.

The compensation package offered to executives or key employees can be broken down into two parts: cash and fringe benefits. Cash compensation includes salaries and bonuses while fringe benefits include items like medical expense insurance, disability insurance, life insurance, and other benefits. The goal of the compensation package is to meet the needs of both the business and key employees. For example, the business may be looking for tax efficiency and the ability to attract, reward, and retain key employees. The fringe benefits are often based on the specific needs of the key employees (who are often the owners). The Section 162 bonus plan may be attractive to key employees who are in need of additional personal insurance and to a business seeking to provide some additional benefits for key employees at a low net cost to the business and with easy administration.

Distinction Between Owner and Employee

For income tax purposes, there is a distinction between "owners" and "employees." Owners are not eligible for many of the tax-advantaged fringe benefits that employees are afforded under the tax law. For fringe benefits (such as Section 162 bonus plans), sole proprietors, owners of partnership interests, LLC members (taxed as a partnership), and greater-than-2% S-corporation owners are treated as owners, rather than employees, even if they actively work for the business. C-corporation owners who also work for the business, however, will be treated as employees. This distinction means that for some types of entities, the goals of a Section 162 bonus plan may not be met when the owners are included in the group of employees receiving the benefits.

Operation of a Section 162 Bonus Plan

Before a Section 162 bonus plan is implemented for a corporation, the board of directors should adopt a corporate resolution to establish reasonableness of compensation (total compensation must be "reasonable" to be tax deductible). Minutes should specify various factors justifying reasonableness, such as the services of the executive are essential to the corporation, or such plan is common for the industry (therefore, the corporation needs a bonus plan in order to retain key employees with a competitive compensation package), or the skills of the executive are unique and contribute to the profitability of the business.

The bonus paid to the executive under a Section 162 life insurance plan will be based on the premiums for the life insurance policy, but it is common for a "double bonus" to be established because the premium amount is taxable income to the executive even if paid directly to the insurance company. The double bonus enables the executive to net a zero tax liability. For example, if the premium is $10,000, and the executive is in the 35% tax bracket, the total bonus would be $15,384 ($10,000 / (1 – .35)), giving the executive $5,384 to pay the taxes and $10,000 for the premiums. Since the bonus amount is treated as salary to the executive, the corporation will be able to take a tax deduction for that amount (as long as total compensation is reasonable).

Each executive covered under the plan will apply for, own, and name the beneficiary on the life insurance policy covering the executive's life, so the executive will have flexibility and control over the policy. The premium amount can be provided as a cash bonus which the executive then pays to the insurance company, or the premium can be sent directly from the employer to the insurance company. If estate taxation is a concern, the policy can have third-party ownership, for example, an irrevocable life insurance trust (ILIT). When the policy is owned by an ILIT, the premiums are still taxed to the executive and are then treated as a gift to the trust under gift tax rules. Estate and gift tax treatment of life insurance is beyond the scope of this textbook, and advice from a knowledgeable estate attorney and CPA is advisable when using trusts in these circumstances.

NONQUALIFIED DEFERRED COMPENSATION

A nonqualified deferred compensation plan (NQDC) may be used as a means to provide retirement, disability, and/or death benefits to a select group of key employees to whom the employer deliberately wishes to confer preferred treatment. In many cases, the nonqualified deferred compensation plan is used to attract or hold a valuable employee.

When NQDC is offered, the employer receives no federal income tax deduction until benefits are actually paid to the employee. All benefits are taxable as ordinary income when paid to the employee and are also subject to Social Security taxes.

Types of NQDC Plans

Salary Reduction Plans

A pure deferred-compensation arrangement provides for a reduction in the employee's current compensation, or a raise is used to provide funding for the future benefit. Thus, under the pure deferred-compensation (salary reduction) plan, the employee delays receipt of some currently available compensation.

Salary Continuation Plans

In a salary continuation plan (supplemental executive retirement plan), none of the employee's current salary is reduced or used to provide the future benefit. The employer's promise of the salary continuation is a benefit in addition to the employee's current salary. Thus, the employer pays the entire cost. These employer promises are often made as an inducement for a valued employee to remain or as an incentive for a new recruit to accept employment.

Note that under a salary continuation plan, the employee promises nothing! The employee may be anxious to remain with the employer because of the attractive continuing salary the employer has promised, but he or she has not promised to stay.

Funding Arrangements

The non-qualified plan may be:

(1) Funded – the employer sets aside specific segregated assets unavailable to creditors
(2) Unfunded – the employer's promise is only secured by the company's general assets.
(3) Informally funded – the employer acquires specific assets which are designed to be liquidated to pay the employee benefits, but the specific assets are commingled with the general assets of the company and thus are available to general creditors.

Under an informally funded plan, the only security or guarantee the employee has of receiving the benefits is the unsecured promise of the employer.

Rabbi Trusts

Deferred-compensation plans can provide for assets to be placed in revocable or irrevocable trusts to pay future benefits. With rabbi trusts, assets to provide benefits are placed in a trust and are kept separate from the company's other assets, but the trust assets are general assets of the company and are still available to the company's general creditors. The IRS has ruled that since the assets of the trust are not currently available to the employee and the trust assets can be taken for the company's general creditors, the employee is not in constructive receipt of the employer's contributions, and no economic benefit is provided the employee; therefore, no current tax is due from the employee. The employee is in receipt of taxable income when payment of benefits is received, presumably after retirement.

There is no guarantee that trust assets will be available to pay the promised benefits to the employee. A rabbi trust can, however, provide for springing irrevocability. Under such a provision, the rabbi trust becomes irrevocable in the event of a change of control or ownership of the employer company. The employer may also be required to make a contribution of the remaining deferred compensation needed to pay benefits.

Insolvency triggers are not permitted with rabbi trusts. An insolvency trigger requires payments to employees or irrevocability of the trust in the event that the employer company's net worth falls below a certain level. Such a provision gives the employees an advantage over general creditors, contrary to the requirements for a rabbi trust. Employees interested in rabbi trusts are usually concerned about their deferred assets being in jeopardy from mergers, acquisitions, or takeovers, so they are interested in the springing irrevocability, even though an insolvency trigger is not permitted.

Secular Trusts

A secular trust is an irrevocable trust used to fund a non-qualified plan. Assets are set aside in the trust for the benefit of the employee and are not subject to creditors. The employee is in constructive receipt and must pay taxes on the amount placed in the secular trust as soon as there is no longer a substantial risk of forfeiture (as discussed in the next section).

Income Tax Treatment

For income to be validly deferred, the employee and employer must conclude a formal deferral agreement *prior* to the employee earning the compensation. If there is no agreement for deferral of income prior to earning the compensation, the IRS will infer constructive receipt, making the income currently taxable. The IRS reasons that if there is no agreement to restrict the distribution of the compensation to the employee, the employee could ask for and obtain the money anytime he or she wished. Such an option for the employee is constructive receipt. An agreement to defer income before it is earned removes the employee's right or power to draw the income; therefore, the income is not available to the employee.

To avoid current income taxes under a formally funded plan (such as a secular trust), the employee must be exposed to a substantial risk of forfeiture. Such risk is present when the deferred-compensation agreement has a provision requiring the employee to give up all rights to the funding assets if the employee fails to comply with certain conditions. The most frequently used risk of forfeiture is the employee's agreement to perform substantial services. For example, a fifty-year-old employee might agree that if the employee terminates service for any reason prior to age 62, he or she forfeits the right to receive the promised deferred income. Thus, the employee has a substantial risk of forfeiture. Since the employee is subject to forfeiting the right, he or she is not in constructive receipt of any economic benefit.

However, when the employee's risk of forfeiture is removed by the employer (or by the lapse of time), the employee will be in constructive receipt of the funding assets. This means on the day the risk of forfeiture ends, the employee is in constructive receipt of income equal to the value of the funding assets.

To avoid constructive receipt, the employee must promise to continue to provide some service. A frequently used device is for the employee to promise to continue to provide consulting services. This arrangement continues the risk of forfeiture and assures that the employee is in receipt of income only to the extent of actual payment.

If the risk of forfeiture is not likely to be enforced by the corporation, the IRS may find that there is no substantial risk. Thus, if a family member is required to perform services for a closely held business and family members are not enforcing the requirement, the IRS may find there is not a substantial risk of forfeiture. The IRS will give special scrutiny to transfers involving a controlling shareholder-employee.

Rabbi Trust	Secular Trust
- General Assets of the Company - Assets segregated in a Trust - No protection from Employer insolvency - Springing irrevocability (merger, acquisitions, etc.) - No current taxation to employee	- Assets segregated in an Irrevocable Trust - Protected from Employer insolvency - Current taxation to employee (can defer with substantial risk of forfeiture – subject to IRS Scrutiny)

Practice Question

A large company has offered Julie a compensation package that will include a non-qualified deferred-compensation plan. Benefits will be based on Julie's performance over the next 5 years. The benefits will not be paid to Julie until she retires as an employee and then completes three years of services as a consultant. When will the benefits from the non-qualified plan be taxed to Julie?

    A. When Julie retires
    B. When Julie earns the benefits during the next 5 years
    C. When the company funds the plan at the end of 5 years
    D. When Julie is no longer required to provide consulting services

Answer:
The benefits from the non-qualified plan will be taxed to Julie when the substantial risk of forfeiture is removed and she is no longer required to provide consulting services. The benefits will be taxed earlier if actually paid to her. The benefits are not taxed when the plan is funded because Julie still has a substantial risk of losing the benefits as long as she has to provide consulting services. In this case, Julie will continue to have the substantial risk of forfeiture until benefits are actually received.
The answer is D.

Under the economic benefit doctrine, an executive must report compensation to the extent the executive has received a benefit with an ascertainable fair market value. Even if the executive has no right to receive the benefit immediately, the executive must report the value of any current economic benefit conferred. Thus, if a contribution is made to an irrevocable trust for the executive and the benefit is not forfeitable, the contribution is an economic benefit to the executive and subject to income tax. To avoid this taxation, assets must remain the property of the employer or must be placed in a rabbi trust, or must remain subject to a substantial risk of forfeiture.

Use of Life Insurance to Fund Plan Benefits

An unfunded plan is essentially a mere promise by the employer to pay a retirement benefit. No reserve is set aside, and no assets are segregated by the employer from its general assets to pay the benefits. The employer's promise is unsecured, and no employer assets guarantee the employee's benefit.

The "funded plan" is not frequently used because the IRS may rule that the employee is in constructive receipt of the assets; therefore, the value of the assets acquired each year must be included in the employee's gross income for the current year. The employee may avoid "constructive receipt" of the funding assets under a funded plan if there is a "substantial risk of forfeiture."

A plan is informally funded when a reserve is established for paying benefits, but the assets in the reserve remain general assets of the employer and can be obtained by creditors in the event of the employer's bankruptcy.

Non-qualified plans are often informally funded by the purchase of:

(1) A life insurance policy
(2) An annuity
(3) Mutual funds

A life insurance policy has the advantage that the internal buildup of cash value will not be taxable to the employer. However, the buildup and the death benefit may be subject to corporate AMT. An annuity has the disadvantage that the employer must pay income tax each year on the income. The annual income on the annuity is subject to current income tax because it is held by the employer corporation (which is a non-natural owner). While individuals do not report the annual income in an annuity, the tax rules require an entity, such as a corporation, to report the annual income.

The NQDC arrangement is often structured to pay retirement benefits to the executive or to pay a death benefit if the executive dies before receiving the retirement benefits. The employer can carry a key person policy on the executive, and be the beneficiary of the death benefit, using the policy proceeds to pay the promised death benefit as a salary continuation payment to the employee's family. If the executive lives to retirement, the employer can pay supplemental retirement income to the retiree out of current company revenue; keep the policy in force after the executive's retirement; and at the executive's ultimate death, recapture the tax-free insurance proceeds to offset the deductible supplemental retirement benefits paid.

The deferred compensation agreement should not make reference to the life insurance policy in order to avoid having the plan treated as "funded." Since the employer owns the policy, the cash value of the policy will be recorded as an asset reserve account on the employer's balance sheet, while the obligation to pay the benefits appears as a deferred liability account. Earnings on assets earmarked to pay the promised benefits are taxable income to the employer each year; however, the use of life insurance has the advantage that the growth of the cash value is tax-deferred.

Practice Question

The GenMed Company wanted to offer a salary continuation plan as an added incentive for a new employee to join the company. GenMed will buy a $1 million variable life insurance policy, and the company will own the policy and pay the premiums. GenMed will be able to use the death proceeds to pay the benefit. Which of the following statements concerning the GenMed plan is correct?

    A. GenMed can deduct the premium payments.
    B. The premium amounts are income to the employee.
    C. This plan is an unfunded, non-qualified deferred-compensation plan.
    D. Benefits paid under this plan to the employee's family would not be taxable income.

Answer:
The GenMed company owns the life insurance policy, so the plan is informally funded or unfunded. The premiums are not deductible, and the premiums are not income to the employee. The premiums would be income to the employee if the

employee owned the policy. GenMed will receive the death proceeds tax-free, but the payments to the employee's family are taxable income.

The answer is C.

DEFINITIONS

Gross Estate – The gross estate is the name given under the federal estate tax laws to all property that a decedent transfers at death. The gross estate includes the total value of all of the assets the decedent owned at death, plus some assets transferred shortly before death and some adjustments for items the decedent did not own but retained control over at death.

Irrevocable Trust – An irrevocable trust gives the grantor (the person who created the trust) no right or power to cancel or change the trust. A revocable trust can become irrevocable if the grantor gives up the power to revoke, becomes incompetent, or otherwise is incapable of revoking.

Transfer Taxes – Transfer taxes include the federal estate tax (upon death) and federal gift tax (on gifts made during lifetime). States may also impose transfer taxes by means of inheritance or death taxes. These transfer taxes are in addition to income taxes.

Business Insurance Summary

Strategy	Goal	Structure of Policy[1]	Income Taxation	Transfer Taxes[2]	Useful for which types of business entities
Stock Redemption Buy-Sell Agreement	To allow for orderly transfer of stock of a deceased, disabled, or retiring shareholder to the corporation at a previously agreed upon price	Owner: corp. Premiums: corp. Beneficiary: corp.	Premiums are not tax deductible Death benefit is income tax free Note: possible corporate AMT on death benefit	Value of the decedent's shares included in decedent-shareholder's gross estate. Arm's length buy-sell can peg value in the estate	C-corp and S-corp
Entity Purchase Buy-Sell Agreement	To allow for orderly transfer of partnership or LLC owner's interest from a deceased, disabled, or retiring owner to the entity at a previously agreed upon price	Owner: business Premiums: business Beneficiary: business	Premiums are not tax deductible Death benefit is income tax free	Value of the decedent's interest in the business included in decedent-owner's gross estate. Arm's length buy-sell can peg value in the estate	Entities other than corporations
Cross Purchase Buy-Sell Agreement	To allow for orderly transfer of stock, LLC, or partnership interest of a deceased, disabled, or retiring owner to the other owners at a previously agreed upon price	Each owner purchases a policy on the lives of the other owners, is responsible for paying the premium on those policies, and is the beneficiary of the policies they own	Premiums are not tax deductible Death benefit is income tax free Purchasing surviving owners get increase in basis of the business equal to purchase price	Value of the decedent's interest in the business included in decedent-owner's gross estate. Arm's length buy-sell can peg value in the estate Value of policies the decedent owned on the lives of the other owners is included in the gross estate (based on replacement cost)	All entities except sole proprietor Note that a sole proprietor can enter into a one-way buy-sell to transfer the business upon death to a successor owner
Wait-and-See Buy-Sell Agreement	Combination of entity and cross-purchase. Offer first made to the business and any shares or ownership interest not purchased by the business is then offered to the surviving owners. Often used in combination with section 303 stock redemption	Entity purchases, owns, pays premiums on, and is beneficiary of a policy on the owner Each owner also owns, pays premiums, and is beneficiary of a policy on the other owners	Premiums are not tax deductible Death benefit is income tax free Note: possible corporate AMT on death benefit for entity purchase	Value of the decedent's interest in the business included in decedent-owner's gross estate. Arm's length buy-sell can peg value in the estate Value of policies the decedent owned on the lives of the other owners is included in the gross estate (based on replacement cost)	All entities except sole proprietor

Strategy	Goal	Structure of Policy[1]	Income Taxation	Transfer Taxes[2]	Useful for which types of business entities
Trusteed Buy-Sell Agreement	A form of cross-purchase arrangement designed to overcome the administrative burden associated with the number of policies required to fund a cross-purchase for more than 3 owners but allowing for the income tax advantages of cross-purchase for the surviving owners	Trustee holds one policy on each owner and keeps the stock certificates subject to the agreement (owners still vote the stock and receive dividends) Premiums can be paid by owners or contributed to the trust by the owners Trustee is beneficiary	Premiums are not tax deductible Death benefits are tax free Purchasing surviving owners get increase in basis of the business equal to purchase price	Value of the decedent's shares included in decedent-owner's gross estate. Arm's length buy-sell can peg value in the estate If the trust is irrevocable (no incidents of ownership) the policy proceeds are not in the gross estate	Entities with two or more owners
Key Person Life or Disability Income Insurance	To protect the business from the economic loss and costs of replacing a key employee upon death or disability	Owner: business Premiums: business Death Benefit/Disability Income: business is beneficiary	Premiums are not tax deductible Death or disability benefits are income tax free Note: possible corporate AMT on death benefit	Proceeds not included in gross estate, but value of business is increased by the proceeds and is included in the estate if the covered key employee is the decedent-owner	All entity types with key employees.

Strategy	Goal	Structure of Policy[1]	Income Taxation	Transfer Taxes[2]	Useful for which types of business entities
Disability Income (DI) Insurance	To provide personal income to a disabled owner	Owner: business owner Premiums: owner Disability Income benefits: owner *note rather than individual policy the owner could be covered under a group DI plan	Premiums are not tax deductible DI benefits are tax free *if group plan, the business will pay premiums and take a tax deduction. Benefits will then be taxable. Also note that sole proprietors, partners, >2% s-corp. owners, and LLC members will be treated as owners rather than employees and will be taxed on the premiums paid by the business. However, this will make the benefits tax-free	Not applicable	All entity types
Business Overhead Expense Insurance	To pay the ongoing expenses of the business in the event the owner becomes disabled. Note that the policy does cover employee salaries but does not cover the owner's salary	Owner: business Premiums: business Benefits: business	Premiums are tax deductible Benefits are taxable, but are used to pay tax deductible expenses	Not applicable	All entity types

Strategy	Goal	Structure of Policy[1]	Income Taxation	Transfer Taxes[2]	Useful for which types of business entities
Buy-Sell Disability	To allow for orderly transfer of a business interest upon the long-term disability of an owner by structuring the disability income policy to coincide with the terms of the buy-sell agreement (e.g., Lump sum and installment payments annually over 5 years)	Entity Purchase: the business owns, pays premium, and is beneficiary of the policy Cross Purchase: each owner owns, pays premium, and is beneficiary of the policy	Premiums are not tax deductible Benefits are tax free	Not applicable	All entity types (sole proprietor can enter into a one-way agreement for disability as well as death)

[1]Changing the structure frequently results in a change in tax treatment.

[2]A detailed discussion of the estate planning impacts of business insurance and buy-sell agreements is beyond the scope of this textbook, but can be found in Keir's Estate Planning textbook.

APPLICATION QUESTIONS

1. The Trent-Harbor Corporation is owned equally by Hugh Trent and Cary Harbor. They are considering a cross-purchase agreement. If the business is worth $500,000, how should the life insurance policy on Hugh Trent be written?

   A. $500,000 face amount, Cary Harbor as owner and beneficiary
   B. $250,000 face amount, Cary Harbor as owner, Hugh Trent as beneficiary
   C. $250,000 face amount, Cary Harbor as owner and beneficiary
   D. $500,000 face amount, Hugh Trent as owner and beneficiary

2. A stock-redemption buy-sell plan would logically be preferred to a cross-purchase agreement by some stockholders under which of the following circumstances?

   (1) If there is a large number of stockholders, and there is a desire to reduce the number of life insurance policies needed
   (2) If equity of results is desired, and a disproportionate amount of stock is owned by one stockholder (pays the lion's share of the plan funding out of earnings)
   (3) If four stockholders of advanced ages owned disproportionate amounts of stock, which would make cross-purchase premium payments financially burdensome for the younger stockholders

     A. (1) only
     B. (2) only
     C. (3) only
     D. (1) and (2) only
     E. (1) and (3) only

3. In the absence of a buy-sell agreement, the heirs of a deceased partner can force surviving partners to take which of the following actions?

   (1) Liquidate the partnership
   (2) Buy the deceased's interest
   (3) Enter into partnership with the deceased's executor

     A. (1) only
     B. (2) only
     C. (3) only
     D. (1) and (2) only
     E. (1) and (3) only

4. Thelma and Louise are equal owners of a business valued at $400,000. They adopted a cross-purchase buy-sell plan over 10 years ago, and now Thelma wants to leave the business to do more traveling. Thelma wants Louise to buy the life insurance policy Thelma owns on Louise. Which of the following statements concerning a sale of the policy is correct?

    A. A sale from Thelma to Louise will be prohibited under the transfer-for-value rule.

    B. If Louise buys the policy, the policy proceeds will be fully excluded from income.

    C. If Louise buys the policy, a portion of the policy proceeds will be ordinary income.

    D. If Louise buys the policy, Thelma will report gain, and Louise will later report capital gain when Thelma dies.

5. Which of the following statements concerning the advantages of a partnership buy-sell agreement is <u>not</u> correct?

    A. If there is a "first-offer" agreement, the price established in the buy-sell agreement will determine the federal estate tax value.

    B. Surviving partners will avoid the conflict of interest in valuing the partnership interest after the decedent's death.

    C. The agreement can be specifically enforced against all parties, so there is no uncertainty about the sale.

    D. The buy-sell agreement assures the heirs of income from the new partnership, even if they elect not to be active partners.

    E. The buy-sell agreement terminates the surviving partners' roles as liquidating trustees and provides liquidity for the deceased's estate.

6. Which of the following situations indicate(s) the need for life insurance for a closely held business or its owners?

    (1) The potential death of a valuable key employee

    (2) The potential death of an owner whose widow(er) would not be a compatible partner for the surviving owner

    (3) The potential death of a minority owner with substantial estate debts, but with no cash

    A. (1) only

    B. (1) and (2) only

    C. (1) and (3) only

    D. (2) and (3) only

    E. (1), (2), and (3)

7. Harry Harth, age 52, is the owner of a successful lawn furniture business near Jacksonville, Florida. Harry was of the opinion that he had adequate life and health insurance but became concerned when he was approached by an insurance agent who inquired concerning Harry's business overhead expense insurance coverage. Which of the following would this coverage provide for Harry that a typical life and health insurance program would not provide?

    (1) Reimbursement for eligible business expenses during a 10- to 12-year period of total disability

    (2) Reimbursement for fixed expenses normal and customary in the conduct of Harry's business, including rent, electricity, heat, water, and employees' salaries

    (3) Replacement of Harry's average monthly salary for the period of total disability

    (4) Salary payments for the person hired to replace Harry during Harry's period of total disability

        A. (1) only
        B. (2) only
        C. (2) and (3) only
        D. (3) and (4) only
        E. None of the above

8. Assume ARCO's board elects to offer the three executives a split-dollar plan with a $100,000 policy owned by ARCO on each of the three executives. Under these assumptions, which of the following statements is (are) true?

    (1) The executive will be taxed on the Table 2001 cost as additional compensation if the executive pays no portion of the annual premium.

    (2) The employer must pay all of the premiums under a split-dollar plan.

    (3) The executive will have to pay interest (or be taxed on this amount) on the outstanding loan balance associated with any premiums paid by the employer.

    (4) All premium payments paid by the employer will be treated as a loan to the employee.

    (5) The executive will be taxed on all premiums paid by the employer in the year paid.

        A. (1) only
        B. (2) only
        C. (1), (3), and (5) only
        D. (2), (4), and (5) only
        E. (3), (4), and (5) only

9. Harry Harth decides to offer his valued assistant, Tom Harvey, a split-dollar life insurance plan on a policy Tom owns. Tom will not be obligated to repay any premiums paid by Harry. Under these assumptions, which of the following statements is true?

    A. Tom will be taxed on the Table 2001 cost as additional compensation if he pays no portion of the annual premium.
    B. Harry and Tom must each pay 50% of the premiums under a split-dollar plan.
    C. Tom will have additional compensation equal to the policy's cash value.
    D. All premium payments paid by Harry will be treated as a loan to Tom.
    E. Tom will be taxed on all premiums paid by the employer in the year paid.

10. In a properly drawn business buy-sell agreement funded by life insurance for a six-person partnership:

    (1) The cross-purchase approach will be found to be more efficient than the entity approach.
    (2) The surviving partners are given the option to buy the interest of a deceased partner.

        A. (1) only
        B. (2) only
        C. Both (1) and (2)
        D. Neither (1) nor (2)

11. In key person life insurance:

    A. The premiums are tax-deductible.
    B. The employee is the beneficiary.
    C. The employer pays the cost.
    D. The employee is the policy owner.

12. All the following statements concerning traditional split-dollar life insurance plans are correct, EXCEPT:

    A. The corporation contributes an amount equal to the annual increase in the cash value.
    B. The corporation receives death proceeds in an amount equal to the net amount at risk.
    C. The plan may be used by the corporation on a discriminatory basis.
    D. The employee is allowed to select the beneficiary for a portion of the death proceeds.

13. (Published question released December, 1996)

Which of the following is (are) true concerning a rabbi trust?

(1) The trust is revocable, and the employer can always rescind it.
(2) The employer may fund the trust from the general assets of the company.
(3) Employer contributions to the trust are exempt from payroll taxes.
(4) The trust's assets may be used for purposes other than discharging the obligation to the employee.

    A. (1), (2), and (3) only
    B. (1) and (4) only
    C. (2), (3), and (4) only
    D. (2) only
    E. (4) only

14. (Published question released December, 1996)

Which of the following is (are) true concerning non-qualified deferred-compensation plans?

(1) They can provide for deferral of taxation until the benefit is received.
(2) They can provide for fully secured benefit promises.
(3) They can give an employer an immediate tax deduction and an employee a deferral of tax.

    A. (1) only
    B. (2) only
    C. (3) only
    D. (1) and (3) only
    E. (2) and (3) only

15. Which of the following factors are desirable when an employee is seeking deferral of a portion of current compensation by means of an informally funded non-qualified deferred-compensation plan?

    (1) The employee's tax bracket will be lower after retirement.
    (2) The employee enjoys a strong personal current financial position.
    (3) The employer is in a strong financial position.
    (4) Assets used to fund the plan are irrevocably committed to the employee.

      A. (1) and (2) only
      B. (1) and (3) only
      C. (2) and (3) only
      D. (1), (2), and (3) only
      E. (1), (2), (3), and (4)

16. Paul's employer has established an informally funded deferred-compensation plan and has purchased a 20-payment whole life policy on Paul's life. To assure the annual premium is excludible from Paul's taxable income, Paul's status should be that of:

      A. The irrevocably designated beneficiary of the policy
      B. A creditor of the firm whose claim is secured by the life insurance policy
      C. An unsecured creditor of the firm
      D. Equitable owner of the bond
      E. The irrevocably designated assignee of the policy

17. If a formally funded non-qualified deferred-compensation plan is used, the employee may still avoid receipt of taxable income if:

      A. Life insurance is the funding instrument.
      B. A substantial risk of forfeiture is associated with the arrangement.
      C. No guarantee is associated with the employer's commitment.
      D. There is assurance of nonforfeitability.
      E. The employee has mere constructive receipt of the funding asset or assets.

18. Which of the following statements concerning a Section 162 bonus plan are correct?

(1) The plan must provide benefits on a non-discriminatory basis.
(2) The life insurance premiums are deductible by the employer.
(3) The employee must pay income tax on the premiums.
(4) The life policy is owned by the employer or a trust set up by the employer.

    A. (1) and (2) only
    B. (1) and (4) only
    C. (2) and (3) only
    D. (3) and (4) only

For practice answering case questions related to Topic 29, please answer the following questions in the cases included in Appendix A at the back of this textbook.

Case	Questions
Black Hills P&L	
Brodinski	
Haurilick	
Beals	
Mocsin	2
Loudon	
Connor	16 and 17
Seidelhofer	18 and 19
Loomis Company	1, 2, 3, and 4
Michael and Diana Eastman	1, 2, 3, 4, and 5
Gary and Judy Parker	41, 42, 43, 44, and 45

ANSWERS AND EXPLANATIONS

1. C is the answer. In a cross-purchase agreement, the owners purchase life insurance on one another. Cary Harbor will buy a life insurance policy in the amount of $250,000 (one-half of the value of the business), and Harbor will own the policy and be the beneficiary.

2. E is the answer. A stock-redemption agreement for a 10-stockholder corporation would mean 10 life insurance policies. A cross-purchase agreement would mean 90 policies (10 x 9). Equity would be maximized if a cross-purchase agreement were used for (2). The stockholders with few shares would buy large amounts of life insurance on the life of the large stockholder. The stockholders with few shares need a large amount of life insurance to buy the large stockholder's shares. This would be equitable but financially burdensome for the low-quantity shareholders. Statement (3) is correct as emphasized above in our evaluation of (2). But, (3) would make the arrangement financially equitable because the younger stockholders need to be paying higher premiums to acquire life insurance to be used to buy shares of the four "oldsters" in case one or more of them dies.

3. A is the answer. Heirs of a deceased partner can force surviving partners to liquidate the partnership. Only if the parties agree, can the heirs sell the deceased's interest to the surviving partners. (3) is incorrect. The executor's duty is to dispose of the deceased's partnership interest.

4. B is the answer. If Louise buys the policy, the policy proceeds will be fully excluded from income. A purchase by the insured is an exception to the transfer-for-value rule.

5. D is the answer. Under a buy-sell agreement, the heirs will sell any interest of the decedent in the partnership and will no longer participate in or receive income from the partnership. A, B, C, and E are correct statements.

6. E is the answer. All three of these situations indicate the need for life insurance for a closely held business or its owners.

7. B is the answer. (1) is not correct because the benefit period is limited to a short term. Ten to twelve years are never offered. (3) and (4) are not correct because there is no replacement of income for the owner (Harry), and no salary payments are provided for the person hired to replace Harry.

8. A is the answer. Under a split-dollar arrangement where the employer owns the policy, the employee will either have to pay the Table 2001 costs or be taxed on this amount if the employer pays it. Thus, (1) is correct and (2) is incorrect. (3) and (4) are incorrect, as these rules apply to policies owned by the employee or a trust created by the employee. (5) is incorrect, as the employee only has to be taxed on the Table 2001 amount and the change in the cash value in the policy.

9. E is the answer. In a split-dollar arrangement where the employee or a trust created by the employee owns the policy and the employee is not obligated to repay any premiums paid by the employer, the employee will recognize income in the year the employer pays the premium. D would be true if Tom were required to repay the premiums. A and C apply to arrangements where the employer owns the policy. B is incorrect, as the employee and employer may allocate the premium payments any way they want.

10. D is the answer. (1) is incorrect. The cross-purchase approach would require (6 x 5 =) 30 separate life insurance policies, versus only six under the entity approach. (2) is also incorrect. The survivors should have a commitment, not an option, to buy the deceased's interest.

11. C is the answer. The premiums are not tax-deductible. The employer is the owner, premium payer, and beneficiary. Therefore, A, B, and D are incorrect.

12. B is the answer. The corporation receives an amount equal to the cash value, not the net amount at risk.

13. C is the answer. (2), (3), and (4) are correct. The employer may fund the trust from general assets; contributions to the trust are exempt from payroll taxes; and the employer may generally use trust assets for other purposes. We should note that this is consistent with the fact that a rabbi trust offers no protection against the possibility that the employer will not have the funds needed to pay promised benefits. It only offers some protection against the employer refusing to pay promised benefits. (1) is not correct because a rabbi trust can be revocable or irrevocable. If irrevocable, the assets are still subject to claims of the employer's general creditors.

14. A is the answer. A properly drafted non-qualified deferred-compensation agreement can defer the receipt of income to covered employees until the deferred benefits are actually received by the employee or otherwise made available. (2) and (3) are incorrect. Funds held for the purpose of paying non-qualified deferred-compensation benefits are subject to the claims of the general creditors of the employer, and the status of a covered employee is that of an unsecured creditor. There is no immediate tax deduction for the employer's obligation to pay future benefits; payments are deducted by the employer when they are actually paid to a covered employee and are included in his or her taxable income.

15. D is the answer. (4) is not correct. If assets are irrevocably committed to the employee, the value of these assets is included in the employee's gross income unless there is substantial risk of forfeiture. (1), (2), and (3) are all desirable factors.

16. C is the answer. As indicated above, as long as the funding asset is a general asset of the employer and the asset is not assigned to the employee, then the employee has no claim on the asset (no right to its value), and the employee avoids taxable income. In this case, the annual premium would not be taxable income to Paul. A, B, D, and E give the employee a claim to the policy and, therefore, are not desirable arrangements.

17. B is the answer. If there is a substantial risk of benefit forfeiture, the employee avoids receipt of taxable income until the funding assets or their dollar values are actually distributed to the employee. A, C, D, and E will do nothing to help the employee avoid receipt of taxable income.

18. C is the answer. A Section 162 bonus plan is usually set up because the employer wants to discriminate by providing an additional benefit to a select number of executives at a corporation. The employer will pay a bonus that equals the premiums on a life insurance policy. The employer can deduct the amount of the bonus as additional salary, and the employee will report it as taxable income. The life insurance policy is owned by the employee or by a trust, such as an ILIT, set up to hold the policy for the employee.

Insurance Needs Analysis (Topic 30)

CFP Board Student-Centered Learning Objectives

(a) Perform an insurance needs analysis for a client, including disability, life, health, long-term care, property and liability.

Insurance Needs Analysis
   A. Introduction to Insurance Needs Analysis.......................................*30.1*
   B. Life insurance needs analysis..*30.2*
       1. Rule of thumb method..*30.3*
       2. Human life value approach..*30.3*
       3. Financial needs analysis...*30.3*
       4. Estimate cash, income, and special goals................................*30.4*
       5. Calculate available wealth..*30.6*
       6. Capital liquidation..*30.6*
       7. Capital retention...*30.7*
   C. Disability, health, long-term care, and property/liability
       insurance needs analysis..*30.7*

INTRODUCTION TO INSURANCE NEEDS ANALYSIS

The insurance conversation can be uncomfortable for many clients because it forces them to think about and acknowledge the possibility of unfortunate events, such as disability, poor health, long-term care, or loss of property, and the certainty of death. While these events are unpleasant to think about, failing to plan responses is certain to make them worse. The insurance needs analysis is an important part of the planning for these events in the risk management process. It can be utilized to identify the appropriate types and amounts of coverage, enabling limited resources to be applied most efficiently and effectively.

The planner often begins the discussion of insurance needs by asking the client to think about what would happen if he or she died (became disabled, lost a home in a fire, etc.) today. While silence is often uncomfortable for both the planner and the client, the silence at the end of the question is the most crucial part of the question. The client needs to have time to picture what life would be like if these events occurred. The client and planner will then be able to determine what goals are important to fund.

In discussing insurance needs analysis, we will begin with an in-depth discussion of life insurance. Other types of insurance needs analysis follow similar approaches.

LIFE INSURANCE NEEDS ANALYSIS

In financial planning, life insurance can be used to replace future income where persons depend on the insured for support, and life insurance can help achieve financial goals, such as making gifts to charity or providing liquidity for payment of estate expenses.

Single people are often told that they do not need life insurance or that the small policy that comes with their work benefits is enough. In many cases, that is correct. However, there are certain instances where a single person may need life insurance, such as to pay off a mortgage, to protect insurability for future dependents, or to leave money to provide for parents, a significant other, relative, friend, or charity.

Blended families (those with children from a previous marriage) and sandwiched families (those who have to provide for minor children, as well as their own parents) tend to have even greater life insurance needs.

There are several approaches that can be used to determine the amount of death benefits needed, including the rule of thumb method, the human life value approach, and the financial needs analysis. In each case, the preliminary determination of the death benefit need should then be reduced by any savings available to fund the same goals.

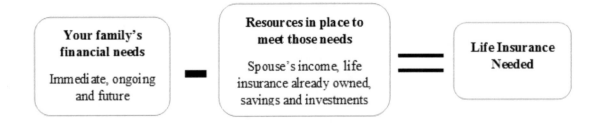

Rule of Thumb Method

The rule of thumb method can provide a rough estimate of death benefit needs using a multiple of earnings such as 6 to 10 times annual income. The biggest advantage to this method is the ease of use. The disadvantage, however, is significant: it appears to be a random number without much meaning to the client. Without a clear understanding of what this death benefit is purchasing, there is little attachment to the policy and the likelihood of the policy eventually lapsing is higher than for a policy where the insured has a clear understanding and emotional connection to the purpose.

Human Life Value Approach

Another approach to determining the amount of death benefit a client should purchase is the human life value approach. A planner who uses the human life value approach will determine the present value of the breadwinner's future earnings that will be used to support dependents.

For example, Jennifer is a 37-year-old single mother who estimates that she will earn an average of $60,000 per year until she retires at age 67. Two-thirds of this income will be used to support her children, so Jennifer will provide an economic value to her dependents of 2/3 x $60,000 = $40,000 per year for 30 years. If the planner uses a 5% rate of interest to discount this amount to a present value needed today to provide for the dependents for 30 years, then the present value is $645,643. In other words, an amount of $645,643 needs to be invested at 5% to provide the $40,000 needed to support Jennifer's dependents at the beginning of each year for the next 30 years. Given these facts, Jennifer's human life value is $645,643.

Like the rule of thumb method, the human life value method has some disadvantages that make it less attractive than the financial needs analysis as a means of determining the death benefit amount. With the human life value approach, there is no capital retention; the life insurance is liquidated at the end of the family's needs. In addition, like the rule of thumb method, there is little emotional attachment to the value of the death benefit. The insured does not have a clear picture of exactly what that death benefit amount is providing.

Financial Needs Analysis

A more comprehensive approach determines life insurance needs by a financial needs analysis. In financial needs analysis, the planner and client determine the total cash needs (burial costs, administrative costs, estate taxes, credit card debt, and other obligations), income needs (during readjustment period, dependency period, life income for surviving spouse, and retirement income), and special needs (mortgage redemption, college costs, emergency fund), then subtract current personal wealth to determine the amount of life insurance needed.

🔑 **KEY SUMMARY 30 – 1** **Life Insurance Needs Approaches**	
Rule of Thumb	6 – 10 times annual income
Human Life Value	Present value of future income support for dependents
Financial Needs Analysis	Total future cash, income, and special goals less current assets

Estimate Cash, Income, and Special Goals

Two key questions should be asked in analyzing personal life insurance needs: (1) How much income would the family need for its various purposes if a breadwinner should die today? (2) When would this income be needed and for how long? The typical needs are described below:

- An estate settlement fund is needed to pay federal and state estate taxes, burial expenses, debts of the estate left unpaid (including the home mortgage), and last illness expenses not paid by medical expense insurance and Medicare. Most of these requirements must be met almost immediately. The federal estate taxes are due nine months after the date of death and are typically a significant amount for those whose estates are large enough to require payment of the tax. In many cases, the client will not be subject to the federal estate tax due to the current high ($5.45 million in 2016) exemption amount, but will be subject to estate taxes at the state level since many states have an exemption amount significantly lower than the federal level. A brief description of state level estate and inheritance taxes can be found at www.kiplinger.com/tool/retirement/T055-S001-state-by-state-guide-to-taxes-on-retirees/. Average funeral costs vary from $7,000 to $10,000, and average cremation costs range from $2,000 to $4,000.

- The readjustment period is the period of time needed by a family to scale down its lifestyle and reduce its standard of living to the income level that will be maintainable after the breadwinner dies. It is desirable for the family to be given adequate time to make this adjustment without undue financial pressure. In addition, with most employers offering only 3 days of paid time off for bereavement, it may be desirable to provide additional death benefits to allow a working surviving spouse to take some additional unpaid time off to be available at home for emotional support of young children. The readjustment period income should be made available immediately, particularly if the family is not well provided with other liquid resources.

- The next need is for an income for the family during the child-rearing years. The total amount needed depends on the number and ages of dependents and their educational objectives. The need occurs at the end of the readjustment period and lasts through the age when children are expected to be financially independent.

- A life income for the surviving spouse is needed to supplement Social Security, retirement plan benefits, and available liquid resources. The need occurs at the end of the dependency or child-rearing period. It may occur prior to the surviving spouse's eligibility for Social Security survivor income benefits at age 60. Also, while the widow/widower benefit under Social Security is available as early as age 60, the benefits will be reduced, and the impact of the surviving spouse having earned income could cause the benefit to be further reduced or eliminated before the surviving spouse's full retirement age (66 or 67). Once the surviving spouse reaches full retirement age under Social Security, however, there will be no additional reduction due to earned income.

- Mortgage redemption funds are needed to pay off the mortgage on the home or any other real estate owned by the deceased. The funds are needed immediately unless other arrangements have been made to pay off or continue monthly payments on any mortgages.

- An education fund may be desired to pay four or more years of college expenses for all children. The funds should first become available when the oldest child is age eighteen.

- A fund for special goals will pay for liquidating a business interest, setting up a trust for children with disabilities or special needs, or making charitable gifts.

- An extra-expense fund should be the lesser of $10,000 or six months of family income. This fund is needed to meet special needs unanticipated or of an emergency nature. The fund should be available immediately. Extra expenses and emergencies are, by definition, unpredictable as to time of occurrence.

EXHIBIT 30 – 1
Typical Family Life Insurance Needs

- Estate settlement fund
- Readjustment period income
- Child-rearing (dependency) period income
- Spouse retirement income
- Mortgage redemption fund
- Education fund
- Special goals fund
- Emergency (extra-expense) fund

A sample needs analysis form can be found in Appendix E of this textbook, and financial planning software may also include an insurance needs analysis form.

Calculate Available Wealth

After the financial need has been estimated, the client and planner will estimate the available assets to fund this need. The personal balance sheet will list the person's or family's assets and liabilities and will show the approximate dollar amounts available to the family if the breadwinner should die today. Not all assets will be available to provide income for the family, however, so the planner needs to prepare a statement of income-producing capital items available today to help meet the family's income needs. This dollar amount is the net amount after deducting debts and obligations. It excludes any non-income-producing property, such as the homestead.

A deficit in family income is determined by subtracting total income that will be available from the total income needed. The income deficit is converted to an amount of capital that will replace the income. For an estate settlement fund or emergency fund, no conversion is required, and the amount is added to the total capital need. The capital amount is then to be provided by life insurance.

Capital Liquidation

The life insurance policy proceeds can be used to provide a lump sum that will purchase an annuity, or the policy settlement options can be used to provide a life income. Either method can be used to avoid the problem of the beneficiary running out of money. With these settlement option choices, the income payments will last for life, regardless of the beneficiary's longevity. This approach results in liquidation of the capital fund.

Capital Retention

A capital retention approach requires purchase of sufficient life insurance to provide the future need entirely from the investment income without liquidation of the capital. This approach preserves the capital. The amount of capital needed is determined by dividing the future income need by the expected after-tax rate of investment return. For example, if the income need is $80,000 per year and the capital can be expected to earn a 5% after-tax rate of return, then the fund needed is $80,000/.05 = $1,600,000.

Note that a combination of approaches can be used. The planner might recommend capital retention for one part of the client's life insurance need and capital liquidation for another part.

DISABLITY, HEALTH, LONG-TERM CARE, AND PROPERTY/LIABILITY INSURANCE NEEDS ANALYSIS

Analysis of the need for other types of insurance, including medical expense insurance, disability income insurance, long-term care insurance, and property and liability insurance has already been discussed in connection with Topics 24-26, and 32 in this textbook.

APPLICATION QUESTIONS

1. Which of the following personal risk exposures can be eliminated by the purchase of adequate life insurance?

(1) A creditor may fear the death of a debtor before the debt is repaid.
(2) If a husband has a straight (pure) life annuity in which all benefits cease upon his death, life insurance on the husband will provide income for the wife.
(3) A person may not be able to accomplish an important financial objective in his or her limited life years. The person may use life insurance on his or her own life to provide death proceeds to finance the achievement of the objective.

    A. (1) only
    B. (1) and (2) only
    C. (1) and (3) only
    D. (2) and (3) only
    E. (1), (2), and (3)

2. Which of the following statements concerning the need for life insurance is correct?

    A. There is no need for a single person to buy life insurance.
    B. Blended families and sandwiched families have the same need for life insurance.
    C. Two-income families have no need for life insurance.
    D. The premature death of a family head in a single-parent family may cause financial insecurity.

3. Which of the following statements concerning the human life value of Bob, the principal breadwinner of his family, is correct?

    A. It does not consider the family's share of income.
    B. It does not consider self-maintenance costs of Bob.
    C. It uses a discount rate to determine present value.
    D. It disregards Bob's average annual earnings over his productive lifetime.

4. David wants to be sure that if he were to die today, there would be enough death proceeds to pay his son's college tuition at the start of each of four years of college. The son is expected to enter college in six years. The current tuition at the school David wants for his son is $12,000 and is expected to rise by 6% per year. If the funds can be expected to earn 8% per year after taxes, how much life insurance should David purchase?

    A. $31,926
    B. $33,004
    C. $36,121
    D. $41,730
    E. $52,908

5. (Published question released November, 1994)

Which of the following is <u>not</u> needed to calculate the client's human life value?

    A. Average earnings to the age of retirement
    B. Estimated annual Social Security benefits after retirement
    C. Costs of self-maintenance
    D. Number of years from the client's present age to the contemplated age of retirement
    E. Selection of the appropriate capitalization rate

6. For which of the following persons can it properly be concluded that there is no need for life insurance at this time?

    (1) A single person
    (2) A married person with no children

    A. (1) only
    B. (2) only
    C. Both (1) and (2)
    D. Neither (1) nor (2)

7. Arnold is 42 years of age and expects to retire in 18 years. A financial planner has used the financial needs analysis to determine that Arnold's family will have an income need of $70,000 annually if he were to die today. Arnold expects that Social Security will pay a retirement benefit of $20,000 to his wife, and he has a 401(k) retirement plan with $250,000. If Arnold assumes assets can be invested to earn 5% returns, what is the amount of life insurance he needs under the capital retention approach?

A. $818,271
B. $1,000,000
C. $1,150,000
D. $1,400,000

For practice answering case questions related to Topic 30, please answer the following questions in the cases included in Appendix A at the back of this textbook.

Case	Questions
Black Hills P&L	
Brodinski	
Haurilick	
Beals	
Mocsin	
Loudon	
Connor	18 and 19
Seidelhofer	20 and 21
Loomis Company	
Michael and Diana Eastman	
Gary and Judy Parker	46, 47, 48, 49, and 50

ANSWERS AND EXPLANATIONS

1. E is the answer. (1), (2), and (3) all describe exposures that can be treated and personal objectives that can be achieved by the purchase of life insurance.

2. D is the answer. A single person needs life insurance for funeral expenses, medical bills, and other unpaid bills. Blended families may involve stepchildren; sandwiched families involve a person caring for an aged parent, as well as for his or her own children. The two-income family needs life insurance because the survivor's income may not be sufficient.

3. C is the answer. As well as considering a discount rate, the human life value considers the family's share; it includes self-maintenance costs of Bob; and it considers average annual earnings over the remaining productive life of Bob.

4. D is the answer. First, compute the expected tuition level when the son enters college 6 years from now. On your financial calculator, enter the following variables:

N = 6
I = 6
PV = 12,000
PMT = 0
FV = ?

Solve for FV which is $17,022.

Now solve for the amount needed in 6 years by entering the following variables:

N = 4
I = (1.08 ÷ 1.06 – 1) x 100 = 1.8868
PV = ?
PMT = 17,022
FV = 0

Solve for PV using begin mode which is $66,220.

Finally solve for the amount needed today by entering the following variables:

N = 6
I = 8
PV = ?
PMT = 0
FV = 66,220

Solve for PV which is $41,730.

5. B is the answer. The human life value is the present value of that portion of a person's future earnings that will go to the support of his or her dependents. A, C, D, and E are used in the calculation, but B is not used.

6. D is the answer. For example, a single person may have dependents and/or a need to cover estate clearance costs. Likewise, a married person with no children may have a dependent spouse or parent, as well as a need to cover estate clearance costs.

7. C is the answer. Arnold's family needs an income of $70,000 and the investment rate is 5%, so the capital retention approach shows that the amount needed at his death is $70,000/.05 = $1,400,000. This amount is reduced by the $250,000 in the 401(k) so the life insurance needed is $1,150,000. Social Security is already considered in the financial needs analysis.

Insurance Policy and Company Selection (Topic 31)

CFP Board Student-Centered Learning Objectives

(a) Define and communicate key insurance policy terms, coverage, conditions, and exclusions.

(b) Recommend appropriate insurance products, given a client's stage in the life cycle, family circumstances, and needs.

(c) Recommend insurance companies based upon an evaluation of service, personnel, financial risks, company ratings and claims processes.

Insurance Policy and Company Selection
A. Insurance Needs During Various Life Cycle Stages.........................*31.1*
B. Life Insurance Policy Selection *31.3*
1. Purpose of coverage *31.3*
2. Duration of coverage *31.4*
a. Temporary needs..*31.4*
b. Permanent needs *31.4*
3. Participating or nonparticipating..*31.5*
4. Cost-benefit analysis..*31.6*
a. Net cost method..*31.6*
b. Interest-adjusted methods *31.7*
5. Other factors *31.8*
C. Insurance Company Selection – Life Insurance *31.9*
1. Financial strength and history of paying claims/
customer satisfaction *31.9*
2. Underwriting...*31.10*
D. Insurance Company Selection – Other Types of Insurance............*31.11*

INSURANCE NEEDS DURING VARIOUS LIFE CYCLE STAGES

As financial planning clients proceed through the stages of the life cycle, insurance needs are likely to change both in types and amounts of coverage. At an early stage, younger clients, approximately age 21-35, will be making their first purchases of auto, tenant, and perhaps homeowner insurance, and may need to insure a growing family against the financial consequences of sickness, injury, disability, or death. These clients will need assistance with selecting policies and amounts of coverage, and may want help with evaluating employee benefits.

Later, when the client reaches an established career stage, roughly between the ages of 35 and 50, a review of existing policies will be necessary to ensure that policy terms and coverage amounts do not get outdated as income and assets increase. If an umbrella liability policy has not been purchased previously, it is likely to be needed at this stage of the client's life cycle in order to protect accumulated assets.

The client will approach peak earnings at about age 50 and will usually be working to accumulate wealth for investment and retirement purposes. As greater amounts of wealth are accumulated, the need for life insurance may dwindle, or the intended uses of life insurance may change from a focus on providing for dependents to other goals, such as charitable giving or payment of federal and state estate taxes at death. During this period, the client will also need to consider the purchase of long-term care insurance.

Approximately 5 or 6 years before the date planned for retirement, the client should begin to make adjustments to transition into retirement. A thorough review of all insurance policies is warranted, and some policies, such as disability insurance, may be discontinued. During this period the client will also be preparing to transition to Medicare for health care coverage and will need guidance on how Medicare works, whether to choose traditional Medicare (Parts A and B) or Medicare Advantage (Part C), and which Part D prescription drug coverage may be most suitable. These clients will also be seeking advice regarding purchase of Medicare Supplement insurance.

> *"Babies haven't any hair.*
> *Old men's heads are just as bare.*
> *Between the cradle and the grave*
> *lies a haircut and a shave."*
> **-Samuel Hoffenstein**

The last stage of the financial life cycle is the period of retirement when the client will be finalizing Medicare and Medigap decisions, reviewing the need or desire to convert cash value life insurance to retirement income (assuming the death benefit is no longer needed), and making decisions regarding conversion of group insurance benefits upon termination of employment.

The nature of life-cycle financial planning requires the planner to keep these different stages of the life cycle in mind and to make adjustments to the insurance plan as the client moves from stage to stage.

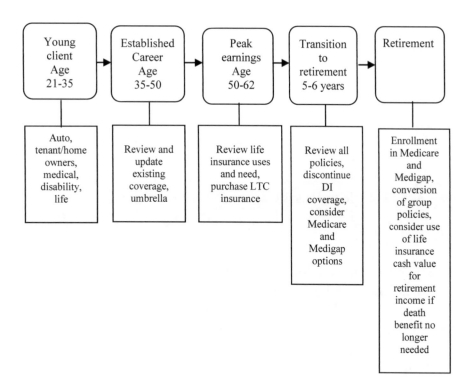

LIFE INSURANCE POLICY SELECTION

Once the amount of life insurance has been determined using the needs analysis discussed in Topic 30 of this textbook, the planner will need to guide the client regarding the selection of a policy. Factors to consider include the purpose of the coverage and the duration of the need. Once it is determined whether a term or permanent policy is desirable, the planner and client will also want to consider whether a participating policy is desirable for the permanent protection.

Purpose of Coverage

While some life insurance agents may be tempted to sell policies based purely on investment and tax features, a life policy will always require mortality expenses. A client purchasing life insurance will be paying for the cost of insurance; therefore, no type or amount of life insurance is suitable for a client to select unless it meets one or more of that client's needs for protection. Those needs, discussed in some detail in Topic 30, typically include several of the following:

- Estate clearance fund
- Emergency fund
- Fund to provide for the insured's survivors

- Debt liquidation fund
- Educational fund for children
- Funds for special goals, such as:

1. Liquidating a business interest
2. Making charitable gifts
3. Implementing a trust arrangement at death
4. Replacing lost earnings due to the death of a key employee
5. Providing for a loved one with special needs
6. Providing for long-term care needs (via a long-term care rider)
7. Providing for end-of-life expenses (via accelerated benefits rider)

- Retirement fund

Thus, the first step in addressing the issue of suitability is to identify and quantify the needs of the client that can be met by life insurance. Then, the question becomes one of determining the best type of life insurance for the client based on risk tolerance, policy features, available riders, and cost.

Duration of Coverage

Temporary Needs

If the needs are purely temporary, such as the need to assure money for the college education of the children, term insurance may be the best solution. However, the term insurance should be renewable, as the need may last longer than originally expected (for example, additional children may come along). Also, if the needs are permanent but the client's ability to pay for life insurance is temporarily lower than it will be later, term insurance may be appropriate. However, the term insurance should be convertible, to assure that permanent insurance will be available to the insured when he or she later is able to afford it.

The size of the policy needed may also affect the decision to buy term insurance. If the need is for a large amount of coverage, the family budget may make term insurance the only affordable option.

Permanent Needs

If the insured's needs are permanent and the insured has the ability to pay for permanent insurance, then the question arises whether to recommend the insured buy permanent insurance or "buy term and invest the difference." There is no easy answer to this highly debatable question, but the main factors to consider are:

- Whether the insured has the specialized expertise in investments and the time to manage a separate investment fund

- Whether the insured will have the motivation needed on an ongoing basis to assure that "the difference" will actually be deposited in a separate investment fund
- Whether the insured is ready to take on the added risks associated with a separate investment fund
- Whether the rate of return from a separate investment fund, after expenses and taxes, will be sufficient to warrant the added risks

If factors such as these suggest that permanent life insurance is more suitable for the client than term insurance, the next question is the type of permanent life insurance that is most suitable. The range of choices is wide, but the most common types to consider are traditional whole life insurance (whether ordinary life or limited-payment life), universal life insurance, and variable universal life insurance. The characteristics of these and other forms of permanent life insurance, and thus the situations in which they are suitable, are described in Topic 28 of this textbook. For example, if inflation protection is important, variable universal life may be suitable. If premium flexibility is needed, universal life may be suitable. Or, if a heavy emphasis on saving through the policy is important, limited-payment whole life may be suitable.

EXHIBIT 31 – 1		
Selection of Life Insurance Coverage		
Short-Term Need	**Long-Term Need**	
Term insurance	*Low Risk Tolerance* Whole life Universal life	*High Risk Tolerance* Variable universal life
	Fixed Premium Whole life	*Flexible Premium* Universal life Variable universal life

If the existing life insurance is exclusively annual renewable group term insurance, the client would be well-advised to consider acquiring an individual permanent policy at an early age. Converting group term at an advanced age can be expensive.

Participating or Nonparticipating

With a whole life policy that is participating, the insurer may return a portion of the owner's premium payment as a dividend. Non-participating policies do not pay dividends. The premiums on a participating policy are typically higher than for those of a nonparticipating policy; however, dividends on participating policies are paid when the insurance company has favorable experience from increased investment returns, decreased mortality expenses, or decreased expenses from operations. Dividends are usually declared annually. Dividends are not guaranteed, and an agent is prohibited from suggesting to applicants that dividends are guaranteed. When dividends are paid out by the insurance company on a regular basis, they have the potential to build significant value over time. The policyowner's options concerning use of dividends are discussed in Topic 28.

Cost-Benefit Analysis

One of the factors affecting life insurance policy selection is the cost of the policy. Determining the true cost of life insurance for the purpose of comparing the net cost of various policies is difficult due to the differing provisions and the differing interest, mortality, and expense assumptions each insurer makes in developing its products.

The National Association of Insurance Commissioners' Life Insurance Disclosure Model Regulation requires that policyowners be provided with a policy summary (titled "Statement of Policy Cost and Benefit Information") showing the premium and benefit patterns for a period of years (including at least one year between age 60 and 65, and policy maturity) and containing, among other items, the following amounts:

- the annual premium for the basic policy
- the annual premium for each optional rider
- the amount payable upon death at the beginning of the policy year, separately showing benefits payable under the basic policy and each rider
- the total guaranteed cash surrender values at the end of each year, separately showing the values for the basic policy and each rider

An example of a Statement of Policy Cost and Benefit Information can be found in Appendix F of this textbook.

In addition to this information, policies that are similar to each other can be compared by evaluating and comparing the net cost of the policies. There are three major methods for determining the net cost of life insurance.

Net Cost Method

The first method is the traditional net cost method. This method is simple, but it is misleading. It starts with a determination of the total premiums to be paid per $1,000 of coverage over a specified period (for example, 20 years) and reduces this dollar amount by the last year's cash value per $1,000 and the total dividends per $1,000 to determine the policyowner's total net cost per $1,000 for the period selected (for example, 20 years). It then divides this total net cost by the number of years to get the net cost per $1,000 per year. The main flaw of this method is that it ignores the time value of money (interest lost by the policyowner because the insurance company has the money).

Interest-Adjusted Methods

The interest-adjusted methods recognize the time value of money. These methods compound the premiums and the expected dividends at a specified rate of interest, usually 5 percent, to reflect the fact that these funds could have earned interest. There are two interest-adjusted methods: the surrender cost index and the net payment cost index.

The surrender cost index is calculated based on the assumption that the policy will be surrendered at a certain period of time, perhaps upon retirement or reaching some other goal where the death benefit is no longer needed. The calculation of the surrender cost index is as follows: (1) solve for the future value of the annual premiums at a 5% interest rate from the year in which it is paid till the end of the 20th policy year; (2) do the same with respect to each year's anticipated dividends; (3) determine the 20th year's cash value; (4) subtract (2) and (3) from (1) to determine the insurance cost. Divide this insurance cost by the future value of an annuity due of $1 for 20 years at 5%, which is $34.72. Divide the result by the number of $1,000 units of face amount of the policy to determine the interest-adjusted surrender cost per $1,000 of coverage. Conceptually, the cost, then, is the amount that was paid in but not returned in the form of the cash surrender value, factoring in time-value-of-money.

Example:

The annual level premium on a $200,000 life insurance policy is $3,000. The policy dividends projected at 5% compound annual interest will total $25,000 by the end of the 20th policy year. At the end of the 20th year, the cash value will be $45,000.

We can calculate the future value of 20 premium payments of $3,000 at 5% compound interest after first setting the calculator to begin mode:

> N = 20
> i = 5
> PMT = 3,000
> FV is calculated to be $104,158

From this amount, we subtract the $25,000 of policy dividends and $45,000 of cash value: $104,158 – $25,000 – $45,000 = $34,158.

The future value of an annuity due of $1 for 20 years is calculated (in begin mode):

> PMT = 1
> N = 20
> i = 5
> FV is calculated to be 34.72

This future value of an annuity due (34.72) is divided into the amount of costs previously calculated of $34,158, and the result is $984. This number is divided by 200, which is the number of units of $1,000 of coverage: $984/200 = $4.92.

Thus, the cost of coverage is $4.92 per $1,000.

If there is no intention to surrender the policy for its cash value, an alternative net cost method, the net payment cost index, may be used. The net payment cost index is calculated in the same way, except that the 20th year's cash value is not deducted in Step (4) above.

🔑 KEY SUMMARY 31 – 1 Methods for Determining Cost of Life Insurance	
Net cost method	Add total premiums, subtract cash value and dividends, divide by number of years. Flaw: Ignores time value of money
Surrender cost index	Add total premiums, subtract cash value and dividends, divide by future value of an annuity due and by number of units of $1,000 coverage. Premiums and dividends are compounded at a rate of interest, such as 5%.
Net payment cost index	Same calculation as in the surrender cost index, except cash value is not subtracted.

Other Factors

Factors other than cost that should be considered when evaluating life insurance policies include the following:

- The financial strength of the insurer
- The company's reputation for claims fairness and policyholder service (Complaint files in the office of the Insurance Commissioner may be revealing in this regard.)
- The dividend history of the insurer
- The level of the guaranteed elements in the policy illustration

---

INSURANCE COMPANY SELECTION – LIFE INSURANCE

Financial Strength and History of Paying Claims/Customer Satisfaction

Due to the long-term nature of life insurance, purchasing a policy from a financially stable insurance company will be in the client's best interest. While there is no surefire way to select a completely safe insurance company or agency, evaluating insurance company ratings according to financial strength can be a good indicator.

In most cases, individuals do not have the resources to do this analysis of financial strength, so they rely on others to do it for them.

There are several companies that rate life insurance companies. One company evaluates insurance companies only – the A. M. Best Co. Three other companies, Standard & Poor's, Moody's Investor Service, and Fitch Ratings are best known for rating corporate debt issues and preferred stock, but they have also entered the arena of rating insurance companies. The newest company to rate insurance companies is Weiss Ratings, Inc. With the exception of Weiss, all the others provide ratings by using public information, as well as internal insurance company information. Weiss uses only public information. Standard & Poor's has one set of ratings that is based only on public information.

One recommended guideline is to choose only a company that has one of the three highest ratings from at least three of the rating services. Dr. Joseph Belth is the proponent of this guideline. He believes that this provides adequate protection.

EXHIBIT 31 – 2
Insurance Company Rating Services

Service	Top Rating
A.M. Best	A++
Standard & Poor's	AAA
Moody's Investor Service	Aaa
Fitch Ratings	AAA
Weiss Ratings	A+

It is important to remember that the various organizations use different letters to rank companies. While A+ is the highest ranking for Weiss, it is the second rank for Best, fifth for Fitch, third for Standard & Poor's, and Moody's doesn't even use it. The third-highest rankings for the various companies are: Best, A; Fitch, A; Moody's, Aa2; Standard & Poor's, A: and Weiss, A-.

Practice Question

What is the service provided by A.M. Best, Standard & Poor's, Moody's, Fitch, and Weiss for clients considering insurance policies?

    A. They rank companies and policies according to costs.
    B. They rate the financial strength of insurance companies.
    C. They report risk-based capital ratios for insurance companies.
    D. They rate insurance companies according to profitability.

Answer:
The rating services of A.M. Best, Standard & Poor's, Moody's, Fitch, and Weiss rate the financial strength of insurance companies so that purchasers will be able to determine the security afforded for their insurance purchase.
The answer is B.

The state insurance department is another good resource for information about insurance companies authorized to do business within the state. Most will list information regarding complaints against the insurers (number, reason, etc), asset and balance sheet information, reserve information, and financial strength.

The NAIC website allows anyone to search for similar information regarding insurance companies in the Consumer Information Source (CIS) area of its website: https://eapps.naic.org/cis/

J.D. Power also provides ratings regarding consumer satisfaction for various types of insurance companies, including life insurance:

    http://ratings.jdpower.com/insurance/index.htm

Underwriting

For some clients, the selection of an insurance company will need to be based on the insurer's underwriting philosophy and standards. Some insurers specialize in insuring identified groups and may offer more favorable classifications or pricing for those groups, and some insurers are willing to insure risks at favorable rates that are viewed as substandard by other insurers. Some insurers may require medical examinations and testing, while others do not.

When a client has a condition that may be of concern in the underwriting process, an insurance broker (as opposed to a captive agent who is limited to products of a particular company) may need to search among many insurance companies to find the best underwriting for the condition.

When underwriting guidelines indicate a higher-than-standard risk, insurance companies have a number of alternative methods to offer for dealing with the increased risk. Rather than simply declining to issue a policy, the insurance company may offer a policy at a higher premium or with restrictions on benefits. One common method of rating policies is through the use of extra percentage tables. These tables may be labeled by letter (for example Table A – Table F, depending on the number of tables used by the insurer), or by number (for example Table 1 – Table 4), with rates stated as increasing percentages of the standard rate (for example, 125% of standard rates, 150% of standard rates, etc.). In some cases, when an insured has a medical condition that is likely to cause an increasing mortality risk, the insurer will issue the policy under a rate-up age method For example, a 35-year-old might have ongoing health characteristics that more closely resemble those of a 45-year-old, and those health characteristics are expected to continue throughout life, so the policy is priced as if the insured were age 45 at issue. On the other hand, when a medical condition exists that is temporary and likely to decrease over time, the insurance company may offer to issue a policy at standard rates but with the stipulation that death benefits will be reduced during the first few years the policy is in force.

Class Discussion 31 – 1

Since marijuana use has become legal in several states, a question has arisen regarding how use of marijuana may impact life insurance underwriting. As a group, students should review and discuss the differences in underwriting for marijuana use in the article found at:

http://www.lifehealthpro.com/2013/06/19/exploring-the-effects-of-marijuana-use-on-life-ins

---

INSURANCE COMPANY SELECTION – OTHER TYPES OF INSURANCE

The following guidelines should be recommended by planners to clients for use in selecting individual property-casualty, health, and other insurance policies.

- Recognize that cost is a constraint for most clients. The amount of money they are able or willing to spend on insurance is finite. This doesn't mean that the cheapest policy is necessarily the best one – only that priorities must be established as to what types of policies will be purchased.

- Take into account the risk tolerance of the particular client. The level of tolerance should have a bearing on which types of loss exposures he or she is willing to assume in their entirety. It should also have a bearing on the amount of certain loss exposures that he or she is willing to retain partially through insurance deductibles and waiting periods.

- Insure first and to high limits against the potentially catastrophic loss exposures. Examples include loss of income for the family due to death or long-term disability of the breadwinner; loss of accumulated assets and perhaps future income due to the high costs of a major illness or the need for long-term care; loss of accumulated assets and perhaps future income due to legal liability arising out of the ownership of land or premises, driving a car, boat, or RV, and the carrying on of a business or profession; and the possible serious reduction in the client's standard of living due to his or her outliving the assets planned to provide a retirement income.

- Obtain an adequate amount of replacement cost property insurance on the client's principal assets (for example, his or her home and jewelry).

- Rely first on the client's group coverages and social insurance, using individual policies to fill the gaps in coverage types and amounts.

- Avoid limited policies and highly restrictive policy provisions.

- Shop around for the best deal, but only among reputable, strong insurers.

- Purchasing home and auto insurance from the same insurer typically results in discounts on premiums for both.

- For LTC insurance, check the insurance company's history of increasing rates for similar LTCI policies.

Additional factors to consider for other types of policies have been discussed in Topics 24-27, and 32 of this textbook.

APPLICATION QUESTIONS

1. Kay, a single mother, has a two-year-old daughter, Corinne. Kay, age 30, is in good health and works as a dietician at a local hospital, earning $24,000 per year. The hospital pays the full premium for group term life insurance equal to one year's salary. Based on this information, which of the following types of additional life insurance is most suitable for Kay?

    A. Universal life
    B. Whole life
    C. Term
    D. Endowment
    E. Universal variable life

2. Ron Halstrum, 58 years of age, is owner of a furniture company and plans to retire in 10 years. He has negotiated with an employee who wants to buy the company when Ron retires. The employee is conservative about investments and has a low risk tolerance. Ron is an aggressive investor and wants some assurances that the employee will be able to buy the company when Ron retires. What type of life insurance policy would be best to buy for the buy-sell agreement?

    A. Variable universal life
    B. Whole life
    C. Yearly renewable term
    D. 10-year level term

3. Which of the following methods of comparing the costs of life insurance policies take(s) into account the time value of money?

    (1) Traditional net cost method
    (2) Surrender cost index method
    (3) Net payment cost index method

        A. (1) only
        B. (2) only
        C. (3) only
        D. (2) and (3) only
        E. (1), (2), and (3)

4. Which of the following is the main difference between the surrender cost index (SCI) and the net payment cost index (NPCI)?

    A. The SCI does not take into account the policy's dividends.
    B. The NPCI does not take into account the face amount of the policy.
    C. The NCPI does not take into account the policy's cash value.
    D. Only the SCI uses a 5% interest assumption.

5. Assume that a life insurance policy has a level annual premium of $14 per $1,000 of insurance. Assume also that projected policy dividends, if invested at 5% compound annual interest, would total $205 per $1,000 of insurance by the end of the 20th policy year. Assume further that the policy provides a 20th year cash value of $180 per $1,000 of insurance. In this situation, which of the following is the policy's annual net surrender cost per $1,000 of insurance?

    A. $5.25
    B. $2.91
    C. $5.05
    D. $6.14
    E. $6.36

6. Sam Vallerio is 45 years of age and needs life insurance for the next 20 years. After he retires, Sam wants to keep the policy in force but withdraw or borrow cash from the policy for living expenses. He is willing to take some risk to obtain more cash value. Which of the following life insurance policies should be recommended for Sam?

    A. Variable universal life
    B. Whole life
    C. Endowment at age 65
    D. Single-premium universal life

7. Which of the following is (are) among the logical guidelines for planners and clients to follow in selecting property-casualty and health insurance coverages?

(1) Insure against losses that are highly likely to occur.
(2) Take into account the risk tolerance of the client.
(3) Purchase individual coverages first, supplementing them with group and social insurance coverages.

    A. (1) only
    B. (2) only
    C. (3) only
    D. (1) and (2) only
    E. (2) and (3) only

8. Which of the following is probably the most important single criterion a financial planner should use in selecting an insurer?

    A. Size of the company
    B. Cost of the products and services
    C. Underwriting standards
    D. Financial strength

9. Which of the following would be the LEAST favorable factor for a life insurance company being seriously considered by a life insurance purchaser of a new $300,000 whole life policy?

    A. The company's A.M. Best's rating is only A.
    B. The policy has a higher cost than other similar policies, based on the surrender cost index.
    C. The company is among the twenty largest life companies as measured by total investment asset values.
    D. The amount of the company's average whole life policy is above the national average.

10. Which of the following statements with respect to the uses of term insurance is (are) correct?

    (1) Term insurance is designed for permanent needs.
    (2) Term insurance can guarantee future insurability.

      A. (1) only
      B. (2) only
      C. Both (1) and (2)
      D. Neither (1) nor (2)

11. Assume that a family breadwinner has a need for a large amount of life insurance but only a modest budget. In this case, which of the following types of coverage would be LEAST appropriate?

      A. Term insurance
      B. Variable universal life insurance
      C. 20-pay whole life insurance
      D. Group life insurance

12. For which of the following needs is term life insurance best suited?

      A. Meeting the estate tax bill of a wealthy client
      B. Retiring an installment debt obligation at death
      C. Providing a life income for the insured's widow
      D. Accumulating funds for retirement

For practice answering case questions related to Topic 31, please answer the following questions in the cases included in Appendix A at the back of this textbook.

Case	Questions
Black Hills P&L	
Brodinski	
Haurilick	
Beals	4
Mocsin	
Loudon	
Connor	20 and 21
Seidelhofer	22 and 23
Loomis Company	
Michael and Diana Eastman	
Gary and Judy Parker	51, 52, 53, 54, and 55

ANSWERS AND EXPLANATIONS

1. C is the answer. Kay badly needs more life insurance for the benefit of Corinne. In light of her low income, renewable and convertible term to supplement her $24,000 of group term coverage is the best solution for her at the present time.

2. B is the answer. The employee will purchase the life insurance, and the employee has a low risk tolerance. The accumulation in cash values with a whole life policy will afford Ron some security that the employee will have the money to buy the company. While the insurance need is short-term, the employee has a need for cash value to buy the company, so term insurance will not satisfy the need.

3. D is the answer. (1) does not take into account the time value of money, which is one of its serious flaws.

4. C is the answer. A is incorrect because both indexes take dividends into account. B is incorrect because both indexes reduce the cost to an amount per $1,000 of face amount. D is incorrect because both indexes use a 5% interest assumption.

5. B is the answer. Calculate the FV of 20 beginning-of-period payments of $14 at 5% compound interest. FV = $486.07. From this, subtract the dividends of $205.00 and the cash value of $180.00. Divide the result, $101.07, by the FVAD of $1 per year at 5%. Enter 20 as the n, 5 as the I, 0 as PV, and $1.00 as the beginning-of-period PMT. Solve for FV, which is $34.72. Divide $101.07 by $34.72 to produce the answer, $2.91 per $1,000 of insurance.

6. A is the answer. The variable universal life insurance policy will provide a variable return on the cash value invested in the separate accounts, but the return is likely to be higher over the 20 years than the return with other policies. The whole life policy provides a guaranteed return that is not likely to give Sam as much cash value after 20 years. The endowment policy has lost its tax advantage under current tax law, and the single-premium universal policy is a MEC, so the loans will be taxable income.

7. B is the answer. In (1), losses that are highly likely to occur are better dealt with through techniques other than insurance. In (3), individual coverages should supplement the group and social coverages of the client.

8. D is the answer. Size is not necessarily the same as strength. Cost and underwriting standards are important, but not as important as sufficient financial strength to pay claims.

9. B is the answer. The higher surrender cost index indicates that the policy is more costly over time than other similar policies. Although an A rating is not A.M. Best's top rating, an A rating is not too bad!

10. B is the answer. Term insurance is designed for temporary protection. Its guarantee of future insurability stems from its renewal feature or conversion feature.

11. C is the answer. The 20-pay whole life policy will require much higher premiums in order to build the cash value to a high enough level that no additional premium payments are needed after 20 annual payments have been made. Less emphasis on saving occurs in variable universal life insurance policy with premiums that continue throughout lifetime. Term insurance, including most group life insurance, would be most appropriate.

12. B is the answer. A and C are incorrect because these are permanent needs. D is incorrect because term insurance does not have a savings component.

Property and Casualty Insurance (Topic 32)

CFP Board Student-Centered Learning Objectives

(a) Identify the primary components of property and casualty insurance and how each component fits into a client's comprehensive financial plan.

(b) Differentiate among the basic homeowners insurance (HO) forms and features and explain how to evaluate and compare policies.

(c) Identify the primary components of automobile insurance and assess any potential property damage or liability exposures.

(d) Explain the role of personal and business liability insurance in comprehensive financial planning and how personal umbrella liability policy (PUP) and business liability insurance interacts with other property and liability insurance products.

Property and Casualty Insurance
  A. *Analysis of insurance policies*......................................32.3
      1. *Basic policy parts*...32.3
      2. *Open perils versus named perils*.............................32.5
  B. *Homeowner insurance*...32.5
      1. *Section I coverages*..32.6
          a. *Coverage A – dwelling*...................................32.6
          b. *Coverage B – other structures*...........................32.6
          c. *Coverage C – personal property*..........................32.6
          d. *Coverage D – loss of use*................................32.8
          e. *Additional coverages*....................................32.9
      2. *Exclusions under Section I*...................................32.10
      3. *Loss settlement under Section I*..............................32.11
          a. *Coinsurance*...32.11
          b. *The loss adjustment process*.............................32.13
          c. *Duties of the insured following a loss*..................32.13
      4. *Section II coverages*...32.14
          a. *Coverage E – personal liability*.........................32.14
          b. *Exclusions specific to Coverage E*.......................32.15
          c. *Coverage F – medical payments to others*................32.15
          d. *Exclusions specific to Coverage F*.......................32.16
          e. *Additional coverages under Section II*...................32.16
          f. *Exclusions to Coverages E and F*.........................32.17
      5. *Miscellaneous provisions in homeowner policies*..............32.19
      6. *Homeowners forms*..32.21
          a. *HO-1 and HO-2*...32.21
          b. *HO-3 Special form and HO-5 Comprehensive*...............32.21

        c. *HO-4 Tenant and HO-6 Condo*..................................32.22
        d. *HO-8 Market value below replacement cost* 32.22
    7. *Endorsements*...32.23
        a. *Scheduled personal property endorsement*.....................32.23
        b. *Personal property replacement cost endorsement*............32.24
        c. *Inflation guard endorsement*..................................32.25
        d. *Guaranteed replacement cost endorsement*...................32.25
        e. *Section II endorsements* 32.25
        f. *Watercraft endorsement*....................................32.26
  C. *Personal automobile insurance* 32.26
    1. *State requirements* 32.26
    2. *Automobile and recreational vehicles insurance*...............32.28
        a. *Part A – Liability coverage*................................32.28
            1.) *Covered auto*...32.28
            2.) *Who is insured?*......................................32.29
            3.) *Split-limits of liability* 32.29
            4.) *Part A Supplementary payments*.....................32.29
        b. *Part A Exclusions*..32.30
            1.) *Less than 4 wheels* 32.30
            2.) *Vehicles not listed in the policy* 32.30
            3.) *Other exclusions*.....................................32.30
        c. *Part B – Medical payments coverage* 32.30
        d. *Part B Exclusions*..32.31
        e. *Part C – Uninsured motorists coverage* 32.32
            1.) *Persons covered under uninsured motorists coverage*.32.32
            2.) *Underinsured motorists coverage*.....................32.33
        f. *Part C Exclusions* 32.33
        g. *Part D – Coverage for damage to the auto*.............32.34
        h. *Part D Exclusions*.......................................32.35
        i. *Deductibles* 32.35
  D. *Umbrella liability insurance*..........................32.36
  E. *Business-related risk exposures*.......................32.39
    1. *Business-related personal loss exposures*.....................32.39
        a. *Loss of profits due to death or disability of a
            key employee* 32.39
        b. *Loss of value due to absence of a ready market in which
            to sell upon death, disability, or retirement*.....................32.40
        c. *Loss of income if the owner becomes disabled*..................32.40
        d. *Loss of income due to business owner's retirement or death*.32.41
    2. *Business-related property and liability loss exposures* 32.41
        a. *Commercial property insurance* 32.41
        b. *Commercial package policy*.............................32.42
            1.) *Basic commercial package policy parts* 32.42
            2.) *Commercial general liability insurance* 32.42
            3.) *Commercial crime insurance*........................32.45

        4.) *Boiler and machinery insurance*................................*32.46*
        5.) *Commercial farm insurance* *32.47*
        6.) *Commercial auto insurance*................................*32.47*
    c. *Specialized commercial policies*...............................*32.47*
        1.) *Businessowners policy*......................................*32.47*
        2.) *Inland marine insurance*...................................*32.48*
        3.) *Ocean marine insurance*...................................*32.48*
        4.) *Surety bonds*..*32.49*
    d. *Commercial umbrella liability policy*.......................*32.49*
    e. *Professional liability policies* *32.49*
        1.) *Professional liability*.......................................*32.49*
        2.) *Physicians professional liability policy* *32.50*
        3.) *Accountants professional liability policy*..............*32.51*
        4.) *Architects and engineers professional liability policy*..*32.51*
        5.) *Other professional liability policies*....................*32.51*
    f. *Workers' compensation and employers liability*..............*32.52*
    g. *Business income coverage* *32.53*

ANALYSIS OF INSURANCE POLICIES

Analyzing present insurance coverage entails assembling all of the client's present insurance policies and riders or endorsements and comparing them against each of the risk exposures identified. The analysis of present coverage should include an assessment of the severity of each loss exposure and of whether risk treatment techniques other than insurance might logically be used.

Basic Policy Parts

For exposures best treated by insurance, present policies should be examined with respect to each of their basic parts:

- Declarations – The planner will want to examine the factual information as to matters such as name and address of the insured, amount of insurance, premium, deductible, and period of coverage.

- Definitions – Defined terms such as "insured," "insured location," "family member," "your covered auto," and "total disability" must provide adequate protection to meet the client's needs.

- Insuring agreements – These are the basic promises of the insurer. Look especially at the covered perils, including whether the policy takes the specified-perils approach (only covering perils specifically named in the policy) or the "all-risks" (now called the open-perils) approach (covering all perils except those specifically excluded in the policy).

- Conditions – A planner will want to review with the client the conditions the insured must meet before a loss occurs so the insurer will be liable if a loss does occur (conditions precedent). Also, look at conditions subsequent, conditions that must be met after a loss occurs to avoid releasing the insurer from liability (for example, notification conditions, preservation of damaged property, not impairing the insurer's subrogation rights, etc.).

- Exclusions – Every policy, even an "all-risks" (open-perils) policy, has exclusions which remove coverage for some losses. Policies contain exclusions because some types of losses are not insurable, some events are too hazardous, some losses are designed to be covered elsewhere, coverage would create excessive moral hazard, or coverage isn't needed by most people. A planner should examine the exclusions to check which perils, activities, property, loss consequences, geographic areas, etc. are not covered and to see if any of them create important coverage gaps for the client.

- Miscellaneous provisions – A planner will want to look at provisions such as those related to cancellation, other insurance, appraisal, coinsurance (property insurance vs. major medical), right of assignment, etc. What rights or responsibilities do these clauses create for the client?

- Endorsements or riders – A planner should examine how these endorsements or riders will change, delete, or add coverage.

Practice Question

Where in the policy would you look to find the amount of insurance provided under a property insurance policy?

- A. Insuring agreements
- B. Declarations
- C. Conditions
- D. Exclusions

Answer:
The amount of insurance is shown in the declarations.
The answer is B.

Open Perils Versus Named Perils

Evaluating homeowner insurance policies also requires that the planner be familiar with the difference between open perils coverage and named perils (basic and broad) coverage.

"Basic" coverage pays for losses caused by certain named perils or causes of loss (fire, lightning, windstorm, hail, explosion, riot, aircraft, theft, damage by vehicles, smoke, vandalism, and volcanic eruption).

"Broad" form coverage provides the same protection as "basic" coverage, and adds coverage for the six additional perils of falling objects; weight of ice, snow, or sleet; accidental discharge of water or steam; freezing; sudden and accidental tearing apart, cracking, burning, or bulging of a heating or air conditioning system; and sudden and accidental damage from electrical current.

"Open-perils" coverage provides coverage for all causes of loss, except those specifically excluded. An open-perils policy typically excludes damage caused by collapse (although it may be covered up to the amount of specified limits), freezing of plumbing and certain fixtures; vandalism damage while the house is vacant or unoccupied; certain losses to fences and patios; theft or vandalism damage to a house under construction; leakage or seepage; wear and tear; smoke from agricultural or industrial operations; mold, fungus, or wet rot; and losses from birds, rodents, insects, smog, rust, and animals of the insured.

HOMEOWNER INSURANCE

Homeowners insurance policies come in several forms; however, all homeowners forms provide both property and liability insurance coverage. The liability coverage is the same for all forms. Loss of use as a result of damage to insured property is also covered.

It is important to note that not all homeowner policies are structured in the same way, so the actual policy being reviewed may look slightly different from that which is discussed in this textbook. It is important to read the actual policy carefully.

Many homeowner policies are broken into two "sections," with Section I covering the dwelling and other property that is part of the dwelling, and Section II covering liability. Each Section is further broken down into "coverage" areas, which are typically lettered Coverage A, Coverage B, Coverage C, Coverage D, Coverage E, and Coverage F.

Section I Coverages

Coverage A – Dwelling

Coverage A – Dwelling of the Homeowners 3 – Special Form (HO-3) provides replacement cost coverage of the dwelling building and anything that is part of the building. The land is not covered.

The purpose of replacement cost coverage on the dwelling is to provide reimbursement to the insured for damage to or destruction of the insured dwelling without deduction for depreciation. If the policy provided for payment to the insured on an actual cash value basis, then depreciation would be deducted. Strictly speaking, the principle of indemnity would require an insurer to pay only actual cash value, but the insurance industry recognizes that an exception to the principle is advantageous. If the insured is reimbursed only the value of a depreciated home, the insured may not be able to rebuild and restore the home. Replacement cost coverage makes it possible for the insured to replace a destroyed home with a new home even though the insurer pays more than the value of the home before the loss.

Full replacement cost is the loss amount payable (up to the face amount of coverage) if the insured carries coverage equal to at least 80% of the current cost of replacement of the dwelling. Additional details regarding the 80% coverage requirement will be discussed on page 32.11 under "Loss Settlement Under Section I".

Coverage B – Other Structures

Coverage B – Other Structures, insures any structures separated from the dwelling by a clear space, such as a detached garage. It may also include nonbuilding structures, such as fences, patios, or even swimming pools. These structures are separately covered for an amount up to 10% of Coverage A. If the other structure is used for business purposes or rented out to anyone other than a tenant of the residence, the other structure is not automatically covered, but it can be covered by endorsement. Thus, if a homeowner turns a garage into a studio for work, the homeowners policy no longer insures the garage, and the owner will need an endorsement in order for the garage to be covered. The endorsement will probably require an additional premium.

Coverage C – Personal Property

Coverage C – Personal Property insures any type of personal property (as opposed to real property) owned or used by a resident, anywhere in the world, for an amount up to 50% of Coverage A. At the insured's option, personal property of guests and residence employees will also be covered.

When evaluating Coverage C, there are several items the planner will want to ascertain:

1. Does coverage apply only to listed perils or is coverage provided on an "open-perils" basis?
2. Are there any high-value items that are subject to special limits on coverage?
3. Are there any items that are excluded from coverage that must be covered by endorsement or by a separate policy?

The HO-2 and HO-3 policies cover personal property only for the perils listed under the broad form. Open-perils coverage can be obtained under an HO-5 policy or by adding an endorsement to an HO-2 or HO-3 policy.

Certain kinds of high-value items have special limits in case of theft, but these limits can be increased by endorsement. The special limits apply to items such as money, jewelry, furs, silverware, guns, electronic car accessories, and coin and stamp collections, which have a high risk of being stolen. For example, the special limit for a loss from a theft of jewelry is $1,500, so if there is a theft of a $5,000 necklace, the insurer will pay no more than $1,500. If the necklace is lost in a fire, however, the insurer will pay the full $5,000. Boats, outboard engines, and trailers have special limits that apply, regardless of the cause of loss. Business property on the premises also has a special limit that applies, regardless of cause.

Coverage C normally does **not** cover the following types of property:

- Items insured under another policy
- Animals, birds, and fish
- Motorized land vehicles (if insurable under auto policies). However, motorized land vehicles used to service the insured's residence or assist the handicapped are covered.
- Equipment powered by motor vehicles
- Aircraft
- Property of roomers, boarders, or tenants
- Property in regularly rented apartments

Practice Question

If the client's detached garage burns down, which of the following items of personal property lost in the fire is <u>not</u> covered by the client's homeowners policy?

    A. The client's boat parked in the garage
    B. Furniture stored by a tenant in the garage
    C. The client's gun collection stored in the garage
    D. Furs stored in the garage in a cedar chest belonging to the client's wife

Answer:

The property of tenants or roomers is not covered by the homeowners policy. Furs, jewelry, and watches are fully covered for fire but are subject to a $1,500 limit for theft. Boats and trailers are subject to a $1,500 limit. Firearms are fully covered for fire but subject to a limit of $2,500 in case of theft.
The answer is B.

Coverage D – Loss of Use

Coverage D, Loss of Use, covers additional living expenses incurred if the dwelling becomes uninhabitable due to damage from an insured peril. In an HO-3 policy, the coverage is on an open perils basis. The coverage pays for the necessary increase in living expenses incurred by the insured in order to continue as nearly as practicable the normal standard of living of the household. Payment is made only for the period of time required to repair or replace the damage or if the insured permanently relocates, for the period required to settle the household elsewhere.

For example, Paul and Marcy rent an apartment for $1,000 a month. There is a fire that makes the apartment uninhabitable, so they have to rent another apartment at $1,200 for three months. The insurance company will pay Paul and Marcy the difference in their rent for the three months or 3 x $200 = $600.

If the insured has been renting out a portion of the premises and the rented-out premises are damaged and become uninhabitable, Coverage D – Loss of Use provides payment for the fair rental value of the rented-out premises. For example, Mary has rented out a portion of her home to a tenant for $600 per month. A fire damages the home so both Mary and the tenant must move out, and Mary must rent an apartment for $900 per month. Mary can recover $600 per month in fair rental value and $900 per month in additional living expenses.

If access to the dwelling is barred by civil authority, Coverage D is applicable, even though the premises are not damaged, as long as the action of the civil authority is a result of damage to neighboring premises by a covered peril. For example, wild fires in the area require the evacuation of Harold's neighborhood for three days. Harold's home is not damaged but other homes are damaged. Harold's additional living expenses and any fair rental value will be covered.

Additional Coverages

When an insured suffers a loss, there may be some additional costs that do not fit specifically into coverages A, B, C, or D, but that are also covered under the policy, but only up to the amount of specific limits. These additional coverages include:

- Trees, shrubs, and other plants (for certain perils only) up to $500 per tree for most policies

- Debris removal (If the cost of replacement plus debris removal exceeds the face amount of coverage, the insurer will make available an additional 5% of the policy limit that may be used for debris removal.)

- Reasonable repairs to protect property from further damage

- Fire department service charges up to $500

- Property removed from premises endangered by a covered peril (maximum period of such coverage is 30 days)

- Credit cards, forgery (limits vary from $0 to $500, depending on the insurance company and riders)

- Loss assessment (if property belonging to a homeowners association or condominium association is damaged and an assessment of all members is made, this coverage pays for a member's assessment when the damage was caused by an insured peril)

- Collapse, but only as provided under the additional coverages in HO-2, HO-3, HO-4, and HO-6 policies (the difference between these types of policies will be discussed later in this topic)

- Breakage of glass or safety glazing material (maximum $100 in HO-1 and HO-8)

- Landlord's furnishings in rental property on the premises (HO-1, HO-2, and HO-3 only)

Practice Question

Which of the following statements concerning the loss of use coverage in homeowners policies is <u>not</u> correct?

    A. There must first be a covered loss to the insured residence premises making it unfit in which to live.

    B. Additional living expense covers the necessary increase in living expenses to maintain the insured's normal standard of living.

    C. Fair rental value is covered if a portion of the residence is not rented out but is being held for rental to others.

    D. There are situations where an insured could collect both additional living expense and fair rental value when the residence premises are unfit to occupy.

Answer:

A covered loss to the insured residence is not required where there is action of a civil authority. Such prohibited use, usually because of a dangerous condition on a neighboring property, is covered.

The answer is A.

Exclusions under Section I

All homeowners policies, even open-perils policies, contain some common exclusions. These exclusions eliminate coverage for damage caused by:

- Ordinance or law (policy can be endorsed to cover) – Ordinances and building codes will sometimes require that when buildings are substantially damaged, the building must be demolished and removed. Building codes may also require that any reconstruction conform to current code requirements. These requirements can make the work very expensive. The unendorsed homeowners policy will not pay for the increased costs required for such demolition or to bring a building up to current building codes. Losses caused by the enforcement of any ordinance or law regulating construction, repair, or demolition of buildings are not covered. Thus, the insurer will not be responsible for reimbursing the insured for any costs incurred in order to comply with the requirements of the municipality's building code.

- Earth movement (policy can be endorsed to cover) – Earth movement, including landslides, mudflow, earth sinking, rising, or shifting, is specifically excluded from coverage.

- Water damage (policy can be endorsed to cover) – Damage caused by flood, backup through sewers or drains, or seepage through basement walls and foundation floors is not covered. (Remember this guide: Rising water is not covered; falling water is covered.)

- Neglect – Losses caused by the neglect of the insured to use all reasonable means to save the property at or after the occurrence of an insured peril are not covered.

- War or nuclear exposure – Losses caused by acts of war or nuclear accident are not covered since they could be catastrophic to the insurance company. However, if fire results because of a nuclear accident, the loss attributable to the fire would be covered.

- Intentional loss

- Power failure – Losses caused by power failure are not covered if the power interruption takes place away from the premises. However, if a covered peril causes the power failure, then losses will be covered. For example, if a tree fell on the insured's home and disrupted electrical power, the cost of food that was ruined due to loss of power to the freezer would be covered.

Certain exclusions apply only to the Dwelling and Other Structures coverage, such as vandalism and malicious mischief and glass breakage (while the dwelling is vacant more than 60 days). Other exclusions in this group applicable only to the Dwelling and Other Structures are seepage or leakage of water and collapse.

Loss Settlement Under Section I

Coinsurance

Loss to property insured under Coverage A will be settled at replacement cost if the dollar amount of the Coverage A limit is at least 80% of the replacement cost of the dwelling building at the time of the loss. If the 80% requirement is met, payment will be, at the option of the insurer, the lesser of:

- Limit of insurance
- Replacement cost
- Actual amount necessary to repair or replace

If the 80% requirement is not met, the payment will be the larger of:

- Actual cash value of damaged property, or

$$\left[\frac{\text{Coverage A}}{80\% \text{ of Replacement cost}} \times \text{Amount of loss} \right] - \text{Deductible}$$

Note that, in HO policies, the deductible is subtracted **after** the fraction is multiplied by the amount of the loss.

The loss settlement provision is also called a coinsurance provision. In property insurance, coinsurance is designed to encourage the insured to carry insurance in an amount at least equal to a high percentage (usually 80%) of the value of the property at the time of a loss. If this amount is carried, the loss will be settled in the normal way, without a coinsurance penalty. If it is not carried, loss settlement will be on the basis of the preceding formula.

Example:

A dwelling will cost $300,000 to replace and has been insured for $200,000. The policy's coinsurance provision requires insurance coverage in an amount that is 80% of the replacement cost. The policy has a $500 deductible. If a fire causes a loss of $40,000, what will the insurance company pay?

The formula for the amount of recovery is:

$$\text{Recovery} = \frac{\text{Amount carried}}{\text{Amount should carry}} \times \text{Loss} - \text{Deductible}$$

The coverage carried was $200,000, and the amount of coverage that should have been carried was $300,000 x 80% = $240,000. The recovery, therefore, is:

$$\text{Recovery} = \frac{\$200,000}{\$240,000} \times \$40,000 - \$500$$

$$= \$33,333 - \$500$$

$$= \$32,833$$

 ***K Study Tip* – The minimum amount of insurance that should be carried is not the full replacement cost; rather, it is 80% (or other coinsurance percentage) of the replacement cost. However, you will need 100% of the replacement cost if you want to be fully covered in the event your home is a total loss.**

The insurer will not pay more than the actual cash value of the damage until the repair or replacement is completed. Thus, an insured who is rebuilding after a fire will not be able to obtain full replacement cost until the work is completed.

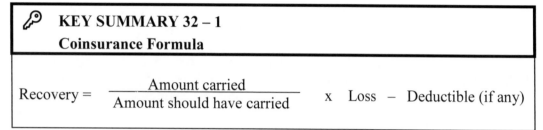

The Loss Adjustment Process

Notice of loss is the act of the insured giving notice to the company that a loss has occurred. Typically, the insured gives notice that a loss has occurred by informing the agent. Most property insurance policies require that the insured give immediate written notice of any loss. However, in practice, property insurers accept notice that is communicated orally, typically by telephone. Notice, however, should be given as soon as possible so that the insurer has ample time to take steps that are in its best interest (including steps to minimize further loss). The policy owner provides the insurer with proof of loss by signing a sworn statement indicating the specific items of property that were lost or damaged. Documentation is required as proof. Typically, the adjuster helps the insured prepare the formal proof of loss papers.

The loss adjustment process is as follows:

(a)   Notice. The insured gives notice that a loss has occurred.

(b)   Investigation. The insurer's investigation is designed to determine whether a loss is covered by the policy and to verify the policyholder's statement of the amount of the loss.

(c)   Proof of loss. The insured is required to file a sworn, written statement that a loss has occurred, the amount of the claim, and the circumstances surrounding the loss.

(d)   Payment of or denial of payment of the claim. The company reimburses the insured for the amount of the loss or denies the claim.

Duties of the Insured Following a Loss

There are seven provisions in the typical property insurance policy that deal with the insured's duties relating to loss settlement:

(1)   Notice of loss. The insured is required to give written notice of loss as soon as possible. Some policies state that immediate written notice must be submitted within 10, 20, or 30 days. However, most insurers will accept telephone notice of loss as temporarily complying with the notice of loss requirement.

(2)   Protection of property. In case of loss, the insured is required to protect the damaged property from further damage.

(3)   Inventory. This provision requires the insured to construct an inventory of the damaged property after a loss. The itemized report must contain the quantity, description, actual cash value, and the amount of the loss to the damaged property. Receipts, bills, and related information that verify the valuations should be attached. It is recommended that a video inventory, along with receipts, bills, etc., be kept in a location outside of the covered property (such as in a safe deposit box at the bank).

(4)   Evidence. Under this provision, the insured may be required to show the damaged property to the insurer as often as is reasonably asked. In obtaining payment for hospital expenses, the insured may be required to submit information concerning the accident or injury and to allow the insurer to acquire medical reports and records pertaining to the accident or injury.

(5)   Proof of loss. Most insurers supply the insured with proof of loss forms to be filled out. The information the insured generally must supply includes the time and cause of loss, the interest of the insured and all others in the property, other insurance covering the loss, all encumbrances on the property, and other pertinent information.

(6)   Assistance and cooperation. This provision requires the insured to cooperate and provide assistance to the insurer when a loss occurs. This requirement includes attending hearings and trials, presenting evidence, and supplying medical reports.

(7)   Appraisal. This provision applies when the insured and the insurer cannot agree on the actual cash value or the amount of the loss. Either party can request an appraisal. Both select a disinterested appraiser. The two appraisers select an umpire. Only differences of opinion of the appraisers are submitted to the umpire to resolve. If there is a dispute as to whether the policy covers the loss, such a dispute is resolved by arbitration.

Section II Coverages

Section II of the homeowners policies includes Coverage E (personal liability) and Coverage F (medical payments to others), along with some additional coverages such as cost of defense, first-aid expenses, damage to property of others, and loss assessment.

Coverage E – Personal Liability

Personal liability coverage applies only to claims made or suits filed against an insured, arising out of bodily injury (BI) or property damage (PD). The BI and PD must also result from an occurrence to which the coverage applies. The occurrences to which the coverage applies are qualified by the exclusions contained in Coverage E. Medical expenses must be incurred within three years from the date of an occurrence that results in BI.

The insurer is obligated to defend the insured, with counsel of the insurer's choice, and to pay any damages, including prejudgment interest, resulting from BI or PD for which an insured is legally responsible. Defense costs are in addition to the coverage limit listed for Coverage E.

Exclusions Specific to Coverage E

 Coverage E – Personal Liability provides bodily injury and property damage coverage for other-than-auto-related liability losses. A single limit, usually $100,000, is provided. This coverage has a number of specific exclusions pertaining to:

- Contractual liability – The policy does not cover liability assumed under contract, except for written contracts relating to ownership, maintenance, or use of an insured location and written contracts in which the insured assumes the liability of others before an occurrence.

- Property owned by an insured – The policy provides liability coverage for BI or PD of people who are not insureds.

- Property in an insured's care, custody, or control – Liability for damage to such property is excluded unless caused by fire, smoke, or explosion (the exception is called fire legal liability coverage).

- Bodily injury to an insured – There is no liability coverage for BI to the named insured, resident relatives, and other residents under age 21 in their care.

Coverage F – Medical Payments to Others

Coverage F – Medical Payments to Others is designed to cover noninsureds injured on the insured premises. There is a limit of $1,000 per person, which can be increased by endorsement. Note that, whereas the personal auto policy, described later, provides medical payments benefits for insureds, the homeowners policies do not provide medical payments for insureds.

Coverage F also provides limited off-premises coverage. Thus, medical expenses for others will be paid when bodily injury is caused away from the insured location, either: (1) by an insured's activities, or (2) by an animal owned by or in the care of an insured.

Exclusions Specific to Coverage F

 While Coverage F provides limited medical payments to others who are injured on the insured property, there are some exclusions under which medical payments will not be payable. These exclusions include:

- Bodily injury to a residence employee off the insured location and not in the course of employment

- Bodily injury of any person, except a residence employee, who regularly resides at any part of the insured location

Additional Coverages Under Section II

Section II of the homeowners policy also includes additional coverages, namely:

- Claims expense – The insurer promises to pay, in addition to the limit of liability, all expenses incurred in the defense of any suit under the policy, interest on judgments, plus certain other legal costs.

- First-aid expenses – The insurer promises to pay, in addition to the limit of liability, expenses incurred by the insured for immediate first aid related to any bodily injury covered under the policy. Such emergency medical services may reduce subsequent claims.

- Loss assessment coverage – The insurer promises to reimburse the insured for any assessments by a condominium association or other cooperative body as a result of bodily injury or property damage not excluded. This insurance is a liability coverage.

- Damage to property of others – This coverage pays for damage to the property of others that is caused by an insured, regardless of whether the insured is legally liable. The insuring agreement states, "We will pay up to $500 per occurrence for damage to property of others caused by an insured." The harm must have been caused by an insured, and the property must have actually been damaged. If an insured borrows a neighbor's golf clubs and loses one, the loss would not be covered.

Practice Question

The HO-3 provides medical payments coverage for all of the following persons, EXCEPT:

A. The insured and family members residing with the insured
B. Any person injured while on the insured premises with the permission of any insured
C. Any person injured away from the insured premises if the injury is caused by the activities of the insured
D. Any person injured away from the insured premises if the injury is caused by an animal owned by or in the care of any insured

Answer:

The medical payments coverage provided by the homeowners forms is not designed to provide health insurance coverage for the insured and the insured's family. The other persons described in this question are covered.
The answer is A.

Exclusions to Coverages E and F

 There are also several exclusions that apply to both Coverage E and Coverage F. Among these are the following:

- Intentional injury – However, most courts have ruled that coverage does apply if the act was intentional, but the result was unintentional.

- Business and professional activities – Hobbies, however, are covered. Also, activities of an insured as a landlord are excluded, except for occasional rental of property as a residence, continuing rental to an individual or family, and rental of space for an office, studio, school, or private garage.

- Uninsured locations – There is no coverage at premises owned or rented by an insured that are not insured locations. Insured locations are the residence premises, other locations shown in the declarations, vacant land other than farmland owned by or rented to an insured, and certain others.

- Motor vehicles – However, certain vehicles are covered, such as those designed for off-road recreational use that do not have to be registered. Golf carts are covered when used while playing golf.

- Watercraft – However, small motorized boats or sailboats are covered.

- Aircraft

- War

- Transmission of a communicable disease

- Criminal activities

- Physical, mental, or sexual abuse

- Use or sale of a controlled substance

- Bodily injury covered by other sources (for example, workers' compensation)

- Nuclear energy

In addition to the exclusions, there are a few policy conditions that apply only to the Section II coverages. One of these relates to the limit of liability. The limit for Coverage E is a per occurrence limit. The limit for Coverage F is the amount payable per person per occurrence.

Other conditions spell out the insured's duties after a loss (such as to notify the insurer, supply information about the claim to the insurer, and assist the insurer in hearings and trials), duties of an injured person under Coverage F (especially, to allow the insurer to obtain medical records), bankruptcy of an insured (which does not release the insurer from liability), and other liability insurance (in most cases, the Coverage E of the homeowners policy is excess over other insurance).

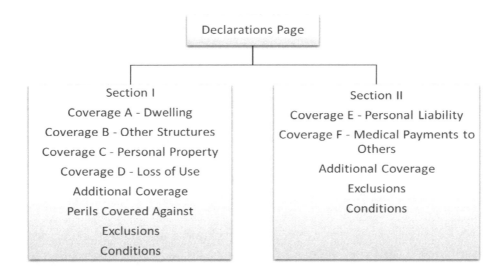

Miscellaneous Provisions in Homeowner Policies

Planners should also be familiar with a number of miscellaneous provisions in homeowners policies. All of these policies contain general policy conditions applicable to both Sections I and II. Among these are:

- Policy period condition – The loss or activity causing the loss must occur during the policy period.

- Concealment or fraud condition – No coverage is provided if the information was material.

- Liberalization condition – At no additional premium, the policy's coverage is broadened when the insurer issues a new edition of the policy with broader coverage.

- Cancellation condition – An insured may cancel at any time by giving notice and returning the policy, in which case a "short-rate" premium refund will be made; insurer may cancel for reasons allowed by law and must give advance written notice, in which case a pro rata premium refund will be made.

- Nonrenewal condition – The insurer must give at least a 30-day advance written notice.

- Assignment condition – The policy may not be assigned to another without the insurer's written consent.

- Subrogation condition – The insurer may take over the insured's rights against a third party who caused the loss, and the insurer can recover to the extent of the insurer's payment for the loss.

Other miscellaneous provisions with which students should be familiar are certain conditions affecting *Section I only*. Among these are the following:

- Insurable interest – The insured's recovery will not exceed the amount of his or her insurable interest.

- Insured's duties following a loss – The insured must notify the insurer, notify police if a theft occurred, notify each credit card company if credit cards were stolen or lost, protect property from further damage, prepare an inventory of damaged property, and file a proof of loss within 60 days.

- Appraisal – If the amount of the loss is in dispute, the insurer and insured each appoint/pay for an appraiser; the appraisers select an umpire; and a decision of any two as to the amount of the loss is binding.

- Other insurance – The policy will pay its pro rata share of any loss unless the property is more specifically covered elsewhere.

- Suit against the insurer – Suit by the insured is allowed only within one year and only if all policy provisions have been complied with.

- Abandonment – The insured may not force the insurer to take over damaged property.

- Mortgage clause – The mortgagee might still recover if the insured's claim is denied. The mortgagee is the lender financing the purchase of the home and may be able to obtain payment from the insurer even when the insured cannot.

- No Benefit to Bailee – Insurer will not pay a claim that benefits a bailee. A bailee is a person who takes temporary possession of property with the understanding that it will be returned, usually after some specific purpose has been accomplished. For example, a watch needing repairs may be left with the jeweler who is a bailee. It is understood that the watch will be returned to the owner when the repairs are completed. If the jeweler fails to return the watch, the insurer will not pay for the loss because the payment benefits the jeweler. The reasoning is that the jeweler should have insurance to pay for the loss.

- Recovered property – If the insured obtains payment for lost or stolen property and then recovers the property, the insured may keep the money or the property, but not both.

In case of a loss to personal property, settlement will normally be made on an actual cash value basis. Actual cash value (ACV) is the property's replacement cost minus physical depreciation (not the depreciation an accountant shows for taxes). Some policies or endorsements, however, pay for the replacement cost (up to the policy's limits) or pay for guaranteed replacement cost (even if more than the policy's limits) with no deduction for depreciation (see Replacement Cost endorsement below). Arguably, paying replacement cost violates the principle of indemnity because the insured receives new property to replace the old. This deviation from the principle of indemnity has been deemed acceptable.

In a few cases, such as for fine arts or jewelry, coverage is written on a valued basis, meaning that in the event of a total loss, a specified dollar amount will be paid, without regard to ACV or replacement cost.

If a pair or set (usually of jewelry) is damaged, the payment will be the lesser of the difference between the actual cash value of the pair/set before and after the loss or the cost to repair or replace.

Homeowners Forms

Most homeowners policies (HO-1, HO-2, HO-3, HO-5, and HO-8) are designed to insure owner-occupants of buildings used for private residential purposes by not more than two families. Incidental office and professional or studio occupancies are permitted.

HO-1 and HO-2

The HO-1 policy covers only basic named perils (fire, lightning, windstorm, hail, explosion, riot, aircraft, theft, damage by vehicles, smoke, vandalism, and volcanic eruption). The HO-2 policy is known as a "broad form" policy because it increased the number of named perils that are covered. In addition to the basic named perils, the HO-2 also covers falling objects; weight of ice, snow, or sleet; accidental discharge of water or steam; freezing; sudden and accidental tearing apart, cracking, burning, or bulging of a heating or air conditioning system; and sudden and accidental damage from electrical current.

HO-3 Special Form and HO-5 Comprehensive

The HO-3 policy, also called a special form policy, provides open-perils coverage on a replacement cost basis for Coverages A, B, and D, but provides broad form coverage on an actual cash value basis for Coverage C, personal property. If open-perils coverage or replacement cost is desirable for Coverage C, an endorsement can be added to increase that coverage. Adding endorsements for both open-perils and replacement cost on Coverage C (known as an HO-15 rider) makes the policy an HO-5 policy, which provides the most comprehensive coverage, but at a higher premium.

The desirability of open-perils coverage, along with premium efficiency, makes the HO-3 policy the most frequently recommended policy for financial planning clients.

Practice Question

Changing from an HO-2 policy to an HO-3 policy will accomplish which of the following improvements to coverage?

    A. Add inflation guard protection
    B. Remove the coinsurance requirement
    C. Change loss settlement from actual cash value to replacement cost
    D. Change coverage from broad form perils to open-perils

Answer:
The change to an HO-3 policy will mean that the coverage is open-perils instead of broad form.
The answer is D.

HO-4 Tenant and HO-6 Condo

In HO-4, which is for tenants, and in HO-6, which is for condominium unit-owners, there is no Coverage A because the insureds do not own their buildings. The principal coverage is Coverage C – Personal Property. HO-4 Tenant's Form provides broad form coverage of personal property. Additional coverage can be purchased for improvements with the Building Additions and Alterations endorsement.

HO-6 Condominiums and Co-Ops provides broad form coverage of personal property and certain building items. The purchase of insurance coverage on the building by the condo association means the individual unit owner must provide coverage only for his or her unit's contents and any improvements he or she installs in the individual unit.

HO-8 Market Value below Replacement Cost

HO-8 is for homeowners who have relatively low-valued dwellings whose replacement costs would far exceed the market values of the dwellings. HO-8 is appropriate coverage for certain types of older property. Some dwellings, for example, were built many years ago, when labor-intensive techniques characterized the home-building industry. These dwellings often involve obsolete types of construction or are too large in relation to the insured's needs. Losses are settled on an actual cash value (ACV) basis, never on a replacement cost basis. The covered perils are fire and lightning, windstorm and hail, explosion, riot and civil commotion, aircraft, vehicles, smoke, vandalism, theft, and volcanic eruption. Contents are covered for up to 50% of the amount on the dwelling.

Practice Question

Which of the following statements concerning homeowners policy forms is (are) correct?

(1) HO-8 covers newer dwellings of high value.
(2) HO-6 covers condominium unit-owners.
(3) HO-4 covers a tenant of rented property.

    A. (1) only
    B. (2) only
    C. (1) and (3) only
    D. (2) and (3) only

Answer:
The HO-8 form is for older dwellings where the cost to rebuild substantially exceeds the dwelling's market value. HO-6 covers condominium unit-owners, and HO-4 covers tenants.
The answer is D.

EXHIBIT 32 – 1
Homeowners Forms – Section I Coverages

	Coverage A – Dwelling	Coverage B – Other Structures	Coverage C – Personal Property	Coverage D – Loss of Use
HO – 1 (Basic)	Named-Perils	Named-Perils	Named-Perils	Named-Perils
HO – 2 (Broad)	Named-Perils (Broad)	Named-Perils (Broad)	Named-Perils (Broad)	Named-Perils (Broad)
HO – 3 (Special)	Open-Perils	Open-Perils	Named-Perils (Broad)	Open-Perils
HO – 4 (Tenants)	None	None	Named-Perils (Broad)	Named-Perils (Broad)
HO – 5 (Comprehensive)	Open-Perils	Open-Perils	Open-Perils	Open-Perils
HO – 6 (Condominium)	None	None	Named-Perils (Broad)	Named-Perils (Broad)
HO – 8 (Modified) For older homes FMV<Replacement	Named-Perils (Basic)	Named-Perils (Basic)	Named-Perils (Basic)	Named-Perils (Basic)

Endorsements

The homeowners broad form and open-perils coverages are designed to meet the needs of the vast majority of America's families. However, some types of property are specifically excluded from coverage under the HO policies, and limits are placed on the coverage available for other items. Homeowners policies can be modified in various ways to meet particular needs. The modifications are made by adding endorsements to the policy. Some of the more common endorsements are discussed below.

Scheduled Personal Property Endorsement

The purpose of the Scheduled Personal Property Endorsement is to provide open-perils coverage on designated items and to permit the insured to arrange for larger dollar amounts of coverage than would otherwise be available. Insureds typically arrange for this endorsement on high value items, particularly for the theft peril. With the Scheduled Personal Property Endorsement, the coverage can be on an open-perils basis anywhere in the world.

The HO-02 and HO-03 have sublimits applicable to certain types of personal property. For example, coverage for theft of jewelry and furs is limited to $1,500. The scheduled coverage endorsement provides coverage beyond the sublimits.

A higher stated limit of coverage can be provided for scheduled items, and the limit can reflect an appraised value. Wealthy homeowners, for example, can obtain stated limits, also called "valued coverage," on such items as fine arts and antiques. These items may be covered under an HO policy by specifically scheduling them with appropriate values as agreed by the insured and insurer. When there is a loss, the insurer uses the stated limit as the maximum coverage available on the item.

In case of a loss to a scheduled item, the insurer will pay the least of the ACV, the cost of repair or replacement, or the stated limit of coverage. The eligible types of property are jewelry, furs, cameras, musical instruments, silverware, golfing equipment, fine arts, and stamp and coin collections. A personal articles floater is a separate policy that provides the same kind of coverage as the Scheduled Personal Property endorsement.

Practice Question

Which of the following is <u>not</u> an advantage of insuring items of fine arts under a Scheduled Personal Property endorsement?

    A. Coverage is on an open-perils basis.
    B. Losses are covered for replacement cost.
    C. The deductible is eliminated.
    D. A higher limit of coverage can be obtained.

Answer:
A Scheduled Personal Property endorsement will provide coverage on an open-perils basis, elimination of the deductible, and higher limits. Losses are not always paid based on replacement cost and, in the case of fine arts, are typically on a valued basis.
The answer is B.

Personal Property Replacement Cost Endorsement

Another available endorsement is the Personal Property Replacement Cost endorsement. It covers most types of personal property for up to their replacement cost, not to exceed the cost of repair and the limit of insurance under Coverage C.

Inflation Guard Endorsement

The inflation guard endorsement provides for automatic increases in the amount of insurance in order to reduce the amount by which coverage falls behind as inflation raises dollar values and the replacement cost of covered property. This endorsement provides for the amount of insurance coverage to increase automatically. The premium for the endorsement increases directly with the percentage increase in the amount of coverage the insured selects. The purpose of the inflation guard endorsement is to help protect the insured against inadvertent deficiencies in the amount of insurance coverage that may result from increases in construction costs. Remember that under the replacement cost coverage, the insured must carry insurance equal to 80% of the dwelling's replacement cost, or he or she will be required to pay for part of the cost of replacement.

Guaranteed Replacement Cost Endorsement

Guaranteed replacement cost coverage can be provided by another endorsement. It pays the full replacement cost of the damage to the dwelling, even if this exceeds the Coverage A limit.

Section II Endorsements

Other endorsements can be added to extend Section II coverages to include business pursuits; to cover home day-care operations; and to add "personal injury" coverage to Section II for such acts as libel, invasion of privacy, and false arrest.

Practice Question

Bill's computer and DVD player were stolen from his home while he was at work. What coverage does Bill have under an HO-3 policy with no special endorsements?

    A. No coverage
    B. Actual cash value
    C. Replacement cost
    D. Agreed value as scheduled

Answer:
The computer and DVD player are personal property covered for actual cash value. Actual cash value is replacement cost less depreciation.
The answer is B.

Watercraft Endorsement

The homeowners policy contains limited coverage for watercraft, and there are exclusions from liability for many watercraft. One reason for the limited coverage is that watercraft are used for recreational purposes, and it is not a common or necessary pursuit for a large number of homeowners. Covering it will increase premiums for those who do not use watercraft. Coverage can be added separately by those who want to engage in the activity. In addition, insurers may feel that covering watercraft is high risk because operators frequently are not careful. There are also few restrictions on the operation of watercraft. Operators generally do not have to be licensed and may have little experience. Watercraft losses may also be caused by "perils of the sea." Perils of the seas include causes of loss such as high winds, waves, rough seas, sinking, collision, and capsizing which are perils associated primarily with the seas or bodies of water.

The Outboard Motorboat endorsement or the Watercraft endorsement may be added to homeowners policies. These endorsements add more physical damage coverage for the watercraft, and the latter extends the liability coverage. In addition, there are specific watercraft policies to handle any exposures for any type of watercraft.

PERSONAL AUTOMOBILE INSURANCE

State Requirements

Automobile accidents are of concern for planning purposes due to their frequency and the potentially high costs involved. Uninsured and underinsured drivers increase uncertainty because they do not pay for the damages and injuries they cause. States in which automobile owners reside have an interest in protecting their residents who become victims of auto accidents. States, therefore, have enacted various laws to help protect those victims. While the methods used to compensate victims of auto accidents vary from state to state, a few of the more common ones are listed here:

- The typical state financial responsibility law requires a driver to show ability after an automobile accident to pay any judgment that may result. Failure of the driver to make such a showing of financial responsibility will cause the driver to have his or her driver's license and automobile registration revoked.

- Compulsory automobile insurance laws require the owners of automobiles registered in the state to have liability insurance. In some instances, instead of insurance, owners can use an approved substitute means of demonstrating financial ability to pay potential judgments. Note that the compulsory auto insurance laws apply to auto owners, not drivers. Today, only 1 state does not have compulsory automobile insurance laws while 49 states and the District of Columbia do have compulsory auto insurance laws. For planning purposes, it should also be noted that the required limits are typically quite low. The following websites offer a breakdown by state:

> http://www.iii.org/issues_updates/compulsory-auto-uninsured-motorists.html

- A few states have unsatisfied judgment funds that provide for payment to persons injured in automobile accidents when the negligent party is unable to pay for the damage. The claimant must proceed against the negligent uninsured motorist as if no fund were available. Only after the court renders a judgment that goes unpaid can the claimant collect from the fund.

- Uninsured motorists coverage pays for bodily injuries to the insured caused by a driver of an uninsured motor vehicle. A vehicle is uninsured when liability insurance is: (i) nonexistent, (ii) less than the amount specified by the state's applicable financial responsibility law, (iii) useless because of denial of coverage or financial failure of insurer, or (iv) useless because of a hit-and-run accident. Uninsured motorists coverage is found in Part C of the personal auto policy.

- No-fault auto insurance is a form of first-party insurance coverage written in conformity with the automobile no-fault laws of the various states. Under "no-fault," payment does not depend on determination of liability. Benefit payments to claimants are based only on economic losses: medical expenses, lost income, and costs of replacing personal services. Under the provisions of a "pure" no-fault law, there would be no tort claims for automobile injuries. All accident victims would be indemnified by their own insurer. No state has a "pure" no-fault law.

  We must distinguish "pure" no-fault insurance from a "modified" no-fault plan. The latter is the only type of law that has been adopted thus far. A modified no-fault plan leaves tort liability in place for injuries meeting specified conditions, notably, for more serious injuries as determined by the nature of the injury or the total amount of medical expense. A monetary or verbal threshold is frequently used, and the threshold must be exceeded before a tort claim may be pursued.

Automobile and Recreational Vehicles Insurance

The personal auto policy (PAP) is designed to provide automobile insurance for individuals and families who own private passenger vehicles such as cars, station wagons, mini-vans, recreational vehicles designed for use on public roads, as well as small trucks and full-size vans not used for business. The policy can be endorsed to cover other types of motor vehicles, such as motorcycles and scooters, and to provide expanded coverage for recreational vehicles. It can also be endorsed to cover a person who does not own a motor vehicle but frequently drives one.

The PAP is broken down into Parts A, B, C, and D with each part providing a different type of protection. Planners will need to review the coverage offered in each part, as well as any limitations or exclusions that may leave a client with uncovered loss exposures.

Part A – Liability Coverage

The first part of the personal auto policy is Part A – Liability. It provides liability coverage for both bodily injury and property damage inflicted on third parties.

This coverage protects the insured in case of a claim or lawsuit due to legal liability for bodily injury or property damage caused by use of or operation of an auto, up to the limits provided in the declarations page. The coverage will apply only to injuries or damages that are the fault (negligence) of the insured. The insurer will pay for the legal responsibility of the insured. The insurer is obligated to defend a claim or lawsuit, even if the insured is not at fault. Defense costs are provided in addition to the limit of coverage.

Covered Auto

The covered auto is the vehicle described in the declarations page. A private passenger auto, pickup, or van acquired during the policy period as an additional vehicle is covered. Notice of such additional vehicle must be given to the insurer within 14 days since an additional vehicle clearly affects the premium.

Replacement vehicles automatically receive the same coverage as the vehicle being replaced. Vehicles being used as temporary substitutes for an insured vehicle are also covered. Such substitute vehicles must not be owned by the insured, but only driven while an insured vehicle is unusable because it has been destroyed or is being repaired or serviced. A utility trailer is also automatically covered under the policy.

Who Is Insured?

The policy covers the named insured, his or her spouse, and family members living with the named insured or spouse (a family member is any person related to the named insured or spouse by blood, marriage, or adoption). Other persons are covered only while using a covered auto with permission. Also insured is any person or organization legally responsible for one who is using a covered auto. For example an employer or charity organization would be an insured while a family member provides a service by driving the covered auto. A spouse who is not a named insured and who ceases to live with the named insured has coverage continued for 90 days.

Split-Limits of Liability

Some earlier versions of the PAP used a single limit of liability for the coverage. The current version, however, uses the split-limits approach. Here, for bodily injury, one limit applies on a per person basis, another limit applies on a per occurrence basis, and a single limit applies for property damage liability. **If the Declarations show that the insured has 100/300/50 of coverage, the automobile policy will pay up to $100,000 per person, but not more than $300,000 in total for the accident, plus up to $50,000 of property damage.**

The most important factor to consider in purchasing automobile liability coverage is what limit one should buy. Whenever possible, one should purchase more than the state's legal minimum. Additional coverage does not cost a great deal beyond the basic premium. Generally, liability insurance "follows the auto." This means that the policy that lists the car involved in an accident has primacy over the policy that covers the driver, but not the specific car, involved in the accident. For example, if Carl borrows a car from his girlfriend Jill and has an accident, the insurance on the car purchased by Jill will pay for the accident. If the limits on Jill's policy are exhausted, however, the policy purchased by Carl will also provide coverage.

Part A Supplementary Payments

Part A also includes some supplementary payments for:

- Bail bonds ($250)
- Appeal bonds
- Postjudgment interest
- Loss of earnings by the insured for testifying (up to $200 per day)
- Reasonable expenses incurred at the request of the insurer

Part A Exclusions

Less than 4 Wheels

The PAP liability coverage excludes vehicles with less than four wheels and vehicles designed for use off public roads. An exception, however, does provide liability coverage for use of golf carts that are not owned by the insured. Another exception provides coverage when such vehicles are used in a medical emergency. If coverage for a motorcycle is desired, the policy can be endorsed to cover such a vehicle, or a separate policy can be purchased. Vehicles having less than four wheels have different risk characteristics, which insurers have decided are more appropriately covered by a separate policy or by a specific endorsement with its own rate structure.

Vehicles not listed in the policy

Motor vehicles not listed in the policy but that are owned or available for the regular use of an insured are excluded. There is coverage for the named insured and spouse when they are driving a non-owned vehicle with the owner's permission.

Other Exclusions

Other exclusions exist primarily because they are not contemplated as part of the risk normally insured under an auto policy or because of the moral hazard involved. Some of these are:

- Intentional injury or damage
- Damage to owned or transported property
- Damage to non-owned property rented to, used by, or in the custody of the insured
- Injury to an employee
- Use in the auto business
- Use of a non-owned auto without permission
- Nuclear energy liability
- Vehicles not designed for use on public roads (but non-owned golf carts are covered)
- Use in prearranged or organized racing or speed contests
- Use as a public livery or conveyance (but use in a share-the-expense carpool is covered)
- Injury covered by workers' compensation

Part B – Medical Payments Coverage

Part B of the PAP is the Medical Payments Coverage and is an optional coverage that can be added to the policy. Usually, there is a low limit, such as $1,000 per injured person, which can be increased by endorsement. It applies without regard to fault and is designed to pay for reasonable expenses of an insured for necessary medical and funeral expenses (within three years of the accident) due to bodily injury caused by an auto accident. A covered person under the Medical Payments Coverage section includes:

- The insured or any family member while occupying an auto or as a pedestrian if struck by a motor vehicle designed for use mainly on public roads.
- Any other person while occupying the covered auto.

If one already has adequate medical expense insurance, the major reason for purchasing automobile medical payments is to cover medical expenses for guest passengers. Automobile medical payments coverage is not as essential as liability coverage. If premium dollars are limited, liability coverage should come first. As with the liability coverage, after the basic premium, increases in coverage do not cost a great deal. This coverage could save the insured a great deal in lawsuits.

Part B Exclusions

Generally, there is no coverage for situations that are excluded from the liability coverage of the policy for the same reasons.

Practice Question

Which of the following statements concerning the Medical Payments Coverage under the personal auto policy is (are) correct?

- (1) Medical Payments Coverage is an optional benefit.
- (2) Medical Payments Coverage excludes payment of the medical expenses of the insured and the insured's family members.

    A. (1) only
    B. (2) only
    C. Both (1) and (2)
    D. Neither (1) nor (2)

Answer:
Medical Payments Coverage under the personal auto policy covers the medical expenses of the insured and the residence family members if they are injured in any motor vehicle accident with a vehicle designed for use on public roads.
The answer is A.

Part C – Uninsured Motorists Coverage

Uninsured motorists coverage is required by most states. This coverage provides compensation to insureds who have suffered bodily injury in an auto accident with an at-fault motorist who had no  insurance or who had insurance below the amounts required by the state's financial responsibility law. This coverage will also pay benefits to the insured who is a victim of a hit-and-run accident, and it will pay benefits when the at-fault driver's insurer denies coverage, or when the other driver's insurer becomes insolvent. In essence, an injured person pays for the insurance an uninsured driver should have purchased.

The losses intended to be covered by the PAP's uninsured motorists coverage are what an insured would be legally entitled to recover from the owner or driver of an uninsured vehicle for bodily injury losses caused by an accident.

Persons Covered under Uninsured Motorists Coverage

Those protected against injuries from an accident with an uninsured motor vehicle are:

- The named insured and any family members

- Other persons occupying the insured's covered auto

- Persons entitled to recover because of bodily injury to the named insured, family members, and occupants. These would be guardians, parents, and executors of covered persons.

Practice Question

Which of the following statements concerning uninsured motorists (UM) coverage is correct?

    A. UM provides medical payments and collision coverages.
    B. UM will pay for property damage when minimum insurance levels carried by the responsible driver are inadequate.
    C. UM will pay an insured hit by an uninsured driver while changing a tire.
    D. UM requires the insured to establish the uninsured driver's identity and lack of liability coverage.

Answer:
UM provides liability coverage, not medical payments or property loss coverages. UM will pay when minimum levels of insurance are not carried. UM will pay in a hit-and-run case, without establishing the identity of the driver or the lack of liability coverage. UM will pay an insured hit while changing a tire.
The answer is C.

Underinsured Motorists Coverage

Underinsured motorists coverage is available to purchasers of uninsured motorists coverage. When added to the uninsured motorist coverage (UM), the underinsured motorists endorsement provides for reimbursement for medical expenses for an insured when a negligent driver who caused the injury has lower liability limits than the limits of the UM of the "good" driver. The insurer for the injured party will pay the amount the insurer of the other vehicle would have paid if the negligent driver had carried adequate liability coverage.

For example, Pearl has a PAP with underinsured motorists coverage in the amount of $100,000, and Helen has a PAP with a liability limit of $50,000. They are in an accident, and it is adjudicated that Helen is at fault. From Pearl's perspective, Helen's auto is an underinsured motor vehicle – its limit is lower than Pearl's underinsured motorists coverage. Pearl's insurer will pay her $50,000 in addition to the $50,000 paid by Helen's policy.

The underinsured motorists coverage is not applicable for a hit-and-run circumstance or when the other motorist is completely uninsured. Only uninsured motorists coverage is applicable for such circumstances.

Part C Exclusions

The following uninsured motorists exclusions apply to the PAP:

- Automobiles used to carry persons or property for a fee
- Vehicles used without a reasonable belief that the user is permitted to do so
- If the injured person settles with the negligent party without the insurer's consent, the injured party can obtain no benefits from the insurer
- The coverage may not be used directly or indirectly to benefit any insurer or self-insurer under a workers' compensation, disability benefits, or similar law. Thus, if an employer makes workers' compensation benefit payments to an injured employee by using self-insurance funds, the employer may not seek reimbursement from the employee's insurer by exercising its subrogation rights.

Part D – Coverage for Damage to the Auto

Part D is Coverage for Damage to Your Auto. This section provides coverage for direct and accidental physical damage (including theft) to the covered auto and any non-owned auto, on an actual cash value basis. Coverage includes: (1) collision, meaning an impact of the covered auto or a non-owned auto with another object, or its overturn; and (2) other-than-collision (formerly known as "comprehensive"), which is a form of open-perils coverage insuring against perils that are not considered collision. Coverage is on an ACV basis, usually subject to a deductible per occurrence.

The PAP specifically designates a number of losses that are categorized as "loss other than by collision." Not deemed collision is any loss involving breakage of glass, loss caused by missiles, falling objects, fire, theft or larceny, explosion, earthquake, windstorm, hail, water, flood, malicious mischief or vandalism, riot or civil commotion, or contact with a bird or animal. (The insured may, however, elect to have breakage of glass treated as loss due to collision.)

 K Study Tip – Collision can be an impact with another car or object, or it can be an upset. Impact with an animal, such as a deer or moose, and objects falling on the car, such as tree branches, are not collisions. Losses from contact with animals and falling objects may be covered under "other-than-collision" coverage.

Transportation expense coverage of up to $20 per day, to a maximum of $600, is automatically included. If the loss was due to a total theft, there is a mandatory 48-hour waiting period; for other cause of loss, there is a 24-hour waiting period. Loss of use and other expenses are covered in this part of the policy for non-owned autos.

A non-owned auto is any private passenger, pickup or van, or trailer (as defined in the policy) that is not owned, furnished, or available for the regular use of the named insured or his or her family member. The auto must be operated by or be in the custody of the named insured or a family member.

Practice Question

Which of the following would be covered as a collision loss under the terms of the physical damage coverage of the personal auto policy?

    A. Falling missiles
    B. Upset
    C. Contact with a bird
    D. Contact with an animal

Answer:
A, C, and D are all considered to be losses other than by collision. Upset is treated as a collision.
The answer is B.

Part D Exclusions

Part D excludes the following:

- Public or livery use (but not a share-the-expense carpool)
- Damage due and confined to wear and tear or freezing
- War and other catastrophic losses
- Campers or trailer bodies owned by the insured but not listed in the declarations
- Governmental action

There are also several equipment-related exclusions that eliminate or exclude coverage for:

- Radios, stereos, tape and CD decks, car phones, CB and mobile radios, CDs, cassettes, tapes, personal computers, and computer discs and diskettes

- Awnings, cabanas, and equipment that create additional living facilities

- Radar detectors and laser-beam detection equipment

- Customizing equipment

The exclusion relating to sound-reproduction equipment does not apply to equipment that is permanently installed in the vehicle or to equipment needed for the operation or monitoring of the vehicle's systems. Also, there is coverage for telephones that are permanently installed in the vehicle.

As for a newly acquired auto that replaces another vehicle, the insured has 14 days to notify the insurer if physical damage coverage is to be continued on the new vehicle. If physical damage coverage is to be added, the insurer must also be notified within 14 days.

Deductibles

Deductible provisions are designed to eliminate small claims from coverage, hold down the premium cost for claims and claim settlement costs, and reduce morale hazard. With a straight deductible, an initial amount of each loss is borne by the insured, as, for example, a $250 deductible in auto collision insurance. However, the insured typically does not have to pay the deductible if he or she is not the party at-fault.

UMBRELLA LIABILITY INSURANCE

An umbrella liability policy provides liability coverage in excess of the limits or exposures set forth in the insured's basic liability policies. The two functions of the umbrella policy are: (a) to provide excess coverage when the limits of the insured's basic coverage are inadequate to cover future judgments, and (b) to provide broader coverage than that provided by the basic policy or policies (the homeowners and the auto policies would both be basic policies). Thus, many losses excluded under the basic policies are covered under the umbrella policy.

If the exposure is not covered by the basic policies, the insured will be required to pay personally an amount specifically set forth in the umbrella policy in the form of a deductible, often called a self-insured retention. In such a case, the umbrella insurer will pay the ultimate net loss in excess of the retained limit, up to the umbrella policy's limit. The additional coverage provided by the umbrella policy is for "personal injury," which is defined to include legal liability for libel, slander, defamation of character, invasion of privacy, false arrest, wrongful entry or eviction, malicious prosecution, and assault and battery not intentionally committed.

 **The umbrella policy requires the insured to maintain specified minimum limits on underlying policies.** Failure to do so will result in a major financial penalty for the insured since the insurer will settle any claim as if the required underlying coverages and amounts had been in force. For example, a typical insurer under a $1 million umbrella policy may insist that the insured have auto liability limits of $100,000 per person, $300,000 per accident, $50,000 property damage, and minimum homeowner Coverage E of $300,000. If the insured carried only $50,000/$100,000/$25,000 coverage and had an accident that resulted in the insured being found liable for $400,000, the underlying PAP would pay $100,000, the insured would have to pay the next $200,000 until the specified minimum for the umbrella was reached, and the umbrella insurer would pay the last $100,000.

Those insureds who have special exposures also are required to arrange basic coverage for those exposures to meet the requirements for the umbrella policy. For example, the owner of a motorized boat that is too large to be covered under the homeowner policy must arrange a special separate policy for the boat before umbrella coverage would be written. Also, underlying professional liability coverage will be required of the professional practitioner who is applying for umbrella coverage.

A comprehensive personal liability (CPL) insurance policy provides liability coverage similar to the liability coverage provided by Section II of the homeowners policies. The CPL policy is designed for individuals who do not purchase a homeowners policy. In that situation, the umbrella policy will stipulate the required insurance under the CPL policy rather than the homeowner policy.

Practice Question

Which of the following statements correctly describe the operation of umbrella liability coverage?

(1) It provides excess coverage when the limits of the insured's basic liability coverage are inadequate.
(2) It provides coverage for some exposures that are not covered by the insured's basic coverage.
(3) A deductible or self-insured retention is typically applied when the loss is covered by the umbrella coverage, but not covered by the basic contract or contracts.

    A. (1) and (2) only
    B. (1) and (3) only
    C. (2) and (3) only
    D. (1), (2), and (3)

Answer:
All three statements are correct.
The answer is D.

EXHIBIT 32 – 2
Individual Insurance Planning Recommendations

Recommendation	Explanation
Upgrade HO-2 to HO-3 or HO-5.	This upgrade improves coverage from broad form perils to open-perils.
Increase the limits of coverage under the homeowners policy.	Increasing coverage will prevent a coinsurance penalty due to inadequate limits.
Increase the deductible on the homeowners policy.	Increasing the deductible will reduce the cost of the insurance, with little reduction of coverage.
Add Scheduled Personal Property endorsement or personal articles floater for jewelry, furs, art objects, etc.	Additional limits are provided for high-value items, and coverage is open-perils. Deductible can be removed. Losses can be paid on a valued basis.
Add Inflation Guard endorsement.	Additional limits are automatically provided to avoid a coinsurance penalty and inadequate coverage.
Add other endorsements as needed.	Endorsements can be added, such as to cover earthquake, personal property for replacement cost (HO-15), or business activities.
Add personal umbrella policy.	This excess liability coverage adds protection to underlying homeowners and auto policies. Coverage is inexpensive and advantageous.
Increase underlying limits to minimums required for the umbrella policy.	Bringing underlying limits up to the minimum required for the umbrella policy will avoid a gap in coverage.
Increase limits for the PAP.	Wealthy clients will especially want higher limits of liability coverage. Limits should be brought up to minimums required by the umbrella policy.
Drop collision or physical damage coverage on low-value cars.	The expense of insuring a low-value car is generally not justified.
Increase the deductible on the PAP.	Increasing the deductible will reduce car insurance premiums.

BUSINESS-RELATED RISK EXPOSURES

Business organizations confront risks relating to personal losses, property losses, and losses due to legal liability that are similar (though probably larger and more complex) to those confronting households and individuals.

Business-Related Personal Loss Exposures

Personal loss exposures tend to be of particular concern to small businesses where one or a few key people are essential to the ongoing success of the business. For example, for an employee of a large corporation, a 60- or 90-day disability is certain to impact their personal financial life, but upon recovery that employee may still rest easy knowing that the business will continue to operate and that the employee will have a job to return to upon recovery. For a small business owner whose business relies on his personal efforts, not only does he have to ensure his salary can be replaced so that the mortgage can be paid and food put on the table, but he also has to make sure the business expenses can be paid and operations can continue so that he still has a business to return to upon recovery. Especially for personal losses confronting small businesses, then the planner should evaluate the following exposures:

- Loss of profits due to the death or disability of a key employee
- Loss of value of the client's business interest because of absence of a ready market in which to sell it if the client dies or becomes totally disabled
- Loss of income and medical care costs if the business owner becomes disabled
- Loss of income due to the business owner's retirement or death

Loss of Profits Due to Death or Disability of a Key Employee

Key employee life insurance is coverage purchased by an employer on the life of a particularly valuable employee whose death would produce a significant financial loss for the employer. The business will be the owner, premium payer, and beneficiary of the life insurance policy on the life of the key employee. The premiums are nondeductible by the employer and death benefits are received income tax-free.

Key employee disability insurance has a similar structure to key employee life insurance, but provides protection for the business in case a key employee becomes disabled for a significant period of time.

Loss of Value Due to Absence of a Ready Market in Which to Sell Upon Death, Disability, or Retirement

A buy-sell agreement is a contract in which a business owner commits his or her estate to a sale of the business interest. There are two common approaches to setting up a buy-sell agreement: an entity agreement and a cross-purchase agreement. Under the entity approach, a partnership or corporation will commit to buying the interest of any deceased owner, and the business will purchase a life insurance policy on each of the owners. With the cross-purchase approach, partners or stockholders will commit to buying the interest of any deceased owner of the firm. With a cross-purchase agreement, each owner will purchase a life insurance policy on the life of each of the other owners. For example, if A, B, and C are all partners in a partnership with a cross-purchase agreement, owner A would purchase life insurance policies on B and C; B would purchase policies on A and C; and C would purchase policies on A and B.

In addition to life insurance, disability income insurance can be used to fund a buy-sell agreement to provide for the purchase of a business interest when the owner becomes disabled. Specialized disability buy-out insurance policies are available to fund the buy-sell agreement. The agreement will typically stipulate a long period of disability, such as one year or longer, must occur before a disabled owner is required to sell his or her share of the business, and the disability buy-out policy will have an elimination period to match that time-frame. The pay-out from the disability policy can be structured to match the terms of the buy-out. For example, the policy might provide a lump-sum down payment of $500,000 followed by 10 annual payments of $100,000 each.

Additional details of buy-sell agreements will be discussed in Topic 29 (Business Uses of Insurance) of this textbook.

Loss of Income if the Owner Becomes Disabled

As mentioned earlier, the long-term disability of a small business owner presents a double challenge: the need to cover personal expenses as well as the need to cover business expenses.

Business Overhead Expense (BOE) insurance policies are available to cover the business's regular expenses when the owner becomes disabled. BOE policies do not, however, cover the owner's salary, so an individual disability policy will also be necessary in order to provide for payment of personal expenses. BOE policies are discussed in more detail in Topic 29 of this textbook, and individual and group disability policies are discussed in more detail in Topic 25 of this textbook.

Loss of Income Due to Business Owner's Retirement or Death

Loss of income to the business at the owner's death can be replaced using a key person life insurance policy, while loss of business income due to the retirement of the owner is often dealt with through sound succession planning. Succession planning strategies are beyond the scope of this textbook; however, key person life insurance is discussed in more detail in Topic 29.

Loss of income to the owner and his family upon death of the owner can be addressed through buy-sell agreements as well as individual and group life insurance policies. Buy-sell agreements are discussed in more detail in Topic 29, and individual and group life insurance are discussed in more detail in Topic 28. Loss of income to the owner upon retirement is best replaced through both individual savings, such as in an IRA or Roth IRA, and contributions to a qualified retirement plan while the owner is still working. Retirement planning strategies are beyond the scope of this text, but are discussed in detail in Keir's Retirement Savings and Income Planning textbook.

Business-Related Property and Liability Loss Exposures

The individual insurance coverage described previously provides only very minor property insurance for business property. For example, the unendorsed homeowners policy covers only up to $2,500 of on-premises ($500 of off-premises) property insurance for business property. It provides no liability coverage for the business activities of an insured. Business owners, therefore, should be encouraged to discuss the need for commercial property and liability insurance policies with their property and casualty insurance agent. While the client will obtain most of their information and recommendations from the P&C agent, financial planners should have at least a basic understanding of the types of policies that may be available and the types of business losses that can be covered under these policies.

Unlike personal insurance, the premiums for these business insurance policies will generally be deductible as a business expense.

Commercial Property Insurance

Commercial property insurance can be written on a specified-perils basis or an open-perils basis. Though the forms may be used for most types of businesses, specialized forms are also available for buildings under construction, for condominium associations, and for commercial condominium unit-owners. The policies may be written on an ACV or replacement cost basis, and many contain an 80% coinsurance clause. Some forms are specifically designed to adjust the coverage for loss exposures whose amounts vary over time.

Commercial Package Policy

The commercial package policy is made up of a standard set of declarations and common policy conditions. To these are added two or more types of coverages, most of them optional. Among the available coverages are commercial property and general liability insurance, crime coverage, boiler and machinery insurance, inland marine coverage, auto insurance, and farm coverage.

Basic Commercial Package Policy Parts

In the Insurance Services Office (ISO) commercial package policy, the declarations page will include the policy number, the name of the insurer, the selling agent, and the insured, the address of the insured, and a description of the insured's business, and the policy's effective date and date of expiration of the policy. There is a statement of the agreement of the insurer to provide the named insured with the requested insurance coverage and the agreement of the insured to pay the required premium.

The common policy conditions form is applicable to all coverages listed in the policy. Those conditions include:

- Cancellation – Cancellation is a policy condition describing the rules and procedures by which the insurer and the insured may cancel the policy.
- Policy Changes – The policy changes condition refers to making changes in the policy after it has been issued. A change can be made only by a written endorsement issued by the insurer. Such changes may occur upon the request of the insured, but with the consent of the insurer.
- Examination of Books and Records – This condition provides the insurer with the right to inspect the insured's books and records to determine the appropriate premium.
- Inspections and Surveys – This condition gives the insurer the right to inspect the insured's premises and operations to determine the insurability of the risk.
- Premiums – The premiums condition asserts that the first named insured in the declarations is responsible for the payment of the premium.
- Transfer of Rights – This condition makes it clear that the insured may not transfer any rights or duties under the policy without the prior consent of the insurer.

Commercial General Liability Insurance

Commercial general liability (CGL) insurance is a policy designed to cover bodily injury and property damage liability, personal and advertising injury liability, and medical payments. The covered loss exposures are for premises liability, business operations liability, products liability, completed operations liability, contractual liability, and vicarious liability due to work performed by others.

A business firm needs commercial general liability insurance coverage to protect the firm against legal liability suits that do not involve automobile accidents or workers' compensation. The following are types of exposures to legal liability that would be classified as "general liability":

- Premises Liability – A visitor to the building is injured because of a hazardous loose board on a stairway.
- Business Operations Liability – The refrigerator repair man negligently leaves tools in the homeowner's hallway, and a child breaks her leg when she trips over the tools.
- Products Liability – Products legal liability may arise out of negligence, breach of warranty (product failed to perform as warranted by manufacturer and person is injured), and strict liability (aspirin becomes contaminated with another lethal drug). This latter example might also present a breach of warranty.
- Completed operations Liability – The contractor installed a defective steam boiler that exploded, injuring several people.
- Contractual Liability – A general contractor may sign a contract with an independent debris removal company, agreeing to hold the debris removal company harmless for any bodily injury or property damage suffered by any third party.
- Vicarious Liability – An employer may be liable for actions of an employee, and a general contractor may be held liable for defective work performed by an independent subcontractor.

The CGL policy may be written on an occurrence basis or, less commonly, on a claims-made basis.

- The **occurrence basis** of coverage in a commercial general liability (CGL) policy protects against liability only for events that occur within the term of the policy, regardless of when the claim for damages is made.
- The **claims-made basis** of coverage in a CGL policy protects against liability only for claims that are made within the term of the policy and during a specified extended reporting period thereafter, regardless of when the event creating the liability occurred.

Occurrence coverage in liability insurance means the "trigger" to make the insurance effective is bodily injury or property damage that happens during the policy period, even though the claim may not be made until after the expiration of the policy period. In some liability coverages, such as products liability, occurrence coverage results in a tail of claims long after the policy period has expired.

Claims-made coverage in liability insurance means that the "trigger" to make the insurance effective is the making of a claim for bodily injury or property damage during the policy period even though the injury or damage may have occurred prior to the policy's inception. This coverage was introduced to overcome the long tail of the occurrence basis policy.

Extended reporting periods extend the time within which the insured may report a claim and be eligible for coverage. On a claims-made policy, the extended reporting period extends coverage to claims that are first reported after the expiration of the policy, but the claims are for bodily injury or property damage that occurred during the period of policy coverage. A number of extended reporting periods may be available, including:

- Sixty-day tail – Tail coverage provided by the CGL extends coverage by sixty days following the expiration of a claims-made policy, during which time claims can be received and recorded. It is provided without cost.

- Five-year tail – This tail coverage is designed to pay claims reported during the five-year period following the expiration of a claims-made policy. The claims must have arisen from occurrences reported to the insurer no later than sixty days after the end of the policy period. This coverage is provided without additional cost.

- Unlimited tail – This coverage extends the sixty-day tail indefinitely. It is not provided automatically, and the insured has the option to purchase it.

The sixty-day and five-year tails, which are automatically included in the policy, are referred to in the policy as the basic extended reporting period (BERP). The unlimited tail, which is not automatically included in the policy, is referred to in the policy as the supplemental extended reporting period (SERP).

An extended reporting period is of no significance for a general liability policy written on an occurrence basis.

In addition to the CGL, a particular type of business may need specialized coverage due to the nature of their business operations. The following are some other types of specialized commercial liability exposures:

(a)   Dram shop legal liability. The various states have passed "dram shop" acts. This legislation imposes strict liability on the seller of intoxicating beverages who, by selling them, causes the intoxication of another who, in turn, causes injury to the person or property of others.

(b)   Pension fiduciary legal liability. The pension plan administrators, trustees, and others who have fiduciary responsibilities associated with the funding of pension plans and other retirement arrangements may be held legally liable individually for failure to perform in accordance with their assumed responsibilities.

(c)   Public officials legal liability insurance. This insurance provides coverage for various wrongful acts or omissions of municipal entities and their public officials.

(d)   Pollution liability insurance. An endorsement to the CGL is usually required. The coverage is not generally available without the endorsement.

(e)   School board legal liability insurance. This insurance covers wrongful acts of school board members.

(f)   Law enforcement legal liability insurance. This insurance provides legal liability insurance for the approved activities of law enforcement agencies.

Practice Question

The Weaver Basket Company used a chemical in its weaving process that seeped into the ground over several years. Although the chemical is no longer used, a claim was recently filed for environmental damage from the chemical. The company has only purchased CGL coverage in the past year and is uncertain as to what kind of CGL coverage it has purchased. If the policy does not exclude coverage for environmental damage, which kind of policy might cover this claim?

A. Claims-made basis only
B. Occurrence basis only
C. Both claims-made and occurrence basis
D. Neither claims-made nor occurrence basis

Answer:
If Weaver Basket Company has a claims-made policy, the claim will be covered because the policy covers claims that are made currently, regardless of when the event occurred. If the company has an occurrence basis policy, the claim will probably not be covered because the damage occurred in the past, before the term of the policy.
The answer is A.

Commercial Crime Insurance

Commercial crime insurance is available to cover various types of property against a number of types of crimes. The company purchases an Employee Dishonesty Bond (also called Fidelity Bond) to cover losses for dishonest employees. The commercial crime insurance policy covers losses from nonemployees. The bond and insurance can insure money, securities, and/or other types of tangible property. It can be written to cover the perils of burglary, computer fraud, disappearance, employee dishonesty, extortion, forgery, alteration, robbery, safe burglary, or theft. Also, the coverage can be written on a discovery basis or on a loss-sustained (occurrence) basis.

Unique provisions in many crime insurance policy forms are as follows:

- No coverage for losses caused by the named insured, officers and directors, or by other employees, unless employee dishonesty coverage is bought
- No coverage for consequential losses
- Requirement that police be notified of a loss
- Loss valuation: Money is valued at its face value, securities at their market value when the loss is discovered, and other property at its ACV.

Practice Question

Commercial Crime Insurance Coverage Forms can be written to insure which of the following types of property?

(1) Money
(2) Securities
(3) Computers

    A. (1) and (2) only
    B. (1) and (3) only
    C. (2) and (3) only
    D. (1), (2), and (3)

Answer:
All three types of property can be covered by crime insurance.
The answer is D.

Boiler and Machinery Insurance

Boiler and machinery insurance covers direct property damage caused by accidental boiler explosion, electrical breakdown, and mechanical breakdown. The boiler and machinery insurance policy covers direct damage to: (a) boilers and fixed vessels, (b) unfixed vessels (for example, electric steam generators, buried vessels, or electrical apparatus within or forming a part of a vessel), (c) refrigerating and air conditioning equipment, (d) engines, (e) turbines, (f) generators, and (g) motors.

Included is damage to the boiler or machine, as well as to other property in the insured's care for which the insured is liable. The heavy emphasis by the insurer on inspection and loss prevention is reflected in the cost of the coverage.

Commercial Farm Insurance

Commercial farm insurance can be written on an open-perils or named-perils basis to cover various types of farm property, including livestock. It can also cover the liability loss exposures of the farmer. A specialized form of farm insurance is crop-hail insurance, written by private insurance or by the federal government.

Commercial Auto Insurance

There are three types of commercial automobile insurance policies:

- The Business Auto Coverage Form provides the same types of coverages as the PAP. Virtually all types of business cars, trucks, and trailers may be covered, depending on the classification of vehicles selected by the insured, such as any vehicle, owned vehicles only, owned private passenger autos only, and non-owned vehicles only.

- The Garage Coverage Form provides liability protection for businesses engaged in selling, servicing, parking, or storing vehicles.

- The Motor Carrier Coverage Form is like the Business Auto Coverage Form, except that it is designed to meet the needs of common carriers, contract carriers, and private carriers who haul their own property or cargo.

Specialized Commercial Policies

Businessowners Policy

The businessowners policy is a property and liability policy designed for small- and medium-sized businesses of certain types. Its property coverage can be written on a named-perils basis or on an open-perils basis for buildings and personal property. The coverage pays for replacement cost and does not contain a coinsurance requirement. The policy also includes business income and extra expense coverage. Standard coverages include debris removal costs, forgery losses, pollutant cleanup costs, and counterfeit currency losses. Coverage for bodily injury, property damage, advertising, and personal injury liability is also included, along with coverage of medical payments to others. A variety of additional coverages can be added for an extra premium, such as accounts receivable coverage, valuable papers and records coverage, and coverage of personal property off the premises.

Inland Marine Insurance

Inland marine insurance is a category of insurance that protects against property losses to goods in transit, property in the hands of bailees, moveable equipment and property, the inventories of certain types of dealers, instrumentalities of transportation and communication, and losses due to "differences in conditions." Differences in conditions (DIC) insurance is a type of inland marine policy that "wraps around" another type of policy to fill in gaps in its coverage, such as the earthquake and flood exclusions, or to provide higher insurance amounts than are available otherwise.

Some inland marine coverages may actually have little or nothing to do with the risks of transportation per se. For example, an inland marine policy will cover theft of a musical instrument while the instrument is in the dressing room of the performing artist.

Ocean Marine Insurance

Ocean marine insurance coverage is available for four types of losses: (i) Hull insurance reimburses the ship owner for direct damage to or loss of the ship; (ii) Cargo insurance reimburses the shipper of the goods for the financial loss if the goods are damaged or destroyed; (iii) Freight insurance reimburses the owner of the ship for the loss of income that occurs because shippers do not pay freight charges for goods that are not delivered; and (iv) Protection and indemnity insurance is basically liability coverage that protects the ship owner if he or she is found to be legally liable for damage to property of others or for bodily injury to others.

Practice Question

Which of the following may not be insured by an inland marine insurance policy?

    A. A small powerboat
    B. A TV antenna tower
    C. The inventory of a jeweler
    D. Property held by a bailee

Answer:
A powerboat will be covered by property and liability policies, not by an inland marine policy.
The answer is A.

Surety Bonds

Surety bonds are contracts with three parties: a surety, a principal, and an obligee. The surety, usually an insurer, guarantees the fulfillment of certain responsibilities by the principal to a third party, the obligee. For example, a landowner hires a contractor to build an office building. The landowner requires the contractor to provide a surety bond for the project. The surety guarantees that the contractor (principal) will complete the project for the landowner (obligee). If the contractor fails to perform, the surety pays for any loss.

Surety bonds have several unusual characteristics. First, if the principal defaults, he or she is liable to the surety for any payments the surety makes. Second, few losses are expected because of the strict underwriting that precedes issuance of a bond. Third, the period of coverage is indefinite. Fourth, a few types of bonds have no maximum dollar limit on the amount payable by the surety. Fifth, the terms of some bonds are prescribed by law.

Commercial Umbrella Liability Policy

Commercial umbrella liability insurance operates in the same way as the personal umbrella policy described earlier (see Page 32.36) by providing catastrophic protection with respect to losses which exceed the underlying coverage and providing protection for unusual losses not covered by primary insurance.

Required underlying policies often include the CGL policy, the business auto policy, and the employer's liability policy. The self-insured retention is often $25,000 or more. The coverage is usually written on an occurrence basis.

Professional Liability Policies

Professional Liability

Professional liability can arise under two different legal theories: breach of contract and negligence. The contractual duties of a professional arise from the contract to provide services for the client. When the professional fails to perform as promised in the contract, the client is entitled to damages based on full performance. The tort-related duty of a professional is the duty to follow a recognized standard of conduct, which is to use reasonable care to avoid causing harm to other persons. Failure to follow this standard will cause the professional to become liable in a negligence action for any damage caused to the other person.

Professional liability insurance provides coverage for legal liability arising from the failure of a person to use the care and the degree of skill expected of a practitioner in a particular profession. The liability

> *"Risk comes from not knowing what you are doing."*
> **Warren Buffett**

coverage available to professionals is twofold: (a) malpractice insurance to cover exposures to bodily injury liability (designed for doctors, dentists, and hospitals), and (b) errors and omissions insurance to cover exposures to property damage liability, including intangible property (designed primarily for insurance agents, attorneys, accountants, architects, and real estate agents).

Most professional liability policies written today do not require the insurance company to obtain permission from the insured to settle a liability claim. The reason for the earlier policy provisions requiring the insured's consent was to protect the professional reputation of the insured. There was apprehension that a voluntary payment could be construed by the public as a confession of guilt. Professionals who are concerned about protecting their professional reputations in such situations may choose to seek a policy that allows the professional to make the final decision regarding settlement of a claim.

Physicians Professional Liability Policy

The physicians professional liability insurance policy covers injury arising out of the physician's negligence. Most policies do not include a definition of "injury" within the policy, so any harm, including property damage, arising from the physician's negligence in rendering professional services is covered.

Liability for Negligent Employees: Like any employer, a physician can become liable for the negligent acts of employees. Should a physician employ a technician to perform X-rays, the physician could be held responsible for the negligent acts of the technician. Similarly, a physician can be held responsible for the negligence of any physician with whom he or she has entered into a partnership or professional association. Some common allegations made against physicians in professional liability cases include surgical error, improper diagnosis, improper testing, lack of informed consent, and improper administration of drugs and anesthetics.

Defenses: Available defenses against medical professional liability include:

- Good Samaritan statutes, which exempt physicians and other licensed health care professionals from liability when they provide gratuitous emergency care. These statutes, however, provide no defense for treatment that is grossly negligent or reckless.

- Informed consent, which provides a defense against technical "battery" since it implies that the patient agreed to the procedure. Informed consent does not provide a defense against professional negligence because it does not constitute acceptance of the physician's negligence by the patient.

Insuring Agreements: The physicians professional liability policy contains two insuring agreements. The individual insuring agreement provides coverage for negligent professional acts of the insured physician, for negligent professional acts of the insured physician's employees or others for whom the insured may become vicariously liable, and for the insured's service on a formal accreditation board. The organization insuring agreement provides coverage for the insured's professional partnership, association, or corporation, and it pays losses arising from the negligent acts of anyone for whom the organization is legally liable.

Accountants Professional Liability Policy

The term "professional services," as used in the insuring agreement of an accountant's professional liability policy, is important because it determines what will and will not be covered under the policy. The definition of this term is not consistent from policy to policy, but it is generally used to mean those activities involved in the practice of an accountant. If an accounting firm offers a broad scope of management advisory services, this information should be disclosed to the insurance company, and the policy language should be modified, if necessary, in order to make sure that the policy covers all of the management advisory services provided by the accounting firm.

Architects and Engineers Professional Liability Policy

The architects and engineers professional liability policy usually places an important limitation on its grant of insured status for the named insured's principals, partners, and employees. The policy will provide coverage for this group only while they are acting in their capacities as such. The effect of this limitation is to exclude coverage for principals, partners, and employees when they are acting as independent contractors for others.

While some professional liability policies exclude coverage for claims involving bodily injury or property damage, an exclusion of this nature would be inappropriate for an architects and engineers professional liability policy. It is entirely possible for the professional negligence of the architect or engineer to result in a structural defect that could cause bodily injury or property damage.

Other Professional Liability Policies

Other important types of professional liability loss exposures and coverages are the following:

- Directors and officers liability insurance – This insurance provides coverage for the directors and officers of a corporation (or non-profit entity) for claims arising from their wrongful acts, and it covers the corporation for amounts it is required or permitted to reimburse directors and officers for claims arising from their wrongful acts.

- Employee benefits liability insurance – This insurance provides coverage for the insured organization and its employees against claims arising from errors and omissions in the administration of the organization's employee benefit plans.

- Fiduciary liability insurance – This insurance provides coverage for the organization and its employees against claims arising from breaches of their fiduciary responsibilities in connection with the organization's employee benefits plans. This insurance can also cover the same errors and omissions covered by employee benefits liability insurance.

- Employment practices liability insurance – This insurance covers the organization, including its directors and officers and other employees, for losses arising from various employment-related offenses, such as wrongful termination, discrimination, and sexual harassment.

Workers' Compensation and Employers Liability

A Workers' Compensation and Employers Liability insurance policy provides two kinds of coverage:

1) Payment of the employer's obligation under state laws to pay workers' compensation benefits for employees
2) Payment for liability claims from employee injuries and illnesses not covered under the workers' compensation laws

The workers' compensation coverage contains the insurer's agreement to pay all workers' compensation benefits that the insured employer is required to pay under state law. There is no specified limit of liability for workers' compensation coverage because state laws set the amount of benefits, and the policy simply pays the amount of benefits required under the state law. The Other States Insurance part of the policy will provide similar coverage for the employer that has operations in different states.

The employers liability insurance is a traditional liability coverage that pays claims when an employer is sued for bodily injury or illness suffered by an employee. The employer can select limits of liability that specify a maximum amount per accident, per employee, and in an aggregate amount for the policy period.

An employer needs the protection of employers liability insurance even if the employer has workers' compensation insurance coverage because the employer may be sued by the employee or the employee's spouse for the negligence of the employer. The employer's negligence may have been perpetrated in the employer's capacity as a business firm that was completely separate from the business firm's position or capacity as the employer of the injured or aggrieved employee. This latter concept is known as the "dual-capacity" doctrine.

A few examples will help clarify the need for employers liability insurance. (a) The spouse of an injured employee is not eligible for workers' compensation benefits, but her lawyer successfully persuades the court that the spouse has suffered a loss because of the employee's injury. (b) "Third-party-over suits" also give rise to suits against the employer. An employee is injured by a visitor to the workplace. The employee successfully sues the visitor. The visitor then seeks to recover part of the court's assessment by taking the employer to court. (c) The employee is injured as the result of a tire blowout, and the defective tire was manufactured by the employee's employer. This third example is an example of the dual-capacity doctrine.

Business Income Coverage

Business income coverage forms available include:

- Business Income (and Extra Expense) Coverage Form – This form covers lost net profits that would have been earned if the shutdown or reduction of operations had not been necessitated by the occurrence of a covered peril; it also covers normal continuing business expenses. In addition, it covers extra expenses needed to avoid or minimize the shutdown or reduction of operations.

- Business Income (Without Extra Expense) Coverage Form – This form is similar to the foregoing form, but with no coverage of most extra expenses.

- Extra Expense Coverage Form – Obviously, this form covers only the extra expenses. It is used by businesses that simply must not shut down, such as banks and newspapers, regardless of the expenses of continuing in operation.

Class Exercise 32 – 1

Using the mini-case information for Steven and Diane Harper, located on Keir's Instructor Website, the class will identify and discuss loss exposures faced by the Harpers for each of the following categories: personal risks, property risks, liability risks, and business-related risks.

APPLICATION QUESTIONS

1. Harry has just experienced a small fire loss to his home and wants to know what his responsibilities are under his homeowners insurance policy. In which section of the homeowners policy will Harry learn what these responsibilities are?

    A. Definitions
    B. Exclusions
    C. Insuring agreements
    D. Conditions
    E. Endorsements

2. Which of the following personal property losses would <u>not</u> be fully covered (less any deductible) by an unendorsed HO-3 policy?

    A. Airline tickets worth $520 were stolen from the insured's handbag as she entered the airline terminal.
    B. The insured's hunting rifles, worth $1,250, were stolen from his tent during a hunting trip.
    C. The insured's laptop computer, used in her professional work and worth $2,400, was taken from her while she was using it during lunch with a client at a restaurant.
    D. The insured's canoe, worth $900, was taken from his garage.
    E. The insured's golf clubs, worth $1,300, were stolen from the trunk of his locked car by someone who forced open the trunk.

3. The most frequently used of the homeowners series is the HO-3. Its coverage for personal property covers most items of personal property owned or used by any insured. Which of the following items of personal property are specifically excluded under the HO-3?

    (1) Animals, birds, or fish
    (2) Property of roomers and boarders
    (3) Articles insured by schedule in this or any other insurance policy

        A. (1) and (2) only
        B. (1) and (3) only
        C. (2) and (3) only
        D. (1), (2), and (3)

4. Mr. and Mrs. Reginald Jackson had their dwelling insured under an HO-3 in the amount of $80,500, which was its current replacement cost. Following a total loss by a covered peril, the Jackson family discovered that the cost to rebuild was indeed, $80,500. The deductible was $500. However, the contractor asked for an additional $3,758 to remove the remains of the destroyed structure. The amount the insurance company will have to pay the insured is indicated by which of the following?

    A. $80,500
    B. 80% of $80,000, or $64,000
    C. $80,000 plus $3,758, or $83,758
    D. $85,000 plus 5% of $80,000, or $89,000
    E. $84,758

5. Which of the following losses would be covered by an HO-3 policy?

    A. As a result of the overflow of a nearby lake, water enters the insured's basement and does $900 damage to floor coverings and the foundation.
    B. During a severe rainstorm, water enters through the wall of the basement and damages stored items worth $444.
    C. The insured, while having a party with many people present, discovers that excessive use of the sanitary facilities has resulted in the backup of water through the sewer, causing more than $2,222 in damage.
    D. While filling the bathtub, the insured's daughter answers the telephone, chats for some 20 minutes, and then discovers that the tub overflowed. The excess water seeps through the bathroom floor, and its weight causes the kitchen ceiling to collapse. Damages exceed $3,333.

6. (Published question released November, 1994)

An HO-3 policy (special form – "all-risks of physical loss" except those specifically excluded) with <u>no</u> endorsements excludes which of the following perils?

    A. Flood
    B. Fire
    C. Collapse
    D. Weight of ice
    E. Volcanic eruption

7. Jack and Robin have their home insured under an HO-3 policy. The amount of the coverage on the dwelling, $100,000, has been left unchanged for several years. Yesterday, the home was struck by lightning, causing $10,000 of damage, as measured by actual cash value, and $18,000 of damage, as measured by replacement cost. The replacement cost of the home at the time of the lightning damage is estimated at $150,000. In this situation, which of the following amounts will Jack and Robin recover from the insurer for this loss?

    A. Nothing, because the insurance is less than 80% of replacement cost
    B. $18,000, the replacement cost of the damage
    C. $10,000, the actual cash value of the damage
    D. $12,000, two-thirds of the replacement cost of the damage
    E. $15,000, five-sixths of the replacement cost of the damage

8. (Published question released November, 1994)

When fine arts or antiques are insured under a homeowners policy by an endorsement:

    A. Coverage is usually on a replacement cost basis.
    B. Coverage is usually on an actual cash value basis.
    C. Coverage is usually provided on a valued basis.
    D. The perils are the same as the homeowners policy to which the endorsement is attached.
    E. Coverage limits are the same as the homeowners policy to which the endorsement is attached.

9. Which of the following statements concerning the liability coverage under the personal auto policy is <u>not</u> correct?

    A. A single limit means that the insurance applies to a given accident, without a separate limit for each person injured.
    B. A split-limit means that the limits for property damage and for bodily injury are different and are applied separately.
    C. If the insurer decides to defend the insured, the defense costs are paid within the limits of liability.
    D. Prejudgment interest is payable within the limits of liability.
    E. The policy covers the insured while using a temporary substitute auto while the insured's car is being repaired.

10. Pat has a personal auto policy, and an accident occurs while she is driving. Which of the following accident circumstances would <u>not</u> be covered under Pat's policy?

    A. Pat is a volunteer driving around her neighborhood to distribute flyers for the local swim and tennis club.

    B. Pat is driving her employer's company car to the office supply store to pick up computer paper.

    C. Pat is driving her own car to collect an executive from her company's home office from the airport for a business meeting.

    D. Pat is a mother picking up four neighborhood children from school as a favor to their parents.

11. Which of the following statements concerning the medical payments coverage under the personal auto policy is <u>not</u> correct?

    A. Coverage will not apply if the medical expenses are incurred by a teenager using a neighbor's car for a joyride without permission.

    B. Coverage will apply if the insured is injured while riding in a car whose owner does not have medical payments coverage.

    C. Coverage will not apply if the insured is injured as a pedestrian by a vehicle lacking medical payments coverage.

    D. Coverage will not apply if the insured is injured in her camper while she is using it as a vacation home.

12. (Published question released January, 1999)

A client recently purchased a new home from a builder for $150,000, including the lot valued at $40,000. How much insurance would you recommend that your client purchase to cover full replacement of the house in the event of a loss?

    A. $88,000
    B. $110,000
    C. $120,000
    D. $150,000

13. Which of the following is covered under the damage to your auto section of a personal auto policy?

    A. Damage from freezing of the operating components of the vehicle

    B. Damage to radar detection equipment

    C. Damage to a laptop computer normally used by the insured while occupying the vehicle

    D. Damage to the vehicle of a neighbor being driven by the insured while her own vehicle is being custom-painted

14. Under which of the following circumstances would the named insured have coverage under the liability section of the personal auto policy?

    A. Damage to the insured's garage door caused by the insured's negligence

    B. Damage to the bicycle of the insured's neighbor being negligently transported in the insured's station wagon

    C. Damage to a business supplier's loading platform when the insured negligently drove the insured auto too close to the platform

    D. Injury to a fellow employee who was making a business trip with the insured in the insured auto to service a customer's computer equipment

15. Which of the following statements concerning auto medical payments coverage is correct?

    A. Coverage applies only to injuries resulting from an insured's negligence.

    B. Its purpose is to provide prompt reimbursement for covered expenses of eligible persons.

    C. Any benefits provided the injured person are deducted from the court's award of damages for the negligence of an insured.

    D. Coverage is restricted to persons injured while occupying a covered auto.

16. Which of the following statements concerning the uninsured motorists coverage under the personal auto policy is correct?

    A. The contract provisions govern the scope of coverage, even if they are not consistent with the applicable state statute.

    B. Coverage applies for bodily injury, as well as for property damage.

    C. There is coverage if the at-fault vehicle has insurance but in an amount less than is required as a minimum by the financial responsibility law of the state where the insured's covered auto is principally garaged.

    D. Coverage does not apply in case of an accident caused by a hit-and-run auto.

17. Which of the following statements concerning the physical damage coverage under the personal auto policy is (are) correct?

(1) An insured with both collision and other-than-collision coverages, both with deductibles, would incur both deductibles if a collision caused both car body and glass damage.

(2) An insured with both collision and other-than-collision coverages, with a deductible for collision only, would have no deductible applicable if a collision loss resulted only in the breakage of glass.

    A. (1) only
    B. (2) only
    C. Both (1) and (2)
    D. Neither (1) nor (2)

18. The other-than-collision coverage will cover losses from which of the following causes?

(1) Vandalism
(2) Impact with a bear
(3) Impact with a telephone pole
(4) Falling objects

    A. (1) and (4) only
    B. (2) and (3) only
    C. (2) and (4) only
    D. (1), (2), and (4) only

19. Brad has purchased an umbrella liability policy requiring that he carry $300,000 per person as the liability limit in his personal auto policy. Brad's auto policy, however, has split-limits of $100,000/$300,000/$50,000. In an auto accident caused by Brad, a pedestrian is injured and is awarded $250,000 by the court. How much will Brad's umbrella liability insurer pay in this situation?

    A. $0
    B. $100,000
    C. $150,000
    D. $250,000
    E. $300,000

20. (Published question released January, 1999)

Terry Underwood purchased a 15-year-old compact car with 100,000 miles for his teenage son who recently received his license. Which of the following auto insurance coverages should be included in the policy for this auto?

(1) Part A – Liability Coverage
(2) Part B – Medical Payments Coverage
(3) Part C – Uninsured Motorists Coverage
(4) Part D – Damage to Your Auto

    A. (1), (2), and (3) only
    B. (1), (2), and (4) only
    C. (1), (3), and (4) only
    D. (2), (3), and (4) only

21. Which of the following statements concerning professional liability insurance is correct?

    A. So-called errors and omissions coverage protects the insured for liability for having negligently caused mental anguish, as well as bodily injury.
    B. Lawyers and accountants are more likely to purchase malpractice coverage rather than errors and omissions coverage.
    C. A surgeon is more likely to purchase malpractice insurance rather than errors and omissions coverage.
    D. A pharmacist is more likely to purchase errors and omissions insurance rather than malpractice coverage.

22. A business that must remain open following occurrence of a covered peril, such as a newspaper publisher, is most likely to purchase which of the following types of business property insurance coverages?

    A. Business Income (Without Extra Expense) Coverage Form
    B. Extra Expense Coverage Form
    C. Ordinary Payroll Exclusion endorsement
    D. Crime insurance

23. The commercial general liability (CGL) policy covers which of the following losses?

    A. Losses to property in the insured's care, custody, or control
    B. Damage to property that is <u>not</u> physically injured
    C. Cleanup costs arising from pollution
    D. Products liability losses

24. Which of the following parts of the Workers' compensation and Employers Liability insurance policy contain(s) a specific dollar limit on the insurer's liability?

    (1) Workers' compensation insurance
    (2) Employers liability insurance
    (3) Other states insurance

        A. (1) only
        B. (2) only
        C. (3) only
        D. (1) and (3) only
        E. (2) and (3) only

25. Which of the following statements concerning the businessowners policy is <u>not</u> correct?

    A. It is designed mainly to cover the loss exposures of restaurants, bars, and places of amusement.
    B. It includes both property insurance and liability insurance.
    C. It contains no coinsurance requirement.
    D. It includes business income coverage.

26. Nathaniel West bought a building two years ago for $700,000. The building is insured under a commercial package policy with limits of $700,000 on the building. The policy is written on a replacement cost basis with an 80% coinsurance requirement and a $2,500 deductible. The current replacement cost of the building is $1 million. If a fire in the building causes damage that will cost $80,000 to repair, what amount will the insurance company pay?

    A. $67,500
    B. $77,500
    C. $70,000
    D. $80,000

27. Dr. Ken Rodalos had an occurrence basis professional liability policy for many years and then last year switched to a claims-made policy. A malpractice claim arose recently for treatment that Ken provided several years ago. Which policy will cover the claim?

    A. Claims-made basis policy only
    B. Occurrence basis policy only
    C. Both claims-made and occurrence basis policies
    D. Neither claims-made nor occurrence basis policy

28. Millie has insured her expensive diamond engagement ring on a valued basis through an endorsement to her homeowners insurance policy. In the event that the ring is stolen, how much will the insurer pay?

    A. The ring's actual cash value
    B. The ring's replacement cost
    C. The difference between the ring's actual cash value and its replacement cost
    D. Nothing
    E. The value of the ring as specified in the endorsement

29. A commercial fire insurance policy on a building has an 80 percent coinsurance requirement. A fire loss occurs involving $40,000 of damage. The building is insured for $120,000. At the time of the loss, the building is valued at $200,000. How much will the insurer pay for the damage? (Ignore any deductible.)

    A. $20,000
    B. $25,000
    C. $30,000
    D. $35,000
    E. $40,000

30. Which of the following is excluded from uninsured motorists coverage?

    A. Hit-and-run vehicles
    B. Out-of-state vehicles
    C. An accident to an insured using a covered auto as a public conveyance
    D. An accident involving another driver whose insurer becomes insolvent before the claim is paid

31. Which of the following are intentional torts?

(1) Invasion of privacy
(2) Negligence
(3) False imprisonment
(4) Libel and slander

    A. (1) and (2) only
    B. (2) and (3) only
    C. (1), (3), and (4) only
    D. (1), (2), (3), and (4)

32. Which of the following is (are) among the causes of or sources of legal liability?

(1) Absolute liability
(2) Intentional tort
(3) Negligence

    A. (3) only
    B. (1) and (2) only
    C. (1) and (3) only
    D. (2) and (3) only
    E. (1), (2), and (3)

33. All the following statements concerning the components of the typical property-liability insurance policies are correct, EXCEPT:

    A. The information provided by the applicant in the declarations section is helpful to the insurer for classifying the risk, determining the premium, and deciding whether to accept or reject the application.
    B. In the insuring agreement, the applicant promises to maintain the property in good condition and to inform the insurer of any significant change in the property's use that might have some impact on the probability of insured losses.
    C. The purpose of the exclusions section is to remove from coverage perils, hazards, properties, persons, and locations the insurer does not wish to cover.
    D. The purpose of the conditions section is to detail the duties and rights of both parties to the contract.

34. All the following statements concerning the elements that must be proven to establish tort liability for negligence are correct, EXCEPT:

    A. There is a duty owed the plaintiff.
    B. There is a failure to act in accordance with the duty owed.
    C. Damage or loss occurs.
    D. The damage or loss must be significant (usually interpreted to mean in excess of $1,000).
    E. The damage or loss results from the breach of the duty owed.

35. Which of the following statements concerning the property insurance loss adjustment process is correct?

    A. Notice of loss must be presented in writing.
    B. An important purpose of the investigation is to determine that the loss is covered by the policy.
    C. The insured's proof of loss may be given orally under oath or in written form.
    D. Appraisal is a viable option only if both parties agree to an appraisal.

36. In case of a loss covered under a property insurance policy, which of the following will be required?

    (1) Notice of loss
    (2) Protection of the undamaged property
    (3) Proof of loss
    (4) Appraisal

        A. (1) and (2) only
        B. (1), (2), and (3) only
        C. (1), (3), and (4) only
        D. (2), (3), and (4) only

37. Which of the following are insurance policy provisions that limit a property insurer's liability in covering insured losses?

(1) Pair or set option available to the insurer
(2) The other insurance provision
(3) The subrogation clause
(4) The aleatory provision

    A. (1) and (2) only
    B. (1), (2), and (3) only
    C. (2), (3), and (4) only
    D. (1), (2), (3), and (4)

38. A commercial building having a replacement cost of $900,000 is insured for only $600,000 under an 80% coinsurance clause with a $3,000 straight deductible. What will the insured receive under the terms of the policy if a fire occurs, causing a $300,000 covered loss?

    A. $100,000
    B. $199,000
    C. $247,000
    D. $300,000

39. Which of the following statements concerning the homeowners series of policies is correct?

    A. Section II of the various homeowners policies covers personal liability and is identical for the entire series of homeowners policies.
    B. Both HO-02 and HO-03 cover losses caused by water damage resulting from seepage of water through basement walls.
    C. The inflation guard endorsement is available and provides that the amount of insurance is automatically increased for any increase in the Consumer Price Index.
    D. Homeowners Form HO-06 provides coverage for older properties, and losses are settled on an ACV basis.

40. Which of the following statements correctly indicates a significant difference between HO-02 and HO-03?

    A. The dwelling and other structures coverage of the HO-02 is "all-risks" (open-perils), while that of the HO-03 is named perils coverage.

    B. The dwelling and other structures coverage of the HO-03 is "all-risks," while that of the HO-02 is named perils coverage.

    C. The HO-02 is designed for a tenant and, therefore, does not cover the dwelling or other structures.

    D. The HO-02 is specifically designed for condominium owners.

41. An insured with an HO-02 or an HO-03 might prefer specific insurance on certain types of personal property by means of a Scheduled Personal Property Endorsement for which of the following reasons?

    A. The HO-02 and HO-03 have sublimits applicable to certain types of personal property.

    B. The insurance rate for scheduled property is usually lower than for blanket coverage.

    C. The HO-02 and HO-03 do not cover loss caused by theft.

    D. These types of personal property are otherwise excluded from coverage.

42. Edward and Mindy Williams have their new suburban dwelling insured by an HO-03 for $80,000, which is exactly its current replacement cost. A nefarious character spots their newly planted valuable trees and returns one night to steal a mimosa tree valued at $800 and 12 walnut trees valued at $300 each. How much will the insurer pay the Williams family for this $4,400 loss?

    A. $0

    B. $4,000

    C. $4,100

    D. $4,400

43. In the event an insured with an HO-03 has a loss, his or her duties after a loss include all the following, EXCEPT:

    A. Giving prompt notice of loss

    B. Preparing an inventory of damaged personal property

    C. Exhibiting the damaged property as often as reasonably required and submitting to examination under oath

    D. Within 30 days following the insurer's request, submitting a signed, sworn statement of loss

    E. Protecting the property from further damage

44. The HO-03 provides medical payments coverage for which of the following persons?

(1) The insured and family members residing with him or her
(2) Any person on the insured premises with the permission of any insured
(3) Any person injured away from the insured premises if the injury is caused by the activities of the insured
(4) Any person injured away from the insured premises if the injury is caused by an animal owned by or in the care of any insured

    A. (1) and (2) only
    B. (1), (2), and (3) only
    C. (1), (3), and (4) only
    D. (2), (3), and (4) only

45. The personal liability coverage of the homeowners series covers bodily injury and property damage liability in which of the following situations?

(1) The liability arises out of the rendering of professional services.
(2) The liability arises out of the insured's use of a motorboat (owned by the insured) powered by an inboard motor.
(3) The liability arises out of the ownership of an aircraft.

    A. (1) only
    B. (2) only
    C. (3) only
    D. (1), (2), and (3)
    E. Neither (1), (2), nor (3)

46. Which of the following statements concerning the homeowners series of policies is correct?

    A. HO-06 is designed for tenants and provides broad form specified perils coverage the same as HO-02, but only for personal property.
    B. HO-02 is the most widely used form.
    C. HO-02 and 03 provide contents coverage up to 50% of the dwelling coverage.
    D. Coverage D (loss of use) would reimburse the insured for the total expenses incurred for accommodations at a motel while the dwelling is being made habitable after fire damage.

47. Which of the following statements concerning specific HO forms is correct?

    A. HO-08 is designed to cover the special exposures of a condominium unit owner.

    B. HO-02 provides "all-risks" coverage for the dwelling and named perils coverage for the dwelling's contents.

    C. If the premium were the same, a rational homeowner would prefer to have the coverage of HO-02 rather than HO-03.

    D. HO-04 provides no coverage on a dwelling or on other structures.

48. Which of the following items of property would be excluded from coverage under the homeowners Scheduled Personal Property Endorsement that a homeowner elects to add to his or her HO-03 policy?

    A. Jewelry and furs

    B. Cameras and musical instruments

    C. Fishing and hunting equipment

    D. Fine arts and antiques

    E. Stamp and coin collections

49. Coverages E and F in a homeowner's policy would provide coverage for which of the following?

    (1) The insured's legal liability for accidental damage to property of others

    (2) The insured's legal liability for personal injury to others arising out of an accident

    (3) Medical payments to others, whether the named insured caused the injury on his or her premises or elsewhere

        A. (1) only

        B. (1) and (2) only

        C. (1) and (3) only

        D. (2) and (3) only

        E. (1), (2), and (3)

50. Which of the following statements correctly describe(s) the operation of the umbrella liability coverage?

    (1) It provides excess coverage when the limits of the insured's basic liability coverage are inadequate.

    (2) It provides coverage for some exposures that are not covered by the insured's basic coverage.

    (3) A deductible or self-insured retention is typically applied when the loss is covered by the umbrella coverage, but it is not covered by the basic contract or contracts.

    A. (1) only
    B. (1) and (2) only
    C. (1) and (3) only
    D. (2) and (3) only
    E. (1), (2), and (3)

51. An unendorsed personal auto policy (PAP) can be used to provide coverage for which of the following?

    (1) Individual and family owners of private passenger autos

    (2) Trucks used by small firms with gross revenues of less than $1 million

    (3) Land motor vehicles, including motorcycles

    A. (1) only
    B. (1) and (2) only
    C. (1) and (3) only
    D. (2) and (3) only
    E. (1), (2), and (3)

52. The insurer's promise to pay all defense costs involving liability of an insured is an important part of the PAP for which of the following reasons?

    (1) Defense costs may exceed the jury's award for property damage and personal injury.

    (2) The insurer has specialized expertise in defending drivers.

    (3) The defense costs are in addition to the policy's liability limits.

    A. (1) only
    B. (1) and (2) only
    C. (1) and (3) only
    D. (2) and (3) only
    E. (1), (2), and (3)

53. Which of the following persons is (are) provided liability coverage under the PAP?

(1) The spouse of the named insured

(2) Any relative by blood or marriage who is a resident of the named insured's household

    A. (1) only
    B. (2) only
    C. Both (1) and (2)
    D. Neither (1) nor (2)

54. Which of the following types of motor vehicles is included for coverage under the liability section of the PAP? (Assume all persons are residents of the named insured's home.)

    A. A motorcycle
    B. A daughter's uninsured Nissan available to the named insured, and accident occurs while named insured is using the vehicle
    C. A son's uninsured BMW used by his sister whenever her brother isn't using it, and accident occurs while sister is using the vehicle
    D. A three-wheel golf cart used for shopping in the family's community area

55. Under which of the following circumstances would the liability coverage of the car owner's PAP be available to the negligent driver?

(1) A neighbor borrows the insured auto for grocery shopping, believing this would be agreeable to the named insured because the neighbor had done the same thing several times previously.

(2) An eighteen-year-old college student, while intoxicated, takes a neighbor's car to show his buddies how he can start the car without an ignition key.

    A. (1) only
    B. (2) only
    C. Both (1) and (2)
    D. Neither (1) nor (2)

56. Under which of the following circumstances would the named insured and spouse be covered under the medical payments of the PAP for injuries suffered?

(1) While occupying an owned, covered auto
(2) While occupying a nonowned auto with fewer than four wheels
(3) When, as pedestrians, they are struck by a vehicle designed for use on public roads
(4) While occupying a nonowned auto

    A. (1) and (2) only
    B. (1), (2), and (3) only
    C. (1), (3), and (4) only
    D. (2), (3), and (4) only

57. Which of the following losses are covered under the physical damage coverage section of the PAP?

(1) Physical damage resulting from breakdown and freezing
(2) Collision damage to an owned auto described in the declarations
(3) Other-than-collision damage to an owned declared auto
(4) Transportation expenses associated with the theft of a covered auto

    A. (1) and (2) only
    B. (1), (2), and (3) only
    C. (1), (2), and (4) only
    D. (2), (3), and (4) only

58. Which of the following would be covered under the physical damage section of the PAP?

    A. Loss of any equipment designed for the reproduction of sound not permanently installed in the covered auto
    B. Damage due to wear and tear
    C. Loss to any custom furnishing or equipment in or upon any pickup, panel truck, or van
    D. Vandalism or malicious mischief damage to tires

59. Automobile medical payments coverage may seem redundant to persons covered by adequate medical insurance. The major reason for purchasing automobile medical payments coverage when one has medical insurance is:

    A. To receive double payments if one is injured
    B. To cover medical expenses for guests or passengers in the car
    C. To increase one's chance of a lawsuit by injured passengers
    D. To follow the principles of risk management and focus on the loss rather than on the effect

60. Which of the following factors is the LEAST important for an auto owner to consider when purchasing automobile physical damage coverage?

    A. The age and value of the car
    B. The financial condition of the insured
    C. Whether the car is financed or not
    D. How low a deductible the insurer will accept (the lower the better)

61. Which of the following statements concerning insurance coverage for dishonest acts occurring at the insured's place of business is (are) correct?

    (1) Protection against the dishonesty of one's employees requires some form of crime insurance.
    (2) Protection against the dishonesty of nonemployees requires the business firm to purchase the appropriate type of bond.

        A. (1) only
        B. (2) only
        C. Both (1) and (2)
        D. Neither (1) nor (2)

62. Which of the following statements concerning package policies available to business firms is correct?

    A. The commercial package policy (CPP) is designed for small firms.
    B. The CPP provides both property and liability insurance coverage.
    C. The CPP provides very broad and comprehensive coverage, but it excludes commercial auto coverage.
    D. The businessowners policy (BOP) is designed primarily for large business firms.
    E. The BOP provides property insurance coverage but no liability insurance coverage.

63. Which of the following statements concerning liability insurance coverage on an occurrence basis or a claims-made basis is correct?

    A. An occurrence basis policy covers claims arising from events that occur during the policy period, and a claim is filed during the same policy period.

    B. Claims-made policies respond to claims whenever the claim is made.

    C. The "long-tail" problem is more acute with claims-made policies than with occurrence basis policies.

    D. The "long-tail" situation creates a problem for the insurer to establish adequate reserves to meet long-tail claims.

64. Which of the following statements concerning the extended reporting period is (are) correct?

    (1) It extends the time for reporting a claim which will be eligible for coverage.

    (2) For a claims-made policy, the period extends coverage to claims that are reported for the first time after the expiration of the policy.

    (3) The period only has significance for an entity insured under a general liability policy if the policy is written on an occurrence basis.

    A. (1) only
    B. (1) and (2) only
    C. (1) and (3) only
    D. (2) and (3) only
    E. (1), (2), and (3)

65. All the following are benefits provided by most workers' compensation laws, EXCEPT:

    A. Medical care costs, without limit
    B. Disability income benefits, subject to a 30-day waiting period
    C. Income benefits to survivors of the covered worker
    D. Rehabilitation benefits

For practice answering case questions related to Topic 32, please answer the following questions in the cases included in Appendix A at the back of this textbook.

Case	Questions
Black Hills P&L	1 and 2
Brodinski	
Haurilick	1, 2, 3, 4, 5, 6, 7, 8, 9, 10, and 11
Beals	5, 6, and 7
Mocsin	3, 4, and 5
Loudon	2, 3, 4, and 5
Connor	22, 23, and 24
Seidelhofer	24 and 25
Loomis Company	
Michael and Diana Eastman	
Gary and Judy Parker	56, 57, 58, 59, and 60

ANSWERS AND EXPLANATIONS

1. D is the answer. The duties of the insured are found among the conditions in the homeowners policies.

2. C is the answer. Electronic business property has a limit of $1,500.

3. D is the answer. (1), (2), and (3) are all excluded under HO-3.

4. C is the answer. The HO-3 provides full replacement cost coverage for damage to the dwelling, up to the face amount of coverage, if the coverage carried is at least 80% of the replacement cost of the dwelling. The $500 deductible is also applied. In addition to providing replacement cost coverage, the HO-3 also provides coverage for debris removal. If the cost of replacement equals or exceeds the face amount of coverage, the insurer provides up to an additional 5% of the limit of liability for debris removal expense.

5. D is the answer. The water damage was accidental and was not among the excluded causes of water damage. A is flood damage, which is not covered. B is excluded because the water seeped through the basement wall. C is not covered because the backup of water through the sewer is not covered.

6. A is the answer. Flood is excluded in the unendorsed HO-3 policy. The other four listed perils are covered.

7. E is the answer. If the amount of insurance carried is less than 80% of the dwelling's replacement cost at the time of the loss, the insurer will pay the greater of the ACV of the loss or the amount produced by this formula:

$$\frac{\text{Amount carried}}{\text{Amount should have carried}} \text{ x Replacement cost of loss}$$

Here, $100,000 ÷ 80% of $150,000 x $18,000 = $15,000. Since this exceeds the $10,000 ACV of the loss, $15,000 will be paid.

8. C is the answer. Fine arts and antiques would be covered on an actual cash value basis, like other personal property, in an unendorsed policy. Since ACV is difficult to determine for fine arts and antiques, an endorsement is often used to provide coverage of such items on a valued basis and to add more covered perils.

9. C is the answer. Defense costs are paid in addition to the limit of liability, although the insurance company is no longer obligated to defend the insured when the limit is reached.

10. B is the answer. Pat's coverage would not pay for an accident in her employer's car if she was using the employer's car for business purposes.

11. C is the answer. Coverage does apply to insureds who are injured as passengers or pedestrians, regardless of whether the vehicle causing the injury had medical payments coverage. Coverage does not apply where the injury occurs to a person using the vehicle without permission, and it does not apply when the vehicle is being used as a residence.

12. B is the answer. While the value of the home, including the land, is $150,000, the value of the home itself is only $110,000, that is, $150,000 – $40,000. In the event the home is totally destroyed, the lot will not have to be replaced.

13. D is the answer. Coverage applies to a vehicle being borrowed as a temporary substitute for the insured's vehicle.

14. C is the answer. The named insured is driving a covered vehicle that he or she owns. A is not covered because vehicle damage to one's own property by an insured is not covered. B is not covered because the bicycle is being transported in the insured station wagon. D is not covered because this would be covered under workers' compensation.

15. B is the answer. A is not a correct statement. The medical payments coverage applies without regard to fault. C is not a correct statement. There is no reduction of the court's award by the amount provided by the medical payments coverage. The two are completely separate. Of course, prompt medical attention provided to the injured person may reduce future medical expenses and thus reduce the injured person's claim for liability damages. D is not a correct statement because the named insured and family members are covered as pedestrians.

16. C is the answer. A is not a correct statement because the policy is assumed to be rewritten to be consistent with the applicable state statute. B is not correct. Coverage applies only to bodily injury. D is not correct. Coverage applies in case of an accident caused by a hit-and-run auto. The insured must only prove that the cause of the accident and the injury were attributable to the hit-and-run auto.

17. B is the answer. (1) is not a correct statement because an insured may elect to have breakage of glass treated as a collision loss. In the situation of (1), we are confident the insured would elect to avoid the double deductible and have both glass and body damage treated as collision losses. (2) is a correct statement because the insured would elect to have the breakage of glass treated as a loss other than by collision and thus have no deductible applicable.

18. D is the answer. Other-than-collision coverage will pay for losses from vandalism, contact with an animal, and falling objects. Impact with a telephone pole is a collision.

19. A is the answer. The umbrella liability insurer will settle the claim as if Brad had $300,000 of coverage under the personal auto policy, not the $100,000 that he did have. Therefore, the umbrella liability insurer will pay nothing.

20. A is the answer. (4) is unneeded, in light of the age of the car, and would be extremely expensive for a new teenage driver.

21. C is the answer. Malpractice coverage is purchased by those whose negligence is likely to cause bodily injury. A surgeon is in this category. A is not a correct statement. Errors and omissions coverage protects the insured for those liabilities that do not include bodily injury. B is not a correct statement. Lawyers and accountants are more likely to purchase errors and omissions coverage. The negligence of lawyers and accountants is not likely to give rise to bodily injuries. D is not a correct statement. A pharmacist is more likely to purchase malpractice coverage. Clearly, negligence on the part of a pharmacist could result in bodily injury to a person whose drug prescription was incorrectly filled.

22. B is the answer. Such a business has to stay open, regardless of cost, so it needs the Extra Expense Coverage Form.

23. D is the answer. Products liability is covered by the CGL policy.

24. B is the answer. (1) and (3) simply pay whatever benefits are required by the applicable state law.

25. A is the answer. These types of businesses are not eligible for this policy.

26. A is the answer. The formula for the recovery is:

$$\frac{\text{Insurance carried}}{\text{Insurance required}} \text{ x Loss } - \text{ Deductible}$$

$$\frac{\$700,000}{(80\%) \ \$1,000,000} \text{ x } \$80,000 - \$2,500$$

$$(7/8) \text{ x } \$80,000 - \$2,500 = \$67,500$$

27. C is the answer. Since the claim arose during the term of the claims-made policy, coverage is provided by that policy. Since the claim arose from events that occurred during the term of the occurrence basis policy, coverage is also provided by that policy.

28. E is the answer. When insurance is written on a valued basis, the specified value is paid, regardless of ACV, replacement cost, or other factors.

29. C is the answer. The amount carried is $120,000. The amount that should have been carried is 80% of $200,000, or $160,000. 120/160 x $40,000 = $30,000.

30. C is the answer. Hit-and-run vehicles are considered to be uninsured vehicles. An out-of-state vehicle is covered if driven by an uninsured motorist. A driver who is held liable but loses coverage because of the insurer's insolvency before the claim is paid is considered an uninsured motorist. An insured is not covered when using the car as a public conveyance.

31. C is the answer. (2) is not an intentional tort. (1), (3), and (4) are all intentional torts.

32. E is the answer. All three items are torts that can be sources of legal liability.

33. B is the answer. B is an incorrect statement. In the insuring agreement, the insurer promises to pay for losses covered by the policy. The insured makes no promises except the promise to pay the initial premium.

34. D is the answer. D is an incorrect statement. The damage or loss does not have to exceed $1,000. A, B, C, and E are all valid elements that must be proven in order to establish tort liability for a negligent act.

35. B is the answer. A is not correct. Notice of loss may be given orally. C is an incorrect statement. Proof of loss must be in writing. An oral statement will not be accepted by the insurer as proof of loss. Documentation is required as proof of loss. D is not correct. Appraisal may be compulsory when requested by either the insured or the insurer.

36. B is the answer. (4) is not correct because appraisal may not be necessary. Appraisal is required only when the parties cannot agree on the amount of the loss. (1), (2), and (3) are all required.

37. B is the answer. (4) is not correct because (4) is not a policy provision. The insurance policy is an aleatory contract, but there is no policy provision providing for this. The insurance policy is an aleatory contract because the insured may obtain benefits more valuable than the premium the insurer receives. (1), (2), and (3) are all policy provisions that limit the property insurer's liability.

38. C is the answer. We apply the formula:

$$\left[\frac{\text{Amount of insurance carried}}{\text{Amount of insurance required}} \times \text{Loss} \right] - \text{Deductible}$$

$$\left[\frac{\$600,000}{80\% \text{ of } \$900,000} \quad x \quad \$300,000 \right] - \$3,000 =$$

$$\left[\frac{\$600,000}{\$720,000} \quad x \quad \$300,000 \right] - \$3,000 =$$

$$\left[\frac{5}{6} \quad x \quad \$300,000 \right] - \$3,000 =$$

$$\$250,000 - \$3,000 = \$247,000$$

39. A is the answer. B is not a correct statement. None of the homeowners policies covers water damage caused by floods, backup through sewers or drains, or seepage through basement walls. C is not a correct statement. The inflation guard endorsement provides for the dollar amount of insurance coverage to increase automatically every quarter. The increase is not tied to the Consumer Price Index. D is not a correct statement. Form HO-08 provides this coverage – not HO-06.

40. B is the answer. A is the reverse of the correct answer. C refers to HO-04. D refers to HO-06.

41. A is the answer. A Scheduled Personal Property Endorsement will not be subject to the sublimits that apply under the HO-02 and HO-03, so a loss will be covered for a higher value. B, C, and D are not correct statements.

42. B is the answer. Trees are covered for up to 5% of the limit for Coverage A, but not more than $500 for any one tree. ($500 + (12 x $300) = $4,100, but the limit is 5% of $80,000, or $4,000.)

43. D is the answer. The sworn proof of loss statement must be filed by the insured without the necessity of any request from the insurance company. A, B, C, and E are among the duties of an insured in the event of loss.

44. D is the answer. (2), (3), and (4) are all covered under the medical payments coverage of the HO-03. (1) is not covered. The medical payments coverage provided by the HO-03 is not designed to provide health insurance coverage for the insured and his or her family.

45. E is the answer. Liability coverage is not provided for any of these activities.

46. C is the answer. A is not a correct statement. HO-04 is designed for tenants, not HO-06, which is designed for condominium owners. B is not correct. HO-03 is the most widely used form. D is not correct. Coverage D would reimburse the insured only for *extra* or additional expenses. This means expenses incurred that are above or in addition to the normal expenses the family would incur if the family were living at home. The policy does not pay the full cost of living at the motel.

47. D is the answer. HO-04 is designed for tenants; it provides only specified-perils coverage for contents. A is not a correct statement. The HO-06 is designed for condominium owners. C is not correct. If the premium were the same, a homeowner would prefer an HO-03, rather than an HO-02. The HO-03 provides "all-risks" coverage on the dwelling. The HO-02 provides only named perils coverage on the dwelling.

48. C is the answer. Fishing and hunting equipment is not covered. A, B, D, and E are all items that are covered by the homeowners Scheduled Personal Property Endorsement.

49. E is the answer. All three items are covered.

50. E is the answer. All three statements are correct.

51. A is the answer. (2) and (3) are not covered under the PAP. (1) is covered. Pickups, vans, and panel trucks are eligible for coverage if not used regularly for business purposes. Miscellaneous motor vehicles, including motorcycles, may be covered by a special endorsement, but only if owned by an individual or by two spouses or by two relatives who are residents of the same household.

52. E is the answer. All three items are logical reasons.

53. C is the answer. Both (1) and (2) are considered to be "insured persons" under the liability coverage of the PAP.

54. B is the answer. The named insured is covered in this situation. However, son's sister is not covered in situation C. A and D are not covered because they are not four-wheel vehicles.

55. A is the answer. (1) is correct because the neighbor has reasonable belief that he or she is permitted to borrow the vehicle. (2) is not correct because the neighbor's eighteen-year-old son does not have reasonable belief that he is permitted to borrow the vehicle.

56. C is the answer. (1), (3), and (4) are all circumstances under which the named insured and spouse would have medical payments coverage under their PAP for injuries suffered. They would not be covered under circumstance (2) because coverage is not available when the vehicle has fewer than four wheels.

57. D is the answer. (2), (3), and (4) are all losses that would be covered under the physical damage coverage section of the PAP. (1) would not be covered because damage caused by breakdown or freezing is excluded.

58. D is the answer. The physical damage coverage is "all-risks" or open-perils coverage. Therefore, since D is not one of the exclusions, it is covered. A, B, and C are excluded under the physical damage coverage of the PAP.

59. B is the answer, as spelled out in the policy.

60. D is the answer. The purchaser of automobile physical damage coverage should use as large a deductible as he or she feels can be handled comfortably in case of an accident. The larger the deductible, the lower the premium. If the car owner were to purchase a policy with a low deductible, he or she would have to obtain the insurance company's approval for all minor repair expenses that exceed a $25 or $50 deductible in order to collect the minor claim payment. This would be a great waste of everyone's time. A, B, and C are factors to consider in purchasing auto physical damage coverage.

61. D is the answer. Neither (1) nor (2) is a correct statement. Protection against the dishonesty of one's employees requires a bond. Protection against the dishonesty of nonemployees requires crime insurance.

62. B is the answer. A is not a correct statement. The CPP is designed for large firms, not small firms. C is an incorrect statement. The CPP includes commercial auto coverage. D is not a correct statement. The BOP is designed for small business firms. E is not a correct statement. The BOP provides both property and liability insurance coverage.

63. D is the answer. In a long-tail situation, claim payments are spread over a substantial period of time (life income for a young person), so the insurer must establish adequate reserves to meet these obligations. A is not a correct statement. For an occurrence basis policy, only the event must occur during the policy period; the claim may be filed anytime. B is not a correct statement. For a claims-made policy, the claim must be filed during the policy period, regardless of when the loss-causing event occurred. C is not a correct statement. The "long-tail" problem is more acute with occurrence basis policies because the event may have occurred many years ago.

64. B is the answer. (3) is not a correct statement. The extended reporting period is of no significance for a general liability policy written on an occurrence basis. (1) and (2) are correct statements. Extended reporting ("tail") periods do *not* extend coverage for occurrences. They extend the time for reporting claims based on occurrences that occurred before the end of the policy period and after the retroactive date.

65. B is the answer. The typical waiting period for disability income benefits under workers' compensation laws is quite short, such as 7 days.

APPENDIX A

BLACK HILLS P&L CASE

The Black Hills Property and Liability Insurance Company is a mutual insurance company domiciled in South Dakota and licensed in ten Midwestern states. The company has always prided itself on expeditious and fair disposition of claims. It emphasizes the importance of an efficient loss adjustment process as a public relations and marketing tool. The agency department makes frequent reference to the company's claims settlement policies and practices in the recruiting of agents and in seeking new business.

Although the company has operated profitably in each of the last ten years, senior management has become concerned in the last three years that an increasing loss ratio has been adversely affecting bottom-line profits. There is a current fear that the company's widespread reputation for expeditious and fair disposition of claims is encouraging claimants to take advantage of the company. A continued worsening of the company's loss ratio could very likely result in a negative bottom-line profit. The company's senior management wants to make a serious effort to reverse the worsening loss ratio and improve the company's profitability.

BLACK HILLS P&L CASE
APPLICATION QUESTIONS

1. All the following are typical property insurance policy provisions that would limit Black Hills' net cash outlay to meet its liability for insured property losses, EXCEPT:

(Topic 22, 32)

    A. The pair-or-set option available to Black Hills
    B. The other insurance provision
    C. The subrogation clause
    D. The aleatory provision
    E. The appraisal provision

2. Y insures a factory building with Black Hills under an 80% coinsurance clause. Y paid $6 million for the building, which now has a replacement cost value of $8 million. Y has insured the building on a replacement cost basis and carries $4,800,000 of coverage on the building. The policy has a $20,000 deductible. How much would the insurer pay Y if a fire does $200,000 of damage?

(Topic 32)

    A. $130,000   D. $175,000
    B. $155,000   E. $200,000
    C. $160,000

BLACK HILLS P&L CASE
ANSWERS AND EXPLANATIONS

1. D is the answer. D is not a policy provision. The insurance policy is an aleatory contract, but there is no policy clause providing for this. The insurance policy is an aleatory contract because the insured may obtain benefits more valuable than the premium the insurer receives. A, B, C, and E are policy provisions that would limit Black Hills' liability.

2. A is the answer.

[($4,800,000 actual coverage/$6,400,000 required coverage) x $200,000 loss] – $20,000

(.75 x $200,000) – $20,000

$150,000 – $20,000 = $130,000

Struggling with Your Financial Calculator?

This is the class you wish you had instead of the manual that comes with the calculator.

Keir online financial calculator class will help ease your mind and teach you the techniques necessary to master your calculator.

- ✓ Interactive, flash multimedia
- ✓ Accessible 24/7
- ✓ Anticipates your errors

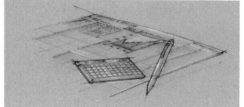

It first introduces you to your calculator and goes into detail when describing the various keys and their functions. It also tells you how to correct all of those "annoying" and inexplicable changes that appear on your display screen.

For more information, or to purchase the class, contact Mary Grace Caudill at 1-800-795-5347 x 101, or visit our website at www.KeirSuccess.com.

Available for the HP-10BII and the HP 12C

BRODINSKI CASE

Florine and Ancil Brodinski have been married twenty-five years and have three children ages 5, 7, and 11. The Brodinskis think of themselves as a middle-class to above-average-income family with typical educational aspirations for the three children. It is assumed that all three will go to the state university, where tuition and other costs will be somewhat less than for a private college or university.

Both Florine and Ancil are employed, but by different employers. Each spouse had a gross income of approximately $40,000 last year. They are each covered by a group term life insurance policy for the amount of their annual income. Each spouse has designated the other spouse irrevocably as the primary beneficiary, and the three children are designated irrevocably as contingent beneficiaries.

In addition to the group term life insurance coverage, Florine has a $50,000 universal life policy on her life, and Ancil has an $80,000 ordinary whole life policy on his life. The two policies have the same beneficiary designations as the group term life insurance coverages.

Florine's employer provides Blue Cross/Blue Shield coverage for all employees and their families under a group contract. Ancil's employer provides medical expense coverage for all employees and their families under a group comprehensive major medical expense insurance policy. Ancil's group comprehensive major medical expense coverage makes use of a stop-loss clause to limit Ancil's out-of-pocket expeneses, including the deductible, to $5,000. Both employers offer the choice of either an HMO plan or a preferred provider organization (PPO) plan to those employees and their families who prefer either of these arrangements.

Ancil has recently purchased an individual disability income policy that uses a split definition of disability. The policy has both an elimination period and a probationary period. The policy has the exclusions usually found in disability income policies, including disability arising out of the insured's occupation. The policy has: (1) a presumptive disability provision, (2) a residual disability benefit clause, and (3) a change of occupation provision.

Although Florine and Ancil will not be eligible for Medicare benefits for another twenty years, they are already considering how Medicare benefits can be integrated and coordinated with their medical expense insurance coverages and how to deal with their long-term care expenses that are likely to pose problems for them in their retirement years.

BRODINSKI CASE
APPLICATION QUESTIONS

1. Assume that Ancil's comprehensive major medical policy provides an initial deductible of $500 and an 80% coinsurance clause. How much will the insurer pay for an appendectomy involving $1,500 of hospital board-and-room charges, a $700 surgical fee, $300 for the anesthetist, and $500 for miscellaneous hospital costs?

(Topic 24)

    A. $2,000   D. $2,750
    B. $2,250   E. $3,000
    C. $2,500

2. In Question 1, assume that medical complications necessitated that Ancil remain in the hospital for several days longer. As a result, total expenses were $30,500. Under these circumstances, how much would the insurer pay?

(Topic 24)

    A. $30,500   D. $25,500
    B. $30,000   E. $25,000
    C. $27,500

3. Which of the following is the most likely wording of the split definition of disability used in Ancil's disability income policy?

(Topic 25)

    A. Inability to perform any occupation, followed by inability to perform his or her own occupation
    B. Inability to perform any occupation for which qualified, followed by inability to perform his or her own occupation
    C. Inability to perform his or her own occupation, followed by inability to perform any occupation for which reasonably suited
    D. Inability to perform any occupation for two years, followed by inability to perform any occupation for which reasonably suited
    E. Presumed disability for two years because of the loss of two bodily members, followed by inability to perform any occupation for which reasonably suited

4. If used in Ancil's individual disability income policy, which of the following definitions of disability would be most favorable for Ancil?

(Topic 25)

    A. Inability to perform any occupation for which fitted by education, training, or experience

    B. Inability to perform his or her own occupation for five years, and then inability to perform any occupation for which fitted by education, training, or experience

    C. Inability to perform his or her own occupation for two years, then inability to perform any occupation for which fitted, but, in fact, does not engage in any occupation

    D. Inability to perform his or her own occupation

    E. Presumed disability for two years because of loss of two bodily members, followed by inability to perform any occupation for which reasonably suited

5. Ancil's individual disability income policy has a presumptive disability provision. Which of the following accidental injuries would usually entitle Ancil to receive disability income benefits under the presumptive disability provision of his disability income policy?

(Topic 25)

    (1) Fracture of one leg and one arm

    (2) Loss of sight in both eyes

    (3) Loss of one leg and one arm

        A. (1) only

        B. (3) only

        C. (2) and (3) only

        D. (1), (2), and (3)

        E. Neither (1), (2), nor (3)

6. Which of the following statements concerning the residual disability benefit clause in Ancil's disability income policy is (are) likely to be correct?

(Topic 25)

(1) The clause provides for the payment of the equivalent of a partial disability benefit for a few days.
(2) A residual disability benefit is typically paid only after the insured recovers from total disability.
(3) If Ancil returns to work after total disability with a 25% reduction in earnings because of his residual disability, he would receive 25% of the benefit to which he was entitled when he was totally disabled.

    A. (1) only
    B. (2) only
    C. (1) and (2) only
    D. (2) and (3) only
    E. (1), (2), and (3)

7. In which of the following ways would the rights of Florine and Ancil, as primary beneficiaries of the various life insurance policies, differ from the rights of their children, who are designated as contingent beneficiaries?

(Topic 28)

(1) If a primary lump-sum beneficiary is living when an insured dies, the contingent beneficiary has no legal right to any of the life insurance lump-sum death proceeds.
(2) Generally, the only circumstances under which a contingent beneficiary would have any legal right to the lump-sum death proceeds would be if the primary beneficiary predeceases the insured.
(3) If the primary beneficiary receives the policy's death proceeds but dies before withdrawing any of the death proceeds, the contingent beneficiary would receive the death proceeds.

    A. (1) only
    B. (2) only
    C. (1) and (2) only
    D. (2) and (3) only
    E. (1), (2), and (3)

8. All the following statements concerning the rights of Florine or Ancil are correct, EXCEPT:

(Topic 28)

A. If he or she were a revocable beneficiary, he or she would have a mere expectancy.

B. As an irrevocable beneficiary, he or she has a vested right.

C. As a policy owner, Florine or Ancil may exercise all of the ownership rights under the individual policy without obtaining the consent of the revocable beneficiary.

D. As a policy owner, Florine or Ancil has the right to assign the policy to whomever he or she wishes without the consent of the designated beneficiary, whether the beneficiary is revocably or irrevocably designated.

E. At time of death of Florine or Ancil, the rights of a revocable beneficiary are no different than those of an irrevocable beneficiary.

9. All the following are likely settlement options available for the life insurance death proceeds of Florine's and Ancil's individual policies, EXCEPT:

(Topic 28)

A. Cash in a lump-sum

B. Installments for a fixed period

C. Installments for a fixed amount

D. Extended term insurance

E. Life income with period certain

10. If they reach retirement age with no other sources of income, the option most appropriate for Florine and Ancil to use for the cash values of their individual life insurance policies would be which of the following?

(Topic 28)

A. Interest option

B. Installments for a fixed period

C. Installments for a fixed amount

D. Joint and last survivor income option

E. Additional paid-up insurance option

BRODINSKI CASE
ANSWERS AND EXPLANATIONS

1. A is the answer. $3,000 is the total health care bill. The $500 deductible reduces this to $2,500. When we multiply $2,500 by 80%, we get $2,000.

2. D is the answer. The $500 deductible reduces the medical expenses total cost of $30,500 to $30,000. Ancil's stop-loss amount is $5,000 including the deductible, so he would pay the $500 deductible and an additional $4,500. The insurer would have to pay $25,500 ($30,500 minus $5,000 that Ancil must pay).

3. C is the answer. It is the only statement that correctly describes the usual split definition of total disability: inability to perform his or her own occupation, followed by inability to perform any occupation for which the person is suited by reason of education, training, or experience.

4. D is the answer. All the other definitions are more severe or more restrictive than D. D is the most liberal of all the definitions of disability.

5. C is the answer. A fracture of one leg and one arm would not indicate presumptive disability. A physician can set the arm and the leg, and the insured can be back in the office in a few days. (2) and (3) would indicate presumptive disability.

6. D is the answer. (1) is not a correct statement. Residual disability is usually more permanent than a few days. Residual disability is the reduction in earnings that persists after the person returns to work. (2) and (3) are correct statements.

7. C is the answer. Both (1) and (2) correctly distinguish the rights of the primary beneficiaries from the rights of the contingent beneficiaries. (3) is not a correct statement because as soon as the primary beneficiary is in receipt of the death proceeds, the contingent beneficiary has no claim to the death proceeds. The heirs of the primary beneficiary will be entitled to the death proceeds.

8. D is the answer. The policy owner must obtain the consent of the irrevocably-designated beneficiary if the policy owner wishes to assign the policy. A, B, C, and E are correct statements.

9. D is the answer. Extended term insurance is not a settlement option for the death proceeds of a life insurance policy. It is an optional use of the policy's nonforfeiture value. A, B, C, and E are all settlement options for a life insurance policy's death proceeds.

10. D is the answer. The joint and last survivor income option assures continuity of income for as long as either spouse lives. E is a dividend option.

HAURILICK CASE

Annuta and Ignas Haurilick live in a four-bedroom, two-story home located on a 1.5-acre lot in suburban Philadelphia. They have insured their home and its contents with an HO-03. They have $200,000 coverage on their dwelling, which is the dwelling's current replacement cost, $20,000 on other structures, $100,000 on personal property, and $40,000 for loss of use. There is a $400 deductible.

The Haurilick family has insured both their Buick LeSabre and their Lincoln Continental under a personal auto policy (PAP). The Haurilick family's PAP has the usual collision coverage, the usual Section II liability coverage, auto medical payments coverage, and both uninsured and underinsured motorists coverage.

HAURILICK CASE
APPLICATION QUESTIONS

1. Which of the following exclusions or limits would be imposed on the property insurance coverage provided by the Haurilick family's HO-03 policy?

(Topic 32)

(1) There would be no coverage for recreational motor vehicles.
(2) Coverage on boats and trailers would be limited to $1,500.
(3) Coverage for theft of jewelry would be limited to $1,500.

    A. (1) only
    B. (1) and (2) only
    C. (1) and (3) only
    D. (2) and (3) only
    E. (1), (2), and (3)

2. Which of the following items of personal property would be specifically excluded under the Haurilick's HO-03?

(Topic 32)

(1) Animals, birds, or fish
(2) Business property on and off the premises
(3) Articles insured by schedule in this or any other insurance policy

    A. (2) only
    B. (1) and (2) only
    C. (1) and (3) only
    D. (2) and (3) only
    E. (1), (2), and (3)

3. Annuta and Ignas have been told that by purchasing an HO-02 policy instead of an HO-03, they could save premium dollars without significantly reducing the effective insurance coverage of their home and its contents. Which of the following statements concerning the HO-02 and the HO-03 is correct?

(Topic 32)

    A. The dwelling and other structures coverage of the HO-02 is all-risks (open-perils), while that of the HO-03 is named perils coverage.
    B. The dwelling and other structures coverage of the HO-03 is all-risks, while that of the HO-02 is named perils coverage.
    C. The HO-02 is designed for a tenant and, therefore, does not cover the dwelling or other structures.
    D. The HO-02 is specifically designed for condominium owners.
    E. Both the HO-02 and the HO-03 require a minimum of $20,000 of coverage for the dwelling.

4. In addition to their HO-03 coverage, Annuta and Ignas might prefer specific insurance on certain types of their personal property by means of a Scheduled Personal Property Endorsement for which of the following reasons?

(Topic 32)

A. The HO-03 has sub-limits applicable to certain types of personal property.
B. The insurance rate for scheduled property is usually lower than for blanket coverage.
C. The unscheduled coverage of the HO-03 does not cover loss caused by theft.
D. The types of personal property covered by the scheduled endorsement are otherwise excluded from coverage under the HO-03.
E. The Scheduled Personal Property Endorsement provides Inflation Guard endorsement coverage for the scheduled personal property.

5. The HO-03 policy of the Haurilick family will provide medical payments coverage for all the following persons, EXCEPT:

(Topic 32)

A. Ignas and all family members residing with him
B. Residence employees
C. Any person on the insured premises with the permission of any insured
D. Any person injured away from the insured premises, if the injury is caused by the activities of an insured
E. Any person injured away from the insured premises, if the injury is caused by an animal owned by or in the care of any insured

6. The personal liability coverage of the Haurilick family's HO-03 would cover bodily injury and property damage liability in which of the following situations?

(Topic 32)

(1) The liability arises out of Ignas's rendering of professional services.
(2) The liability arises out of Ignas's use of a motorboat (owned by Ignas) powered by an inboard motor.
(3) The liability arises out of Ignas's ownership of an aircraft.

A. (1) only
B. (2) only
C. (1) and (2) only
D. (1), (2), and (3)
E. Neither (1), (2), nor (3)

7. Which of the following residents of the Haurilick household would be provided liability coverage under the family's PAP?

(Topic 32)

(1) Annuta, the spouse of the named insured

(2) Any relative by blood or marriage who is a resident of the named insured's household

(3) An eighteen-year-old daughter who is away at school for nine months of each year

    A. (1) only
    B. (2) only
    C. (1) and (2) only
    D. (2) and (3) only
    E. (1), (2), and (3)

8. All the following statements concerning the auto medical payments coverage provided by the Haurilick family's PAP are correct, EXCEPT:

(Topic 32)

    A. Coverage applies without regard to fault.
    B. Its purpose is to provide prompt reimbursement for covered expenses of eligible persons.
    C. The coverage may reduce or eliminate liability claims.
    D. Coverage is restricted to persons injured while occupying a covered auto.
    E. Coverage is not available for a fellow employee.

9. Which of the following statements concerning the medical payments coverage for Annuta and Ignas under the family's PAP is (are) correct?

(Topic 32)

(1) They are covered while occupying an owned covered auto.

(2) They are covered when, as pedestrians, they are struck by a vehicle designed for use on public roads.

(3) They are covered while occupying a nonowned auto.

    A. (1) only
    B. (2) only
    C. (1) and (2) only
    D. (2) and (3) only
    E. (1), (2), and (3)

10. In the event of theft of the Haurilick family's Lincoln Continental, transportation expenses provided under the physical damage coverage of the PAP are for:

(Topic 32)

    A. $10 a day, up to $450, beginning 24 hours after total theft of a covered auto
    B. $10 a day, up to $300, beginning 48 hours after total theft of a covered auto
    C. $20 a day, up to $600, beginning 48 hours after total theft of a covered auto
    D. $20 a day, up to $500, beginning 48 hours after total theft of a covered auto
    E. $150 a day, up to $600, beginning 48 hours after total theft of a covered auto

11. Which of the following would be considered a collision loss under the terms of the physical damage coverage of the Haurilick family's PAP?

(Topic 32)

    A. Falling tree branch hits insured vehicle
    B. Upset of insured vehicle
    C. Dent from a stone thrown by a passing car
    D. Contact with an animal
    E. Windshield cracked by a poorly hit golf ball

HAURILICK CASE
ANSWERS AND EXPLANATIONS

1. E is the answer. All three items indicate actual exclusions or limitations on the coverage provided by the Haurilick family's HO-03 policy.

2. C is the answer. (1) and (3) are excluded. HO-3 does provide a limited amount of coverage of business property on and off the premises.

3. B is the answer. Since B is correct, then A is incorrect. C is incorrect because HO-02 is not designed for tenants. HO-02 does provide dwelling coverage. D is incorrect because HO-02 is not designed for condominium owners. E is incorrect because HO-02 permits a minimum of $15,000 of coverage on the dwelling.

4. A is the answer. B, C, D, and E are all incorrect statements.

5. A is the answer. The medical payments coverage provided by the HO-03 is not designed to provide health insurance coverage for the insured and his or her family. B, C, D, and E indicate people who would be eligible for benefits under the HO-03 medical payments coverage.

6. E is the answer. Liability coverage is not provided for any of these activities.

7. E is the answer. All three would be considered insured persons under the liability coverage of the Haurilick family's PAP.

8. D is the answer. D is not a correct statement because the named insured and family members are covered as pedestrians. A, B, C, and E are correct statements.

9. E is the answer. (1) and (3) are correct because the named insured and spouse are covered while occupying any four-wheel vehicle. (2) is correct because both Annuta and Ignas would be covered as pedestrians.

10. C is the answer. In the event of theft, the insured is entitled to receive payment of transportation expenses equal to $20 per day, up to a total of $600, and the expenses begin to accrue 48 hours after the theft.

11. B is the answer. A, C, D, and E are all considered to be losses other than by collision.

BEALS CASE

James and Anne Beals had been married for 24 years and are now separated. James, who is 55 years of age, is a funeral director and is the owner of two funeral parlors. Anne is 51 years of age and owns and operates a graphics design business. The couple has two children: Ronald, age 16, and Christine, age 13. All of the Beals are in good health. James and Anne have simple wills leaving their entire estates to each other.

Anne Beals started her graphics design business about 8 years ago. The business is called Beals Designs, and Anne is the sole owner. In order to expand her business, Anne took out a loan about five years ago from the Mellon Bank in the amount of $50,000, and James Beals cosigned the loan. Anne has paid back $5,000 of the original loan amount, leaving a balance of $45,000. Anne makes monthly payments on the loan. The business has done well, and Anne nets about $50,000 annually after paying her expenses.

Anne has three employees. She has adopted a profit-sharing Keogh plan for herself and her employees. Although the plan offers several different investment options, Anne has her account balance invested through the plan in guaranteed investment contracts (GICs). In addition, she has invested IRA money in a balanced mutual fund. She describes herself as a conservative investor. Anne has named James as the beneficiary of her profit-sharing plan and of her IRA.

James Beals has moved out of the home that he owns with Anne as tenants by the entirety. He is currently renting an apartment for $800 per month. Since Anne and James have agreed that she will keep the house in her name, Anne makes the monthly mortgage payment. James and Anne bought the house for $80,000 and have spent $40,000 on capital improvements.

The children will remain with Anne and spend vacations with their father. Anne is currently receiving child support and alimony from James. James earns approximately $120,000 annually from his business. He is also the owner of two buildings that are rented to the Beals Funeral Home, Inc. One building was purchased 22 years ago for $175,000, and the other was built 12 years ago for a cost of $350,000. Each building is now worth approximately $500,000. James is the sole stockholder and president of the Beals Funeral Home, Inc., which is an S corporation.

Beals Funeral Home, Inc. has a 401(k) plan that matches employee contributions at a rate of 50 cents for each dollar contributed by an employee, up to 6% of each employee's compensation. The company has eight employees in addition to James. The 401(k) plan offers different investment options, and James has invested his 401(k) plan contributions in a balanced mutual fund. James describes himself as a conservative investor. James has named Anne the beneficiary of his 401(k) plan account balance and of his IRA account assets.

<u>Appendix A – Beals Case</u>

James Beals owns a whole life insurance policy with a face amount of $200,000 and term life insurance in the amount of $300,000. Anne Beals owns a universal life insurance policy with a face amount of $200,000. James and Anne have named each other as beneficiaries of these policies. James has a disability income insurance policy that will pay him $1,000 monthly if he is disabled.

Since James Beals is a funeral director, he would like to have a lavish funeral. The costs of his funeral will be in the range of $40,000. Assuming he dies today, the administrative expenses for his estate are expected to be $30,000.

JAMES BEALS
Personal Balance Sheet

Assets

Invested Assets

Cash/cash equivalents	$ 14,500
Marketable securities	250,000
Business interest	800,000
Life ins. cash value	35,000
	$1,099,500

Use Assets

Business real estate	$1,000,000
Personal property	45,000
Automobiles	30,000
	$1,075,000

Retirement Plan Assets

IRA	$ 25,000
401(k)	175,000
	$ 200,000

Total Assets	$2,374,500

Liabilities

Auto loan	$ 7,000
Mortgage *	200,000
Lawyers' fees	8,000
	$ 215,000

Net Worth	$2,159,500

Total Liabilities and Net Worth	$2,374,500

---

* Business real estate: 15 years at 9 %.

ANNE BEALS
Personal Balance Sheet

Assets

Invested Assets

Cash/cash equivalents	$ 2,500
Marketable securities	150,000
Business interest	300,000
Life ins. cash value	30,000
	$482,500

Use Assets

Primary residence	$200,000
Personal property	52,500
Automobiles	25,000
	$277,500

Retirement Plan Assets

IRA	$ 24,500
Profit-sharing plan	75,000
	$ 99,500

Total Assets	$859,500

Liabilities

Auto loan	$ 7,500
Lawyers' fees	7,000
Business loan	45,000
Mortgage *	50,000
	$ 109,500

Net Worth	$750,000

Total Liabilities and Net Worth	$859,500

---

* Principal residence: originally 30 years @ 8%

JAMES BEALS
Projected Monthly Cash Flow Statement

Cash Inflows

Salary – S corporation	$ 8,000
Distribution – S corporation	2,000
Net rental income	2,600
Interest income (tax-exempt)	400
Dividend income	250
Interest income (taxable)	200

Outflows

Rent	800
Food	150
Utilities	125
Transportation (gas, oil, maintenance)	150
Car payment	400
Clothing	250
Entertainment	400
Travel	500
Life insurance	200
Disability insurance	100
Auto insurance	150
Family gifts	500
Charitable gifts	300
Federal income tax	2,800
State income tax	600
Social Security and Medicare taxes	600
401(k) contribution	700
Savings and Investment	
Miscellaneous	100
Alimony	700
Child support	500

ANNE BEALS
Projected Monthly Cash Flow Statement

Cash Inflows

Business income	$4,200
Interest income (tax-exempt)	500
Dividend income	50
Interest income (taxable)	100
Alimony *	700
Child support	500

* Payments cease upon Anne's death or remarriage.

Outflows

Mortgage	1,100
Food	350
Utilities	175
Transportation (gas, oil, maintenance)	130
Car payment	300
Clothing	350
Entertainment	250
Travel	250
Life insurance	150
Auto insurance	150
Family gifts	300
Charitable gifts	100
Federal income tax	900
State income tax	200
Social Security and Medicare taxes	600
Savings and Investment	
Miscellaneous	100

JAMES BEALS – Investment Portfolio

Common Stock	Fair Market Value
Disney	$ 15,000
DuPont	10,200
Exxon	20,000
Intel	41,400
Lucent	16,200
PepsiCo	12,800
Walmart	11,200
Beals Funeral Home, Inc.	800,000
Common stock mutual fund	13,200
Balanced fund (401(k))	175,000

Municipal Bonds	
Dreyfus General Municipal Bond Fund	$ 70,000

Bonds	
Vanguard High Yield Corporate Bond Fund	$ 40,000
Income Fund (IRA)	25,000

Cash and Equivalents	
Cash	$ 4,500
Cash equivalents, incl. money markets	10,000

TOTAL	$1,264,500

ANNE BEALS – Investment Portfolio

Common Stocks	Fair Market Value
Cisco Systems	$ 40,000
Common stock mutual fund	10,000
Balanced fund (IRA)	24,500

Municipal Bonds	
Merrill Lynch Long-Term Municipal Bond Fund	$ 90,000

Bonds	
Scudder High-Yield Bond Fund	$ 10,000

Cash and Equivalents	
Cash	$ 2,500
GICs – Profit-sharing plan	75,000

TOTAL	$252,000

BEALS CASE
APPLICATION QUESTIONS

1. All the following methods can be used by the Beals family to reduce the amount of risk to which the family is currently exposed, EXCEPT:

(Topic 22)

A. They could sell their home and both spouses rent property.
B. They could remove the deductibles they currently have on all their automobile insurance policies.
C. Anne could incorporate her graphics design business.
D. James could change the S corporation to a conventional C corporation.
E. James could implement additional loss prevention methods for his two buildings rented to Beals Funeral Home, Inc.

2. Which of the following statements concerning the disability income insurance policy owned by James are correct?

(Topic 25)

(1) A split definition of disability will likely mean that benefits will be paid during an initial benefit period of two years only if James is unable to engage in his own occupation, followed by inability (after two years) to perform any occupation for which James is reasonably suited.
(2) The most liberal definition of disability for James is defining total disability to mean the inability of James to perform his own occupation.
(3) If the policy contains a presumptive disability provision, disability benefits would likely be paid if James fractured both his right arm and his right leg.
(4) If the policy contains a residual disability clause, it is likely that the policy benefit will be payable only after James makes a partial recovery from total disability.

    A. (1) and (2) only
    B. (2) and (3) only
    C. (3) and (4) only
    D. (1), (2), and (4) only
    E. (1), (2), (3), and (4)

3. In which of the following ways does Anne's universal life (UL) policy differ from James' whole life (WL) policy?

(Topic 28)

    A. The UL policy provides for tax-deferral of investment income.

    B. The UL policy permits Anne to use the policy's cash value to pay one or more future premiums.

    C. The UL policy's cash value may be increased by increasing the amount of each future premium payment.

    D. The UL policy's cash value is more predictable than the cash value of the WL policy because of the guaranteed investment results.

    E. The UL policy's investment results can be expected to exceed the investment results of the WL policy.

4. Which of the following statements concerning the life insurance coverages for James and Anne Beals are correct?

(Topic 31)

    (1) James does not need additional life insurance either to provide liquidity for his estate or to assure payment of the child support and alimony.

    (2) James should not replace his $300,000 of term insurance with variable life insurance.

    (3) Anne should purchase an additional $250,000 of term insurance to provide for her children's college education since James will not be responsible for paying for the children's education.

    (4) If James agrees to carry life insurance in an amount sufficient for the children's education, then Anne can allow her universal life policy to lapse after the divorce because she will then have no need for life insurance.

    A. (1) and (2) only

    B. (1) and (3) only

    C. (2) and (3) only

    D. (2) and (4) only

    E. (3) and (4) only

5. Assume Anne becomes sole owner of the Beals' residence home and has HO-3 insurance coverage equal to the home's current market value. Why might Anne rationally decide to purchase a specific personal property endorsement for the HO-3?

(Topic 32)

    A. She considers the sub-limits of the HO-3 that are applicable to certain types of personal property to provide inadequate coverage.

    B. The insurance rate for scheduled property is typically lower than for blanket coverage.

    C. One reason for the low rates on scheduled coverage is that theft losses are not covered.

    D. The types of personal property usually covered by scheduled coverage are excluded from coverage under the basic HO-3.

    E. The departure of James from the home means less security for personal property and also higher rates for theft, vandalism, and other crime exposures.

6. Assume Anne becomes sole owner of the Beals' home and has HO-3 insurance coverage on the home. Which of the following persons will have personal liability coverage provided by Anne's HO-3?

(Topic 32)

    (1) Both Anne and James

    (2) Son Ronald while he is away at college

    (3) Daughter Christine who marries Maxwell Turner at age 16 because Christine is pregnant and lives at Maxwell's parents' home

    (4) A 19-year-old friend of son Ronald to whom Anne loaned the family's small outboard motorboat

    A. (1) and (2) only

    B. (1) and (3) only

    C. (2) and (3) only

    D. (2) and (4) only

    E. (3) and (4) only

7. Which of the following statements concerning insurance coverage for the Beals family members is correct?

(Topic 32)

    A. Anne's HO-3 provides all-risks coverage for both the dwelling and Anne's personal property.

    B. The dwelling policy program should be recommended for James.

    C. An HO-4 would provide adequate coverage for James.

    D. Anne would be eligible for HO-6 coverage, and the annual premium would be less than for an HO-3.

    E. An HO-4 should be recommended for Ronald while he is away at college.

BEALS CASE
ANSWERS AND EXPLANATIONS

1 D is the answer. A conventional C corporation could do nothing to reduce risk for James that could not be done just as well and just as effectively by an S corporation. Statements A, B, C, and E describe methods that Anne or James could implement to reduce risk.

2. D is the answer. (3) is not a correct statement. There is a high probability that after a competent physician sets James' arm and leg, James would be back at work in a few days. (1), (2), and (4) are correct statements.

3. C is the answer. James may increase his premium payments for the WL policy, but this is shown as premiums paid in advance and not as an increase in the cash value of the WL policy. A is not correct because both policies provide for tax-deferral of investment income. B is not correct because James may arrange for a policy loan for the premium payments for the WL policy. D is not correct because the UL policy does not guarantee investment results. Statement E is not correct because there is no reason to assume that investment results for the UL policy will exceed the guaranteed investment results for the WL policy.

4. A is the answer. James does not need additional life insurance to provide liquidity for his estate. He already has $500,000 of life insurance and over $200,000 in liquid assets. His debts are less than $250,000, and there will be no estate tax if the entire estate passes to Anne. Of course, after he is divorced, he may need to reconsider liquidity since there will then be a potential estate tax owed. There is no need to obtain life insurance for the child support and alimony obligations. Replacement of the term insurance with variable life insurance is not recommended for James because the term insurance will most likely be discontinued after his children complete their educations. The term insurance is temporary insurance for a temporary need, and variable insurance is a more permanent insurance that James does not need at this time. Moreover, the variable insurance will require a higher premium. James will be equally responsible for the children's education with Anne, so she has no need to buy additional life insurance to pay for their educations. Moreover, she and James already have enough life insurance to provide for the education of their children. Anne should not allow all of her life insurance to lapse since she owes $45,000 on the business loan and $50,000 on the mortgage on the residence. She should have some life insurance to pay these debts and for the needs of her estate.

5. A is the answer. The HO-3 imposes special limits of liability under Coverage C (personal property). For example, watercraft and their equipment have a $1,000 limit, loss caused by theft of jewelry has a $1,500 limit, and loss by theft of silverware has a $2,500 limit. The Beals are likely to have personal property exposures that exceed the limits of coverage provided by the basic HO-3. A specific personal property endorsement could be added to the HO-3 to provide specific desired coverage.

Obviously, this means an increase in the annual premium. The insurance premium rate for scheduled property is higher than for blanket coverage. Theft of jewelry and other personal property may be insured with scheduled coverage. The basic HO-3 policy limits the dollar amount of coverage for some items but does not exclude coverage completely. The insurer would not raise rates merely because of James's departure.

6. **D** is the answer. (1) is not correct. James is not covered because he is no longer a resident of Anne's home. (3) is not correct because Christine is married and no longer a resident of Anne's home. (2) and (4) are covered.

7. **C** is the answer. HO-4 is designed to provide coverage for personal property of persons renting an apartment or a house. A is not correct because an HO-3 does not provide all-risks coverage for personal property. B is not correct because an HO-4 should be recommended for James. D is not correct because an HO-6 is designed to provide coverage for condominium owners. E is not correct because Ronald would be covered by Anne's HO-3.

MOCSIN CASE

PERSONAL INFORMATION

Richard Mocsin is 46 years old, and his wife Gloria is 37 years old. Richard and Gloria were married 8 years ago; it was Richard's second marriage and Gloria's first marriage. Richard and Gloria have one child Charles, who is 6 years of age. Richard has two children by his prior marriage: Laura, who is 14 years of age, and Elaine, who is 12. All of the children attend public schools.

Richard is a biology professor at the university and is a partner in Wizard Research Associates, a biotechnology firm that Richard started with three of his associates from the university.

ASSET INFORMATION

The Mocsins own their personal residence in joint tenancy with right of survivorship, and it is valued currently at $250,000. They purchased the home seven years ago for $175,000. They have finished the basement and added a room and bathroom at a cost of $40,000. They have a mortgage balance of $150,000. The Mocsins' household furnishings are valued at $70,000, and Gloria's jewelry and furs are valued at $30,000. Richard and Gloria live in a state that follows the common-law forms of property ownership.

Richard and Gloria have a joint checking account that contains $7,000 and a joint savings account that contains $15,000. Interest income on the savings account last year was $450. The Mocsins also have $12,000 in money market mutual funds that paid dividends last year of $515. Richard owns shares in a growth stock mutual fund that he purchased three years ago for $5,000, is now worth $5,750, and paid dividends last year of $100. Dividends on these shares are expected to grow by 8% per year, and Richard believes that a 10% rate of return would be appropriate for these shares with their degree of risk. Gloria owns shares in a municipal bond fund purchased for $6,300, currently valued at $7,000, and yielding $400 per year tax-free. The Mocsins jointly purchased 500 shares in Power Station, Inc., a public utility company. These shares were acquired at a cost of $6,250, are currently valued at $8,000, and pay annual dividends of $480.

Richard's father died two years ago, and his mother died last year, leaving Richard an inheritance of $150,000 in U.S. Treasury securities, paying 8% interest ($12,000 annually), and a one-half interest in common with his brother in a Florida condominium. The condominium was valued in his mother's estate at $120,000 and was purchased six years ago for $125,000. Real estate taxes on the condominium, half of which Richard includes among his itemized deductions for federal income tax purposes, total $1,000. Both of Gloria's parents are still living.

The Mocsins are also joint owners of a parcel of undeveloped land in the mountains, where they plan to build a vacation home. The parcel of land cost them $75,000 and is currently valued at $70,000. They have a $30,000 mortgage on the property. Interest on the mortgage is $2,700 per year. Real estate taxes are $700.

Richard owns an apartment building near the university that he rents to students. The apartment building was purchased four years ago for $95,000 and is currently valued at $125,000. The annual gross rental income from the property is $11,000. Richard has a mortgage balance of $60,000, and his interest payments total $4,950. His real estate taxes and maintenance expenses are $3,000, and depreciation is $2,850.

The Mocsins are joint owners of two automobiles. The cars are valued at $25,000 and $17,500. Richard owns a sailboat which he bought for $35,000 and is valued now at $40,000.

Richard has a one-fourth interest in the partnership Wizard Research Associates, which is engaged in research for genetic engineering of various plants. There are no employment contracts for the partners. In addition to the partners, the firm has eight employees, including four research assistants, two secretaries, and two maintenance/hothouse workers. The research assistants are paid $30,000 each, the secretaries are paid $18,000 each, and the other workers are paid $20,000 each.

Richard and his partners believe that the value of Wizard Research Associates is approximately $1 million. There has been no objective valuation, however. The largest assets of the firm are its building and grounds, where the firm has a laboratory, hothouses, and fields for growing experimental plants. The building and land were purchased for $250,000, and $150,000 was allocated to the building and $100,000 to the land. Additional buildings have been added at a cost of $75,000, and the current value is estimated to be $400,000. The firm has a mortgage balance on the building and land of $150,000. The partnership has been depreciating the building for tax purposes under the original accelerated cost recovery system.

INCOME TAX INFORMATION

Richard earns $60,000 in annual salary from the university, and he reports another $48,000 of net taxable income from the biotechnology firm. Gloria earns $30,000 working in public relations for a hospital. She also receives $5,000 at the beginning of each year from a trust established by her grandfather, with securities valued currently at $100,000. At Gloria's death, the trust income will be paid to Charles, or if Charles is over age 25, the corpus will be distributed to him. The Mocsins file joint tax returns.

Richard pays child support for his two daughters in the amount of $400 each per month, and these payments are probably 75% of their support annually. Richard's daughters are in the custody of their mother and live with her for approximately nine months of the year. Richard is required by his divorce decree to maintain a $100,000 life insurance policy to provide child support in the event of his death.

Several years ago, Richard established custodian accounts for Laura and Elaine. Laura's account generates annual income of $900, and Elaine's account has annual income of $850.

Richard and Gloria incur home mortgage interest costs of $12,000 per year. Real estate taxes on their home are $2,500. They will pay $4,500 in state income taxes this year and $150 in personal property taxes. Their contributions to charities totaled $2,000.

RETIREMENT INFORMATION

Gloria owns IRA accounts totaling $17,000. She is now an active participant in a defined-contribution pension plan through the hospital where she works, and her vested account value is $35,000. Eight percent of Richard's gross salary at the university is deducted each year and contributed to a tax-deferred annuity. The university contributes an additional six percent dollar for dollar on a tax-deferred basis. The plan is projected to pay Richard $2,500 per month when he retires at age 65 or to Gloria at his death.

One of the partners in Wizard Research Associates is age 65 and about two years away from retirement, and two partners are age 55. The partners would like to prepare for the expected retirement of the age-65 partner, as well as the unexpected death or disability of any partner. The partners are also contemplating a retirement program for the firm and would like advice concerning the design.

INSURANCE INFORMATION

The university provides disability income coverage for one-third of Richard's salary, group medical expense insurance covering Richard and his family through a health maintenance organization, and group term life insurance for Richard, with a death benefit of $50,000. Richard owns a whole life insurance policy that will pay a death benefit of $100,000 and has a cash value of $5,500, and he owns a universal life policy with a face value of $150,000 and a cash value of $3,000. The annual premium on the whole life policy is $2,000, and the annual premium on the universal life policy is $800. Gloria has group term life insurance through her employer in a face amount that is equal to her salary.

Property and liability insurance that insures the Mocsins' house for its replacement cost has an annual premium of $1,200. The Mocsins' cars are insured under a personal auto policy providing limits for bodily injury of $100,000/$300,000, property damage of $25,000, uninsured motorists coverage of $10,000/$20,000, no-fault benefits, and a collision deductible of $250. Richard's sailboat is insured under a yacht policy.

ESTATE PLANNING INFORMATION

Richard's will leaves his entire estate to Gloria, but if Gloria predeceases Richard, the estate will be left in trust for Richard's three children equally. Gloria's will leaves her entire estate to Richard or, if he predeceases her, to Charles.

MOCSIN CASE
APPLICATION QUESTIONS

1. Which of the following statements concerning the various life insurance policies owned by Richard and Gloria is correct?

(Topic 28)

A. As the cash value of Richard's whole life policy increases, the face amount of the policy payable declines.

B. The annual premium per $1,000 of coverage is $4.00 for the whole life policy and $5.33 for the universal life policy.

C. The investment yield is known for the policy's duration for both the whole life policy and the universal life policy.

D. Richard might successfully elect to pay no premiums for three years on his universal life policy.

E. Gloria has the option of converting her group term life insurance to a cash value permanent type of coverage on any date she chooses.

2. Richard Mocsin and the other owners of Wizard Research Associates are considering an insured cross-purchase buy-sell agreement funded by life insurance. Which of the following statements concerning the partners' use of an insured cross-purchase buy-sell agreement is correct?

(Topic 29)

A. Richard must pay higher premiums on the life insurance policies he purchases than will the other owners.

B. The premiums for the life insurance policies will be paid with before-tax dollars and are deductible.

C. The death proceeds from insurance owned by Richard on the life of a deceased partner will be includible in the gross estate of the decedent.

D. The tax basis for interests held by Richard and the other surviving owners will not be affected by the sale of the decedent's partnership interest.

E. The decedent's estate will have to pay capital gains tax on the sale of the partnership interest.

3. Which of the following statements concerning the Mocsins' use of other or additional insurance coverages is correct?

(Topic 32)

A. They could provide all-risks coverage for contents by replacing their HO-03 policy with an HO-04 policy.

B. They could provide coverage for the contents of their condominium in Florida by adding an H0-06 as an endorsement to their HO-03 policy.

C. They could have provided all-risks coverage for both their dwelling and its contents if they had purchased an HO-02 instead of an HO-03.

D. They could have provided contents coverage up to 50% of the dollar amount of the dwelling coverage if they had purchased either an HO-02 or an HO-03.

E. They could reduce the premium cost for their homeowners coverage by insuring their home for its replacement cost under an HO-08.

4. Which of the following items of personal property would be excluded under the Mocsin family's HO-03 policy?

(Topic 32)

(1) Animals, birds, and fish
(2) Business property
(3) Loss caused by the negligent use of the dwelling fireplace
(4) Loss of $2,000 of clothing in a hotel fire while the family is vacationing in Paris

A. (1) only
B. (2) and (3) only
C. (1), (2), and (3) only
D. (2), (3), and (4) only
E. (1), (2), (3), and (4)

5. Which of the following would be excluded from liability coverage under the Mocsin family's personal auto policy (PAP)?

(Topic 32)

(1) Richard's use of a motorcycle recently acquired for weekend recreation purposes

(2) Richard's use of one of the family's cars for business purposes

(3) Richard's use of one of the family's cars in the neighborhood car pool, for which service each passenger pays Richard $5.00 weekly

A. (1) only
B. (1) and (2) only
C. (2) and (3) only
D. (1), (2), and (3)
E. Neither (1), (2), nor (3)

MOCSIN CASE
ANSWERS AND EXPLANATIONS

1. D is the answer. No premiums need be paid for either policy if Richard elects to use the cash values of the policies to pay annual premiums (if the policies cash values are adequate). A is not correct. As a whole life policy's cash value increases, the net amount at risk declines, not the face amount. B is not correct. The whole life's premium per $1,000 of coverage is $20, not $4. C is not correct. The investment yield on the universal life policy is not known for the policy's duration. The investment yield for the universal life policy varies with the investment success of the insurance company. E is not a correct statement. Conversion of group term life insurance is only permitted at termination of employment or at termination of the master contract.

2. A is the answer. Richard must pay higher premiums on the policies he purchases than will the other owners. The other owners are older, so the premiums for policies on their lives will be greater. The premiums for the life insurance policies will be paid with after-tax dollars and are not deductible. The death proceeds from life insurance owned by Richard on the life of a deceased partner will not be included in the estate of the decedent because the decedent had no incidents of ownership at the time of death. Note that the policies owned on the other partners will be includible in the decedent's estate. The basis for interests held by Richard and the other surviving owners will be increased by the sale of the decedent's partnership interest. The decedent's estate will not have to pay capital gains tax on the sale of the partnership interest because the partnership interest receives a step-up in basis to date-of-death value.

3. D is the answer. A is not a correct statement because HO-04 is for tenants and provides broad form coverage for contents. B is not a correct statement because the HO-06 is a separate policy covering condominiums, but it is not added as an endorsement to another policy. As a matter of fact, the family's HO-03 would provide coverage for the condominium's personal property up to 10% of the contents coverage provided at the insured residence. C is not a correct statement because an HO-02 does not provide all-risks coverage for the dwelling or the contents. The HO-02 provides only broad form coverage covering 17 perils. E is not a correct statement because under an HO-08, losses are settled on an actual cash value (ACV) basis. Losses are not settled on a replacement cost basis.

4. A is the answer. HO-3 covers business property up to $2,500 on premises and up to $250 off premises. (3) would not be excluded because negligence on the part of the insured is never the basis for an insurer to deny a homeowner's loss. Negligence is the cause of many covered kitchen fires. (4) would not be excluded. The HO-03 contents coverage is worldwide. Fire is a covered peril.

5. A is the answer. Only four-wheel vehicles are covered. Coverage is provided for all other items. (2) is covered. Although most vehicles used for business purposes would be excluded, the exclusion does not apply to private passenger cars owned by an insured. (3) is covered. Carpool use of a covered auto is approved.

LOUDON CASE

PERSONAL INFORMATION AND BACKGROUND

Dennis and Sarah Loudon have been married for 8 years and have one child who is 5 years old. Dennis has one child by a previous marriage. The Loudons own a three-bedroom home, 2 cars, a motorboat, and a dog. Dennis operates a restaurant with his two brothers, and Sarah works as a credit analyst for a bank. The Loudons are all in good health.

Dennis Loudon

Dennis Loudon is age 38 and is a partner in a restaurant called The Blue Elf. Dennis and his two brothers operate the restaurant, and Dennis is the youngest of the three brothers. One brother is two years older, and the other brother is four years older. In addition to the three brothers, the restaurant has four full-time and five part-time employees. The full-time employees have been with The Blue Elf for two to four years and range in ages from 23 to 37. Each of the part-time employees works less than 1,000 hours annually. Two of the part-time workers are 60 years of age, and the others are under 21. Dennis and his brothers devote full-time to the restaurant.

Sarah Loudon

Sarah Loudon is age 35 and has been employed by Nationsbank as a credit analyst for 9 years. She has an MBA in finance from the state university.

Tracy Loudon

Tracy Loudon is age 5 and attends the local public elementary school where she is in kindergarten. She goes to the daycare center for the afternoons.

Thomas Loudon

Thomas Loudon is age 10 and lives with his mother Frances, Dennis's first wife. Thomas attends public elementary school and goes to an after-school program.

PERSONAL AND FINANCIAL GOALS

The Loudons have the following financial goals, in order of priority:

1. Send Tracy and Thomas to private colleges away from home.
2. Minimize their current income taxes.
3. Save for retirement to provide a standard of living that is 75% of their preretirement earnings.
4. Save for a vacation home.
5. Develop an estate plan to minimize estate taxes.

ECONOMIC INFORMATION

1. The Loudons expect that inflation will average 3% per year.
2. The Loudons expect Dennis' income from The Blue Elf to increase 4% annually.
3. The Loudons expect Sarah's salary to increase 5% annually.
4. Current mortgage rates are 6.5% for 15 years and 7% for 30 years. Lenders are requiring three "points" for mortgage loans.

INSURANCE INFORMATION

Life Insurance	Policy #1	Policy #2
Insured	Dennis	Sarah
Face amount	$100,000	$100,000
Type	Whole life	Group term
Cash value	$15,400	$0
Annual premium	$2,000	Employer-paid
Beneficiary	Sarah	Dennis
Contingent beneficiary	Tracy	Tracy
Owner	Dennis	Sarah
Settlement options	Life income	None

Medical Expense Insurance

The Loudon family is covered under a group major medical plan through Sarah's employer. The annual family deductible is $500, and above the deductible, the plan pays 80% of covered medical expenses. The cap on out-of-pocket medical expenses per illness or injury is $2,000, including the deductible.

Disability Insurance

Dennis has a personal disability income policy that will pay $2,000 per month after a 30-day elimination period. This policy has an "own occupation" definition of disability. The policy has a benefit period to age 65. The annual premium is $700.

Sarah has a disability income policy arranged for by her employer. The definition of disability is "own occupation," and the policy will pay 50% of her gross pay after a 90-day elimination period. The annual premium is $450, and the employer pays one-half and Sarah pays one-half.

Homeowners Insurance

The Loudons have a homeowners HO-3 policy providing $150,000 of coverage on the dwelling. The personal liability coverage has a $100,000 limit, and medical payments coverage has a $1,000 limit per person. The premium is included in their monthly mortgage payment.

Automobile Insurance

Both of the Loudons' cars are insured under a personal auto policy (PAP) with bodily injury liability limits of $100,000/$300,000 and a $50,000 limit for property damage liability. The medical payments coverage is $5,000 per person per accident. Uninsured motorists coverage is in the amount of $50,000 per accident. The deductible on their collision coverage is $250, and the deductible on the other-than-collision coverage is $250. Their annual premium is $1,100.

INVESTMENT INFORMATION

The Loudons describe themselves as having a moderate level of risk tolerance in investments. Their expected and required rate of return is 9%. They expect to become more conservative as they approach retirement age.

INCOME TAX INFORMATION

The Loudons are currently in the 25% income tax bracket for federal income tax purposes. The state income tax is 2%.

RETIREMENT INFORMATION

The Loudons plan to retire in 27 years when Dennis is age 65. They would like to have a standard of living that is equal to 75% of their preretirement income. At the time they retire, the Loudons plan on selling their interest in the restaurant and moving to Florida or Texas. They expect that they will live in retirement for 25 years.

The Loudons expect to receive Social Security benefits at the time they retire. Dennis expects to receive $13,000 per year in full retirement benefits at age 67. Sarah expects to receive the same amount.

Dennis has an IRA through the credit union where he does his banking. Dennis has contributed $2,000 each year to the IRA for the past ten years. The returns on the account have declined from 10% to 6% over the past ten years.

Sarah has a 401(k) plan through the bank where she works. The bank contributes $0.50 for every $1 contributed by Sarah, up to 6% of her salary. Sarah can contribute a maximum of 10% of her salary. She has been contributing 6% for the past six years. The annual return on the 401(k) investments has averaged 9% over the past six years. Sarah has named Dennis as the beneficiary.

GIFTS, ESTATES, TRUSTS, AND WILL INFORMATION

The Loudons have simple wills leaving their estates to each other.

Dennis and Sarah Loudon
Statement of Cash Flows

January 1 – December 31, 20XX

Annual Inflows

Dennis's net income from the restaurant (Partnership income)	$ 58,000
Sarah's salary	54,000
Dividend income	880
Savings interest income	275
Certificate of deposit interest income	300
Total Inflows	$113,455

Annual Outflows

Mortgage (PITI)	$ 14,700
Utilities and phone	2,450
Food	3,800
Clothing	3,400
Car payments	9,600
Car maintenance, gas, and oil	2,875
Boat maintenance, gas, and oil	2,150
Entertainment	4,000
Vacation	3,200
Child care – Tracy	3,600
Life insurance	2,000
Health and dental	2,400
Disability insurance	925
Car insurance	1,400
Federal income tax	25,250
State income taxes	2,200
Social Security and Medicare taxes	13,000
Charitable contributions	2,000
401(k) contributions	3,240
IRA contributions	2,000
Frances Loudon	7,200
Total Outflows	$ 111,390
Discretionary Funds	$ 2,065

DENNIS AND SARAH LOUDON
Personal Balance Sheet

December 31, 20XX

Assets
Cash/Cash Equivalents

JT	Checking account	$ 4,320
H	Money market fund	5,200
JT	Savings account	9,170
	Total Cash/Cash Equivalents	$ 18,690

Invested Assets

H	Certificate of deposit	$ 5,000
JT	Growth stock mutual funds	15,600
H	Stock	8,800
H	IRA (Dennis)	21,800
W	401(k) (Sarah)	35,160
H	Partnership in restaurant	160,000
H	Life insurance cash value	15,400
	Total Investments	$261,760

Personal-Use Assets

JT	House (land is $25,000)	$160,000
JT	Volvo	27,000
JT	Explorer	35,000
H	Boat	12,000
W	Jewelry	9,000
	Total Personal-Use Assets	$243,000
	Total Assets	$523,450

Liabilities

Current Liabilities

JT	Credit card balances	$ 4,200
JT	Car Loans	40,000
	Total Current Liabilities	$44,200

Long-Term Liabilities

JT	Mortgage (9% for 30 years)	$111,500
JT	Business loan*	33,333
	Total Long-Term Liabilities	$144,833

Total Liabilities	$189,033
Net Worth	$334,417
Total Liabilities	$523,450

* The business loan is at 10% for 10 years.

H = Husband
W = Wife
JT = Joint tenancy

INFORMATION ON ASSETS AND LIABILITIES

Personal Residence

The Loudons purchased their home with a 30-year mortgage at a 9% rate of interest. The house is a 3-bedroom ranch and has a burglar alarm.

Stock

Dennis received 100 shares of EXXON stock as a gift from his father. His father bought the stock in 1996 for $50 per share and gave the stock to Dennis in 1998 when the shares sold for $60 per share. Dennis has reinvested his dividends in additional shares of EXXON stock. The total amount of reinvested dividends is $1,000. No dividends were reinvested this year. The stock currently sells for $72 per share (as of the date of the balance sheet).

The Blue Elf

Dennis and his brothers bought the restaurant 10 years ago. The restaurant has a fair market value of $480,000. The building and property have been appraised at $300,000. The restaurant is expected to increase in value at the rate of 4% per year. The Loudons have cosigned a note with Dennis' brothers for a loan taken out three years ago to improve the restaurant. The balance on the note is $33,333.

Frances Loudon

Dennis pays his first wife Frances $600 per month for child support. This payment will drop to $200 per month when their child Thomas reaches age 18. Thomas is now 10 years old. Thomas attends an after-school program for which his mother pays $700 per school year.

EDUCATION INFORMATION

The Loudons would like to start college funds for Thomas and Tracy. The current cost of the private colleges where they expect to send their children is $25,000 per year, including tuition, room, board, and books. They expect that the children will begin college at age 18 and will attend for four years. The Loudons expect that the rate of inflation in the costs for private colleges will be 7%.

LOUDON CASE
APPLICATION QUESTIONS

1. Which of the following statements concerning Sarah Loudon's disability income insurance policy is correct?

(Topic 25)

A. The "own occupation" definition is the most liberal definition of disability.
B. The "any occupation" definition is the best definition of disability.
C. The 90-day elimination period is more expensive than a 30-day elimination period would be.
D. Sarah would receive disability benefits equal to her current salary.
E. Disability benefits Sarah would receive would be 100% income-tax-free.

2. As you review the insurance coverages maintained by the Loudons, which of the following areas of concern should you point out to them?

(Topic 25, 28, 32)

(1) The need to add a Scheduled Personal Property Endorsement to their HO-3 policy for jewelry
(2) The need for Sarah to add to her group life insurance the same settlement option as Dennis has on his whole life policy
(3) The need to replace the "own occupation" definition in both disability income policies with the more liberal to the insured "any occupation for which suited" definition

A. (1) only
B. (2) only
C. (3) only
D. (1) and (2) only
E. (1) and (3) only

3. The dog owned by the Loudons recently bit a neighbor's child while the child was in his own backyard. Because treatment of the child's injury was not provided promptly, complications set in, and the child's medical bills totaled $1,800. In this situation, which of the following statements is correct?

(Topic 32)

A. The Loudons have no insurance coverage for this loss because they have not taken out an umbrella liability policy.
B. The medical payments coverage in the Loudons' HO-3 policy will not pay because the neighbor's child is not an insured.
C. The medical payments coverage in the Loudons' HO-3 policy will not pay because the injury occurred away from the covered premises.
D. The personal liability coverage in the Loudons' HO-3 policy will not pay because injuries caused by pets of an insured are specifically excluded.
E. The loss will be covered under medical payments up to $1,000 and for $800 under liability.

4. Which of the following statements concerning the coverage provided by the Loudons' HO-3 policy is correct?

(Topic 32)

(1) The Loudons carry too much coverage on the dwelling.
(2) HO-3 provides all-risks/replacement cost coverage on the dwelling.
(3) HO-3 provides all-risks coverage/ replacement cost coverage on contents coverage.

    A. (1) only
    B. (2) only
    C. (3) only
    D. (1) and (2) only
    E. (1), (2), and (3)

5. Assume that, at your recommendation, the Loudons purchase a personal liability umbrella policy with a $500 self-insured retention. The policy specifies that the Loudons must maintain in force a PAP with limits of at least $100,000/$300,000/$25,000 and personal liability coverage through their homeowners policy of at least $300,000. Now assume that the Loudons are held liable for $125,000 in damages when a guest is seriously injured on the Loudons' premises due to negligence on their part. In this case, how much will be paid by the HO-3 insurer and the umbrella insurer?

(Topic 32)

A. Nothing by either insurer
B. $100,000 by the HO-3 insurer and nothing by the umbrella insurer
C. $125,000 by the HO-3 insurer and nothing by the umbrella insurer
D. $62,500 by the HO-3 insurer and $62,500 by the umbrella insurer
E. $100,000 by the HO-3 insurer and $24,500 by the umbrella insurer

LOUDON CASE
ANSWERS AND EXPLANATIONS

1. A is the answer. "Own occupation" is the most generous type of coverage because the definition is more liberal. If the insured does not fit the very narrowly defined specifics of her occupation, then the insured can collect benefits and continue to work in another area if need be. "Any occupation" is the most restrictive type of coverage because the insured will receive no benefits if Sarah can hold any job. A 90-day elimination (waiting) period would be less expensive than a 30-day period. Sarah would receive only $2,000 per month, which is less than her current $2,700 per month salary. Since the premium payments are split between Sarah and the employer, benefits would not be 100% income-tax-free.

2. A is the answer. (1) is correct because the endorsement will provide open-perils ("all-risks") coverage for the full value of Sarah's jewelry. The HO-3 covers jewelry for only $1,500 if the loss is due to theft. (2) is incorrect. A life-income option pays only for as long as the beneficiary is alive. Although it provides the most periodic income per $1,000 of death proceeds, it would provide nothing for the children or others if either beneficiary should die soon after the insured. We think a pure life-income option is inappropriate for either policy. (3) is incorrect because the "own occupation" definition is more liberal to the insured (though more expensive) than the "any occupation for which suited" definition.

3. E is the answer. A is incorrect because an umbrella policy, even if the Loudons owned one, would not cover a loss as small as this one that is covered by an underlying policy, the HO-3, as explained below. B is incorrect because medical payments coverage in the HO-3 applies to persons other than the insureds, the Loudons. C is incorrect because the injury need not occur on the Loudons' premises to be covered by the HO-3 policy. D is incorrect because the HO-3 policy does not exclude loss caused by a pet of an insured. The personal liability coverage will pay for damages for which the insured is legally liable, which presumably is the case here. Also, the medical payments coverage specifically applies to off-premises bodily injury caused by an animal owned by or in the care of an insured. Therefore, the loss will be covered by the medical payments portion of the policy up to $1,000 and by the personal liability portion for the balance.

4. D is the answer. The Loudons only need to carry $135,000 of coverage since land is valued at $25,000. $150,000 would be too much coverage. HO-3 policies provide all-risks/replacement cost coverage on the dwelling and actual cash value coverage on the contents. An HO-5 policy provides all-risks/replacement cost coverage on the contents.

5. B is the answer. The Loudons did not carry the required underlying liability amount on their HO-3. Therefore, the umbrella insurer will pay only the amount for which it would have been liable, namely, zero, if the required amount had been carried on the HO-3 policy. The HO-3 insurer, on the other hand, is responsible for the loss, but only up to its $100,000 limit of liability. Note that the self-insured retention is irrelevant in this case. It applies only to losses not covered by an underlying policy but covered by the umbrella policy.

CONNOR CASE

Greg and Darcie Connor have worked with Danielle Jacobs, a local CFP®
professional, for the last several years. The Connors met with Danielle yesterday to
update their financial plan as Greg recently inherited $2.5 million from his father.
According to the engagement letter, Danielle is to prepare and implement for a fixed
fee a comprehensive financial plan for the Connors within the next 3 months. The
engagement letter specifically mentions that Danielle is also responsible for the
preparation of any income, gift, or trust tax returns as she is also a CPA and has
prepared the Connors' returns since she started working with them. Danielle will
receive additional compensation related to the tax preparation. Likewise, Danielle
will receive commissions related to the purchase of any insurance as she is a licensed
insurance agent. Furthermore, Danielle receives a quarterly asset management fee for
managing the Connors' portfolio. The engagement will automatically continue as the
Connors have asked Danielle to check in with them once a year for the next five
years to make sure their financial plan is still achieving their goals and objectives.
Danielle will receive separate compensation based on the amount of work required
every year to update their plan. Greg and Darcie gave Danielle $2,500 as a retainer
for her services. Danielle captured the following information during her meeting with
the Connors and by reviewing the relevant financial documents including her notes
from previous meetings with the Connors over the last few years.

PERSONAL INFORMATION AND BACKGROUND

Greg and Darcie Connor live in Hattiesburg, Mississippi near the University of
Southern Mississippi campus. They met at Southern Miss where Greg majored in
graphic design and Darcie majored in political science. They moved to Washington,
DC after Darcie graduated so she could follow her dream of working for a Senator.
After living her dream for 10 years, Darcie was ready to settle down and become a
mother. Greg and Darcie decide to return to Gulfport, Mississippi to be near Darcie's
parents. However, after surviving several major hurricanes, they decided to move
farther inland back towards Southern Miss in Hattiesburg. Upon returning to
Hattiesburg, Greg reconnected with David, a fraternity brother who started a business
when they were in college called Whatever You Want To Say T-Shirt Co. Greg was
looking for a job at the time and accepted an offer to help David until he could find
something more permanent. Greg enjoyed working with David so much that he
stayed on full time and is now a 25% owner of the business.

Name	Relationship	Age	Occupation	Health	Comments
Greg	Husband	47	Owner/T-Shirt Co.	Excellent	Plays on a co-ed softball team
Darcie	Wife	45	Mother	Excellent	Wants to return to work part time once her daughter is in high school
John	Son	12	Student	Excellent	Plays on a traveling soccer team
Sheila	Daughter	10	Student	Excellent	Wants to pursue a dancing career

Greg's mother died 10 years ago in a car accident. Greg's father died earlier this year from liver cancer. Darcie's parents downsized their home a couple of years ago when they retired. They are avid members of the local book club and enjoy doing crossword puzzles in addition to spoiling their grandchildren. Darcie believes her parents saved enough money for retirement. Darcie recently learned her parents each have a long-term care policy that provides a $100 daily benefit. However, she is not sure if this will provide them with adequate coverage. Darcie's parents are in relatively good health for being in their mid 70's.

GOALS AND OBJECTIVES

1. Greg wants to make sure his company will continue to operate if anything happens to Greg or David.
2. They want to pay for both children to attend Southern Miss.
3. They want to take a trip to Washington, DC next summer.
4. They want to spend $20,000 to remodel their kitchen this year.
5. They want 80% of their current income in today's dollars per year in retirement.
6. They want to minimize income, gift, estate, and GST taxes.

INCOME TAX INFORMATION

Greg and Darcie had an adjusted gross income of $175,000 last year and paid $30,000 in income taxes to the federal and state governments. They anticipate their adjusted gross income this year will be the same. They are in the 25% and 5% marginal federal and state tax bracket, respectively, for the current year.

RETIREMENT INFORMATION

Greg participates in his company's SIMPLE IRA plan and contributes $10,000 per year. The company matches dollar-for-dollar on the first 5% of Greg's salary. The employer contributions vest immediately.

Darcie contributes $5,000 to an IRA every year. She never participated in a qualified plan when she was in the workforce.

Greg and Darcie assume they will live for 35 years in retirement. Danielle previously determined the Connors will need 80% of their current income in today's dollars when they retire.

BUSINESS INFORMATION

Whatever You Want to Say T-shirt Co. currently has 2 full-time employees (including Greg) and 3 part-time employees. The company was set up as a corporation, but Danielle has recommended making an S corporation election. David owns 75% of the business and Greg owns the other 25%. Greg purchased his 25% interest three years ago when David was going through a nasty divorce from his wife Mary. David needed the cash in order to give the money to Mary as part of the divorce settlement.

Whatever You Want to Say T-shirt Co creates and sells t-shirts, sweatshirts, and other items for Southern Miss organizations including the fraternities, sororities, athletic teams, and academic groups. Their designs have been so popular that they are now the main supplier for several national fraternities and sororities in addition to several universities in the southeast. Last year, they had over $600,000 in sales. This year they are projecting over $750,000 in sales. They will spend the additional income on a nationwide marketing campaign. If they end up with a profit at the end of the year, David and Greg take it as a year-end bonus. The salary numbers below include the anticipated year-end bonuses.

The employee census is as follows:

	Age	Length of Employment	Salary
Full Time:			
David Poston	47	27 years	$225,000
Greg Connor	47	8 years	$185,000
Part Time:			
Amanda Klink	20	2 years (works 20 hours per week)	$9.00 per hour
Paige Kemmit	20	1 year (works 15 hours per week)	$8.50 per hour
Mark Smith	19	6 months (works 5 hours per week)	$8.00 per hour

The business has adequate insurance coverage for liability, property damages, automobile, and overhead expense insurance. The business also has all required employment insurance policies.

David has told Greg that he would like Greg to buy the business if David should become disabled or pass away. David would buy back Greg's interest if Greg should become disabled or pass away. They have not yet put any of their discussions in writing. They have also not had the business valued since Greg's divorce when it was worth $1 million. They believe it has increased in value to around $1.2 million.

EDUCATION INFORMATION

Greg and Darcie want to fund their children's education to Southern Miss. Currently the cost is $15,000 per student per year including room and board. According to Southern Miss newsletters, they anticipate the cost will increase 8% a year. Greg and Darcie anticipate both children will take five years to complete their undergraduate degree. They also hope both children will complete a two year masters program.

ESTATE PLANNING INFORMATION

Greg and Darcie updated their wills shortly after Greg's dad died. Their wills create a Bypass trust and a QTIP trust with provisions to reduce their estate tax liability to zero and a 30 day survivorship requirement for the surviving spouse. The QTIP trust names the surviving spouse as the beneficiary of the trust with the remainder going to John and Sheila, *per stirpes*. The Bypass trust names the surviving spouse, John and Sheila as discretionary beneficiaries until the surviving spouse passes away. At that time, all remaining assets will be divided equally between John and Shelia, *per stirpes*.

The surviving spouse is named as the executor of each estate. If the surviving spouse is unable or unwilling to serve, Larry Rabun, their estate planning attorney, will serve as the executor.

Greg and Darcie have both executed Powers of Attorneys naming each other. They also executed Advanced Medical Directives stating they do not want life support.

In regard to any gifts or bequests, they want to treat their children equally. Thus far, they have made no taxable gifts.

INHERITANCE INFORMATION

Greg was named as the sole heir of his father's estate in his will and all beneficiary designation forms. After paying all expenses, taxes, and outstanding debts, Greg received $2.5 million dollars which consisted of the following items:

Asset	Proceeds	Father's Basis	Notes
Home	$500,000	$295,000	His father owned the home for over 20 years.
MEC	$250,000	$100,000	Purchased 10 years ago
Life insurance	$500,000	$200,000	The premiums were paid entirely by Greg's father's employer. The $200,000 basis represents the amount of premiums his father reported for income taxes.
Brokerage account	$1,150,000	$800,000	His father always enjoyed following the stock markets
Checking account	$25,000	$25,000	
Personal property	$75,000	$150,000	Majority of proceeds from antique china set from Greg's great grandmother
Total	**$2,500,000**	**$1,570,000**	

Greg's father also owned a life annuity with a 10-year period certain. Greg's father bought the deferred annuity 7 years ago for $60,000 but only received two yearly payments of $5,000 before he passed away. Greg's father anticipated receiving payments for 20 years based on his life expectancy.

INVESTMENT INFORMATION

Greg and Darcie have managed to save $100,000 in their brokerage account. They originally had over $250,000, but they had to liquidate the bulk of their account in order for Greg to purchase his 25% interest in the T-shirt Company. Danielle worked with the Connors to come up with their asset allocation. They now need to revisit their asset allocation as Greg just received the $2.5 million cash distribution from his father's estate. Greg gave the check to Danielle to deposit in their account during their meeting. Their account balances at the end of last year immediately following their yearly reallocation were as follows:

Name	Allocation Percentage	Basis	FMV (End of Last Year)
Short-Term Bond Fund	10%	$9,000	$10,000
S&P 500 Index Fund	40%	$42,000	$40,000
Mid-cap growth fund	20%	$17,000	$20,000
Small-cap fund	10%	$7,000	$10,000
International fund	20%	$12,000	$20,000
Total	**100%**	**$87,000**	**$100,000**

Greg and Darcie have their SIMPLE IRA and traditional IRA, respectively, invested for long-term growth with a moderate overall investment risk. Danielle helped them come up with the asset allocations inside each account.

ECONOMIC INFORMATION

Greg and Darcie want to make the following assumptions.

Long-term inflation rate	3%
Education inflation rate	8%
Current mortgage refinancing rates – 30 year loan	7.0%
Current mortgage refinancing rates – 15 year loan	6.5%
Maximum loan value on mortgages	80%
Home equity line of credit rates	8.25%
Rate of return on investments	7%
Risk free rate of return	4%

Greg and Darcie Connor
Projected Cash Flow
For the Current Year

Cash Inflows

Greg's salary	$185,000
Investment income	unknown
Total	**$185,000**

Cash Outflows

Taxes (income and payroll)	$ 40,000
Retirement plan contributions	$ 15,000
Mortgage (principal and interest)	$ 36,000
Property taxes (home and cars)	$ 4,000
Medical and dental expenses	$ 2,000
Utilities	$ 6,000
Lifestyle expenses	$ 45,000
Insurance premiums	$ 10,000
Vacations	$ 5,000
Trips for John's soccer team	$ 2,000
Savings	$ 12,000
Unknown	$ 8,000
Total	**$185,000**

Statement of Financial Position
Greg and Darcie Connor
as of December 31st Last Year

ASSETS

Cash and Cash Equivalents

Checking account: JT [1]	$	15,000
Savings account: JT [2]	$	25,000
Total Cash and Cash Equivalents	$	40,000

Invested Assets

SIMPLE IRA plan: H [3]	$	132,000
IRA: W [4]	$	68,000
Whatever You Want to Say T-shirt Co.	$	300,000
Annuity: H [5]	$	100,000
Brokerage account: JT [6]	$	100,000
Total Invested Assets	$	700,000

Personal-Use Assets

Home: JT [7]	$	500,000
Jewelry: W	$	12,000
Nissan: H	$	25,000
Minivan: W	$	32,000
Furniture and household items: JT	$	100,000
Total Personal-Use Assets	$	669,000

Total Assets	**$1,409,000**	

LIABILITIES AND NET WORTH

Liabilities

Mortgage – JT [8]	$	400,000
Credit cards [9]	$	10,000
Total Liabilities	$	410,000

Total Liabilities	**$**	**410,000**

Net Worth	**$**	**999,000**

Notes to the Financial Statements

H = Husband
W = Wife
JT = Joint tenancy

[1] Account pays 1.5% annual interest.

[2] Account pays 3.0% annual interest.

[3] Darcie is the primary beneficiary. John and Sheila are equal contingent beneficiaries.

[4] Greg is the primary beneficiary. John and Sheila are equal contingent beneficiaries. Darcie has deducted $20,000 of her contributions.

[5] Greg bought the annuity with funds he inherited when his mother died. He paid $25,000 for the annuity. Starting at age 65, Greg will receive a $10,000 annual annuity payment for life.

[6] See Investment Information for account detail.

[7] The land is worth $80,000. Their basis is $460,000 in the home.

[8] The 30-year mortgage has 22 years remaining; the fixed interest rate is 7.0%.

[9] They used the credit card when Greg needed to buy a new piece of equipment for the business at the end of last year as it had the lowest interest rate of 3.9% for three years. The company reimburses Greg for each monthly payment.

INSURANCE INFORMATION

The Connors had the following insurance claims over the last few months:

1. John was practicing penalty shots at the local soccer field when his foot slipped and he kicked the soccer ball into his coach's windshield. The windshield shattered due to the force with which John kicked the ball. The coach filed a claim with his insurance company, National Insurance, to get his windshield replaced and all of the glass removed from inside his car. National Insurance has filed a claim with Greg's insurance company to recover their loss.

2. Greg caused a three car accident when he swerved to miss a dog running loose on the freeway. Greg did not damage his car as the other cars crashed when they swerved to miss Greg's car. The drivers filed the following claims against Greg:

   - Car #1 – Driver was not hurt, but there was $5,000 of damage to his car.
   - Car #2 – Driver and passenger were both seriously injured and each filed a $150,000 claim. The driver also filed $35,000 of damage to the car.
   - Car #3 – Driver had minor injuries and filed a $50,000 claim. The driver also filed $15,000 claim for damage to the car.

3. Sheila had her tonsils taken out last month after having five episodes of Strep throat within six months. The total cost of the surgery and extended hospital stay due

to complications was $10,000. Sheila's doctor also charged her $2,000 for office visits and $500 for lab tests.

4. John and his best friend Eli were working on a science experiment in the garage which unfortunately caught fire. John and Eli quickly ran out of the garage and called 911 on John's cell phone. Although the fire department arrived within 10 minutes, the fire spread from the garage to a portion of the house. It cost $75,000 to repair the fire damage.

5. The Governor of Mississippi issued mandatory evacuations due to a category 3 hurricane heading directly to the Mississippi coast. The Connors evacuated their home for 4 days and incurred $1,200 in hotel room charges. Luckily, their home did not incur any damage although other homes in their neighborhood were not as lucky. They have filed a claim for those expenses under section D of their HO-3 policy.

The Connors also spent $5,000 to add burglar-proof windows during the year following a string of break-ins in their neighborhood.

The Connors recently read an article about buying life insurance on children. They are seriously considering the idea to not only provide coverage for their children but to also use it as a learning tool with their children about financial planning.

The following charts summarize the key information about the Connors' insurance coverages.

Life Insurance

Insured	Owner	Primary Beneficiary	Contingent Beneficiaries	Face Amount	Type	Annual Premium	Notes
Greg	Greg	Darcie	John and Sheila	$500,000	20 year convertible term	$1,500	Purchased 5 years ago
Darcie	Darcie	Greg	John and Sheila	$500,000	20 year convertible term	$1,250	Purchased 5 years ago

Disability Insurance

Insured	Current Benefit Amount	Benefit Period	Inflation Rider	Premium	Notes
Greg	$7,500/month	5 years	None	$1,000/year	Policy uses split definition of disability. Greg's company pays the premium with after-tax dollars.

Medical Insurance

Insured	Plan Type	Copayments	Coinsurance	Deductible	Stop-Loss	Premium
Greg (family coverage)	PPO	$0	20%	$2,000 per person/ $3,000 family	$5,000	$650 per month. Greg's company pays $200 per month of the premium and does a payroll deduction for the other $450.

Long-Term Care Insurance

Insured	Current Benefit Amount	Benefit Period	Inflation Rider	Premium	Date of Issue
Greg	None				
Darcie	None				

Homeowners Insurance

Type	Dwelling Amount	Contents Coverage	Liability	Premium	Deductible
HO-3	$350,000	$100,000 ACV	$500,000	$3,000/year	$1,000
Earthquake	$350,000	$100,000	n/a	$750/year	$1,000
Flood	$350,000	$100,000	n/a	$1,000/year	$1,000

Automobile Insurance

Vehicle	Type	Liability Limits	Collision	Comprehensive (Other-Than-Collision)	Premium
Greg's Nissan	Personal auto policy	50/100/25	$500 broad form deductible	$500 deductible	$350/month
Darcie's Minivan	Personal auto policy	50/100/25	$500 broad form deductible	$500 deductible	$275/month

CONNOR CASE
APPLICATION QUESTIONS

1. What insurance principle is National Insurance using to get reimbursed for the damage to the windshield caused by the soccer ball?

(Topic 22)

    A. Adverse selection
    B. Law of large numbers
    C. Risk reduction
    D. Subrogation

2. What risk management technique did the Connors implement this year related to the break-ins in their neighborhood?

(Topic 22)

    A. Risk avoidance
    B. Risk retention
    C. Risk reduction
    D. Risk transfer

3. Which of the following risk exposures should Greg treat as his first priority for insuring?

(Topic 23)

    A. Business related
    B. Death
    C. Disability
    D. Retirement

4. Which of the following risk exposures should Darcie treat as her first priority for increasing insurance coverage?

(Topic 23)

    A. Additional life insurance coverage
    B. Additional property coverage for her furniture and other household items.
    C. Additional liability coverage for her car
    D. Additional liability coverage for her home

5. How much will the insurance company pay related to Sheila's episodes with Strep throat and the surgery to remove her tonsils?

(Topic 24)

    A. $8,000

    B. $8,400

    C. $10,000

    D. $10,500

6. How much does Greg have to include into his taxable income each month related to the health insurance premiums paid by his employer?

(Topic 24)

    A. $0

    B. $200

    C. $450

    D. $650

7. Which of the following is the best recommendation Danielle can give Greg related to his disability policy?

(Topic 25)

    A. Greg should replace the policy with one that uses the "educated and trained for" definition of disability.

    B. Greg should have his company pay the premium with pretax dollars.

    C. Greg should replace the policy with an identical policy but has a longer benefit period.

    D. Greg should replace the policy with an identical policy but that also includes an inflation rider.

8. Which of the following is the best recommendation Danielle can give Darcie related to a disability policy?

(Topic 25)

    A. Darcie should purchase an own occupation policy with a 30 day elimination period.

    B. Darcie should purchase an own occupation policy with a 30 day waiting period.

    C. Darcie should purchase an own occupation policy with a 30 day waiver-of-premium provision.

    D. Darcie is not eligible to purchase a disability policy.

9. Which of the following is the best advice Danielle can give Darcie about her parent's long-term care coverage?

(Topic 26)

    A. Darcie's parents have adequate long-term care insurance as their policies will cover most of their daily expenses.

    B. Darcie's parents should consider purchasing additional long-term care insurance, if they can afford the premium.

    C. Darcie's parents most likely will need additional long-term care insurance, but they can easily wait 10 years before purchasing additional coverage.

    D. Darcie's parents most likely will need additional long-term care insurance but they are too old to be underwritten for a new policy.

10. What is the total amount Greg will receive from his father's annuity?

(Topic 27)

    A. $0

    B. $10,000

    C. $40,000

    D. $60,000

11. What amount did Greg's father have to report as income related to the annuity payment he received in the year he died?

(Topic 27)

    A. $0

    B. $2,000

    C. $3,000

    D. $5,000

12. Which of the following is the best recommendation Danielle can give Greg regarding his life insurance?

(Topic 28)

    A. He should not convert the insurance policy.

    B. He should convert to a whole life insurance policy.

    C. He should convert to a deferred annuity.

    D. He should convert to a variable life insurance policy.

13. If Greg predeceases Darcie by 15 days, which of the following is correct concerning Darcie's life insurance?

(Topic 28)

   A. The death benefit will be paid out to the Bypass Trust established under Greg's will.

   B. The death benefit will be paid out to the Bypass Trust established under Darcie's will.

   C. The death benefit will be paid out to the QTIP Trust established under Darcie's will.

   D. The death benefit will be paid out directly to John and Sheila.

14. How much must Greg report as taxable income related to the MEC distribution?

(Topic 28B)

   A. $0

   B. $100,000

   C. $150,000

   D. $250,000

15. How much must Greg report as taxable income related to the life insurance distribution?

(Topic 28B)

   A. $0

   B. $200,000

   C. $300,000

   D. $500,000

16. What type of buy-sell agreement should Danielle recommend to Greg and David?

(Topic 29)

   A. A one way cross-purchase

   B. A two way cross-purchase

   C. An entity redemption

   D. A stock redemption

17. Which of the following correctly describes the ramifications of David purchasing Greg's convertible term insurance for purposes of the buy-sell agreement?

(Topic 29)

   A. David will be able to deduct the premium payments as a business expense.

   B. David will receive the death benefits as tax-free income when Greg dies.

   C. David will have to pay income taxes on the death benefits that exceed his basis.

   D. David meets the exception to the transfer-for-value rules as a shareholder.

18. Which of the following expenses should the Connors consider when determining the amount of life insurance coverage they should carry?

(Topic 30)

(1) Education fund
(2) Mortgage redemption fund
(3) Readjustment period income
(4) Special needs fund

    A. (1) and (2)
    B. (3) and (4)
    C. (1), (2), and (3)
    D. (1), (2), (3), and (4)

19. Which of the following insurance policies should the Connors consider purchasing first?

(Topic 30)

    A. Business overhead expense insurance
    B. Split-dollar life insurance
    C. Unemployment insurance
    D. Umbrella insurance

20. What policy would be the most appropriate vehicle for a buy-sell agreement between Greg and David?

(Topic 31)

    A. 15 year term life insurance
    B. Renewable term life insurance
    C. Universal life insurance
    D. Variable universal life insurance

21. Which of the following would be the most appropriate vehicle for providing life insurance coverage for John and Sheila?

(Topic 31)

    A. 10 year term life insurance
    B. 20 year term life insurance
    C. Whole life insurance
    D. Deferred annuity

22. How much will the insurance company pay related to the fire caused by John and Eli?

(Topic 32)

    A. $64,625
    B. $65,525
    C. $74,000
    D. $75,000

23. How much will the insurance company pay related to the automobile accident caused by Greg?

(Topic 32)

    A. $125,000
    B. $275,000
    C. $290,000
    D. $405,000

24. Which of the following statements is correct about the homeowners insurance coverage the Connors have related to the hurricane?

(Topic 32)

    A. The insurance company will not cover the expense as there was no actual damage to the Connors' home.
    B. The HO-3 policy does not pay for this type of expense.
    C. The Connors would need hurricane insurance in order for the loss to be covered.
    D. The Connors' insurance claim will be approved.

CONNOR CASE
ANSWERS AND EXPLANATIONS

1. **D** is the answer. The insurance company is stepping into the soccer coach's place under the principle of subrogation in order to be reimbursed for their expense to fix the windshield and clean up the car. Adverse selection is the tendency of those individuals most likely to incur a loss to seek to obtain coverage. Law of large numbers specifies that the more units exposed to loss, the greater will be the predictability of future loss results. Risk reduction occurs when the client does something to reduce the loss frequency or loss severity.

2. **C** is the answer. The Connors installed burglary-proof windows which is a technique to reduce risk. An example of risk avoidance would be not putting a swimming pool in the backyard. An example of risk retention would be an increase in the deductible on a homeowner's policy. An example of risk transfer is purchasing insurance to cover the potential loss.

3. **A** is the answer. Greg's first priority should be to create a buy-sell agreement with David and purchase the life insurance policy on David. Greg currently has $500,000 of convertible life insurance. He also has a disability policy and retirement accounts.

4. **C** is the answer. Darcie only has $50,000 of liability coverage per person up to $100,000 per accident on her automobile policy. Increasing these amounts should be treated as her top priority. She has $100,000 of coverage on her property which is its current value. She also has $500,000 of life insurance already in place that can be converted to a permanent policy. She has $500,000 of liability coverage on her home. Although she might also want to increase her home liability coverage, her top priority should be to increase the automobile coverage.

5. **B** is the answer. Sheila incurred a total of $12,500 in medical bills ($10,000 + $2,000 + $500). The insurance policy requires the Connors to pay a $2,000 deductible and then 20% of any additional charges up to a total $5,000 out-of-pocket for the year. This means the Connors will pay the first $2,000 plus 20% of the remaining $10,500 which is $2,100 for a total of $4,100. The insurance company will pay the $8,400 difference.

6. **A** is the answer. The company payments of the health insurance premiums are nontaxable. As a result, Greg does not need to include the $200 per month in his income. **Editor's Note:** The business is currently structured as a C-corporation, but the planner has recommended that they make an S-corp. election. If the clients follow that advice, Greg should be aware that, as a greater-than-2% S-corp. owner, he will have the medical insurance premiums that were paid by the corporation included on his W-2, but will then be permitted to take an above-the-line deduction for 100% of those premiums on his tax return.

7. C is the answer. The best advice is to replace the policy with one that has a longer benefit period as Greg is only 47 years old. If he were injured today and unable to work, he would only receive benefits for 5 years which would be until age 53. He might also want to consider adding the inflation rider but the longer benefit period would provide a larger benefit. Greg should not replace the policy with one that uses the "educated and trained for" definition of disability as he already has a split definition policy which provides the "own occupation" definition for a certain period of years and then the "educated and trained for" definition. Greg should not have his company pay the premiums with pretax dollars as that would cause the benefits to be taxable. The current payment structure will allow Greg to receive the disability benefits on a tax free basis.

8. D is the answer. Darcie is currently not working so she is not eligible to purchase a disability policy as the disability benefits are always based on a percentage of current earnings.

9. B is the answer. Although Darcie's parents are in their mid 70s, most insurance companies will issue new long-term care policies as long as the insured is under age 80 (depending on the insurance company). As a result, they should not wait 10 years before deciding to purchase additional coverage. Their current policy only provides benefits of $100 per day which most likely will not cover most of their daily expenses especially since there is no mention of an inflation rider in the fact pattern.

10. C is the answer. His father's annuity had a 10-year period certain feature. His father received two $5,000 yearly payments before passing away. As the heir named on the beneficiary designation form, Greg will receive the 8 additional guaranteed payments under the period certain feature. Thus, he will receive $40,000 ($5,000 x 8).

11. B is the answer. Greg's father paid $60,000 for the deferred annuity and expected to receive 20 payments of $5,000 each for a total of $100,000. As a result, Greg's father would treat a portion of each annuity payment as a nontaxable return of basis using the following exclusion percentage formula: Exclusion % = Basis/expected return, which is 60% ($60,000/$100,000) in this case. This means that $3,000 (60% of the $5,000 payment) is treated as a tax free return of basis. The other $2,000 is treated as taxable income.

12. B is the answer. Greg has a $500,000 convertible term life insurance policy. Since the term insurance is not a permanent solution, Greg should convert the policy to a permanent product. However, term insurance can typically only be converted to a whole life insurance policy or an endowment policy, although some insurance companies now allow conversion to universal life insurance as well. Term insurance cannot be converted to a deferred annuity, as there is no cash value in a term policy.

13. D is the answer. Greg is the primary beneficiary of Darcie's life insurance policy and John and Sheila are named as contingent beneficiaries. As a result, the death benefits will be paid out directly to John and Sheila. The life insurance proceeds are excluded from Darcie's probate estate as the proceeds pass under contract to the named beneficiaries.

14. A is the answer. The MEC distribution is a death benefit distribution. As a result, the entire distribution is income tax free.

15. A is the answer. The death benefit of a life insurance policy is always income tax free to the beneficiary regardless of whether the insurance premiums were paid by the insured or the insured's employer.

16. B is the answer. Greg and David are both relatively young, but they have disproportionate ownership in the business. The cross-purchase arrangement works best due to the different ownership percentages as it is more equitable for both shareholders. It needs to be a two way cross-purchase as both Greg and David are interested in buying out the other shareholder. A one way buy sell agreement is used if only one party owns the stock and a second party is agreeing to purchase the stock (e.g., father owns 100% of the stock and the son will buy out the father). An entity redemption and a stock redemption are the same thing where the company buys out the deceased shareholder's stock. The entity redemption works best when there are multiple owners or disproportionate ownership by the oldest owner.

17. C is the answer. David tripped the transfer-for-value rules when he purchased Greg's life insurance policy because the business is a corporation. As a result, David will have to pay income taxes on the amount of the death benefit that exceeds his basis. If David and Greg were both partners in a partnership, David would have been able to avoid the transfer-for-value rules.

18. D is the answer. If the Connors should die today, they would want money to fund their children's education, repay their mortgage, provide income to the family while they adjust their living expenses and lifestyles, and they need special funds for the business.

19. D is the answer. The Connors could use an umbrella policy to provide them with expanded liability protection. The T-shirt business already has overhead expense insurance and unemployment insurance. The split-dollar life insurance requires the business to pay all or a portion of the life insurance premiums on a policy. The income tax ramifications of the split-dollar plans are no longer as favorable for the taxpayer. Moreover, this is probably not the first policy they should purchase because the umbrella policy is a better choice.

20. C is the answer. A buy-sell agreement should be funded with a permanent life insurance product in order to have a build-up in the cash value of the policy. However, a variable universal life insurance policy is not the best answer as the cash value will depend on the investment performance of the assets selected by the insured. Thus, the universal life insurance policy is the best option of the four answers provided.

21. C is the answer. John and Sheila are both children. As a result, the premiums on a whole life policy would be reasonable. The term policies would not provide any coverage when they are most likely to need it. A deferred annuity does not make sense given their young ages.

22. C is the answer. The Connors' home is worth $420,000 after reducing the $500,000 value by the $80,000 of land. The Connors carry $350,000 of insurance on their home which exceeds the 80% threshold to avoid a reduction in benefits ($420,000 x 80% = $336,000). As a result, their homeowners policy will pay the $75,000 claim for the fire damage less the $1,000 deductible for a total of $74,000.

23. A is the answer. Greg's insurance company will pay up to $50,000 per person but no more than $100,000 per accident plus $25,000 in property damage. The total claims against Greg are $350,000 for liability and $55,000 for property. His insurance company will pay only the $125,000 as limited by his policy.

24. D is the answer. The Connors had to evacuate ahead of a hurricane. Part D of their homeowners' policy covers expenses of having to evacuate a home. As a result, the insurance claim will be approved. There is no separate hurricane insurance. The Connors already have the only two separate insurance policies, which are the earthquake and flood insurance policies.

SEIDELHOFER CASE

PERSONAL INFORMATION AND BACKGROUND

Maxwell and Margery Seidelhofer have had a roller coaster life. They started a bar and restaurant in a historic tavern but then lost it when the construction of a new highway forced them to move the tavern to an out-of-the-way location. They were successful with a flower shop for several years until a larger flower shop opened at the mall and took a substantial part of their business. They tried various jobs for several years while they were raising their children before trying their latest business venture – a dry cleaner, Mainstreet Cleaners. They became owners in the business with another couple and have been successful with the dry cleaning business, although it was slow going for them in the first couple of years. They have continued with the dry cleaning operation and recently celebrated their 7th year in operation. They are both on their second marriages, and Max has a son named JD from his previous marriage. Max and Margery have had two children together, Karen and Samuel. The Seidelhofers live in Indiana, Pennsylvania, which has remained the idyllic, small town America, just as it was when Jimmy Stewart lived there. They also own a farmhouse with 200 acres of farmland.

Maxwell celebrated his 59th birthday last week, and his wife gave him a present of a complete financial plan. Both Maxwell and Margery have wanted a complete financial plan for a long time, and Margery decided that it was time to do something while they were still riding on top. They collected a lot of family information for this meeting.

Name	Relationship	Age	Occupation	Health	Comments
Maxwell	Husband	59	Business owner	Good	Very involved with local sports teams
Margery	Wife	57	Manager	Good	Wants to have a candy shop
Karen	Daughter	26	Computer programmer	Excellent	Married; one child
Samuel	Son	23	Graphic artist	Excellent	Not married
JD	Son	35	Account manager	Excellent	Maxwell's son from his first marriage

Samuel is not married and is considering alternative careers. He is investigating the possibility of going back to business school and might apply to study at night. He would like to buy a car so he does not have to borrow his parents' or sister's car. Karen's daughter is eight months old, and Margery would like to take more time away from the dry cleaning business to spend with her granddaughter. Karen's husband, Steve Lee, has mentioned that they might be interested in buying the dry cleaning business in a few years.

During the past year, Maxwell contracted Lyme disease, probably from working in the fields at the farm. His doctor's bills were $250, and the tests and antibiotics to treat the disease were another $600. Margery recently had pneumonia that required hospitalization. Her doctor's fees were $2,500, and the hospital expenses were $5,000. She made a full recovery after a long period of bed rest and rehabilitation. Earlier in the year, Margery broke her finger at work, when the finger was caught in the clothes conveyor track. The cost of the doctor was $700, and X-rays and medical bills were $700.

Max's mother lives in a retirement home near Pittsburgh. Margery's parents live in the same house where she grew up but are considering custodial care for Margery's father, who is showing the first signs of Alzheimer's disease.

Max's brother lives in California. Margery's brother lives in New York and has two children. He would like to move out of the city and back to the farm. Max and Margery have been considering renting out 200 acres of their farmland to a local farmer, or they may sell it to Margery's brother. Margery's sister lives in Virginia and has three children. Max's son by his first marriage is a banker and lives in Baltimore.

GOALS AND OBJECTIVES

1. Max wants to retire in 7 years and move to a warmer climate, where there is spring training for a professional baseball team.
2. Margery wants to retire in 6 months and spend more time with her grandchild.
3. Max and Margery want to minimize gift and estate taxes.
4. They want to have $90,000 per year in today's dollars in retirement.
5. They want to buy an RV and travel around the western United States and Canada.
6. They would like to help pay for their grandchildren's college expenses.

INCOME TAX INFORMATION

Max and Margery had an adjusted gross income of $220,000 last year and paid $39,000 in taxes to the federal government. They anticipate their adjusted gross income this year will be $250,000. They are in the 28% marginal federal tax bracket for the current year.

RETIREMENT INFORMATION

Max and Margery are participants in the profit-sharing plan established at the dry cleaning business. The plan contributes up to 6% of participant payroll and is cross-tested. They are both fully vested in the plan. The other employee participants in the plan are generally several years younger than Max and Margery.

Max and Margery assume they will live for 30 years in retirement. They also assume a 3.5% inflation rate and a 6% rate of return on their investments in retirement.

EDUCATION INFORMATION

Max and Margery would like to set some money aside to help pay for their granddaughter's education. They want to give the grandchild the amount of money required for an education at the state university. For planning purposes, they assume that the current annual cost of an education at the university is $16,000 per year and that it will increase 5% per year. They would also like to be able to do the same for future grandchildren.

Margery would like to transfer money from her IRA into a 529 plan for Karen's child. Maxwell has agreed to gift-splitting for gift tax purposes.

ESTATE PLANNING INFORMATION

Max and Margery each have basic wills that leave everything to the surviving spouse. Max set up an irrevocable life insurance trust with a $100,000 variable life policy for his son from his first marriage. The policy recently lapsed due to nonpayment of premium.

As already mentioned, Max and Margery are considering making gifts to fund their grandchildren's education. They are also considering contributing their family farmhouse to a QPRT for the benefit of their children. Max anticipates the QPRT would terminate after 10 years. They have not yet made any taxable gifts.

BUSINESS INFORMATION

Maxwell is a 50% owner of the stock in the dry cleaning business, Mainstreet Cleaners. The corporation has not been valued recently, but the Seidelhofers have read about sales of similar businesses for $1.5 million. They would like some advice about planning for a sale of the business when they retire. The other stockholders at Mainstreet Cleaners would like to arrange for a buy-sell agreement. The other stockholders, Sarah Bukowsky and Olga Helmholz, are ages 42 and 38. They each own 25% of the stock. Maxwell would like to have a cross-purchase or entity buy-sell plan for his business interest and would transfer his existing life insurance policy to a person or entity that would be a party to the plan.

BROKERAGE ACCOUNT INFORMATION

Max and Margery have paid very little attention to their brokerage account. They have given their broker discretionary powers to trade in their account, and they receive confirmations and account statements from him. They contact him annually to review the results.

Max considers himself a moderately conservative investor, and Margery is conservative.

Name	Basis	FMV (End of Last Year)
U.S. Treasuries	$50,000	$56,600
Municipal bonds	$20,000	$24,600
S&P 500 Index Fund	$50,000	$57,200
Large-cap value fund	$33,000	$41,400
Mid-cap fund	$22,000	$30,300
Small-cap growth fund	$15,000	$22,500
Global growth fund	$45,000	$64,400
Total	**$235,000**	**$297,000**

Max has been considering rolling his IRA into a self-directed IRA so that he can invest in commodities. The IRAs are currently invested in a small-cap international fund.

ANNUITY INFORMATION

Maxwell purchased the life annuity 7 years ago for $50,000. It is invested in a balanced fund subaccount. Maxwell will begin receiving $4,700 annual benefits next year. His life expectancy will be 24 years at the time he starts receiving distributions.

Maxwell and Margery Seidelhofer
Projected Cash Flow
for the Current Year

Cash Inflows

Max's salary	$125,000
Margery's salary	75,000
Dividends – Mainstreet Cleaners stock	40,000
Investment income	Reinvested
Total	**$240,000**

Cash Outflows

Taxes (income, payroll, real estate)	$ 48,000
Lifestyle expenses	$130,000
Insurance premiums	$ 12,000
Savings	$ 24,000
Unknown	$ 26,000
Total	**$240,000**

Maxwell and Margery Seidelhofer
Statement of Financial Position
as of December 31st Last Year

ASSETS

Cash and Cash Equivalents

Checking account: JT	$ 26,000
Savings account: JT	$ 50,000
Life insurance cash value: H	$ 75,000
Life insurance cash value: W	$ 16,000
Total Cash and Cash Equivalents	$ 167,000

Invested Assets

Profit-sharing plan: H [1]	$ 123,000
Profit-sharing plan: W [2]	$ 94,000
IRA: H [3]	$ 121,000
IRA: W [4]	$ 141,000
Variable annuity: H [5]	$ 65,000
Mainstreet Cleaners stock: H	$ 750,000
Brokerage account: JT [6]	$ 297,000
Total Invested Assets	$1,591,000

Personal-Use Assets

Indiana home: JT [7]	$ 450,000
Farmhouse: JT [8]	$ 600,000
Baseball memorabilia collection: H [9]	$ 28,000
Jewelry: W	$ 41,000
Ford F-150 truck: H	$ 25,000
SUV: W	$ 33,000
Furniture and household items: JT	$ 100,000
Total Personal-Use Assets	$1,277,000

Total Assets   **$3,035,000**

LIABILITIES AND NET WORTH

Liabilities

Mortgage – Indiana home: JT [10]	$ 220,000
Credit card debt [11]	$ 7,000
Car loan [12]	$ 20,000
Total Liabilities	$ 247,000

Total Liabilities   **$ 247,000**

Net Worth   **$2,788,000**

Notes to the Financial Statements

H = Husband
W = Wife
JT = Joint tenancy

[1] Margery is the primary beneficiary. Karen and Samuel are the contingent beneficiaries.

[2] Maxwell is the primary beneficiary. Karen and Samuel are the contingent beneficiaries.

[3] Maxwell's parents are the primary beneficiaries. Maxwell was able to deduct all of his contributions.

[4] Margery's parents are the primary beneficiaries. Margery was able to deduct all of her contributions.

[5] See Annuity Information for account detail.

[6] See Brokerage Information for account detail.

[7] The land is worth $100,000. Their current basis is $350,000.

[8] The land is worth $450,000. Their current basis is $450,000.

[9] The memorabilia is valued at auction prices.

[10] There are 10 years remaining on the mortgage. The interest is fixed at 6.25%.

[11] The credit card carries a 6% interest rate for the next 24 months.

[12] This car loan has an 8% interest rate and will be paid off in 4 years.

INSURANCE INFORMATION

Life Insurance

Insured	Owner	Beneficiary	Face Amount	Type	Cash Value	Annual Premium	Notes
Maxwell	Maxwell	Margery	$250,000	Whole Life	$75,000	$2,200	Bought 25 years ago; loan taken for $5,000
Margery	Margery	Maxwell	$150,000	Universal Life	$16,000	$1,200	Bought 10 years ago
Maxwell	ILIT	JD	$100,000	Variable	Unknown	$1,000	Policy lapsed

Disability Insurance

Insured	Current Benefit Amount	Benefit Period	Inflation Rider	Premium	Notes
Maxwell*	$3,000/month	5 years	3% per year	$300/year	100% of premium paid by Maxwell

* Maxwell's disability income policy is guaranteed renewable and has a split definition of disability, a 60-day elimination period, and a cost-of-living adjustment rider. Maxwell is interested in increasing his protection for the disability risk.

Margery would like to get a disability policy that has a low premium and will pay her in the event that she is unable to work for a long period of time due to illness or injury.

Health Insurance

Insured	Plan Type	Deductible	Coinsurance	Stop-Loss	Premium
Maxwell	Major medical	$500	20%	$6,000 (includes deductible)	Paid by employer
Margery	Major medical	$500	20%	$6,000 (includes deductible)	Paid by employer
Karen	HMO	None ($10 copayment per visit)	N/A	N/A	Paid by employer
Samuel	None	N/A	N/A	N/A	None

Long-Term Care Insurance

Insured	Current Benefit Amount	Benefit Period	Inflation Rider	Premium	Date of Issue
Maxwell	$150/day*	3 years	5% simple	$700/year	8 years ago
Margery	$150/day*	3 years	5% simple	$700/year	8 years ago

* Maxwell and Margery have both purchased qualified long-term care policies that have a waiting period of 100 days.

Homeowners Insurance

Type	Dwelling Amount	Contents Coverage	Liability	Premium
HO-3 (Indiana home)	$450,000	$150,000 ACV	$1,000,000	$1,500/year
HO-3 (Farmhouse)	$600,000	$100,000 ACV	$1,000,000	$1,200/year

Automobile Insurance

Vehicle	Type	Liability Limits	Collision	Comprehensive (Other-Than-Collision)	Premium
Maxwell's F-150	Personal auto policy	50/100/25	$500 broad form deductible	$250 deductible	$150/month
Margery's SUV	Personal auto policy	50/100/25	$500 broad form deductible	$250 deductible	$200/month
Karen's Passat	Personal Auto Policy	50/100/25	$500 broad form deductible	$500 deductible	$200 month

Mainstreet Cleaners carries a businessowners' policy with the limits recommended by its insurance broker and also has workers' compensation and employers' liability coverage. Mainstreet Cleaners covers its employees under a major medical insurance policy.

SEIDELHOFER CASE
APPLICATION QUESTIONS

1. Which of the following members of the Seidelhofer family are using the risk management technique of avoidance for the "pure" risk of loss from first-party automobile property damage?

(Topic 22)

A. Maxwell
B. Margery
C. Karen
D. Samuel

2. Which of the following statements best describes the principle of risk and insurance that applies to Margery Seidelhofer's disability income exposure?

(Topic 22)

A. Margery is not an insurable risk because her losses will not be definite in amount when she cares for her grandchild.
B. Margery can continue retention because loss severity is likely to be low while caring for her grandchild.
C. Margery can continue to self-insure through her employer while caring for her grandchild.
D. Margery's insurance transfer for this exposure can be continued when she stops working.

3. If the Seidelhofers rent out farmland to a local farmer, which of the following risk management techniques would be most appropriate for their liability exposure for this land?

(Topic 22)

A. None, they are already insured under their homeowners policy.
B. Retention
C. Additional limits on their homeowners policy
D. Noninsurance transfer

4. Which of the following loss exposures is in most need of attention by Maxwell?

(Topic 23)

A. Auto liability
B. Poor health
C. Business liability
D. Personal property

5. Of the following risk exposures, which should present Margery with the most concern about her coverage?

(Topic 23)

    A. Unemployment
    B. Poor health
    C. Death
    D. Negligence liability

6. What amount will Margery Seidelhofer receive in reimbursement from her health insurance for medical expenses this year?

(Topic 24)

    A. $3,580
    B. $5,600
    C. $6,000
    D. $6,720

7. Based on the medical expenses incurred in the past year by Maxwell and Margery Seidelhofer, which type of health insurance plan would provide benefits with the least out-of-pocket expense to them?

(Topic 24)

    A. Maxwell's coverage
    B. Karen's coverage
    C. Samuel's coverage
    D. Comprehensive major medical policy

8. Which of the following statements concerning the income tax treatment of Maxwell's disability income insurance policy is correct?

(Topic 25)

    A. Maxwell will not have to report any benefit payments as taxable income.
    B. If Maxwell uses the benefits to pay for business overhead, he can deduct the premiums.
    C. If Maxwell does not use the benefits for business expenses, he will have to report the benefit payments as taxable income.
    D. Maxwell can deduct a portion of the premiums, whether he uses the benefits for business expenses or not.

9. Which of the following recommendations to Maxwell concerning his disability income policy is the most important?

(Topic 25)

A. Change the definition of disability to any occupation.
B. Change the benefit period to 10 years.
C. Change the elimination period to 90 days.
D. Change the renewal to noncancellable.

10. Which of the following statements concerning the Seidelhofers' long-term care insurance coverage is correct?

(Topic 26)

A. Maxwell and Margery will not have cash surrender values when they retire.
B. Maxwell and Margery cannot deduct the premiums for their policies.
C. Maxwell and Margery should add an inflation protection rider for their benefit payments.
D. Maxwell and Margery are overinsured for long-term care because their coverage will reduce Medicare and Medicaid payments.

11. Which of the following options would be the least expensive way for the Seidelhofers to deal with the possibility that long-term care costs may exceed their coverage?

(Topic 26)

A. Change their long-term care coverage to provide lifetime benefit periods.
B. Increase their long-term care coverage to $250 per day.
C. Add an accelerated benefits rider to their life insurance policies.
D. Add custodial and home health care benefits to their medical insurance coverage.

12. What federal income taxes will Maxwell owe next year on the annuity payments?

(Topic 27)

A. $583
B. $733
C. $995
D. $2,617

13. If Maxwell requested a distribution of $20,000 from the variable annuity today, what additional income taxes would he need to pay for this transaction?

(Topic 27)

A. $4,200
B. $4,620
C. $5,700
D. $7,600

14. In the event that Maxwell predeceases Margery, how will the proceeds of her life insurance policy be paid?

(Topic 28)

    A. To her primary beneficiary
    B. To her contingent beneficiaries
    C. By intestacy
    D. By will to her children

15. Which of the following statements describes the major drawback to Maxwell of replacing his whole life insurance policy?

(Topic 28)

    A. Mortality costs will be reduced.
    B. The incontestability clause will be renewed.
    C. Dividends will be reduced.
    D. The policy can only be reinstated except with special permission of the insurer.

16. How much can Margery withdraw from her universal life policy without income tax consequences?

(Topic 28B)

    A. $0
    B. $12,000
    C. $16,000
    D. $150,000

17. If Maxwell surrenders his life insurance policy for its cash value, what will he report for income tax purposes?

(Topic 28B)

    A. $20,000 capital gain
    B. $20,000 ordinary income
    C. $25,000 capital gain
    D. $25,000 ordinary income

18. Which of the following persons could acquire Maxwell's policy as part of the Mainstreet Cleaners buy-sell agreement and not be subject to the transfer-for-value rule?

(Topic 29)

(1) Olga Helmholz
(2) Steve Lee
(3) Mainstreet Cleaners
(4) Karen Lee

    A. (3) only
    B. (1) and (3) only
    C. (2) and (4) only
    D. (1), (2), (3), and (4)

19. Which of the following statements concerning a buy-sell agreement for the Seidelhofers' business interest in Mainstreet Cleaners is correct?

(Topic 29)

    A. A cross-purchase agreement will be preferred because there are many owners.
    B. A cross-purchase agreement will be preferred by the Seidelhofers due to the differences in age and ownership interests.
    C. An entity agreement will be preferred if the business will be sold by the surviving owners soon after a redemption under the agreement.
    D. An entity agreement will be preferred by the Seidelhofers due to the corporation's lower tax bracket.

20. In determining the personal life insurance needs for the Seidelhofers under a financial needs analysis, the amount of Maxwell's current life insurance is most likely based on which of the following future needs?

(Topic 30)

    A. A mortgage redemption fund
    B. A life income supplement for the surviving spouse
    C. An education fund
    D. A special-needs fund for liquidating a business interest

21. Under a rule of thumb for the human life value approach, Maxwell would need to purchase at least how much additional life insurance?

(Topic 30)

    A. $0
    B. $250,000
    C. $500,000
    D. $750,000

22. Which of the following life insurance policies would be most appropriate to recommend for the proposed buy-sell agreement for Mainstreet Cleaners?

(Topic 31)

    A. Whole life

    B. Yearly-renewable term life

    C. Variable life, invested in a growth subaccount

    D. Variable universal life, invested in an international subaccount

23. Which of the following life insurance policies would be most appropriate for the irrevocable life insurance trust for JD?

(Topic 31)

    A. A universal life policy

    B. A yearly-renewable term life policy

    C. A participating whole life policy

    D. A survivorship life policy

24. Which of the following statements concerning the property, casualty, and liability insurance coverage for Maxwell and Margery Seidelhofer is most likely correct?

(Topic 32)

    A. They are overinsured for property loss coverage on their homes.

    B. They have adequate personal liability coverage.

    C. They have inadequate first-party property loss coverage for their cars.

    D. They have inadequate coverage for business activities conducted at home.

25. Which of the following recommendations is most appropriate for the Seidelhofers' property, casualty, and liability insurance program?

(Topic 32)

    A. They should drop collision and comprehensive coverage on their lower-value car and increase their deductibles.

    B. They should add uninsured motorists coverage to their auto policies and inflation guard endorsements to their homeowners policies.

    C. They should add a $1 million umbrella liability policy, reduce their homeowners liability limits, and increase their auto liability limits.

    D. They should change their homeowners policies from broad form coverage to open-perils coverage on their dwellings.

SEIDELHOFER CASE
ANSWERS AND EXPLANATIONS

1. D is the answer. Samuel does not own a car, so he does not have exposure to the risk of loss from damage to an automobile owned by him. The other members of the family own cars and are insured for the loss from damage to their cars.

2. B is the answer. When Margery leaves her employment to care for her grandchild, the loss severity from the disability income exposure will be reduced. A disability will not cause her to lose the income from her employment. Margery will still be an insurable risk because she is still capable of working and earning income. Margery's disability income exposure is not currently self-insured by her employer, nor is it insured at all.

3. D is the answer. The Seidelhofer homeowners policy excludes business activities, such as renting land, so they do not have coverage for the rental activity. Additional limits would not change the exclusion of coverage. They can elect retention, but a more effective risk management technique for this activity is a noninsurance transfer. They can require the tenant to assume the liability risk for losses occurring on the property while the tenant is renting it. The tenant can be required to accept all liability and to hold the Seidelhofers harmless. The lease could even require the tenant to obtain insurance naming the Seidelhofers as additional insureds.

4. A is the answer. Maxwell has only minimum automobile liability coverage and should obtain increased limits. Maxwell has adequate health insurance, and Mainstreet Cleaners has business liability coverage in its businessowners policy. Maxwell's personal property is adequately insured through homeowners policies.

5. D is the answer. Margery has only the minimum coverage for liability in the event that she is negligent in the operation of an automobile. She needs the additional protection of increased limits. She cannot insure unemployment, and she has adequate health insurance. Her life insurance may or may not be adequate.

6. B is the answer. Margery's pneumonia treatment cost $7,500. Her deductible is $500, and her coinsurance is 20% of the remaining $7,000. She will pay $500 + $1,400 = $1,900, so the insurer will pay $7,500 − $1,900 = $5,600. The broken finger occurred at work, so it will be covered by workers' compensation.

7. B is the answer. With an HMO plan like Karen's, the Seidelhofers would have had out-of-pocket expenses for the copayments for each visit, but they would not have had any coinsurance requirement. The Seidelhofers did not have a large number of visits, so the copayments would have been less than the deductibles under the major medical or comprehensive major medical policies.

8. A is the answer. Since Maxwell owns the policy and pays the premiums, the benefits will be received free of income tax. The premiums are not deductible, so the benefits are not taxable.

9. D is the answer. Maxwell's policy is currently guaranteed renewable, which means that the insurer can increase the premiums. A noncancellable policy means that the contract will stay in force, and the insurer cannot increase premiums. The change in definition to any occupation is a more restrictive definition of disability and should not be recommended. The change in benefit period is not worthwhile because Maxwell is already 59 years of age and he wants to retire in 7 years. The change in elimination period will reduce his premiums but will also reduce his benefits.

10. A is the answer. The long-term care policies purchased by the Seidelhofers are qualified long-term care contracts, so they must meet certain requirements for income tax purposes. One of the requirements is that the policy not offer a cash surrender value. Since the policy is qualified, they can deduct their premiums. The policy already has an automatic inflation rider. D is an incorrect statement, as Medicare payments are not impacted by long-term care insurance coverage.

11. C is the answer. Adding accelerated benefits to their life insurance policies should not require any additional premium. The addition of lifetime benefit periods, additional coverages, and additional benefit amounts will increase premiums.

12. B is the answer. The expected return on the annuity is 24 years x $4,700 = $112,800. Maxwell's basis is $50,000. The exclusion percentage is $50,000/$112,800 = 44.33%. The excluded amount is (44.33%) x ($4,700) = $2,083. The taxable income is $4,700 – $2,083 = $2,617. Maxwell is in the 28% income tax bracket, so he will owe an additional $733. No penalty will be due because Maxwell will be 60 years of age next year.

13. C is the answer. Maxwell purchased the annuity for $50,000, and it has a current value of $65,000, so the annuity has earned $15,000. The tax rules require the earnings to be distributed first, so the $15,000 of earnings will be taxed as ordinary income. The additional $5,000 will be treated as a tax-free return of capital. Since Maxwell is younger than 59½, he will have to pay a penalty of 10% on the $15,000 distribution. Maxwell will owe 28% of the $15,000, or $4,200. The penalty is $1,500, so the total owed in taxes will be $5,700.

14. C is the answer. Margery has named Maxwell as her beneficiary. There is no contingent beneficiary, so if Maxwell predeceases Margery, the policy will be payable to her estate. Margery's will passes her estate to Maxwell. If he predeceases Margery, her will fails to dispose of the estate. The estate will pass by intestacy to Margery's heirs.

15. B is the answer. With a replacement policy, the incontestable clause starts anew. Maxwell has held his policy past the original contestable period, but with a replacement, the insurer under the new policy will have a new contestable period in which to challenge the validity of the policy. The reduction in mortality costs is not a drawback to Maxwell and may mean reduced premiums. Maxwell receives no dividends on his existing policy, so this is not a drawback of the replacement. D is an incorrect statement, as the whole life policy is being replaced rather than reinstated.

16. B is the answer. Margery can withdraw the amount of her premiums without income tax consequences. She has paid premiums of $1,200 for 10 years, so the total she has paid is $12,000.

17. D is the answer. In the surrender of a life insurance policy for its cash value, the owner must report the difference between the cash value and the premiums paid as ordinary income. Any policy loan is added to cash value. In this case, the cash value is $75,000 and there is a $5,000 loan, so the total cash value is $80,000. The premiums paid are $2,200 for 25 years, for a total of $55,000, so the ordinary income is $25,000.

18. A is the answer. The transfer-for-value rule does not apply if the purchaser is the insured, the insured's partner, the insured's partnership, or a corporation in which the insured is an officer or shareholder. Maxwell is a shareholder in Mainstreet Cleaners (a corporation), so the transfer-for-value rule will not apply if the policy is acquired by that entity.

19. B is the answer. A cross-purchase agreement will be preferred by the Seidelhofers because Maxwell is older and has a larger interest than the other owners. The entity agreement would be unfair to Maxwell because more premiums will be paid out of the company's earnings to buy his interest. If the business will be sold soon after a shareholder dies, the cross-purchase agreement is preferable because the surviving owners will have a higher cost basis, as their basis is increased by the purchase price. The surviving owners' basis is not increased with an entity agreement.

20. A is the answer. The payment of the home mortgage with the insurance proceeds will help reduce Margery's immediate income needs. Margery will not need a life income supplement for retirement because the Seidelhofers already have ample assets for retirement. Their children are grown, so they do not need an education fund. While liquidating the business may require some time and expense, the facts do not suggest that the expense will be great. The buy-sell agreement that is under consideration will remove these costs.

21. C is the answer. The rule of thumb for the human life value approach recommends 6 to 10 times the insured's annual income. Maxwell's annual income is $125,000, so the minimum required is 6 x $125,000 = $750,000. Since he has $250,000, he needs an additional $500,000.

22. A is the answer. Maxwell is a moderately conservative investor, so the variable life policies would be too aggressive. The whole life policy will guarantee that there will be cash value available for the sale of the business under the buy-sell agreement. Term insurance is not a permanent solution for the buy-sell agreement, and the premiums could get very expensive.

23. A is the answer. The universal life policy will help to avoid the problem of the policy lapsing for nonpayment of premium because the policy provides for flexible payment of premiums. The universal life policy will have cash values, and the premiums will probably be less than for the participating whole life policy. With a participating whole life policy, the policy will be owned by the trust, so dividends will be paid to the trustee and not to Maxwell.

24. A is the answer. Both of the Seidelhofers' homes are overinsured. The value of the Indiana home is $450,000, with a land value of $100,000, and the farmhouse is valued at $600,000, with the land value of $450,000. Both homes are insured at full value. The land will not be affected by fire or other insured perils. The Seidelhofers do not have adequate personal liability coverage when they operate a car. They have only minimum liability coverage under a PAP. Their physical damage coverage is adequate for the value of their cars. They do not conduct business activities at home, so they do not need additional coverage for business activities conducted at home.

25. C is the answer. The Seidelhofers do not have an umbrella liability policy but have $1 million of liability coverage under their homeowners policy. They should add the umbrella to cover larger liability losses for auto liability, as well as the additional coverage provided by the umbrella. The umbrella will require them to increase auto liability to specified minimums but will allow them to reduce the liability coverage on the homeowners policy. Their cars are not low enough in value to drop collision and comprehensive coverage, and their deductibles are not very low. The facts do not indicate that the Seidelhofers lack uninsured motorists coverage, and this coverage is required by most states. They do not need to add inflation guard to their homeowners policy since they are overinsured on the farmhouse. They do not need to change to open-perils coverage in the homeowners policy because they already have that coverage with an HO-3.

LOOMIS COMPANY CASE

The Adrian Loomis Company (ALCO) is a small wood products manufacturing corporation located in the suburbs of Denver, Colorado. The corporation has 32 employees, all between the ages of 19 and 53, with annual compensation between $12,000 and $80,000. Employee turnover is low, with several employees receiving their pins for fifteen years of service.

George Adrian is the principal stockholder of the 30-year-old business, with Frank Loomis, the only other stockholder, owning 40% of the stock. A profit-sharing plan was established six years ago, but the employees are unhappy because George and Frank have elected to make contributions to the plan only for three out of the six years the plan has been in existence. Some employees have asked if the profit-sharing plan could be replaced by a defined benefit pension plan. George and Frank would like to establish a nonqualified executive benefit plan that could be used to increase their own monthly retirement benefits without having to increase the retirement benefits for any other employees. They also believe they could use the nonqualified plan to provide increased retirement and other benefits for three executives they would like to add to their management and marketing teams. These three people are highly qualified professionals who are being courted by some other companies that recognize the obvious talents of these people.

LOOMIS COMPANY CASE
APPLICATION QUESTIONS

Editor's Note: Questions 1, 2, and 3 are based on the assumption that ALCO establishes a non-qualified executive benefit plan.

1. Which one of the following statements concerning the basic characteristics of nonqualified deferred compensation plans is <u>not</u> correct?

(Topic 29)

A. The employer generally has no tax deduction until benefits are paid to the employee.

B. During his or her working years, the employee receives the same tax treatment for any employer contributions under a nonqualified plan as under a qualified plan.

C. Under both an unfunded plan and an informally funded plan, the only security or guarantee the employee has is the unsecured promise of the employer.

D. Under both a funded plan, and an informally funded plan, the IRS may likely rule that the employee is in constructive receipt of income unless there is a substantial risk of forfeiture.

E. Nonqualified plans are designed to be discriminatory.

2. Which one of the following statements concerning specific types of nonqualified deferred compensation plans is <u>not</u> correct?

(Topic 29)

A. A pure deferred compensation plan provides for a reduction in the employee's current compensation or a refusal of a raise.

B. Under the typical salary continuation plan, the employee promises to remain with the employer for a specified time period.

C. The employee has an unsecured debt against the company.

D. SERPs can be used to provide extra retirement benefits for selected employees.

E. Under the terms of the typical salary continuation plan, the employee gives up none of his or her current salary.

3. An employee of ALCO will avoid current receipt of taxable income under all the following circumstances, EXCEPT:

(Topic 29)

A. ALCO makes an irrevocable, but unfunded, promise to pay the employee $300 a month for life, beginning at age 65.

B. ALCO makes an unsecured promise to pay the employee $500 a month beginning at age 65 if the employee does not leave before age 65.

C. The employee is given a nonforfeitable right to $10,000 a year at age 67 to be paid out of ALCO's cash flow.

D. ALCO pays the annual premiums for an ordinary life policy which is assigned to the employee for the purpose of providing the employee with $200 a month after age 65.

E. An unfunded and an unsecured promise is made by ALCO to pay the employee $5,000 a month for as long as the employee lives.

4. If ALCO establishes a funded nonqualified deferred compensation plan, participating employees may still avoid current receipt of taxable income provided there is:

(Topic 29)

A. life insurance as the funding instrument.

B. substantial risk of forfeiture associated with the arrangement.

C. no guarantee associated with the employer's commitment.

D. assurance of nonforfeitability.

E. only common stock used for funding benefits.

LOOMIS COMPANY CASE
ANSWERS AND EXPLANATIONS

1. D is the answer. D is not a correct statement because there is little likelihood that under an informally funded plan, the IRS will rule there has been constructive receipt by the employee. As long as the specific asset remains a general asset of the corporation, there is no constructive receipt by the employee. A, B, C, and E are correct statements.

2. B is the answer. B is not a correct statement because the employee makes no promises or commitments. All promises and commitments are made by the employer. A, C, D, and E are correct statements.

3. D is the answer. D is an incorrect statement because the employee does not avoid current receipt of taxable income if the life insurance policy is assigned to the employee and the employer continues to pay the annual premiums. A, B, C, and E are correct statements.

4. B is the answer. If there is a substantial risk of benefit forfeiture, the employee avoids receipt of taxable income until the funding assets or their dollar values are actually distributed to the employee. None of the other options indicates that there is substantial risk of benefit forfeiture.

MICHAEL AND DIANA EASTMAN CASE

PERSONAL INFORMATION AND BACKGROUND

Michael, age 39, and Diana Eastman, age 38, live in Big City in the Midwest and have been married for 15 years. They have two children: a daughter, age 9, and a son, age 5. Their daughter attends public school, and their son is enrolled in a private kindergarten.

Michael Eastman

Michael is a 6% owner of Software Services, Inc., a company he started with several others. Michael is a vice president and is chairman of the benefits committee and has an annual salary of $250,000.

The company is closely held, has 15 employees, and has an estimated value of $10 million. Software Services, Inc. is in the highest corporate tax bracket. The company has several employee benefit plans, including a qualified plan for its employees, and wants to continue to reward its key employees and strengthen its corporate position in the industry. The 401(k) provides a safe harbor 4% nonelective contribution.

Five years ago, the company established a split-dollar insurance plan for the top five executives, using the collateral assignment method. With the new regulations for split-dollar plans, Michael knows that Software Services will discontinue their use, and yet the corporation wants to help employees secure adequate life insurance coverage to protect their families. Michael is exploring whether a Section 162 executive bonus plan would accomplish the company's goal.

Michael has elected the maximum dependent care as a Flexible Spending Account (FSA) benefit. The annual costs for his son are going to be $7,000, and his daughter's after-school program is $4,000 this year.

Diana Eastman

Diana is employed at Big City Bank and Trust Company. She is a vice president, has worked there for six years, and is to be promoted to senior vice president at the end of the year. Her salary has increased in $5,000 increments each year for the past four years. This year her salary is $90,000. She participates in the bank's 401(k) plan, and the bank matches up to 4% of salary and vests on a 2- to 6-year graded schedule.

With the promotion, Diana's salary will increase to $130,000, and she will receive 5,000 non-qualified stock options and 4,000 incentive stock options. Her plan is to exercise the options, when the price of the stock is $24, in five years and sell the stock at a price of $33 four years later. She plans to use the proceeds for her daughter's freshman year in college.

In keeping with the bank's policy of encouraging stock ownership, along with rewarding long- term employees, the bank's board of directors adopted a restricted stock plan. Diana was not eligible to participate in the restricted stock plan but will be eligible to receive shares when she receives her promotion. Diana is optimistic about the bank's stock and expects it to appreciate in value. She also expects the bank will stay in business for many years to come.

Now that Diana has secured her promotion, she feels protected by the golden parachute plan, which provides executives with 3.2 times their base amount of compensation, in the event of a takeover.

SOFTWARE SERVICES, INC.

Michael's company offers the following employee benefits:

Benefit	Key Provisions
Group term life insurance: Basic	Noncontributory Formula: One times salary Maximum: $200,000
Group term life insurance: Supplemental	Premium: Paid by employer Maximum: $1,000,000, including basic group term life insurance Available in the cafeteria plan
Dependent group term life insurance	Premium: Paid by employee Spousal coverage: Maximum $100,000 in $25,000 increments Children's coverage: $2,000 per child, up to age 19 (25 if a full-time student)
Sick pay	Two weeks
Short-term disability insurance	Duration: 26 weeks Benefit: 70% income replacement, up to a maximum weekly benefit of $1,500
Workers' compensation	Covers all absence due to work-related injury or illness
Long-term disability insurance: Basic	Definition of disability: Own occupation Elimination period: 180 days Benefit period: Until age 65 Percentage of income replacement: 60%, up to a maximum benefit of $3,000 per month Premium: Paid by employer Integrated with Social Security Plan is guaranteed renewable

Benefit	Key Provisions
Long-term disability insurance: Supplemental	Definition of disability: Own occupation Elimination period: 180 days Benefit period: Until age 65 Percentage of income replacement: 60%, up to $15,000 per month, including basic Not integrated with Social Security Michael has elected maximum supplemental LTD through the cafeteria plan, using after-tax contributions
Comprehensive major medical insurance	Premium: Paid by employer Coinsurance: 80% Coinsurance stop-loss limit (after deductible): $5,000 Initial annual deductible: $1,000 per person, $2,000 per family
Health Savings Account (HSA)	Under consideration
Cafeteria plan and Flexible Spending Account benefits	Benefit dollars furnished by employer: 4% of salary, with a maximum of $10,000 per year Eligible benefits: (1) Supplemental group life (2) Supplemental group long-term disability (pretax or after-tax) (3) Flexible Spending Account: $2,550 maximum for health care, plus $5,000 maximum for dependent care
Supplemental executive retirement plan	Covers all owner-employees Benefit is $50,000 per year for 10 years at normal retirement, age 65 Contains a clause requiring consultation to the company for five years after retirement, as well as a provision that the retiree will not compete with the company during that time Starting this year, new enrollees' benefits are integrated with Social Security

BIG CITY BANK AND TRUST COMPANY

Diana's company offers the following employee benefits:

Benefit	Key Provisions
Group term life insurance	Premiums: Paid by employer Benefit: 2 times annual income, up to $100,000
Group long-term disability insurance	Premiums: Paid by employer Benefit: 60% of salary, maximum of $5,000 per month Integrated with Social Security and workers' compensation
Group long-term care insurance	Selective plan for senior vice presidents and above Premiums: Paid by employer Benefit: $300 daily benefit Tax-qualified
Non-qualified stock options	Grant: Diana will receive options on 5,000 shares this year Exercise price: $16 per share (FMV at the date of grant) Exercise period: 10 years When vested: Two years
Incentive stock options	Grant: Diana will receive options on 4,000 shares this year Exercise price: $16 per share (FMV at the date of grant) Exercise period: 10 years When vested: Immediately
Restricted stock	Grant: Diana will receive 3,000 shares of restricted stock Grant price: $0 per share ($16 FMV at the date of grant) When vested: 5 years
Employee stock purchase program	Each participant has the right to buy shares at 95% of the FMV, up to a $10,000 maximum per year
Key person life insurance	Selective plan for senior vice presidents and above Benefit: 3 times annual salary Owner: Bank Beneficiary: Bank Premiums: Paid by the bank Employee can buy the policy at retirement for its cash value
Non-qualified deferred-compensation plan	Unfunded Eligibility: Senior vice president and above Benefits: $100,000 per year for 10 years at death, disability, or retirement
Golden parachute plan	Provides executives with 3.2 times their compensation, in the event of job loss due to a takeover

REAL ESTATE BUSINESS

Michael also owns an interest in a real estate business partnership with his sister Elizabeth and father William. His father and sister make the day-to-day business decisions, but Michael is very much involved in the decisions relating to property development. Michael's father is approaching 65 and wants Michael and his sister to continue the business. There are three employees in addition to the family. The family members have asked for your recommendation regarding insurance planning issues. Michael owns 20%, his sister owns 30%, and his father owns 50%.

The real estate business has business overhead disability insurance which is paid by the company. The policy covers normal business expenses for the office, including rent and utilities and employees' salaries for a time period of up to two years. The premiums are tax-deductible. Some of the family's goals have been to provide protection for William's income, to provide for overhead costs of the business for a reasonable length of time, as well as to control insurance costs.

ESTATE PLANNING INFORMATION

About five years ago, Michael and Diana each executed wills, placing the maximum amount that they can transfer free of estate taxes in a bypass trust, with the rest of their assets going into a QTIP trust. The surviving spouse is a discretionary beneficiary of the bypass trust. Their children are the remainder beneficiaries of the bypass and the QTIP trusts. Michael and Diana also executed nonspringing durable powers of attorney and living wills at the same time.

Statement of Financial Position
Michael and Diana Eastman
12/31 of Last Year

Assets			Liabilities	
Checking: JT	$	10,000	Credit cards	$ 12,000
Money market funds: JT		5,000	Car loans	9,000
Bond funds: JT		35,000	Mortgage[1]	127,000
Mutual funds: JT				
U.S. equity		150,000		
Small-cap		40,000		
Mid-cap		60,000		
Michael: 401(k)[2]		144,000		
Diana: 401(k)[3]		68,000		
Residence: JT		200,000		
Real estate partnership: H		125,000		
Software Services, Inc. stock: H		600,000		
Life insurance cash value: H		15,000		
Personal property: JT		75,000		
Automobiles: JT[4]		40,000		
TOTAL ASSETS		$1,567,000	LIABILITIES	$148,000
NET WORTH		**$1,419,000**		

H = Husband
W = Wife
JT = Joint tenancy with right of survivorship

---

[1] Original loan term is for 30 years at 6%.
[2] Diana is the primary beneficiary, and the children are contingent beneficiaries.
[3] Michael is the primary beneficiary, and the children are contingent beneficiaries.
[4] Michael's $25,000 SUV and Diana's $15,000 SUV.

Cash Flow Statement
Michael and Diana Eastman
for the Period 1/1 through 12/31
Annualized Projection

INFLOWS

Michael: Salary	$250,000
Diana: Salary	130,000
Interest income	Reinvested
Dividend income	Reinvested
Capital gains	Reinvested

TOTAL INFLOW **$380,000**

OUTFLOWS

Mortgage payment (P & I)	$ 18,900
Real estate taxes	4,000
Homeowners insurance	2,400
Federal income tax	68,000
State income tax	19,000
FICA	17,520
Life insurance premiums	1,200
Disability insurance premiums	2,700
Automobile insurance premiums	1,900
Michael's 401(k)	14,000
Diana's 401(k)	14,000
Food	6,500
Utilities	3,500
Telephone	1,700
Laundry	500
Clothing	7,500
Car expense	2,600
Car repairs	1,900
Home repair/maintenance	3,400
Charitable gifts	20,000
Entertainment	5,000
Vacations	3,000
Support/dependents	22,000
529 plan contributions	20,000
FSA contributions	5,000
Savings/investment	74,000
Unknown	39,780

TOTAL OUTFLOW **$380,000**

MICHAEL AND DIANA EASTMAN CASE
APPLICATION QUESTIONS

1. Which of the following is correct about Diana's non-qualified deferred-compensation plan once she is promoted to senior vice president?

(Topic 29)

   A. Michael would receive $100,000 per year for 10 years at Diana's death, taxed as ordinary income.
   B. If Diana became totally and permanently disabled, the benefits payable to Diana would reduce the group long-term disability plan she is otherwise entitled to receive.
   C. Since the plan is inherently discriminatory, it will have an adverse effect on any qualified plan established by the bank.
   D. Benefits payable to Diana in retirement will be eligible for long-term capital gains treatment.

2. What is the impact on Diana if the bank funds the non-qualified deferred-compensation plan with a rabbi trust?

(Topic 29)

   A. Immediate income taxation on any funds allocated to her account in the trust
   B. $100,000 ordinary income, due to constructive receipt
   C. No current impact
   D. Removal of the substantial risk of forfeiture

3. Which of the following is most likely a suitable financing method for Diana's non-qualified deferred-compensation plan?

(Topic 29)

   A. General revenues of the bank
   B. A secular trust to assure payments to executives on a tax-favored basis
   C. The golden parachute arrangement
   D. A universal life policy with a waiver-of-premium benefit, owned by the bank

4. Which of the following is a disadvantage to the Big City Bank and Trust Company's use of an annuity to informally fund the non-qualified deferred-compensation plan?

(Topic 29)

    A. The executives will incur current taxation on the amount of the annuity funding.

    B. The bank must pay corporate income tax on the annual increase in the annuity values.

    C. A lifetime income cannot be guaranteed because the corporation theoretically has perpetual life.

    D. The death benefit under the annuity is income-tax-free only to the extent of earnings within the annuity.

5. Which of the following is correct regarding Michael's SERP?

(Topic 29)

    A. If Michael fails to honor the consulting agreement, he will forfeit his benefits.

    B. If Michael dies, Diana is entitled to benefits, as long as she honors Michael's consulting agreement.

    C. Michael's benefit will be integrated with Social Security.

    D. The noncompete clause will not be enforced.

MICHAEL AND DIANA EASTMAN CASE
ANSWERS AND EXPLANATIONS

1. A is the answer. Big City Bank and Trust Company's non-qualified deferred-compensation (NQDC) plan provides, among other benefits, death benefits to Michael, which would be taxed as ordinary income. B is wrong because there is no indication of any integration with group long-term disability. C is wrong because NQDC plans are specifically designed (and allowed) to be discriminatory. D is wrong because the benefits are taxed as ordinary income.

2. C is the answer. In a rabbi trust, the assets are still available to the general creditors of the company. As a result, the rabbi trust continues to provide a substantial risk of forfeiture. A is wrong because of the lack of creditor protection. B is wrong because constructive receipt has not occurred. D is wrong because the substantial risk has not been removed.

3. D is the answer. The universal life policy, including the waiver-of-premium benefit, provides benefits in the event of death, disability, or retirement. A is wrong because the general revenues will quite likely be inadequate to fund the benefits projected. B is wrong because a secular trust involves immediate income taxation to the executive. C is wrong because the golden parachute would be operative only at the time of a takeover.

4. B is the answer. An annuity owned by a nonnatural person, like a corporation, loses the tax deferral of the annual interest or gains. A is wrong because it overstates the adverse impact of the annuity funding. C is wrong because the corporation is not the annuitant. D is wrong because the earnings will be income in respect of a decedent.

5. A is the answer. A provision in Michael's SERP is the requirement for ongoing consultation services. If Michael fails to honor the consulting agreement, he will forfeit his benefits. B is wrong because the consultation requirement is imposed on Michael, not Diana. C is wrong because the SERP is not integrated. D is wrong because there is no indication that the corporation will not enforce the noncompete provision.

GARY AND JUDY PARKER

PERSONAL INFORMATION AND BACKGROUND

Gary and Judy Parker live in Missouri and have been married for 19 years. They have 2 children, John and Julie Parker, ages 17 and 15, respectively. The Parkers own two cars and a five-bedroom home located at 1425 Clayton Road. Gary owns an independent insurance agency, Parker Risk Management, and Judy works as the vice president for Computer Solutions, a local computer consulting firm.

Judy's mother, Sandy Thompson, was recently diagnosed with cancer and is currently living with Gary and Judy. The Parkers also have a local college student, Tim Wilson, living with them. Gary's estranged aunt, Martha Ritchey, has recently reunited with Gary after 10 years.

Gary Parker
Gary is 47 years old and started Parker Risk Management (PRM) 12 years ago. Gary works as an insurance broker and has 4 employees working for him. He owns the building where Parker Risk Management is located. Frank Thomas, a friend of Gary's and a fellow insurance broker, recently approached Gary about combining their businesses. Frank is 55 years old and is planning to retire in ten years. Frank and Gary are currently in discussions about a buy-sell agreement. Frank's biggest concern is whether Gary will have enough money to buy the business in ten years when Frank wishes to retire. Gary is a moderately aggressive investor, while Frank is more conservative.

Judy Parker
Judy is 44 years old and has been the vice president for Computer Solutions for five years. Prior to working for Computer Solutions, Judy worked as an assistant vice president for Network Consultants. While Judy was working at Network Consultants, the company took out and paid the premiums on a key person life insurance policy on Judy. Network Consultants remains the owner and beneficiary of the policy on Judy's life, but Judy has the right to buy the policy for its cash value when she retires.

Sandy Thompson
Judy's mother Sandy is 71 years old and has been retired for 10 years. Prior to retirement, Sandy worked at the local courthouse as a stenographer. Sandy's husband Robert died two months ago. Sandy will receive $500,000 from Robert's life insurance proceeds. Sandy's main concern upon Robert's death was having enough money to pay her increasing medical bills. Five months ago, Sandy was diagnosed with lung cancer. Her health is quickly declining, and the doctors have given her 18 – 24 months to live.

Tim Wilson

Tim is 22 years old. Tim is a family friend and pays $200 per month to live with the Parkers. He has been living with the Parkers for four years, although he recently notified Gary and Judy that he would be moving out because he is getting married and buying a house. Tim recently graduated from college and started his first job. Tim's salary is $27,000 per year, and he is struggling with a limited budget. Tim just purchased a used car for $2,000. Tim has the minimum PAP liability limits of 25/50/10 and has an HO-2 policy for the new house.

Martha Ritchey

Gary's Aunt Martha is 64 years old. Twelve years ago, Martha won the lottery and collected a lump-sum payment of $800,000. Martha was wise with her investing and is now worth nearly $2,500,000. After winning the lottery, Martha moved to the Caribbean because too many people were asking her for money. Martha has recently moved back to the U.S. and reunited with her remaining family. She purchased a beachfront house in Florida for $800,000 and a $50,000 convertible. Martha also owns a small yacht that she purchased while in the Caribbean. Martha's father Robert Ritchey is 85 years old and in declining health. Martha is the sole source of support for her father. Robert applied for long-term care insurance two years ago, but he was unable to qualify for coverage.

John and Julie Parker

The Parkers estimate that the cost of educating John and Julie at the state university will be approximately $45,000 and $55,000, respectively.

Parker Risk Management

Parker Risk Management provides property, casualty, life, and health insurance for its clients. Gary also holds his Series 6 license for variable product sales and is considering the Series 7 licensing. PRM's life insurance needs analysis guideline is to use the human life value approach. ABC Insurance Company asked Gary to offer its life insurance products. Gary is interested in researching ABC's financial strength.

Gary and a colleague, Rick Moore, are presently in discussions about some business continuation planning for PRM. Gary would like Rick to buy PRM when Gary dies because Judy has no interest in running the business. Rick is willing to buy PRM, but he does not currently have the cash available to purchase PRM if something happened to Gary.

Gary was recently notified that Great Mutual Life Insurance Company, one of the companies where Gary places life insurance policies, has become insolvent.

PROPERTY AND CASUALTY INSURANCE POLICY INFORMATION

Car

100/300/50	Liability Limits
$10,000	Medical Payments
$250	Comprehensive Deductible
$500	Collision Deductible
100/300	Uninsured Motorists
100/300	Underinsured Motorists

Gary is the principal driver.

Truck

50/100/50	Liability Limits
$10,000	Medical Payments
50/100	Uninsured Motorists
50/100	Underinsured Motorists

Judy is the principal driver.

Boat

Boat Owner's Package
$2,000 franchise deductible for losses up to $10,000

Gary and Judy are also in the process of purchasing a 12-year-old car for their son John to drive as his primary vehicle. Gary and John have applied and paid for insurance, and the coverage has been bound.

1425 Clayton Road[1]

HO-3 Policy Form	$1,000 Deductible
$256,000	Dwelling
$25,600	Other Structures
$100,000	Liability
$1,000	Medical Payments
$2,000	Personal computer coverage on a valued basis[2]

Earthquake endorsement

---

[1]The replacement cost is $370,000.
[2]Depreciation on the computer equals $1,000.

LIFE INSURANCE POLICY INFORMATION

Gary Parker

Gary owns a universal life policy that he bought 12 years ago when he started Parker Risk Management. The face value of his policy is $500,000. The policy currently has $61,000 in cash value. Gary has paid $5,000 per year in annual premiums since the policy's inception. Judy is the primary irrevocable beneficiary, and John and

Julie are the contingent beneficiaries. Gary also owns a deferred annuity that will make payments for 10 years. Gary purchased this deferred annuity several years ago.[3] The annuity is currently worth $50,000, and annual payments are expected to be $6,000 per year starting on Gary's 62nd birthday. Gary is also shopping for some additional life insurance so that money would be available to fund college educations for John and Julie if something were to happen to Gary.

Judy Parker

Judy owns a whole life policy that she bought 8 years ago. The face value of her policy is $250,000. The policy currently has $1,200 in dividends and $5,500 in cash value. Judy has paid $1,000 per year in premiums since the policy's inception. Gary is the primary beneficiary of the policy. Judy also participates in a split-dollar insurance plan for executives at Computer Solutions. The plan was set up five years ago when Judy joined the company. Judy owns this policy, and Gary is the beneficiary.

Sandy Thompson[4]

Sandy owns a whole life policy that she purchased 32 years ago. The face value of her policy is $600,000, and the policy also has a waiver-of-premium rider before age 70. The policy currently has $525,000 in cash value. Sandy has paid $9,000 in annual premiums since the policy's inception. Judy is the primary beneficiary of the policy. Because Sandy is concerned about having enough money to pay her increasing medical bills, she is considering a viatical settlement. Greentree Investors has offered Sandy a viatical settlement payment of $540,000. In addition to pursuing the viatical settlement, Sandy also considered the accelerated benefits offered by her insurance company, but she was recently informed that she is ineligible for accelerated benefits.

Martha Ritchey

Martha has recently considered purchasing permanent life insurance. The factors most important to Martha are only paying premiums for the next 10 years and using her dividends to purchase additional life insurance.

---

[3]Annuity was purchased with a $35,000 lump-sum payment.
[4]Three months ago, Sandy applied for additional life insurance and was denied coverage.

Robert Ritchey

Martha's father Robert owns a whole life policy with a face value of $200,000. Robert has paid $4,000 in annual premiums since the policy's inception 10 years ago. The cash value in the policy is currently $30,000. Robert has recently been diagnosed with Parkinson's disease and is expected to live three more years. Robert has contacted a viatical settlement company about selling his life insurance policy for $140,000.

HEALTH INSURANCE POLICY INFORMATION

Gary Parker

Gary recently purchased an individual disability income policy that uses a split definition of disability. The policy has a 60-day elimination period and a benefit period of 5 years. Gary is also interested in purchasing long-term care insurance and has recently priced some policies. He is most interested in purchasing a long-term care policy with the lowest possible premiums and a short waiting period.

Judy Parker

Judy carries major medical coverage for the entire family through Computer Solutions. The family calendar-year deductible is $500, and the policy has an 80% coinsurance provision. The coinsurance stop-loss provision limits the Parker's total out-of-pocket cost per calendar year to $5,000 plus any deductibles. Judy has recently considered purchasing a disability income policy. Her primary concern is a reduction in her income due to total disability or a less-than-total disability and decreased work capacity. Her goal is to keep premiums relatively low.

Sandy Thompson

Sandy is currently receiving Medicare benefits, and she also has a Medicare supplement plan in place. Sandy has owned a disability policy for 20 years that has an own occupation definition of disability. Her policy provides a base benefit of $1,500 per month and a Social Security rider that will provide replacement of her projected $1,000 Social Security disability benefit for life. Ten years ago, Sandy lost the use of her right hand because it was shut in a car door. She was unable to resume her stenographer duties, so she retired from her position and filed for disability.

Four years ago, Sandy purchased a tax-qualified, guaranteed-renewable long-term care policy. Her policy provides a daily benefit amount of $100 and has a 3-year benefit period, an elimination period of 60 days, and an annual inflation protection endorsement of 5%, compounded annually.

Martha Ritchey

Martha currently carries a high-deductible health insurance plan and participates in a Health Savings Account. Martha's deductible and annual expenses equal $2,900. She contributes $200 per month to her HSA. In the current year, she received distributions of $2,200 from her HSA for qualified medical expenses. $2,000 of the distribution was the return of Martha's contributions; $200 of the distribution was earnings from her contributions.

Tim Wilson

Tim is currently shopping for a disability income insurance policy. Tim's main concerns are keeping his premiums low and level and having a policy that cannot be cancelled by the insurance company. Tim is also shopping for health insurance coverage because his employer does not provide this coverage. He would like broad health insurance coverage with low deductibles and co-pays, and he is willing to give up physician choice flexibility.

PERSONAL INSURANCE: LOSS HISTORY

September 2015 – John was driving the truck when he pulled into an intersection and hit another car. Two teenage girls were in the other car. One girl sustained injuries totaling $65,000, and the other girl sustained injuries totaling $23,000. The girls were driving a car that also sustained $12,000 in damage. John sustained injuries totaling $4,000, and damages to the truck totaled $3,000.

March 2015 – Judy's friend Elaine was visiting their home. As Elaine was walking down the front steps to leave, she tripped, fell down the stairs, and broke her ankle. Elaine's medical bills totaled $15,000.

January 2015 – Gary was driving the car when a deer jumped in front of it. Gary hit the deer, lost control of the car, and ran into a fence in a neighbor's yard. Damage to Gary's car from hitting the deer totaled $4,000, and damage to the fence totaled $2,500.

November 2014 – Judy caught pneumonia and was hospitalized for 3 weeks. Judy's hospital bill totaled $22,000.

June 2014 – Gary and Judy were hosting a barbeque in their backyard, when the fire in the barbeque pit escalated out of control and caused $64,000 of fire damage to their house. The neighbor's house also suffered damages of $10,000. The neighbor collected from his own homeowner's insurance policy for damages to his house. His insurer then brought action against Gary and Judy for repayment.

February 2014 – Julie was feeling ill and was admitted to the hospital. It was determined that she had appendicitis, and an appendectomy was performed. Julie's hospital bill totaled $7,000, including $100 for books Julie bought from the hospital gift shop.

December 2013 – An earthquake erupted in Missouri, and the Parker house was totally destroyed. Most of the Parkers' personal property was destroyed, including their personal computer. The reconstruction took 8 months, and temporary housing was found until all repairs were made. Temporary housing cost $2,000 per month. Damages totaled $230,000.

May 2013 – Julie was in the Parkers' detached garage, starting the lawn mower, when the lawn mower caught fire and burned the garage. Damages to the garage totaled $10,000.

April 2012 – Gary was boating at a nearby lake when he lost control of his boat and crashed the boat into a rock. Damages totaled $7,500.

COMMERCIAL INSURANCE POLICY INFORMATION

Parker Risk Management currently carries commercial property insurance coverage for $300,000 on the business building.[1] The policy is written on a replacement cost basis with an 80% coinsurance requirement and a $2,000 deductible. Gary also carries business income coverage[2] for PRM.

Parker Risk Management had carried an occurrence-basis general liability policy since the company's inception but switched to a claims-made basis policy in January 2015.

COMMERCIAL INSURANCE LOSS HISTORY AND INFORMATION

February 2015 – A former client at PRM, Millie Davis, filed a lawsuit against the company for a fall she sustained 2 years ago while walking out of the office. Millie sued to recover medical expenses recently incurred to get a hip replacement. Damages totaled $43,000.

January 2015 – Victor Kent, a client at PRM, applied for variable life insurance through PRM. Gary neglected to give Victor a prospectus as part of the sale.

January 2015 – Tony, an employee at PRM, was caught stealing insurance premiums from PRM. Damages totaled $3,000.

---

[1] The replacement cost for the building was determined to be $500,000.
[2] PRM's average gross income per day is $1,000, and average net income per day is $600.

Appendix A – Gary and Judy Parker Case

December 2014 – Tonya Watkins, a client at PRM, came into the office to apply for a $100,000 life insurance policy. Tonya's husband was named as the beneficiary. Gary was unsure of whether Tonya would meet underwriting requirements, so the policy was submitted without any premium. As Tonya was leaving PRM, she had a heart attack and died instantly.

September 2014 – Heather Roberts, a client at PRM, filed a $3,000 claim on a car she still had insured but had just sold to her neighbor. The insurance company denied the claim.

March 2014 – A candle was accidentally left burning at the office overnight, and one section of the office was completely destroyed by fire. PRM was unable to resume business operations for 6 business days. Damages to the building totaled $70,000. Gary also incurred expenses totaling $1,000 to minimize the shutdown period.

November 2013 – Doug Tillman, a client at PRM, was in the office paying his insurance premiums, when a ceiling tile fell and hit him on the head. He suffered a concussion, and damages totaled $6,000.

April 2013 – Kim Wilson, a 16-year-old student, purchased a life insurance policy on herself. Gary submitted the application and premium to the life insurance company, and the policy was issued.

GARY AND JUDY PARKER CASE
APPLICATION QUESTIONS

1. Following the June 2014 homeowners loss, the neighbor's insurance company demonstrated what principle?

(Topic 22)

A. Indemnity
B. Insurable interest
C. Adverse selection
D. Subrogation

2. Which of the following is a *risk reduction* technique Gary could use to help lower his insurance premiums?

(Topic 22)

A. Increase the deductible on his auto insurance policy.
B. Use hold-harmless agreements in leases.
C. Install a security system in his home.
D. Cover employee theft losses out of business income.

3. Which of the following is the best risk management technique for Tim's recent car purchase?

(Topic 22)

A. Insurance for the property and liability loss exposures
B. Avoidance for the property loss exposure and retention for the liability loss exposure
C. Retention for the property loss exposure and transfer for the liability loss exposure
D. Retention for the property loss exposure and reduction for the liability loss exposure

4. Which of the following is the best risk management technique for Martha's recent home purchase?

(Topic 22)

A. Reduction for the property loss exposure and insurance for the liability loss exposure
B. Retention for the property loss exposure and transfer for the liability loss exposure
C. Transfer for the property and liability loss exposures
D. Reduction for the property and liability loss exposures

5. Which of the following correctly describes the policy PRM wrote on Kim in April 2013?

(Topic 22)

    A. The policy never existed at all.

    B. The policy can be cancelled by either Kim or PRM.

    C. The policy is not enforceable because Kim is a minor.

    D. The policy is valid if both parties fulfill the policy requirements.

6. Which of the following risk exposures should Tim Wilson treat as a priority for insuring?

(Topic 23)

    A. Poor health

    B. Liability losses

    C. Unemployment

    D. Death

7. Which of the following is Gary Parker's biggest area of risk exposure?

(Topic 23)

    A. Death

    B. Disability

    C. Retirement

    D. Poor health

8. Which of the following loss exposures should most concern Martha?

(Topic 23)

    A. Property losses to her home

    B. Life insurance

    C. Long-term care costs for her father

    D. Liability losses from her car, home, and boat

9. For which coverage is Tim Wilson most likely to buy an amount of insurance based on the maximum possible loss from the risk exposure?

(Topic 23)

    A. Life insurance

    B. HO-2 property insurance

    C. PAP coverage

    D. Disability income insurance

10. If Gary wants to add a $1 million umbrella policy, where would he look in the policies providing the primary coverage to make sure there is no coverage gap?

(Topic 23)

   A. Declarations
   B. Insuring agreement
   C. Exclusions
   D. Conditions

11. What was the insurance company's payout for Julie's hospital stay in February 2014?

(Topic 24)

   A. $7,000
   B. $5,600
   C. $5,200
   D. $5,120

12. During Judy's November 2014 hospital stay, how much out-of-pocket expenses were incurred for that claim?

(Topic 24)

   A. $17,200
   B. $4,800
   C. $4,400
   D. $3,720

13. Which of the following claims would NOT be excluded under the Parkers' current medical insurance coverage?

(Topic 24)

   A. Eyeglasses for Julie
   B. Injuries Gary sustains during a trip to Italy
   C. John's cosmetic surgery after his auto accident
   D. Injuries related to a fall Judy has at work

14. What is the tax result of Martha's contributions to her Health Savings Account in the current year?

(Topic 24)

   A. $2,400 itemized deduction
   B. $2,400 above-the-line deduction
   C. $2,900 itemized deduction
   D. $2,900 above-the-line deduction

15. What is the tax result of Martha's distributions from her Health Savings Account in the current year?

(Topic 24)

    A. $0

    B. $200 ordinary income

    C. $200 capital gain

    D. $2,000 capital gain

16. Which of the following disability income policy provisions should be recommended to Judy based on her objectives?

(Topic 25)

    A. Own occupation definition of disability

    B. Partial disability benefits with no elimination period

    C. Residual disability benefits with a 90-day elimination period

    D. Any occupation definition of disability with a 1-year benefit period

17. How much disability income did Sandy receive from the insurance company when she injured her hand, assuming that she was receiving a Social Security disability benefit of $400?

(Topic 25)

    A. $0

    B. $1,500

    C. $2,100

    D. $2,500

18. Which of the following changes would help Gary lower his disability insurance premiums with the least effect on his coverage?

(Topic 25)

    A. Changing his definition of disability to an own occupation definition

    B. Changing his definition of disability to an any occupation definition

    C. Changing his benefit period to 10 years

    D. Changing his elimination period to 90 days

19. Which of the following disability income policies should be recommended to Tim?

(Topic 25)

    A. Any occupation definition of disability with a guaranteed renewable provision

    B. Any occupation definition of disability with a noncancelable provision

    C. Own occupation definition of disability with a noncancelable provision

    D. Split definition of disability with a guaranteed renewable provision

20. Which of the following statements is correct concerning the tax treatment of Sandy's disability income insurance policy?

(Topic 25)

    A. The benefit is free of income taxation.

    B. A portion of the benefit is taxable income.

    C. The total premiums paid can be deducted for income tax purposes.

    D. A portion of the premiums paid can be deducted for income tax purposes.

21. Which of the following long-term care policies would be most appropriate for Gary?

(Topic 26)

    A. $100 daily benefit with a two-year benefit period and a 90-day elimination period

    B. $250 daily benefit with a five-year benefit period and a 30-day elimination period

    C. $100 daily benefit with a one-year benefit period and a 30-day elimination period

    D. $150 daily benefit with a three-year benefit period and no elimination period

22. If Sandy is admitted for 180 days to a long-term care facility that charges $130/day, how much will Sandy's policy pay?

(Topic 26)

    A. $8,814

    B. $12,000

    C. $14,586

    D. $15,600

23. Sandy is concerned with reducing her long-term care policy premiums. Which of the following would help Sandy reduce her premiums?

(Topic 26)

    A. Changing her elimination period to 30 days

    B. Changing her benefit period to 4 years

    C. Changing her inflation protection to 4%

    D. Changing her daily benefit to $125

24. Which of the following statements is correct regarding Sandy's long-term care policy?

(Topic 26)

A. Upon admission to a long-term care facility, Sandy is immediately released from paying any further premiums.

B. Sandy must wait 60 days from the date the policy was written for her policy to be issued.

C. Sandy must be unable to perform two activities of daily living (ADL) for her coverage to begin.

D. Sandy's current daily benefit is $105.

25. Which of the following is the least suitable financing option Martha can use for Robert's long-term care expenses?

(Topic 26)

A. Taking an accelerated death benefit from his life insurance policy

B. Entering the viatical settlement agreement

C. Taking a life insurance policy loan against the cash value in his life insurance policy

D. Giving away his assets to qualify for Medicaid

26. Which of the following statements concerning the payout from Gary's annuity is correct?

(Topic 27)

A. Gary assumes the risk that the payout will not increase as expected.

B. Gary can be certain that the payout from the annuity will exceed the amount he invested in it.

C. If Gary lives past age 70, the payout from the annuity will end.

D. The annual payout would have been larger from a joint life annuity with Judy.

27. If Gary were to take a $25,000 withdrawal from his annuity this year, what would be his income tax consequences?

(Topic 27)

A. $16,500 ordinary income

B. $15,000 capital gain and $2,500 penalty

C. $15,000 ordinary income and $2,500 penalty

D. $15,000 ordinary income and $1,500 penalty

28. When Gary takes payments from his annuity, how much of his annual payment is includible in gross income?

(Topic 27)

   A. $1,000
   B. $2,500
   C. $3,500
   D. $5,000

29. When Gary reaches age 69, which of the following statements concerning the annuity payments will be correct?

(Topic 27)

   A. Gary will receive the same amount of taxable income annually as at age 62.
   B. The return of capital portion of the annuity payments will be discontinued.
   C. The annuity payments will consist entirely of taxable ordinary income.
   D. No more payments will be made from the annuity.

30. If Gary dies the day after his 65th birthday, which of the following statements concerning the annuity will be correct?

(Topic 27)

   A. Payments to a beneficiary will be tax-free if Judy is the beneficiary.
   B. Payments to a nonspousal beneficiary will consist entirely of ordinary income.
   C. Payments to a beneficiary will continue as during Gary's life and must continue for six years.
   D. Payments to a beneficiary will continue from the date of death for 10 years.

31. Which of the following is correct concerning Gary's current beneficiary designation on his life insurance policy?

(Topic 28)

   A. If Judy and the children are still living when Gary dies, the life insurance death benefit will be split evenly among them all.
   B. If Judy predeceases Gary, the children will receive the life insurance proceeds after Gary dies and must pay estate taxes on the proceeds.
   C. Gary has the right to assign his policy to whomever he wishes without the consent of any of his beneficiaries.
   D. If John predeceases Gary, Judy will receive the life insurance proceeds when Gary dies.

32. Which of the following life insurance policies should be recommended to Martha, given her objectives?

(Topic 28)

 A. 10-year term

 B. 10-year limited payment whole life policy with dividends purchasing paid-up additions

 C. 10-year limited payment whole life policy with dividends accumulating at interest

 D. Single-premium whole life policy with dividends accumulating at interest

33. Which settlement option should Sandy select for the life insurance proceeds from her husband Robert's life insurance policy?

(Topic 28)

 A. Lump-sum payment

 B. Straight life annuity

 C. Life annuity with refund feature

 D. Life annuity with period certain

34. When Sandy became disabled ten years ago, which of the following happened with her life insurance policy?

(Topic 28)

 A. The insurance company paid the death benefit to Sandy.

 B. The insurance company began making the premium payments.

 C. The insurance company surrendered the policy and paid Sandy her cash value.

 D. The insurance company cancelled the policy.

35. Gary has recently talked to Tim about purchasing life insurance. One policy Gary plans to propose is a universal life policy. Which of the following riders would be most appropriate for the universal life proposal Gary is preparing for Tim?

(Topic 28)

 A. Waiver-of-premium rider

 B. Long-term care rider

 C. Guaranteed insurability

 D. Accelerated death benefits

36. If Gary surrenders his life insurance policy for its cash value, what would he report on his income tax return?

(Topic 28B)

    A. $1,000 ordinary income
    B. $1,000 capital gain
    C. $3,500 ordinary income
    D. $3,500 capital gain

37. If Judy takes the dividends from her life insurance policy, what would she report on her income tax return?

(Topic 28B)

    A. $0
    B. $1,000 ordinary income
    C. $1,200 capital gain
    D. $1,200 ordinary income

38. What taxable gain must Robert Ritchey report if he sells his life insurance policy to the viatical settlement company?

(Topic 28B)

    A. $0
    B. $60,000
    C. $100,000
    D. $110,000

39. If Sandy elects to accept the viatical settlement offered by Greentree, what amount must Greentree report for tax purposes in the year of Sandy's death, ignoring future premiums paid by Greentree?

(Topic 28B)

    A. $15,000 ordinary income
    B. $15,000 capital gain
    C. $60,000 ordinary income
    D. $60,000 capital gain

40. If Sandy accepts the viatical settlement and lives past her life expectancy, what portion of the viatical settlement payment is taxable to Sandy?

(Topic 28B)

    A. The difference between the cash value in her policy and the payment from Greentree
    B. The entire payment Sandy receives from Greentree
    C. The cash value in her original policy
    D. None of it

41. If Judy Parker dies next year, which of the following statements is correct?

(Topic 29)

    A. The key person policy on her life is payable to Gary income-tax-free.

    B. Gary can buy the key person policy at Judy's death for its cash value.

    C. Network Consultants can deduct the premiums on the key person policy up to the first $50,000 of coverage.

    D. Network Consultants will receive the proceeds of the key person policy income-tax-free but possibly subject to the corporate alternative minimum tax.

42. If, at retirement, Judy buys the key person life insurance policy owned by Network Consultants, which of the following statements is correct?

(Topic 29)

    A. The policy will be transformed into a split-dollar arrangement.

    B. The purchase will constitute a transfer for value with adverse income tax consequences.

    C. Network Consultants must pay ordinary income tax on any gain from the sale.

    D. The death benefit will lose its income-tax-free character after the transfer, due to a lack of insurable interest.

43. Which of the following statements concerning the split-dollar arrangement that Computer Solutions offered to its executives is correct?

(Topic 29)

    A. The employer owns the cash value, but the death benefit minus the cash value is paid directly to the executive's beneficiary.

    B. All premiums are paid by the employer, and the cash value accrues to the employer, with the death benefit minus the cash value paid to the executive's beneficiary.

    C. The employer owns the cash value up to the amount of the premiums paid; the executive owns the cash value amounts over the cost of the premiums paid and is taxed on the cash value according to Table 2001.

    D. The executive owns the balance of the cash value over the premiums paid by the employer, and the employer receives from the death proceeds its premiums paid. The executive will have to include the deemed interest payments in taxable income each year.

44. Which of the following persons has a need for business overhead expense disability income insurance?

(Topic 29)

A. Gary Parker
B. Judy Parker
C. Tim Wilson
D. Robert Richey

45. If Gary uses cross-purchase buy-sell agreements with Frank Thomas and Rick Moore for business continuation planning, which of the following statements is correct?

(Topic 29)

A. The buy-sell agreement between Rick Moore and Gary is likely to be inequitable due to the different ages and interests of the parties.
B. When Frank retires, Rick will likely have to buy substantial additional life insurance coverage on Gary.
C. The agreement will require a large number of life insurance policies that will make it administratively burdensome.
D. An entity agreement would be preferable to a cross-purchase agreement in the event the merger occurs.

46. What is Gary NOT taking into consideration when he completes an insurance needs analysis with clients?

(Topic 30)

A. Determining expected income taxes for the client
B. Determining a reasonable discount rate
C. Determining personal family expenditure needs
D. Determining Social Security benefits expected

47. What would NOT be a benefit of Gary's using the capital retention approach to insurance needs analysis versus the current approach he uses?

(Topic 30)

A. Consideration of the capital needed to provide income
B. Consideration of other income sources available
C. Consideration of the dividends available in the policy
D. Consideration of when income would be needed by the beneficiaries

48. What could make Gary's life insurance needs analysis more comprehensive?

(Topic 30)

 A. Considering capital retention, if appropriate
 B. Considering the value of future earnings
 C. Considering tax expenditures
 D. Considering inflation and a reasonable discount rate

49. What business continuation strategy should be recommended to Gary and Rick for PRM?

(Topic 30)

 A. Gary and Rick should enter into a buy-sell agreement for PRM.
 B. Judy and Rick should enter into a buy-sell agreement for PRM.
 C. Judy should purchase life insurance on Rick and enter into a one-way buy-sell agreement.
 D. Rick should purchase life insurance on Gary and enter into a one-way buy-sell agreement.

50. What would NOT be a benefit of Gary's using the financial needs approach to life insurance needs analysis versus the current approach?

(Topic 30)

 A. Consideration of current personal wealth
 B. Consideration of other life insurance resources
 C. Consideration of total cash needs
 D. Consideration of the cash value generated by the policy

51. Gary is considering a purchase of a life insurance product for John and Julie. Which of the following would be most appropriate?

(Topic 31)

 A. 10-year term
 B. 30-year term
 C. Whole life
 D. Deferred annuity

52. Which of the following policies should Gary purchase to fulfill his additional life insurance needs?

(Topic 31)

 A. $100,000, 5-year term
 B. $100,000, 10-year term
 C. $150,000, universal life
 D. $200,000, yearly-renewable term

53. What policy would be the most appropriate vehicle for a buy-sell agreement between Gary and Frank?

(Topic 31)

    A. Variable universal life
    B. 10-year level term
    C. Universal life
    D. Yearly-renewable term

54. Tim has asked Gary for advice on what life insurance policy would be most appropriate, given Tim's financial situation. What policy is most suitable?

(Topic 31)

    A. Convertible term
    B. Variable life
    C. Universal life
    D. Whole life

55. Which of the following health insurance products should be recommended to Tim?

(Topic 31)

    A. Hospital-Surgical-Medical policy
    B. Major Medical Expense policy
    C. Preferred Provider Organization (PPO) policy
    D. Health Maintenance Organization (HMO) policy

56. What was the insurance company's payout to the Parkers for the May 2013 loss to the garage?

(Topic 32)

    A. $9,000, under Coverage A
    B. $9,000, under Coverage B
    C. $7,649, under Coverage A
    D. $7,649, under Coverage B

57. For the February 2015 liability claim filed against PRM, which commercial general liability policy will cover the claim?

(Topic 32)

    A. Claims-made policy
    B. Occurrence-basis policy
    C. Both claims-made and occurrence-basis policies
    D. Neither claims-made nor occurrence-basis policies

58. Regarding the September 2015 truck accident in which John sustained injuries totaling $4,000, what is the amount of the Parkers' out-of-pocket cost for John's medical bills?

(Topic 32)

A. $0
B. $500
C. $700
D. $1,200

59. Gary and Judy are considering the purchase of a personal umbrella liability policy. Which of the following underlying policies' liability coverage must be matched to the requirements stated in the umbrella policy in order to ensure there is no coverage gap?

(Topic 32)

(1) HO3 policy
(2) PAP
(3) Boat owner's policy
(4) Property insurance on the Parker Risk Management building

A. (1) and (2) only
B. (2) and (3) only
C. (1) and (4) only
D. (1), (2), and (3) only

60. Which of the following perils is not covered under the Parkers' homeowner policy?

(Topic 32)

(1) Flood
(2) Earthquake
(3) Mold

A. (1) only
B. (3) only
C. (1) and (3) only
D. (1), (2), and (3)

GARY AND JUDY PARKER CASE
ANSWERS AND EXPLANATIONS

1. D is the answer. The principle of subrogation allows the insurer that paid the claim to take over the rights of the insured claimant to receive reimbursement from the third party.

2. C is the answer. Risk reduction is a management technique that lowers probable loss frequency or probable loss severity. Installing a security system in his home is one way Gary could reduce his chance of loss and lower his insurance premiums.

3. C is the answer. The property loss exposure for Tim's car is low because the car is only worth $2,000, so Tim should retain that loss exposure. The liability and financial loss exposure for Tim is potentially very high, so insurance is appropriate for transferring the potential loss exposure.

4. C is the answer. The property loss exposure for Martha's home is high because the home is worth $800,000, so Martha's property loss exposure should be transferred to an insurance company. The liability loss exposure for Martha's home is also high because Martha has a high net worth, and liability losses arising from Martha's home could be financially devastating. The liability loss exposure should also be transferred to an insurance company.

5. D is the answer. A voidable policy is one that may be voided by only one of the parties. It is a binding contract unless the party with the right to void the policy elects to void it. Because Kim is a minor, she has the right to void the policy. If Kim does not elect to void the policy, it is a valid contract.

6. A is the answer. Poor health is one of Tim Wilson's most significant risk exposures, and his employer does not offer health insurance. In addition, the Affordable Care Act requires Tim to purchase minimum essential coverage or pay a penalty tax. Tim has liability insurance with the PAP and the HO-2. Unemployment insurance is provided through his work and cannot be purchased from a private insurer. Life insurance is not a priority for Tim's situation and budget. Tim can delay purchasing life insurance but should not delay getting health insurance.

7. C is the answer. Gary has life insurance, disability insurance, and major medical insurance through his wife's employer. He does not have a retirement plan, and he does not yet have long-term care insurance. He has an annuity that will pay benefits of $6,000 annually, so he needs some additional planning for his retirement years.

8. D is the answer. Martha's biggest asset is her net worth, and the major loss exposure Martha faces are liability losses from using her car, home, or yacht. Liability losses have virtually unlimited magnitude. Even the high cost of long-term care for Martha's father does not exceed her liability loss potential.

9. B is the answer. The HO-2 property insurance will insure Tim's new home, and he will be required to insure the house for its full value because the mortgagee will require protection for its mortgage. The maximum possible loss for Tim from the loss of the house is the value of the house. Tim is looking for disability insurance that is low cost so he will not be buying coverage for the maximum possible loss. The PAP coverage is at the minimum level for liability so Tim is not buying for protection against the maximum possible loss. He will probably not cover the car for collision since the car is worth only $2,000. There is no mention of Tim buying life insurance.

10. A is the answer. The umbrella policy requires a minimum amount of liability coverage in the underlying policies, such as $300,000, before the umbrella will pay for any losses. The amount of liability coverage provided in the underlying policies is listed in the declarations pages of those policies. If the amount of liability coverage in the PAP and homeowners is not up to the requirement of the umbrella policy, there will be a coverage gap.

11. D is the answer. The books purchased from the hospital gift shop are not a covered medical expense. The coinsurance clause indicates that the insurer pays 80% of the total covered medical expenses, $6,900, less the deductible, $500:

($6,900 – $500) x 80% = $5,120

Note that the deductible is subtracted first, before application of the coinsurance.

12. D is the answer. During Julie's hospital stay in February 2014, the Parkers paid their $500 calendar-year deductible, so no deductible is applied to this loss since it is in the same calendar year. Considering the 80% coinsurance requirement on their family medical plan, Judy would be responsible for $22,000 x 20% = $4,400. However, their policy's stop-loss limit means that $5,000 is the maximum out-of-pocket expenses the Parkers must incur in one calendar year. Since the out-of-pocket expenses for Julie's February 2014 hospital stay totaled $1,280 (excluding the $500 deductible). Judy is only required to pay $3,720 for her November 2014 hospital stay:

$1,280 + $3,720 = $5,000.

13. C is the answer. Major medical health insurance policies will cover cosmetic surgery when necessitated by injuries. A, B, and D are typical exclusions to major medical insurance policies.

14. B is the answer. Contributions to an HSA are an above-the-line deduction, and Martha is eligible to deduct all contributions made to her HSA account during the year.

15. A is the answer. Distributions from an HSA account are tax-free if used to pay for qualified medical expenses.

16. C is the answer. Residual disability benefits pay a portion of total disability benefits, based on a reduction in income due to a part-time return to work. By taking a 90-day elimination period, Judy can keep her costs a little lower. Answer A would have very high premiums. Answer B would be expensive with the absence of an elimination period. Answer D would be the least expensive, but the coverage would be highly restrictive.

17. C is the answer. Because Sandy was receiving a Social Security disability benefit of $400, the benefit she received from the insurance company under her Social Security rider was reduced by $400 ($1,500 + $1,000 – $400 = $2,100).

18. D is the answer. Taking a longer elimination period will cause Gary's premiums to decrease. If Gary opted to take an *any occupation* definition of disability, his premiums would decrease, but his coverage would become highly restrictive.

19. B is the answer. An *any occupation* definition of disability policy is the most restrictive but also carries the lowest premiums, which is one of Tim's primary concerns. A noncancelable policy is one that provides level premium payments and cannot cancel, as long as the insured continues to pay the premiums.

20. A is the answer. Disability insurance benefits are generally free of income taxation because the premiums paid are not deductible.

21. C is the answer. By keeping the daily benefit low and the benefit period short, Gary can lower the cost of his long-term care insurance. Gary was also concerned with having a small wait time between when he is eligible for LTC benefits and when he can start receiving benefits. A 30-day elimination period will help him minimize the waiting period.

22. C is the answer. Sandy's policy has a 60-day elimination period, so benefits will not be payable until day 61. The policy will pay for 120 days at $121.55 per day, with the inclusion of Sandy's inflation rider (5% annual increase for the four years the policy has been in force). Total benefits paid by the policy will be $14,586. To calculate the $121.55 per day: original purchase was four years ago with a benefit of $100 per day and compound inflation at 5%. N = 4, I = 5, PV = 100, solve for FV.

23. C is the answer. By reducing the automatic inflation increase in Sandy's daily benefit from 5% to 4%, Sandy could reduce her policy premiums.

24. C is the answer. Most long-term care policies allow coverage to begin once the insured is unable to perform at least two ADLs.

25. D is the answer. Medicaid benefits are only available to individuals at federal poverty guidelines. If Robert transferred his assets to become eligible for Medicaid benefits, he would become subject to a 5 year look-back period for assets transferred.

26. B is the answer. Gary's payout will be $6,000 annually for 10 years, so he is guaranteed $60,000. Gary paid $35,000 for the annuity per footnote 3. Gary does not bear the risk of varying payout because the annuity payments are fixed. The annuity was not described as a variable annuity. The payout starts at age 62 and will continue for 10 years certain. Thus, if Gary lives past age 70, the annuity will make one more payment (the 10 payments will be made on his 62nd to 71st birthdays).

27. D is the answer. Since the gain in the annuity was $15,000 ($50,000 – $35,000 = $15,000), that portion of the withdrawal is subject to ordinary income tax. Because Gary has not reached age 59½, his withdrawal is also subject to a 10% penalty tax for early withdrawals.

28. B is the answer. Gary's cost of the contract is $35,000, and his expected return is $60,000 ($6,000 yearly payment for 10 years). The exclusion ratio is 58.33% ($35,000 contract cost/$60,000 anticipated return), so 41.67% of each annuity payment is includible in Gary's gross income. $6,000 x 41.67% = $2,500.

29. A is the answer. The amount of the payments is fixed at $6,000 per year for ten years. The portion of each payment that is includible in ordinary income will not change. D is incorrect as the payments will continue until age 71.

30. C is the answer. The payments from the annuity will continue for six years after Gary's death because it has a 10-year period certain (the 10 payments will be made on his 62nd to 71st birthdays). The amount of the payments and the taxation of the payments will not change.

31. D is the answer. Because Judy is the primary beneficiary, she will receive the insurance proceeds if she is living when Gary dies. Because Judy is also the irrevocable beneficiary, Gary needs consent from Judy to change his beneficiary designation. B is an incorrect answer because the children will not be required to pay taxes on the death benefit received.

32. B is the answer. A 10-year limited payment whole life insurance policy is the only policy that provides permanent life insurance protection that is paid-up after 10 years. By taking the dividends as paid-up additions, Martha could purchase additional life insurance with her dividends.

33. A is the answer. Because Sandy's main concern is having the money to pay her immediate medical bills, a lump-sum payment would be most appropriate for Sandy. An annuity is not appropriate for Sandy because her life expectancy is extremely short, given her recent cancer diagnosis.

34. B is the answer. Sandy's waiver-of-premium rider states that if she becomes totally and permanently disabled before age 70, premiums on her life policy will be waived, and the insurance company will begin making the premium payments for Sandy.

35. C is the answer. As a young man about to get married, the most appropriate rider to add to Tim's policy is the guaranteed insurability rider. The guaranteed insurability rider gives Tim the option to buy additional amounts of insurance at specified dates, without having to provide evidence of insurability. This rider is ideal for young families who are likely to have children or for young families who expect a higher future income potential.

36. A is the answer. If a policyholder surrenders a life insurance policy for the cash value, and the cash value exceeds the total aggregate premiums paid, the policyholder recognizes ordinary income on the difference. The difference here is $1,000.

37. A is the answer. Life policy dividends are considered by the IRS to be a return of excess premiums and are free of income taxation. If the dividends exceed the total premiums paid, subsequent dividends paid are included as ordinary income for tax purposes.

38. C is the answer. For proceeds from a viatical settlement to qualify as though the benefits were paid by reason of death, the policyholder must be terminally ill and expected to die within 24 months. Because Robert's life expectancy is three years, he does not qualify as terminally ill, and the proceeds from a viatical settlement will be taxable gain. The amount taxable to Robert is the amount he receives from the settlement, less the premiums paid on the policy:

$140,000 settlement payout – $40,000 premiums paid = $100,000 taxable gain

39. C is the answer. Greentree must report the total gain as ordinary income:

$600,000 policy proceeds – $540,000 settlement payout = $60,000 ordinary income

40. D is the answer. If Sandy lives beyond the 24 months, she is not subject to income tax liability on the benefits. The terminal illness condition must only be satisfied when the viatical settlement payment is made to the insured.

41. D is the answer. Although income-tax-free, the death benefit payable to the corporation may attract the corporate AMT. A is wrong because the benefits are payable to Network Consultants. B is wrong because Judy will have already died, thus generating the death benefit. C is wrong because the premiums are not deductible.

42. C is the answer. Upon the sale of the policy, the company must recognize ordinary income on any gain. A is wrong because split-dollar would not be involved unless Network Consultants and Judy entered into an agreement. B is wrong because the transfer-for-value rules do not apply when the insured buys his or her own policy. D is wrong because it is not a transfer for value. Although the insurable interest requirement is met at the time of the inception of the life policy, it is irrelevant here.

43. D is the answer. The split-dollar plan uses the collateral-assignment method, so the executive owns the cash value but has collaterally assigned it to the employer to the extent of its premiums. The premium payments by the employer are treated as loans. The executive can either pay the interest on the loans each year or be taxed on the deemed interest payments as additional income.

44. A is the answer. Gary Parker has a small insurance broker's business and would benefit from a business overhead expense disability income insurance policy that would pay for the business' expenses in the event of his disability. The other persons do not own small businesses.

45. B is the answer. At the time Frank retires, Gary will be the owner of the combined businesses operated by Frank and Gary. The buy-sell agreement with Rick will then require a larger purchase price. The agreement will require additional life insurance to fund the purchase. The cross-purchase agreement usually produces greater equity of results, so the arrangement will not be inequitable. Since there are only two parties to each agreement, the number of life insurance policies will not be burdensome. An entity agreement is not likely to be a better way of arranging the sale after the merger. The facts do not indicate what the interests will be, so it is difficult to say whether the entity or cross-purchase agreement will be preferable.

46. D is the answer. The human life value approach does not consider other income sources, such as Social Security or personal wealth.

47. C is the answer. The capital retention approach and all other life insurance needs analyses do not consider the dividends available. Because dividends are not guaranteed, it cannot be determined how much dividends the policy will have when the insured dies.

48. A is the answer. The human life value approach Gary currently uses does not consider capital retention. Considering capital retention would make Gary's needs analysis more comprehensive. Choices B, C, and D are all considered under the human life value approach.

49. D is the answer. Because Judy will not be able to run the business if something happens to Gary, Rick needs cash readily available to purchase PRM if something happens to Gary. Rick should purchase a life insurance policy on Gary's life so he can use the tax-free proceeds from the life insurance policy to purchase the business. The agreement is a one-way buy-sell because Rick owns none of the business now.

50. D is the answer. Life insurance financial needs analyses do not consider the cash value a policy will generate. The cash value generated by a policy is a living benefit and is irrelevant when determining how much death benefit a client will need. The financial needs analysis considers the total cash, income, and special needs present and subtracts current personal wealth to determine how much life insurance is needed.

51. C is the answer. Because John and Julie are young, a whole life policy would provide appropriate coverage at a reasonable price. Term policies would not protect John and Julie when they are most likely to die. Annuities are not a reasonable option, given their young ages.

52. B is the answer. If Gary is concerned with having additional life insurance protection to fund his kids' education, a term policy would be most appropriate because his need is temporary. The 10-year term policy is Gary's best choice because John will be attending college in one year, and Julie will be attending college in three years. A 10-year term policy will cover the years that John and Julie would need college funding.

53. C is the answer. The universal life policy is most appropriate for Gary to purchase on Frank's life. The universal life will allow for a cash value accumulation so Gary will have the cash to purchase Frank's business interest when Frank wishes to retire. A term policy is not appropriate because the term policy does not allow for any buildup of cash values. The variable universal life is too aggressive for a buy-sell agreement because the cash value might not be available if the separate account does not perform well.

54. A is the answer. Because Tim is planning to buy a house, Tim has a need for life insurance protection for his mortgage. In light of his limited budget, a convertible term life insurance policy would be the most appropriate recommendation for Tim. Tim's income will most likely increase in the future, and Tim might be able to afford permanent life insurance coverage at that time. A convertible policy will allow Tim to eventually convert his term policy to a permanent policy.

55. D is the answer. An HMO policy is most appropriate for Tim because deductibles and copayments are generally lower with HMOs. HMOs also provide very broad coverage, but the disadvantages of HMO plans are limited physician and hospital choices, but that is acceptable to Tim.

56. D is the answer. Gary and Judy should be carrying at least $296,000 in coverage on their house ($370,000 x 80% = $296,000). Because Gary and Judy did not carry the 80% coinsurance requirement, their recovery from the insurance company is computed as follows:

$$\frac{Did}{Should} \ \text{x} \ \text{Loss} - \text{Deductible} = \text{Recovery}$$

$$\frac{256,000}{296,000} \ \text{x} \ \$10,000 - \$1,000 = \$7,649$$

Because the garage is not attached to the main dwelling, it is covered under Coverage B – Other Structures.

57. C is the answer. Since the claim arose during the term of the claims-made policy, coverage is provided by that policy. The event occurred during the term of the occurrence-basis policy, so coverage is also provided by the occurrence-basis policy.

58. A is the answer. John is a covered person under the personal auto policy (PAP) for the truck, therefore, the medical payments coverage of the PAP, which has a $10,000 limit, will cover all of his $4,000 medical bills related to the accident.

59. D is the answer. A separate commercial umbrella policy must be purchased to provide coverage for the business-owned property. The personal umbrella policy will require that all underlying personal property insurance policy types (home, auto, boat, RV, ATV, etc.) maintain a specific amount of liability coverage. It is important to ensure that these liability coverage requirements are met in order to prevent gaps in coverage between the underlying policy and the umbrella policy.

60. C is the answer. All three are exclusions in the HO-3 policy; however, the Parkers have purchased an Earthquake endorsement to ensure that the earthquake peril is covered.

Appendix B – Sample Life Insurance Declarations Page

Policy Specifications

Owner	Jane Buck	**Policy Number**	XY00244658
Insured	Jane Buck	**Date of Issue**	October 10, 2012
Face Amount	$650,000	**Age at Issue**	40
Sex	Female	**Beneficiary**	See Application
Underwriting Class	Preferred Non-Tobacco	**Conversion Available To**	October 10, 2032

Schedule of Benefits and Premiums

Benefits	Benefit Amounts	Annual Premium	Level Premium Period
Life Insurance	$650,000	$461.50	20 Years*
Waiver of Premium		$105.10	20 Years*
Policy Fee		$64.00	
Total Initial Annual Premium		$630.60	

*Annual renewal premiums are shown in the Table of Premiums on page 5. On the twentieth policy anniversary and any later policy anniversary, we have a right to change the premium. See the Right to Change Premium provision.

Expiry Dates. The initial Expiry Date is October 10, 2032. Subsequent expiry dates will occur at the end of each one year renewable term period. The final expiry date is October 10, 2067.

Inquiries regarding your policy should be directed to your agent, or, if he or she is not available to the Fictitious Life Insurance Company administrative office: 1-888-888-8888

Modal Factors

For premium modes other than annual, multiply the annual premiums by the appropriate modal factor given here:

	Direct Bill	Pre-Authorized Check
Annually	1.0	1.0
Semi-annually	.53	.51
Quarterly	.285	.257
Monthly	Not Available	.0875

APPENDIX C

Sample Summary of Benefits and Coverage

Insurance Company 1: Plan Option 1
Summary of Benefits and Coverage: What this Plan Covers & What it Costs

Coverage Period: 01/01/2014 – 12/31/2014
Coverage for: Individual + Spouse | Plan Type: PPO

 This is only a summary.

Important Questions	Answers	Why this Matters:
What is the overall deductible?	**$500** person / **$1,000** family Doesn't apply to preventive care	You must pay all the costs up to the **deductible** amount before this plan begins to pay for covered services you use. Check your policy or plan document to see when the **deductible** starts over (usually, but not always, January 1st). See the chart starting on page 2 for how much you pay for covered services after you meet the **deductible.**
Are there other deductibles for specific services?	Yes. **$300** for prescription drug coverage. There are no other specific **deductibles.**	You must pay all of the costs for these services up to the specific **deductible** amount before this plan begins to pay for these services.
Is there an out-of-pocket limit on my expenses?	Yes. For participating providers **$2,500** person / **$5,000** family For non-participating providers **$4,000** person / **$8,000** family	The **out-of-pocket limit** is the most you could pay during a coverage period (usually one year) for your share of the cost of covered services. This limit helps you plan for health care expenses.
What is not included in the out-of-pocket limit?	Premiums, balance–billed charges, and health care this plan doesn't cover.	Even though you pay these expenses, they don't count toward the **out-of-pocket limit.**
Is there an overall annual limit on what the plan pays?	No.	The chart starting on page 2 describes any limits on what the plan will pay for *specific* covered services, such as office visits.
Does this plan use a network of providers?	Yes. See **www.[insert].com or call 1-800-[insert]** for a list of participating providers.	If you use an in-network doctor or other health care **provider,** this plan will pay some or all of the costs of covered services. Be aware, your in-network doctor or hospital may use an out-of-network **provider** for some services. Plans use the term in-network, **preferred,** or participating for **providers** in their **network.** See the chart starting on page 2 for how this plan pays different kinds of **providers.**
Do I need a referral to see a specialist?	No. You don't need a referral to see a specialist.	You can see the **specialist** you choose without permission from this plan.
Are there services this plan doesn't cover?	Yes.	Some of the services this plan doesn't cover are listed on page 4. See your policy or plan document for additional information about **excluded services.**

Insurance Company 1: Plan Option 1

Summary of Benefits and Coverage: What this Plan Covers & What it Costs

Coverage Period: 01/01/2014 – 12/31/2014

Coverage for: Individual + Spouse | **Plan Type:** PPO

⚠️

- <u>Copayments</u> are fixed dollar amounts (for example, $15) you pay for covered health care, usually when you receive the service.
- <u>Coinsurance</u> is *your* share of the costs of a covered service, calculated as a percent of the **allowed amount** for the service. For example, if the plan's **allowed amount** for an overnight hospital stay is $1,000, your **coinsurance** payment of 20% would be $200. This may change if you haven't met your **deductible.**
- The amount the plan pays for covered services is based on the **allowed amount**. If an out-of-network **provider** charges more than the **allowed amount**, you may have to pay the difference. For example, if an out-of-network hospital charges $1,500 for an overnight stay and the **allowed amount** is $1,000, you may have to pay the $500 difference. (This is called **balance billing**.)
- This plan may encourage you to use participating **providers** by charging you lower **deductibles, copayments** and **coinsurance** amounts.

Common Medical Event	Services You May Need	Your Cost If You Use a Participating Provider	Your Cost If You Use a Non-Participating Provider	Limitations & Exceptions
If you visit a health care provider's office or clinic	Primary care visit to treat an injury or illness	$35 copay/visit	40% coinsurance	—————none—————
	Specialist visit	$50 copay/visit	40% coinsurance	—————none—————
	Other practitioner office visit	20% coinsurance for chiropractor and acupuncture	40% coinsurance for chiropractor and acupuncture	—————none—————
	Preventive care/screening/immunization	No charge	40% coinsurance	
If you have a test	Diagnostic test (x-ray, blood work)	$10 copay/test	40% coinsurance	—————none—————
	Imaging (CT/PET scans, MRIs)	$50 copay/test	40% coinsurance	—————none—————

Insurance Company 1: Plan Option 1

Summary of Benefits and Coverage: What this Plan Covers & What it Costs

Common Medical Event	Services You May Need	Your Cost If You Use a Participating Provider	Your Cost If You Use a Non-Participating Provider	Limitations & Exceptions
If you need drugs to treat your illness or condition More information about **prescription drug coverage** is available at www. [insert].	Generic drugs	$10 copay/prescription (retail and mail order)	40% coinsurance	Covers up to a 30-day supply (retail prescription); 31-90 day supply (mail order prescription)
	Preferred brand drugs	20% coinsurance (retail and mail order)	40% coinsurance	———none———
	Non-preferred brand drugs	40% coinsurance (retail and mail order)	60% coinsurance	———none———
	Specialty drugs	50% coinsurance	70% coinsurance	———none———
If you have outpatient surgery	Facility fee (e.g., ambulatory surgery center)	20% coinsurance	40% coinsurance	———none———
	Physician/surgeon fees	20% coinsurance	40% coinsurance	———none———
If you need immediate medical attention	Emergency room services	20% coinsurance	20% coinsurance	———none———
	Emergency medical transportation	20% coinsurance	20% coinsurance	———none———
	Urgent care	20% coinsurance	40% coinsurance	———none———
If you have a hospital stay	Facility fee (e.g., hospital room)	20% coinsurance	40% coinsurance	———none———
	Physician/surgeon fee	20% coinsurance	40% coinsurance	———none———

Insurance Company 1: Plan Option 1

Summary of Benefits and Coverage: What this Plan Covers & What it Costs

Coverage Period: 01/01/2014 – 12/31/2014

Coverage for: Individual + Spouse | Plan Type: PPO

Common Medical Event	Services You May Need	Your Cost If You Use a Participating Provider	Your Cost If You Use a Non-Participating Provider	Limitations & Exceptions
If you have mental health, behavioral health, or substance abuse needs	Mental/Behavioral health outpatient services	$35 copay/office visit and 20% coinsurance other outpatient services	40% coinsurance	——none——
	Mental/Behavioral health inpatient services	20% coinsurance	40% coinsurance	——none——
	Substance use disorder outpatient services	$35 copay/office visit and 20% coinsurance other outpatient services	40% coinsurance	——none——
	Substance use disorder inpatient services	20% coinsurance	40% coinsurance	——none——
If you are pregnant	Prenatal and postnatal care	20% coinsurance	40% coinsurance	——none——
	Delivery and all inpatient services	20% coinsurance	40% coinsurance	——none——
If you need help recovering or have other special health needs	Home health care	20% coinsurance	40% coinsurance	——none——
	Rehabilitation services	20% coinsurance	40% coinsurance	——none——
	Habilitation services	20% coinsurance	40% coinsurance	——none——
	Skilled nursing care	20% coinsurance	40% coinsurance	——none——
	Durable medical equipment	20% coinsurance	40% coinsurance	——none——
	Hospice service	20% coinsurance	40% coinsurance	——none——
If your child needs dental or eye care	Eye exam	$35 copay/ visit	Not Covered	Limited to one exam per year
	Glasses	20% coinsurance	Not Covered	Limited to one pair of glasses per year
	Dental check-up	No Charge	Not Covered	Covers up to $50 per year

Excluded Services & Other Covered Services:

Services Your Plan Does Not Cover (This isn't a complete list. Check your policy or plan document for other excluded services.)

- Cosmetic surgery
- Dental care (Adult)
- Infertility treatment

- Long-term care
- Non-emergency care when traveling outside the U.S.
- Private-duty nursing

- Routine eye care (Adult)
- Routine foot care

Other Covered Services (This isn't a complete list. Check your policy or plan document for other covered services and your costs for these services.)

- Acupuncture (if prescribed for rehabilitation purposes)
- Bariatric surgery

- Chiropractic care
- Hearing aids

- Most coverage provided outside the United States. See www.[insert]
- Weight loss programs

Insurance Company 1: Plan Option 1
Summary of Benefits and Coverage: What this Plan Covers & What it Costs

Your Rights to Continue Coverage:

** Individual health insurance sample –

Federal and State laws may provide protections that allow you to keep this health insurance coverage as long as you pay your **premium**. There are exceptions, however, such as if:

- You commit fraud

- The insurer stops offering services in the State

- You move outside the coverage area

For more information on your rights to continue coverage, contact the insurer at [contact number]. You may also contact your state insurance department at [insert applicable State Department of Insurance contact information].

OR

** Group health coverage sample –

If you lose coverage under the plan, then, depending upon the circumstances, Federal and State laws may provide protections that allow you to keep health coverage. Any such rights may be limited in duration and will require you to pay a **premium**, which may be significantly higher than the premium you pay while covered under the plan. Other limitations on your rights to continue coverage may also apply.

For more information on your rights to continue coverage, contact the plan at [contact number]. You may also contact your state insurance department, the U.S. Department of Labor, Employee Benefits Security Administration at 1-866-444-3272 or www.dol.gov/ebsa, or the U.S. Department of Health and Human Services at 1-877-267-2323 x61565 or www.cciio.cms.gov.

Your Grievance and Appeals Rights:

If you have a complaint or are dissatisfied with a denial of coverage for claims under your plan, you may be able to **appeal** or file a **grievance**. For questions about your rights, this notice, or assistance, you can contact: [insert applicable contact information from instructions].

Does this Coverage Provide Minimum Essential Coverage?

The *Affordable Care Act requires most people to have health care coverage that qualifies as "minimum essential coverage."* **This plan or policy [does/ does not] provide minimum essential coverage.**

Does this Coverage Meet the Minimum Value Standard?

The *Affordable Care Act establishes a minimum value standard of benefits of a health plan. The minimum value standard is 60% (actuarial value).* **This health coverage [does/does not] meet the minimum value standard for the benefits it provides.**

———— *To see examples of how this plan might cover costs for a sample medical situation, see the next page.* ————

About these Coverage Examples:

These examples show how this plan might cover medical care in given situations. Use these examples to see, in general, how much financial protection a sample patient might get if they are covered under different plans.

This is not a cost estimator.

Don't use these examples to estimate your actual costs under this plan. The actual care you receive will be different from these examples, and the cost of that care will also be different.

See the next page for important information about these examples.

Having a baby
(normal delivery)

- **Amount owed to providers: $7,540**
- **Plan pays $5,490**
- **Patient pays $2,050**

Sample care costs:

Hospital charges (mother)	$2,700
Routine obstetric care	$2,100
Hospital charges (baby)	$900
Anesthesia	$900
Laboratory tests	$500
Prescriptions	$200
Radiology	$200
Vaccines, other preventive	$40
Total	**$7,540**

Patient pays:

Deductibles	$700
Copays	$30
Coinsurance	$1320
Limits or exclusions	$0
Total	**$2,050**

Managing type 2 diabetes
(routine maintenance of a well-controlled condition)

- **Amount owed to providers: $5,400**
- **Plan pays $3,520**
- **Patient pays $1,880**

Sample care costs:

Prescriptions	$2,900
Medical Equipment and Supplies	$1,300
Office Visits and Procedures	$700
Education	$300
Laboratory tests	$100
Vaccines, other preventive	$100
Total	**$5,400**

Patient pays:

Deductibles	$800
Copays	$500
Coinsurance	$500
Limits or exclusions	$80
Total	**$1,880**

Note: These numbers assume the patient is participating in our diabetes wellness program. If you have diabetes and do not participate in the wellness program, your costs may be higher. For more information about the diabetes wellness program, please contact: [insert].

Questions and answers about the Coverage Examples:

What are some of the assumptions behind the Coverage Examples?

- Costs don't include **premiums**.
- Sample care costs are based on national averages supplied by the U.S. Department of Health and Human Services, and aren't specific to a particular geographic area or health plan.
- The patient's condition was not an excluded or preexisting condition.
- All services and treatments started and ended in the same coverage period.
- There are no other medical expenses for any member covered under this plan.
- Out-of-pocket expenses are based only on treating the condition in the example.
- The patient received all care from in-network **providers**. If the patient had received care from out-of-network **providers**, costs would have been higher.

What does a Coverage Example show?

For each treatment situation, the Coverage Example helps you see how **deductibles**, **copayments**, and **coinsurance** can add up. It also helps you see what expenses might be left up to you to pay because the service or treatment isn't covered or payment is limited.

Does the Coverage Example predict my own care needs?

- ✗ **No.** Treatments shown are just examples. The care you would receive for this condition could be different based on your doctor's advice, your age, how serious your condition is, and many other factors.

Does the Coverage Example predict my future expenses?

- ✗ **No.** Coverage Examples are **not** cost estimators. You can't use the examples to estimate costs for an actual condition. They are for comparative purposes only. Your own costs will be different depending on the care you receive, the prices your **providers** charge, and the reimbursement your health plan allows.

Can I use Coverage Examples to compare plans?

- ✓ **Yes.** When you look at the Summary of Benefits and Coverage for other plans, you'll find the same Coverage Examples. When you compare plans, check the "Patient Pays" box in each example. The smaller that number, the more coverage the plan provides.

Are there other costs I should consider when comparing plans?

- ✓ **Yes.** An important cost is the **premium** you pay. Generally, the lower your **premium**, the more you'll pay in out-of-pocket costs, such as **copayments**, **deductibles**, and **coinsurance**. You should also consider contributions to accounts such as health savings accounts (HSAs), flexible spending arrangements (FSAs) or health reimbursement accounts (HRAs) that help you pay out-of-pocket expenses.

APPENDIX D

Sample Employee Notice and Consent Form

FORM FOR EMPLOYER-OWNED LIFE INSURANCE
NOTICE AND CONSENT REQUIREMENTS

Internal Revenue Code Section 101(j) creates new Notice and Consent requirements that must be met before a policy is issued. Following is a form you may use to comply with these requirements. If you submit an application for an employer-owned life insurance policy, you should make sure that this form is signed and submitted to the insurance carrier *before* the policy is issued. <u>Failure to comply with the new law means that part of the death benefit may be taxed as ordinary income.</u>

Definition.

The law defines "employer-owned life insurance" broadly. It includes any policy if:

- The owner engages in a trade or business, <u>and</u>
- The owner (or a related party) is a beneficiary (direct or indirect), <u>and</u>
- The insured is an employee at the time of policy issue, <u>and</u>
- The insured is a U.S. citizen or resident.

Four Safe Harbors.

The form deals only with the Notice and Consent requirement. Both the Notice and Consent <u>and</u> at least one of the four safe harbors specified in the new law must be in place to keep the death benefit income tax free.

Safe Harbor 1: Key Person

The insured is a key person at policy issue. This safe harbor (unlike the others) provides certainly at the time the policy is issued that the death benefit will continue to be income tax free. The employer must keep good records. Possibly many years from now, when the employee dies, the employer may have to prove that the employee satisfied the key person rules when the policy was issued.

A key person for these purposes is someone who, at policy issue:

- Was a director of the employer.
- Was a 5% or greater owner in the year before policy issue.
- Received compensation of $95,000 or more (adjusted for inflation).
- Was one of the five highest paid officers.
- Was among the 35% highest paid employees.

You cannot know if the remaining safe harbors are available <u>until the employee dies</u>. Until then, the employer won't know for sure if the death benefit is taxable or not taxable.

Safe Harbor 2: Current Employee

The insured was an employee any time in the 12-month period before death.

Safe Harbor 3: Death Benefit Paid to the Insured's Heirs

- A member of the insured's family (spouse, parents and grandparents, children and grandchildren, brothers and sisters).
- An individual the insured named (other than the employer).
- A trust set up for anyone in those first two groups of people.
- The insured's estate.

Although this may avoid income tax on the death benefit, it does create a split dollar arrangement. If the employer owns the policy and the person named as beneficiary is any of these people, the arrangement is, by definition, split dollar. The employee will be taxed on the economic benefit provided by the policy.

Safe Harbor 4: Buy-Sell Funds

Death benefits remain income tax free if used to buy the insured's interest in the employer (equity, capital or profits) from someone listed in Safe Harbor 3.

Reporting Requirements.

The IRS has released Form 8925 that is required to be filed by employers (with their income tax return) that own "employer-owned life insurance contracts". The form itself contains the instructions. The form asks if the employer has a valid consent form for each covered employee. If not, then the number of employees for whom a valid consent does not exist must be listed.

DISCLAIMER.

These materials may not be used for penalty protection.

NOTICE AND CONSENT TO EMPLOYERS
APPLICATION FOR LIFE INSURANCE

NAME AND ADDRESS OF CARRIER:

_____

_____

_____

1. EMPLOYEE (PROPOSED INSURED) INFORMATION

Full Name (First, Middle, Last. Include maiden name in parentheses.)		Gender ☐ F ☐ M	Date of Birth MM/DD/CCYY	Social Security Number
Street Address	City		State	Zip Code
Occupation				

2. EMPLOYER (OWNER) INFORMATION

Full Legal Name

Street Address	City		State	Zip Code

3. NOTICE BY EMPLOYER (OWNER)

a. Employer intends to apply for insurance on the life of the Employee (Proposed Insured).

b. The maximum face amount the Employee (Proposed Insured) could be insured for at the time the contract is issued is $_____

c. The Employer will be the Owner of any policy issued and a beneficiary of any proceeds payable upon the Employee's (Proposed Insured's) death.

4. CONSENT OF EMPLOYEE (PROPOSED INSURED)

a. I consent to being an insured under the life insurance policy for which my Employer intends to apply.

b. I consent to my Employer continuing coverage, after my employment ends, under any policy issued.

c. I understand that my Employer will own the policy. Unless provided in a separate agreement, my Employer will receive all of the death proceeds, and my personal representative, next of kin, and heirs at law will have no beneficial interest in the policy or its death proceeds.

AGREEMENT AND AUTHORIZATION

This form is provided as a convenience to the Employer and to obtain information that may be needed for information reporting services. By providing this form, the carrier makes no representation that completing it will constitute compliance with any law or regulation, tax or otherwise. Federal tax law specifies that the death benefits of certain employer-owned life insurance contracts will not be completely excluded from federal gross income of the Employer unless notice-and-consent requirements and other requirements specified in the law are fulfilled.

The carrier and its representatives and distributors do not provide tax or legal advice. The carrier did not accept this form for use by any taxpayer to avoid any Internal Revenue Service penalty. You should ask your independent tax and legal advisors for advice based on your particular situation.

A photocopy of this form shall be as valid as the original.

_____   _____
Signature of Employee (Proposed Insured)   Date

_____   _____
Signature of Employer (Owner)   Date

_____
Title

APPENDIX E

Sample Life Insurance Needs Analysis Form

IF _____ Died Today:	
Funeral costs	$
Estate taxes and administration	$
Final medical expenses	$
Mortgage pay-off	$
Other debts	$
Readjustment period income	$
Income replacement during child dependency period	$
Income replacement for surviving spouse after dependency period and before retirement	$
Retirement period income for surviving spouse	$
Extra expense fund	$
Special Goals:	$
Education funding	$
Support of dependents with special needs	$
Charitable contributions	$
Care of pets	$
Other	$
Total Need	$
Less available assets	–
Total Need to be Funded with Life Insurance	$
Amount to be funded with term insurance	$
Less existing term insurance	–
Additional term insurance needed	
Amount to be funded with permanent insurance	$
Less existing permanent insurance	–
Additional permanent insurance needed	

APPENDIX F

Example of Statement of Policy Cost and Benefit Information

Date Statement Prepared: January 20, 2011   Policy Number: U12345678

Insured: John Q. Sample   Age: 60   Sex: Male

Insurance Class: Preferred Plus Non-Nicotine

Owner: John Q. Sample

Agent: Bess C. Landers
        1234 Main St.
        Anytown, PA 11111

Insurance Company: A-One Life Insurance and Annuity Company
                   Individual Life Operations, PO Box 567, Anytown, MN 22222

IMPORTANT NOTICE

The projected result of your insurance program may change drastically with variations in the interest rates, cost of insurance rates, and the frequency, timing and amount of your premium payments. You should read and study your policy and policy summary very carefully.

COVERAGE

Base Policy: $250,000 Flexible Premium Universal Life Policy
Death Benefit Option: A – Level Option
Riders: Policy Protection Rider

ANNUAL PREMIUMS UNDER COST OF INSURANCE

POLICY YEAR	TOTAL	BASIC	RIDER 1	RIDER 2	RIDER 3	RIDER 4
			ALLOCATED TO:			
1	$16,111.36	$16,111.36	$0.00	$0.00	$0.00	$0.00
2	$ 3,111.36	$ 3,111.36	$0.00	$0.00	$0.00	$0.00
3	$ 3,111.36	$ 3,111.36	$0.00	$0.00	$0.00	$0.00
4	$ 3,111.36	$ 3,111.36	$0.00	$0.00	$0.00	$0.00
5	$ 3,111.36	$ 3,111.36	$0.00	$0.00	$0.00	$0.00
10	$ 3,111.36	$ 3,111.36	$0.00	$0.00	$0.00	$0.00
20	$ 3,111.36	$ 3,111.36	$0.00	$0.00	$0.00	$0.00
Age 65	$ 3,111.36	$ 3,111.36	$0.00	$0.00	$0.00	$0.00

ANNUAL PREMIUMS UNDER MAXIMUM COST OF INSURANCE

POLICY YEAR	TOTAL	BASIC	RIDER 1	RIDER 2	RIDER 3	RIDER 4
			ALLOCATED TO:			
1	$16,111.36	$16,111.36	$0.00	$0.00	$0.00	$0.00
2	$ 3,111.36	$ 3,111.36	$0.00	$0.00	$0.00	$0.00
3	$ 3,111.36	$ 3,111.36	$0.00	$0.00	$0.00	$0.00
4	$ 3,111.36	$ 3,111.36	$0.00	$0.00	$0.00	$0.00
5	$ 3,111.36	$ 3,111.36	$0.00	$0.00	$0.00	$0.00
10	$ 3,111.36	$ 3,111.36	$0.00	$0.00	$0.00	$0.00
20	$ 3,111.36	$ 3,111.36	$0.00	$0.00	$0.00	$0.00
Age 65	$ 3,111.36	$ 3,111.36	$0.00	$0.00	$0.00	$0.00

Example of Statement of Policy Cost and Benefit Information
(Continued)

Insured: John Q. Sample   Policy Number: U12345678

POLICY YEAR	DEATH BENEFITS		CASH SURRENDER VALUES	
	UNDER CURRENT COST OF INSURANCE AND CURRENT INTEREST RATE	UNDER MAXIMUM COST OF INSURANCE AND MAXIMUM INTEREST RATE	UNDER CURRENT COST OF INSURANCE AND CURRENT INTEREST RATE	UNDER MAXIMUM COST OF INSURANCE AND MAXIMUM INTEREST RATE
1	$250,000.00	$250,000.00	$2,494.23	$2,423.80
2	$250,000.00	$250,000.00	$4,018.72	$1,159.06
3	$250,000.00	$250,000.00	$5,390.94	$0.00
4	$250,000.00	$250,000.00	$8,025.16	$0.00
5	$250,000.00	$250,000.00	$10,581.46	$0.00
10	$250,000.00	$250,000.00	$19,770.79	$0.00
20	$250,000.00	$250,000.00	$18,336.61	$0.00
AGE 65	$250,000.00	$250,000.00	$10,581.46	$0.00

BASIC INFORMATION

Projection based upon current interest assume a rate of 3.00% for all years. The current interest rate is subject to change at any time; however, it will never drop below the minimum account value interest rate. Guaranteed projections are based on the minimum account value interest rate of 3.00%.

Policy loans. The loaned account value will be credited with interest at a rate of 3.00%. The rate charged on any loaned account value is 5.00% in years 1-10 and 4.00% beginning in year 11. The rates charged on loaned account values are subject to change at any time; however, they will never exceed 5.00% in years 1-10, or 4.25% thereafter.

Preferred loans are available after the 10th policy year. The amount available is the excess of the account value over the premiums paid since issue. For preferred loans, the rate charged on loaned account value is 3.00%, and the rate charged on loaned account value will never exceed 3.25%.

During the first nineteen policy years, a surrender charge is applied to any full surrenders.

The premium level chosen may result in expiration of coverage under guaranteed assumptions.

This summary is not a contract. Refer to your policy for a complete description of your coverage. If you have any questions regarding your coverage, please contact us at the address shown on the previous page.

Example of Statement of Policy Cost and Benefit Information
(Continued)

LIFE INSURANCE COST INDICES

	NET PAYMENT COST INDICES		SURRENDER COST INDICES	
	10TH YEAR	20TH YEAR	10TH YEAR	20TH YEAR
CURRENT BASIC POLICY	$18.86	$16.42	$12.87	$14.31
GUARANTEED BASIC POLICY	$18.86	$16.42	$18.86	$16.42

An explanation of the intended use of these indices is provided in the Insurance Buyer's Guide.

2016 Key Facts and Figures

Keir Educational Resources compiled the following key facts and figures for the CFP® Certification Examination to assist you with your preparation for this comprehensive exam.

Please note the following items:

1. This list is not intended to be an all-inclusive listing of facts and figures tested on the CFP® Certification Examination.

2. Very few of the figures included in this list will be provided during your CFP® Certification Examination. **<u>Only the items underlined will be provided</u>** (electronically as an exhibit button on the bottom of the computer screen). For example, all of the underlined Personal Exemption and Standard Deduction information listed on the next page are provided. However, the provided information on the exam does not include information about the self employment taxes or kiddie taxes. As a result, you will need to know how to calculate both taxes. Likewise, you will need to memorize all the other items that are not underlined.

Personal Exemption	**2016**

Personal exemption amount per person	4,050

*Phaseout of 2% for every $2,500 ($1,250 MFS) or
fraction thereof that AGI exceeds the following amounts*

Single	259,400
Married filing jointly or surviving spouse	311,300
Married filing separately	155,650
Head of household	285,350

Standard Deductions	**2016**

Single	6,300
Married filing jointly or surviving spouse	12,600
Married filing separately	6,300
Head of household	9,300

*Additional standard deduction amount if age 65 or older
or blind*

Married (per person)	1,250
Unmarried	1,550

Taxpayer is claimed as a dependent

No earned income	1,050
Earned income (earned income plus amount)	350
Maximum deduction using earned income	6,300

Phaseout of Itemized Deductions

*Phaseout of 3% of the amount by which AGI exceeds the
threshold:*

Single	$259,400
Married filing jointly or surviving spouse	$311,300
Married filing separately	$155,650
Head of household	$285,350

Employment Taxes	**2016**
Social Security tax rate	
Employer's portion	6.2%
Employee's portion	6.2%
Total for self-employed individual	12.4%
<u>Maximum amount of earnings subject to Social Security taxes (wage base)</u>	$118,500
Medicare tax rate	
Employer's portion	1.45%
Employee's portion (on all net self-employment income)	1.45%
Total for self-employed individual (on all net self-employment income)	2.9%
<u>Employee's additional Medicare surtax on earnings above $200,000 ($250,000 MFJ, $125,000 MFS)</u>	<u>.9%</u>
Maximum amount of earnings subject to Medicare taxes	Unlimited
Total employment taxes	
Employer's portion	7.65%
Employee's portion	7.65%
Total for self-employed individual	15.3%
Percentage of self-employed earnings subject to SE taxes	92.35%
Percentage of SE taxes deducted above-the-line	50%

Kiddie Tax	**2016**
Amount not subject to tax due to personal exemption	1,050
Amount taxed at child's rate of 10%	1,050
Unearned income above these amounts taxed at parents' marginal tax rate	Unlimited

Child Tax Credit	**2016**
Child tax credit per child	1,000

Phaseout of $50 for every $1,000 or fraction thereof that AGI exceeds the following amounts (completely phased out if AGI exceeds threshold by $20,000 per child):

Single	75,000
Married filing jointly or surviving spouse	110,000
Married filing separately	55,000
Head of household	75,000

Child or Dependent Care Credit	**2016**

Maximum amount of qualifying expenses

One child or dependent	3,000
Two or more children or dependents	6,000
AGI amount when credit reduced to 20% level	43,000

Maximum credit, assuming taxpayer's AGI at 20% level

One child or dependent	600
Two or more children or dependents	1,200

American Opportunity Tax Credit (formerly called Hope Credit)	**2016**

Credit percentage amounts

First $2,000	100%
Second $2,000	25%
Maximum credit	$2,500

Phaseout starts at the following AGI amounts:

Single	80,000
Married filing jointly or surviving spouse	160,000
Married filing separately	0
Head of household	80,000

Credit completely phased out at the following AGI amounts:

Single	90,000
Married filing jointly or surviving spouse	180,000
Married filing separately	0
Head of household	90,000

Lifetime Learning Credit   **2016**

Credit percentage amounts
First $10,000   20%

Maximum credit $2,000

Phaseout starts at the following AGI amounts:
Single   55,000
Married filing jointly or surviving spouse   111,000
Married filing separately   0
Head of household   55,000

Credit completely phased out at the following AGI amounts:
Single   65,000
Married filing jointly or surviving spouse   131,000
Married filing separately   0
Head of household   65,000

Education Expenses   **2016**

Above-the-line deduction for educational loan interest payments   2,500

Phaseout of educational loan interest deduction starts at the following AGI amounts:
Single   65,000
Married filing jointly or surviving spouse   130,000
Married filing separately   0
Head of household   65,000

Educational loan interest deduction completely phased out at the following AGI amounts:
Single   80,000
Married filing jointly or surviving spouse   160,000
Married filing separately   0
Head of household   80,000

Education Expenses	**2016**
Above-the-line deduction for tuition and related expenses	$4,000

AGI limitations to claim up to the full $4,000 above-the-line deduction

Single	$65,000
Married filing jointly or surviving spouse	$130,000
Married filing separately	$0
Head of household	$65,000

AGI limitation to claim up to $2,000 above-the-line deduction if AGI exceeds the limits above for the $4,000 deduction

Single	$80,000
Married filing jointly or surviving spouse	$160,000
Married filing separately	$0
Head of household	$80,000

Tax-free treatment on Series EE bonds

Phaseout of tax-free treatment on Series EE bonds starts at the following AGI amounts:

Single	77,550
Married filing jointly or surviving spouse	116,300
Married filing separately	77,550
Head of household	77,550

Tax-free treatment on Series EE bonds completely phased out at the following AGI amounts:

Single	92,550
Married filing jointly or surviving spouse	146,300
Married filing separately	92,550
Head of household	92,550

Coverdell Education Savings Accounts	**2016**
Coverdell Education Savings Account (ESA) contribution limit	2,000

Phaseout of ESA contribution starts at the following AGI amounts:

Single	95,000
Married filing jointly or surviving spouse	190,000
Married filing separately	95,000
Head of household	95,000

Coverdell Education Savings Accounts	**2016**

ESA contribution completely phased out at the following AGI amounts:

Single	110,000
Married filing jointly or surviving spouse	220,000
Married filing separately	110,000
Head of household	110,000

Section 179 Deduction	**2016**

Section 179 deduction amount	500,000
Limit on property placed in service	2,010,000

Health Savings Accounts	**2016**

High deductible health plan minimum deductible amounts

Single	1,300
Family	2,600

Maximum out-of-pocket limits

Single	6,550
Family	13,100

Contribution Maximums

Single	3,350
Family	6,750
Catch-up contributions (age 55 or older)	1,000

Income Tax Rates	**2016**

Marginal tax rate ends at the following income levels:

Single

10%	9,275
15%	37,650
25%	91,150
28%	190,150
33%	413,350
35%	415,050
39.6%	Unlimited

Income Tax Rates	2016

Married filing jointly or surviving spouse

10%	18,550
15%	75,300
25%	151,900
28%	231,450
33%	413,350
35%	466,950
39.6%	Unlimited

Married filing separately

10%	9,275
15%	37,650
25%	75,950
28%	115,725
33%	206,675
35%	233,475
39.6%	Unlimited

Head of household

10%	13,250
15%	50,400
25%	130,150
28%	210,800
33%	413,350
35%	441,000
39.6%	Unlimited

Trusts

15%	2,550
25%	5,950
28%	9,050
33%	12,400
35%	n/a
39.6%	Unlimited

Income Tax Rates	**2016**

Tax rates for capital gains and dividends

Taxpayers in the 39.6% bracket	20%*
Taxpayers in the 25%, 28%, 33%, and 35% tax brackets	15%*
Taxpayers in the 10% or 15% tax bracket	0%
IRS Section 1250 depreciation recapture	25%
Collectibles	28%

*For single taxpayers with AGI over $200,000 ($250,000 MFJ; $125,000 MFS) an additional 3.8% Medicare Contribution tax will apply to capital gains to the extent that Net Investment Income exceeds the threshold level.

Alternative Minimum Taxes (AMT)	**2016**

AMT exemption amounts

Single	53,900
Married filing jointly or surviving spouse	83,800
Married filing separately	41,900
Head of household	53,900
Estates and trusts	23,900

Phaseout of AMT exemption of 25% of AMTI that exceeds the following amounts:

Single	119,700
Married filing jointly or surviving spouse	159,700
Married filing separately	79,850
Head of household	119,700
Estates and trusts	79,850

AMT tax rates
Single, married filing jointly, head of household, and estates and trusts

26% on income up to	186,300
28% on income over	186,300

Married filing separately

26% on income up to	93,150
28% on income over	93,150

Alternative Minimum Taxes (AMT)   **2016**

Maximum tax rate on capital gains and dividends   20%**
**The maximum tax rates on capital gains and dividends
   used in computing the regular tax are used in computing
   the tentative minimum tax as well (15% for most taxpayers,
   20% for high-income taxpayers)

Estate and Gift Taxes   **2016**

Annual gift tax exclusions
Gifts to any person   14,000
Gifts to a U.S. citizen spouse   Unlimited
Gifts to a noncitizen spouse   148,000

Lifetime gifts
Applicable exclusion amount   5,450,000
Applicable credit amount   2,125,800

Bequests at death
Applicable exclusion amount   5,450,000
Applicable credit amount   2,125,800

Top estate tax rate   40%
Top gift tax rate   40%

Generation-skipping transfer (GST) tax
Annual GST exclusion   14,000
Lifetime GST exemption amount   5,450,000
Flat GST tax rate   40%
Special-use valuation limit   1,110,000
Section 6166 special 2% interest rate   1,480,000

Retirement Plans   **2016**

Taxpayer or employee contribution limits
IRA (combined traditional and Roth IRA limit)   5,500
401(k) plans   18,000
403(b) plans   18,000
457 plans   18,000
SIMPLE plans   12,500

Retirement Plans   **2016**

Catch-up contribution limits
IRA (combined traditional and Roth IRA limit)	1,000
401(k) plans	6,000
403(b) plans	6,000
457 plans	6,000
SIMPLE plans	3,000

Defined-contribution plan limitations
Participating payroll	25%
Maximum percentage of employee's compensation	100%
Participant's contribution not to exceed	53,000
Maximum compensation to be considered	265,000

Defined-benefit plan limitations
Maximum annual benefit	210,000
Maximum compensation to be considered	265,000

SEP plan limitations
Maximum percentage of employee's compensation	25%
Participant's contribution not to exceed	53,000
Minimum compensation needed to participate	600
Maximum compensation to be considered	265,000

Qualified plan definitions

Highly-compensated employee
Any employee who owns 5% or more of the company	
Any employee among the top 20% highest-paid and paid more than	120,000

Key employee
Any officer earning	170,000
Any employee who owns 5% or more of the company	
Any employee who owns 1% or more of the company and makes	150,000

Phaseout of IRA deduction starts at the following amounts:
Single	61,000
Married filing jointly or surviving spouse	98,000
Married filing separately	0
Head of household	61,000

IRA deduction completely phased out at the following amounts:
Single	71,000
Married filing jointly or surviving spouse	118,000
Married filing separately	10,000
Head of household	71,000

Retirement Plans   **2016**

Phaseout of IRA deduction with an active participant spouse

AGI limit when phaseout starts	184,000
AGI limit when completely phased out	194,000

Phaseout of Roth IRA contributions starts at the following amounts:

Single	117,000
Married filing jointly or surviving spouse	184,000
Married filing separately	0
Head of household	117,000

Roth IRA contribution completely phased out at the following amounts:

Single	132,000
Married filing jointly or surviving spouse	194,000
Married filing separately	10,000
Head of household	132,000

Social Security Benefits   **2016**

Limit on earnings before the reduction of benefits of $1 for every $2 earnings above limitation ($1 for every $3 in the year of full retirement age)

Under full retirement age	15,720
Persons reaching full retirement age	41,880
Over full retirement age	n/a
Amount needed to earn one Social Security credit	1,260

Medicare   **2016**

Part A deductibles for hospital stays

Days 1-60 (total deductible for all 60 days)	1,288
Days 61-90 (deductible per day)	322
Days 91-150 (deductible per day)	644

Part A deductibles for skilled nursing facility

Days 1-20	0
Days 21-100 (deductible per day)	161.00

Part B monthly premium (monthly premiums will be higher if AGI exceeds $85,000 for single taxpayers or $170,000 MFJ taxpayers)	121.80
Part B annual deductible	166

Editor's Note: A sheet of formulas such as those presented below is provided electronically on the CFP® Certification Examination as an aid to the person taking the test. However, the formulas are not labeled. For your information in preparing for the test, we have indicated what the formulas may be used for.

Value: Constant Dividend Growth Model

$$V = \frac{D_1}{r - g}$$

Rate of Return Based on Current Price

$$r = \frac{D_1}{P} + g$$

Covariance

$$COV_{ij} = \rho_{ij}\, \sigma_i\, \sigma_j$$

Two-Asset Portfolio Standard Deviation

$$\sigma_p = \sqrt{W_i^2\, \sigma_i^2 + W_j^2\, \sigma_j^2 + 2W_iW_jCOV_{ij}}$$

Beta

$$\beta_i = \frac{COV_{im}}{\sigma_m^2} = \frac{\rho_{im}\sigma_i}{\sigma_m}$$

Population Standard Deviation

$$\sigma_r = \sqrt{\frac{\sum_{t=1}^{n} (r_t - \bar{r})^2}{n}}$$

Sample Standard Deviation

$$S_r = \sqrt{\frac{\sum_{t=1}^{n} (r_t - \bar{r})^2}{n - 1}}$$

Req. Rate of Return:
Security Market Line (CAPM)

$$r_i = r_f + (r_m - r_f)\, \beta_i$$

Jensen Performance Index

$$a_p = \bar{r}_p - [\bar{r}_f + (\bar{r}_m - \bar{r}_f)\beta_p]$$

Treynor Performance Index

$$T_p = \frac{\bar{r}_p - \bar{r}_f}{\beta_p}$$

Duration

$$D = \frac{1 + y}{y} - \frac{(1 + y) + t(c - y)}{c[(1 + y)^t - 1] + y}$$

Percentage Change in a Bond's Price, Given a Change in Interest Rates

$$\frac{\Delta P}{P} = -D \left[\frac{\Delta y}{1 + y}\right]$$

Information Ratio

$$IR = \frac{R_P - R_B}{\sigma_A}$$

Effective Rate

$$EAR = \left(1 + \frac{i}{n}\right)^n - 1$$

Taxable Equivalent Yield

$$TEY = r/(1-t)$$

Arithmetic Mean

$$AM = \frac{a_1 + a_2 + a_3 + \ldots + a_n}{n}$$

Sharpe Performance Index

$$S_p = \frac{\bar{r}_p - \bar{r}_f}{\sigma_p}$$

Geometric Mean

$$GM = \sqrt[n]{(1 + r_1) \times (1 + r_2) \times \ldots (1 + r_n)} - 1$$

Unbiased Expectations Theory

$$_1R_N = [(1 + _1R_1)(1 + E(_2r_1)) \ldots (1 + E(_Nr_1))]^{1/N} - 1$$

Holding Period Return

$$HPR = [(1 + r_1) \times (1 + r_2) \times \ldots (1 + r_n)] - 1$$

TAX TABLES

A set of tax tables similar to the ones provided below will be provided electronically during the July 2016 CFP® examination.

Income Tax Rate Tables					

SCHEDULE X: Single

2016

Taxable Income				% on	of the
Over	But Not Over	Pay	+	Excess	amount over
$ 0 –	9,275	$ 0		10%	$ 0
9,275 –	37,650	927.50		15	9,275
37,650 –	91,150	5,183.75		25	37,650
91,150 –	190,150	18,558.75		28	91,150
190,150 –	413,350	46,278.75		33	190,150
413,350 –	415,050	119,934.75		35	413,350
Over 415,050		120,529.75		39.6	415,050

SCHEDULE Y-1: Married Filing Jointly and Surviving Spouse
2016

Taxable Income Over	But Not Over	Pay	+	% on Excess	of the amount over
$ 0 –	18,550	$ 0		10%	$ 0
18,550 –	75,300	1,855.00		15	18,550
75,300 –	151,900	10,367.50		25	75,300
151,900 –	231,450	29,517.50		28	151,900
231,450 –	413,350	51,791.50		33	231,450
413,350 –	466,950	111,818.50		35	413,350
Over 466,950		130,578.50		39.6	466,950

SCHEDULE Y-2: Married Filing Separately
2016

Taxable Income Over	But Not Over	Pay	+	% on Excess	of the amount over
$ 0 –	9,275	$ 0		10%	$ 0
9,275 –	37,650	927.50		15	9,275
37,650 –	75,950	5,183.75		25	37,650
75,950 –	115,725	14,758.75		28	75,950
115,725 –	206,675	25, 895.75		33	115,725
206,675 –	233,475	55,909.25		35	206,675
Over 233,475		65,289.25		39.6	233,475

SCHEDULE Z: Head of Household

2016

Taxable Income		Pay	+	% on Excess	of the amount over
Over	But Not Over				
$ 0 –	13,250	$ 0		10%	$ 0
13,250 –	50,400	1,325.00		15	13,250
50,400 –	130,150	6,897.50		25	50,400
130,150 –	210,800	26,835.00		28	130,150
210,800 –	413,350	49,417.00		33	210,800
413,350 –	441,000	116,258.50		35	413,350
Over 441,000		125,936.00		39.6	441,000

2016 Net Investment Income Tax

The net investment income tax is applied at a rate of 3.8%.

For Individuals

The 3.8% tax applies to the lesser of:
* the net investment income, OR
* the excess of modified adjusted gross income (MAGI) over the following threshold amounts:
  - $250,000 for married filing jointly or qualifying widow(er) with dependent child
  - $125,000 for married filing separately
  - $200,000 for single or head of household

For Trusts and Estates

The 3.8% tax applies to the lesser of:
* the undistributed net investment income, OR
* the excess of the adjusted gross income over $12,400

2016 Additional Medicare Tax

The additional Medicare tax is applied at a rate of .9%

Filing Status	Threshold Amount
Married filing jointly	$250,000
Married filing separately	$125,000
Single, head of household, or qualifying widow(er)	$200,000

2016 Long-Term Capital Gain Rates

	Maximum LTCG Rate
Taxpayers in the 10% or 15% ordinary income tax bracket	0%
Taxpayers in the 25%, 28%, 33%, or 35% ordinary income tax bracket	15%
Taxpayers in the 39.6% ordinary income tax bracket	20%
IRC Section 1250 depreciation recapture	25%
Collectibles	28%

CORPORATE INCOME TAX RATES

2016

Taxable Income Over	But Not Over	Pay	+	% on Excess	of the amount over
$ 0 –	50,000	$ 0		15%	$ 0
50,000 –	75,000	7,500		25	50,000
75,000 –	100,000	13,750		34	75,000
100,000 –	335,000	22,250		39	100,000
335,000 –	10,000,000	113,900		34	335,000
10,000,000 –	15,000,000	3,400,000		35	10,000,000
15,000,000 –	18,333,333	5,150,000		38	15,000,000
18,333,333 –	………..…			35	0

ESTATES AND NONGRANTOR TRUSTS INCOME TAX RATES

2016

Taxable Income Over	But Not Over	Pay	+	% on Excess	of the amount over
$ 0 –	2,550	$ 0		15%	$ 0
2,550 –	5,950	382.50		25	2,550
5,950 –	9,050	1,232.50		28	5,950
9,050 –	12,400	2,100.50		33	9,050
12,400 –	……….	3,206.00		39.6	12,400

STANDARD DEDUCTION AND PERSONAL EXEMPTIONS

2016

Standard Deduction*:

Single	$6,300
Married filing jointly/ Qualifying widow(er)	12,600
Married filing separately	6,300
Head of household	9,300
Dependent	1,050**

* increased by $1,250 for a married taxpayer age 65 or older or blind ($2,500 if both 65 and blind); by $1,550 for a single taxpayer age 65 or older or blind ($3,100 if both 65 and blind)

** or $350 plus earned income, if greater

Personal Exemption: $4,050

2016 Retirement Plan Contribution Limits and Phase-Outs	
Elective deferrals – 401(k), 403(b), 457, and SARSEP	$18,000
Catch-up contributions	$6,000
Defined contribution limit	$53,000
Defined benefit limit	$210,000
SIMPLE plan elective deferral limit	$12,500
Catch-up contributions	$3,000
Maximum includible compensation	$265,000
Highly compensated employee	
Look-back to 2015	$120,000
Look-back to 2016	$120,000
Key employee (top heavy plan)	>$170,000
SEP participation limit	$600
IRA or Roth IRA contribution limit	$5,500
Catch-up contribution	$1,000
IRA deduction phaseout for active participants	
Single	$ 61,000 – $ 71,000
Married filing jointly	$ 98,000 – $118,000
Married filing separately	$ 0 – $ 10,000
Spousal	$184,000 – $194,000
Roth IRA phaseout	
Single	$117,000 – $132,000
Married filing jointly	$184,000 – $194,000

2016 Estate and Gift Tax Rates and Exemptions	
Applicable credit for gift/estate taxes	$2,125,800
Applicable exclusion amount	$5,450,000
Maximum estate/gift tax rate	40%
Maximum Generation-Skipping Transfer Tax (GSTT) rate	40%
Annual gift tax exclusion	$14,000

2016 Social Security Wage Base and Earnings Limits	
Wage base	$118,500
Earnings limitations:	
Below full retirement age	$15,720
Persons reaching full retirement age	$41,880

2016 Social Security Full Retirement Ages			
Year of Birth	Social Security Full Retirement Age	Year of Birth	Social Security Full Retirement Age
1943 – 54	66	1958	66 and 8 months
1955	66 and 2 months	1959	66 and 10 months
1956	66 and 4 months	1960 and later	67
1957	66 and 6 months		

2016 Health Savings Account Limits	
High Deductible Health Plan	
Minimum Deductible Amounts	
Single	$1,300
Family	$2,600
Maximum Out-of-Pocket Limits	
Single	$6,550
Family	$13,100
Contribution Maximums	
Single	$3,350
Family	$6,750
Catch-up contributions (age 55 and older)	$1,000

2016 Education Phase-Outs	
EE Bonds for education – exclusion phaseout	
Single	$77,550 – $92,550
Married filing jointly	$116,300 – $146,300
Coverdell Education Savings Account – contribution phaseout	
Single	$95,000 – $110,000
Married filing jointly	$190,000 – $220,000
Lifetime Learning Credit – AGI phaseout	
Single	$55,000 – $65,000
Married filing jointly	$111,000 – $131,000
American Opportunity Tax Credit – AGI phaseout	
Single	$80,000 – $90,000
Married filing jointly	$160,000 – $180,000
Education Loan Interest Deduction – AGI phaseout	
Single	$65,000 – $80,000
Married filing jointly	$130,000 – $160,000

2016 Alternative Minimum Tax (AMT) Exemptions and Phase-Outs

Filing Status	Exemption	AMTI Phaseout
Single	$53,900	$119,700
Married filing jointly	$83,800	$159,700
Married filing separately	$41,900	$79,850
Trusts and estates	$23,900	$79,850

2016 AMT Rates

AMTI up to $186,300	26%
AMTI over $186,300	28%

2016 CHILD TAX CREDIT

Modified AGI Beginning Phase-Out Range for Child Tax Credit

Married Filing Jointly	$110,000
Single/Head of Household	$ 75,000
Married Filing Separately	$ 55,000

Phase-out complete when MAGI exceeds applicable threshold by $20,000 per child

The tables below will be provided on the exam if needed, or the necessary factors will be provided within the question.

**Table VI – Ordinary Joint Life and Last Survivor Annuities;
Two Lives – Expected Return Multiples**

Ages	65	66	67	68	69	70	71	72	73	74
65	25.0	24.6	24.2	23.8	23.4	23.1	22.8	22.5	22.2	22.0
66	24.6	24.1	23.7	23.3	22.9	22.5	22.2	21.9	21.6	21.4
67	24.2	23.7	23.2	22.8	22.4	22.0	21.7	21.3	21.0	20.8
68	23.8	23.3	22.8	22.3	21.9	21.5	21.2	20.8	20.5	20.2
69	23.4	22.9	22.4	21.9	21.5	21.1	20.7	20.3	20.0	19.6
70	23.1	22.5	22.0	21.5	21.1	20.6	20.2	19.8	19.4	19.1
71	22.8	22.2	21.7	21.2	20.7	20.2	19.8	19.4	19.0	18.6
72	22.5	21.9	21.3	20.8	20.3	19.8	19.4	18.9	18.5	18.2
73	22.2	21.6	21.0	20.5	20.0	19.4	19.0	18.5	18.1	17.7
74	22.0	21.4	20.8	20.2	19.6	19.1	18.6	18.2	17.7	17.3
75	21.8	21.1	20.5	19.9	19.3	18.8	18.3	17.8	17.3	16.9
76	21.6	20.9	20.3	19.7	19.1	18.5	18.0	17.5	17.0	16.5
77	21.4	20.7	20.1	19.4	18.8	18.3	17.7	17.2	16.7	16.2
78	21.2	20.5	19.9	19.2	18.6	18.0	17.5	16.9	16.4	15.9

from Reg. Sec. 1.72-9

One-Life-Expected Return Multiples

Age	Multiples Life Expectancy	Age	Multiples (Life Expectancy)	Age	Multiples (Life Expectancy)
5	76.6	42	40.6	79	10.0
6	75.6	43	39.6	80	9.5
7	74.7	44	38.7	81	8.9
8	73.7	45	37.7	82	8.4
9	72.7	46	36.8	83	7.9
10	71.7	47	35.9	84	7.4
11	70.7	48	34.9	85	6.9
12	69.7	49	34.0	86	6.5
13	68.8	50	33.1	87	6.1
14	67.8	51	32.2	88	5.7
15	66.8	52	31.3	89	5.3
16	65.8	53	30.4	90	5.0
17	64.8	54	29.5	91	4.7
18	63.9	55	28.6	92	4.4
19	62.9	56	27.7	93	4.1
20	61.9	57	26.8	94	3.9
21	60.9	58	25.9	95	3.7
22	59.9	59	25.0	96	3.4
23	59.0	60	24.2	97	3.2
24	58.0	61	23.3	98	3.0
25	57.0	62	22.5	99	2.8
26	56.0	63	21.6	100	2.7
27	55.1	64	20.8	101	2.5
28	54.1	65	20.0	102	2.3
29	53.1	66	19.2	103	2.1
30	52.2	67	18.4	104	1.9
31	51.2	68	17.6	105	1.8
32	50.2	69	16.8	106	1.6
33	49.3	70	16.0	107	1.4
34	48.3	71	15.3	108	1.3
35	47.3	72	14.6	109	1.1
36	46.4	73	13.9	110	1.0
37	45.4	74	13.2	111	0.9
38	44.4	75	12.5	112	0.8
39	43.5	76	11.9	113	0.7
40	42.5	77	11.2	114	0.6
41	41.5	78	10.6	115	0.5

Uniform Table of Applicable Distribution Periods
for Required Minimum Distributions

Age of the Employee	Applicable Divisor	Age of the Employee	Applicable Divisor
70	27.4	93	9.6
71	26.5	94	9.1
72	25.6	95	8.6
73	24.7	96	8.1
74	23.8	97	7.6
75	22.9	98	7.1
76	22.0	99	6.7
77	21.2	100	6.3
78	20.3	101	5.9
79	19.5	102	5.5
80	18.7	103	5.2
81	17.9	104	4.9
82	17.1	105	4.5
83	16.3	106	4.2
84	15.5	107	3.9
85	14.8	108	3.7
86	14.1	109	3.4
87	13.4	110	3.1
88	12.7	111	2.9
89	12.0	112	2.6
90	11.4	113	2.4
91	10.8	114	2.1
92	10.2	115 and older	1.9

CERTIFIED FINANCIAL PLANNER BOARD OF STANDARDS, INC.

2015 Principal Knowledge Topics (72 Topics)

The following Principal Knowledge Topics are based on the results of CFP Board's 2015 Job Analysis Study.

The Principal Knowledge Topics serve as the blueprint for the March 2016 and later administrations of the CFP® Certification Examination. Each exam question will be linked to one of the following Principal Knowledge Topics, in the approximate percentages indicated following the general category headings.

The Principal Knowledge Topics serve as a curricular framework and also represent subject topics that CFP Board accepts for continuing education credit, effective January 2016.

Eight Principal Knowledge Topic Categories

A. **Professional Conduct and Regulation** (7%)

B. **General Financial Planning Principles** (17%)

C. **Education Planning** (6%)

D. **Risk Management and Insurance Planning** (12%)

E. **Investment Planning** (17%)

F. **Tax Planning** (12%)

G. **Retirement Savings and Income Planning** (17%)

H. **Estate Planning** (12%)

A. Professional Conduct and Regulation

A.1.   CFP Board's Code of Ethics and Professional Responsibility and Rules of Conduct

A.2.   CFP Board's Financial Planning Practice Standards

A.3.   CFP Board's Disciplinary Rules and Procedures

A.4.   Function, purpose, and regulation of financial institutions

A.5.   Financial services regulations and requirements

A.6.   Consumer protection laws

A.7.   Fiduciary

Professional Conduct & Regulation

1425 K STREET NW #800 ■ WASHINGTON, DC 20005 ■ P 800-487-1497 ■ F 202-379-2299 ■ CFP.NET

B. General Principles of Financial Planning

B.8.	Financial planning process
B.9.	Financial statements
B.10.	Cash flow management
B.11.	Financing strategies
B.12.	Economic concepts
B.13.	Time value of money concepts and calculations
B.14.	Client and planner attitudes, values, biases and behavioral finance
B.15.	Principles of communication and counseling
B.16.	Debt management

General Financial Planning Principles

C. Education Planning

C.17.	Education needs analysis
C.18.	Education savings vehicles
C.19.	Financial aid
C.20.	Gift/income tax strategies
C.21.	Education financing

Education Planning

D. Risk Management and Insurance Planning

D.22.	Principles of risk and insurance
D.23.	Analysis and evaluation of risk exposures
D.24.	Health insurance and health care cost management (individual)
D.25.	Disability income insurance (individual)
D.26.	Long-term care insurance (individual)
D.27.	Annuities
D.28.	Life insurance (individual)
D.29.	Business uses of insurance
D.30.	Insurance needs analysis
D.31.	Insurance policy and company selection
D.32.	Property and casualty insurance

Risk Management & Insurance Planning

E. Investment Planning

E.33.	Characteristics, uses and taxation of investment vehicles
E.34.	Types of investment risk
E.35.	Quantitative investment concepts
E.36.	Measures of investment returns
E.37.	Asset allocation and portfolio diversification
E.38.	Bond and stock valuation concepts
E.39.	Portfolio development and analysis
E.40.	Investment strategies
E.41.	Alternative investments

F. Tax Planning

F.42.	Fundamental tax law
F.43.	Income tax fundamentals and calculations
F.44.	Characteristics and income taxation of business entities
F.45.	Income taxation of trusts and estates
F.46.	Alternative minimum tax (AMT)
F.47.	Tax reduction/management techniques
F.48.	Tax consequences of property transactions
F.49.	Passive activity and at-risk rules
F.50.	Tax implications of special circumstances
F.51.	Charitable/philanthropic contributions and deductions

G. Retirement Savings and Income Planning

G.52.	Retirement needs analysis
G.53.	Social Security and Medicare
G.54.	Medicaid
G.55.	Types of retirement plans
G.56.	Qualified plan rules and options
G.57.	Other tax-advantaged retirement plans
G.58.	Regulatory considerations
G.59.	Key factors affecting plan selection for businesses

G.60. Distribution rules and taxation

G.61. Retirement income and distribution strategies

G.62. Business succession planning

H. Estate Planning

H.63. Characteristics and consequences of property titling

H.64. Strategies to transfer property

H.65. Estate planning documents

H.66. Gift and estate tax compliance and tax calculation

H.67. Sources for estate liquidity

H.68. Types, features, and taxation of trusts

H.69. Marital deduction

H.70. Intra-family and other business transfer techniques

H.71. Postmortem estate planning techniques

H.72. Estate planning for non-traditional relationships

Contextual Variables

In addition to the Principal Knowledge Topics, other important variables are to be considered when dealing with specific financial planning situations. These are referred to as "Contextual Variables" and are used as part of content development for the CFP® Certification Examination or other case-based scenarios.

More specifically, financial planning situations require the application of financial planning knowledge for different types of clients. Important client details to consider as part of financial planning situations are:

- **Family Status** (traditional family, single parent, same-sex couples, blended families, widowhood)
- **Net Worth** (ultra-high net worth, high net worth, mass affluent, emerging affluent, mass market)
- **Income Level** (high, medium, low)
- **Life or Professional Stage** (student, starting a career, career transition, pre-retirement, retirement)
- **Other Circumstances** (health issues, divorce, change of employment status, aging parents, special needs children)

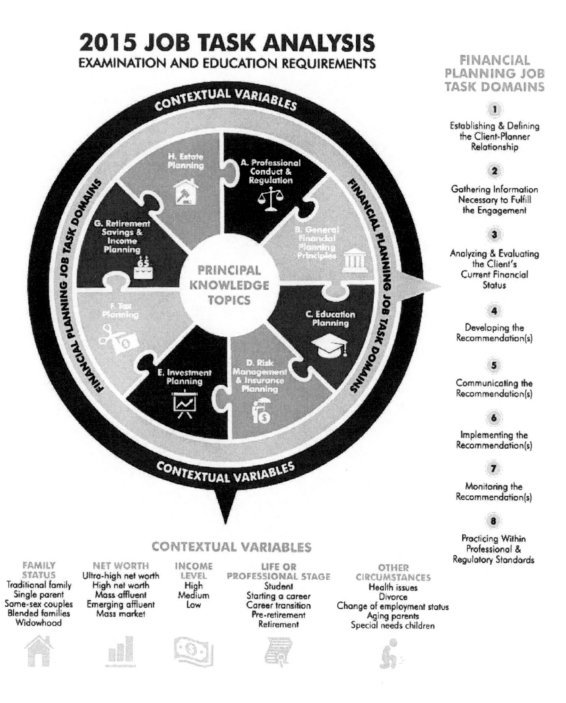

2015 JOB TASK ANALYSIS
EXAMINATION AND EDUCATION REQUIREMENTS

CONTEXTUAL VARIABLES

FINANCIAL PLANNING JOB TASK DOMAINS

PRINCIPAL KNOWLEDGE TOPICS

- H. Estate Planning
- A. Professional Conduct & Regulation
- G. Retirement Savings & Income Planning
- B. General Financial Planning Principles
- F. Tax Planning
- C. Education Planning
- E. Investment Planning
- D. Risk Management & Insurance Planning

CONTEXTUAL VARIABLES

FINANCIAL PLANNING JOB TASK DOMAINS

1 Establishing & Defining the Client-Planner Relationship

2 Gathering Information Necessary to Fulfill the Engagement

3 Analyzing & Evaluating the Client's Current Financial Status

4 Developing the Recommendation(s)

5 Communicating the Recommendation(s)

6 Implementing the Recommendation(s)

7 Monitoring the Recommendation(s)

8 Practicing Within Professional & Regulatory Standards

CONTEXTUAL VARIABLES

FAMILY STATUS	NET WORTH	INCOME LEVEL	LIFE OR PROFESSIONAL STAGE	OTHER CIRCUMSTANCES
Traditional family	Ultra-high net worth	High	Student	Health issues
Single parent	High net worth	Medium	Starting a career	Divorce
Same-sex couples	Mass affluent	Low	Career transition	Change of employment status
Blended families	Emerging affluent		Pre-retirement	Aging parents
Widowhood	Mass market		Retirement	Special needs children

GLOSSARY

RISK MANAGEMENT AND INSURANCE PLANNING

A 12b-1 fee is an annual distribution or marketing fee that may be assessed in the subaccounts of variable annuities and mutual funds. 12b-1 fees can also be used to provide ongoing compensation to sales agents.

A Section 401(k) plan is a defined contribution qualified retirement plan established by an employer and allows employees to save money for retirement in a tax-advantaged way through payroll deductions. Employers typically match a portion of employee contributions as a way to encourage employees to contribute.

A Section 403(b) plan is a retirement plan established by tax-exempt organizations (employers described in Sec. 501(c)(3) of the IRC) and public school districts, and the plan allows employees to save money for retirement in a tax-advantaged way through payroll deductions.

A Section 457 plan is a retirement plan established by governmental units, agencies, and tax-exempt organizations, and the plan allows employees to save money for retirement in a tax-advantaged way through payroll deductions.

In the formula for calculating income taxes, certain deductions, called above-the-line deductions, may be used to reduce the taxpayer's adjusted gross income. Above-the-line deductions may be taken by all taxpayers who qualify for them, regardless of whether they choose to take the standard deduction or itemized deductions later in the tax return.

Absolute liability For certain torts, the law imposes "liability without fault." A person who maintains a dangerous condition on his or her premises, such as keeping a wild animal, or who engages in an activity that involves a high risk of harm to others or to their property in spite of all reasonable care, such as blasting, will be strictly liable for any harm that results. Thus, absolute liability will apply to the keeping of wild animals, manufacturing of explosives, oil well drilling, crop spraying by plane, and containment of water.

An abstract of title is a document containing the results of a historical search of the title to a piece of real property. The abstract will contain a record of all owners or others with an interest in the particular piece of real estate. Included will be such things as transfers of the title to the property that have occurred over time and any encumbrances or liens held by individuals or organizations against the title to the property.

Acceptance of an offer signals the formation of a contract. Acceptance means that there is agreement as to the terms of a contract and the parties are bound. In property insurance, the applicant makes the offer by signing the application for coverage. The insurer accepts the applicant's offer by issuing the policy.

Accidental bodily injury is physical injury to the insured, resulting from an accident. The means is not necessarily accidental.

The accidental death benefit in a life insurance policy specifies that, in addition to the face amount, an extra amount, often equal to the face amount, will be paid to the beneficiary if the insured's death occurs as a result of an accident.

An accumulation unit is a unit in a variable annuity purchased by the annuitant with his or her premium contribution prior to the start of the annuity's liquidation period. As stock market values rise during the accumulation period, the policy owner's contribution buys a smaller number of accumulation units, whereas if stock values fall, a larger number of accumulation units is purchased with the policy owner's contribution. At the end of the accumulation period, the total number of accumulation units that have been purchased is exchanged for annuity units.

Activities of daily living (ADLs) include dressing, walking, bed-to-chair transfer, toileting, bathing, and continence maintenance. Recognizable impairment of the ability to perform two or three ADLs qualifies an insured for the benefits provided by the long-term care insurance policies offered by some companies. Other companies are more severe and require complete inability to perform two or three ADLs for the insured to be eligible for benefits under a long-term care policy.

Actual cash value (ACV) of the loss is the maximum reimbursement that will be provided the claimant under most property insurance contracts. In most cases, ACV is the property's replacement cost minus physical depreciation, not the depreciation the accountant shows in the financial statements.

Additional living expenses are the extra expenses incurred in living elsewhere during the period of time it is impossible to remain in a dwelling that has been damaged by fire or another insured peril. The additional living expense coverage provides reimbursement to the insured and family if the dwelling described in the policy is damaged by an insured peril and thereby becomes uninhabitable. The additional living expense reimbursement is paid only for the length of time necessary to repair or replace the damaged residence. For example, if fire damages the home of the insured, the extra expense incurred to obtain suitable living accommodations at a motel would be covered by the additional living expense coverage.

An additional purchase option, also sometimes referred to as a guaranteed insurability option, is a rider that may be added to a life insurance contract, giving the insured the option of purchasing additional amounts of insurance on specified dates during the life of the policy without having to provide evidence of insurability.

Most insurance policies are contracts of <u>adhesion</u>. This means the contract is written by one party, and the second party either adheres to (or accepts) the contract as written or rejects it. The second party is given no opportunity to modify the language or the terms of the contract.

<u>Adjustable life insurance</u> is a policy designed to provide the insured premium payer with considerable flexibility in the amount of the coverage and the amount of the premium payment, and it permits him or her to lengthen or shorten both the premium-paying period and the protection period. At a given date, the policy may be either term insurance or a limited-payment policy (or some combination of these two types of policies). Increases in the coverage amount usually require evidence of insurability.

In the formula for calculating income taxes, the <u>adjusted gross income</u> is total income minus certain deductions (called above-the-line deductions). Adjusted gross income is the last line on the front of the Form 1040 and the first line on the back of the Form 1040.

<u>Adverse selection</u> is selection against the insurance company. It refers to the tendency of poorer-than-average risks or less-than-desirable entities to seek or to continue insurance to a greater extent than do the better risks. For example, people with health impairments seek life insurance. Homeowners in river valleys seek flood insurance.

An <u>agency</u> is the relationship that exists when one person, the agent, acts on behalf of another person or entity, known as the principal.

In property and casualty insurance, an <u>agent</u> is a person authorized by a company to solicit insurance sales. Such agents are typically authorized to bind the insurer to the contract, which is effective until canceled. In life insurance, an agent is a sales and service representative of the company but has no authority to bind the company.

An <u>aleatory contract</u> is one that may permit one party to receive benefits greatly in excess of the benefits to be received by the other party. Thus, gambling contracts are aleatory contracts. An insurance contract is aleatory because the insured may receive benefits far in excess of the premium paid. On the other hand, a typical sales contract is commutative. Both parties will receive equivalent benefits.

American Agency System is the term used to refer to the system of insurance marketing in which the agent is free to place business with whatever insurer he or she chooses. The agent has no commitment to any one insurer.

The amount of life insurance needed is based on an analysis of the various needs of the insured's dependents, should the income-producer die today.

An annuity is a specified amount of money, paid or received at a specified uniform interval, for a specified period of time. An ordinary annuity makes or receives the payments at the end of each period, such as mortgage payments at the end of each month or dividends received at the end of each quarter.

An annuity due is an annuity in which the first payment is made or received immediately upon inception of the annuity contract or policy. For example, assume a monthly annuity is entered into on June 1, 20XX. If it is an ordinary annuity, the first payment would be made (or received) on July 1, 20XX. On the other hand, if it is an annuity due, the first payment would be made (or received) on June 1, 20XX.

Annuity options A purchaser of an annuity has several options or choices as to types of payout arrangements he or she may select. The five primary annuity options are: (a) straight or pure life annuity, (b) fixed period annuity, (c) fixed amount annuity, (d) period certain and life annuity, and (e) installment refund or cash refund life annuity.

Any occupation definition Under this harsh and severe definition of "total disability," the insured is considered totally disabled only if he or she is unable to perform any and every duty pertaining to any gainful occupation.

Apparent authority is not an authority the principal confers on the agent; rather, this authority arises from appearances the principal has created that led a third party to reasonably believe authority existed. The agent goes beyond his or her expressed and implied authority. Two conditions are necessary for apparent authority to exist: (a) The principal creates the appearance of authority or makes no effort to prevent the agent from overstepping his or her authority. (b) The third party has no way of knowing that the agent has overstepped his or her authority.

The appraisal provision of the typical property insurance policy requires each party to select an appraiser. The two appraisers select an umpire, who resolves disputes when the two appraisers cannot agree.

Assistance and cooperation Most liability insurance policies require the insured to assist the insurer in its defense of a liability claim. The cooperation of the insured will obviously be important to the insurer in building its defense. The insured usually has more information about the event than anyone else and can be helpful in finding witnesses who were present at the time the event occurred.

Assumption of risk A plaintiff cannot recover if he or she had knowledge of the risks involved and voluntarily accepted the exposure to the danger(s) involved. Legally, "no legal wrong is done to one who consents."

An attractive nuisance is any dangerous instrumentality (place, condition, or object) that is likely to entice or allure children (for example, earth-moving equipment or an automobile junkyard). Property owners are expected to recognize the hazardous nature of such instrumentalities and exposures and take special precautions to prevent children from gaining entrance to the property. The property owner may be held liable for failure to take prudent steps to prevent children from having access to the attractive nuisance.

The automatic premium loan provision is an option available to a life insurance policy owner that specifies that if the policy owner fails to pay the premium due by the end of the grace period, a loan against the policy's cash value in the amount of the premium will automatically be established by the insurance company. The purpose of the automatic premium loan provision is mainly to prevent an inadvertent lapse of the policy through failure of the policy owner to pay each premium on a timely basis.

Automobile liability insurance is a form of liability insurance that is designed to protect the insured parties for legal liability arising out of the ownership or use of a covered auto. An owner or operator of an auto may be held liable for bodily injury to occupants or other third parties, as well as for property damage. An operator of an auto may drive negligently, cause a collision with another auto, and injure the other driver and damage the other auto. The operator of an auto, in assisting a passenger to enter the auto, may accidentally close the auto door on the passenger's hand, causing a permanent injury.

The relation of earnings to insurance or the average earnings clause is sometimes used in disability income policies. The typical clause states that if at the time disability commences, the insured's total disability income benefit exceeds the insured's earned income, or average earned income for the preceding two years (whichever is greater), the income benefits under the policy will be reduced proportionately.

Benchmark figures showing cost per $1,000 of life insurance by age group were derived by Dr. Joseph Belth from certain United States population death rates. The benchmark figures can be used to determine if the life insurance protection offered by a life insurance company is reasonably priced. If the insurer's price per $1,000 is close to the death claim or the benchmark figure, the coverage is reasonably priced.

The benefit period in a disability income policy is the maximum period of time during which benefits may be payable. Short-term disability income coverages usually have benefit periods of up to two years. Long-term disability income coverages, on the other hand, may have benefit periods as long as the lifetime of the insured or until the insured reaches a specified age, such as age 65. The term "benefit period" is also used in the field of long-term care coverage to specify the maximum duration over which the costs of long-term care will be reimbursed by a policy. Some such policies provide a lifetime benefit period. Others provide a shorter benefit period but may contain a restoration of benefits clause that restores some or all of the policy's benefit after the insured is out of a care facility for a specified number of days.

A binder is an agreement (either written or oral) whereby one party agrees to provide insurance coverage for another party pending a final underwriting processing of the application. Thus, the binder may "bind" coverage for a temporary period of time.

Blue Cross is an independent, nonprofit corporation providing service benefits in the form of hospital care for its membership in a limited geographical area. Blue Cross plans operate in the United States on a prepayment basis and offer hospital service benefits. Each plan has a contractual pricing arrangement with the hospitals for services provided by the latter.

Blue Shield is similar to Blue Cross, except the former provides medical services other than hospital care. Thus, surgery and other physician services are provided by Blue Shield. The Blue Shield plan arranges contractual pricing agreements with participating area physicians. "Reasonable and customary" surgical charges are paid in full.

Bodily injury by accidental means Accidental means are means that are set in motion unintentionally by the injured party (the insured). If I jump from a tree and break my leg, the means of the injury are not accidental. In jumping from the tree, I did exactly as I intended.

A breach of warranty is an act that is contrary to the terms of one's promise or agreement. Thus, it is a broken promise. For example, the insured warranted that a watchman would be on duty at all times. Actually, the watchman went home at 4:00 a.m. every morning. This would be a breach of warranty.

A broker is a person who is legally the agent of the insurance buyer. Although he or she represents the buyer, the broker is paid a commission by the insurance company.

The Business Auto Coverage Form is a form under which commercial automobile insurance is written. The Business Auto Coverage Form insures the business against loss arising out of ownership, operation, and other relationships to vehicles used for business purposes. The policy also provides coverage for medical payments, physical damage, and for the uninsured motorists exposure.

The <u>Business Income Coverage Form</u> protects against loss arising from the necessary interruption or suspension of business caused by damage to or destruction of property at the described location by a covered peril.

<u>Business interruption insurance</u> is the name formerly used to describe what is now called business income coverage.

The <u>businessowners policy (BOP)</u> is a package policy designed specifically for small and medium-size retail stores, office buildings, apartment buildings, and similar firms. It covers the business building, business personal property, loss of income for the business, and liability exposures. It may also be endorsed to cover employee dishonesty, outdoor signs, plate glass, earthquake, and boiler and machinery exposures.

A <u>business pursuit</u> is any activity related to the person's trade, profession, or occupation. Such activities are normally excluded from the liability coverage of homeowners policies.

A <u>cancellable</u> health insurance policy is a contract that may be terminated by the insurer at any time during its term. Five days written notice is required. The unearned premium must be returned. Cancellation of the coverage has no effect on any outstanding claim.

When property is held longer than one year and is sold for a gain, it receives special tax treatment as a <u>capital gain</u> rather than being taxed as ordinary income, which is taxed at the taxpayer's highest marginal tax bracket. The long-term capital gain rate is 15% for most taxpayers (0% for those in the 10% and 15% marginal brackets; 20% for those in the 39.6% marginal bracket).

A <u>captive agent</u> represents exclusively one company and its affiliates.

The <u>capture theory</u> holds that in some industries, regulators tend to become dominated by those they regulate. For example, in some cases, regulators are selected from the industry to be regulated and later return to it.

A <u>career agent</u> is a life insurance agent representing one or a few insurers. Career agents usually are supported by an agency in the form of office space, help, and education and training programs.

A <u>cash refund annuity</u> is an annuity that promises to pay a life income to the annuitant but that also promises that should the annuitant die before receiving benefits in an amount equal to the purchase price paid for the annuity, the difference, without interest, will be refunded to the annuitant's heirs in a lump sum.

A life insurance policy's cash surrender value is the amount available in cash upon voluntary termination of the policy. The typical life insurance policy has a schedule showing the cash value available at each age of the insured.

Causes of loss forms are used under the commercial package policy to indicate the perils for which coverage is provided. There are four such forms: (a) basic form, (b) broad form, (c) special form, and (d) earthquake form.

Disability income policies typically include a change of occupation provision that permits the insurer to reduce the benefit payable in the event the insured changes to a more hazardous occupation. The benefit is reduced to the benefit the premium paid purchases at the more hazardous employment classification. If the insured changes to a less hazardous occupation, the premium is reduced, but the benefit remains the same.

Claims expense. Under the Additional Coverages of Section II, the homeowners policy commits the insurer to pay (above and beyond the limit of liability) any expenses incurred in defending the insured against any suit covered by the policy, plus interest on any judgments and some other specified legal costs.

The claims-made form is used in commercial liability insurance. It makes coverage applicable if a claim is filed with the insurer during the policy period. The older occurrence-basis general liability policy makes coverage applicable if the injury or damage occurs during the policy period, regardless of when suit is filed.

A client profile is a description of the client that sets forth the factors that should be taken into account in trying to develop an appropriate life insurance program for him or her. The profile will set forth the client's age, income, health, wealth accumulation, and other pertinent information.

Code definition of life insurance To qualify for the favorable federal income tax treatment accorded life insurance, a policy must meet either one of two tests. (a) The cash value accumulation test requires that the policy's cash surrender value must never exceed the net single premium the insurer would charge to have the policy paid up (if the insured's age 95 is the earliest age of policy maturity for the policy's face amount). The net single premium computation can be made using either 4% interest or the policy's guaranteed interest rate if it is larger. (b) The second test is really two tests: (i) a guideline premium test, and (ii) a cash value corridor test. The guideline premium test is met if the sum of the premiums that the policy owner must pay does not exceed: (a) "the guideline single premium," or (b) "the sum of the guideline level premiums." The calculation of "the guideline single premium" must be made using the larger of 6% interest or the policy's guaranteed interest rate. The guideline level premium is the annual level premium required to fund the policy's future benefits, assuming the time period for funding extends to at least the insured's age 95. Thus, the premium fails the guideline premium test if the premium exceeds the amount needed to fund the policy's death benefit.

A policy will fail the cash value corridor test if the policy's death benefit is less than a specified percentage of the policy's cash surrender value.

From all this detail, it is important to remember that the government's objective is to prohibit policy owners from being able to accumulate on a tax-deferred basis excessive cash values relative to the amount of pure life insurance or death protection provided by the policy.

Coinsurance In property and liability insurance, the coinsurance clause is a policy provision requiring the insured to maintain coverage equal to at least a specified percentage of the value of the property insured. Normally, there is a rate reduction for purchasing insurance to the specified percentage of the value of the property. If the insured fails to comply with the clause by failing to maintain the required percentage of coverage to the property's value, he or she will suffer a penalty in the event of an insured loss. The penalty is in the form of reduced claim payment. The insurer will pay only that percentage of the loss that the amount of coverage carried bears to the amount of coverage specified. (Usually, the coverage specified is 80% of the property's value at the time of the loss.) See also next Glossary term.

A coinsurance provision in health insurance requires the insured to pay a percentage of each medical expense that is in excess of the deductible. This provision (clause) is frequently referred to as the "percentage participation" clause.

Cold lead advertising is the use of a marketing method that fails to clearly disclose that the purpose of the marketing is to solicit insurance and that contact will be made by an insurance agent. Cold lead advertising is a prohibited sales practice.

The collateral source rule holds that legal damages assessed against a tortfeasor should not be reduced by the amount of any other recovery available to the injured party.

Collision is damage to an auto caused by upset or impact with another vehicle or object.

The commercial general liability (CGL) policy provides coverage for those liability risks to which most commercial firms are exposed (including premises and operations, products and completed operations, liability arising out of independent contractors, and contractually-assumed liabilities).

The <u>commercial package policy (CPP)</u> is a multi-line policy providing property and liability coverage in the one policy. The CPP includes commercial auto insurance, among other coverages.

The twelve <u>Commercial Property Coverage Forms</u> provide coverage for different types of losses to commercial property. Some forms are appropriate for covering direct loss to commercial property. Other forms are appropriate for covering indirect or consequential losses for commercial firms.

<u>Commercial property floater risks</u> are personal property that is mobile and thus exposed to loss caused by the perils of transportation. The 1977 definition of inland marine commercial property floater risks lists twenty-two types of coverage. These twenty-two commercial property floater risks might be divided into four subclasses (Business Floater Policies, Dealers' Forms, Bailee Forms, and Miscellaneous Policies).

<u>Common carriers</u> are agencies of transportation (such as trucks or railroads) that carry goods by offering a scheduled service between specific locations. Common carriers are distinguished from contract carriers that provide transport service under contracts arranged with individual customers.

<u>Common Conditions Form</u> The commercial package policy contains substantial standardization for the commercial line forms. The structure of each of the policies is basically the same. Each commercial package policy includes a standard common declarations part, a Common Conditions Form, and the specific forms appropriate for the particular line of coverage. The Common Conditions Form includes provisions such as how to cancel the policy, who is responsible for paying premiums, and how to make changes to the policy.

A <u>common disaster clause</u> is a clause in a life insurance policy designed to settle the question of who is to receive the proceeds in the event that the insured and the beneficiary both die in a single occurrence and there is no evidence as to which survived the other. The question is whether the proceeds go to the beneficiary or to the estate of the deceased insured. Common disaster clauses typically follow the Uniform Simultaneous Death Act of the state, which specifies that if there is no evidence as to which person survived the other, it will be presumed that the insured survived the beneficiary. The clause may also be worded so as to provide the reverse presumption if that is the wish of the policy owner.

<u>Comparative negligence</u> means that when two parties are at fault, damages are to be apportioned between them. There are currently three variations:

(a) Under the pure type, the claimant's recovery is diminished by his or her proportion of total negligence.

(b)   Under the 50% rule, the claimant may recover as long as his or her negligence is not greater than that of the defendant (the plaintiff does not recover anything if he or she is found to be 51% responsible).

(c)   Under the 49% rule, the plaintiff is permitted to recover reduced damages as long as his or her negligence is "less than" or "not as great as" that of the defendant (no recovery for the plaintiff if his or her negligence is found to be 50%).

Competent parties are one of the four requirements for a legal contract. A person would lack legal competency to enter into a binding contract if he or she were a minor, mentally incompetent, or intoxicated. Within a reasonable time after reaching his or her majority, a person may disaffirm a contract entered into during his or her minority. A minor's contracts are voidable at his or her option at any time. Many states have reduced the legal age for purposes of negotiating a contract for life and health insurance. Therefore, if the applicant resided in one of the states permitting the reduced legal age for life insurance, the minor applicant could negotiate a binding contract.

The term comprehensive is used in insurance to refer to broad, all-inclusive coverage. For automobile insurance purposes, the comprehensive coverage is available for all damage to the insured vehicle (not excluded) except collision damage.

Comprehensive automobile coverage is coverage for physical damage to the insured auto other than damage caused by collision (unless the damage is excluded).

Comprehensive major medical is usually written on a group insurance plan and is designed to provide the protection offered by a combination of a basic plan and major medical coverage. It is characterized by low deductible amounts and coinsurance with the insured paying a portion of cost above the deductible and the insurance company paying the remainder. Some comprehensive major medical policies have no coinsurance above a stated maximum amount of medical expenses.

The comprehensive personal liability (CPL) insurance policy provides liability coverage similar to the liability coverage provided by Section II of the homeowners policies. The CPL policy is designed for individuals who do not purchase a homeowners policy. The coverage is "comprehensive" in that it provides protection against all types of liability exposures included within the broad insuring agreement, except those specifically excluded.

Compulsory automobile liability insurance laws require the owner of automobiles registered in the state to have liability insurance or, in some instances, an approved substitute form of security.

Concealment is the intentional omission of material information in completing an application for insurance. The information omitted is considered material if the insurer would have made a different underwriting decision if the withheld information had been disclosed.

A conditionally renewable health insurance policy is a continuous term policy that the insurer may terminate by not renewing it under certain conditions stated in the contract. From the insured's point of view, this type of policy gives greater security as to renewability than does an optionally renewable policy (under the latter, renewability may be refused for no reason) but is less secure than guaranteed renewable or noncancellable policies.

Conditions Policy conditions set forth certain limitations on the insurer's liability for covered losses or specify specific duties and obligations for the insured. The purpose of the specified conditions is to make more definitive the specific coverage that is being provided. They provide the ground rules for the continuance of the insurance agreement. Those conditions that relate to the policy owner's duties and obligations are designed to protect the insurer and assure the company that the arrangement will be carried out as contemplated when the contract was accepted.

Condominium owner's form: HO-6 covers the unique exposures that confront the typical condominium unit owner. The purchase of insurance coverage on the building by the condo association means the individual unit owner must provide coverage only for his or her unit's contents and any improvements he or she installed in the individual unit. HO-6 generally parallels the coverage of HO-4, providing protection against loss by the same broad form perils.

The consideration is that which is given to one party as an inducement for the completion of a contract. For insurance contracts, the consideration provided by the applicant is the premium, the statements in the application, and the promise to abide by the conditions of the contract. The insurer's consideration is the promise to pay valid claims submitted for losses incurred.

Consumer-Directed Health Plans (CDHPs) are a combination of a high deductible health insurance plan and a Health Savings Account (HSA).

A contingent beneficiary is the person or persons designated to receive a life insurance policy's death benefit if the primary beneficiary dies prior to the death of the insured.

Continuing care retirement communities (CCRCs) provide long-term care in an apartment-house setting. The person pays a single premium initially. The person also pays a continuing monthly maintenance fee, which amount varies (usually upward) as inflation has its impact.

Contractual liability is liability a person acquires because he or she signs a contract agreeing to accept liability for acts of others or for circumstances involving others. For example, manufacturers frequently sign a contract agreeing to hold a railroad harmless for any negligence of the railroad in operating a side track the railroad builds leading to the manufacturer's loading platform.

Contributory negligence means that the plaintiff was responsible for the plaintiff's own injury to some extent. It is conduct by the plaintiff that falls below the standard required for his or her own protection. In some jurisdictions, the plaintiff could not recover even if his or her negligence was slight when compared to that of the defendant. A more reasonable approach to the concept of contributory negligence is comparative negligence. (See Glossary Term, "comparative negligence," above.)

A coordination of benefits clause is a provision in a medical expense insurance policy designed to prevent the insured from collecting from more than one insurance policy in such a way as to recover more than 100% of the eligible expenses that he or she has incurred. The clause typically establishes either that the different policies will share in the reimbursement of the insured in some proportion or that one policy shall be primary, meaning that it pays the full amount up to its limit of liability, and any other policy will be secondary.

A corridor deductible is a deductible in a medical expense insurance policy that applies after benefits from a basic or underlying coverage have been exhausted and before benefits from a supplemental, or major medical, plan begin to be available.

Cost-of-living adjustments are provisions available through riders to disability income policies. Such riders provide increases in disability income benefits after a disability starts, thereby providing some means of preserving the real purchasing power of the benefits once a disability has begun.

Covered charges in a medical expense insurance policy refer to types of expenses that are eligible for reimbursement. For example, the costs of lab tests while in a hospital would be covered charges, whereas, typically, the cost of a television set in one's hospital room is not a covered charge.

Covered persons are persons whose property, life, health, or activities are insured by a particular type of insurance. For example, for a list of covered persons see those identified as "insured" under the liability section of the PAP or the uninsured motorists coverage of the PAP.

Crime insurance The commercial crime policy is composed of the standard parts used for all the commercial property coverage policies: the common policy declarations, the common policy conditions, a Commercial Crime Declarations Form, a Crime General Provisions Form, and one or more crime coverage forms and endorsements. In total, there are fourteen crime coverage forms, Forms A through N.

In order to be eligible to receive benefits under Social Security, a worker must be currently or fully insured. <u>Currently insured status</u> allows a deceased, retired, or disabled worker to receive limited benefits. To be currently insured, a worker must have earned 6 of the last 13 credits available (a worker can earn a maximum of 4 credits per year, and one credit is earned for each $1,260 earned in 2016).

<u>Custodial care</u> is the third level of care provided by long-term care institutions. This is care for which medical services are not needed. The main services provided are food preparation, food service, bathing, and moving patient from bed to chair and, subsequently, from chair to bed.

<u>Custodianships</u>, or custodial accounts, are accounts in which property is placed under the care of a third party, who manages it for the benefit of a child-beneficiary. Custodial accounts are authorized under the state's UGMA or UTMA statutes.

<u>Damage to property of others</u> is one of the four additional coverages under Section II (Liability Section) of the homeowners policy. It is a non-liability coverage that pays for damage to the property of others that is caused by an insured, regardless of whether the insured is legally liable. The insuring agreement states, "We will pay up to $500 per occurrence for property damage to property of others caused by an insured." **Note:** The harm must have been caused by an insured, and the property must have actually been damaged. If an insured borrows a neighbor's golf clubs and loses one, the loss would not be covered. There are four exclusions relating to this coverage: (a) losses covered under Section I; (b) intentional damage; (c) damage to owned and rented property; and (d) business pursuits, uninsured locations, and vehicles.

The <u>declarations</u> section of an insurance policy contains the representations of the applicant concerning the location, condition, and other features of the property or exposure being covered by the policy.

A <u>deductible</u> provision in a property insurance or health insurance policy requires the policy owner to pay part of each loss. The insurance benefit provided by the insurer is the excess of the loss or claim over the amount of the deductible. It operates in the same manner as the deductible in automobile physical damage coverage.

In calculating income taxes for the year, <u>deductions</u> are certain types of expenses incurred throughout the year that taxpayers are permitted to use to reduce income. Deductions may be broken down into above-the-line deductions and below-the-line deductions. For below-the-line deductions, taxpayers can choose to take a standard deduction amount, or they can choose to itemize deductions, such as qualified mortgage interest, state and local income taxes, and charitable contributions.

A deferred annuity is an annuity whose liquidation period does not begin until more than one benefit payment interval has elapsed after purchase. For example, an annuity that is purchased by a 30-year-old athlete with a single premium under which the benefits are to begin when he or she is age 50 is a deferred annuity.

A defined-contribution plan is a qualified retirement plan established by an employer in which individual accounts are established for participating employees, and the employer contributes a percentage of each employee's compensation. Benefits are based on amounts contributed to each participant's account and the returns earned on the accounts.

A delay clause is a clause inserted into a life insurance settlement arrangement to resolve the possible problem where a beneficiary outlives the insured by a short period of time, both of whom die as a result of a common accident. The delay clause typically states that the beneficiary will be entitled to the proceeds only if he or she outlives the insured by at least some minimum period of time, such as 30 days. Otherwise, the proceeds belong to the estate of the insured or to a named contingent beneficiary.

A direct writer is an insurance company whose agents, as salaried salespersons, sell directly to prospects. Direct writers are distinguished from those companies that use commission agents who may represent more than one insurer. The term is also frequently used to refer to carriers that operate through exclusive agents. In reinsurance, the term "direct writer" refers to the company that originally writes the business to be reinsured.

Directors and officers errors and omissions insurance provides coverage for corporate officers and directors for suits claiming that these officials are guilty of mismanagement. The policy contains a deductible, and there is typically a 5% coinsurance provision applicable to any loss above the deductible.

Dividend options Participating life insurance policies permit the policy owner to elect from among several forms as to how he or she will take the policy's annual dividend. Thus, dividends may be taken in cash, applied toward payment of the policy's current premium, applied to the purchase of paid-up additions to the policy, or left on deposit with the insurance company to accumulate at interest. The "fifth" dividend option allows use of all or part of the dividend to purchase term life insurance up to the amount of any policy loan or cash value.

Dollar cost averaging is an investment strategy requiring an investor to make purchases of the same dollar amount at regular intervals, such as monthly or quarterly. Rather than investing a lump sum in the market all at once when the market may be at a high point, investments are spread over time to reduce the risk of buying at the wrong time. By investing at regular intervals, some dollars are invested when market prices are higher, and some dollars are invested when market prices are lower, creating the potential for a lower average cost per unit (share). Dollar cost averaging does not, however, eliminate the risk of loss.

A dram shop liability policy provides coverage for the insured's liability arising out of the sale or serving of alcoholic beverages. Coverage may be purchased on either an occurrence or a claims-made basis.

The dual-capacity doctrine is of significance for an employer who may be liable in its capacity as an employer of employees and liable as a business firm, which liability is completely separate from the business firm's position or capacity as the employer of the injured or aggrieved employee. For example, an employee may be injured as the result of a tire blowout, and the defective tire was manufactured by the employee's employer.

Due care is the process a financial planner must follow in obtaining the available information and transmitting this information to his or her client, along with a carefully prepared, objective analysis.

The elimination period (waiting period) specified in a disability income policy makes the insured bear the burden of the first few days of lost income arising out of disability. It is a deductible that requires the insured to absorb the loss of earnings for the first few days of any disability.

Employers liability and workers' compensation insurance are needed by the employer because the employer may be sued by the employee's spouse, as well as being responsible for injuries to the employee arising out of and in the course of the employee's employment.

An endorsement is language added to an insurance policy that is designed to modify the insuring agreement, the exclusions, or the conditions of a policy. When such amendments are added to a life insurance policy, they are usually referred to as "riders."

The entire contract clause is a provision included in a life insurance policy that states that the policy and the application attached to the policy constitute the entire contract between the parties. In other words, parol (oral) evidence may not be introduced to show that the terms of the policy are other than as written.

Errors and omissions insurance is professional liability insurance coverage for individuals working in such professions as accounting, insurance, law, or real estate, where there is a possibility of legal liability resulting from the rendering, or failure to render, professional services.

An estate tax is a tax imposed on a decedent's right to transfer property to heirs and beneficiaries at death.

Exclusion is a condition, peril, hazard, or event that is specifically eliminated from the coverage of an insurance policy. For example, "war" is an event that is typically excluded in property insurance policies.

Existing insurance means the amount of life insurance the client has in force at the present time. A listing of each specific policy showing the amount of insurance by policy number is desirable. The client must recognize that his or her group coverage is only temporary since a change of employment status may mean reduced coverage.

Express authority is the authority or power given by the insurance company to its agents as set forth in the agency agreement or contract.

The extended term option is a nonforfeiture option in a life insurance policy that provides that the cash surrender value will be used as a single premium to buy term insurance in an amount equal to the original face amount of the policy. The length of the term will depend upon the size of the cash value and the attained age of the insured at the time the option is selected.

Extra Expenses are one of the additional coverages provided by the Business Income Coverage Form. Extra Expenses are expenses that would normally not be incurred but that are necessary and are incurred during the period of restoration.

The facility of payment clause provides that the insurer may pay a life insurance policy's death benefit to any relative by blood or marriage of the insured or beneficiary whom the company believes is entitled to receive it, if the death benefit does not exceed $1,000. This provision is designed to relieve the insurer of the problem of finding an authorized and legitimate payee for the death proceeds when the dollar amount is very small.

A family income policy is a whole life policy combined with decreasing term insurance for the first several (usually 20) years of coverage. The term insurance is designed to provide income for the remainder of the child-rearing years, following the early death of the breadwinner.

A family maintenance policy is like the family income policy, but the term coverage is level, rather than decreasing.

A family protection policy is a package policy covering both parents and the children. Usually, the package consists of whole life on Dad, term to Dad's age 65 on Mom, and convertible term to age 21 on each child.

Under the family purpose doctrine, the owner of an automobile is held liable for the negligent acts of members of his or her family or household in their operation of the family car. The rationale is that the family member is acting in the capacity of agent for the car owner. The principal (the car owner) is liable for the acts of his or her agent.

Fidelity bonds provide coverage for a business firm for exposure to loss resulting from employees' dishonesty. They cover an employer's loss of money, securities, or other personal property as a result of fraud, forgery, embezzlement, and theft by employees.

The Financial Planning Process is a six-step process that is used to develop comprehensive strategies to assist clients in achieving their goals and objectives. The six steps in the financial planning process are:

1. Establish and define the client-planner relationship
2. Gather information, including goals and priorities
3. Analyze and evaluate the client's current financial status
4. Develop and present the financial plan
5. Implement the financial plan
6. Monitor the plan

Financial responsibility laws Typical state financial responsibility laws require that any driver involved in any manner in an automobile accident that causes bodily injury or property damage to other than the property of the owner or driver will have his or her driver's license and automobile registration revoked unless such driver can demonstrate financial ability to pay any judgment that may result from that particular accident. Most states require that the driver must also provide evidence of financial responsibility for any future accidents.

FINRA is a self-regulatory organization whose members are broker-dealers. FINRA oversees broker-dealers and writes and enforces rules for sales of securities and for those who sell them. Anyone who represents buyers or sellers of securities must register with FINRA under the sponsorship of a broker-dealer.

Fire and allied lines refers to the property insurance coverage that was provided business firms in earlier days. The coverage provided indemnity for loss caused by the traditional property perils that property insurance policies contained.

Fire legal liability insurance provides liability coverage for damage to rental property caused by the renter's negligence. Because of the exclusion of coverage for property under the care, custody, and control of the insured, the owner may seek to recover for a fire loss by suing the tenant. The tenant may have a need for legal liability insurance.

First-aid expense is a coverage included in Section II of the homeowners policy under Additional Coverages. The insurer promises to pay, in addition to the policy's limit of liability, expenses incurred by the insured for immediate medical services deemed necessary at the time of an accident involving the insured.

First-dollar coverage means that the insured pays no part of certain medical expenses. There is no deductible and no coinsurance. This approach is used in some insurance company comprehensive plans to compete with the Blues, whose traditional philosophy has been to provide "first-dollar" coverage.

First-to-die life insurance policy See Glossary term, "joint life insurance policy," below.

A franchise or payroll deduction life insurance plan is the offering of individual life insurance products to employees of a common employer. Employees electing to purchase one or more of the available insurance coverages are offered the same types of policies available from an agent. The employer deducts the premium from the employee's paycheck and mails an aggregate premium to the insurer for all the employees.

Freight insurance reimburses the owner of a ship when the ship is lost at sea and the ship owner does not receive payment for carrying the goods that also sank.

In order to be eligible to receive benefits under Social Security, a worker must be currently or fully insured. Fully insured status allows a deceased, retired, or disabled worker to receive a full range of benefits. To be fully insured, a worker must have earned 40 credits during their lifetime (a worker can earn a maximum of 4 credits per year, and one credit is earned for each $1,260 earned in 2016).

A Garage Coverage Form provides comprehensive liability insurance for garages and other commercial firms engaged in the sale of automobiles and automotive products and services. It also provides physical damage coverage for the insured's property.

A "gatekeeper" physician is a primary care physician. In a typical HMO plan, if the subscriber wishes to consult with a specialist for further care, the primary physician, or gatekeeper physician, must give his or her consent.

General agents assist the insurer in performing its marketing functions. In life insurance, a pure general agency would be owned by the general agent who would be granted an overriding commission that provides funds to pay a commission to the sales people and salaries to the office staff. A life insurance general agency should be contrasted with a branch office, which is owned and operated by the insurer. In property and liability insurance, the general agent takes some responsibility for underwriting and claims administration. When the general agency is specialized in the handling of particular property or liability lines, the underwriting function becomes an extremely important part of its overall duties.

A general damage is a catch-all category for liability claims that traditionally include such intangible injuries or grievances as pain and suffering, disfigurement, mental anguish, and loss of consortium.

A general liability insurance policy provides liability coverage for business firms. It is designed to provide protection against nonautomobile liability exposures that do not involve injuries to employees. It provides coverage against two major exposures: (a) premises and operations, and (b) products and completed operations.

A grace period is a period (usually 31 days) following the premium due date during which if the premium is unpaid, the contract continues in full force. Upon death during the grace period, the amount of the premium in default is deducted from the proceeds of the policy. The premium may be paid during the grace period to prevent lapse of the policy.

The gross estate is the name given under the federal estate tax laws to all property that a decedent transfers at death. The gross estate includes the total value of all of the assets the decedent owned at death, plus some assets transferred shortly before death and some adjustments for items the decedent did not own but retained control over at death.

A guaranteed insurability rider may be included in life and health insurance policies and, more recently, in long-term care insurance policies. Such riders permit the insured to acquire additional units of coverage at specific dates in limited amounts without having to provide the insurer with evidence of insurability.

A guaranteed renewable disability income policy gives the insured the right to continue the policy in force by the timely payment of premiums to a specified maximum age, during which time the insurer has no right to increase the premium for an individual insured, but only for the entire classification in which the insured was placed when the policy was issued.

Guest laws are state statutes that limit the right of a guest to sue the host automobile driver for negligence. These statutes were designed to minimize collusion between the host driver and his or her injured guest. A host driver may be sued only for "gross, willful and wanton negligence." He or she may not be sued for mere "ordinary negligence."

A hazard is any condition that creates or increases the probability of the occurrence of a loss or increases the magnitude of loss from a given peril. A can of lighter fluid near a fireplace is a hazard. A loose board in a stairway is a hazard. A faulty engine in a passenger airplane is a hazard.

Health insurance is a broad term that includes both medical expense insurance and disability income insurance.

Health insurance exchanges (a.k.a. heath insurance marketplace) were established under the Affordable Care Act as a means to create an organized and competitive market in which individuals may purchase health insurance. Some Marketplaces are operated by the states, while others are run for the states by the federal government at www.healthcare.gov.

A health maintenance organization (HMO) is a prepaid medical group practice plan providing health care benefits. The individual subscribers pay an annual fixed fee that permits the subscribers and their families to receive comprehensive health care services without an additional charge. Preventive health services are emphasized by the HMOs.

Home care is the lowest level of care provided for patients needing long-term care. Home care is a realistic option when the person is capable of providing basic services for himself or herself and thus can be permitted to reside at home with or without someone living with him or her. Home care is more economical and cost-effective than institutional care. In some cases, a daily visit to the person's home by a nurse is necessary. In other cases, a nurse comes to the home only once or twice a week.

Homeowners broad form: HO-2 is for homeowners, with a minimum of $15,000 of insurance on the dwelling. The policy provides coverage against all the perils insured under HO-1 and also protects against loss caused by the following perils: falling objects; weight of ice, snow, or sleet; heat or air conditioning damage; water damage; freezing of plumbing; and injury by artificially generated electricity. These are the broad form perils.

Homeowners modified coverage form: HO-8. This provides homeowners coverage to owners of certain types of older property. Some dwellings, for example, were built many years ago, when labor-intensive techniques characterized the home-building industry. These dwellings often involve obsolete types of construction or are too large in relation to the insured's needs. Losses are settled on an actual cash value (ACV) basis, never on a replacement cost basis. Theft coverage is provided for the premises only with a $1,000 maximum per occurrence. Theft losses are also subject to a $250 deductible.

Homeowners special form: HO-3 is for homeowners, with a minimum of $20,000 of insurance on the dwelling. The coverage for the dwelling and other structures is open-perils coverage, while the perils covered for personal property are the broad form perils. This policy is called the "special form."

Homeowners form: HO-5 is similar to HO-3, except that it provides open-perils coverage on personal property.

Homeowners tenant's form: HO-4 provides no coverage on a dwelling or on other structures. The coverage, with a minimum of $6,000, is on personal property and loss of use. The perils are the same as for the broad form HO-2. The coverage provided by HO-4 is designed for tenants.

A hospital reimbursement contract is an insurance policy designed to pay to the insured (sometimes to the hospital) all or a substantial part of the cost of room and board when the insured is confined to a hospital.

A hospital service benefit contract provides hospital services to the insured and family members for a stated number of days, rather than providing cash indemnity. Blue Cross has traditionally operated under this type of arrangement.

The human life value of a person is the present value of that portion of a person's future total earned income that, barring death or disability, will be used for the financial support of his or her dependents.

An immediate annuity is an annuity that begins one payment interval after the purchase is made. For example, an immediate annuity that provides an annual income of $50,000 and that is purchased with a single premium would begin to provide income one year after the purchase is completed.

Implied authority The law attributes to agents those powers the public reasonably may believe an agent to have.

The incontestable clause is a provision in a life insurance policy that denies the insurer the right to contest the validity of the policy because of misrepresentation by the insured after a specific period of time, usually two years. This means that even deliberate misrepresentations by the applicant will not be grounds for contesting the validity of a life insurance policy after the expiration of the contestable period.

Indemnity means reimbursement. In property insurance, much attention is given to enforcing the principle of indemnity. This means that property insurance policies are strictly contracts of indemnity. That is to say, the insurer will reimburse the insured for the amount of his or her financial loss, but no more. It can be argued that settling a property insurance claim on the basis of the replacement cost of the building destroyed is not indemnity. This is because the replacing of an old building with a new building places the insured in a better financial position than before the loss.

An independent adjuster adjusts property and liability losses on behalf of several insurance companies. Such adjusters are paid a fee for each loss adjusted, rather than a salary by one insurer.

An independent agent generally represents several insurers, has his or her own office staff, and can afford to spend as much effort on keeping business as getting it. Commonly, the agent has some claims-payment authority. The unique status of the independent agent enhances his or her ability to help select insurers and provide other services for clients.

An indeterminate premium policy refers to a life insurance policy having a specified maximum premium, but whose initial premium is well below this maximum. The insurer reserves the right to adjust the initial premium up or down, subject to the specified maximum premium. The low premium charged for the first year is typically guaranteed for two to ten years.

An indexed whole life policy is a basic whole life policy whose face amount rises with the Consumer Price Index, with or without an increase in the premium.

An Individual Retirement Account (IRA) is a retirement savings vehicle that can be set up by individuals with earned income, and the IRA provides special tax advantages. Individuals are limited in the amount they can contribute.

The inflation guard endorsement provides for automatic increases in the amount of insurance to reduce the amount by which coverage falls behind as inflation raises dollar values and the replacement cost of covered property. This endorsement provides for the amount of insurance coverage to increase automatically every quarter by some percentage of the original face amount. The insured selects a quarterly percentage increase in the amount of coverage (for example, 1%, 2%, or 3%). The premium for the endorsement increases directly with the percentage increase in the amount of coverage the insured selects.

Inland marine insurance may be purchased as a separate policy or as endorsements to other coverages. For example, the homeowners Scheduled Personal Property Endorsement provides coverage for nine classes of property under the same coverage as if a separate policy were purchased for each of the nine classes of property. Inland marine insurance is used extensively in writing coverage for mobile personal property for commercial firms. We have previously mentioned the commercial property floater risks and the four subclasses (Business Floater Policies, Dealers' Forms, Bailee Forms, and Miscellaneous Policies).

An <u>installment refund annuity</u> is an annuity in which the insurance company promises to pay a life income to the annuitant and also promises that should the annuitant die before recovering benefits in an amount equal to the purchase price paid for the contract, the difference will be paid in continuing installments, without interest, to the annuitant's heirs.

An <u>insurable interest</u> (in property insurance) is such a relationship between the insured and the subject matter of the insurance that the insured will suffer a financial loss if the subject matter is damaged or destroyed. For example, a homeowner has an insurable interest in his or her home because he or she would suffer a financial loss if the home was damaged or destroyed.

An <u>insurable risk</u> is one possessing the following four characteristics: first, a large number of homogeneous exposure units so that future losses are reasonably predictable; second, losses that are definite as to cause, time, place, and amount; third, losses that are fortuitous or accidental, meaning that they are beyond the control of the insured; and fourth, losses that are not catastrophic.

<u>Intentional torts</u> include such infringements on the rights of others as assault and battery, libel, slander, false arrest or imprisonment, trespass, or invasion of privacy. Persons who suffer injury as a result of these intentional torts have the right to sue for damages.

<u>Interest-adjusted cost methods</u>. Two forms of the "interest-adjusted method" of life insurance policy cost comparisons are:

(a)   Surrender Cost Index (SCI). Assume a $10,000 whole life policy having a $240 annual premium. Dividends for the 20 years are projected to total $1,300. The 20th year cash value for the policy is $3,420. If we assume the $240 annual premium could be invested at 5%, we would have $8,333 at the end of 20 years. Assume that the dividends invested at 5% would accumulate to $2,256. Subtracting the $2,256 dividend accumulation amount from the $8,333 premiums, we have $6,077 as the net outlay. When we subtract the 20th year policy cash value of $3,420 from $6,077, we have $2,657 (the cost of the $10,000 coverage). The SCI is calculated on the assumption that the policy will be surrendered at the end of the 20th year.

The next step is to divide the $2,657 cost of insurance by the value to which a deposit of $1 per year would accumulate at 5% interest. This means we divide $2,657 by $34.719. The result (known as the interest-adjusted Surrender Cost Index per $1,000 at the end of 20 years) is $7.65.

(b)   The Net Payment Cost Index (NPCI) differs from the SCI because no deduction is made for the policy's 20-year cash value. Thus, in the preceding example, we divide $6,077 by $34.719 to obtain the NPCI of $17.50 per year per $1,000 of coverage.

The <u>interest option</u> is a settlement option in a life insurance policy that specifies that the insurance company is to pay only the interest earnings on the proceeds, not the proceeds themselves, to the named beneficiary. The interest option may give the beneficiary full or partial withdrawal rights with respect to the principal. Any undistributed principal remaining upon the death of the primary beneficiary under the interest option will then be paid to the named secondary beneficiary.

The <u>interest rate per compounding period (i)</u> is the portion of the annual interest rate applicable to each compounding period. For example, if the annual rate is 12% and interest is compounded quarterly, the interest rate per compounding period is 12% divided by 4 = 3% each quarter.

The <u>interest rate per discounting period (i)</u> is the portion of the annual interest rate applicable to each discounting period. For example, if the annual rate is 9% and interest is applied monthly, the interest rate per discounting period is 9% divided by 12 = 0.75% each month.

An <u>interest-sensitive whole life</u> policy is one whose annual dividends are responsive to the current level of money rates. This is a departure from the traditional dividend allocation method, where excess investment earnings are allocated at the same rate for all policies, without regard to the level of premiums paid by the policy owners during past years. In a period of rising interest rates, this traditional "portfolio average method" will have an average investment return that is below the high current money rates.

<u>Intermediate care</u> is the second level of care provided by long-term care institutions. It is below the level of care provided by "skilled nursing care." Intermediate care uses fewer nurses per 100 persons for whom nursing care is provided.

<u>Inventory</u> The homeowners policy requires the insured, in case of loss, to furnish a complete inventory of the destroyed, damaged, and undamaged property, showing in detail quantities, costs, actual cash value, and amount of loss claimed. Thus, when used in this sense, the term "inventory" means a listing of personal property items.

An <u>invitee</u> is a person who has been "invited" to come onto the land or premises for the purpose or benefit of the property owner. Customers in a store are invitees. The duty owed to an invitee is to keep the premises in a safe condition or to warn the invitee of any dangerous conditions. Thus, the property owner must make a diligent effort to discover any unsafe conditions and thus be able to warn the invitee of those unsafe conditions.

An irrevocable beneficiary designation is one that may not be altered by the policy owner without the permission of the beneficiary. The policy owner has relinquished the right to change the beneficiary designation.

An irrevocable trust gives the grantor (the person who created the trust) no right or power to cancel or change the trust. A revocable trust can become irrevocable if the grantor gives up the power to revoke, becomes incompetent, or otherwise is incapable of revoking.

Itemized deductions are specified expenses that individual taxpayers can use to reduce taxable income for the year. Among other expenses, itemized deductions include the ability to deduct qualified medical expenses to the extent that they exceed 10% of the taxpayer's adjusted gross income for the year (7.5% of AGI if the taxpayer or spouse is over age 65 as of the end of the tax year).

A joint life annuity provides periodic payments only for the period of time that both annuitants live. The contract is terminated when the first annuitant dies. A joint and survivor annuity, on the other hand, continues the payments until the second annuitant dies.

A joint life insurance policy commits the insurer to paying the face amount of the policy upon the death of one or more persons insured by the policy. The policy pays the face amount when the first person dies. The policy is then terminated.

Joint and several liability refers to the type of liability a partner has in a partnership. In the event the partnership incurs debts, or even if an individual partner incurs a business debt, all of the partners are liable jointly, meaning proportionately, for the debts. In addition, each partner is liable severally, meaning that he or she may be held responsible for the entire debt. In the latter event, that partner would have a right of action against the remaining partners.

A joint and survivor annuity is an insurance contract that provides a life income while both of two designated annuitants are alive, and it continues at the same or a reduced amount of income to the surviving beneficiary, following the death of the first beneficiary.

The large-loss principle emphasizes that the consumer will use his or her premium dollars most effectively by absorbing small losses through careful budgeting and arranging insurance coverage for those losses that will have a serious financial impact on the consumer. For example, insurance should not be used to replace garbage can covers that are blown away in a windstorm! Insurance should be used to meet substantial financial loss. Since most perils cause only small loss, consumers should pay for the frequently occurring small losses and let the insurer indemnify them only for their major or severe losses. The use of the deductible in property insurance and medical expense insurance is based on the large-loss principle.

The doctrine of "last clear chance" is often applied in negligence cases to establish negligence on the part of the defendant if he or she had a last clear chance to avoid the accident and did not seize that clear opportunity. The defendant with a last clear chance is held to be guilty of negligence even though there was contributory negligence on the part of the plaintiff.

The law of large numbers (also referred to as the "law of averages") states that the larger the number of events, the closer the actual results will be to expected or probable results. If we tossed 50 coins one at a time, we probably would not have 25 heads and 25 tails. However, if we tossed a single coin 5 million times, the number of heads would be very close to 2.5 million.

Legal capacity means being legally capable of entering into a valid and enforceable contract. Persons lack legal capacity if they are minors, mentally incompetent, intoxicated, or under the influence of drugs.

Legal form To be legal in form, an insurance contract must use language that approximates that prescribed by the state, and the insurer must follow the proper legal procedure for filing and gaining acceptance as prescribed by the state regulatory authority.

Legal object For an insurance contract to have a legal object means it must have a legal purpose. Providing coverage for illegal drugs being smuggled into the U.S. would not be a legal purpose. An insurable interest provides an insurance policy with a legal purpose.

The level of care refers to the degree or intensity of care required of a patient. In long-term care coverages, these levels of care range from skilled care, which is the most comprehensive and expensive, through intermediate care, custodial care, and simple home care. The last requires the least comprehensive services and entails the lowest care.

Level premium term refers to term policies with periods of protection of 5, 10, 20, or more years, and with level premiums during the period of protection. Level premium term policies have become increasingly popular and potentially very profitable to insurers unless they lapse before acquisition costs are recovered. The NAIC's Regulation XXX requires insurers to have higher reserves than formerly and, so, to charge higher premiums on level premium term policies of more than 5 years.

Liability risk is one of the four classifications of pure risk. The basic peril in the liability risk is the unintentional injury of other persons or damage to their property through negligence or carelessness. However, liability may also result from intentional injuries or damage. Under our legal system, the law provides that one who has injured another or damaged another's property through negligence or otherwise can be held responsible for the harm caused. Liability risks, therefore, involve the possibility of loss of present assets or future income as a result of damages assessed or legal liability arising out of either intentional or unintentional torts or invasion of the rights of others.

A licensee is a person who comes onto the property of another person with the presumed approval or permission of the owner but for no purpose of, or benefit to, the latter. The property owner is under no duty to make property safe for a licensee but must only give the licensee reasonable warning of unsafe conditions known to the property owner. A more severe standard of care is owed the "invitee." For the latter, the property owner must make an intensive effort to discover any hazards and then remove them or warn the invitee. For the licensee, no special intensive effort is required of the property owner to discover existing hazards.

Life insurance See, Code definition of life insurance, above.

Limited-payment whole life insurance is a form of whole life insurance whose premiums are payable only for a limited number of years. The policy becomes a paid-up policy at the end of the premium-paying period. Thus, continuous protection is provided for the whole of life, but premiums are paid only for a limited period. The policy's cash value may be obtained by the policy owner at any time. Most companies offer limited-payment policies of 10, 15, 20, 25, or 30 years or policies that become paid-up at age 55, 60, 65, or 70.

Linton yield The Linton yield is derived by subtracting the annual cost of pure insurance (pure protection) from the annual premium (minus the annual dividend). The residual amount is the annual savings deposit. The Linton yield is the ratio of this annual addition to savings over the policy's cash surrender value at the beginning of the year.

The annual cost of the pure protection is typically derived by calculating an average cost of term insurance by using the published term insurance premiums of a few competitive companies. The term insurance rate per $1,000 thus calculated is applied to the net amount at risk (face amount of the policy minus the policy's cash surrender value).

Living benefit riders are included in some life insurance policies, with or without requiring an additional premium. Such riders commit the insurer to pay a portion of the policy's death benefit at the request of the policy owner when the insured is terminally ill. The negative aspect of this use of life insurance cash values prior to the death of the insured is that the beneficiary is deprived of the benefits of the policy whose primary purpose presumably was to meet financial needs of the policy beneficiary.

Loading refers to the dollar amount the insurer adds to the net premium and the premium payer pays to cover the insurer's expenses (for example, marketing costs and administration expenses). The terms "loading" and "loads" are frequently used to mean the same.

Long tail When professional liability policies (and other commercial liability coverages) are written on an occurrence basis, the insurer may be required to pay claims for negligence that occurred many years ago. This extended period prior to the surfacing of liability claims is known as the "long tail."

The Long-Term Care Partnership Program is a program whereby states encourage the purchase of private LTC insurance by offering consumers access to Medicaid under special eligibility rules should they need additional LTC coverage beyond what the policy provides. The state benefits from the delay of Medicaid claims during the initial phase of long-term care covered by the insurance policy. The consumer benefits by the ability to retain assets equal to the amount of long-term care benefits purchased in the partnership policy, while still qualifying for Medicaid once the policy benefits have been depleted.

Long-term care riders Individual long-term care insurance policies may have varying riders. These include automatic increase riders, return of premium riders, spousal discount riders, and riders permitting restoration of benefits after extensive use of policy benefits may have nearly exhausted future benefits.

Long-term disability coverage refers to a disability income policy whose benefit period is 5 years, 10 years, or until age 65. A few long-term policies provide lifetime replacement of income for disabilities caused by accident. Some very liberal policies will pay lifetime benefits for both accident and sickness total disabilities.

Loss of use coverage, designated as Coverage D in the homeowners policies, pays additional living expenses incurred on account of loss of covered property. It also pays loss of rental value of portions of the premises rented to others. Coverage is also provided when civil authorities bar access to the premises because of damage to neighboring premises by a peril insured against in the insured's policy.

Low-load life insurance is a conventional life insurance product whose premium contains small expense margins, especially for various acquisition costs, including the agent's commission. It may even be marketed directly to purchasers without an agent. Advantages are lower premiums and higher cash values; a disadvantage is lack of an agent's expertise, advice, and motivational skills.

Major medical insurance policies are designed to reduce the family's financial burden of heavy medical expenses resulting from catastrophic or prolonged illness or injury. These policies provide benefit payments for 75%-80% of all types of hospital care or medical treatment by a physician above a certain deductible amount that must be paid by the insured person.

Malpractice insurance is a liability insurance coverage for professional people that provide protection for the liability exposures involving bodily injury.

A taxpayer's marginal tax rate is the highest rate applied to their income, and represents the tax that will be paid on the next dollar of income for that year. U.S. income taxes are imposed on a progressive tax scale, which means that the higher the income, the higher the amount of tax that is paid. Taxpayers pay first at 10%, then 15%, 25%, 28%, 33%, 35%, and 39.6%.

The market failure theory of regulation emphasizes that the purpose of regulation is to correct market failures by placing restrictions on the actions of firms in an industry. The restrictions are designed to make the firms behave in a manner that will produce results as near as possible to those that would prevail under conditions of competition in the marketplace.

A market-value-adjusted (MVA) annuity is one that offers a higher guaranteed interest rate than most fixed-dollar annuities. However, if it is surrendered prior to a specified time, and if the market value of the underlying securities has declined, the purchaser pays a whopping surrender charge, perhaps as high as 30%.

A material fact is important information relevant to the subject matter or property being insured. Information withheld by an applicant for insurance is material when, if known, the information would change the underwriting basis of the insurance or would cause the insurer to refuse the application, charge a higher rate, or offer a modified policy.

Maximum benefit payment is the maximum dollar amount of benefits that an insurer will pay under a major medical expense policy. The maximum benefit may have been stated for a calendar year or a benefit year and some policies had a lifetime maximum. The Affordable Care Act eliminated lifetime benefit maximums for policies issued or renewed after September 23, 2010, and eliminated annual maximums on most covered benefits beginning January 1, 2014. Some individual plans, however, were "grandfathered" and permitted to continue to have annual maximums.

The maximum payment period is the maximum benefit period for a disability income policy. Short-term disability income policies may have maximum benefit periods of only 3, 6, or 24 months. Long-term policies may have 5-year, 10-year, or even lifetime benefit periods.

Medicaid is a joint health care coverage program of the federal and state governments. Benefit levels and qualifications vary from state to state, but in all states, benefits are available only to low-income individuals.

Medical payments coverage is one of the coverages provided under the personal auto policy. This coverage provides payment for reasonable expenses incurred for necessary medical and funeral services because of bodily injury caused by an auto accident and sustained by a covered person. The coverage applies without regard to fault. The covered persons are the named insured, any family member, and other persons who suffer bodily injury while occupying a covered auto. The named insured and family members are also covered as pedestrians if they are injured by any car designed for use on a public road.

Medical payments to others coverage is one of the coverages provided under the homeowners policies. An important point of differentiation between the medical payments coverage in homeowners policies versus auto policies is that in homeowners policies, the medical expenses of insureds are not covered. Rather, coverage applies only to persons other than insureds.

Medicare-approved expenses are medical expenses of various types that are eligible for reimbursement under the federal Medicare program.

A Medicare supplemental policy is designed to fill the gaps in coverage left by the Medicare coverage. Commercial insurers and Blue Cross/Blue Shield organizations have developed special policies for this purpose. For example, the Medicare supplement policies cover the Medicare deductibles and the coinsurance amounts the covered person otherwise would be required to pay.

A misrepresentation is an untrue statement. If the misrepresentation is material, it usually is grounds for voiding a property-liability insurance policy. Remember that usually after two years, a life insurance policy may not be declared invalid because of misrepresentation. All states require the inclusion of the incontestable clause in life insurance policies.

A misstatement of age clause in life and health insurance is a policy provision requiring an adjustment in the amount of coverage when the insured has misstated his or her age. The coverage is adjusted to provide the benefit that the premium paid would have purchased if the age had been stated correctly.

The modified any occupation definition is a definition of disability found in disability income policies that specifies that the claimant is disabled only if he or she is unable to engage in any occupation for which he or she is reasonably suited by education, training, experience, and prior economic status.

A modified no-fault plan leaves tort liability in place for automobile injuries meeting specified conditions, notably for more serious injuries as determined by the nature of the injury or the total amount of medical expense. A monetary or verbal threshold is frequently used. The threshold in no-fault laws is the standard that injuries must exceed before a tort claim may be pursued.

Moral hazard refers to the increase in the probability of loss arising out of or associated with character weaknesses of people. The dishonest tendency on the part of an insured may induce that person to attempt to defraud the insurance company. A dishonest person may intentionally cause a loss or may exaggerate the amount of a loss in an attempt to collect more than the amount to which he or she is entitled.

A morale hazard exists whenever the attitude, carelessness, and lack of discipline of the people associated with an exposure to loss are such as to increase the probability or severity of loss. Poor housekeeping practices, slovenly disregard for trash and vermin, and general failure to police the premises suggest the existence of a morale hazard.

A multi-employer trust is established by a group of employers to provide tax advantaged benefits for employees and owners. When established to provide healthcare and other benefits for the welfare of employees, they may be referred to as Multiple Employer Welfare Arrangements (MEWAs).

The National Association of Insurance Commissioners is a national organization of those state officials who are responsible for the regulation of insurance in their respective states. Although the organization has no official power, it has been effective in making insurance regulation surprisingly uniform throughout the 50 states. The permanent staff of the organization is continuously researching ways to improve insurance regulation and operations in the public interest in all 50 states.

Needs determination is the process of evaluating all the variables that have an impact on a family's need for life insurance coverage. It involves recognizing and evaluating subjective goals; present and future needs and earnings; assets and liabilities; Social Security and pension benefits; income, estate, and gift taxes; and the expected future impact of inflation.

Negligence is behavior or conduct that does not meet the standard expected of a reasonable and prudent person. If one's negligence leads to the injury of another or to damage of another's property, the negligent party may be held legally liable for the damage.

Negligence per se. Negligence "as a matter of law" may exist where a person violates a statute. Negligence per se would exist if the injured party is one of a class of persons whom the statute was intended to protect, and the harm that has occurred is a type that the law was intended to prevent. An example is the automobile speed limit established by law. These speed limits amount to the establishment of rules that no reasonable person should violate. If the rules are violated, the violation is referred to as "negligence per se," and the injured party is relieved of the obligation of proving that the speed was unreasonable.

Negligent entrustment is a basis on which mere ownership of property, such as an automobile, may render the owner legally liable even though he or she had nothing to do with the use of the vehicle involved in the accident. For example, a parent who negligently entrusts the use of an automobile to a very young, unskilled, or otherwise incompetent child may be held responsible for any damage the child does in using the automobile.

The net single premium is what an insurance company would need to collect from each insured in the group to provide the insurer with enough dollars to pay death benefits as deaths occur. The net single premium is assumed to be paid at the inception of the policy and earns compound interest for as long as the policy remains in force. The net single premium is calculated by use of only the mortality cost and the interest factor. The net single premium has no loading for expenses.

No-fault insurance is a form of first-party insurance coverage written in conformity with the automobile no-fault laws of the various states. Under "no-fault," payment does not depend on determination of liability. This is a major device for accelerating claim settlements. Benefit payments to claimants are based only on economic losses: medical expenses, lost income, and costs of replacing personal services (up to the policy limits–for which there are statutory minima). Under the provisions of a "pure" no-fault law, there would be no tort claims for automobile injuries. All accident victims would be indemnified by their own insurer.

A noncancellable disability income policy guarantees the insured the right to renew the disability income policy for a stated number of years or until a stated age, with the premium at each renewal date guaranteed. The insurer has no right to cancel the coverage or to increase the scheduled premium rates.

Nonforfeiture options refer to the alternative ways that a policy owner may receive the policy's cash value upon surrender of the policy. The options usually available include: (a) lump-sum payment in cash, (b) extended term insurance, (c) a reduced amount of paid-up life insurance, or (d) one of the installment annuity options.

The nonforfeiture value in a life insurance policy is its cash surrender value. The nonforfeiture value may be taken in cash, as a reduced amount of paid-up insurance, or as extended term insurance.

Nonoccupational disability is disability whose cause is not associated with the person's occupation. Short-term disability income policies usually do not cover disabilities from accidents or sickness arising out of or in the course of the insured's employment or covered under any workers' compensation law. Many long-term disability income policies cover disabilities that are either occupational or nonoccupational.

A nonparticipating life insurance policy charges a premium that realistically anticipates the cost of the insurance protection and expenses for the classification to which the insured is assigned. Since the premium reflects expected costs and some profit, no dividends are paid to the owners of such policies.

Notice of loss Most property insurance policies require the insured to give immediate written notice to the insurer of any loss and to protect the property from further damage. Thus, notice of loss is one of the requirements that the insured must meet to be reimbursed in case loss occurs.

Nursing facility requirements Long-term care insurance policies frequently require that the insured must receive policy benefits from a facility licensed by the state. A minority of policies specify that policy benefits must be received at a Medicare-certified facility. This latter requirement obviously limits the availability of facilities for the insured.

Occupational disability is disability that arises out of and in the course of one's employment. Since occupational disabilities are covered under workers' compensation, most short-term disability income policies exclude such disabilities from coverage. However, long-term policies tend to provide coverage for such disabilities.

The occurrence form of a liability policy is one that will pay for liability claims that arise from incidents that occur during the policy period, regardless of when the legal action is filed. As a consequence, the occurrence form of liability coverage may result in a "long tail" of claims possibilities for the insurer.

Ocean marine insurance covers four types of losses: (a) Hull insurance insures the vessel or ship. (b) Cargo insurance insures the ship's cargo. (c) Freight insurance insures the ship owner against loss of income when cargo is lost when the ship sinks. (d) Protection and indemnity provides liability insurance coverage for the ship owner.

Ordinary income tax rates are the rates assessed on income that is not treated as a capital gain. Taxpayers add all of their ordinary income, such as wages and business income, for the year, subtract certain allowable reductions, and pay tax at progressive rates as income increases: first at 10%, then 15%, 25%, 28%, 33%, 35%, and 39.6%.

Organic-based mental illness coverage usually means long-term care insurance coverage only for specifically-named illnesses caused by impairment of body organs. Among such illnesses that are typically covered are Alzheimer's disease, Parkinson's disease, and senile dementia.

Ostensible authority is another term for apparent authority. Thus, ostensible authority means the principal has created the appearance that the agent has the powers the public has come to expect the agent to have.

The ownership clause in a life insurance policy states that the person designated as the owner has the right to assign or transfer the policy, receive the policy's cash values and dividends, and borrow against the policy's cash values.

Own occupation definition Under this definition of total disability, the insured is considered totally disabled if he or she is unable to engage in any and every duty of his or her own occupation.

A package policy is the insurance coverage resulting from combining the coverages of two or more separate policies into a single contract.

The paid-up reduced amount option is a nonforfeiture option in a life insurance policy. This option gives the insured the right to take the nonforfeiture value as fully paid-up permanent insurance in a reduced face amount that is determined by the attained age of the insured and the size of the nonforfeiture value at the time the option is selected.

The parol evidence rule is a rule that when a written contract is made, all previous oral agreements are considered included in the written contract, and no changes are permitted.

Partial disability benefit is a coverage provision found in most accident and in some sickness policies that promise to pay a reduced benefit if the insured can perform some but not all the important daily duties of his or her occupation. The benefit usually is available only after the insured has recovered from total disability.

A participating life insurance policy entitles the policy owner to receive dividends. Dividends return to the policy owner some of the difference between the premium charged and the actual operating expenses and mortality cost of the company.

A peril is a potential cause of loss. Loss-producing agents, such as fire, hail, theft, and windstorm, are all perils.

Permissive-use statutes are state laws that impose liability on the owner of an automobile for any liability where the owner gave permission to someone to operate the automobile, regardless of the operator's age.

The personal auto policy (PAP) is the currently marketed automobile insurance policy that insures private passenger automobiles and certain types of trucks owned by an individual or by a husband and wife.

Personal contract Property and liability insurance policies are said to be "personal contracts." This means that the policy is personal to the insured and may not be assigned to anyone else without the approval of the insurer. This prohibition against assignment is logical because the insurer underwrites the character and the morals of the insured as carefully as the insurer underwrites the features and exposures of the property insured. The insurer gives considerable attention to the credit standing, character, conduct, and capacity of the insured and wants to have an opportunity to review these qualities in case the property changes hands. The insurer should have the right to exercise control over who will be insured and, thus, be in a position to eliminate undesirable insureds.

Personal injury, as a liability insurance coverage, means "bodily injury," which is defined as "bodily harm, sickness or disease, including required care, loss of services, and death resulting from." The term also is used sometimes to describe a group of offenses that injure a person's character, such as libel, slander, or invasion of privacy.

A personal producing general agent (PPGA) is a life insurance general agent who is engaged primarily in personal selling, rather than agency building. Frequently, the PPGA receives an expense allowance from the insurance company.

The personal property floater is a type of insurance coverage providing "all-risks" coverage on unscheduled personal property. It resembles Coverage C of a homeowners policy that has been endorsed with a special personal property coverage endorsement.

Under the physical damage coverage of the PAP, the insurer will pay for direct and accidental loss to the covered auto, including its equipment, minus any applicable deductible shown in the declarations. The physical damage coverage includes collision loss or damage and loss other than by collision (the so-called comprehensive coverage).

A physical hazard is a physical condition of property that creates or increases the probability or severity of loss. Examples of physical hazards that increase the probability or severity of loss from the peril of fire are the type of construction, the location of the property, and the occupancy of the building.

The policy cost per thousand of life insurance coverage may be determined by use of the following formula:

$$\frac{P + CVP\,(1 + i) - (CSV + D)}{(F - CSV)\quad(.001)}$$

In this formula:

F is the policy's face amount.
CSV is the cash surrender value at the end of the present year.
CVP is the cash surrender value at the end of the previous year.
P is the annual premium.
D is the dividend.
i is the discount rate selected.
.001 is the factor to convert to a policy cost per $1,000.

This is the most direct and effective way to evaluate the cost of a policy being offered by a life insurance company.

The policy loan provision in a life insurance policy is a clause that allows the policy owner to borrow up to the full amount of the policy's cash or loan value at any time. The loan bears a specified rate of interest. The loan need not be repaid according to any schedule. In fact, if the insured dies without having repaid all of any policy loan outstanding, the policy loan, plus unpaid interest, will be deducted from the death proceeds.

Post-claim underwriting refers to the decision within an insurance company's underwriting department as to whether to renew or revise the rates on an existing insured at the time of renewal.

A preexisting condition is a physical condition that the insured "enjoyed" before the medical expense or disability income policy was issued. Such preexisting conditions are usually excluded from coverage under individual medical expense or disability income policies.

Preexisting conditions waiting period is a period of time at the start of a health insurance policy during which there is no coverage for medical conditions that existed prior to the inception of the policy.

A preferred provider organization (PPO) is a business entity established to deliver health care services to the purchaser of such services (typically an employer or an insurance company.) The PPO may offer special pricing discounts, and the employer or insurance company may agree to promote greater utilization of the PPO's services.

Premium tax credits may be available to taxpayers with moderate incomes who purchase health insurance coverage through the Health Insurance Marketplace. The premium subsidies were designed to assist millions of Americans who could not otherwise afford health insurance.

Presumptive disability is a coverage provision included in disability income policies that provides that the loss of the use of two bodily members or the loss of one's sight will be considered as total disability, regardless of whether or not the insured can do any work.

The primary beneficiary is the person or persons designated to receive the death proceeds of a life insurance policy.

A prior hospitalization requirement is a requirement in some long-term care insurance policies specifying that no benefits are payable for long-term care unless such care follows a period of hospital confinement.

Under the terms of the PAP, a private passenger auto is a four-wheel motor vehicle, other than a truck type, owned or leased under contract for a continuous period of at least six months.

The probation period is the period of time after issuance of a health insurance policy, usually fifteen to thirty days, during which time no sickness coverage is effective. Thus, the provision will deny coverage for a sickness that may have been in the incubation stage when the policy was issued. Note that coverage still applies during the first few days for any bodily injuries arising out of accidents.

Probate is the legal process through which a decedent's will is validated, claims against the estate are paid, and assets are distributed to beneficiaries.

A producer is a person who produces sales for an insurance company.

A producing general agent (PGA) is a general agent who produces the majority of his or her income by selling insurance personally. Unlike a conventional general agent, a producing general agent often does not have a specified territory for which he or she is responsible and often is not charged with the responsibility for hiring agents to work for him or her.

Professional liability refers to the liability that an investment adviser may have to a client, to the SEC, to the FINRA, or even to state regulatory authorities under the various laws and regulations governing the adviser's conduct.

Professional liability insurance provides coverage for legal liability arising from the failure of a person to use the care and the degree of skill expected of a practitioner in a particular profession.

Proof of loss The requirements for filing proof of loss under the Standard Fire Policy begin at Line 27 "...and within sixty days after the loss, unless such time is extended in writing by this Company, the insured shall render to this Company a proof of loss signed and sworn to by the insured, stating the knowledge and belief of the insured as to the following...." (Similar requirements are set forth in other property insurance policies.)

Property risk is one of the four categories of pure risk. Anyone who owns property faces property risks simply because such possessions can be destroyed or stolen. Property risks embrace two distinct types of loss: (a) direct loss, and (b) indirect or "consequential" loss.

The proximate cause is the cause that directly and independently of all other causes produces the event or result in question.

The public choice theory views regulation as a part of a political-economic system that attempts to redistribute wealth among competing groups based on preference expressed in the political-economic marketplace.

Punitive damages are the additional dollars a court awards to the injured party in addition to the compensatory damages sought by the plaintiff. Such awards are sometimes made because of malicious or wanton misconduct on the part of the tortfeasor (wrongdoer) to serve as a punishment for the wrongdoer and possibly as a future deterrent to others. Today, lawyers for plaintiffs frequently seek punitive damages for their injured clients.

A purchasing group is an entity established for the purpose of purchasing liability insurance coverage for the members of a group that typically includes business firms, professional organizations (for example, doctors, dentists, lawyers), and other organizations with above-average exposures to liability risk (for example, day-care centers and municipalities).

Qualified retirement plans are retirement plans established by employers in order to receive special tax treatment, such as the ability to deduct contributions made to the plan and tax-deferred growth prior to when distributions are made to employees. In order to receive the special tax treatment, certain rules must be followed.

Rebating is the illegal (in most states) return of part or all of the premium to the buyer of insurance.

Reformation is the changing of a contract to state what the parties originally intended. It is the correction of an error, not the writing of a new contract.

Regular (basic) medical expense insurance pays for medical, surgical, and hospital expenses up to a modest specified amount. Because the maximum benefit is so low, major medical coverage is necessary to supplement this basic coverage.

The life insurance policy's reinstatement provision permits the policy owner to restore the policy to good standing after premium payments have been discontinued. Evidence of insurability is required.

Renewable at the company's option This refers to a disability income policy that can be renewed at the end of the term period of coverage at the option of the company. Thus, by optionally refusing to renew, the insurer can effectively cancel the coverage at renewal date. The insurer may not cancel during the policy term and obviously must pay all claims that are outstanding at the time of refusal to renew.

Replacement cost means the cost of replacing or repairing damaged or destroyed property at current cost without a deduction for depreciation.

"Replacement cost" is also the gift tax value of a paid-up life insurance policy. It is equal to what a person would pay (single premium) for a comparable paid-up policy issued at the insured's current age.

The following are the requirements for an enforceable contract: (a) offer and acceptance, (b) consideration, (c) legal object, (d) competent parties, and (e) legal form.

Res ipsa loquitur is translated "the thing speaks for itself." Under this concept, a person may be found to be negligent because the accident could not have normally happened without negligence on the part of the person being charged. In the eyes of the law, the fact the accident occurred is prima facie evidence that the defendant was negligent. No additional proof of wrongdoing is needed.

Rescission is a legal remedy for a contract that one party shows to be void because the contract was negotiated by fraud, misrepresentation, or concealment, or there was a mutual mistake of a material fact. When an insurance contract is terminated by rescission, the insurer is required only to return the premiums paid by the policy owner.

Reserves are a measure of the liability of the insurance company to its policy owners. For a whole life policy, the policy reserve is the difference between the level premiums to be paid by the policy owner (increased by interest and reduced by the expense loading) and what is needed to pay death benefits because some insureds die prematurely. A policy's cash value is approximately equal to the policy's reserve. From the point of view of the policy owner, he or she thinks in terms of what the insurance company owes if he or she surrenders the policy. The insurance company thinks in terms of how much it owes the policy owner (the amount of the reserve). The reserve is not an asset of the insurer, it is a liability. To be solvent, the insurer must have assets at least equal to its liabilities. The reserve arises because of the level premium method of paying for life insurance. The level premium method is what also gives rise to a life insurance policy's cash value.

Residual disability benefits are designed to make up income lost because a partial disability prevents the insured from working at full-income capacity. Residual disability is typically measured by the ratio of a person's reduction in earnings after recovery from total disability to his or her earnings before disability. Thus, the residual disability coverage will provide that percentage of the maximum policy benefit as indicated by the ratio described above.

Respite care is a type of care for a long-term care patient that allows a primary caregiver a "vacation" periodically. Respite care would provide for the cost of care provided by a temporary substitute for the primary caregiver.

Respondeat superior A literal translation would be, "Let the master answer." This means that the principal is liable in certain cases for the wrongful acts of his or her agent. The concept is usually not applicable if the wrongdoing occurs outside the normal range of the employee's duties.

A return-of-premium or return-of-cash-value policy is a combination of whole life and increasing term insurance. The latter is equal to either the sum of the premiums paid to date or the present cash value. At death, the policy pays the basic face amount plus either the total premiums already paid or the cash value.

A revocable beneficiary is one designated to receive the death proceeds. However, the policy owner retains the right to change the beneficiary designation at any time.

Riders are provisions or endorsements that are added to a life insurance policy to amend the policy. Riders may be used to increase or decrease benefits, waive a condition, or amend the original contract in some specific way. The terms rider and endorsement are synonymous.

Risk avoidance is the elimination of loss exposures either by refusing to acquire property that might expose the entity to loss, or if property is possessed already, the entity disposes of the property.

Risk management is a scientific approach to the problems of dealing with the pure risks facing an individual or a business. The concept of risk management is based on the desirability of reducing the cost of safeguarding an entity against financial loss by the most appropriate means.

Risk reduction is any method or technique designed to reduce risk. Two common ways to reduce risk are: (a) reduction of the probability of the occurrence of loss (loss prevention), and (b) reduction of the severity of loss (loss reduction).

Risk retention When an entity does not take possible action to avoid, reduce, or transfer the risk of loss, the exposure to loss is retained. Risk retention may be voluntary or involuntary. Voluntary risk retention is characterized by the recognition that the risk exists and the conscious assumption of the future losses that may occur. The decision to retain a risk voluntarily is made presumably because there are no alternatives that are more attractive. An exposure to loss may be retained involuntarily because: (a) insurance coverage is not available (for example, flood insurance is not available in some communities), (b) the property owner can't afford the premium for coverage, (c) no insurance company is willing to provide the coverage for the entity for underwriting reasons, or (d) the person is unaware of the existence of a risk exposure.

A risk retention group is a "mini-insurance company" that provides liability insurance coverage for its member-shareholders. The membership of a specific risk retention group is composed exclusively of organizations that are engaged in similar businesses or have similar exposures to liability risks. The risk retention group really provides self-insurance for its membership. It does not purchase coverage from commercial insurers.

Risk sharing A basic characteristic of insurance is the sharing or spreading of risk among the members of the group. The sharing of losses through the use of the insurance mechanism is sometimes referred to as the pooling of risk. A corporation is also an example of risk sharing. Each stockholder accepts a small percentage of the total business risk.

Risk tolerance refers to the client's attitude toward uncertainty and exposures to loss. The person who has a low risk tolerance would tend to avoid life insurance policies whose cash values are invested in common stocks and other equities. Instead, he or she would prefer a policy whose cash value is invested primarily in bonds, mortgages, and other fixed-dollar investments. The person with a high tolerance for risk would be willing to buy variable life insurance and a variable annuity. The person with a low tolerance for risk would likely reject term insurance because of the uncertainty concerning his or her insurability at the end of the elected term. The conversion privilege and the renewable feature of term insurance, of course, do eliminate some of the risk of future insurability.

Risk transference is a method of removing an exposure to loss from one party and placing the responsibility for dealing with the exposure on the shoulders of another who is more willing to bear the risk. An example is hedging, which is used by commodity processors to protect themselves against an unfavorable change in market price between the time the hedger buys a product and the time the finished or processed item is sold. The risk is transferred to a speculator by means of a contra transaction. For example, when the flour manufacturer buys wheat, he or she sells the same quantity of wheat for future delivery.

The scheduled personal property endorsement to a homeowners policy is used when a specific dollar amount of "all-risks" coverage is desired on designated items. Valuables such as jewelry and furs, silverware, musical instruments, cameras, and stamp and coin collections may be scheduled under the endorsement, thus providing "all-risks" coverage on these items.

Second-to-die life insurance provides life insurance on two or more lives and pays the death proceeds upon the death of the second or last person to die. (See also survivorship whole life policy.)

The Securities and Exchange Commission (SEC) is the government agency holding primary responsibility for enforcing securities laws and regulating stock exchanges and other key participants in the securities industry.

Self-employment tax includes both the employee and employer portion of the Social Security and Medicare tax. Individuals who are self-employed include sole proprietors, partners in a partnership, and LLC members.

Self-insurance is a method of risk retention that has two requirements: (a) A large number of homogeneous exposure units must exist so that losses can be predicted based on the law of large numbers. (b) A source of funds must be arranged for paying losses. The source of funds can be accumulated liquid assets, the cash flow generated from operations, or sources of credit, such as banks or other institutions. To establish a self-insurance plan, the self-insurer must have the financial strength to fund the plan and to absorb losses.

The use of one of the settlement options is one of the ways, other than immediate payment in a lump sum, in which the policy owner or beneficiary of a life insurance policy may choose to have the policy proceeds paid. The usual settlement options are: (a) fixed amount each month, (b) payable in equal installments over a fixed period of years, (c) life income with no minimum period guaranteed, and (d) life income, guaranteed for some minimum period.

Severability of insureds means that a liability insurance policy applies separately to each insured. For example, assume that a homeowner's gardener negligently runs over the homeowner while operating an insured tractor in the course of the gardener's employment. The homeowner (the named insured) could bring suit against the gardener and possibly collect under the homeowner's own policy. We should emphasize that the concept of severability does not give each insured the full limit of the policy's coverage for any one occurrence. The injured insureds must share the policy's dollar limit.

Short-term disability coverage is the coverage provided by so-called short-term disability income policies. The period of time of benefit payments varies by company. Some companies provide short-term benefits for a maximum of six months – some for only three months. More and more companies are extending the benefit period to a maximum of two years.

Single limit of liability The automobile liability insurance coverage may be written with a single limit to cover both property damage liability and bodily injury liability. As an alternative, the automobile liability insurance coverage may be written as a separate limit for property damage liability and a separate limit for bodily injury liability.

A single-premium deferred annuity (SPDA) is purchased with a single premium, but the periodic annuity or liquidation payments are deferred, typically until age 65 or some other specified retirement age. It is possible for a person to purchase a separate SPDA each working year. Thus, for a working career of 50 years, the person would have 50 such SPDA contracts.

A single-premium immediate annuity (SPIA) is purchased with a single premium, and periodic annuity payments usually begin one month after the payment of the single premium.

A single-premium whole life policy is a whole life policy purchased with a large, lump-sum premium. These were once very attractive investments because the cash value grew on a tax-deferred basis, like other whole life policies. Since 1988, however, such policies are likely to be classified by the IRS as modified endowment contracts (MECs), in which case withdrawals are taxed on a last-in, first-out basis. This means the first distributions from a policy will be of the investment earnings and will be included in the policy owner's gross income. However, no taxation occurs as long as no distributions occur. If there is a distribution, there is a 10% penalty tax on withdrawals before age 59½ in addition to any income taxes assessed.

Skilled nursing care is the most comprehensive level of long-term care provided and the most expensive. This top-of-the-line care usually means that a registered nurse, who is under a licensed physician's supervision, is available 24 hours a day.

Specific damages refer to the dollars awarded to the plaintiff in a negligence case to reimburse the injured party for his or her measurable loss. Such losses include expenses incurred for medical care and loss of income resulting from bodily injury.

A spendthrift clause is a clause contained in a life insurance policy's settlement arrangement that is designed to protect the proceeds from the claims of creditors of the beneficiary. The clause takes away from the beneficiary any power to assign, transfer, or otherwise encumber the payments that are to be made to him or her under the settlement option. A spendthrift clause may be elected only for beneficiaries other than the policy owner and may be elected only by the policy owner.

A split definition is one that uses a liberal definition of total disability for a short period of time and then applies a more severe definition thereafter. For example, total disability might be defined for two years as the inability to perform one's own occupation. Thereafter, total disability might be defined as the inability to perform any occupation for which the person is suited by reason of education, training, and/or experience. Under this latter definition, a dentist who has lost one hand could be expected to accept employment as a salesperson of dental supplies and equipment, but not to accept employment selling pencils on a street corner.

State high risk pools are programs that were set up in 35 states from 1976 to 2009 to assist uninsurable individuals. The health care reform act of 2010 provided additional funding to all 50 states to either expand existing programs or to create new programs. States can choose to continue to run their own programs or can defer to the federal government to run their programs.

A stock redemption agreement is a binding contract arranged among a corporation's owners, committing the corporation to purchase the ownership interest of a deceased owner. The deceased's estate is committed to selling the business interest of the deceased. The agreed upon price is specified in the agreement, or a valuation formula sets forth the method to be followed to determine the price. The owners arrange for adequate life insurance on their lives so that the terms of the agreement may be fulfilled at the time of the death of an owner.

Stop-loss insurance provides protection against catastrophic or unpredictable losses for employers who have chosen to self-insure their health care plans for employees. Under the stop-loss policy, the insurance company will become liable for losses over a certain dollar amount (the deductible).

A structured settlement is an agreement, often arising out of negligence lawsuit settlements, to pay the injured party a periodic income for a specified period or even for life. Often, the payments are made by an insurance company, and their amount is determined actuarially.

Subrogation is a common-law right of the insurer to acquire the legal rights of the insured against any third party who may have caused a covered loss. This right of the insurer is also specifically stated in the subrogation clause of the typical property insurance policy. For example, the insurer pays for collision damage under the automobile policy and then has subrogation rights against the negligent third party. An insurance company may step into the legal shoes of an insured after paying the amount of the loss caused by a negligent third party.

The suicide exclusion in a life insurance policy is a clause specifying that if the insured dies by suicide within the first year or two of the policy's existence, the insurance company's liability will be limited to a return of the premiums paid.

A Summary of Benefits and Coverage (SBC) must be provided to health insurance plan participants. The SBC is provided in an easy-to-read format to help consumers to better understand the coverage they have and allow them to compare their coverage options across different types of plans.

The Supplemental Extended Reporting Period endorsement gives the CGL insured an additional 60 days after the expiration of the CGL policy to report a claim under a claims-made basis CGL policy.

The CGL insured has 60 days after the expiration of the policy to purchase a Supplemental Extended Reporting Period endorsement for an additional premium. This endorsement gives the insured an unlimited period of time for reporting a liability claim.

A surgical reimbursement insurance contract reimburses the insured according to a schedule that lists the amounts the policy will pay for a variety of surgical procedures.

Surgical service plans. Participating physicians agree to accept the benefit payable by Blue Shield as their total compensation without additional charge to the subscriber, provided that the subscriber's income does not exceed a certain level.

Surplus or excess-line brokers are persons licensed to acquire for the insured coverage beyond what the usual local (domestic) regulations allow. Brokers so licensed are responsible for carrying out the local regulations specifically applicable to these special transactions; very important among these is collection of the local premium tax. A surplus agent would be a person performing the same functions but doing so as a representative of the insurer.

A survivorship whole life (second-to-die life) policy covers two insureds, with the face amount payable only at the death of the second one to die. It is often used to meet the estate tax liability at the death of the second spouse to die, at which time there is no marital deduction because, barring remarriage, there will be no surviving spouse.

The survivors' needs for a client's family include the education needs of the children, the income needs of the client's family and parents, and emergency fund needs. The magnitude of the dollar amount required to meet the client's survivor needs depends on the number of his or her dependents, their financial resources, their ages, and their health.

Term insurance provides protection for a definite but limited period of time. If death occurs during the term for which the policy is written, the death proceeds are payable. If the insured survives the term, the policy expires.

The liability insurance policy is referred to as third-party coverage because the policy provides compensation to someone who is not a party to the contract. Only the insured policyholder and the insurance company are parties to the liability insurance contract. Third-party coverage means a liability insurance coverage that promises to pay, up to the policy limits, the injured party to whom the insured is legally liable.

Title insurance reimburses a property owner if some defect in the deed causes him or her to lose the property or suffer financial loss. This type of insurance policy is written primarily by companies specializing exclusively in this type of coverage.

A tort is any civil wrong inflicted upon a person other than by breach of contract. The person or entity committing the tort is called a "tortfeasor." We should note that criminal behavior may give rise to criminal legal action by the state and also may involve a civil suit by the injured party.

A tort exposure is a potential liability for loss arising out of an accident or arising out of an activity. Examples of tort exposures are possible liability for damages caused by driving an automobile or boat or carrying on a profession.

Under the traditional net cost method, the life insurance policy's net cost is determined by totaling the gross annual premiums for a given number of years (usually 10 or 20 years). If the policy is a participating policy, dividends for the 10- or 20-year period are subtracted. From this amount, we subtract the policy's cash value at the end of the 10 or 20 years. We then divide this residual amount by the number of years (10 or 20), which gives us the cost per year for the coverage. To obtain the cost per $1,000 of coverage per year, we divide by the number of thousands of dollars of coverage.

Transfer taxes include the federal estate tax (upon death) and federal gift tax (on gifts made during lifetime). States may also impose transfer taxes by means of inheritance or death taxes. These transfer taxes are in addition to income taxes.

A trespasser is one who is on the property of another without the owner's permission.

TRICARE is a health insurance plan offering civilian benefits for military personnel, military retirees, and their dependents.

Twisting is persuading an insurance policy owner to replace an existing policy with a similar policy issued by the same or another company, to the detriment of the insured. If it can be shown that the switch is beneficial to the policy owner, the change is not twisting. Twisting is illegal. Incomplete or misleading comparisons of policies by the agent attempting to achieve a replacement are considered by the courts to be "twisting."

An umbrella liability policy provides liability coverage in excess of the limits or exposures set forth in the insured's basic liability policy.

Underinsured motorists coverage provides coverage for a vehicle with at least the minimum insurance required by the financial responsibility law, but less insurance than the limit of underinsured motorists coverage carried by another vehicle. For example, Pearl has a PAP with underinsured motorists coverage in the amount of $100,000, and Helen has a PAP with a liability limit of $50,000. They are in an accident, and it is adjudicated that Helen is at fault. From Pearl's perspective, Helen's auto is an underinsured motor vehicle–its limit is lower than Pearl's underinsured motorists coverage.

Underwriting is the functional area within an insurance company in which applicants for coverage are either accepted or rejected and, if accepted, placed in an appropriate rating classification.

The Uniform Simultaneous Death Act is a statute that has been adopted in most states to resolve the question as to who is entitled to the proceeds in the event that the insured and the beneficiary of a life insurance policy die in a common accident where there is insufficient evidence to determine which one died first. The typical state statute in this regard specifies that the proceeds will be distributed as if the insured outlived the beneficiary.

The Uniform Transfers to Minors Act is another type of state statute authorizing the creation of custodial accounts for the benefit of minor beneficiaries. UTMA accounts are similar to UGMA accounts, the main difference being that UTMA custodial accounts are subject to fewer restrictions on the permissible types of investments.

A unilateral contract is an agreement for an exchange of an act for a promise. The typical insurance contract is unilateral because only the insurer has made a binding promise. The insured pays a premium in exchange for the insurer's promise to indemnify the insured in case the event insured against actually occurs. The insured has made no legally enforceable promise and cannot be held for breach of contract.

Uninsured motorists coverage provides coverage for an uninsured motor vehicle. Such a vehicle is defined as a land motor vehicle or trailer for which liability insurance is: (a) nonexistent, (b) less than the amount specified by the state's applicable financial responsibility law, (c) useless because of denial of coverage or failure of the insurer, or (d) useless because of a hit-and-run accident (PAP Part C).

Unintentional torts are those that arise out of negligence or carelessness. There is no malice, premeditation, or plotting to carry out the wrongdoing.

Universal life insurance is a flexible premium life insurance policy that permits the policy owner to change the death benefit from time to time (with satisfactory evidence of insurability for increases) and vary the premium payments. A fixed percentage of the gross premium is allocated to the insurer's expenses. The remainder is credited to the policy's cash value. This is appreciated monthly at money market rates of interest and reduced by the policy owner's share of mortality costs for his or her classification. Under one form of UL, a level death benefit is provided until the policy's cash value exceeds this amount. Under a second type of UL policy, the death benefit is a minimum level amount (for example, $50,000) plus the policy's increasing cash value. After the first year, the policy owner may use the interest income from the policy's cash value to keep the policy in force. Thus, the policy may be used as term insurance, ordinary whole life insurance, or made into a paid-up policy by accelerating premium payments, at the policy owner's option.

Unoccupancy means that a building has personal property contents in it, but the building has no occupants.

Usual, customary, and reasonable (UCR) tables are tables developed by means of a formal survey of charges made by purveyors of medical services in a given geographic area. Insurers typically agree to pay for services charged by 90 percent of the professional practitioners in the area. Consequently, a physician or hospital that charges more than the UCR fees for the service in question may have to receive some or all of its payment from the patient himself or herself.

The insurance contract is said to be a contract of utmost good faith. Both parties must behave honestly. However, the concept probably has greater application to the honesty of the insured. In making its decision whether to insure and how to rate an applicant, the insurer relies on the complete truthfulness of the applicant in providing information about the loss exposure. If the information provided by the applicant is false or incomplete, the insurer may be able to avoid the contract on grounds of breach of warranty, misrepresentation, or concealment.

Vacancy A building is vacant when it has neither occupants nor contents.

A <u>valued policy</u> is a policy that promises to pay a specified amount in the event of a loss, regardless of the actual cash value or other measure of the precise amount lost. For example, a disability income policy promising to pay $2,000 per month as a benefit is a valued policy.

A <u>variable annuity</u> is an annuity contract whose payout benefits vary directly with the investment results achieved on the assets supporting the annuity contract.

The <u>variable life insurance</u> policy provides for the policy's death benefit and cash value to vary with the investment experience of a segregated investment account maintained by the insurer. Since the investments selected are primarily common stocks and other equities, the death benefit is supposed to increase as inflation increases the family's need for more life insurance protection.

<u>Variable universal life insurance</u> is a combination of a standard universal life policy with the investment characteristics of variable life insurance. This means the periodic premium in excess of the amount needed to pay mortality costs and expenses usually is invested to a large extent in common stocks or other equities.

A <u>viatical agreement</u> is one in which the insured sells an existing life insurance policy to another person or organization, usually for 50% to 85% of the face value, depending on the insured's life expectancy. The sale provides the insured with needed cash to pay medical expenses under circumstances where the health impairment is terminal.

<u>Vicarious liability</u> is liability ascribed to one person or entity because of the acts of another. A principal has vicarious liability because of the tortious conduct or negligence of his or her agent.

A <u>void contract</u> is one without legal effect. In essence, it lacks one of the requirements specified by law for a valid contract. A void contract cannot be enforced by either party.

A <u>voidable contract</u> is one that may be set aside by one of the parties. A contract is binding unless the party having the right to void the contract elects to do so. Most contracts business firms make with minor children are voidable by the minor child.

Form <u>W-2</u> is the income tax form used to report taxable earnings and income tax withheld for an employee of a business. It is mailed to the employee by January 31st of the following calendar year and is used to report earnings and withheld taxes when filing the individual income tax return.

Waiver and estoppel are similar. A waiver is a voluntary relinquishment of a known right. In practice, this means words or actions which reasonably indicate to another that a particular right has been given up.

Estoppel occurs when there has been conduct which leads another to believe, reasonably, that a right will not be asserted, and that the other party acts in reliance on such reasonable belief. The doctrine of estoppel holds that a right cannot subsequently be asserted to the detriment of "that other person." For example, an insurer only smiles when a construction company tells the insurer that it is storing dynamite in one of its buildings. The insurer would be estopped from asserting its rights under the policy if the dynamite explodes and the ensuing fire destroys the building. The insurer's smile led the insured to believe such storage would be all right.

A waiver-of-premium provision is a provision that may be added by a rider to a life insurance policy. The rider specifies that the annual premium for the life insurance policy is waived by the insurer during the insured's total disability, as defined in the rider. The waiver provision takes effect after the insured has been disabled for six months, but the waiver often is retroactive to the date of disability after the six months have passed.

The waiver provision is a clause in a property-liability insurance policy protecting the insurer. The insurer's agent may not make promises to the insured without the insurer's approval. The agent may not orally agree to permit the insured to store dynamite on the insured's property.

A warranty is a statement or guarantee in an application for insurance, the mere falsity of which renders the contract voidable at the option of the other party. Note that a warranty technically need not relate to a material fact in order to render the contract voidable.

Whole life insurance is a type of life insurance that provides for payment of the face amount upon the death of the insured, no matter when that may occur, as long as the policy is kept in force up to that point.

Yearly renewable and convertible term insurance is a form of life insurance that provides for payment of the face amount if death occurs within the one-year period of coverage. In addition, the policy gives the policy owner the right to renew the coverage for additional periods of the same duration without having to provide evidence of insurability. The policy also gives the policy owner the right to convert the term insurance to a permanent form of life insurance without having to provide evidence of insurability.

For purposes of the personal auto policy (PAP), the words "your covered auto" mean the specific automobile owned by the insured and shown in the policy's declarations, as well as any auto or trailer an insured does not own while used as a temporary substitute for an insured auto.

INDEX

ACA 24.30

Accumulation Phase 27.14

Actual Cash Value 22.24

ACV 22.24

Adverse Selection 22.19

Affordable Care Act 24.30

     Minimum Essential Coverage (Individual) 24.32

Affordable Care Act, Impact on Coverage and Exclusions 24.9

Age, Misstatement of 25.13

Agents and Brokers, Functions of 22.22

Aggregate Deductible 24.6

Analysis and Evaluation of Risk Exposures 23.1

Anchoring, Avoid 27.34

Annuities 27.1

     Classifying 27.5

     Uses 27.4

Annuities, Evaluating 27.33

Annuities, Nonnatural Owners 27.28

Annuities in Retirement Planning 27.30

Annuitization Options 27.9

Annuitization Phase 27.15

Annuity Fees and Charges 27.11

Annuity Tax-Free Distribution to Pay for Long-Term Care Insurance 27.26

Archer Medical Savings Accounts (MSA) 24.15

Assets, Transfers to Reduce 24.28

Beneficiaries 28.27

     Common Disaster Clause 28.29

     Revocable vs. Irrevocable 28.29

Boiler and Machinery Insurance 32.46

Business Entities, Types of 29.6

     Accumulated Earnings Tax 29.10

     Alternative Minimum Tax (Corporate) 29.9

     C-Corporation 29.8

     General Partnerships 29.7

     Limited Liability Companies (LLCs) 29.8

     Limited Partnerships 29.8

     LLC 29.8

Index

Business Entities, Types of, continued

    Partnerships...29.7

    Perpetual Life of a C-Corporation 29.10

    S-Corporations...29.11

    Sole Proprietorship..29.6

    Transferability..29.10

Business Income Coverage 32.53

Business Overhead Expense Insurance.................................29.31

Business Uses of Insurance...29.1

Business-Related Personal Loss 32.39

Business-Related Risk Exposures..32.39

Buy-Sell Agreements 29.15

Buy-Sell Agreements, Types of and funding with Insurance..............29.20

Cadillac Health Insurance Plans 24.32

Cafeteria Plans 24.62

Cap on Insured's Payments...24.6

CCRC...26.22

COB (Coordination of Benefits)...24.47

COBRA AND HIPPA...24.58

Coinsurance..24.6

COLA...25.15

Commercial Auto Insurance 32.47

Commercial Farm Insurance...32.47

Commercial Package Policy 32.42

Commercial Property Insurance 32.41

Commercial Umbrella Liability Policy...................................32.49

Complications of Closely Owned and/or Family Owned Business........29.3

    Ability to Attract and Retain Key/Highly Skilled Employees..........29.3

    Lack of Diversification 29.5

    Management/Personnel Issues....................................29.5

    Risk of Lost Income Due to Death or Disability of a Key Employee...29.3

    Risk of Lost Income due to Disability of the Owner.......29.3

    Succession Planning Issues..29.4

Comprehensive Major Medical Policy 24.7

Consumer-Directed Health Plans...24.45

Continuing Care Retirement Communities (CCRCs)................26.22

Contract Requirements...22.27

Coordination of Benefits (COB)...24.47

Cost of Living Adjustment (COLA).......................................25.15

Index

Cross Purchase Agreements 29.21

Cross Purchase and Entity Purchase Agreements, Choosing 29.25

Deductibles 24.5

Deferred Annuities, Two Phases...27.4

Definitions..24.69, 26.23, 27.37, 28B.12, 29.39

Dental Insurance 24.65

Disability Income Insurance (Individual) 25.1

Disability Income Insurance Policies..25.5

Disability Income Needs, Creating a Plan 25.24

Disability Income Policies, Analyzing 25.6

Disability Income Policies, Individual...25.6

    Benefit Amount..25.9

    Benefit Period 25.9

    Disability, Definitions of 25.7

    Elimination Period 25.8

    Exclusions..25.6

    Probationary Period 25.7

    Renewability Provisions 25.11

    Short-Term vs. Long-Term Coverage.....................................25.9

    Underwriting 25.10

Disability Insurance as an Employee Benefit 25.17

Disability, Health, Long-Term Care and Property/Liability

    Insurance Needs Analysis 30.7

Disputes...22.25

Distributions to Beneficiaries, rules for 27.27

Dividends 28.31

Domestic Partner, Health Coverage for 24.46

Embedded Deductible...24.37

Embedded Versus Non-Embedded Deductible 24.36

Embedded Versus Non-Embedded Deductible MOOP 24.40

Employee Benefit Analysis..25.23

Employer Shared Responsibility..24.55

Employer-Provided Health Insurance, Regulation of.........................24.49

Endorsements..32.23

    Guaranteed Replacement Cost Endorsement............................32.25

    Inflation Guard Endorsement...32.25

    Personal Property Replacement Cost Endorsement.....................32.24

    Scheduled Personal Property Endorsement 32.23

Endorsements, continued

    Section II Endorsements 32.25

    Watercraft Endorsement 32.26

Endowment Life Insurance 28.22

Entity Purchase (Stock Redemption) Agreements....................29.23

Equity-Indexed Annuities 27.17

Estoppel..22.25

Exclusions in Medical Expense Insurance Policy 24.8

Family Medical Leave Act (FMLA)..24.51

Financial Planning Process, Six-step process 22.35

Fixed Annuities...27.13

Fixed Annuity vs. Variable Annuity 27.8

Flexible Spending Accounts (FSA) 24.63

FMLA 24.51

FSA 24.63

GIO 25.15

Group Long-Term Care Insurance 26.19

Group Medical as an Employee Benefit 24.45

Guaranteed Insurability Option (GIO)...................................25.15

Health Care Costs, Planning for in Retirement......................24.66

Health Care Reform 24.30

Health Care Reform and Employer-Provided Coverage 24.53

Health Insurance and Health Care Cost Management 24.3

Health Insurance for Seniors..24.16

Health Insurance Marketplace 24.33

Health Insurance Policy Types 24.4

Health Maintenance Organizations (HMO)............................24.11

Health Reimbursement Arrangements (HRA)..........................24.16

Health Savings Accounts (HSA's)..24.13

HIPPA 24.61

HIPPA AND COBRA..24.58

HMO 24.11

Homeowners Forms 32.21

    HO-1 and HO-2...32.21

    HO-3 Special Form and HO-5 Comprehensive 32.21

    HO-4 Tenant and HO-6 Condo.......................................32.22

    HO-8 Market Value below Replacement Cost 32.22

Homeowner Insurance 32.5

Hospital, Surgical, and Physicians' Expense Insurance 24.4

HRA 24.16

HSA 24.13

HSA, Rules for 24.13

Hybrid Annuity/Long-Term Care Products 27.32

Immediate Annuity vs. Deferred Annuity 27.6

Income Replacement, the need for..................................25.2

Indemnity, The Principle of..22.23

Inland Marine Insurance 32.48

Insurable Interest...22.26

Insurable Risks: Ideal Risk Characteristics....................22.18

Insurance Company, Selecting..25.26

Insurance Contracts..22.29

Insurance Definitions and Concepts 22.15

Insurance Needs Analysis 30.1

Insurance Needs During Various Life Cycle Stages.........31.1

Insurance Policy and Company Selection........................31.1

Insurance Policy Components..22.32

    Beneficiary Designations 22.33

    Conditions 22.32

    Declarations 22.32

    Exclusions 22.32

    Insuring Agreement 22.32

    Policy Ownership..22.33

    Riders and Endorsements..22.33

Insurance Policy, Analysis of 32.3

Insurance Transfer 22.12

Insurance, Types of Producers in the Marketing of..........22.20

Intentional Torts..23.6

Interest Crediting Methods 28.32

Internal Limits...24.5

Key Person Insurance 29.28

Law of Large Numbers 22.16

Legal Aspects of Insurance..22.23

Liability Risk Exposures..23.5

Life Insurance (Individual) 28.1

Life Insurance as an Employee Benefit 28.44

    Contributory vs. Noncontributory Plans 28.45

    Conversion Analysis 28.48

    Dependent Coverage 28.46

    Group Ordinary Plan 28.47

    Group Permanent Insurance 28.47

    Group Term Life Insurance 28.44

    Group Universal Life Insurance Programs (GULP) 28.47

    GULP 28.47

    Nondiscrimination Rules 28.45

    Portability of GULPS 28.48

    Tax Treatment 28.46

Life Insurance Company Selection 31.9

    Other Types of Insurance 31.11

Life Insurance for Long-Term Care 26.21

Life Insurance Needs Analysis 30.2

    Financial Needs Analysis 30.3

    Human Life Value Approach 30.3

    Rule of Thumb Method 30.3

Life Insurance Policy

    Illustrations 28.36

    Policy Replacement 28.37

Life Insurance Policy Selection 31.3

Life Insurance Premiums 28.4

Life Insurance Uses and Benefits 28.3

Life Insurance, Group Carve-Out 28.48

    Death Benefit Only Plan 28.49

    Premium Bonus Plan 28.48

Life Insurance, Income Taxation of Life Insurance Death benefits 28B.6

    Transfer-for-Value Rule 28B.6

Life Insurance, Income Taxation of Lifetime Benefits from 28B.1

    Determining Basis 28B.3

    Dividends 28B.2

    Life Settlements 28B.5

    Loans 28B.2

    Premiums 28B.1

    Surrender 28B.4

    Tax-Free Exchange – Sec. 1035 ....28B.4

    Withdrawals 28B.2

Life Insurance, Other Strategic uses of...28.43
    Business Uses...28.44
    Charitable Giving..28.43
    Installment Note Protection 28.43
    Pension Maximization 28.43
Life Insurance, the Contract...28.23
    Declarations Page..28.23
Life with Cash refund 27.10
Life with Installment Refund 27.10
Life with Period Certain..27.10
Long-Term Care Expenses, paying for 26.2
Long-Term Care Insurance (Individual)...26.1
Long-Term Care Insurance (LTCI) 26.5
Long-Term Care Insurance Partnership Program 24.28
Long-Term Care Insurance Partnership Program 26.20
Long-Term Care Need 26.3
Long-Term Care Planning, the need for 26.2
Loss, Maximum Possible and Maximum Probable 23.2
LTCI...26.5
LTCI as Part of the Financial Plan...26.5
LTCI, Designing 26.6
LTCI Laws – HIPPA rules and NAIC Model Legislation.......................26.6
LTCI Policy Features and Provisions
    Benefit Amount..26.13
    Benefit Periods...26.13
    Cost 26.16
    Covered Services 26.11
    Eligibility and Underwriting...26.9
    Eligibility to Receive Benefits 26.10
    Inflation Protection 26.14
    Nonforfeiture Benefits 26.15
    Reimbursement vs. Indemnity 26.14
    Renewability Provisions 26.16
    Waiting (Elimination) Periods 26.12
    Waiver of Premium..26.14
LTCI Premiums from Other Plans...26.18
Major Medical Insurance 24.5
Managed Care 24.45
Managed Care Plans 24.10

Marketplace or Non-Marketplace 24.35

MECs 28B.7

    Sec. 1035 Exchanges 28B.10

    7-Pay Test for MEC 28B.8

    Taxation of Lifetime Benefits 28B.9

Medicaid 24.27

Medicare 24.16

Medicare, Eligibility 24.18

Medicare, Funding 24.17

Medicare, Parts A and B 24.21

    Out-of-Pocket Cost 24.22

Medicare Part C, Medicare Advantage 24.23

Medicare Part D, Prescription Drug Benefits 24.24

Medicare Tax and Medicare Tax on Investment Income 24.30

Medicare, Taxation of Premiums and Benefits...........................24.24

Medigap Coverage 24.25

Mental Health Parity 24.51

Misrepresentation...22.26

Modified Endowment Contracts (MECs) 28B.7

Mortality 28.5

MSA..24.15

Negligence 23.5

Non-Embedded Deductible...24.38

Nonforfeiture Options..28.33

Non-insurance Transfer 22.11

Nonqualified Deferred Compensation 29.33

    Types of plans 29.33

Nonwaiver Provision 22.25

Ocean Marine Insurance 32.48

Open Enrollment..24.34

Other Insurance Provision..22.24

Parol Evidence Rule 22.25

Payment..25.13

Period Certain 27.10

Personal Automobile Insurance 32.26

    Automobile and Recreational Vehicles Insurance 32.28

    Deductibles 32.35

    Part A – Liability Coverage 32.28

    Part A Exclusions..32.30

Index

Personal Automobile Insurance, continued
    Part B – Medical Payments Coverage 32.30
    Part B Exclusions 32.31
    Part C – Uninsured Motorists Coverage 32.32
    Part C Exclusions 32.33
    Part D – Coverage for Damage to the Auto 32.34
    Part D Exclusions 32.35
    Split-Limits of Liability 32.29
    State Requirements 32.26
Personal Risk Exposures 23.3
Point-of-Service Plans (PPO) 24.13
Policy Reserves 28.6
PPO 24.12
Preferred Provider Organizations (PPO) 24.12
Premium Tax Credits 24.33
Premiums and Strategies to Reduce Household Insurance Costs 22.33
Presumptive Disability 25.12
Professional Liability Policies 32.49
    Accountants Professional Liability Policy 32.50
    Architects and Engineers Professional Liability Policy 32.50
    Physicians Professional Liability Policy 32.50
Property and Casualty Insurance 32.1
Property Risk Exposures 23.4
Pure Annuity vs. Refund Annuity 27.7
QLAC 27.31
Qualified Annuity vs. Nonqualified Annuity 27.8
Qualified Longevity Annuity Contracts (QLACs) 27.31
Rabbi Trust 29.34
Recurrent Disability 25.12
Reformation 22.26
Refund Annuities 27.9
Regulation of Annuities 27.19
Retention 22.11
Riders 28.29
Riders to Disability Income Policies 25.14
    Partial Disability 25.14
    Residual Disability 25.14
Riders to Variable Annuities 27.15
Risk Avoidance 22.10

Risk Management and Insurance Planning................................22.1

Risk Management and Insurance, Purpose and benefits of 22.2

Risk Management Process 22.2

    Step 1: Establish the Risk Management Objective 22.3

    Step 2: Gather Information to Identify the Loss Exposures 22.4

    Step 3: Analyze and Evaluate the Loss Exposures

        and the Risk Management Techniques Available.................22.7

    Step 4: Develop a Plan, Selecting the Best Risk Management

        Techniques to Achieve the Objectives................................22.8

    Step 5: Implement the Plan 22.9

    Step 6: Monitor the Plan 22.10

Risk Management Techniques (Responses to Risk)........................22.10

Risk Management, Three Basic Rules 22.14

Risk Reduction................................22.11

Sec. 101(j) Forms for Business-Owned Life Insurance......................29.24

Sec. 162 Bonus Plans................................29.32

Section 1035 Exchange................................27.26

Section I Coverages 32.6

    Additional Coverages................................32.9

    Coverage A – Dwelling 32.6

    Coverage B – Other Structures 32.6

    Coverage C – Personal Property 32.6

    Coverage D – Loss of Use 32.8

    Exclusions................................32.10

    Loss Settlement................................32.11

Section II Coverages 32.14

    Additional Coverages................................32.16

    Coverage E – Personal Liability 32.14

    Coverage F – Medical Payments to Others................................32.15

    Exclusions – Coverage E 32.15

    Exclusions – Coverage F 32.16

Secular Trust................................29.35

Self-Funded Plans 24.49

Self-Insurance 22.20

Settlement Options................................28.35

SHOP (Small Business Health Options Program)............................24.56

Short-Term Disability and Sick Pay Plans................................25.19

Sick Pay Plans and Short-Term Disability................................25.19

Single Life vs. Joint Life Annuity................................27.7

Single Premium Annuity vs. Periodic Premium Annuity......................27.6

Small Business Health Options Program (SHOP)..............................24.56

Social Security Disability Backpay 25.20

Social Security Disability Benefits 25.3

Social Security Offset 25.20

Social Security Rider 25.16

Specialized Commercial Policies..32.47

Split-Dollar Life Insurance 29.30

Straight Life Annuity 27.9

Strict Liability 23.6

Structured Settlements 27.29

Subrogation 22.23

Summary Plan Descriptions and Summary of Benefits and Coverage.....24.50

Superannuation 27.30

Surety Bonds 32.49

Survivorship Life Insurance...28.23

Tax Advantage of Employer-Provided Health Plans..........................24.52

Taxation for Partners and S-Corporation Owners 25.22

Taxation of Employer Sponsored Group Disability 25.21

Taxation of Long-Term Care Insurance Premiums and Benefits 26.17

Taxation of Nonqualified Annuities 27.22

    Accumulation Period 27.22

    Aggregation Rules 27.24

    Annuitization Period 27.24

    10% Penalty Tax on Early Distributions 27.23

    Withdrawals After Age 59½..27.22

Taxation of Premiums and Benefits for

    Individual Disability Insurance.....................................25.17

Taxation of Premiums and Benefits for Individual

    Health Insurance Policies...24.29

Taxation of Premiums and Benefits for Individuals

    and Self-Employed Individuals.......................................24.29

Taxation of Qualified Annuities 27.21

Temporary Annuity...27.11

Term Insurance 28.7

    Advantages and Disadvantages..28.9

    Renewal and Conversion 28.7

Traditional Indemnity (Fee-for-Service)...................................24.45

Trusteed Agreements 29.26

Index

Umbrella Liability Insurance 32.36

Underwriting 22.19

Universal Life Insurance 28.18

    Advantages and Disadvantage 28.20

    Flexible Death Benefits 28.19

    Unbundling the Elements of the Policy 28.18

Utilization and Costs, Control of 24.10

Utmost good Faith, Principles of 22.30

Variable Annuities 27.14

Variable Annuities, Advantages of 27.16

    Disadvantages of 27.17

Variable Life Insurance 28.15

    Advantages and Disadvantages 28.16

    Inflation Hedge 28.16

    Regulation of 28.17

    Separate Accounts 28.15

Variable Universal Life Insurance 28.21

VEBA 24.64

Viatical Settlements 28.38

    Ethical Issues 28.42

    Tax Rules Sec. 101(g) 28.39

Vision Insurance 24.66

Void vs. Voidable Contracts 22.29

Voluntary Employees Beneficiary Associations 24.64

Wait-and-See Agreements 29.27

Waiver-of-Premium Provision 25.12

Waiver 22.25

Whole Life Insurance 28.11

    Advantages and Disadvantages 28.13

    Cash Values 28.13

    Premiums 28.11

Workers' Compensation and Employers Liability 32.52